WOMEN'S STUDIES ENCYCLOPEDIA

Volume I

VIEWS FROM THE SCIENCES

EDITED BY Helen Tierney

PETER BEDRICK BOOKS
NEW YORK

This edition first published in 1991 by
PETER BEDRICK BOOKS
2112 Broadway
New York, NY 10023

WOMEN'S STUDIES ENCYCLOPEDIA, Volume 1: Views
from the Sciences, edited by Helen Tierney, was originally
published in 1989 by Greenwood Press, an imprint of
Greenwood Publishing Group, Inc., Westport, CT.
Copyright © 1991 by Helen Tierney. Paperback edition
published with permission of the editor and Greenwood
Publishing Group, Inc. All rights reserved.

Library of Congress Cataloging-in-Publication Data

Women's studies encyclopedia / edited by Helen Tierney.
    Reprint. Originally published: New York : Greenwood Press, 1989-.
    Includes bibliographical references and index.
    Contents: v. 1. Views from the sciences.
    ISBN 0-87226-244-8
    1. Women–United States–Encyclopedias. 2. Women–Encyclopedias.
  3. Feminism–Encyclopedias.   I. Tierney, Helen.
  HQ1115.W645   1991
  305.4'03–dc20   90-56478
                                                         CIP

Printed in the United States of America

5 4 3 2 1

Contents

Acknowledgments

This encyclopedia is a collaborative effort of many women and men who have given generously of their time, experience, and expertise. Acknowledgment and special thanks are due first to all those who contributed articles and to the consultants whose advice and counsel were essential in choosing topics, in recommending professionals to write articles, and in reviewing articles. Thanks also go to the very many whose encouragement helped to keep things going in times of discouragement and to those whose advice I followed and to those whose advice I should have followed.

Acknowledgments are due to the University of Wisconsin System for the sabbatical that allowed me to launch the project and to my colleagues in the Women's Studies Program and the History Department for their understanding and support. I am indebted to a large number of individuals who were especially generous with their assistance along the way. To Valerie Lagorio, Susan Mitchell, Susan Searing, and Jacqueline Ross; to Janet Boles, Susan Carter, Geraldine Forbes, Patricia Rozee-Koker, Allen Scarboro, Ann Waltner, Elaine Wheeler, and many others I owe a debt of gratitude. My thanks also to Julie Brewer for her clerical assistance and, finally, to my mother, who will not read this book but who in many ways is responsible for it.

Consultants and Contributors

CONSULTANTS

Robin L. Bartlett, Economics, Denison University
Janet K. Boles, Political Science, Marquette University
Marilyn J. Boxer, Associate Dean of Arts and Sciences, San Diego State University
Susan B. Carter, Economics, Smith College
Judith Leavitt, History of Medicine, Wisconsin Medical School
Illene Noppe, Human Development, Wisconsin-Green Bay
Barbara J. Price, Dean, Graduate Program, John Jay College, CUNY
Patricia Rozee-Koker, Psychology, California, Long Beach
Allen Scarboro, Sociology, Millsaps College
Beth E. Schneider, Sociology, California, Santa Barbara
Ethel Sloane, Biosciences, Wisconsin-Milwaukee
Cecilia V. Tierney, CPA, Accounting, Phoenix, Arizona
Rhoda Unger, Psychology, Trenton State College
Mariamne Whatley, Curriculum and Instruction, Wisconsin-Madison
Elaine Wheeler, R.N., Platteville, Wisconsin

CONTRIBUTORS

Barry D. Adam, Sociology, University of Windsor
Jilda M. Aliotta, Political Science, Miami University
Judith L. Alpert, Psychology, New York University
Rima D. Apple, History of Medicine, Wisconsin School of Medicine

Richard D. Ashmore, Psychology, Rutgers University

Nancy S. Barrett, Economics, American University

Pauline Bart, Psychiatry, University of Illinois at Chicago

Susan Basow, Psychology, LaFayette College

Phyllis Jo Baunach, Bureau of Justice Statistics, Department of Justice

Cheryl Becker, Library, University of Wisconsin–Platteville

Barbara R. Bergmann, Economics, University of Maryland

Mary Kay Biaggio, Psychology, Indiana State University

Francine D. Blau, Institute of Labor and Industrial Relations, University of Illinois

Kathleen M. Blee, Women's Studies, University of Kentucky

Susan Bordo, Philosophy, Le Moyne College

Marilyn J. Boxer, Associate Dean of Arts and Letters, San Diego State University

Dorothy H. Bracey, Anthropology, John Jay College, CUNY

Rose M. Brewer, Sociology, University of Minnesota

J. Brooks-Gunn, Senior Research Scientist, Educational Testing Service

Victoria Brown, Sociology, San Diego State University

Alyson L. Burns, Psychology, University of California–Davis

Anthony R. Caggiula, Psychology, University of Pittsburgh

Susan J. Carroll, Egleton Institute for Politics, Rutgers University

Susan B. Carter, Economics, Smith College

Carol Christy, Political Science, Ohio University–Lancaster

Pauline Rose Clance, Psychology, Georgia State University

Jane F. Collier, Anthropology, Stanford University

Jane M. Connor, Communications Studies, SUNY-Binghamton

Ellen Piel Cook, Psychology, University of Cincinnati

Nancy Datan, Human Development, University of Wisconsin–Green Bay

Janice Delaney, Library of Congress, Washington, D.C.

Frances K. Del Boca, Psychology, Bard College

Kenneth L. Dion, Psychology, University of Toronto

Ed Donnerstein, Psychology, University of California–Santa Barbara

Lorah D. Dorn, Individual & Family Studies, Pennsylvania State University

Jacquelynne S. Eccles, Psychology, University of Michigan

Wendy Eisner, Eisner Associates, Bergenfield, New Jersey

Steven L. Ellyson, Psychology, Youngstown State University

Claire Etaugh, Psychology, Bradley University

Sara M. Evans, History, University of Minnesota

Reza Fazel, Anthropology, University of Massachusetts–Boston Harbor

Clarice Feinman, Criminal Justice, Trenton State University

Margaret Fenn, Business Administration, Emeritus, University of Washington

Marianne A. Ferber, Economics, University of Illinois

Kathy E. Ferguson, Political Science, University of Hawaii at Monoa

Iris G. Fodor, Psychology, New York University

Rita Jackaway Freedman, Private Clinical Practice, Scarsdale, New York

Irene H. Frieze, Psychology, University of Pittsburgh

Frances Garb, Biology, University of Wisconsin–Stout

Alma M. Garcia, Anthropology, University of Santa Clara

Clarke Garrett, History, Dickinson College

Robert L. Griswold, History, University of Oklahoma

Ellen Gruenbaum, Department of Anthropology, California State University–San Bernardino

Esther Heffernan, Sociology, Edgewood College

Gregory M. Herek, Psychology, City University of New York

Beth Hess, Sociology, County College of Morris

Marjorie Honig, Economics, Hunter College, CUNY

Kathleen B. Jones, Women's Studies, San Diego State University

Brigitte Jordan, Anthropology, Michigan State University

Evelyn Fox Keller, Mathematics, Northeastern University

Don Quinn Kelley, History, Medger Evers College, CUNY

Louise H. Kidder, Psychology, Temple University

Deborah K. King, Sociology, Dartmouth College

Diane Kravetz, School of Social Work, University of Wisconsin–Madison

Marianne LaFrance, Director of Women's Studies, Boston College

Melissa Latimer, Sociology, University of Kentucky

Ellen Lewin, San Francisco, California

Alison Klairmont Lingo, History, University of California–Berkeley

Mary Lou Locke, History, University of California–San Diego

Marian Lowe, Chemistry, Boston University

Mary Jane Lupton, English, Morgan State University

Penelope A. McLorg, Lexington-Fayette Health Department, Lexington, Kentucky

Dayle Mandelson, Affirmative Action Director, University of Wisconsin–Stout

Susan Marshall, Sociology, University of Texas–Austin

Nan L. Maxwell, Economics, California State University–Hayward

Martha T. Mednick, Psychology, Howard University

Jill G. Morawski, Psychological Laboratory, Wesleyan University

Marietta Morrissey, Sociology, Texas Tech University

Barbara J. Nelson, Hurbert H. Humphrey Institute, University of Minnesota

Sarah M. Nelson, Anthropology, University of Denver

Betty A. Nesvold, Political Science, San Diego State University

Andreé Nicola McLaughlin, Women's Studies, Medger Evers College, CUNY

Illene Noppe, Human Development, University of Wisconsin–Green Bay

Jill Norgren, Government, John Jay College, CUNY

Maureen O'Toole, Psychology, Georgia State University

Vivian Paley, Education, University of Chicago

Michele A. Paludi, Psychology, Kent State University

Lynn Paringer, Associate Dean, Business and Economics, California State University—Hayward

Kathy Peiss, History, University of Massachusetts at Amherst

Carol O. Perkins, Women's Studies, San Diego State University

Anne Petersen, Individual and Family Studies, Pennsylvania State University

Nicole Hahn Rafter, Criminal Justice, Northeastern University

Janice G. Raymond, Women's Studies, University of Massachusetts at Amherst

Sue Tolleson Rinehart, Political Science, Texas Tech University

Sylvia Robertson, Women and Children in Crisis, Bartlesville, Oklahoma

Robert Rosenthal, Psychology, Harvard University

Elyce Rotella, Economics, Indiana University

Patricia Rozee-Koker, Psychology, University of California–Long Beach

Diana E. H. Russell, Sociology, Mills College

Arlene Scadron, Media Communications, Pima County Community College

Allen Scarboro, Sociology, Millsaps College

Beth E. Schneider, Sociology, University of California–Santa Barbara

Stephanie A. Shields, Psychology, University of California–Davis

Jodi L. Sindelar, Epidemiology & Public Health, Yale School of Medicine

Sarah Slavin, Political Science, SUNY–Buffalo

Natalie J. Sokoloff, Sociology, City University of New York

Barbara Sommer, Psychology, University of California–Davis

Gloria Stephenson, English, University of Wisconsin–Platteville

Diane E. Taub, Sociology, Southern Illinois at Carbondale

Carol Tavris, Psychology, University of California–Los Angeles

Leonore Tiefer, Urology, Beth Israel Medical Center

Carole Wade, College of Marin, Larkspur, California

Lynn Walter, Anthropology, University of Wisconsin–Green Bay

Jennifer L. Warlick, Economics, Notre Dame University

Maria-Barbara Watson-Franke, Women's Studies, San Diego State University

Elaine Wheeler, R.N., Platteville, Wisconsin

Juanita H. Williams, Psychology, Professor Emeritus, South Florida University

Nanci Koser Wilson, Center for the Study of Crime, Delinquency and Corrections, Southern Illinois at Carbondale

Anne Woollett, North East London Polytechnic, London, United Kingdom

Nancy Worcester, Women's Studies, University of Wisconsin–Madison

Mary Ann Zettelmaier, R.N., Chesterton, Indiana

Introduction

Those who have organized courses in women's studies are familiar with the need for information from other disciplines and the difficulty of finding such information in an easily usable format—a concise account that incorporates the most recent feminist research and is written in a style and vocabulary a nonspecialist can understand. My complaints to a friend about the need for some sort of handy reference work, containing information from other fields, to which a historian could turn for help in trying to clarify and illuminate women's role in history were met with the not very sympathetic reply, "So write one." Thus began the Women's Studies Encyclopedia Project, an effort to create for those interested in learning about women, for students, general readers, scholars from other disciplines, a reference tool that includes the results of feminist research on women from various academic perspectives.

The project soon outgrew its original unrealistic goal of a one-volume desk reference touching on all disciplines. The present volume, the first of three, is limited to subjects from fields that can be considered, in some sense, as "science": natural, behavioral, and social sciences, health and medicine, economics, linguistics, political and legal sciences. It is, necessarily, partial and incomplete in its coverage: the volume of scholarship on topics related to and affecting women is so enormous, the research fields, subfields, and specialties so prolific, that one volume could scarcely scratch the surface of a single discipline, let alone of all the "sciences." An early decision in favor of contributed articles in the 750 to 1,500 word range, so as to allow for a fuller discussion of most topics, severely limited the number of individual articles. Limiting the number of entries meant that painful decisions had to be made as to what was to be included and what not included. Aside from a few instances in which promised material could not, for various reasons, be delivered in time for publication, all final decisions on content are my own.

The reader may find an overconcentration of articles in some areas and gapping omissions in others. In general, articles on health and medicine are limited to women's most common problems (e.g., cystitis, vaginitis) or problems that affect women much more than men (e.g., depression, agoraphobia); articles on women's employment, to fields in which women predominate (e.g., health professions, teaching, librarianship, clerical occupations). A few topics of major importance to women (e.g., the family, socialization) are treated in more than one article, from different disciplinary perspectives.

The articles are meant to convey information to an educated audience without expertise in the subject area of the individual entry. They are not intended for use in research. The bibliographic apparatus is, therefore, very limited. The few references included at the end of some articles are meant primarily to direct readers to works from which they may obtain a fuller explanation or more detailed information on the subject.

The major focus of the work is on the American experience. Most articles are limited just to the United States. Some include the wider compass of the industrialized West, but very few include nonindustrial cultures. This narrow focus was dictated by space limitations. For most articles it was impossible, given the constraints on length, to take the discussion beyond the borders of the United States without too great a sacrifice of content. Unless otherwise specified, therefore, discussion is limited to the United States.

There is no single feminist perspective informing the entries. One aim, in inviting contributions, was to incorporate as wide a variety of feminist approaches as possible, so that all shades of opinion, from those so conservative that some will deny they are feminist to the most radical, are represented. Since I did not believe that my own agreement with opinions expressed was necessary, or even always desirable, contributors had the widest possible latitude in developing their articles as they saw fit.

The lack of a uniform feminist perspective may bother some readers. So too may the lack of uniformity of organization. The wide variety of subjects and approaches made a uniform system of organization and structure impossible—it was not always possible to begin with a definition, or to incorporate the entry heading into the lead-off sentence. Most entries begin with a definition, but for those kinds of entries for which a definition was not appropriate, no effort was made to force a uniform structure over disparate material.

Cross-references have been reduced to a minimum because of space limitations. When a word or phrase for which there is an entry in this volume is used as a noun in another entry, the cross-reference is indicated by an asterisk. In cases in which major topics might be listed under several different headings, a cross-reference to the heading used is given.

The names of the authors of entries follow the entry and are also listed in Consultants and Contributors. Those articles that do not carry the name of an author were written by the editor.

WOMEN'S STUDIES ENCYCLOPEDIA

A

ABORTION is loss of a fetus* before the potentiality of independent life has been attained, legally in the United States before the twenty-eighth week of menstrual age (28 weeks after the last menstrual period). After the twenty-eighth week, the death of the fetus is called *premature* or *still birth*. *Fetal death* is death before the fetus is expelled or extracted from the mother, regardless of the length of the pregnancy.

Spontaneous abortion is the body's mechanism for expelling fetuses that, for a variety of causes, cannot complete the period of gestation*. The term *miscarriage* is usually limited to a spontaneous abortion before the third trimester (twenty-eighth week of menstrual age), although it is sometimes used of induced abortions as well. The great majority of spontaneous abortions occur early in gestation, due to abnormal development or death of the ovum or its membrane. They often occur before the woman realizes she is pregnant and are assumed to be menstrual irregularities.

Spontaneous abortions occur most frequently among the very young and those over 30. A higher frequency among nonwhites may be the result of environmental factors. Causes usually stem from physical or physiological problems of the cervix or uterus, the great majority of which (around 90 percent) cannot be corrected medically. Common causes include congenital abnormalities, uterine fibroids, incompetence of the cervix (usually from its having been overstretched), and deficiency of progesterone. Other causes include uterine infections, radiation and chemotherapeutic drugs used in cancer treatment, and, although rarely, general diseases or infections that result in high body temperatures.

Induced abortion is the interruption of a pregnancy, by the mother or some other person, under conditions that are not spontaneous. Where induced abortions are illegal, exceptions are sometimes allowed for *therapeutic abortions*, to save the life or the health of the mother.

Evidence of induced abortion exists in every society with written records and in nearly all contemporary primitive societies. Although various methods have been used and advocated to induce abortion, ranging from the completely worthless, such as eating raspberries or applying sympathetic magic, to the extremely dangerous, the technique remained basically unchanged from ancient times until the latter nineteenth century when industrialization and urbanization made efforts to control human fertility a major social problem in all Western nations.

The two basic methods can be traced back to ancient medical texts. The *herbal method* is the ingestion of substances toxic to the cell nucleus. The fetus will be killed, but the woman, hopefully, will recover. The best-known, most commonly used substance is oil of juniper: savin (*Juniperus sabina*) was used by the Greeks and Romans and was spread from the Mediterranean to Northern Europe. Its use is mentioned in seventeenth-century English writings, including Nicolas Culpepper's *The Complete Herbal*. It is the main ingredient in Buchanan's Pills, best known of the nineteenth century cures for "women's ailments." "Female correctives" sold everywhere, but especially in poorer countries, still contain oil of juniper. The commonest time for administering it is within a few days of the missed period.

The *mechanical method* is relatively simple: to enter the uterus and completely remove the products of conception by the use of probes and instruments. The cervix must be dilated to pass the instruments into the uterus. The fetal membrane is then ruptured and natural expulsion of the conceptus invariably follows. The fifth century B.C. Hippocratic Corpus describes a graduated set of dilators, and probes and instruments which have remained basically unchanged were found in the ruins of Herculaneum and Pompeii (destroyed A.D. 79). Great care is needed and risks are serious. Dilation of the cervix by inserting unsterilized plant material that will absorb moisture and swell, causing a slow and even dilation, can cause infection. The position of the uterus and its extremely soft wall when pregnant makes perforation and severe bleeding very easy. Raw areas, and especially any placental material not expelled, form ideal sites for infection.

As the demand for abortions greatly increased in the nineteenth century, and before social-purity laws drove physicians and more or less open advertisements from the scene in many Western countries, the kind of abortion probably varied with the income level of the woman. Physicians and midwives probably used mechanical techniques. Products were advertised and sold as emmenogogues, correctives to bring on delayed menstruation. Herbalists sold their remedies to the poor.

Some progress in methods began to appear in the nineteenth century. The curette, a spoon-shaped instrument for scraping a wound clean, developed by the French in the eighteenth century, in the nineteenth began to be used for inducing or treating incomplete abortions. Bleeding and infection are reduced by curettage to remove all products of conception. Dilation and curettage (D&C) remains a basic technique.

The chief advances in dilation were laminaria tents, dried, compressed seaweed which can be sterilized, and the use of anesthesia to block the pain of cervical dilation.

"Drycupping," the forerunner of vacuum aspiration, was known as early as 1863. However, progress in acceptance was slow—the technique was known in Russia in 1927 and in China during World War II. By the late 1950s and early 1960s it had spread to Japan and Eastern Europe. Czech glassmakers were able to make excellent suction curettes, but the West did not adopt drycupping until the late 1960s. After it was combined with local anesthetic in Yugoslavia in 1966, it began to be used in England in 1967 and after this spread rapidly.

In 1961 Harvey Karman, an illegal abortionist who could not use anesthesia, developed a very small-bore tube so that the cervix would not need dilation for it to be passed into the uterus. With soft, flexible tubing this simple abortion catheter (about 4 mm diameter), which needs no or only local anesthesia, reduced the costs of abortion and was simple and safe. It can be used for pregnancies of up to six or eight weeks.

Today vacuum aspiration is most common for first trimester abortions. A thin tube, or cannula, with openings on one end and attached to an aspirator, is introduced into the uterus. As suction is applied, the cannula is rotated and drawn in and out of the uterus, drawing out the products of conception. The diameter of the cannula depends upon the age of the fetus. D&C, once the standard method for first trimester abortions, today is still used for treating all incomplete abortions. The cervix is dilated, a preliminary curettage is preformed, then the placental tissue is detached by forceps.

Induction methods, which became the most widely used techniques for later abortions until the mid–1980s, began to be developed in the 1920s and 1930s. Special soaps or pastes were introduced in Germany in the 1920s and used, particularly in Germany and Denmark, in the interwar period. Medicated soap is introduced through the vagina into the extraovular space (between uterine wall and membrane). The soap spreads around the fetal sac and normally induces an abortion within 48 hours. Cases of infection led to decline in its use in Europe, but it is still used in developing countries.

After abortion was legalized in the United States, the common procedure for late abortions was the two-step method: first, the cervix was dilated and the normal reproductive process interrupted; hours later contractions began and the conceptus was expelled. A D&C was usually performed to make sure that all the products of conception were removed.

The most used two-step induction abortion method was by injection, under local anesthetic, of a liquid into the amniotic sac to kill the placenta and thus induce an abortion. The first steps in developing the method date to the 1930s when liquids were injected into the amniotic cavity or into the fetal membrane. When abortion laws were liberalized, interest in the use of injection led to experiments with different substances: formalin, glucose, saline solution, urea, prostaglandins. (Prostaglandins are a family of long-chain fatty acids found in men and women. They play an important role in menstruation, spontaneous abortions, and labor.) Prostaglandin or prostaglandin and urea solutions were most commonly used in Europe, but saline solutions, or saline with urea and/ or prostaglandins, continued to be preferred in the United States. However, injection carries risks to the mother. Saline solutions introduced into the mother's system, for instance, can be fatal. And this method is more traumatic than is evacuation.

Since the mid–1980s, dilation and evacuation (D&E) has replaced injection. After dilation, vacuum aspiration and forceps and curettage are used to remove the products of conception. The method is safer and takes much less time than the introamniotic injection technique. Today it is the method used for late first trimester and second trimester abortions.

For later abortions, hysterotomy (also called miniature cesarean section), dating from the nineteenth century, was the usual method for therapeutic abortions before the development of the two-step technique. It is now rarely used except in conjunction with sterilization. Through an abdominal incision the uterus is opened and emptied.

A hysterectomy, totally removing uterus and pregnancy, is used when uterine disease is present. Abdominal entrance is made in the presence of fibroids; vaginal, in cases of prolapse.

Menstrual regulation (menstrual aspiration, menstrual interruption, preemptive abortion) is the name given to surgical evacuation of uterine contents shortly after the first missed period (usually within 14 days). Vacuum aspiration with a Karman curette is the common method. Certain feminist groups use menstrual regulation monthly for fertility regulation and personal hygiene. (The long-range effects of this practice are not yet known.) Emptying the uterus before one knows for certain whether or not she is pregnant can help to avoid the negative emotional response that sometimes accompanies abortion. It can also change the legal rules (e.g., abortion is illegal in Argentina but menstrual regulation is not considered a crime).

The first "morning-after pill" was a five-day course of synthetic estrogen (DES), which must be started within 72 hours of intercourse, to prevent the implantation of a fertilized ovum in the uterus. DES use has side effects: nausea, vomiting, headache, disturbed menstrual pattern. There is also an increased incidence of ectopic pregnancies* (pregnancies outside the uterus) and indications of serious problems, including cancer, in children when the drug is used during pregnancy. Research in the use of progestins, or a combination of estrogen and progestin, continues. The use of Orval, a contraceptive pill with high progestational activity, is safer and probably more effective than DES.

Two very important developments, originating in the United States, are outpatient or day care abortions and abortion counseling. Out-patient treatment, quick, cheap, and reasonably safe, is used increasingly in Europe, Australia, Singapore, and India. Abortion counseling, done properly, enables women to accept early termination, which is much safer than later termination (or than pregnancy), and to accept it with no or only local anesthesia.

Further Reference. Boston Women's Health Book Collective, *The New Our Bodies, Ourselves* (New York, 1984).

ABSENTEE RATES, SEX DIFFERENTIALS IN. Among women in 1979 the incidence of absenteeism was significantly higher than that among men. About 8.6 percent of women experienced an absence during a work week compared to 5.5 percent of men. About 3.4 percent of hours worked by full-time wage and salary workers in the United States is lost due to absences resulting from illness, injury, and personal reasons. About 1 in 15 workers experienced one or more absences in a week for one or more of these reasons. Women lost 4.3 percent of their usual work time in May 1979 compared to 3.0 percent for men (D. Taylor, "Absences from Work among Full-Time Employees," *Monthly Labor Review*, March 1981, 68–70).

Exactly why the absentee rate of women is higher than that of men has been the subject of recent research. Some economists have attributed the higher absence rates of women to their role as family caregivers. Women miss work not only to care for their own illnesses but to care for family members as well. Other economists have attributed the differences to the occupational and wage distribution of the sexes. Women may be more heavily concentrated in those occupations which experience high absentee rates for both men and women.

Table 1 shows the proportion of time lost from work by race, sex, and marital status in May 1979. It is interesting to note that married men with spouses and never-married men have the same absentee rates, while married women have significantly higher rates than never-married women. This suggests that the presence of family responsibilities may affect the probability that women miss work for ill health and personal reasons. This could result for two reasons. First,

Table 1
Percent of Time Lost from Work for Illness and Personal Reasons

	Total	Married Spouse Present	Never Married
Women	4.3	4.5	3.4
White			
Men	2.8	2.9	2.8
Women	4.0	4.3	3.0
Black			
Men	4.6	4.3	5.0
Women	6.0	6.3	6.3

SOURCE: D. Taylor, "Absences from Work among Full-Time Employees," *Monthly Labor Review*, March 1981, 68–70.

women may serve as caregivers so that when a spouse, child, or older family member is ill, the wife or mother may miss work to care for the needs of the family member. Second, to the extent that women assume more household production responsibilities than men, they may be less willing to continue to work while ill and risk getting an even more serious illness.

Black women miss significantly more time from work than white women, and there is little variation in work loss by martial status among black women. The lack of variation in absentee rates by marital status may reflect the fact that single black women are more likely to be heads of households than single white women. Consequently, the family responsibilities assumed by single black women may not be significantly different from those faced by their married counterparts.

Carol Leon examined the incidence of week-long absences among labor force participants in 1980. She found that during an average week 1.5 percent of women missed the entire week of work for health reasons compared to 1.4 percent of men ("Employed But Not at Work: A Review of Unpaid Absences," *Monthly Labor Review*, November 1981, 18–21). However, women were twice as likely as men (.9 percent compared to .5 percent) to miss work for reasons other than vacation, illness, bad weather, or a labor dispute. This finding further supports the idea that the higher absentee rates of women are due primarily to their role as family caregivers.

Leon also found that men were much more likely to be paid for weeks missed from work than were women. In 1980, men received pay for two-thirds of their week-long absences. In contrast women were paid for about half of their full-week absences.

The National Health Interview Survey collects annual data on the number of work-loss days associated with short-term illness. The number of loss days for males and females by major diagnostic category is shown in Table 2.

Women workers miss an average of 3.7 days from work every year for ill health compared to 2.7 for men. For both sexes the number of work-loss days is lower for workers over 45 than for those age 18 to 44. Women miss more days from work for respiratory conditions and infective diseases, and men miss more for injuries and diseases of the digestive system. Among women under age 45, about .52 days per year of work loss can be attributed to pregnancy. Thus, excluding pregnancy considerably narrows the difference in work-loss days between men and women.

This evidence suggests that women experience more illness-related absences than men. However, the tables do not take into account earnings differences between males and females, differences in the occupational distribution of the sexes, and the availability of fringe benefits such as sick leave which reduce the cost to an employee of missing a day from work for health reasons.

Steve Allen found that once he controlled for the wage rate, the availability of sick leave, the availability of income from other sources, and union membership, there were no significant differences in unscheduled absence rates between men and women ("An Empirical Model of Work Attendance," *Review*

Table 2
Work-loss Days per Person Resulting from Acute Health Conditions—1985

Condition	Males			Females		
	All	18-44	45+	All	18-44	45+
All Acute	2.62	2.73	2.36	3.70	4.00	2.94
Infective & Parasitic Diseases	.17	.22	.06	.34	.40	.19
Respiratory Conditions	.85	.90	.72	1.38	1.37	1.38
Digestive Conditions	.17	.09	.34	.20	.18	.25
Injuries	1.22	1.37	.85	.83	.94	.5

SOURCE: National Center for Health Statistics, U.S. Department of Health and Human Services, "Current Estimates from the National Health Interview Survey, United States, 1985," Vital and Health Statistics, Series 10, No. 160, DHHS Pub. No. (PHS) 86–1588.

of Economics and Statistics 63 [1981]: 77–87). He also found that while women were more likely than men to miss a day of work for illness, the amount of time lost per absent worker was lower for women. He attributes this to the possibility that women may recognize and treat health problems at an earlier stage than men. Supporting this idea is the fact that while women miss more days from work at early ages, after age 55, absentee rates for women are lower than they are for men. Women may thus be making early investments in their health which they recapture over their working lives. By staying home and taking care of their illnesses when they first occur, women may increase their productive work lives.

Lynn Paringer examined work-loss differences between men and women for specific illnesses. She also found that once earnings, sick leave, occupation, age, and health status of a worker were controlled, there were no significant differences between the sexes in terms of work loss. Paringer found that days of work loss for a given illness increased with age, but that the increase was significantly higher for men than for women ("Women and Absenteeism: Health or Economics?" American Economic Review 73 [1983]: 123–127).

These research findings suggest that while women experience significantly higher absentee rates than men, most of the differential can be explained by occupation and earnings variables. A worker's sex is not a determining factor in work loss. This is an important finding since an employer looking at summary absentee data may conclude that women workers, by virtue of their higher absentee rates, are less dependable than their male counterparts. Research simply does not support this conclusion. Absentee rates are dependent on earnings, occupation, and age. They are not affected by a worker's sex.

Further References. J. Hedges, "Absence from Work—Measuring the Hours Lost," *Monthly Labor Review*, October 1977, 16–23. J. Sindelar, "Differential Use of Medical Care by Sex," *Journal of Political Economy* 90 (1982): 1003–1019. D. Taylor, "Absent Workers and Lost Work Hours, May 1978," *Monthly Labor Review*, August 1979, 49–52. D. Wingard, "The Sex Differential in Mortality Rates: Demographic and Behavioral Factors," paper presented at the annual meeting of the Society for Epidemiologic Research, Minneapolis, Minn., June 1980.

LYNN PARINGER

ACQUIRED IMMUNE DEFICIENCY SYNDROME (AIDS) is the disease of the decade. Sorting the implications of this sexually transmitted disease* for women is a process that will continue for years. Initially it was thought that AIDS was only a problem for gay men and IV drug users, but later even lesbians* were recommending rubber dams and plastic gloves to prevent the spread of AIDS between women. With continued analysis of the proportionately few women who have been diagnosed as having AIDS, a risk pattern has emerged. Women who use IV drugs and share needles are at great risk of exposure. Women who have sexual intercourse with men who use "dirty" needles for IV drug use are at significant risk. Women who have been the recipients of blood products or donor semen not certified free from AIDS antibodies are at risk. Women who have penile-vaginal or anal sex with large numbers of men without benefit of a barrier such as a condom increase their risk. Lastly, women comprise 90 percent of health care workers with an occupational risk of exposure to the AIDS virus.

It is becoming increasingly clear that women are much more likely to contract AIDS from men than men are from women and that women are at much greater risk of exposure to the AIDS virus when they have genital sex with men than when women have sex with women.

AIDS does affect women differentially, however. In analysis of patients diagnosed with AIDS (G. Kolata, "Women with AIDS Seen Dying Faster," *New York Times* [October 19, 1987], 1, 10) it was noted that women diagnosed with AIDS are more likely to suffer from multiple infections resulting in earlier death than men diagnosed with AIDS. Women with AIDS are more likely than men to be black or Hispanic. Attempts to explain these findings have pointed to women's relatively lower income status and limited access to health care, and to the prevalence of drug use in the communities of color. The role of women's hormones is also unknown. It appears that AIDS may be exacerbated by pregnancy, and it is clear that AIDS can be transmitted from mother to fetus*. It is then vital that women contemplating pregnancy know whether they have been

exposed to the AIDS virus. However, it is important to question blanket elimination of childbearing for women who test positive to the presence of antibodies
to AIDS until it is known whether a percentage of antibody-positive people can
live without developing the syndrome itself and what antibody-positive status
means in regard to maternal transmission.

Women concerned about possible exposure to the AIDS virus can be tested
at confidential, low-cost testing sites available in many areas. (They can be
located through the local health department.) Because of the hysteria surrounding
AIDS and because the primary risk groups are among the most socially oppressed
groups in our society, women should be careful to seek testing only where it is
anonymous and voluntary, accompanied with personal counseling and education.
Notification of test results should be undocumented to avoid possible cancellation
of health or life insurance, loss of employment, or other discriminatory actions
that are frequently not subject to legal intervention (J. S. Zones, "AIDS: What
Women Need to Know," *Network News* [National Women's Health Network],
November/December 1986).

The AIDS era presents heterosexually active women with new decisions about
birth control. Oral contraceptives provide no protection against sexually transmitted diseases, a threat with new potency since AIDS is fatal. Using oral
contraceptives when condoms are necessary as well puts contraceptive selection
in a whole new light.

Safe sex guidelines have become widely publicized wherever people will
tolerate disclosure of frank talk about sexual behavior. Most important is the
admonition that women avoid sharing needles if they are IV drug users and that
women having sex with men who are not known to be safe from infection should
require them to use condoms when having penile-vaginal sex or penile-anal sex
and when giving men oral sex. The challenge is to preserve sexual pleasure
while minimizing one's risk of AIDS and other sexually transmitted diseases.

Very little is written about young women (and men) coming of age in a time
when sexual interactions have become increasingly associated with the risk of
a deadly disease. Youngsters frequently ask their parents and teachers if they
can get AIDS from a kiss. In an era of AIDS adolescents face their own mortality
with the prospect of sexual interactions.

ELAINE WHEELER

ADDICTION is habitual or obsessive behavior that continues despite adverse
emotional, medical, and financial consequences. The behavior may be the use
of a substance (e.g., alcohol, drugs, cigarettes), activities (e.g., exercise, gambling), or destructive relationships.

Because addictions generally have been studied individually and from individual perspectives (biological, psychological, or sociological), there is little
agreement about the causes of addictive behavior. It is clear, however, that
gender plays an important, but widely varying, role. Gender may influence the
"addiction of choice" through variance between genders in the economic ability

to support different addictions (gambling costs more than food addictions), access to substances (housewives are more likely to be prescribed tranquilizers than are their husbands), and social expectations (there is more pressure on women to be thin).

Chemical substance abuse is more common among men than among women, except in two instances: more young women now smoke than do young men, and more women than men take prescribed psychoactive drugs. Why more young women than young men now smoke is not clear. But women visit physicians more often than do men and are much more likely to be prescribed mood-altering drugs. They are also less likely to ask the doctor, or be told by the doctor, what the drugs are and what their effects. Problems arising from unintended misuse of drugs by the elderly affect women more than men because of the greater number of elderly women.

Causes of Female Addictions. Research has discovered genetic influences in alcohol addiction and, to a lesser extent, in smoking, but in neither case are they the only influences. Other factors, often gender specific, are involved. Basic to all addictions, whether drugs, food disorders, or destructive relationships, seems to be low self-esteem. Since women are rarely encouraged to develop a strong sense of identity, their self-image and sense of self-worth tends to be weak.

Common problems among women include depression*, loneliness, family problems, serious illness, unexpected divorce*, sexual abuse, lack of support in nontraditional roles, and the pressures and stresses of the home and of the workplace. When problems become overwhelming, some women turn to religion; others, to therapy or devotion to work or outside activity; still others, to addictive behaviors.

Addiction is least among traditional women at ease in traditional roles. Women who challenge the system or are in any sort of vulnerable position are much more at risk. Incest and rape victims form a disproportionate percentage of the female alcoholic population; Native American women have a higher rate of alcoholism than white women; over one-third of all lesbians* have alcohol problems.

Women who do not enjoy the traditional housewife role may feel isolated and alone. They may seek relief from feelings of frustration, anger*, and/or guilt for wanting a life beyond dishes and diapers, in alcohol, pills, other drugs, or destructive relationships. So may the female head of household with a full-time job, home and child care*, and inadequate finances. As career women face the pressures and stresses of the job, some the same as those that drive men to addiction, some unique to women entering "nontraditional" areas of employment, they tend to meet those pressures the same way men have. Being one of the boys may equate with drinking like a man.

Fears, anxieties, and peer pressures of adolescent girls have made anorexia, bulimia, and other food disorders a growing problem. Also, advertising to encourage use of cigarettes by this age group seems effective. The ads picture women who are young, independent, and thin, the model most adolescent girls aspire to.

Cocaine, long believed to be nonaddictive, might seem at first the answer to many problems. Without mess, smell, or needle marks, it suppresses the appetite, helping to control weight, releases inhibitions, and gives a feeling of great energy. Many women are introduced to it by husbands or men friends—it has become part of the dating ritual in some circles.

Cross-Addiction. One addiction can reinforce or lead to another. To cope with depression and anxiety caused by cocaine, women may use alcohol or Valium. Bulimics use speed or coke to lose weight. In 1983, 40 percent of female Alcoholics Anonymous (AA) members (64 percent of those under 30) reported addiction to another drug. Chemical dependency and destructive relationships are a particularly frequent combination. Sex and Love Addicts Anonymous, based on the AA model, was begun by recovered alcoholics.

Effects of Addiction. The health problems associated with chemical addictions are serious and generally well known. They also can differ by gender. Alcohol affects women more rapidly and with greater intensity than it affects men. The differing ratios of water and fat in women's and men's bodies cause a difference in the metabolism of alcohol. Equal amounts consumed by a man and a woman of equal weight result in higher concentrations of alcohol in women's tissue. Estrogen may also increase the rate of absorption and may be the cause, or a major cause, of women's suffering greater liver damage sooner, and at lower consumption levels, than men. And addicted women are much more vulnerable to rape* and other sexual exploitation. Food disorders may result in health problems from rotting teeth to sterility to starvation.

Chemical addictions can cause sexual dysfunction and greatly increases the health risks to pregnant women and their offspring. Opiates and cocaine can cause complications leading to injury or death of the pregnant woman and spontaneous abortion or infant death. The infant death rate is four times higher for heroin addicts than for the general population.

Chemical substances may cross the placenta and affect the fetus, which may become addicted and/or suffer developmental problems from low birth weight to serious physical and mental anomalies. Nicotine may lead to low birth weight and subsequent health problems. Tranquilizers during the first trimester have been blamed for congenital defects such as cleft palate. Heavy drinking can result in fetal alcohol syndrome (FAS)—any, or a combination of several, physical and mental defects including small head, problems with the joints, serious heart defects, and mental retardation.

Addictions affect the nonaddicted. Inhaling others' tobacco smoke can be harmful. Effects of alcohol are especially tragic: one person dies every 20 minutes from automobile accidents caused by drunk driving. Alcohol plays a prominent part in wife battering (perhaps one-half of all reported cases) and rape. The victims may try to cope by turning to alcohol.

The effects of addiction on the families of the addicted are receiving increasing attention. Support groups have been organized for the spouses, children, and adult children of addicts, Al-Anon and Alateen programs for family members in alcoholic homes, Adult Children of Alcoholics groups for adults struggling with problems rooted in their growing up with an alcoholic parent.

Difficulty of Getting Women into Treatment. Although fewer women than men are addicted to chemical substances, they have a harder time breaking their dependency and are less likely to seek treatment: one in three alcoholics is a woman; one in five in treatment is a woman; one in three cocaine users is thought to be female; one in ten in treatment is female. One reason fewer women seek treatment is probably the stigma attached to alcoholism and drug abuse. That stigma is much greater for women than for men. The nineteenth-century appointment of the woman as the moral repository for society affects late twentieth-century attitudes. Women addicts are judged by harsher standards than are men; the low self-esteem of the addict is lowered still further as she internalizes society's judgment. Seeking treatment would mean acknowledging the addiction to herself and exposing herself to society's censure. Society too is less ready to suspect or acknowledge addiction in women. Doctors frequently misdiagnose it as depression and prescribe drugs that make the situation worse.

Another problem is that the agencies that funnel addicts into the treatment system tend to miss women. One is the traffic court, but women are less likely to be arrested for drunkenness than are men. If a woman is with a man in a car, chances are he is driving. If a woman is stopped for drunk driving, she may be driven home instead of being arrested.

Corporate programs feed into the system, but seldom include women. Most women in the workforce are underemployed in routine jobs than can be done well enough without being sober. Those, mostly males, with jobs on the career ladder are most valuable to employers and are most likely to be spotted for treatment. Also, frequent absences of women are more likely to be credited to "female problems" than to chemical addiction. For their part, women are less likely to admit need for help—because of the greater stigma of their addiction, fear of losing child custody, or lack of any arrangements for child care during treatment.

Housewives are even harder to get into the system than women in the workforce. They are usually farther into addiction before they, or other family members, are aware of the problem. And the family's fear of the "disgrace" may make them deny that a problem exists or to try to hide it within the home. A husband or male friend may even resist or actively oppose treatment if the addiction increases his control over the woman.

Although women smoke less and inhale less deeply than men, they are less successful in breaking nicotine addiction. One reason may be concern about gaining weight. Another may be less support in their attempts to quit. The irritability common to the withdrawal period and the expression of negative feelings that nicotine had controlled may cause some family members to encourage women to go back to smoking.

Treatment. Women face special problems in treatment. Health care professionals are not immune from stereotypes. Clinicians define "mental health" in terms of men. By definition a "mentally healthy" female is a mentally unhealthy human. Whereas men will be counseled to break those associations that led to the addiction, counseling for women may stress "adjustment." Women's anger may be labeled "pathological" because "healthy females" don't express anger. The gender of the therapist is probably not as important as her/his sensitivity to the special problems and needs of female clients.

When most of the addicted are male, treatment programs are designed with their needs in mind. Most alcohol and drug programs, then, are designed for men and may not meet women's needs. Females are likely to have associated medical problems that the treatment center may not be equipped to handle. Services like vocational education, job placement, and child care may be more necessary for the rehabilitation of women—the lack of child care facilities in conjunction with treatment programs is an especially important problem for women. In-patient treatment programs cannot be utilized by women with family responsibilities.

Most treatment programs include both men and women, but women's therapy groups are becoming more numerous as the need for programs that will meet the special needs of women is recognized. There are some Alcoholics Anonymous groups for women in larger population centers, and the number of separate therapy programs has increased as professionals and patients realize the need for them.

A women's program must be oriented toward meeting needs unique to women. It should include counseling and group therapy on issues of female sexuality; it should be able to treat on a five-day or out-patient basis and include a child care component, vocational training, and job placement. Rape counseling may be needed. Women of color need programs that take problems unique to them into account. Also more study is needed to better understand women's body chemistry. More data needs to be collected to better understand the etiology of women's addiction and to improve the diagnosis and treatment of women.

Further References. "Issues Related to Alcohol and Drug Abuse and the Mental Health of Women: Executive Summary," *Public Health Reports* 100 (1985): 95–98. H. B. Milkman and H. J. Shaffer, *The Addictions: Multidisciplinary Perspectives and Treatments* (Lexington, Mass., 1985).

ADDITIONAL WORKER EFFECT/DISCOURAGED WORKER EFFECT. The neo-classical model of women's labor force participation* implies that women may respond to an increase in the unemployment rate in one of two ways. They may increase their labor force participation to compensate for the fact that male breadwinners are out of work. This is termed the Additional Worker Effect. Alternatively, they may decrease their labor force participation because the higher unemployment rate makes finding a job more difficult. This is termed the Discouraged Worker Effect. Empirical studies find that for women the Discouraged Worker Effect dominates the Additional Worker Effect. This is one reason why women's unemployment rates fall relative to men's during recessions.

SUSAN B. CARTER

ADULTERY is voluntary extramarital intercourse with a person of the opposite sex, whether unmarried (single adultery) or married (double adultery). Ancient patriarchal societies (e.g., Amorite, Assyrian, Hebrew, Greek, Roman) did not consider extramarital intercourse adultery unless a married woman (or a concubine) was the offender. In some societies no distinction was made between seduction of a woman and rape* (laws of Middle Assyria, Athens). In Rome, after adultery was made a crime at law (lex Julia de adulteris, 17 B.C.), the married woman's offense was adultery; the married man's, the lesser crime of vice.

The double standard*, that only the woman's infidelity deserves serious punishment, has permeated thinking in all patriarchal societies. It rests in large part on the idea of woman as property. The male's property right in the female is an important factor in completely forbidding extramarital intercourse for females in about half of all human societies. In others, extramarital sexual activities may be allowed, or even required, in certain instances (e.g., in fertility rites or with guests as a sign of hospitality). In few has extramarital sex been freely permitted for women, although there have been periods when women's adultery in the upper levels of society, if discreet, has been quietly tolerated (e.g., eighteenth-century Western Europe).

In most patriarchal societies, a couple caught in the act of adultery could be killed with impunity by the offended husband or the woman's relatives (in Assyria and Rome the man could not be killed unless the wife were also). In fact, juries have refused to convict "wronged husbands" in some U.S. jurisdictions into the twentieth century. Legal punishment varied, but, when not capital, usually involved some form of public humiliation for the woman.

The Christian church officially insisted that adultery was as wrong for a husband as for a wife and that a wife's adultery could not be used as grounds for divorce*. However, the idea that married men should be subjected to the same restrictions as married women was never translated into the general consciousness of the Christian community or into the laws of medieval jurisdictions. As grounds for legal separation, one instance of a wife's adultery was usually sufficient, but a husband's adultery was grounds only if it created a public scandal. In fourteenth-century Perugia, an adulterous wife was flogged out of town and exiled; an adulterous husband was fined 50 pounds if the adultery was committed in his own house and was public knowledge. In thirteenth-century Spain a married man's sleeping with a Moslem or Jewish woman was not considered an offense. For a woman, adultery with a Moslem or Jew was the most disgraceful, most harshly punished act she could commit.

The Protestant emphasis on the patriarchal family tended to strengthen the emphasis on the need for female purity. Wherever divorce was allowed, adultery was a cause. And for a century after the Reformation, laws against adultery were tightened up in both Protestant and Catholic countries, with severe flogging or death frequent penalties for female offenders. Afterwards, the laws were generally relaxed, and seldom enforced. However, adultery was still a crime. In the United States after World War II only three states had no criminal penalties for it. In other states, the penalties ranged from a $10 fine to imprisonment for one offense.

In the twentieth century, with more openness about sexual matters, extramarital intercourse (EMI) has become a subject of serious study. The Kinsey reports (A. Kinsey et al., *Sexual Behavior in the Human Male* [Philadelphia, 1948] and A. Kinsey et al., *Sexual Behavior in the Human Female* [Philadelphia, 1953]) laid the groundwork for all subsequent study of EMI. Morton Hunt, in his follow-up study *Sexual Behavior in the 1970s* (Chicago, 1974), proposed an estimate of the incidence of EMI that indicated little change since the Kinsey studies: that the percentage of men who have ever engaged in EMI is close to, but not over, 50 percent; that of women, 18 percent. For men, he found little overall increase since 1948 and only a modest increase in the youngest (18 to 24 year old) cohort of his sample. For women in the under 25-year-old group, however, he found an increase from 8 to 24 percent, a change of "historic dimensions." This approach toward equality in extramarital activity by young men and women would indicate a radical repudiation of the double standard by young women. Studies since Hunt's (e.g., C. Tavris and S. Sadd, *The Redbook Report on Female Sexuality* [New York, 1977] and P. Blumstein and P. Schwartz, *American Couples* [New York, 1983]) indicate that the trend toward equal participation in extramarital affairs between men and women has continued: EMI rates among women continue to increase slightly, especially among the college educated. Husbands' rates are still higher than wives' but have remained fairly constant.

Despite the assault on the double standard, however, wives were still more often accepting of the extramarital activity of husbands than were husbands of extramarital activity by wives. Men were more likely to engage in relationships that they label as purely sexual than were women and to approve of extramarital affairs than were women. They reported more desire for extramarital sex and engaged in it earlier in their marriages, had more partners, and were more likely to consider their actions justified and to feel less guilt than were women. Women more often reported that their extramarital affairs stemmed from emotional involvement or grew out of marital dissatisfaction. They also reported more guilt feelings (S. P. Glass and T. L. Wright, "Sex Differences in Type of Extramarital Involvement and Marital Dissatisfaction," *Sex Roles* 12 [1985]: 1101–1120).

Despite the explosion of literature, and talk, advocating sexual freedom of marriage partners, group sex, mate-swapping, etc., the "permissiveness" of the 1970s was much more in evidence among the single than among the married (Hunt, 270–274). The spread of herpes and the fear of AIDS brought a change of atmosphere in the 1980s, with "permissiveness" giving place to caution, "swinging" to talk of "safe sex."

Nearly all those engaging in extramarital intercourse still attempt to keep it secret from their marriage partner. If discovered, it can be devastating. To the marriage partner it may cause feelings of intense anger*, profound hurt, loss of self-esteem, trust, and confidence. In the perpetrator, it can cause inner conflict, guilt, and, if revealed, shame, and sometimes relief. It often either destroys or irreparably damages the marriage. The modern marriage, unlike most marriages in previous ages, is based on emotional involvement. The discovery of marital infidelity can destroy that emotional cement the keeps this important human relationship together.

AFFIRMATIVE ACTION is a term first officially used in a 1961 executive order, issued by President Kennedy, requiring a nondiscrimination statement in all federal contracts. Title VII* of the Civil Rights Act of 1964 authorized the courts to "order such affirmative action as may be appropriate" in order to remedy the results of discrimination*. Executive Order 11246* (1965) and the associated regulations of Revised Order Number 4 (1971) identified for the first time specific actions to be taken by federal contractors to eliminate the effects of present and past discrimination.

Generally, affirmative action is considered to be an active form of nondiscrimination that is comprised of identifying the underrepresentation in all conditions of employment of qualified women, racial/ethnic minorities, and other protected groups, and then taking specific actions to enable an employer to utilize the protected groups according to their availability (that is, to achieve affirmative action goals). These actions may include, for example, additional recruitment and advertising for qualified members of protected groups as well as developing, implementing, and monitoring employment policies that are designed to encourage increased protected group representation. Affirmative action does *not* involve the setting of quotas, which are illegal unless assigned by the courts when discrimination is found; nor does it mean the hiring of less qualified women, racial/ethnic minorities, or other members of protected groups. The person most qualified for a position should be hired, promoted, etc., without regard to race, sex, national origin, or other non–job-related characteristic; however, the employer must be able to document that good faith efforts were made to recruit qualified women, racial/ethnic minorities, or others.

Further References. E. Kirby, *Yes You Can: The Working Woman's Guide to Her Legal Rights, Fair Employment, and Equal Pay* (Englewood Cliffs, N.J., 1984). U.S. Department of Labor Women's Bureau, *A Working Woman's Guide to Her Job Rights (Leaflet 55)* (Washington, D.C., 1984).

DAYLE MANDELSON

AGE-EARNINGS PROFILES are plots of workers' earnings over their life-times. Men's age-earnings profiles tend to rise steeply from their labor force entry until about age 55 and then decline slightly. Women's age-earnings profiles tend to be flat.

SUSAN B. CARTER

AGE OF CONSENT is the age fixed by law at which one's consent to certain acts, such as sexual intercourse and marriage*, is valid. The age of consent for females has generally been younger than that for males, but in the United States all except three states now have the same age for both. Over time the age of consent has risen, from 12 for women and 14 for men in the Middle Ages to 18 in most states of the United States today (exceptions: in Louisiana it is 21 and in Mississippi 15 for women, 17 for men).

AGING of women is a topic of scholarly and popular interest. In part, this interest is the result of the significant and continuing increases in life expectancy for women in modern industrial societies, so that today, on average, women may expect to live 7.3 years longer than men. This means that our rapidly growing older population will be largely composed of women who have outlived their husbands; indeed, at age 85 and over, there are 42 men for every 100 women. Thus, the problematic aspects of old age—appropriate housing, adequate income, health status, loneliness, and the likelihood of institutionalization—will be primarily experienced by elderly women, and most acutely by black women.

The other spur to interest in women and aging comes from the new feminist movement. As part of a general revisioning of women's lives, many male-defined stereotypes of the female experience were subject to practical and scholarly analysis and found wanting. The great majority of women do *not* go into mental depression during midlife, mourning their lost reproductive capacities. To the contrary, the postmenopausal period today is one of renewed vitality and enhanced self-esteem. This positive shift is even more pronounced in nonindustrial societies, where women's social power and personal freedom expand greatly once the women are past the reproductive years.

The picture that emerges is, therefore, quite mixed. On the one hand, although negative images of older women remain deeply embedded in popular culture and medical literature, the situation for most middle-aged women in our society has greatly improved over the past two decades, thanks to changes wrought by the new feminist movement. Compared to their mothers and grandmothers, women entering midlife today have higher levels of educational attainment, a history of relatively continuous labor force participation*, and a wider range of choice in combining the various strands of their lives: family*, work, friendships, community service. As a consequence, their mental health status has dramatically improved.

On the other hand, many midlife women and most of the very old will be subject to extraordinary stress, due not to aging per se but to particular social and economic deprivations. Given the high rate of divorce*, large numbers of middle-aged women will become "displaced homemakers" without marketable skills (having devoted themselves to home and husband), too young for social security benefits, and with children too old to qualify for Aid to Families with Dependent Children. When they do find jobs, these are typically low-wage as well as low-skill. Few will be awarded, and even fewer receive, support payments from the ex-spouse. Women's chances of remarriage at age 40 are relatively low and decline steadily with age, in contrast to men's (whose remarriage rates remain high and stable until very old age).

Very old women also have a special set of constraining conditions. At age 75 and over, fewer than one in four women are living with a spouse (compared to 71 percent of males age 75 +). Two-thirds will be widowed, having spent several years monitoring the terminal illness of their husband. In some respects, however, elderly widows have an advantage over widowers, in that they are better able to construct supportive interpersonal networks out of surviving friends and relatives, including their own adult children. Because of liberalizing amendments to the Social Security Act in 1965 and 1972, including Medicare, most widows can remain independent, in their own household, until very old age.

But survival as an elderly widow still carries certain economic penalties; a widow's benefit is roughly two-thirds of what the couple received, while fixed living costs do not decrease. Further, the original benefits for most people over age 75 today were computed on a smaller base of earnings than for later retirees, so that their incomes are at the lower end of the distribution. Although the poverty rate for all persons age 65 + is slightly below that for the nation as a whole, the rate for elderly women is almost double that of their male age peers. Older women most likely to have incomes below poverty level are those "unrelated individuals" living in single-person households. For black female unrelated individuals age 65 +, the poverty rate is two in three.

An additional concern of the very old is health. While older men are more likely than older women to have serious "killer" conditions, it is women who live long enough to develop debilitating chronic ailments that eventually sap their strength and savings. But the age of onset of such illnesses has been pushed back, thanks to better nutrition and health habits in successive cohorts of elderly, as well as improved medical care at earlier ages. Therefore, older women in the future will not only live longer but do so with fewer functional limitations.

Nonetheless, caregiving to the frail elderly will remain a major problem for women—for the recipient of care as well as the adult daughter who typically provides it. Having to relinquish one's hard-won independence will be increasingly difficult for future cohorts of very old women. When a parent reaches the point of needing full-time daily care, her children will themselves be entering old age. But as the fastest growing segment of the older population today is the age group 85 + , we may expect that at least one in four adult women will provide home care to an elderly relative for an average of five years.

For these reasons, every public program for America's older population is a feminist issue. Income maintenance, housing, transportation, health care, nursing home regulation, community-based home health services, respite care for the homebound—each of these is crucial to the quality of life of women of both older generations, for it is they more than men who benefit from any increase in the level of public commitment. Conversely, it is they who will be dispro-portionately harmed by any cutbacks. Policy toward the aged is not gender neutral. And whatever is not provided through public sources will become the exclusive responsibility of other women: their daughters and daughters-in-law or the poorly paid employees of the institutional care system.

Further References. J. K. Brown, V. Kerns, and Contributors, *In Her Prime: A New View of Middle-Aged Women* (South Hadley, Mass., 1985). M. R. Haug, A. B. Ford, and M. Sheafor (eds.), *The Physical and Mental Health of Aged Women* (New York, 1985). B. B. Hess and E. Markson (eds.), *Growing Old in America: New Perspectives on Old Age*, 3rd ed. (New Brunswick, N.J., 1985). E. Markson (ed.), *Older Women* (Lexington, Mass., 1983).

BETH B. HESS

AGORAPHOBIA is the most frequently occurring clinical phobia with a high prevalence rate for females (65 to 85 percent female). The American Psychiatric Association (*Diagnostic and Statistical Manual of Mental Disorders* [3rd ed., Washington, D.C., 1980], 226–230) defines agoraphobics as showing: "A marked fear of being in public places. . . . Normal activities are increasingly restricted as the fears or avoidance behaviors dominate the individual's life . . . behaviors may occur with or without panic attacks. . . ." Clinical symptoms include (1) "fear of fear": worry about the physical symptoms escalating to panic attacks; (2) avoidance behaviors (the phobias); (3) self-sufficiency problems (needing others to be with them); (4) unassertiveness; and (5) depression* (D. Chambless and A. Goldstein [eds.], *Agoraphobia: Multiple Perspectives on Theory and Treatment* [New York, 1982]).

For many women, agoraphobia begins in the late teens or soon after marriage* or motherhood and may last a lifetime (mean age of onset is mid-twenties). Agoraphobic symptoms appear to be related to stress associated with marital or interpersonal conflict.

In the past ten years, with the advent of behavior therapy and the documented success of exposure treatment and the use of psychopharmacological drugs for alleviating the major symptoms of agoraphobia, there has been an enormous increase in the research and clinical literature on agoraphobia and anxiety dis-orders.

The major treatments can be categorized as the biological versus the more sociocultural and the psychodynamic versus the behaviorial. There have been attempts recently to integrate the various approaches. On one end of the spectrum are (1) biological theories that stress constitutional factors that predispose individuals to panic disorders and anxiety attacks. One popular theory, which has no research support, is that women have an inborn constitutional deficit (mitral valve prolapse [MVP]) that lowers their threshold for panic attacks. (2) Psychopharmacological theories, which consider physiological arousal deficits as primary, are gaining in popularity as more positive research findings are reported. On the other end of the spectrum are (1) psychodynamic theories that consider early attachment problems, conflict, and/or sexual repression as primary, (2) learning theories that favor a conditioning model, and (3) social/cultural feminist theories that stress familial learning and societal factors.

Most theorists agree that agoraphobia runs in families, although they differ on the attention paid to familial factors in treatment. Agoraphobics are typically found to have mothers and even grandmothers who are classified as having agoraphobia or anxiety disorders themselves. (In one study 34 percent had a phobic mother, whereas only 6 percent had a phobic father.)

Phobic symptoms are reported to coexist with personality patterns of dependency and avoidance. Generally, mothers have been blamed for the presumed childhood overprotection linked to the symptoms, with little attention directed toward fathers. Feminist writers and therapists who addressed the issue of why agoraphobics are predominantly female argue against a constitutional factor. They stress that both parents create a climate for the inculcation and continued fostering of an agoraphobic ideology of extreme helplessness and dependency that results from overtraining in the stereotypic aspects of the female role. Researchers on female agoraphobics report low scores on sex-role stereotyping scales that measure instrumentality, activity, and assertiveness. The low scores support the link between phobias and stereotypic feminine behavior.

Whereas agoraphobia has been characterized as a high prevalence disorder for women and linked to a stereotypic female socialization pattern, the most popular treatments have been some variant of behavior therapy that generally do not put women's issues in the foreground. While psychoanalysts have been interested in treating agoraphobics, such treatment stresses the lifting of sexual repressions and/or conflict resolution. These traditional therapies have not been demonstrated to be effective. Instead, the majority of female agoraphobics seek out treatments at behaviorally oriented anxiety disorder clinics and self-help programs. The main features of such programs are variants of behavioral treatment entailing assessment and treatment for the fear of fear, anxiety or panic attack. The client is taught anxiety management techniques, i.e., relaxation and breathing exercises. Sometimes antianxiety drugs are used. Next there is treatment for phobic avoidance through exposure to feared situations. This may involve imaginal or real-life exposure treatment that teaches the client to confront rather than avoid the feared situation. (In imagination she constructs a hierarchy of her fears, from least to most frightening, and then works out a program of assignments to confront these feared situations in real life.) A key goal is the acquisition of coping, problem solving, and assertiveness skills. Most behavioral programs also feature some variant of cognitive therapy, that is, the client is enabled to get in touch with irrational or unproductive thinking about her anxieties and phobias (e.g., "I can't handle myself when anxious") and taught to either combat it or substitute more productive thinking (e.g., "I can learn how to cope with anxiety").

For the most part, behavior therapists have been somewhat successful in designing short-term treatments that feature exposure to the feared stimuli as primary. In most studies, 60 to 70 percent of the cases are reported to be improved. Yet for some agoraphobics such programs may not be as helpful as promised. There are reports of high dropout rates, resistance, and dissatisfaction with behavioral treatment.

Since feminists have argued that agoraphobics were socialized to be "stereotypically female," behavior therapy can be construed as a model therapy for remediation of the avoidant, dependent behaviors through the development of more independent coping strategies. However, given the high dropout rate and the resistance of many agoraphobics to behavioral treatment, there is need for an expanded cognitive/behavioral treatment for agoraphobics that takes account of ongoing interpersonal stresses, e.g., being in the wife role. Consequently, increasing attention is being paid to interpersonal variables through work with couples in phobic treatment programs. Given the importance of the therapist in teaching the female agoraphobic client new ways of behaving, feminist therapists have also focused on the therapist-client process as an additional ingredient for fostering change.

Further References. K. A. Brehony, "Women and Agoraphobia: A Case for the Etiological Significance of the Feminine Sex Role Stereotype," in V. Franks and E. Rothblum (eds.), *The Stereotyping of Women: Its Effects on Mental Health* (New York, 1983). I. G. Fodor, "The Phobic Syndrome in Women," in V. Franks and V. Burtle (eds.), *Women in Therapy* (New York, 1974). I. G. Fodor, "Cognitive/Behavior Therapy for Agoraphobic Women: Toward Utilizing Psychodynamic Understanding to Address Family Belief Systems and Enhance Behavior Change," in M. Braude (ed.), *Women, Power and Therapy* (New York, 1987). G. Thorpe and I. Burns, *The Agoraphobic Syndrome* (New York, 1983).

IRIS G. FODOR

ALIMONY (SPOUSAL SUPPORT) is an allowance for support or maintenance. The use of the term is now confined almost exclusively to payments made to support one party to a marriage* after the dissolution of the marriage by separation or divorce*. Alimony may be granted for a term of years or until the death of one of the parties or the remarriage or cohabitation with a member of the opposite sex by the recipient.

By the eleventh century the medieval church had succeeded in making marriage indissolvable, but in a few instances it permitted separation. Since the couple were still legally married and the husband continued to control the wife's property, maintenance for the wife had to be provided. The husband, unless the wife was living openly in adultery, had to provide the wife's necessaries, which would vary according to the status and wealth of the erstwhile partners.

With the Reformation, in all Protestant countries marriage became a civil contract, and except in England, divorce became possible on very restricted grounds (chiefly adultery and impotence). Since the divorce proceedings were adversarial, alimony became tied to the idea of guilt and innocence.

In the United States marriage was regulated by the colonies, then by the individual states. After the American revolution, grounds for divorce were expanded in many states by the legislatures and/or by judicial interpretation of "cruelty." By the opening of the twentieth century women were receiving far more divorces than men, but few were granted alimony, and even fewer actually received it—a pattern which persists.

Through the nineteenth and early twentieth centuries a welter of laws that differed widely and a rising divorce rate were the subjects of concern and debate among liberal and conservative reformers, but little change was made in the granting of alimony (by World War II three states allowed alimony to husbands under certain circumstances). The movement for divorce reform that began in the late 1960s, however, did address this issue, and a new standard, "rehabilitation," was adopted as the goal of alimony in the Uniform Marriage and Divorce Act of 1974, a model law approved for state adoption. Since the late 1960s almost every state has made some changes in its divorce laws. About one-third have moved in the direction of "rehabilitative" alimony.

With rehabilitative alimony, if the dependent partner, whether male or female (in 1979 the Supreme Court struck down gender-based alimony laws), is deemed capable of becoming economically self-sufficient, alimony is provided for a limited time period and includes, in addition to maintenance, a sum sufficient to pay for education or training* that is supposed to allow for earnings that will approximate the person's economic status during marriage.

In 1986, all states made provision for alimony except Texas. Many states had eliminated consideration of fault, but two, Louisiana and Idaho, specifically limit the possibility of alimony to the innocent party, while 14 others take misconduct into account. Florida, Georgia, North Carolina, South Carolina, and Virginia prohibit the granting of alimony to anyone guilty of adultery*.

Fourteen states had, with varying degrees of explicitness, moved in the direction of temporary alimony. For example, in Delaware, for anyone married less than 20 years, alimony is limited to 2 years. In New Hampshire, if there are no minor children, alimony is limited to 3 years, and will cease three years after the youngest child reaches its majority.

Rehabilitative alimony, although it has, at least to some extent, reduced the fraud and cheating that pervade the whole system of child support and alimony payment, has not been entirely successful, especially from the viewpoint of the dependent (with few exceptions, the female) partner. The premise that after a few years of training the ex-wife will be able to find entry-level employment allowing her a standard of living in any way comparable to her ex-husband's is ludicrous. Older women, in particular full-time homemakers, are especially left high and dry. Those without other income and marketable skills have little likelihood of earning enough to stay above the poverty level. The need has led to displaced homemaker laws in many states, but the quantity and quality of the services provided vary widely.

ALTERNATIVE LIFE-STYLES. See SEXUAL ORIENTATION

AMNIOCENTESIS is a procedure that can be used to detect fetal health problems, both genetic and environmental, through tests performed on amniotic fluid. By the early 1980s amniocentesis could be used to assess the sex and maturity of the fetus* and to diagnose around 90 prenatal health problems through a variety of biochemical tests on and the karotyping of fetal cells in the fluid. Among the anomalies that can be detected or diagnosed are Down's syndrome, Tay-Sachs disease, and neural tube defects. Anomalies such as cleft palate and clubfoot cannot be detected. Women should recognize the potential for abuse of amniocentesis, especially in its use in determining the sex of the fetus. (See also REPRODUCTION, ETHICS OF.)

ANDROCENTRISM places man in the center and woman on the periphery. In 1903 Lester F. Ward defined androcentric theory as "the view that man is primary and woman secondary, that all things center, as it were, about man, and that woman, though necessary to the work of reproduction, is only a means of continuing the human race, but is otherwise an unimportant accessory" (*Pure Sociology*, p. 292). Feminists picked up the word from Charlotte Perkins Gilman's use of it in *The Man-Made World: Our Androcentric Culture* (1911), and use it as a term signifying man's assumption of superiority over females and other "defective" beings and man's biases in conflating and confusing the masculine with the generic. Other words meaning essentially the same thing are "masculinist," "masculist," "phallism," and "male chauvinist."

ANDROGYNY is the combination of masculine and feminine characteristics within a person. The idea of androgyny is an ancient one rooted in classical mythology and literature. Since the early 1970s it has been widely adopted as a new sex-role alternative to the dichotomous psychological characteristics and roles traditionally prescribed for the sexes. In its most generic sense, androgyny signifies an absence of any sex-based differentiation, including unisex dress styles, bisexuality*, and hermaphroditism. Social scientists generally restrict usage of "psychological androgyny" to describe an individual who manifests in personality or behavior a combination of characteristics labeled as masculine and feminine in our society.

The concept of psychological androgyny is based in previous ideas about the nature of psychological differences between the sexes, but reflects tolerance of a much broader range of sex-role options for men and women. Traditional notions of sex differentiation held that the sexes were or ideally ought to be as different psychologically as they were physically. The core of those characteristics stereotypically associated with women (femininity*) is sensitivity, emotionality, selflessness, and interrelationships with others (expressive/communal). Characteristics associated with men (masculinity) center around goal orientation, assertiveness, self-development, and separation,from others (instrumental/agentic). The association of these instrumental/agentic characteristics exclusively with men and expressive/communal characteristics with women was considered typical, expected, and psychologically healthy. Individual deviation either through failure to exhibit attributes typical of one's sex or through endorsement of some characteristics atypical of one's sex implied psychological maladjustment of some sort.

This traditional model did not account for the presence of similarities across the sexes or differences within the sexes in feminine and masculine characteristics. Also with the resurgence of the feminist movement, the sex-role values embodied within this model increasingly appeared to be overly restrictive and outdated. The concept of psychological androgyny provided a way to frame sex-role alternatives in terms of masculinity and femininity without the prescriptive, sex-specific values of more traditional views.

Proponents of psychological androgyny generally assume that masculinity and femininity are independent but not mutually exclusive groups of characteristics existing in everyone to varying degrees. Individuals can be meaningfully described by the extent to which they endorse each group as self-descriptive. Both masculinity and femininity have a unique and positive but not sex-specific impact upon a person's psychological functioning (e.g., both sexes benefit from being feminine). Thus, possession of high levels of both sets of characteristics, or androgyny, should represent the most desirable, even ideal, sex-role alternative.

Descriptions of psychological androgyny differ considerably according to what types of psychological characteristics are emphasized. All of the descriptions portray a blending of or an ultimate transcendence of sex-linked dichotomies of personality characteristics and behavior. Androgynous persons have been frequently defined as those who possess both masculine and feminine personality traits. Other descriptions have emphasized possession of socially appropriate, observable behaviors, or thought processes that do not rely upon sex-related cues or meanings. The manner in which masculinity and femininity might work together to produce androgyny has also been variously explained. Androgyny may mean the balancing or moderating of masculinity and femininity by each other, a beneficial summation of the positive qualities of femininity and masculinity, the emergence of new qualities, or elimination of sex-stereotypic standards in an individual's perceptions and decisions, thus making masculine/feminine distinctions irrelevant.

An especially influential early description of androgynous persons proposed by Sandra Bem portrays them as flexible and adaptable, with an ability and willingness to engage in either masculine or feminine behavior as the situation warrants. In contrast, predominantly feminine or masculine (sex-typed) individuals presumably use sex-based standards to guide their behaviors, resulting in a seriously limited repertoire of options.

Research on psychological androgyny indicates that researchers have somewhat succeeded in capturing the expressive/communal and instrumental/agentic nature of femininity and masculinity through their newly developed femininity and masculinity measures. However, individuals' masculinity and femininity self-descriptions often do not strongly relate to other aspects of sex roles (e.g., attitudes or behaviors). Masculinity has proven to be much more closely related to individuals' self-esteem and psychological adjustment than is femininity. Masculinity's greater strength in this area probably stems from the more positive valuing of masculine characteristics in American society.

Numerous studies have attempted to demonstrate that androgynous individuals enjoy mental health benefits not shared with those who are sex-typed, or those who see neither set of characteristics as particularly self-descriptive. Androgynous persons do tend to score as the best adjusted on a variety of measures, although the data are not conclusive. Contrary to researchers' early expectations, individuals who are high in masculinity (and low in femininity) often appear to be as well off as androgynous persons. However, individuals low in both masculinity and femininity are clearly disadvantaged. Evidence for sex differences in the androgyny literature suggests that the process, likelihood, and implications of becoming androgynous may be different for men and women. Finally, sex-role related characteristics are probably very complex and affected by a variety of factors. For example, an individual who is androgynous in self-description could appear to be quite traditional in attitudes, behavioral preferences, actual behaviors, and so on, depending upon the person and the situation. Today because of the nature of the research results and new refinements in sex-role theory, researchers are less likely to consider androgyny to represent a particular type of person who can be expected to behave in a consistent, predictable manner across a variety of situations.

Despite ambiguities suggested by research, mental health practitioners have found androgyny to be useful in naming new personality and behavioral alternatives for individuals coping with widespread social changes in how the sexes view themselves and each other. As a value and goal in counseling and psychotherapy, androgyny represents the desirability of moving away from prescriptions based upon biological sex alone toward enhancing of individual adaptability and choice.

Further Reference. E. P. Cook, *Psychological Androgyny* (Elmsford, N.Y., 1985).

ELLEN PIEL COOK

ANGER was viewed by Freud as an outgrowth of the destructive drive. Accordingly, traditional psychiatric and psychological formulations have regarded anger as an unruly emotion that must be subdued, as a problem that resides within the individual. This approach has, however, ignored some other important considerations about anger: the social context of anger and anger expression as an instrument for social change. Anger is a justifiable reaction to oppression and is a common experience among disfranchised persons. The failure to recognize the anger of disfranchised groups in the context of oppressive societal conditions has serious ramifications. If anger is viewed as a problem within the individual, then it becomes the domain of mental health professionals, who can then treat angry persons for their "personal" problem.

The experience of anger and societal reactions to it have special significance for disfranchised persons. Any individual who is frequently subjected to oppression and subjugation is likely to react with anger. When the traditional Freudian model is applied to analyze this anger, the culturally instigated anger comes to be viewed as an inherently dangerous drive, one which should be controlled and suppressed. For disfranchised individuals and groups the traditional perspective of anger has translated into a denial of the anger experience. This invalidation of anger can be viewed as a subtle means of social control in that there is no attempt to consider the social context in which anger arises. The focus is not on addressing the *source* of the anger—which may be injustice—but on removal or suppression of the *individual's* anger.

Further, anger expression is not considered acceptable behavior for women, and, in fact, women experience higher levels of anxiety and guilt over the experience and expression of anger and aggression than do men. Thus, women may be more likely to experience and to give in to the pressure to suppress their anger.

Some contend that even if anger is a justifiable reaction to oppression, it is a destructive emotion. Anger can, however, be experienced and expressed without being destructive; in fact, it can be a force for constructive change. For instance, if one person in a relationship feels anger over a sense of unfair treatment, an assertion of this anger that is designed to inform the other and to introduce an atmosphere of cooperative problem solving is more likely to lead to fruitful discussion than is either a stormy accusation or an attempt to suppress the anger.

On the other hand, anger that is expressed with the intent of injuring or insulting another is likely to have a destructive effect on interpersonal relationships since it may affect the capability of each person to trust the other. This instrumental anger manifests itself in attempts to control another, as in instances of intimidation. When the purpose of anger is to control another, the intimidator tends to evidence a lack of respect for others, presuming a right to control them. Typically, there is confusion over personal boundaries, such that the intimidator does not take personal responsibility for his/her reactions and refuses to understand and respect the rights of other persons.

For many, however, the concern is not how to express anger but whether to express it. Persons who are not aware of their oppression are not likely to experience anger over it. Women and other disfranchised persons are especially vulnerable to pressures to suppress their anger—pressures which may be imposed by themselves as well as by others. The cost of this suppression may, however, be lowered self-esteem, a sense of powerlessness, and fear of responding to or of even recognizing oppressive conditions. It must be recognized that anger may be a justifiable response to social-political injustice and, as such, may represent an individual or group attempt to challenge that injustice. An important contribution of the feminist analysis is an examination of the broader social context in which anger arises and the validation of anger as a justifiable response to oppressive social-political conditions.

MARY KAY BIAGGIO

ANOREXIA NERVOSA AND BULIMIA. Two eating disorders found primarily among young, white, affluent women in modern, industrialized countries. Anorexia nervosa is purposeful starvation alone or in combination with excessive exercising, occasional binge eating, vomiting, and/or laxative abuse. Twenty to 25 percent of initial body weight is lost. Bulimia denotes a regular pattern of binge eating followed by vomiting or purging with laxatives. Bulimics' weight is usually normal or close to normal. Both eating disorders involve a fear of fatness and a distorted body image. Elements of socialization relating to culture, family*, and sex roles clarify why anorexia nervosa and bulimia are most prevalent in certain groups.

Cultural Socialization. In developing countries, fatness is a symbol of wealth and a desired body shape. However, in modern, industrialized nations, fatness no longer signifies affluence because people generally have an adequate supply of food. In fact, it is possible to eat too much. Slimness therefore symbolizes discretionary eating, and appearance norms shift from plumpness to thinness.

Among vulnerable groups, the slim body ideal is accompanied by a fear of fatness and an urgent pursuit of slimness. The affluent tend to value slimness more and to be thinner than other individuals. With whites composing most of the upper strata, eating disorders are more prevalent among whites. As blacks become more upwardly mobile, eating disorders among them should increase.

The prevalence of anorexia nervosa and bulimia among women can be explained by the emphasis society places on women's appearance. Role models as portrayed in magazines and television advertisements are uniformly slender. Traditional beauty standards also reflect the slimness norm. Since 1959, *Playboy* centerfolds and Miss America have become progressively thinner; since 1970, Miss America has been slimmer than the average contestant. Because they are viewed as visual objects, women try to fulfill society's expectations about their appearance by conforming to the thinness orientation. Although a slimness norm for men exists, it is overridden by a strength/muscularity norm.

One indication of how urgently women pursue the thin body ideal is the national obsession with dieting. Over the last decade, there has been a vast increase in weight-reducing centers and diet plans, aids, and books. In a recent survey, more than half the women aged 24 to 54 had dieted at least once in the previous year; three-quarters dieted for cosmetic rather than health reasons.

Individuals who develop eating disorders are responding to the cultural norm of thinness and can be seen as extensions of the slim body ideal.

Family Socialization. Anorexics and bulimics are also socialized by their families to value thinness. Their siblings and parents are often preoccupied with eating, exercising, and body weight and shape. These issues become matters of rivalry among family members. In addition, parents of anorexics and bulimics emphasize achievement and perfection. Many individuals with eating disorders maintain near-perfect grades and fulfill high expectations. However, their accomplishments are not recognized by their family because such achievements are considered normal.

Another element of socialization within these families is the valuing of conformity. Anorexics and bulimics are negatively sanctioned for not adhering to parents' expectations of attractive appearance, diligence, and obedience. However, emotions, especially negative ones, are generally not verbalized; family members rarely express antagonism or anger*. Although these families appear to be close and supportive, their underlying interaction is impaired due to a lack of meaningful communication.

Families of individuals with eating disorders also exhibit excessive interdependency. Anorexics and bulimics are reluctant to make decisions without consulting their parents, especially their same-sex parent. This parent, in turn, reinforces dependency by encouraging the child's need for approval and discouraging efforts toward independence. Dependency and the desire to satisfy others' expectations maintain low self-esteem among those with eating disorders.

Anorexics and bulimics perceive their bodies and eating behavior as areas of autonomy. In order to cope with their families' enforced dependency and extreme emphasis on appearance, achievement, and conformity, anorexics starve and bulimics binge and vomit/purge. For females, dependency, conformity, and concern for appearance are compounded by cultural and sex-role socialization*.

Sex-Role Socialization. With divergent adaptations, individuals who have eating disorders are responding to sex-role expectations. Anorexics' girlish appearance is interpreted as a rejection of femininity* and womanhood. In contrast, bulimics are characterized as overconforming to traditional female roles.

By becoming progressively slimmer, anorexics lose breast and hip development, stop menstruating, and assume the body of prepubescence. In their reversion to a childlike appearance, anorexics remove themselves from the sexual arena and postpone adulthood. Through denial of hunger, adolescent females, those most likely to be anorexic, regain a feeling of control in the upheaval and powerlessness caused by changing bodily processes and social roles.

Despite their quest for power and control, anorexics actually become more dependent because of their weakness and frailty. Their extreme slimness parodies feminine appearance norms of delicacy and petiteness. Paradoxically, while anorexics reject female sexuality with their asexual bodies, they epitomize the idealized feminine traits of fragility and smallness.

Bulimics conform more thoroughly than anorexics to stereotyped femininity. Overidentifying with traditional female sex roles, bulimics have an intense need for validation from males. They seek approval from men and are exceedingly compliant to their partners' wishes. Dependent and passive, bulimics have a minimal sense of control in their lives.

Always striving to fulfill the idealized feminine role, these women expect to be rewarded by males' wanting and pursuing them. When they perceive rejection, bulimics blame the appearance of their bodies. Believing that they are not thin enough to please men, they begin to diet. When dieting fails to result in male companionship, bulimics use binging as a release from frustrations and from their strictly controlled lives. However, the fear of becoming fat from binging leads to vomiting or purging. The use of binging for a release and vomiting/ purging for weight control and purification becomes a self-perpetuating cycle. Thus, through different processes, bulimics and anorexics embody sex-role socialization. (See also FOOD AND EATING DISORDERS.)

Further References. M. Boskind-Lodahl, ''Cinderella's Stepsisters: A Feminist Perspective on Anorexia Nervosa and Bulimia,'' *Signs* 2 (1976): 342–356. S. Orbach, *Fat Is a Feminist Issue* (New York, 1979).

DIANE E. TAUB AND PENELOPE A. MCLORG

ANTIFEMINIST MOVEMENTS are organized opposition to feminist demands for equality of treatment under the law. Antifeminist movements have a largely female constitutency, although males appear to provide considerable financial support. Their major ideological theme is the defense of the traditional family, consisting of a breadwinning husband and nonemployed wife. This sexual division of labor is perceived as the basis of family stability and female privilege. According to the antifeminist argument, universalistic laws will deny women the special protections they have always enjoyed: the right to be exempt from military service*, to be financially supported by their husbands, and especially the right to be a full-time homemaker.

There have been two major waves of antifeminist activity in the United States: opposition to woman suffrage and more recently to the proposed Equal Rights Amendment*. Antisuffrage organizations existed before the twentieth century, but the founding of the National Association Opposed to Woman Suffrage in 1911 marked the heyday of the countermovement. This organization claimed 350,000 members and 25 state chapters, mostly in the northern and midwestern states. Between 1912 and 1916, they helped defeat 15 of the 21 state woman suffrage referenda before the male electorate. By 1917, however, antisuffrage momentum was lost as New York, long considered a key state by both sides, added a woman suffrage amendment to its state constitution; this event was quickly followed by presidential endorsement, congressional passage, and state ratification of the Nineteenth Amendment enfranchising 26 million American women in 1920.

   The anti-ERA movement was more successful than its predecessor. It began to coalesce in 1972, the first year of the ERA ratification process. Twenty-two states ratified the ERA in that year, and eight more followed in 1973; in most states, there was strong consensus on the amendment and political observers predicted that ratification by the required 38 states would occur long before the March 1979 deadline. But this did not happen. Despite a congressional extension to June 1982, the Equal Rights Amendment lapsed three states short of ratification. Significantly, no additional states ratified the ERA after January 1977, and several states attempted to rescind their ratification.

   The credit for reversing the momentum of the amendment goes to Phyllis Schlafly and her STOP ERA organization. While there have been other contemporary antifeminist organizations with such eye-catching names as Eve Reborn, HOT DOG (Humanitarians Opposed to Degrading Our Girls), and HOW (Happiness of Womanhood), STOP ERA overshadows all others in political influence. Schlafly founded STOP ERA in October 1972 and operated it with no paid staff, no membership dues, and minimal bureaucratic structure. But it had a charismatic leader who could mobilize her loyal constituency on a moment's notice and who proved adept at turning the liabilities of a housebound constituency into a strategic advantage.

   Phyllis Schlafly is an accomplished woman with extensive political experience. She put herself through college, did graduate work at Radcliffe and, after raising six children, earned a law degree. Long active in the Republican party, Schlafly served as speechwriter for presidential candidate Barry Goldwater, several times ran unsuccessfully for Congress, and before the ERA issue was best known for her writings in favor of a strong U.S. defense policy. After being defeated in a bitter contest for the presidency of the National Federation of Republican Women in 1967, she launched *The Phyllis Schlafly Report* to communicate with her loyal followers and the Eagle Trust Fund to receive donations for the support of conservative causes. Since 1968, Schlafly has held annual training conferences for her top lieutenants; in 1975, she began publication of the *Eagle Forum Newsletter*, which provides detailed instructions on antifeminist strategy. This includes emphasizing the differences between "libbers" and themselves by appearing in ladylike attire, holding bake sales, and lobbying state legislators with gifts of homemade jam. Telephone trees and letter-writing campaigns maximized the resources of homemakers who were difficult to mobilize for collective action. Schlafly also orchestrated clever media events including skits, original songs, props such as caskets for burying the ERA, and colorful quotes to keep the issue before the public.

   The success of STOP ERA derives also from its coalition building. Schlafly capitalized on her broad political network to forge links with such conservative organizations as the Moral Majority, the American Farm Bureau Association, and the John Birch Society, as well as single-issue groups against abortion*, pornography*, gun control, and unions. The strategy of integrating STOP ERA with the so-called New Right increased its available resources and enabled the adoption of more sophisticated tactics, such as the use of computer-generated mailing lists, political action committees, and highly coordinated campaign strategies targeting profeminist candidates for defeat.

Compared to feminist activists, anti-ERA women were older, less educated, more religious, more likely to be married, and less likely to be married to professionals or to be in professional occupations themselves. These background characteristics were more weakly associated with ERA opposition among the general population, who were more influenced by the anticipated consequences of the amendment: those who thought the ERA would harm male employment opportunities and lower family incomes were more likely to oppose it. Such findings suggest that the defeat of the Equal Rights Amendment was effected in part by the economic downturn of the 1970s, which may have increased its perceived threat.

Further References. J. K. Boles, *The Politics of the Equal Rights Amendment: Conflict and the Decision Process* (New York, 1979). S. E. Marshall and A. M. Orum, "Opposition Then and Now: Countering Feminism in the Twentieth Century," in Gwen Moore and Glenna D. Spitze (eds.), *Research in Politics and Society* (Greenwich, Conn., 1986), 2: 13–34. G. D. Spitze and J. Huber, "Effects of Anticipated Consequences on ERA Opinion," *Social Science Quarterly* 63 (1982): 323–331.

SUSAN E. MARSHALL

ASSERTIVENESS TRAINING, when popularized as part of the self-help movement for women, tended to be regarded as a means for women to "act like men" or "become aggressive," and as a result some people lamented the loss of "femininity*." The theoretical and clinical basis for assertiveness training rests on the assumption not that women (or men) should be more aggressive but rather that being assertive is different from being either passive or aggressive.

People's beliefs about a psychologically "healthy adult," "healthy man" and "healthy woman" reveal some striking contradictions. Most people describe a "healthy adult" and a "healthy man" in similar terms, saying they are strong, independent, capable of being a leader. By contrast, a "healthy woman" is described as weak, dependent, a better follower than leader. Being a "healthy woman" means not being a "healthy adult" (I. K. Boverman, D. M. Broverman, F. E. Clarkson, P. S. Rosenkrantz, and S. R. Vogel, "Sex Role Stereotypes and Clinical Judgements of Mental Health," *Journal of Consulting and Clinical Psychology* 34 [1970]: 1–7).

Assertiveness training addresses these contradictions. It provides training* in some of the attributes previously associated with being a "healthy adult."

How assertive behaviors are taught differs from one trainer to another, but the foundation is similar. Learning to be assertive involves recognizing what one's feelings and wishes are, developing insight into what one would like to say or do, and learning to express one's wishes directly and clearly. Assertive behavior is not intended to harm others, though it may include expressing anger and other negative feelings. It also includes setting limits and saying "no."

Assertiveness trainers often present their trainees with a "Bill of Rights," which includes such items as (1) you have a right to make your wants known to others and (2) you have a right to say "no" and to set limits on what you will permit.

Assertiveness training has focused more on women than men in part because women need to counteract their traditional upbringing. Women have traditionally been taught to pay attention to other people's needs and feelings rather than their own. As wives, mothers, and even daughters, women and girls are expected to nurture others and "be nice." Many of the problems women bring to assertiveness training concern their inability to express some of their own wishes—to ask someone else to do something for them or to refuse someone else's request. Unassertive behavior—not knowing how to make requests of others and not being able to say "no" to others—does not create good social or interpersonal relations if the woman subsequently feels resentful.

In assertiveness training women learn to distinguish among several kinds of behavior: (1) unassertive, (2) indirect aggressive, (3) direct aggressive, and (4) assertive.

Unassertive behaviors are accessions to another person's wishes, often against one's will and without a clear expression of one's own wishes. The unassertive person does what she's told, but grudgingly and perhaps ineffectively. An office worker who repeatedly works late against her will might put in time but not the necessary care and attention. Her unassertive accession undermines both her own and the other person's wishes.

Indirect aggressive behaviors are refusals to go along with another's wishes by offering an excuse or in some way deflecting the responsibility for one's choice. A woman asked to work overtime against her will might say she can't because her husband or members of the car pool would be inconvenienced and upset. "If you make me stay late again all those other people will be upset, and it will be your fault" is an example of indirect aggression if the woman does not assume responsibility for her own preferences, and it is direct aggression if she accuses the other persons of acting to harm her.

Direct aggressive responses impugn the other's motives or character: "You treat me like a servant . . . you seem to think I don't have anything better to do than stay late every day."

In contrast to the above modes of reacting, a woman behaving assertively acknowledges the wishes of the other person but also states her own needs and wishes: "I understand that you need someone to work overtime, but I count on being able to leave at 5:00 and do not want to work later than that." By assertively setting her own limits, she might hurt or anger the other person even though that is not her intention. She can be prepared for that consequence without assuming responsibility for the other person's reactions.

In the examples chosen above, the woman faces different types of risks. By complying unassertively, she risks feeling unworthy in her own estimation and appearing unworthy in the other's eyes. She appears to be cooperative but unenthusiastic and ungenuine. By refusing in an indirect aggressive manner, she risks angering the other person both because she did not comply and because she did not assume responsibility for her noncompliance. By refusing in a direct aggressive manner, she risks seeming hostile and provoking a hostile counterresponse. An assertive refusal is also risky if the other person is her boss. The worker might appear noncompliant and uncooperative and could risk losing a job or promotion. Assertiveness training does not change those power imbalances, but it does provide practice in the direct expression of one's needs and wishes without hostile accusations.

In these examples, the woman's position of power vis-à-vis the person making the request affects the objective risk she faces by making an assertive statement. If the woman is dependent on the other person for financial or other resources, she encounters greater risks for whatever actions she chooses. Assertiveness training does not encourage women to risk their jobs or other relationships at all costs. It rather provides alternatives to the other three modes of acting.

Scholars have studied the effects of assertiveness training to understand how it affects a woman's subsequent actions and feelings and how it affects other people's perceptions of the woman. Assertive women are often evaluated more negatively than assertive men. Being assertive, therefore, creates greater risks for women than for men. On the other hand, being unassertive or passive means not acting like a "healthy adult." Assertive women contradict the traditional sex-role stereotype, and that is part of the goal of assertiveness training.

Further References. N. Costrich, J. Feinstein, L. H. Kidder, J. Marecek, and L. Pascale, "When Stereotypes Hurt: Three Studies of Penalties for Sex-Role Reversals," *Journal of Experimental Social Psychology* 11 (1975): 520–530. M. Crawford, "Gender, Age, and the Social Evaluation of Assertion," *Behavior Modification* 11 (1987): 8–87. L. S. Kahn, "Group Process and Sex Differences," *Psychology of Women Quarterly* 8 (1984): 261–281. J. A. Kelly, J. M. Kern, B. G. Kirkley, and J. N. Paterson, "Reactions to Assertive Versus Unassertive Behavior: Differential Effects for Males and Females and Implications for Assertiveness Training," *Behavior Therapy* 11 (1980): 670–682.

LOUISE H. KIDDER

B

BATTERED WOMEN are women who are beaten by their husbands or male companions in a repeating pattern. Lenore Walker (*The Battered Woman* [New York, 1979], 55–77) has called this pattern the cycle of violence. This cycle encompasses the tension-building phase, the acute battering incident, and the phase of kindness and contrite loving behavior. While the problem of violence against women is not new, awareness of the scope of the problem has grown since the 1970s. The women's movement brought to attention the amount of violence perpetrated on women by men. Unbiased measurements have confirmed that evaluation. FBI statistics estimate that 1.8 million women are severely beaten each year by men with whom they live. An incident of wife abuse takes place every 18 seconds in the United States. Women are more likely to be injured in their homes than in any other place, but violence in the home has been seen as a private matter. Injuries to women have been minimized by those who have not wished to deal with the problem. Further, blame for the violence has frequently been placed on the victim, not only by the perpetrator but by society at large.

In the early 1970s Erin Pizzey, working with an advice center in London, became aware that many of those seeking assistance were battered women. Chiswick Women's Aid, the first shelter for battered women, grew from her awareness. In the United States the interest of women's groups led to the formation of local self-help groups and subsequently to state and national coalitions working to end violence against women. In the mid-1980s there are approximately 900 crisis intervention programs and shelters nationwide, most of which receive some state funding through welfare or mental health budgets. The most common approach to working with battered women is that of advocacy based on the value of self-determination and respect for the dignity of each individual. A typical program will provide a 24-hour hot line, safe shelter for women and their children, supportive advocacy, and access to social and legal resources. Information is provided about the dynamics of battering and the cycle of violence. In daily interaction and support groups women share their experiences, thus breaking their isolation. Counseling provides a safe place for women to express their feelings and to make choices about their lives. Child advocacy services emphasize the needs of children and teach parenting skills to mothers. Additionally, many shelter programs are developing counseling services for abusive men.

The experiences of shelter programs and research studies have given rise to a growing body of knowledge about violence between mates. The problem of battering crosses all socioeconomic and racial boundaries. Battering may be of a physical, psychological, or emotional nature. Physical violence may be pushing, shoving, slapping, punching, choking, biting, hitting with an object, or injuring with a weapon. Women entering shelters may carry bruises, cuts, black eyes, or broken bones. They may have been raped, held at gun or knife point, or thrown from vehicles. Women may come to shelter following hospitalization. Children may have been forced to watch or listen to abuse of their mothers. They also may have been physically abused. Psychological violence may take the form of continual verbal degradation of women and their capabilities. Over time constant criticism and policing of actions result in loss of self-respect and the conviction that the abuse is deserved. Emotional abuse in the form of threat of physical injury, loss of support, loss of life, or loss of children is incapacitating. Fearful women may feel forced to go along with the abuse to avoid harm to themselves or others.

Battering men typically have low self-esteem. They believe in the traditional role expectations that place men in the dominant position in the family. They believe that they are justified in confining women to a place men have defined and that violence is permissible to control their families. Women are an available target for the unleashing of feelings of anger* or of loss of control. Battering men are jealous and blame others for their problems. They may or may not batter while drinking alcohol. Alcohol or drugs become convenient excuses to unleash violence. Battering men frequently have been raised in homes where they were abused or saw their mothers abused. They strongly deny the need for a change in their behavior and are difficult to motivate in treatment.

Battered women are victims of violent crime, yet many stay in or return to abusive relationships. This behavior has been grossly misunderstood in the past as clinicians have speculated that these women enjoyed the abuse. It is now known that women stay or return for a variety of reasons. Many women are economically dependent on men. They frequently have no money for housing, transportation, or basic needs. They may lack job skills and have no information about job training, low-income housing, or financial assistance. They have often exhausted their support networks of family and friends. They may fear loss of their children or retaliation for having dared to try to leave, and they cannot depend on law enforcement to keep the abuser away. Women with financial resources may have different barriers to leaving an abusive marriage and different resources for surviving that marriage. They may fear loss of status, style of life, or educational opportunities for their children. They may be able to flee to a hotel or travel if abuse threatens or until injuries heal. Women are taught that they are responsible for their mate's happiness, successes, and failures. They believe their husband's judgment that they deserve his treatment—that they are responsible for the violence they receive. Many women have come from families of origin where manipulation, intimidation, and battering have been the accepted pattern of relationships between men and women, and religious and cultural constraints reinforce their belief that they must keep the marriage intact. They carry a load of guilt for the failure of the marriage. Most women love their mates and hope that they will change. The loving days with accompanying remorse following a violent incident lead to the hope that this time the change will be real. In *The Battered Woman*, Walker postulated a theory to explain the experience of many women. She used the concept of learned helplessness* developed by behaviorists. In effect, if women have enough experience of being degraded for attempting to assert themselves, they will grow to believe that they are in fact helpless to change anything and will try no longer.

There are several stages in the experience of battered women. Initially they deny the abuse or the severity of the abuse to themselves and to others. When they acknowledge the abuse, women blame themselves and hope for change. At some point they may seek help by choice or by being forced to flee. At this time, safe from the abuser, with appropriate intervention women may experience growth in self-esteem and enhancement of survival skills. Out of ambivalence about ending the relationship women may use counseling to try to end the violence or may go in and out of the relationship several times. The ultimate goal is that they will one day live nonviolently.

Further References. D. Martin, *Battered Wives* (San Francisco, 1976). E. Pizzey, *Scream Quietly or the Neighbors Will Hear* (London, 1974).

SYLVIA ROBERTSON

BETROTHAL is a formal agreement of marriage* at a later date made between the parties whose consent is necessary for the marriage to take place. In many premodern societies the betrothal was legally necessary for a valid marriage and could be as binding. After the financial and other arrangements were decided upon by the husband-to-be or his guardian and the guardian of the wife-to-be, a public betrothal, involving ceremonial acts (e.g., pouring perfume over the girl's head in ancient Mesopotamia; placing an iron ring on her finger in ancient Rome), took place. The marriage, sometimes occurring without further formality, might follow within a few weeks or, in the case of infant betrothals, not for years.

In some societies the couple did not have the right to refuse marriage (e.g., India, Greece); in others, they could, at least theoretically, refuse consent (e.g., Hebrew, Roman). In Roman and medieval law generally the betrothed couple had to be old enough to understand what was being said (age seven) and could not be forced to marry without their consent. However, many infant betrothals are recorded, and young men could much more easily evade marriage than could young women. In Rome a girl could refuse marriage only if she could prove the young man morally unfit. Under Germanic law, a daughter could not escape from a betrothal entered into by a parent on her behalf.

Through the early modern period betrothal remained a binding contract. In rural areas in Europe and America and in other cultures throughout the world many young couples began sexual relations after betrothal, but generally this was not considered a serious offense. However, for a betrothed person to have relations with a third party could be considered adultery*, for which the penalty was severe.

Betrothal could be dissolved for cause or by mutual consent of the young man and the woman's guardian, but unilateral failure to honor the contract could have serious consequences. Even when betrothal was not legally required for a valid marriage, as in England, a suit for breach of promise could be brought against a man for defaulting on a betrothal. In the United States 28 states still recognize breach of promise suits, although some have limited the recovery of damages.

Where the arranged marriage has given way to the marriage of choice, and where dowry* or bridegift* is not a concern, the betrothal, with its signification of parental control and family alliances, has disappeared, sometimes being merged into the marriage ceremony (e.g., Russian Orthodox, Judaic), generally leaving behind a residue of customs and informal practices.

BIOLOGICAL DETERMINISM. See SOCIOBIOLOGY

BIOPSY: Removing living tissue from the body and subjecting sections of it to microscopic examination. Biopsies can be performed on almost any tissue and are done whenever there is a possibility that cancer* might be present. In women tissue from the breast, cervix, cervical canal, vulva, and endometrium, along with skin growths, are most frequently subject to biopsy. The procedure is used whenever an abnormal Pap smear* or the discovery of a lump in the breast indicates the need for examination. It is used during cancer operations to try to determine whether the cancer has spread beyond the area known to be involved. Endometrial biopsies are also useful in diagnosing menstrual and infertility problems.

Methods include, among others, scraping cells with a spoon-like curette (as in endocervical and endometrial curettage), inserting a needle into a lump in the breast and aspirating the fluid or, with hard lumps, using a hollow needle to withdraw the core of the tumor (needle biopsy) or by surgical procedure. Tissue is sent to a pathology laboratory where it is sectioned and examined. Most procedures can be performed in the doctor's office under local anesthesia.

Formerly, when breast cancer was suspected, a one-step procedure was used. The woman was prepared for surgery and given a general anesthesia; the biopsy performed; the excised material sent to the laboratory where it was sectioned and one or more sections quick-frozen and examined. Within 10 to 15 minutes word was sent back to the operating room, and if cancer was present, an immediate operation was performed. The woman did not know when she went under anesthesia whether she would wake up with one breast or two.

A two-step procedure is preferable and can be used for almost all biopsies unless the tissue is so deep that major surgery is necessary to get to the tissue (e.g., in ovarian biopsies). There should be no need for a one-step procedure in breast cancer. With the two-step method, biopsy is an out-patient procedure. A permanent section, which takes several days, is done. It is more accurate and yields more information. With more time and information, the woman can better make informed decisions about the need for further tests, or for getting a second opinion, and about the type of treatment to be used.

BIRTH CONTROL. See CONTRACEPTIVES

BIRTHING ALTERNATIVES (ALTERNATIVE BIRTH MOVEMENT). The development in the United States of a range of choices in childbearing services and techniques in contrast to, and as a critique of, an essentially monolithic, highly mechanized Western health care system, which has largely shaped prevailing patterns of childbirth*. Many choices are based on evaluation of nonmedical traditions for management of childbirth in the United States as well as on identification and examination of management modalities in non-Western cultures. In general, alternatives are (1) to hospital-based birth, insofar as that implies loss of maternal autonomy in the childbearing experience; (2) to escalating costs of childbirth; and (3) to what can be perceived as an inadequate response to the universal sense of physical and psychosocial vulnerability experienced by mothers and significant others at the time of childbirth.

In the last twenty years, this movement has precipitated, and continues to precipitate, major changes in the management of childbirth. Major categories of choice, or alternatives, while not discrete, are birth setting, childbirth attendants, birth position, and pharmacologic and technologic support.

Setting. The model is the home, rather than the hospital; the rationale, that childbearing is best experienced in a setting that is, or approximates, the context of the childbearing woman's life and that maintains nonseparation of the infant from the mother and significant others. Alternatives range from home birth through birth centers and birthing rooms. Birth centers are freestanding or hospital-affiliated. The model and demonstration project for freestanding birth centers, the Maternity Center Association, New York, has demonstrated that safety can be maintained and cost-effectiveness accomplished for healthy women and infants attended by certified nurse-midwives. Hospital-based birth alternatives may be autonomous, though contiguous, birth centers, but in some settings may be birthing rooms in labor and delivery suites. In the former, essentially the same principles apply as in freestanding centers; in the latter, labor, birth, and immediate recovery take place in one room, after which time mothers and infants may be moved to separate hospital areas (postpartum suites for mothers and newborn nurseries for infants). In some settings mothers and infants are not moved from the room of birth; in these instances the birth setting is usually referred to as a single-unit delivery system (SUDS).

Childbirth Attendants. A case can be made for differing emphases between nursing/midwifery and medicine relative to childbirth. Because the tradition and science of nursing and midwifery* emphasize holism and health as characteristic of human reproductive phenomena, therapeutics is based on maintenance and enhancement of the social, cultural, and physiologic protective mechanisms surrounding childbearing. By contrast, because emphases in the tradition and science of Western medicine have been on detection and treatment of disease, therapeutics in based on employment of diagnostic methodologies and technologies to discover and correct instances of disease or dysfunction in mother and fetus/infant.

A third category of birth attendant is the lay midwife or attendant who acquires training* by experience and/or apprenticeship and who sees her role as "standing by" or being "with woman" (the generic meanings of obstetrics and midwifery, respectively). The rationale commonly employed by those selecting lay attendants is that there is, thereby, no influence of pathology-oriented training (which some perceive to extend to formally trained and licensed nurses and midwives) that can result in use of technologies judged to be nonphysiologic, invasive, unnecessary, inhumane, unsafe, or otherwise inconsistent with maternal autonomy in childbearing.

While birth attendants can function in varieties of settings, the usual pattern is that lay- or nurse-midwives attend home births and nurse-midwives and/or physicians, plus nurses, attend women in birth centers and birthing rooms.

Birth Position. Rather than adhering to a single standard position (i.e., dorsal lithotomy [lying prone with legs elevated]), alternative birth settings, by their lack or limitation of hospital equipment, facilitate the mother's use of whatever activity or position she perceives to be most beneficial for herself and her infant. Research indicates that maternal freedom of movement during labor and some variation of upright position for birth (e.g., standing, squatting, sitting) are safe for both mother and infant and produce the least risk of iatrogenic (therapy-induced) circulatory complications for both.

Pharmacologic and Technologic Support. Concern is with the routine, nondiscriminate employment of any or all anesthetic, analgesic, amnesic, or stimulant medications, and routine use of attendant-dominated technologies (e.g., continuous or intermittent electronic fetal monitoring equipment, stirrups, high-technology infant care equipment) that interfere with spontaneous processes of labor, birth, and recovery; that shift control over the childbearing experience from the mother and significant others to the birth attendant(s); and/or that pose a threat to the safety of the mother and infant. Although some kind of technology, however simple, is a concomitant of most birth settings worldwide, the general approach in alternative birth settings is to employ minimum, or no, medication and simple technologies.

VBAC. An emerging development that might be considered under the aegis of birthing alternatives is vaginal birth after previous cesarean birth (VBAC). The rationale for VBAC, in addition to the philosophic bases for other birthing alternatives, is threefold:

1. Surgical technique for cesarean birth that involves cutting the uterus in the lower, noncontractile portion does not jeopardize contractile activity in subsequent labors.

2. Frequently, reasons for cesarean management of childbirth are not necessarily repeatable (e.g., breech presentation; "failure to progress" as a diagnosis). "Failure to progress," in particular, reflects the fact that the etiology of the onset and progress of labor remains incompletely understood, and there is little reason to presume that the conduct of one labor will be repeated in subsequent labors.

3. Vaginal birth after cesarean birth, other things being equal, is safer than repeat cesarean birth for both mother and infant.

Criticism. Negative criticism of the alternative birth movement usually proceeds from the premise that advances in Western medical science have decreased maternal and infant morbidity and mortality, that issues of maternal and infant safety cannot be adequately addressed outside the hospital setting, and that not all women enter childbearing in a healthy state. Each of these issues (including the last, which may seem the most incontrovertible) requires reexamination and clarification to determine its accuracy, validity, and applicability. For those reasons most responsible practitioners in the United States will view the alternative birth movement as an opportunity to engage in ongoing evaluation of the premises on which the care of childbearing women and their infants is based.

Further References. B. Jordan, *Birth in Four Cultures* (Montreal, 1983). J. W. Mold and H. F. Stein, "The Cascade Effect in the Clinical Care of Patients," *New England Journal of Medicine* 314 (1986): 512–514. National Association of Childbearing Centers, Box 1, RD #1, Perkiomenville, Pa. 18074.

MARY ANN ZETTELMAIER

BISEXUALITY within the feminist community is often defined as the sexual orientation* of women who devote their primary energy to other women but whose affectional and sexual preference includes both women and men.

Bisexuality was recognized in the early sex research of Alfred Kinsey at Indiana University as including more persons than homosexuality*.

Women who name themselves bisexual often get criticism from both the community-at-large and the lesbian community. Homophobia* (fear of homosexuality) and especially the threat that lesbian relationships present to male dominance affect bisexual women as well as lesbian women. Lesbian women sometimes criticize bisexual women for not accepting their "true" sexuality (assumed to be lesbian by the lesbian community), for not being able to make a decision, for stealing energy from the lesbian community, for utilizing heterosexual privilege. Support groups for bisexual women are often well attended but cloistered because of the vulnerability women feel about the issues surrounding bisexuality.

During the era of AIDS (Acquired Immune Deficiency Syndrome*) the term *bisexuality* has come to be associated with people who provide a conduit of HIV virus between the gay and larger communities. Bisexual men are in a position to transmit the HIV virus responsible for AIDS from higher risk male-to-male sexual interactions to women in heterosexual interactions. Bisexual women are at greater risk in their sexual interactions with men. Transmission of the HIV virus between women has been demonstrated only under extreme circumstances. Bisexual women, therefore, are needlessly blamed as links in the HIV transmission chain.

ELAINE WHEELER

BLACK WOMEN AND FEMINISM. A long tradition of black female competence, leadership, and self-determination forms the bases of black women's relationship to feminism. Black women have shared many of the general concerns of the women's movement such as suffrage and education in the nineteenth century, and equal pay and child care* in the twentieth. Yet they have not readily identified with a movement defined in terms of the experiences of white, middle-class women nor have they participated en masse in its organizations and activities. Their absence is not, as often mistakenly assumed, from a lack of feminist consciousness*, but rather from their invisibility within, and the racism of, the movement's ideology and politics. Black feminist thought, organizations, and activism have existed and continue to exist independent of the women's movement. Black feminism is an active commitment to struggle against the multiple and simultaneous oppressions black women face and is articulated through the perspectives of African-American women's cultural heritage.

Patricia Hill Collins ("Learning from the Outside Within: The Sociological Significance of Black Women's Feminist Thought," *Social Problems* 33 [1986]: S14-S32) has identified three recurring themes in black feminist thought: (1) the affirmation of self-definitions and self-valuations; (2) attention to the interlocking nature of race, gender, and class oppressions; and (3) an awareness of the cultural heritage which has enabled generations of black women to resist these discriminations. The first theme stresses the importance of black women's establishing positive individual and collective images; discovering their own perspective on their life circumstances; and applying their own standards of beauty, thought, and action. In asserting self-determination, a single black female perspective, image, or feminism is not presumed. Just as the realities of black women's lives differ, so too does the acceptable range of their political and social expression. Maria Stewart, perhaps the first woman to speak publicly in this nation, wrote in 1831 of the importance of black women describing and naming themselves (see Bert James Loewenberg and Ruth Bogin [eds.], *Black Women in Nineteenth-Century American Life* [University Park, Pa., 1976], 183–200).

The second persistent theme in black feminism is the recognition of the multiple jeopardies of race, class, gender, and sexuality which circumscribe black women's lives. Anna Julia Cooper, who was born in slavery in 1858 and became a noted educator, earning a Ph.D. at the age of 63, spoke of black women being "doubly enslaved" and of their confronting both "the women question and a race problem" (see selections from her writings in Loewenberg and Bogin and in Gerda Lerner's *Black Women in White America: A Documentary History* [New York, 1972]). Today, black female scholars and writers still examine the issue of these dual discriminations (see DOUBLE JEOPARDY). This acknowledgment of simultaneous oppressions necessitates a more encompassing, humanist vision in their feminist theorizing. Black women have continually insisted that their liberation must entail the liberation of all black people. At the First National Conference of Colored Women in 1895, activist Josephine St. Pierre Ruffin stated, "Our woman's movement is a woman's movement that is led and directed by women for the good of women and men, for the benefit of all humanity, which is more than any one branch or section of it" (see Lerner, 440–443).

This note of universalism is heard in the voices of contemporary black feminists such as Bell Hooks, who states that "feminism . . . is a commitment to eradicating the ideology of domination that permeates Western culture on various levels—sex, race, and class, to name a few—and a commitment to reorganizing U.S. society so that the self-development of people can take precedence over imperialism, economic expansion, and material desires" (*Ain't I a Woman: Black Women and Feminism* [Boston, 1981], 194).

Black feminism always entails a recognition of community. Feminist concerns are manifest in work for religious, health, educational, cultural, and other community institutions through such organizations as the National Association of Colored Women and the National Council of Negro Women. In the economic arena, black women have organized mutual benefit associations like the Independent Order of Saint Luke, which founded the longest continuously operating black bank in the country, labor unions such as the Tobacco Workers Union, and community development foundations.

A recognition of black feminism's historical origins in African-American women's culture is the third theme. Black females learn skills, values, and attitudes for maintaining collective efforts and perpetuating positive self-concepts. The wisdom born of resistance has encouraged the development of dignity, strength, independence, and imagination which has been continued through generations (Angela Davis, *Women, Race and Class* [New York, 1983]). Through informal work, local service groups, and a national club movement, black women labor together seeking emancipation. Their political activism and savvy were developed in such groups as the Women's Era Club of Boston, founded in the 1890s, which through its newsletter, *The Women's Era*, denounced lynching and advocated woman suffrage; the Combahee River Collective (1974); the National Black Feminist Organization (1973); the National Political Congress of Black Women

(1984); and the Black Women's Liberation Committee of the Student Non-Violent Coordinating Committee.

This collective consciousness is preserved, studied, and shared through the scholarship of black feminists. There are black women's courses, programs, and conferences; research centers such as the Center for Research on Women at Memphis State University or the National Institute on Women of Color in Washington, D.C.; journals such as *Sage: A Scholarly Journal on Black Women*; and publishing companies such as Kitchen Table: Women of Color Press. A decidedly prowoman culture enriches and empowers black women to create choices even in the face of external constraints.

The historical continuity of black feminist expressions can be traced from the 1833 address of Maria Stewart, "What if I am a woman," to Sojourner Truth's famous "Ain't I a Woman?" speech in 1851, to Amy Garvey's 1925 editorial "Women as Leaders," to Alice Walker's "womanist"* (see *In Search of Our Mothers' Gardens: Womanist Prose* [San Diego, 1983]), a concept which comes closest to encompassing the range of ideologies and praxis of black women's feminism: "a womanist acknowledges the particularistic experiences and cultural heritage of black women, resists systems of domination, and insists on the liberty and self-determination of all people" (quoted from Womanist, Womanism, Womanish, *infra*).

Further References. G. I. Joseph and J. Lewis, *Common Differences: Conflicts in Black and White Feminist Perspectives* (New York, 1982). B. Smith (ed.), *Home Girls: A Black Feminist Anthology* (New York, 1983).

DEBORAH KING

BLACK WOMEN'S STUDIES (also Africana Women's Studies) as an "autonomous academic discipline" was popularized by African-American feminists in the middle 1970s. Its first major publication was *All the Women Are White, All the Blacks Are Men, But Some of Us Are Brave: Black Women's Studies* (1982).

Definition. (1) An interdisciplinary field of theoretical and practical studies in race, gender, and socioeconomic class from the perspective of women of African descent, and including teaching, research, advocacy and informal education in feminist theory* and world cultures, women's history, studies in sexuality and public policy, social change and social movements, and the philosophy and methodologies of science. (2) Studies in the empowerment of women of African descent and/or Asian/Pacific descent, their histories and cultures, focused on issues of human freedom, self-awareness and positive self-concept, cultural identity, community development, and self-determination for racially/nationally oppressed peoples worldwide. (3) A political and intellectual imperative stemming from the expansion and combining of the disciplines of Black/Africana Studies and Women's Studies.

Origins. In the United States, the nineteenth-century Afric-American Female Intelligence Society of Boston, the Colored Women's Progressive Association, and the National Association of Colored Women were early promoters of the study of African-American women through theory, advocacy, and informal education. In 1939, the National Council of Negro Women launched an Archives-Museum where, according to founder Mary McLeod Bethune, "the records, letters, books, pictures, medals and other authentic materials, suggestive of the struggles and accomplishments of Negro women [could] be assembled" (Bettye Collier-Thomas, "Towards Black Feminism: The Creation of the Bethune Museum Archives," in Suzanne Hildenbrand [ed.], *Women's Collections: Libraries, Archives and Consciousness* [New York, 1986]. In 1977, this became the National Archives for Black Women's History and the Mary McLeod Bethune Memorial Museum, the only independent repository of black women's history established by African-American women.

Human Rights and Feminism. Formal education about women of color* remained scarce and limited to the historically black colleges and universities until the late 1960s. This was changed by two phenomena. First, the struggle for human rights by African-Americans sparked a movement for black studies as a political struggle against racist distortions, omissions, and abuses at all levels of education. Second, during the new feminist movement, women's studies were developed to counter the devaluation of women and the trivialization of their lives, work, and history. Although both were concerned with "mainstreaming" into existing curricula, by and large black studies concentrated on males, and women's studies excluded black women and other women of color.

In 1969, under the rubric of black studies at the University of Pittsburgh, Sonia Sanchez introduced a course, "The Black Woman," employing new theoretical constructs, "diarchy" (vis-à-vis matriarchy* and patriarchy*) and "secondary consciousness" (i.e., the dominant culture's gender suppositions about blacks as perceived by blacks), in the describing of the black female experience in the Americas. This groundbreaking effort to unify the study of gender, race, and socioeconomic class in relation to Africana women was followed in 1971 with a programmatic effort in Women's Studies by predominantly black female Bennett College of Greensboro, North Carolina. Throughout the 1970s, scholarly examination of women in the African diaspora paralleled the burgeoning African-American feminist movement, yet by the mid 1970s, only about 1 percent of women's studies courses in U.S. higher education provided instruction about black women.

Milestones. The United Nations Decade for Women (1976–1985) boosted American black feminist efforts to institutionalize black women's studies. Significant developments in curriculum include the first doctoral program in Africana women's studies (Atlanta University, 1984), pilots of a minor in black women's studies (Spelman College, 1982) and of a cross-cultural black women's studies curriculum (Medgar Evers College of the City University of New York, 1985), the Culture of Southern Black Women Project (University of Alabama, 1980), and the first course in Canadian higher education on black women (Concordia University, 1983).

Milestones in research and development during the era of the push for black women's studies include the Schlesinger Library Black Women Oral History Project (Radcliffe College, 1976), the Association of Black Women Historians (1978), a national Scholarly Research Conference on Black Women (National Council of Negro Women, 1979), a Third World Women's Caucus in the National Women's Studies Association (1981), the Kitchen Table: Women of Color Press (New York, 1981), the Black Women in the Middlewest Archives Project (Purdue University, 1983), a national Black Women's Studies Conference (Bennett College, 1984), the publishing of *Sage: A Scholarly Journal on Black Women* (Atlanta, 1984), the Southern Women's Working Paper Series (Memphis State University, Spelman College, and Duke University of North Carolina, 1984), and an international conference on "Black Women Writers in the Diaspora" (Michigan State University, 1985).

Further References. Atlanta University Africana Women's Center, Africana Women's Studies Series (Atlanta, 1984). G. T. Hull et al. (eds.), *All the Women Are White, All the Blacks Are Men, But Some of Us Are Brave: Black Women's Studies* (New York, 1982).

ANDRÉE NICOLA MCLAUGHLIN AND DON QUINN KELLEY

BONA FIDE OCCUPATIONAL QUALIFICATION (BFOQ). In interpreting Title VII* of the Civil Rights Act of 1964, the Equal Employment Opportunity Commission (EEOC) has determined the extent to which sex can be considered a bona fide occupational qualification (BFOQ). Sex is a BFOQ if the employer can prove business necessity, but it is not to satisfy customer or employee preference. Neither marital status, existence of preschool children, nor general assumptions about women's capabilities or commitment to the labor force may be a basis for failure to employ on the basis of sex.

A major problem in nondiscriminatory hiring was state protective legislation*. The EEOC Guidelines of 1968 affirmed the belief that Title VII did not overturn state differential legislation, but refused to recognize a protective legislation BFOQ that was discriminatory rather than protective in effect. After the *Rosenfeld* v. *Southern Pacific Company* (293 F. Supp. 1219 CD Cal. 1968) decision struck down most state sex-specific laws, the Guidelines read that when protective legislation conflicts with EEOC regulations, the regulations supersede. According to the 1972 Guidelines, protective legislation must not be sex-specific but must cover all workers.

Without the EEOC's stringent interpretation of sex as a BFOQ, Title VII would have been meaningless insofar as combating discrimination* in the hiring of women is concerned.

BREASTS. See MAMMARY GLANDS (BREASTS)

BRIDEGIFT/BRIDEWEALTH is a form of marriage payment in which wealth in the form of property, money, goods, or services is given by the groom or his family* or kin group to the bride or her family or kin group. Anthropologists no longer use the term *brideprice* because of its connotation of buying a wife. A distinction may be made between bridewealth and bridegift, using bridewealth to refer to gifts to the bride's family or kin group and bridegift to refer to gifts part or all of which are given to the bride.

This form of marriage payment has been found in many societies throughout history, but is more characteristic of small preindustrial egalitarian or polygamous societies than of highly stratified or monogamous ones.

BRIDESERVICE. A term used by some feminist anthropologists for a type of sex-gender system found among many foragers and hunter-horticulturists. Because marriage* organizes relations of privilege and obligation in societies where labor is divided only by sex, age, and kinship position, not by caste or class, a classification scheme that distinguishes different ways of validating marriages can highlight relationships among gender, productive relations, political processes, and cultural representations. In "brideservice" societies, where grooms are expected to work for their in-laws or provide gifts the groom obtains with his own labor, marriages do not create long-term relations of debt among adults. All adults control the distribution of their produce; ongoing relationships depend upon the continued willing exchange of goods and services through which people organize the distribution of food. In less egalitarian "bridewealth" societies, where grooms are expected to present in-laws with gifts obtained through the labor of someone other than the groom himself, the acquisition of gifts puts young men in debt to the elders who help them marry. Elders who have helped many youths marry control the distribution of many people's products. They become political leaders who help less fortunate elders, organize trade and warfare, and sponsor public ceremonies.

In common anthropological usage, "brideservice" refers not to a type of society but to a mode of marriage found in many types of societies, including complex, archaic civilizations. It is defined as a mode of obtaining a wife in which the groom works for the bride's kinsmen. The term belongs to a contrast set that includes bridewealth (in which the groom or his relatives provide substantial gifts for the bride's kin), token bridewealth, gift exchange, dowry* (in which the bride's relatives transfer property to the bride, the groom, or the groom's kinsmen), the direct exchange of one woman for another, and the absence of exchange.

Further Reference. J. Collier and M. Rosaldo, "Politics and Gender in Simple Societies," in S. Ortner and H. Whitehead (eds.), *Sexual Meanings* (New York, 1981).

JANE F. COLLIER

C

CANCER is one of the leading causes of death in women, being responsible for more deaths now than in our grandmothers' day largely because communicable diseases and deaths from childbearing have been reduced significantly. Changes in our environment, especially in the work environment, as well as increased cigarette smoking put women at greater risk of cancer now than earlier.

Women of color* have a greater incidence of cancer and are more likely to die of cancer than white women. Reductions in cancer mortality have not benefited women of color as much as white women. For example, black women continue to have twice the rate of cervical cancer as white women even though the rate of cervical cancer for all women has dropped substantially. Esophageal cancer declined sharply in white males (it was never very high in white females), but continues to increase in black women (and men).

Cancer treatment has been controversial for women. Hysterectomy (removal of the uterus) has been used to treat uterine cancer but has also been done when, in fact, cancer was not found to be present. Radical surgery of the breast has been done for decades when more conservative treatment produces the same life expectancy.

Lung Cancer. Recently a 50-year trend was changed when lung cancer beat out breast cancer as the leading cause of cancer deaths in women. This change resulted not from lower incidence or fewer deaths from breast cancer but largely from increased smoking by women. Although more men and women continue to become ex-smokers, there is disturbing evidence that more teenaged women than men are starting to smoke and that women may find it more difficult to quit.

Lung cancer has no early symptoms, and survival rates have not improved significantly during the 1980s. The best way to deal with lung cancer is to prevent it by avoiding cigarette smoking, avoiding "passive smoking," i.e., inhaling the secondhand smoke of family* or coworkers, and avoiding occupational exposure to fumes from rubber and chlorine and dust from cotton and coal. Exposure to asbestos plus cigarette smoke increases the lung cancer risk nearly 60 times.

Cigarette advertising has been successful at targetting women consumers and has used camaraderie among women and even women's progress as a tactic to sell the product. It is important that women not be deluded into thinking that a risk-free cigarette exists. Low tar and nicotine cigarettes may be useful as a transition to quitting, but not as a safeguard against lung cancer. Quitting completely lowers risk over time unless irreversible changes in lung tissue have occurred.

As social and work settings become less tolerant of smoking behavior, women can take the initiative in breaking the association between smoking and sophistication that advertising seeks to promote and that teen women are buying.

Breast Cancer. Until recently breast cancer was the number one cause of cancer deaths in women. The increase in smoking among women has been the main factor causing lung cancer to surpass breast cancer in its effect of cancer mortality. The incidence of breast cancer is actually increasing, probably related at least in part to environmental contaminants. Deaths have not been reduced in spite of campaigns to encourage breast self-examination and in spite of aggressive surgical intervention.

A number of factors have been identified as increasing a woman's risk of breast cancer. Overall, 1 in 11 women is estimated to develop breast cancer in her lifetime. Women with a family history of breast cancer (e.g., in mother or sister[s]), those who have a greater number of menstrual cycles in a lifetime (e.g., women with early onset of menses, late menopause*, women with no children or children born later in life)—these women are at greater risk of breast cancer. Also, women who have fibrocystic changes in their breasts may find it difficult to detect changes indicative of breast cancer.

Examination of the breast by the woman herself or by her spouse/lover is important in detecting changes such as a lump or thickening or nipple discharge. These signs need to be investigated by a physician skilled in detection and management of breast disease.

Mammography, low dose x-ray of breast tissue, is more sensitive than manual examination in the detection of breast changes, especially in women over 40, the age at which the risk of breast cancer increases greatly. If "dedicated" x-ray machines (machines used only for mammography and never adjusted upward to greater doses of x-ray) are used, then the risk of exposure to x-ray is outweighed in women over 40 and in women who are at special risk.

The American Cancer Society recommends the following schedule for the use of mammography:

Ages 35–39   one baseline mammography

Ages 40–49   mammography every 1–2 years

Ages 50+   mammography every year

Women who find they have an early localized breast cancer (under 5 mm in size) should insist on surgical removal of the lump only. For many years surgeons have continued to perform radical mastectomies, i.e., removal of the entire breast, lymph nodes under the arm, and sometimes muscle from the chest wall, leaving a woman disfigured. Research in Europe and later in the United States confirmed that women with localized disease do not live longer with the radical procedure than if the lump alone is excised (lumpectomy). Only women's demands will change surgeons' practice.

For women with breast tumors greater than 5 mm in size, lumpectomy accompanied by chemotherapy and/or radiation may still be the treatment of choice. Treatment for cancer of the breast that has spread to the lymph nodes or other areas is more complicated. Women need to focus on detection of early changes in breast tissue and treatment choices. This focus may help allay fear of surgical disfigurement, which has kept women from early intervention.

Uterine and Cervical Cancer. Uterine and cervical cancer are often considered together, but they present different risk patterns. The cervix, the lower portion of the uterus which can be felt at the back of the vagina, is more susceptible to cancerous changes in women who have exposure to sperm. Young women in early puberty (e.g., 13 years old) and girls who have been subjected to repeated sexual abuse are especially at risk. When young girls and women have sex with a number of men, their risk of cervical cancer is increased as well.

Use of barrier methods of birth control, especially condoms and the diaphragm, reduces the risk of cervical cancer. The Pap smear* is highly effective in detecting early cervical cell changes. Recommendations regarding the frequency of Pap smear testing vary from every year to every three years after two normal annual results. It makes sense that women at higher risk get Pap smears more often. Lesbian or celibate women often mistake their risk of cervical cancer as zero and get Pap smears rarely or never. Cervical cell changes that are detected early can be treated by removal of a localized area on the cervix, avoiding the need for hysterectomy while preserving childbearing ability, if valued. Therefore, regular Pap smears are essential to the health of all women.

The risk of cervical cancer is more likely in women who have had herpes genitalis* or chlamydia*. These women should follow the recommendation of annual Pap smears according to the advice of a gynecologist.

Uterine cancer, or cancer of the endometrium, the lining of the uterus, occurs more often in women over 40 years of age, women who are significantly overweight (20 percent above weight range for height), women who have taken sequential birth control pills, women who have taken estrogen replacement for long periods, and women with irregular or absent ovulation.

The Pap smear is not a good method of detecting uterine cancer. Women at risk who have irregular or unexplainable uterine bleeding should have an endometrial biopsy*. A second opinion regarding the advisability of hysterectomy is essential and even required by some insurance companies because of the frequency of removal of normal uteri in the past.

Women sometimes discontinue regular gynecological care after the "child-bearing years" when actually the risk of uterine and breast cancer increases. It is important to continue gynecological visits throughout the later years of life.

Colon and Rectal Cancer. Deaths from colon and rectal cancer in women have been noticeably reduced in recent years. Even so, colon and rectal cancer occurs more often in women than in men and is the third leading cause of cancer deaths in women.

The American Cancer Society recommends the following schedule for early detection: (1) a rectal exam as part of an annual checkup after age 40; (2) a test for blood in the stool every year after age 50; (3) the procto, a visual exam of the lower bowel, every three to five years after two annual negative tests, after age 50.

People at risk of colon and rectal cancer are those with a personal or family history, a history of intestinal polyps or of ulcerative colitis. Persons who eat a diet high in processed foods and low in fiber may be at greater risk. High fat diets have also been suggested as a risk factor for colon cancer.

ELAINE WHEELER

CASTRATION. See CIRCUMCISION (FEMALE)

CHICANA FEMINISM, developed during the 1960s within the context of the Chicano movement, is a social movement characterized by a politics of social protest. Various struggles evolved within this movement, including the United Farm Workers unionization efforts, the Chicano Student movement, and the Raza Unida party. Chicanas, who participated actively within each of these struggles, by the end of the sixties began to assess their participation in the Chicano movement. The 1970s witnessed the development of Chicana activists who addressed issues related to the Chicano movement from a feminist perspective. They responded to the constraints they experienced as women within this social movement. In the same way that the men were reinterpreting the historical and contemporary experience of Chicanos in the United States, Chicanas began investigating the ways in which race, class, and gender shaped their lives as women of color* in American society.

Through their writings and political activities Chicana feminists raised a series of questions concerning their status in U.S. society and the Chicano movement. A key feminist concern involved the relationship between a Chicana feminist movement and the Chicano movement. Other central issues of concern to Chicana feminists include the origins and consequences of racial and gender stereotypes directed against Chicanas; machismo, its origins and extent within Chicano communities; the nature of the Chicano family and the role of women within it; and, lastly, the problematic relationship between Chicana feminists and white feminists.

Chicana feminist activity increased on many university campuses throughout the United States. Workshops on Chicanas were included as part of the Denver Youth Liberation Conference held at the Crusade for Justice in 1969, 1970, and

1971. Martha Cotera, a leading Chicana feminist, organized an informal Chicana caucus at the Raza Unida Conference held in Austin, Texas, in July 1970. The Comision Femenil Mexicana developed as a direct result of a women's workshop at the Mexican American National Issue Conference held in Sacramento, California, in October 1970. The first national conference organized by and for Chicanas met in May 1971, in Houston, Texas: La Conferencia de Mujeres por la Raza. In addition to discussions related to education, employment, health care, immigration, and a wide range of other topics, Chicana feminists responded to antifeminist attacks from within the Chicano movement.

Feminist writings appeared in newspapers, journals, newsletters, and pamphlets. The Chicana feminist newspaper from Long Beach, California, *Las Hijas de Cuauhtemoc*, carried an article in one of its early issues dealing with various aspects of feminism. This newspaper later expanded into *Encuentro Femenil: The First Chicana Feminist Journal*. A historical search for the roots of feminism can be found in other documents published and disseminated during the 1970s. The June 1971 issue of *El Grito del Norte*, for example, devoted a special section to Chicanas. In 1977, Martha Cotera published *The Chicana Feminist* (Austin), a collection of essays dealing with the development of Chicana feminism.

Chicana activists believed that a feminist perspective required a focus on the interconnectedness of the multiple sources of oppression facing Chicanas. A key component of Chicana feminism clearly emerged from this community of feminist discourse in the 1970s. Chicana feminists argued that race, class, and gender interact simultaneously in explaining the life experiences of Chicanas in American society.

Chicana feminism sparked an outgrowth of research studies by and about Chicanas. A direct connection exists between the development of Chicana feminism and a growing body of research that focuses on the effects of race, class, and gender. Contemporary Chicana feminism continues to evolve; conferences and organizations continue to deal with feminist issues and questions. The 1984 conference of the National Association for Chicano Studies (NACS) held in Austin, Texas, adopted the theme "Voces de la Mujer" (Voices of Women). Women from throughout the United States met in Austin to discuss their research on Chicanas as well as to discuss specific political questions. Selected papers have been collected in a volume entitled *Chicana Voices: Intersection of Class, Race and Gender*. Chicana feminists viewed this conference as a turning point for the movement although much work needs to be done in its building.

Further Reference. Alma M. Garcia, "Studying Chicanas: Bringing Women into the Frame of Chicano Studies," in Teresa Cordova et al., *Chicana Voices: Intersection of Class, Race and Gender* (Austin, 1986).

ALMA GARCIA

CHILD ABUSE. See DOMESTIC VIOLENCE; INCEST

CHILDBIRTH cross-culturally, is an event of enormous personal and societal significance. It is, after all, the process through which new members are recruited into a society. Apart from the changes the birth of a child engenders in the lives of a couple, birth also constitutes a rite of passage which transforms their status within the family and the community. Indeed in many societies a female is not considered a woman until she has borne a child and a union is not considered a legitimate marriage* until a child has been produced.

It is useful to draw a distinction between "parturition,"* the physiological aspects of birthing, and "childbirth," the ways in which this process is experienced, endowed with meaning, and behaviorally managed. Parturition, determined by human anatomy and physiology, is universal. The growth of the fetus*, the beginning of uterine contractions at the end of the pregnancy, the opening up of the birth canal, the eventual expulsion of baby and placenta, and finally lactation, happen for all women no matter where they give birth, be that in a hut in jungles of South America or in a modern hospital. It would be reasonable to expect that these panhuman characteristics of parturition would have led, in the course of evolution, to some optimal way of bringing a baby into the world, and that this method would have spread to all human groups because of its survival value.

Cross-cultural variation begins with ideas about conception. For example, there are societies where the baby is thought not to be conceived at one point in time but rather as "built up" through the efforts of the couple. The mother contributes the red parts of blood (which therefore no longer flows during pregnancy), while the father contributes the white parts, e.g., skin, bones, and intestines, through his semen. In such societies, continued intercourse is considered necessary for building a healthy baby. In other cultures, particularly those who believe in the reincarnation of ancestors, conception is believed to occur because a "spirit child" wants to be born and finds itself a mother. Australian aborigines believe that the child may enter the woman either through the vagina (if, for example, she squats at certain springs frequented by spirit babies) or through the mouth, if, for example, she eats a fish prepared by the father into which a spirit child has entered because it wants to be born. Similar cross-cultural differences are evident in all aspects of pregnancy, birth, and the postpartum period.

Because of the universally acknowledged significance of birth, people everywhere have regulated its conduct: each culture, each subculture has developed a distinct set of beliefs and practices which constitute a "birthing system." These practices and beliefs are grounded in the culture in which they arose and are congruent with people's ideas about the world, the supernatural, their attitudes to their bodies, their view of women's roles and competencies, and their concept of a human being. What happens in birth has to make sense in the society at large, so that if, for example, a society is highly technologized, we are likely to find technologized birth. If the society treats women as important and autonomously functioning members, it is also likely that women get treated that way during birth. Thus birth both reflects and reinforces the shared values that people hold.

In the United States and most other industrialized countries birth has come to be defined as a medico-technological event and has passed from the women's domain into the realm of specialist medicine. This comparatively recent view sees birth as (at least potentially) pathological and makes pregnant women into patients requiring treatment by physicians in hospitals where the resources of biomedical technology, pharmacology, and surgery are available. In most industrialized countries the biomedical model of birth has supplanted the traditional view of birth as a marked but common life cycle event which women are competent to manage. Increasingly, however, countermovements to the pathological view of birth are emerging in industrial societies.

Everywhere in the industrialized world birthing is currently the subject of intense debate. This debate is generated, in part, by the often harmful outcomes of overly technologized birth, but also, especially in the United States, by the women's health movement. Increasingly, women now insist that they can and should be active participants in the birth process rather than passive patients who give their care over into the hands of technical specialists. This has resulted, in the last decades, in the rise of the natural childbirth movement; the re-emergence of lay and nurse-midwifery and home birth; and the growing popularity of hospital birthing rooms, freestanding birthing centers, and the concept of family-centered perinatal care. In the last few years some of the methods used by traditional practitioners have been revived in the West. Some practitioners now recommend walking and upright position during labor, physical and emotional support by family and friends, and sometimes even use the technique of external cephalic version, by which a baby that is in the wrong position for birth is turned around before labor begins.

In developing countries modernization efforts overwhelmingly rely on the biomedical model of birth, in spite of the fact that in the impoverished Third World the practice of hospital-based, physician-dependent, technology-intensive perinatal management is severely hampered by insufficient supplies of drugs, inadequately trained staff, nonrepairable machinery, and the like. This endemic lack of resources, coupled with culturally motivated resistance to hospital birth by indigenous communities, has prevented Western-style obstetrics from replacing traditional ways of birthing. Today, outside of the frame of Western medicine, the birth of children is still seen as a normal (rather than a pathological) life cycle event that should be handled by the family and the women's community. Where indigenous ethno-obstetrics has not been replaced by biomedical obstetrics, the conduct of birth relies on an empirically grounded and often supernaturally sanctioned repertoire of practices and a network of traditional birth attendants who subscribe to a body of beliefs about the nature of birth that they share with childbearing women (and often with men).

In spite of the extensive cross-cultural variation in birthing practices and beliefs, there are some general principles to which traditional birthing systems tend to adhere. These emerge from the view that birth is a normal, physiologic life cycle event and thus stand in contrast to routine obstetric management in technologized birth.

The first of these is that birth is women's business. Until recently, the conduct of normal birth has been almost exclusively in the hands of childbearing women themselves, assisted by women of the family and community midwives. Outside of Western medicine, male specialists (curers, shamans, medicine men) are consulted only in severely pathological cases. The categorical exclusion of males from the birth chamber (sometimes with the exception of the father of the child) has been nearly universal. While there are a few societies where men can become birth attendants, it is only in the United States and similarly technologized countries that men are considered the most appropriate decision-makers at normal births.

Cross-culturally, most births take place on the woman's territory, either her own house or hut, or, on occasion, the house of her mother. Most people believe it is important that the woman give birth in a familiar place, where she feels comfortable and protected. Even today, 60 to 80 percent of all births around the world are attended by midwives at home.

Another cross-cultural regularity is that women do not give birth alone or with strangers but are attended by other experienced women who provide physical and emotional support. Biomedical research in hospitals in Guatemala and the United States has shown that the presence of other women (doulas) not only influences the experience of birth but also shortens labor and positively affects neonatal mortality and morbidity. This "doula effect" may be one reason why midwife-attended births tend to produce better outcomes than births attended by physicians under similar conditions.

Decisions about the management of labor, which the biomedical model locates in the physician, are, in ethno-medical systems, made collaboratively by the woman and her attendants. In nontechnologized birth, information about the progress and nature of labor comes primarily from the wisdom of experienced women who have themselves successfully borne children. By contrast, medical decision-making is based on test results, machine output, and conformity of the labor pattern to a pre-established ideal norm which only medical specialists are thought to be competent to interpret.

Cross-culturally, women are mobile during the early stages of labor. In most societies it is the rule that they carry out their normal activities until labor is well established. Almost everywhere women are free to assume whatever position they feel most comfortable in during the period when the baby descends and the birth canal opens up. During full labor, women tend to assume a great variety of positions, such as walking, standing, kneeling, and sitting. During the second (pushing) stage as well, vertical rather than horizontal positions are most common, and these not only provide the aid of gravity in the descent of the fetus but also lead to active involvement of the woman in the birthing of her baby. The passive on-the-back position with legs immobilized, which is common in technologized birth, was unknown before Western obstetrics. It increases the control of the physician in the active management of labor but leads to a series of negative effects, such as lower oxygen saturation, circulatory problems, slowing down of labor, and lack of participation by the woman.

In most societies, the baby is cleaned, wrapped, and otherwise made presentable before being given to the mother. The afterbirth is almost universally treated with great care and is often thought to hold some mystical connection to the baby. It may be buried or burned with some ritual. Universally, it is thought important that mother and baby undergo a period of rest and seclusion, most typically lasting from a week to a month. During this time breastfeeding is established, mother-infant attachment takes place, and the mother recuperates from the exertions of giving birth. The mother adheres to a special diet and observes culturally determined rules of behavior, which often focus on replacing "heat" lost during childbirth. The seclusion period is often terminated by a coming-out event, during which the mother in her new status and the newborn baby are introduced to the community. Naming of the baby and according it full human status may take place at this time or may be delayed even longer.

A cross-cultural approach to birth outlines the range of variation as well as important unifying principles in the management of parturition. Exploring the range of options which different cultures have taken up can provide important alternatives to an overly narrow biomedical view of childbirth.

Further References. B. Jordan, *Birth in Four Cultures*, 3rd ed. (Montreal, 1983). B. Jordan, "The Hut and the Hospital: Information, Power and Symbolism in the Artifacts of Birth," *Birth: Issues in Perinatal Care and Education* 14 (1987): 36–40. M. Mead and N. Newton, "The Cultural Patterning of Perinatal Behavior," in S. Richardson and A. Guttmacher (eds.), *Childbearing—Its Social and Psychological Aspects* (Baltimore, 1967).

BRIGITTE JORDAN

CHILD CARE. The "looking after" of children. With urbanization and industrialization old ways of tending the children of working mothers were no longer always possible, as residential and work patterns changed and employment no longer centered in the home. As a result, in the eighteenth and nineteenth centuries, private and public services were created to help parents who worked outside the home care for their children.

Child care policy refers to various public and private sector benefits and programs, actual or desired, to influence the care of young children. Most familiar are group and family day care programs provided by either the government or the employer. But child care programs may also encompass tax policies, such as child care deductions and credits, or direct cash grants to facilitate and encourage childrearing. Employment-related policies include not only the place and number of day nurseries but also the option of paid maternity and parent leave with job protection and seniority and medical benefits. Flexible work hours and job-sharing opportunities for parents also come within the contemporary understanding of child care policies.

   The nature of child care reflects societal attitudes toward families, parenting, and, in particular, women. Although the number of women working in paid employment outside the home has increased dramatically in the past several decades, childrearing has remained primarily the mother's responsibility. Curiously, however, societal responses to child care needs have turned less on service to women and children than on concerns over decreasing population and labor needs, especially in wartime.

   Families need child care for many reasons, the most familiar being to enable parents to work. But parents might also need day care while they complete their education, if they become chronically ill, or when they need what psychologists call "quality" adult time. Increased labor force participation* of women has stimulated the demand for day care and other child care policies that permit families to care well for their children. In countries like the United States, the larger number of single women raising children alone has drawn attention to the inadequacies of child care benefits. So have the needs of an increasing number of homeless families whose children would benefit from the services often part of a good day care program.

   Child care benefits and services vary widely from country to country. For a number of reasons, including the tremendous loss of population in World Wars I and II and the influence of social democratic parties, European governments have far more extensive child care policies than the United States. In Europe it is far more common to find public creche and nursery school programs open to children regardless of family income. Paid maternity leave is also part of the European agenda. The average leave is five months at full pay. In Sweden fathers as well as mothers may elect to take paid parent leave. Parents may also adopt a six-hour workday until a child is eight years old. West Germany offers a monthly housework day. Italian women receive substantial credit toward job seniority with the birth of each child.

   The situation in the United States is sharply different. With population steady through much of the twentieth century, neither employers nor government has perceived a need to encourage a higher birth rate or higher workforce participation through child care policies. Until major changes in tax policy, introducing first a child care tax deduction and then, in the mid-1970s, a tax credit, most child care policy consisted of income-tested day care programs. Families not considered "needy" were thought properly beyond receiving aid for child care. Indeed, President Nixon in his 1971 veto of comprehensive child care legislation described this kind of government intervention as "family weakening."

   Influenced by the women's movement, the realities of female employment, and a birth rate now below replacement level, employers and government in the United States are beginning to discuss "adaptation" to feminization of the workforce. Alarmed at the weakening of the family, officials now speak of child care as "something that supports family life." There is considerable argument, however, about the nature of such supportive policies. Contention centers on whether tax policies or a family wage to encourage women with children to stay home should prevail over freely available day care centers that permit women to work out of the house after bearing children. Child care policy is, and will be, as it has been, a means of influencing not only children's but women's lives and well-being.

Further References. S. B. Kamerman and A. J. Kahn, *Child Care, Family Benefits and Working Parents* (New York, 1981). J. Norgren, "Child Care," in Jo Freeman (ed.), *Women: A Feminist Perspective*, 3rd ed. (Palo Alto, 1984). J. Norgren, "The Voteless Constituency: Children and Child Care," in J. K. Boles (ed.), *The Egalitarian City: Issues of Rights, Distribution, Access, and Power* (Westport, Conn., 1986).

JILL NORGREN

CHILDREN: THEIR EFFECT ON LABOR SUPPLY. With few exceptions, the presence of children reduces the amount of paid labor supplied by women; and, at the same time, working women* have fewer children. This complex relationship makes it difficult to estimate the exact impact of children on paid labor supply.

The presence of children can alter labor supply in two ways—labor force participation* and hours of work. First, women with children are less likely to be "in the labor force" (defined as employed for pay for at least one hour in the last week or actively seeking employment), although much of the recent growth in female labor force participation has been due to the entrance of married women with children. Second, women with children reduce employment through hours worked. Aside from school-aged youth, the largest group of part-time workers is women with children, and this group is increasingly opting for part-time employment.

Conversely, employment decreases the number of children a woman has since women devoting time to labor market activities may substitute, first, education and, later, market work for children. Since investing in and maintaining market skills often requires continuous labor force attachment, women specializing in labor market activities reduce childbearing to facilitate labor market work. Employed women are more likely to be childless or have only one child than women who are not engaged in labor market activities.

While aggregate trends portray work habits of females with children, they mask varying patterns among sociodemographic groups. Black women have higher fertility rates and greater labor force participation than white women. Educated women are more labor force committed, have fewer children, and work more hours than women with lower levels of education.

Employment, fertility, and their interrelationship change over time. While females have increased labor market activities since 1900, they have decreased their fertility. At the turn of the century, the average woman had nearly four children over her lifetime. While fertility rates fell for generations, around 1921 the decline quickened and fertility fell by more than a third in the next 12 years with birth rates reaching historic lows during the Depression. In 1947, birth rates jumped and continued to rise until 1957 (the baby boom). At this time, birth rates began to fall again, until today the average woman has about 1.8 children—far below the population replacement level of 2.2.

Four principal hypotheses, each with some empirical support, explain these phenomena. First, the presence of children makes women less able or willing to take employment outside the home. Employment and motherhood are inherently incompatible because of the time and emotional energy needed for both. Therefore, continued decreases in childbearing will facilitate increased employment.

Second, women restrict childbearing to be more actively involved in paid employment. Because labor market employment requires investing in training* (e.g., education) that is not needed for childraising, and because dropping out of the labor force to raise and/or bear children depreciates their skills, women specializing in labor market employment reduce the number of children they have or forgo childbearing. Thus, continued increases in female employment will decrease fertility.

Third, outside or antecedent factors (e.g., education, family background, or attitudes) explain both employment and the number of children a woman bears, with the decision changing when these factors change. Attitudes (e.g., views toward sex roles, work, children, or religion), family background (e.g., socioeconomic status of family of origin, mother's employment status, parental encouragement in school), and personal family characteristics (e.g., woman's wages, education, spouse's income, marital duration), all independently affect both the fertility and employment decision, with the outcome determining the number of children and hours of paid employment a woman undertakes. Changing attitudes toward women, work and education, and changing relative wages in the market will alter both employment and fertility.

Fourth, couples (or the single woman) decide about employment and children at the same time, based on antecedent/outside factors; however, once a decision is made, it is followed throughout their lifetime. For example, a couple decides to have two children and have the female drop out of the labor force during childbearing years (or the couple also may decide to forgo children so that both partners can work). This decision becomes the basis for action in the marriage and workplace and is rarely altered. Therefore, changes in attitudes or employment have little impact on the fertility decisions of those women currently of childbearing age; however, changing attitudes will impact future generations of women.

While empirical and theoretical explanations for the inverse employment-fertility relationship differ, a few generalizations can be made. First, changing social attitudes toward women's working facilitate increased employment, and increased education of females make it costly (in terms of market wages forgone) for a woman to engage exclusively in household production. Thus, both social and economic forces operate to increase women's paid labor market activities and to decrease the number of children a woman bears.

Second, the inverse relationship between fertility and paid labor market activity suggests that historically women specialized in childbearing or labor market work. However, historic specialization and current increased female labor market activities caused women in America to underestimate the time they spend in the labor market. Although young females express a desire to be "taking care of children" at age 35 (say), many more are engaged in paid labor market activities than initial desires indicate. This misperception causes women to underinvest in labor market skills and puts them at a disadvantage once they are working.

Finally, increases in women working part-time indicates declines in the specialization of earlier times. The workplace needs to respond by increasing adequate child care facilities and by expanding the number of part-time positions. Females need to respond by investing in labor market skills. Both children and female employment are here to stay, and both women and employers need to respond accordingly.

Further References. L. W. Hoffman and F. I. Nye, *Working Mothers* (San Francisco, 1974). C. Lloyd (ed.), *Sex Discrimination and the Division of Labor* (New York, 1975).

NAN L. MAXWELL

CHLAMYDIA TRACHOMATIS, a sexually transmitted disease, is more prevalent than gonorrhea* in the United States. As with gonorrhea, women rarely have symptoms to warn them of infection. Unrecognized and untreated chlamydia can result in pelvic inflammatory disease, scarred Fallopian tubes resulting in infertility* or ectopic pregnancy*, spontaneous abortion (miscarriage), stillbirth, and postpartum infection. Women who are troubled with chronic bladder infections may find that chlamydia is the responsible organism. Infants born to chlamydia-infected mothers may suffer blindness (chlamydia is a major cause of blindness in newborns in Third World countries). Pneumonia may also result.

In the absence of symptoms it is difficult to determine when to seek testing for chlamydia. Women who experience pain or bleeding with sex, especially cervical contact, pain with urination, or low abdominal pain need be tested for chlamydia. Even though it is only marginally supported by the literature at this point, the experience of nurse practitioners indicates that women on oral contraceptives who experience "breakthrough bleeding" (bleeding when taking medicated pills, without having missed pills) need to be tested for chlamydia. Women with multiple partners, and women whose partners have multiple partners, are at greater risk of chlamydia.

No reliable research is available on chlamydia in lesbian women. It is speculated by clinicians who provide care for large numbers of lesbian women that the chlamydia found in lesbian women is related to the number of lesbians* who have been sexual with men at some time. Heterosexually active women, especially those with more than one partner, may benefit from annual screening for chlamydia. At the occasion of an annual Pap smear*, the presence of an inflamed cervix which bleeds upon contact would indicate the need to test for chlamydia.

Self-visualization of the cervix between annual examinations can provide information about the need for testing.

Women who test positive for chlamydia (and their partners) should be treated with a regimen of tetracycline. A test of cure is recommended after two to three weeks. Chlamydia is not responsive to home remedies. Condoms are an effective barrier to the spread of chlamydia trachomatis.

ELAINE WHEELER

CIRCUMCISION (FEMALE). A euphemistic but widely used term for several forms of genital surgeries performed on girls and women. The commonest form is that known as clitoridectomy, or excision, which consists of amputation of the clitoris and removal of the surrounding tissues such as the prepuce (clitoral hood) and part of the labia minora. Also included in the term is the less damaging practice, often referred to as sunna circumcision, which consists of the removal of the prepuce only (analogous to male circumcision). Caution should be exercised in interpreting the label *sunna*, however, as some practitioners extend the term to removal of part of the clitoris and even more drastic surgeries. The most severe form of the surgeries is that commonly known as pharaonic circumcision, in which the entire clitoris, prepuce, and labia minora are removed, along with the adjacent parts of the labia majora, after which the two sides of the vulva are stitched shut (infibulated), occluding the urethra and most of the vaginal opening, but preserving a single tiny opening for the passage of urine and menses.

Although medically unnecessary and often very harmful, female genital surgeries continue to be performed in many of the world's cultures, but the prevalence of and rationales for the practices vary a great deal. Until the 1950s, for example, clitoridectomies were performed on female mental patients in the United States who were considered chronic masturbators. In other situations, the surgeries are more widespread, being done on large percentages of the female population simply because they are female. While sometimes thought of as a puberty rite, it is more common for the operations to be performed on much younger girls, ages four to nine. In most cultures it is performed by older women, often midwives.

Where these surgeries are commonly performed, they are usually considered to be justified by customary and/or religious values concerning gender-role expectations, and are therefore often referred to as "ritual" genital surgeries. There is, however, no single religion or ethnic group through which the custom is perpetuated. Forms of these surgeries are found widely, in many countries of Africa and the Middle East especially, among Muslims, Christians, and followers of other religions. For those who do practice some form of circumcision, there is often some ambivalence about it. But in many cases it forms a strong element of national and gender identity, for both women and men, and outsiders who criticize the surgeries have often been attacked for their insensitivity to the desire for cultural self-determination. Reasons given for the practice include ideas of purification and the protection of virginity through the reduction of sexual desire and (in the case of infibulation) the creation of a barrier to intercourse, but the range of symbolic meanings in the various cultures cannot be generalized.

The surgeries are known by a variety of names, and there is some problem of shifting nomenclature as people who practice one form are taught that another is preferable. Therefore, caution should be exercised in interpreting the labels used. The term *sunna circumcision*, for example, is from the Arabic for "tradition," i.e., following the traditions of the Prophet Mohammed, who is supposed to have permitted his followers to "reduce, but do not destroy." Sunna has therefore become the term preferred by those Muslims who practice it, and the unfortunate religious association of this term may serve to justify a practice not specifically required and not practiced by most followers of Islam.

Common health consequences following the surgeries include hemorrhage (bleeding), shock, infections, septicemia (blood poisoning), injury to adjoining structures, and retention of urine, as well as less well-documented psychological effects. These are exacerbated when the surgeries are performed as they often are in unhygienic circumstances—often in homes with dirt floors, by untrained midwives using unsterile instruments and without antiseptics, anesthesia, or pain relievers—and deaths sometimes result. The infibulated state can also cause many health problems later in life, including scarring, abcesses and cysts, dysmenorrhea, chronic pelvic infections, recurrent urinary tract infections, infertility*, difficulty with urination, and vasico-vaginal fistula. First intercourse is often painful and difficult, and childbirth can result in complications from obstructed labor. Childbirth requires a long incision, reinfibulated after delivery, by a birth attendant.

Both local and international efforts to discourage these practices are underway, primarily focused on publicizing the harmful health effects. Some analysts feel that fundamental changes in the status of women in the affected societies will be necessary, allowing women themselves to determine what changes they desire.

Further References. R.H.D. Abdalla, *Sisters in Affliction: Circumcision and Infibulation in Africa* (London, 1982). A. El-Dareer, *Woman, Why Do You Weep? Circumcision and Its Consequences* (London, 1982). E. Gruenbaum, "The Movement against Clitoridectomy and Infibulation in Sudan: Public Health Policy and the Women's Movement," *Medical Anthropology Quarterly* 13 (1982): 4–12.

ELLEN GRUENBAUM

CIVIL RIGHTS ACT OF 1964. See TITLE VII

CLERICAL OCCUPATIONS are the largest class of female-dominated occupations in the United States and in other Western countries. Currently, one out of every three employed American women is in a clerical job, and nearly 80 percent of all clerical workers are women.

In the middle of the nineteenth century clerical work was a man's job. The first U.S. women hired into clerical positions were employed by the Treasury to clip currency because of the shortage of qualified male workers during the

Civil War. The success of this experiment, in which women were paid half the male wage, led to the hiring of more female clerks by the federal government. In 1870, there were fewer than 2,000 female clerical workers, and under 3 percent of all U.S. clerical workers were women.

The situation changed rapidly in the 1870s with the invention and adoption of the typewriter. Use of the typewriter spread quickly, leading to a demand for trained operators. Perhaps because of similarities between the typewriter and the sewing machine, typewriter operation was early seen to be an appropriate job for women. Although there was considerable public debate about the suitability of office employment for women, women typists soon became common, and their employment increased rapidly as use of the writing machine spread. By 1890, women were 20 percent of the much larger clerical labor force, and nearly one-third of women clerical workers were employed as stenographers and typists whereas only 4 percent of men were so employed.

As the economy grew and became more complex, clerical employment increased rapidly. In 1870, only 1 of every 100 nonagricultural workers was in a clerical job. By 1930, 1 of every 10 was so employed; and by 1980, 1 in 5 workers was in a clerical occupation. As clerical employment grew, women's share of the clerical labor force also grew from under 3 percent in 1870, to 53 percent in 1939, to nearly 80 percent in 1980.

The expansion of women's employment in clerical jobs was due to a number of factors. Technological change in the office created conditions that fostered the employment of more women. As new machines and organizational schemes were adopted, clerical operations were standardized and broken into smaller parts. Jobs in the larger, more technologically sophisticated offices required skills that were transferable between employers, could be learned in schools, and were therefore appropriate for women workers who were expected to have short-term attachment to the firm. This differed markedly from the situation that prevailed in earlier days when offices had a few male clerks who were trained by the firm and hoped to work their way up to a managerial position. Because of the extremely rapid growth of total clerical employment, there was very little actual displacement of male office workers by women. Both male and female clerical employment has increased over time with substantial segregation by sex among the clerical occupations. Women found work in the new routinized and mechanized office jobs, while men's clerical employment was concentrated in supervisory positions and jobs, such as shipping clerk, with substantial manual components. Men continued to be able to use clerical jobs as the first rungs on the ladder to upward mobility long after most women in offices were confined to dead-end jobs.

Wars also played an important role in opening opportunities in office employment for women. Wartime labor shortages led employers to experiment with hiring women in jobs which they had not previously held. In clerical occupations, these remained women's jobs after the wars ended. During the Civil War the federal government hired the first female clerks. World War I saw the opening of many clerk positions to women. Bank telling became a woman's occupation during World War II.

As the demand for clerical workers increased, employers found women eager and able to take the new jobs. Women's educational levels increased as more and more attended and graduated from high schools. The number of private business schools grew rapidly, and public high schools began to offer instruction in clerical skills. Women enrolled in these courses in large numbers.

Women were attractive to employers because their lack of other opportunities meant that they worked for lower pay than did men. Clerical jobs were attractive to women because the pay and working conditions were superior to those in most other jobs available to women. In the nineteenth century, earnings of women clerical workers were higher than those of almost all other employed women. Over time the pay of women clerical workers fell relative to the pay of women in other occupations but generally remained above the pay of women in manufacturing jobs. Even as the relative pay of clerical workers fell, the jobs remained attractive to many women because of the better working conditions and higher social status of office jobs.

The women who went into clerical jobs prior to World War II were mostly young, single, native-born whites. Many were the unmarried daughters of the respectable middle class who eschewed blue-collar jobs. Employers commonly had regulations against the employment of married women clerical workers. As time went on older women, married women, black women, and working-class women found jobs as clerical workers. However, as late as 1930, 82 percent of all female clerical jobholders were unmarried, and more than half were under age 25. Black women were not hired into clerical jobs in substantial numbers till the mid-1960s when some racial barriers fell.

In the 1960s and 1970s, office work was changed by the introduction of computers, but employment continued to grow at a rapid pace. In the 1980s, office work is again being transformed by the adoption of microcomputers, which may have as profound an impact as did the typewriter in the late nineteenth and early twentieth centuries.

Further References. M. W. Davies, *Woman's Place Is at the Typewriter: Office Work and Office Workers, 1870–1930* (Philadelphia, 1982). H. A. Hunt and T. L. Hunt, *Clerical Employment and Technological Change* (Kalamazoo, Mich., 1986). E. J. Rotella, *From Home to Office: U.S. Women at Work, 1870–1930* (Ann Arbor, Mich., 1981).

ELYCE J. ROTELLA

CLIMACTERIC is the gradual ending of ovarian activity until it completely ceases at menopause*. The process extends over a period that may last for ten years or more, usually beginning in the early forties and ending sometime between the ages of 45 and 55. The period of the climatric is marked by menstrual irregularity, and as menopause nears, ovulation during the menstrual cycle* becomes less frequent.

COGNITIVE ABILITIES, SEX DIFFERENCES IN. There have been two quite different approaches to the study of sex differences in cognitive abilities. One approach has assessed sex differences in performance on various indicators of cognitive skills such as grades in school and scores on tests of mathematical, scientific, verbal, and spatial skills. The other approach has investigated sex differences in cognitive style (the ways males and females approach cognitive tasks and their response to challenge and difficulty).

Cognitive Abilities. In what is acknowledged as the most comprehensive review of sex differences*, E. E. Maccoby and C. N. Jacklin (*The Psychology of Sex Differences* [Stanford, Calif., 1974]) concluded that there are reliable sex differences in only four areas, three of which are cognitive: mathematical, spatial, and verbal skills. Since that date, several more sophisticated studies and research syntheses have been done. In general, these studies and reviews suggest the following conclusions: (1) Males outperform females, especially after the age of 14, most consistently on timed tests of spatial perception and mental manipulation of objects (measures of spatial skills), and on timed tests involving mathematical problem solving and proportional reasoning. (2) Sex differences (with females outperforming males) on timed tests of verbal skills are quite weak, and in most cases, insignificant, and more likely to occur prior to age 17. (3) Females outperform males slightly in school grades for verbal skills and there are no sex differences in grades for mathematics and science. (4) The general pattern of sex differences may emerge somewhat earlier and may be somewhat large among gifted and talented students.

It should be noted, however, that except for the sex differences on spatial skills, which account for as much as 8 percent of the variance, the obtained sex differences are not very large (accounting for only 1 to 4 percent of the variance). In addition, the magnitude of the differences is influenced by a variety of factors including age, previous course enrollment patterns, ethnic background, maturational rate, the particular test given, the historical period in which the study was done (differences are much smaller in more recent studies than in earlier studies), test-taking strategies, and the domains in which the problems are couched. Finally, the variance within sex on all measures is much greater than the variance between the sexes.

Given that sex differences in quantitative and scientific reasoning occur most consistently on timed tests rather than on other indicators of achievement such as school grades, tests and test taking should be discussed in a bit more detail. Performance on tests of mathematical and proportional reasoning depends on the individual's familiarity with the domain in which the questions are couched. An individual's reasoning capacity can be assessed with problems from several different domains (e.g., biology, physics, population genetics, cooking, etc.). Since how well one does on a particular problem is influenced by the extent to which one is familiar with the domain in which the problem is couched, and since many reasoning problems are couched in domains more familiar to males than to females (e.g., physics), tests of mathematical reasoning may be biased in favor of demonstrating male superiority.

Sex differences in variables linked to test-taking behavior may also be important mediators of the sex differences that emerge on timed tests. Females are more likely to use the response option "I don't know" rather than guessing, especially on difficult items. Females also report higher levels of test anxiety than males and are less likely to be risk takers, especially in male sex-typed domains. Each of these differences could have a negative impact on females' test-taking behavior sufficiently large to account for the sex differences on tests of mathematical and scientific reasoning.

Origins of Sex Differences on Cognitive Tests. Several explanations have been provided for the obtained sex differences on tests of mathematical reasoning and spatial skills. These include a sex-linked recessive gene for spatial skills, differential patterns of brain lateralization, hormonal influences, differential social and educational experiences both at home and in school, and differences in psychological characteristics (such as achievement motivation, confidence, interest, anxiety, cognitive style, autonomous learning behaviors, and mastery orientation). The evidence is least consistent for the biological explanations and most consistent for the social factors: males receive more and perhaps better math and science instruction, and more encouragement to develop these skills. Parents and teachers also have higher estimates of adolescent and adult males' mathematical and scientific talent, often in the face of contradictory information. Evidence regarding the psychological factors varies across the particular construct being considered with the strongest evidence supporting the importance of stereotyped sex differences in confidence, interest, and anxiety. In each case, however, the relationship of these antecedents varies across outcome measures; thus, it is likely that performances on spatial, mathematical, verbal, and scientific reasoning tasks is differentially influenced by various antecedents. Biological factors, for example, may have their largest influence on tests of particular spatial skills while social and psychological factors may be more influential on tests of knowledge.

Cognitive Styles/Orientation. Several investigators have suggested that males and females differ in a set of characteristics that influence their general orientation to cognitive tasks. For example, J. H. Block (*Sex Role Identity and Ego Development* [San Francisco, 1984]) argues that males are more likely to exhibit an "accommodative" mode of interacting with the world while females are more likely to exhibit an "assimilative" mode. The accommodative mode is characterized by cognitive efforts to create new mental structures and new strategies when confronted with new information or with disequilibrating experiences, and by a general orientation to explore and exploit the environment. In contrast, the assimilative mode is characterized by efforts to fit new information into existing mental structures, by relying longer on familiar strategies, and by a generally conservative orientation to one's environment. A somewhat similar distinction has been offered by C. S. Dweck ("Motivational Processes Affecting Learning,"

American Psychologist 41 [1986]: 1040–1048). She argues that females are less likely to seek out intellectual challenges and are more likely to resort to familiar strategies, to seek outside help, or to give up when faced with difficult intellectual problems. The evidence regarding these hypotheses is quite weak at present but research in this area is just beginning. I suspect, however, that sex differences on these types of variables, as on sex differences on cognitive skills, will be quite small and that the overlap of males' and females' scores will be quite large.

Further References. J. E. Eccles, "Sex Differences in Achievement Patterns," in T. B. Sonderegger (ed.), *Psychology and Gender: Nebraska Symposium on Motivation, 1984* (Lincoln, 1985). D. F. Halpern, *Sex Differences in Cognitive Abilities* (Hillsdale, N.J., 1986). J. S. Hyde and M. C. Linn (eds.), *The Psychology of Gender: Advances through Meta-Analysis* (Baltimore, 1986).

                                                                                    JACQUELYNNE S. ECCLES

COLOR, WOMEN OF. Women in the United States who are of African, Asian, Hispanic, and American Indian heritage. These categories are umbrella terms which can be further broken down into finer divisions within each racial-ethnic category. Divisions within the African category include black Americans, Afro-Caribbeans, and other women from the African diaspora who now live in the United States. Asian women include Japanese, Chinese, South Asians, Pacific Islanders, and new immigrants from Southeast Asia. Hispanic women include Mexican-Americans, Puerto Ricans, Cubans, and immigrants from South and Central America. And American Indian women encompass over 300 tribal affiliations crosscutting reservation and urban Indian life.

Increasingly, scholars point out that black/white comparisons can no longer dominate the discussion of gender, race, and ethnicity in America. While discussions of race and ethnicity have focused on men and discussions of gender have focused on white women, a third category, women of color, is emerging as a legitimate theoretical and conceptual framework for viewing a range of racial-ethnic women in America. The term has also been applied cross-culturally, but for purposes of this discussion the analysis will be restricted to the American case.

While women of color are distinct from the white majority in terms of race and ethnicity, there are historical differences between the groups that make them not strictly comparable. These differences are anchored in unique experiences involving culture, language, racism, and sexism*. Nonetheless, it is their common experiences of racial and sexual discrimination* in a society defined in terms of whiteness and maleness that is the major unifying feature of their existence.

Thus in this essay the focus in on contrasting and comparing two major dimensions in the lives of women of color. The first emphasis is on a shared theoretical lens through which to view their history and current-day status. This theoretical framework is the intersection of race, class, and gender in their lives. The second focus involves looking at women of color's deep embeddedness in family and work relations. They are central forces in the social construction of racial-ethnic family life, and their economic positioning in labor markets is a reflection of race and gender inequality.

The central theoretical theme in the analysis of women of color is race, gender, and class inequality. These inequalities are interconnected. This means that the ideology of racism, economic inequity, and gender inequality are distinctive but interrelated forces in their lives. Women of color often occupy unique economic, cultural, and gender niches. Hence, their evolution as women is somewhat separate from that of Anglo and other white ethnic women.

Regarding race, women of color suffer from the cultural and symbolic definitions and practices of white supremacy. Thus, in a related sense, the self, language, religion, and family practices of women of color have been stigmatized and treated as inferior. In addition, gender has been the basis of inequality in their lives. Women, generally, do not fair well in a society organized along patriarchal lines. Yet, in a society crosscut by racial inequality, women of color are doubly at risk. For example, in the economic sphere, even though all women are heavily ghettoized in clerical positions, when supervisory positions are held by women, white women tend to be in the supervisory positions and women of color tend to be supervised. Another case in point is that while political, economic, and social power are monopolized by white males, women of color must rely largely upon innovative political strategies and resistance. These tools have been part of the arsenal of black women's struggle since the time of the slave trade. Other women of color have been more submerged politically, but are beginning to come into their own, defining their interests and organizing to achieve these goals.

In terms of class and economic relations, women of color are disproportionately poor. This is especially true for Mexican-American, American Indian, and black women. It is somewhat less so for certain Asian women, such as the Japanese, but the new Southeast Asian immigrants, such as the Hmong, are often impoverished. Nevertheless, these women share in common gender experience with all women because of their connection to the range of gender inequality: distinctive gender socialization and gender discrimination.

Finally, crosscutting race, class, and gender issues are the domains of work and family. Family is essential in the lives of women of color. The feminist critique of the family as a site of oppression has been challenged by these women. Feminists from these groups argue that the family is central to their existence and often serves as a haven in a society which demeans them (B. Hooks, *From Margin to Center* [Boston, 1984]). For example, black women have centered their lives in family and community as well as paid work. This tradition continues to the present. Historically, Hispanic women have not been as involved in paid work as black women have, but this is changing as a growing number of Hispanic women enter the paid labor force. Home, however, has been quite essential to them. M. Baca-Zinn and D. S. Eitzen (*Diversity in American Families* [New York, 1987]) note that Mexican-American women have been powerful forces within their homes. Family has also been central in the lives of Asian women.

Furthermore, extensions and kin-shared family relations are also indicative of American Indian family life.

As working women*, each group faces discrimination in the labor market. This discrimination has varied somewhat by group since the women are rather differently located in the labor force. Yet, overall, women of color have been in sex/race categories with job ceilings and disproportionately occupy jobs at the bottom of the labor market, this positioning profoundly shaped by race, ethnicity, and sex. Only in the last 20 years have the labor market experiences of women of color increasingly converged with the experiences of white women. Now all groups of women are sex segregated in the labor force, primarily in service and clerical work. Even so, white women are more likely to be employed in executive and managerial levels than are other groups.

More specifically, black women are still overrepresented in service and non-household domestic work. Mexican women are involved more than others in seasonal work, and skilled Mexican-American women are centered in the low-paying clerical, operative, and service occupations. American Indian women predominate in low-level service work but confront the dilemma of obtaining any kind of employment since unemployment rates tend to be high on reservations and in urban areas. Japanese, Filipino, and Cuban women are at the top of the professional work categories, but Asian women dominate in garment, piecemeal, and semiconductor work in this country (E. M. Almquist, *Minorities, Gender and Work* [Lexington, Mass., 1979]). Neither group is free from race and sex discrimination in the workplace.

In short, there is unity in diversity in the context of these women's work and family lives. For all, there remains the difficult struggle of maintaining a sense of self and a degree of personal integrity in hostile environments. Yet, through their innovations, struggles, and resistance, women of color are a positive and notable force in American society.

ROSE M. BREWER

COMMUNITY PROPERTY is a system of property ownership and control in which marriage* is treated as an economic partnership to which each spouse makes an equal but different contribution, and in which each is entitled to an equal share of the assets.

Community property was introduced into the United States in territories formerly held by Spain and France: Arizona, California, Louisiana, New Mexico, and Texas. Idaho, Nevada, and Washington also use the system; some others adopted it briefly because of its income tax advantages but reverted to common law when the Revenue Act of 1948 ended the advantage.

In general, under the community property system, property brought to the marriage and property acquired by one of the spouses through gift, devise, or inheritance during the marriage remain under individual ownership. All other property belongs equally to both spouses. Originally the husband controlled the common property and, in some cases, the wife's separate property as well. The wife's rights in the joint property, then, were of practical importance only at the dissolution of the marriage.

During the marital property reform movement of the late nineteenth century, the husband's absolute control was weakened. He could not encumber or sell real property without his wife's knowledge and consent, or transfer any property to defraud his wife. Where she did not have it before, the wife gained the right to manage her own property and, in some states, to control her own wages.

In the reforms of the 1960s and 1970s, husbands lost the sole right of management of joint property. In 1967 Texas adopted a "gender-neutral" system of control according to which spouse held title, in effect leaving most husbands in control of most assets. The Washington reform in 1972, however, gave equal management and control to both parties. The other six states adopted the Washington pattern over the next seven years.

The community property system has decided advantages over a separate property system for most married women in matters of credit, contract, and management and control of property. In property settlements at the death of the husband or in cases of divorce*, community property's equal division contrasts with the widow's third that is usually the norm in cases of intestacy and is often used as a guideline in "equitable division" divorce settlements in common law states.

Courts in common-law property states found community property rules helpful in determining property settlements at divorce. When in the 1970s and 1980s common-law states moved to erase sex discrimination in credit and contract and to reform divorce and inheritance laws, community property rules were again consulted. Feminists in common-law property states have worked for and supported the adoption of the community property (marital property*) concept.

COMPARABLE WORTH (also called "Pay Equity") is a wage policy requiring equal pay within a jurisdiction or firm for job classifications that are valued equally in terms of skill, effort, responsibility, and working conditions. In practice, implementing this policy requires the application of a *single* job evaluation system to all job classifications within the jurisdiction or firm. The job evaluation system measures in detail the skill, effort, responsibility, and working conditions of every job classification and combines the scores in each area to produce a *single* overall score for every classification. Job classifications with equal overall scores are considered to have equal value to the jurisdiction or firm. Under a comparable worth wage policy, classifications of equal value are paid equivalently. All individuals holding the same jobs within equal classifications would not be paid the same wages, however, because seniority, merit, or quantity or quality of work done would continue to differentiate individuals' wages within equivalent classifications.

Comparable worth became controversial when an analysis of the relationship between current wages and points revealed differences in compensation related to gender, race, and ethnicity. A large number of studies have shown that if two job classifications have the same value according to the job evaluation system, but one is held primarily by men and the other held primarily by women, or one is held primarily by whites and the other by people of color, the job held by men or whites usually pays more. For example, the State of Minnesota used the results of a Hay Associates point-factor job evaluation to determine whether, at equivalent point levels, female-dominated and male-dominated jobs were paid equivalently. At equal Hay point values, jobs dominated by women paid less than those dominated by men. Minnesota's analysis did not extend to comparisons of race and ethnicity because the state of Minnesota's workforce, like the state's population, has fewer than 3.5 percent people of color. Using a somewhat different methodology, the comparable worth analysis undertaken for state of New York employees included race, ethnicity, and gender comparisons and showed parallel findings.

Opponents of comparable worth, relying on a neo-classical view of economics, believe that wages should be established not by the value of a job to the firm or jurisdiction, but rather by what the marketplace pays for each type of job. Comparable worth supporters respond, in the tradition of institutional economics, that the market embodies the customs and practices that encourage low wages for jobs filled by women and minorities. The gender-, race- and ethnicity-based wage differences found within jurisdictions and firms for equally valued jobs are evidence that the market does not properly value the work traditionally done by women and minorities.

The movement for comparable worth arose from the persistence of wage differentials between women and men, differentials that were exacerbated for women of color*. In 1984, figures for full-time workers showed that white women earned 64¢, black women earned 58¢, and Hispanic women earned 54¢ for every dollar earned by white men. In that same year, black men earned 74¢ and Hispanic men 71¢ in comparison to the dollar earned by white men. While the earnings differentials between minority and white workers had become narrower after World War II, earnings differentials between women and men remained fairly stable. The Equal Pay Act of 1963 and Title VII* of the Civil Rights Act of 1964 did little to reduce the overall earnings differentials between women and men.

One of the major reasons the Equal Pay Act and Title VII did not change earnings differentials is that women and men do not for the most part hold the same kinds of jobs. According to 1980 census data, women workers, regardless of race or ethnicity, were likely to work in occupations that were two-thirds filled by women, and men were likely to work in jobs whose incumbents ranged from 69 to 79 percent male, depending on color. The more an occupation is filled by women or people of color, the lower its wage rate.

The history of comparable worth began soon after World War I when the newly created International Labor Organization called for "equal pay for work of equal value." In the United States during World War II the War Labor Board created a policy of equal pay for equal work and very briefly supported a policy of equal pay for jobs of equal content, regardless of the sex of the worker. Sustained interest in equal pay and comparable pay did not survive the war years. Not until 1963, when Congress passed the Equal Pay Act, did the "equal pay for equal work" standard become law, eschewing the comparable worth standard proposed in earlier versions of the bill. In 1964, Title VII of the Civil Rights Act created a general national prohibition against employment discrimination*. Section (h) of Title VII, referred to as the Bennett Amendment, reconciled the provisions of the Equal Pay Act and Title VII with regard to women's wage discrimination claims. Title VII has become particularly important in the implementation of comparable worth because it prohibits not only intentional discrimination but also neutral policies having an adverse impact on protected groups.

One of the legal questions yet to be decided under the incorporation of the Equal Pay Act into Title VII of the Civil Rights Act of 1964 is whether Title VII accepts a comparable worth wage standard. In 1981, in *County of Washington* v. *Gunther*, the Supreme Court ruled that Title VII was not restricted to the equal work standard of the Equal Pay Act. Although the Court explicitly chose not to rule on the "controversial concept of 'comparable worth,' " advocates agreed that the Court had not precluded further consideration of comparable worth cases.

The *Gunther* opinion offered a boost to local, state, and national activists. Working from a base of several years of grass-roots efforts, public employee unions, particularly the American Federation of State, County and Municipal Employees, joined women's organizations, minority groups, and others to form the National Committee on Pay Equity in 1979. Opponents also organized, primarily through business associations like the National Association of Manufacturers, to lobby against the policy.

Litigation, legislation, and collective bargaining have been used to achieve comparable worth. Like many equity reforms, the early efforts have focused on the public sector. A growing number of state and local governments use or plan to use pay equity as the basis for compensation of public employees. As of April 1987, 28 states had conducted job evaluation studies for state workers, and 17 states had begun to make some kind of comparable worth wage adjustments, using legislative appropriations. The cost has generally been in the range of 2 to 5 percent of total payroll. In 1984, Minnesota became the first state to require all local jurisdictions to prepare plans to implement comparable worth policies for their public employees. Some cities like Los Angeles and San Jose have approached comparable worth through collective bargaining. Between 1980 and 1988, efforts to study or implement comparable worth for the federal workforce stalled due to partisan divisions.

SARA M. EVANS AND BARBARA J. NELSON

CONCUBINAGE is a legally and socially recognized union of a man with a woman who does not have the full status of a wife. In many monogamous societies, although a man could have only one wife, he might have one or more concubines of inferior status. Ancient Rome differed in that, although concubinage was recognized, a man could not have a wife and a concubine at the same time. Areas recognizing legal concubinage have slowly dwindled: Eastern Europe ceased recognition with the spread of orthodox Christianity, Western Europe in the sixteenth century, China in the early twentieth.

Concubines or secondary wives might be procured for various reasons. Princes and aristocrats might take secondary wives, or might be offered concubines, to form family alliances. If a marriage was childless, the husband might take a concubine rather than divorce and remarry. Young concubines were taken for pleasure, especially as the wife got older. Widowers, instead of remarrying, might take a concubine so as not to produce new heirs.

The concubine is usually of much lower social status than the husband. She is often a slave or a freedwoman, but could be an alien whose marriage with a citizen was not legal, a free woman in a union with a member of the nobility or from a family* too poor to pay a dowry*. The concubine and her husband might live together in all respects as a married couple, or she might live in the same household with a wife and possibly other concubines as well. In the latter case, she would be in an inferior position and would have to show proper respect to the legal wife. Her inferior position did not prevent her being subject to the same punishment as a legal wife for sexual misconduct.

There are usually few or no guarantees of permanency for the union or for the concubines' future maintenance. The fate of a slave concubine was likely to be sale to a brothel. The fate of a free woman dismissed without maintenance, even if she had a family to grudgingly receive her, would not be enviable. In Athens a daughter given in concubinage might bring a gift, similar to a dowry, which, since the gift would have to be returned if the woman were dismissed, helped to assure the stability of the union. In medieval Spain the *barragania* was protected by a contract. If dismissed, she had the right to maintenance for life and sometimes the right of inheritance.

Children of the union were usually considered illegitimate and inherited their mother's status. They did, however, have some legal rights and might inherit in the absence of children by the wife. In Rome the father had to maintain them, and in the absence of legitimate heirs, they inherited one-sixth of his estate. In China, the children of concubines were accounted children of the principal wife and shared equally. The children of a *barragania* inherited their father's status.

Although considered very improper, some free women lived in concubinage with slaves. In Rome from the mid-first century A.D. a woman who did so could be reduced to the status of freedwoman, or even enslaved. Her children, until the time of Hadrian (d.138), were slaves.

In Roman law only a thin line separated marriage and concubinage, the *affectio maritalis* (the intention of being married). A dowry was a sign of intent to marry. Many people who could not marry (e.g., Roman soldiers until A.D. 197, members of the senatorial class with freedpersons) lived together permanently in all respects as man and wife. Soldiers commonly married their concubines upon retirement.

The Eastern, or Byzantine, Empire ceased to recognize concubinage under Leo the Philosopher (d.911), but it remained legal in the West. The position taken by the Council of Toledo (c.400), that a married man who kept a concubine was subject to ecclesiastical punishment but an unmarried man who did so was not (canon 17), was restated, in full or by implication, in councils and synods through the mid-eleventh century.

By the nineth century, after the church had gained ground in its fight against multiple wives and/or concubines and repudiation of wives, it attacked quasi-marriages by portraying concubines as loose women and seductresses. However, its general acceptance of concubinage for single laymen remained the same. Civil law in various areas of thirteenth-century Europe also attest to the legality of the institution.

In fact, as long as "word of mouth" marriages, vows exchanged without witnesses, were accepted, there could be no sharp distinction between marriage and concubinage. It was not until the Reformation in the sixteenth century when, in both Protestant and Catholic areas, strict conditions for a lawful marriage were imposed and enforced that concubinage ceased to be a legally recognized form of union in Western Europe.

CONSCIOUSNESS RAISING is the process of transforming the personal problems of women into a shared awareness of their meaning as social problems and political concerns. Through consciousness raising (CR), women come to understand the intricate relationships between the individual aspects of their experience and public, systemic conditions; that is, the personal become political. For feminists, changed consciousness is a fundamental component of social change.

Consciousness raising is the cornerstone of feminist theory* and practice. It is a core component of feminist activities and organizations, including the large national women's organizations; women's caucuses and political action groups; women's studies courses and scholarship; feminist service agencies; feminist music, theater, art, and literature; and women's CR and support groups.

Through consciousness raising, feminist theorists and activists redefine and reinterpret the meaning of women's social experience. In women's organizations, understanding the nature of female oppression is essential for assessing needs, establishing goals, providing alternative programs and services, and working toward social change. Also, significant personal change occurs for women through understanding themselves as part of a larger social group and through viewing personal problems within the context of common social roles and social conditions.

The primary mechanism for consciousness raising in the contemporary feminist movement has been the CR group. In their early stages, mid–1960s to the early 1970s, CR groups consisted primarily of radical feminists, and group discussions focused on political analyses and the development of feminist ideology. Also, these early CR group members educated themselves and others through projects such as writing pamphlets and newsletters, serving as a "speakers' bureau," planning demonstrations and protests, and organizing other women's CR groups. Proliferation of CR groups during this period and public awareness of feminist thought can be largely attributed to their efforts. These early groups served as mechanisms for educating and radicalizing women and for creating a broad-based social concern with women's issues.

By the mid–1970s, the political education functions of activists in these groups became less salient. The presence of gender bias and discrimination* and the principles and goals of the feminist movement were increasingly discussed in society at large. At the same time, the appeal of the personal growth and support aspects of CR groups became prevalent. CR became widely identified as a way for women to examine issues in their own lives in terms of their social conditioning. By altering women's perception of themselves and of society at large, CR groups were seen as effective mechanisms for personal and social change.

In CR groups, institutional structures and social norms, as well as individual attitudes and behaviors, provide the framework for analysis. Through sharing, CR groups help women understand and deal with personal problems as they are related to their gender-role conditioning and to their experiences with bias, discrimination, and victimization. Through this process, personal attitudes, behaviors, roles, and relationships, as well as social policies and practices, become targets for change. Although literature may be used to provide additional information, the personal experiences of group members are the central ingredients for understanding problems and for devising solutions, both private and public.

CR groups epitomize feminist theory and method. Based on equal sharing of resources, power, and responsibility, they are generally leaderless and stress principles of sisterhood and the authority of personal experience. There is an assumption of shared experience and shared difficulties. CR groups emphasize being supportive and nonjudgmental toward members' behaviors and attitudes but critically examine social values and political beliefs.

Studies indicate that CR group outcomes include (1) increased self-awareness, self-respect, and self-esteem; (2) increased awareness of the effects of traditional gender roles* and sexism*; (3) increased awareness of a commonality with other women; (4) improved relationships and a sense of solidarity with other women; (5) development of a sociopolitical analysis of female experience and the nature of female oppression, and the development of a feminist identity; (6) changes in interpersonal relationships and roles; and (7) participation in a range of activities designed to change women's political and social circumstances. The most prevalent findings concern changed perceptions, attitudes, and beliefs in a pro-feminist direction.

By the late 1970s, with women having multiple sources for heightening their awareness of female subordination, many CR groups emerged as a result of women's feminist identity. These groups (often referred to as women's support groups) provide women with support, validation, and assistance as they work to incorporate feminism into their everyday lives. In these groups, women continue to explore the social structural nature of their problems and share strategies for dealing with them; they develop feminist alternatives to apply in their work and in their personal relationships. For women who are not actively involved in the movement, CR groups continue primarily as a means for personal growth through shared understandings of problems common to women.

Consciousness raising is an integral part of the services offered by feminist agencies, including women's counseling centers, rape crisis centers, and shelters for battered women*. Also, feminist workers in traditional agencies design programs and services to help female offenders*, women who abuse alcohol and drugs, women with eating disorders, incest victims, etc., and include consciousness raising as an important part of their overall efforts. The goal is to help women understand how traditional gender roles and gender inequality have contributed to their distress and victimization.

Also, consciousness raising is a central component of feminist approaches to therapy. Feminist therapists believe that it is growth producing for women to evaluate the ways in which cultural ideology and structural realities shape female experience. Feminist therapists often use all-women groups, which facilitate the consciousness-raising aspects of their work. These groups de-emphasize the authority of the therapist and help the group members share and understand the experiences that have influenced them collectively as women.

For many women, redefinition of gender roles* and new attitudes toward women have translated into political activism. For all women, personal change from consciousness raising has political significance. Female oppression is supported by women's internalizing cultural views that devalue women and legitimate women's powerlessness and victimization. By helping women understand the multifaceted ways in which their personal difficulties are inextricably linked to their subordinate social status, consciousness raising significantly alters how women view themselves, women as a group, and their social circumstances. By altering these internalized views, consciousness raising challenges one of the primary ways in which oppression is maintained.

Similarly, many of the changes that occur in women's values, attitudes, and behaviors are in opposition to the dominant cultural ideology. When the nature of personal change conflicts with the dominant values of society, personal change becomes political and holds broad social implications. The transformation of the meaning of personal experience through consciousness raising creates feminist supporters and activists and thereby remains the core of feminist approaches to social change.

Further References. M. L. Carden, *The New Feminist Movement* (New York, 1974). M. M. Ferree and B. B. Hess, *Controversy and Coalition: The New Feminist Movement* (Boston, 1985). D. Kravetz, "The Benefits of Consciousness-Raising Groups for

Women,'' in Claire Brody (ed.), *Women's Therapy Groups: Paradigms of Feminist Treatment* (New York, 1987).

DIANE KRAVETZ

CONTRACEPTIVES are methods, devices, chemicals, or hormones used to prevent conception or implantation of a fertilized ovum as a result of vaginal intercourse. No one method combines 100 percent effectiveness, complete safety, and reversibility. The woman (or the couple) must decide which method is best for her (them) in light of health risks, ethical considerations, and sexual needs. Acquired Immune Deficiency Syndrome (AIDS)* has introduced a new factor to be considered in the choice of contraceptive. Unless there is certainty about the health of her partner, the woman must protect herself not just from possible pregnancy but from a fatal disease as well.

Natural methods, which do not involve the use of outside agents, are the least effective. One of the oldest is *coitus interruptus*, or withdrawal of the penis immediately prior to ejaculation. Withdrawal has a low effectiveness, but some couples use it successfully. When no other method is available, it might be "better than nothing."

Rhythm Methods are based on the natural cycle of the woman's reproductive system*. Theoretically, if the time of ovulation can be pinpointed with any accuracy, then, by factoring in the length of time that the ovum and sperm within the woman's vaginal area remain viable, a monthly schedule of "safe" and "unsafe" periods for intercourse can be determined and conception avoided. All the rhythm methods require careful record keeping and long periods of abstinence. Because each person's body rhythms are different, and subject to change, none of the rhythm methods has an effectiveness approaching methods using outside agents. They are especially unreliable during cycle changes, as when women stop breastfeeding and as they approach menopause*.

The calendar rhythm method is based on the assumption that ovulation takes place at the midpoint between menstrual periods. It has been superseded by more sophisticated methods of determining time of ovulation. The thermal, or basal body temperature (BBT), method is based on a rise of temperature of from 0.4 to 0.5 degrees F that occurs at ovulation and persists until menstruation. Daily records of temperature are kept, and a "safe period" is charted. The Billings method is based on observing changes in the cervix and cervical mucus. As ovulation nears, the cervix softens and mucus increases. The "safe periods" will be periods of dryness before and after menstruation.

The sympto-thermal method, combining the cervical mucus and the BBT methods, increases effectiveness beyond that obtained by either one used alone. For any success in the use of these natural methods of birth control, careful instruction by a trained counselor is essential.

Methods employing outside agents are intended to control women's reproductive cycles or to prevent conception or implantation of a fertilized ovum during periods of fertility. They include the use of barriers, intrauterine devices, hormones, and surgical techniques. They do not require the cooperation of the other partner. Condoms and vasectomy are male methods of contraception. The other methods are used by women.

Barrier Methods require the use of material agents to block the passage of sperm or to prevent implantation of fertilized ova. Chemical barriers contain a spermicide in a foam, jelly, cream, or ointment base. Inserted about a half-hour before intercourse, they form an occlusive seal, holding the sperm while the spermicide kills them. The woman must remain lying down from the time of insertion until after the coital act. There is some possibility that conception during or shortly after using a spermicide increases the risk of birth defects.

Barrier devices include the condom, used by men, and the diaphragm, vaginal sponge, and cervical cap, used by women. The condom is a thin sheath of latex or animal membrane that fits over the penis, containing the ejaculate—about a half inch needs to be left at the tip to catch the seminal fluid. It is important to make sure that the condom has no cracks or imperfections. Since use of a latex condom can help prevent the spread of sexually transmitted diseases*, it is strongly recommended as a defense against transmission of the AIDS virus.

The diaphragm is a rounded cup of latex with a flexible rim that is fitted between the pubic bone and the back of the vagina, with the rim going beyond the cervix to rest on the vaginal cul-de-sac. Since it does not completely seal the cervix, a chemical barrier must also be used: spermicidal cream or jelly is placed around the rim, and some in the center of the diaphragm. Any sperm getting around the rim will be immobilized and killed by the spermicide. Proper size and rim style to fit the individual, proper placement, and an adequate amount of spermicide are essential to the effectiveness of the diaphragm. It should be left in place for eight hours after intercourse, but a longer period will increase the risk of toxic shock syndrome*, and probably vaginitis*.

In 1983 the Food and Drug Administration (FDA) approved over-the-counter sale of the vaginal sponge. It is a disposable disk (about 3/4 inch thick) of polyurethane that is moistened, then inserted into the vagina so that the indentation on the top of the cylinder fits over the cervical opening (OS). It is held in place by the walls of the vagina and contains a spermicide that releases slowly. A loop of tape on the bottom of the cylinder allows easy removal. Although less effective than the diaphragm, it does not need to be fitted, does not leak, and can be left in place for 24 hours (it must be left in place for 6) and used for repeated intercourse. The results of long-term use are not yet known.

The cervical cap, a latex device that fits over the cervix, was approved for use by the FDA in May 1988. The cervical cap, which has been used in various areas of the world for centuries, was available in the United States earlier in the century but at the time of FDA approval had to be imported. Thimble shaped, it comes in several sizes and fits over the cervix, forming an almost airtight seal around the OS. It can be left in place for two or three days but cannot be used during menstruation. Most clinics advise the use of small amounts of spermicide;

some instructions call for none. Cervical caps must be fitted, and some women may have difficulty finding a proper fit from the sizes available.

Intrauterine Devices (IUD) have been recognized as effective contraceptives for thousands of years, although the way they work is not clear. The prevalent theory is that a foreign object in the uterus stimulates the production of prostaglandins, thereby preventing successful inplantation of the fertilized ovum by increasing uterine contractions. IUD use became practicable with the development of plastics and improved insertion techniques in the twentieth century. Plastic devices of various shapes, some with copper or progesterone, were marketed. They appeared so highly effective that in the 1970s they were promoted as an alternative to the—it was thought—more dangerous hormonal method (oral contraceptives).

Pelvic infections, sometimes life threatening (especially in the case of pregnancy), occur at twice the rate of infections with barrier devices. It is possible to perforate the uterine wall at insertion, and occasionally the device will migrate through the uterine wall after its insertion. Ectopic pregnancies are abnormally high among IUD users. Pregnancy while the IUD is in place, or removal of the IUD once pregnancy is determined, runs a high risk of spontaneous abortion. Complaints about serious problems arising from the use of IUDs led the FDA to ban the Dalkon shield. As lawsuits against its manufacturer mounted, other companies withdrew their products. In the late 1980s IUDs were not available in the United States (although at least one manufacturer was planning to market a new device). They may still be obtained in other countries, but their risks are considerable.

The Hormonal Method, oral contraception or ''the pill,'' was approved by the FDA in 1960 and was first hailed as the final answer. These contraceptives contain an estrogen and progestin that together act to prevent conception by suppressing ovulation or, if ovulation does occur, impeding the fertilization and implantation of the ovum. The pill is taken daily for three weeks, then use is discontinued for seven days.

The use of the pill can have side effects, some minor, some likely to disappear after several cycles of use, some life threatening. The latter include increased blood pressure, the possibility of heart attack, cancer*, and problems with the liver and gallbladder. The possible dangers led to a ''pill scare'' and reduction of use in the mid–1970s. Most of the side effects are related to the estrogen. A reduction in the amount of estrogen from a high of 150–100 micrograms to 50, or, in low-dose pills, to 35–30 micrograms, has reduced the risks. In the low-dosage pills, the amount of progestin has also been lowered. The lowered hormone levels have not decreased the effectiveness.

Groups of women at risk have also been identified: women who smoke, older women (risks rise after age 30), those who are diabetic, seriously overweight, or who have a history of heart, liver, or gallbladder problems. Prolonged use combines with other factors to increase the risk. Hence, a healthy nonsmoker under age 35 can use oral contraceptives for 10 to 15 years without accumulating additional risk. Before a woman begins use of the pill, a careful assessment of benefits and risks in light of the individual's medical history, a thorough physical examination, especially a Pap smear*, and familiarity with the symptoms of the possible serious side effects are essential. So too are a three-month assessment and regular six-month checkups for as long as pill use continues. For those young, healthy women for whom the pill poses no serious problems there are additional benefits in its use: reduced risk of ovarian cancer, reduced chance of pelvic inflammatory disease, very regular periods, reduction of menstrual cramping and of blood flow, and, for some, reduction of premenstrual tension.

Minipills, containing only progestin, have been marketed in the United States since 1973 for women who should not, or do not wish to, take estrogen. The low-level progestin pills, which are taken daily, are safer than, but not quite as effective as, low-dose combined pills, and cause spotting and irregular bleeding. Few women use the minipill.

A postcoital or morning-after type contraceptive is the use of combined pills with high progestional activity (Orval). They must be taken as soon as possible after intercourse (no later than 72 hours) and repeated in 12 hours.

Surgical Methods, or sterilization, prevent reproduction by preventing the delivery of sperm or of ova. Sterilization is an increasingly popular form of fertility control, especially for those over 30 years of age. More women are sterilized than men. The most frequent form of sterilization is tubal ligation or salpingectomy, which can be performed under local anesthesia. Through an abdominal or vaginal incision, the Fallopian tubes are cut, then tied or cauterized, thus breaking the passage from the ovaries to the uterus. Although there are very occasional failures in which the cut ends of the tube rejoin, the procedure should be considered irreversible.

Vasectomy, a sterilization procedure for men, is even easier and safer than tubal ligation and is also cheaper. The procedure takes about five minutes under local anesthesia. The vas is tied above the testes, shutting off the sperm portion of the seminal fluid. Theoretically, the operation is reversible, but for all practical purposes should be considered irreversible. Vasectomy and tubal ligation do not interfere with sexual pleasure or menstrual function.

CORRECTIONAL OFFICERS AND SUPERINTENDENTS. Women who guard inmates in prisons and jails and those who are in charge of prisons and jails. Until the 1960s those who served as guards were called matrons, whereas those who were in charge were called superintendents (or head matrons); since then they have been referred to as correctional officers and superintendents (or wardens) respectively. In the United States, careers for women in the correctional system (known as the prison system before the 1960s) started after 1873 when the federal government and states began to establish separate all-female prisons. Until the 1960s women could work only in all-female institutions but thereafter have been employed, in limited numbers, as correctional officers and superintendents in all-male institutions. The history of women in the correctional system reflects, in general, changes that have taken place in the role of women in society since the mid-nineteenth century and, in particular, the attitudinal changes of feminists toward that role.

Careers for women in the correctional system evolved largely through the efforts of women involved in the reform activities of the 1820s to 1870s; some were feminists who participated in the women's movement. These white, well-educated, middle-class women turned to community service as an accepted activity when they found little opportunity to utilize their education and leadership ability. Many focused their attention on the redemption of fallen women, the prostitutes, vagrants, and alcoholics whose numbers had increased markedly with the growth in immigration, urbanization, and industrialization that followed the Civil War. Evoking a stereotypical view of woman as highly moral, pious, and virtuous nurturer, they argued that women were better able than men to redeem fallen women and children and that this process should be undertaken in all-female institutions. The first such institution, the Indiana Reformatory for Women and Girls, opened in 1873, creating nontraditional career opportunities for women in what had been an almost exclusively male system. The reformers had, by arguing that women were innately different from men, succeeded in creating a matriarchal enclave within the correctional system in which women neither worked with nor competed with their male counterparts.

This system of separate male and female correctional institutions, in which the only employment opportunities for women were in the relatively small number of female institutions, persisted for almost a hundred years. Not only did women receive lower salaries than men for similar positions, but they found themselves virtually excluded from positions of high authority in the correctional system. By the late 1960s, however, the voice of a new women's movement began to be heard in opposition to a system that offered limited opportunities to women. The civil rights and women's rights movements stimulated court decisions and legislation (Civil Rights Act, Title VII*, 1964) that outlawed discrimination based on race and sex. Women now had the legal basis upon which to demand equality of opportunity, and they did so, attempting to compete directly with men for all positions in the heretofore sex-segregated, male-dominated correctional system. They further bolstered their appeal for equal employment opportunities in the system by again invoking the stereotypical image of woman, arguing that women, being more humane, sensitive, and caring, were better able than men to create an atmosphere conducive to the rehabilitation of male as well as female criminals.

In their attempts to achieve equality of opportunity women have met intense opposition both from male staff and male inmates. The former argued that female correctional officers posed security risks in male prisons because of their weakness and vulnerability to rape*, a position that was upheld by the U.S. Supreme Court (*Dothard* v. *Rawlinson*, 1977) when it agreed that the bona fide occupational qualification* exception in Title VII allowed women to be barred from employment in certain male correctional facilities for security reasons. Male inmates had some success in arguing that the presence of women violated their right to privacy until a federal court decided (*Griffin* v. *Michigan Department of Corrections*, 1982) that male inmates have no constitutional right to privacy when balanced against the objective of providing equal job opportunities for women.

As a result of the *Dothard* decision, and because of continued opposition from male staff, women have made only limited inroads in the correctional system. Most of the gains were made after 1972 when the Equal Employment Opportunity Commission was given jurisdiction over government employment. Thereafter, departments of corrections were obliged to establish integrated staffs and develop unisex personnel policies and practices. By the mid–1980s the federal system and almost all the states had women officers in selected male institutions (female officers constituted about 8.5 percent of the correctional staff in male institutions), a few women had become superintendents of male facilities, several had been assigned to central administrative offices in positions of authority, and one woman became a commissioner of corrections. Black women, in particular, gained after the U.S. Supreme Court declared unconstitutional segregation based on race (*Brown* v. *Board of Education*, 1954). When racial segregation in prisons and jails ended, black women were hired and became eligible for promotion, and in 1983 constituted almost a third of the entire female correctional officer staff.

Despite antidiscrimination policies and practices the correctional system continues to be a male-dominated area of employment. Consequently, women who have sought employment and advancement in the system have had to overcome opposition from male staff. From the mid-nineteenth century to the 1970s women often used sex-role stereotypes to justify their role in the system despite the fact that many of them have been feminists actively involved with women's movements. However, in the 1980s a significant change took place in the position taken by female correctional officers and superintendents. Rejecting stereotypical woman, they argued that women had the right to equal employment opportunities in the correctional system because they were professionals capable of doing the job.

Further References. C. Feinman, *Women in the Criminal Justice System* (New York, 1986). B. Olsson (ed.), *Women in Corrections* (College Park, Md., 1981).

CLARICE FEINMAN

COUVADE, from the French *couver*, "to sit on," "to hatch," is a term that encompasses a wide variety of customs, including activities and restrictions upon activities and diet, by which fathers in a given society ritually take the part of the mother or join with her in childbirth* and the period of recuperation after childbirth.

Such customs have been noted from ancient times. The geographer Strabo in the first century B.C. and travelers in the nineteenth century A.D. wrote of the customs of the Basques in Spain; Marco Polo remarked on the customs of Chinese

Turkestan; other medieval and modern travelers amazed and amused readers with reports of men groaning in pain while their wives were in labor. Modern anthropologists have given more staid accounts of practices that stem from what seems a virtually universal concept.

The father's participation in the birth ritual and the duration and severity of the ritual vary widely. The father may perform acts that imitate those of the mother at the various stages of labor, delivery, and recuperation; may be prohibited foods or activities that, if eaten or engaged in by the mother, might harm the child; or may undergo prescribed activities thought to be of benefit to the mother or child. In some cases the father's ritual role may be more important than the mother's. Or both parents may be restricted from work and certain foods for a period, with the mother being more restricted for a longer period.

Couvade emphasizes the importance of the male in the creation and birth of the child but apparently may also assist the wife in having a safe delivery. By refraining from such actions as smoking, scratching, and eating the flesh of animals, the father may be protecting the child from the harm that such actions on the part of the birth-giver might cause. By imitating the actions of the wife in delivery, the father may attract to himself the evil spirits that interfere with delivery, thus keeping them from the wife and child.

COVERTURE is the English law term for the condition of women during marriage*. "[T]he very being or legal existence of the woman is suspended during the marriage, or at least is incorporated and consolidated into that of her husband, under whose wing, protection and cover, she performs everything" (Blackstone's *Commentaries*, 18th c.). In England and the common-law states of the United States, this concept of the married couple as a single person at law placed such constraints on the wife as inability to contract, sue, or be sued in her own right and inability to control her own property. It also meant that husband and wife could not contract with, or testify for or against, each other. The disabilities coverture places upon the married woman were fought by early English and American feminists, and are still being fought by their late twentieth-century descendants.

CRIMINAL JUSTICE. Women participate in the criminal justice system (CJS) in two ways: as professionals working within the system or as change-agents working outside the system. In the CJS women serve in increasing numbers in policing, in corrections, and in the courts.

The number of sworn police officers has crept up from 1.4 percent female in 1971 (the first year sex data were reported) to 6.3 percent in 1984 (FBI, *Uniform Crime Reports*, annually). Improvement arose from affirmative action suits in which height and weight requirements were struck down. Too, research indicates that women perform successfully on the job (P. B. Bloch and D. Anderson, *Policewomen on Patrol* [Washington, D.C., 1974] and S. E. Martin, *Breaking and Entering* [Berkeley, 1980]). Even a small but growing number of women are in administrative positions, in corrections and courts, particularly. Police chiefs are still almost exclusively male. But as increasing numbers of entry-level women move up through the ranks, more women police can be expected to attain administrative positions.

In corrections, problems for women are intensified because some 95 percent of all prisoners are male. Thus if women want to enter this area in significant numbers, they will have to be allowed to work in all-male facilities. (See CORRECTIONAL OFFICERS.)

Courts are staffed at the professional level by attorneys and judges. Here too are increases; in 1960, 2 percent of all U.S. law degrees were awarded to women; by 1983, 36 percent were (U.S. Department of Justice, *Civil Rights Forum*, 1985). No count is available of women defense attorneys and prosecutors, though Edith Flynn's observation in "Women as CJ Professionals" (in N. H. Rafter and E. A. Stanko, *Judge, Lawyer, Victim, Thief* [Boston, 1982]) that women prosecutors mostly try cases such as domestic and juvenile that give them little public visibility holds true for defense attorneys as well. In the judiciary, women holding federal judgeships rose from 10 in 1977 to 108 in 1984. Of 25,000 state-level judges only 564, or 2.3 percent, were female in 1984. Variation from state to state is wide, from none in New Hampshire to Hawaii's 125. Most sit on courts of limited or special jurisdiction, as do 61 percent of women federal judges. In state courts, 36 percent sit on general trial courts; a scant 8.5 percent on appellate courts (Linda Sanders, "Female Judges," unpublished paper, Southern Illinois University, 1986).

The women appearing in increasing numbers in the CJS face common problems: a lack of women in the higher, administrative positions, a pattern of specialization and isolation for women, and gender stereotypes. The first two problems are interrelated. Lines of advancement require movement up through the ranks, especially in corrections and police work. Rarely do persons occupying staff positions move up. Yet women are more likely to be received as workers in specialized areas: in police work as juvenile and vice detail officers or as officers dealing with female suspects and victims; in the judiciary, in matrimonial or juvenile courts; in corrections, in sex-segregated adult women's facilities and in juvenile facilities. The problem is twofold. First, women are being "ghettoized" into special "women's" areas of the CJS, from which advancement into line positions is difficult. Second, areas in which women have specialized have been accorded less prestige.

Gender stereotypes present a more difficult problem. Barriers in the CJS go beyond the simple exclusion found in other occupations. Lack of equal opportunity in criminal justice is less amenable to reform because it cuts to the core of important gender stereotypes. Cultural stereotypes of what it means to be a man are deeply embedded in images of what it means to be a crime fighter. Traditional ideal attributes of the status of woman and of crime fighter conflict with one another.

The degree of difficulty in overcoming gender stereotypes varies widely. First, if an agency follows an organizational model of service rather than crime control, women are likely to be less disadvantaged. Second, if the occupational subculture within an agency is male-oriented only in the sense of the exclusivity of an all-male club, rather than being fashioned from such occupational imperatives as physical force, women will be more accepted. Finally, if occupational specialties amounting to "male only" and "female only" jobs are allowed to continue to develop within an agency, women will achieve a short-run gain at the expense of long-term loss (N. K. Wilson, "Women in the CJS," in Rafter and Stanko, cited above).

Women have been much more effective working *outside* the criminal justice system than within. In the last two decades the feminist movement has concentrated much of its effort on ameliorating the situation of women as victims*. Ironically enough, this often has meant women have become crime fighters; women have indeed played the role gender stereotypes prohibit.

Efforts on several levels include, first, the feminist push for legislative change in rape law reform, police powers to enforce protection of battered women*, and recently, with less success, legislative protection for victims of pornography*; second, feminist pressure for changes in the CJS response to female victims (through publicity and direct work with CJS agencies, feminists have helped to improve significantly the response of hospitals, police agencies, and, with less success, the courts, to rape and wife battery); and, third, women have established aid for female crime victims entirely outside the CJS—shelters for victims of wife battery and crisis hot lines and counseling services for victims of rape and other female-victim crimes.

Feminist lobbying and direct political action demonstrate that not only have women had more impact on the CJS as outsiders than as "insiders" but also that feminists have had more impact on criminal justice practice than has any other single reform group.

Ultimately the largest impact women can have on the criminal justice system will come from changes they may be able to effect in woman's general socio-economic situation. Decreased rates of wife battery, rape, incest*, sexual harassment*, and dissemination of violent, antifeminine erotic materials (pornography) depend upon increasing women's political and economic power. When and if this empowerment occurs, women's victimization will lessen, and feminist efforts outside the system of criminal justice will be less necessary, because at that time women will approach 50 percent parity in all levels of the criminal justice professions.

NANCI KOSER WILSON

CULTURAL FEMINISM is the feminist theory* that stresses the differences between women and men and the superiority of the feminine. Basically nonpolitical, it concentrates on developing a separate life-style, a Womanculture.

According to Brooke ("The Retreat of Cultural Feminism," in Redstockings [ed.], *Feminine Revolution: An Abridged Edition with Additional Writings* [New York, 1978]), socialist feminists first used the term (c.1972) in attacking radical feminism* as nonpolitical. The name was then taken up by nonpolitical women within radical feminism, some of whom were coming in at that time from the counterculture. Cultural feminism does not concern itself with political action to attain equal rights or to ameliorate women's class oppression, but concentrates on individual self-realization through the creation of an alternative life-style. Women are, in the cultural feminist view, more nurturing, more peaceloving, less violent—because they are women. Eschewing biological determinism, they look to women's traditional culture as the source of their superior values and believe that by re-creating that culture they can transform society, replacing the aggressive values of patriarchy* with the nurturing values of women, hence their interest in matriarchy* and goddess worship, in developing woman's religion, art, and literature.

Josephine Donovan (*Feminist Theory: The Intellectual Traditions of American Feminism* [New York, 1985], Chapter 2) traces the roots of contemporary cultural feminism to the influences of romanticism and evolutionary theory in nineteenth-century feminist thought. She credits Margaret Fuller as the initiator of cultural feminism and considers Matilda Joselyn Gage and Charlotte Perkins Gilman as two of its most important theorists. Contemporary cultural feminist theory, e.g., Mary Daly's *Gyn/Ecology* (1978), Adrienne Rich's *Of Woman Born* (1977), and Susan Griffin's *Woman and Nature* (1978), is an important aspect of second-wave feminism.

CYSTITIS (inflammation of the bladder) is woman's most common urinary tract infection, one that occurs and recurs frequently. Although not usually serious, it is painful and can be embarrassing. The woman may feel the need to urinate frequently. The urine burns painfully during discharge and may also contain blood or pus.

Since a woman's urethra is relatively short (c. 2 in.), it is fairly easy for bacteria to get into the bladder and cause inflammation. Other factors that seem to promote or aggravate cystitis are caffeine, alcohol, decreased fluid intake, not urinating for long periods, and pressure on the urethra from sex.

Cystitis may disappear without treatment or may respond to self-treatment. However, it should not be allowed to persist beyond 48 hours without medical treatment since it could spread to the kidneys, causing a much more serious infection. If untreated, it could also lead, especially in girls, to muscle damage resulting in inability to "hold urine." In any case, whenever there is blood in the urine medical attention should be sought within 24 to 48 hours.

Further Reference. A. Kilmartin, *Cystitis: The Complete Self-Help Guide* (New York, 1980).

D

DECONSTRUCTION. In the latter part of the 1960s, literary theory shifted from structuralism to poststructuralism. Jacques Derrida in "Structure, Sign and Play in the Discourse of the Human Sciences" (1966) and *On Grammatology* (1967) founded the new critical movement called deconstruction, which criticized semiology and structuralism for the continuance of the basic Western philosophical belief in "logocentrism": the concept of structure that depends on stabilizing, fixed, "centers," such as truth, God, consciousness, being, essence, etc., and the inferior axiological oppositions, such as lie, Satan, unconscious, nonbeing, appearance, etc. Derrida is primarily concerned with the opposition of speech and writing. He argues that although the spoken word has always been viewed as a "center," with privileged status over its axiological opposite, writing, this is a "violent hierarchy," not only because the two are so similar but also because the hierarchy can be reversed. Reversing such hierarchical opposites is the first stage of deconstruction; the second is to resist asserting a new "violent hierarchy."

Feminists have been attracted to Derridean deconstruction because it demonstrates that thinking in terms of binary opposition has always implied the subordination of the second term to the first. Deconstruction exposed "man" as always occupying the privileged position, as always having set himself up as the central reference point. As deconstruction sought to expose and dismantle the terms and logic through which these claims have been made, many feminist critics have responded to it.

Several French feminist critics have used deconstruction theory in creative ways. For example, Julia Kristeva has looked closely at the opposition between the masculine (and therefore privileged) "closed" rational systems and the feminine, pre-Oedipally formed (hence a characteristic males also have but in most cases devalue) "open" disruptive irrational systems, the former aligning with her use of the term "symbolic" and the latter with her term "semiotic." The

"violent hierarchy" is deconstructed in Kristeva's theories as the poet and rev-
olutionary are shown to rely on that which emanates from the drives associated
with the body of the mother.

Hélène Cixous mapped out the binary oppositions that privilege man and calls
for remapping that places the woman as the "center." She advocates only the
first stage of deconstruction: the "violent hierarchy" can stay in place, with the
females body's plenitude occupying the place of privilege.

Derridean deconstruction has presented two major problems to feminists. First
of all, Derrida's resistance to "centers" lies at the base of his theories. Language,
he believes, should be—and often is—in constant "play," with no fixed terms
or elements that are beyond subversion. Such "play" can disrupt the delimiting
effects of "centers." Furthermore, he dismisses linguistic determinacy of form
and meaning and stresses that words are constantly deferred as to their meaning.
Inasmuch as Derrida believes not only that these things should be operative, but
also that they have been, he denies what many feminists wish to stress, i.e.,
that men almost totally control the meaning of language.

The second major problem is related to the first in that Derrida gave primary
status over all human activities to writing and hence to textuality and the inter-
textuality of all things. In deconstructionist theory, only writing allows full
referrals and shows true differences between and among things because our minds
are linguistic. Feminists question how they can imagine a relation between
linguistic play and deferral (this engrossing involvement with the signifying
processes) and the political and economic action necessary to gain the power
for change. Regardless of these drawbacks, feminist critics have found deconstruction a contemporary literary theory that serves them well.

GLORIA STEPHENSON

DEPENDENCY is the state of needing someone or something for support,
comfort, or aid. In Anglo-American culture, dependency is a dirty word, a
negative condition, associated with female weakness and helplessness, in contrast
to the ideal emotional condition of "independence," associated with male
strength and autonomy. But in other cultures, such as the Japanese, dependence
is regarded as essential in social life; Japanese even has a special word for the
need to be attached to and dependent on others (*amaeru*).

Popular books in recent years have debated whether men or women are the
"dependent sex," but the evidence shows that all human beings are dependent
on others, though for different things at different times in their lives. In a family*,
for example, the spouse who isn't earning an income is financially dependent
on the one who is; the spouse who cannot express feelings is emotionally dependent on the one who can; the spouse who has the flu is temporarily dependent
on the one who doesn't.

The stereotype of the emotionally self-reliant, independent male and the cling-
ing, dependent female has a kernel of truth, but it is not the whole cob. Because
women have traditionally been financially dependent on men, some observers

have concluded that men have not "needed" women as much as women "needed" men. In *The Cinderella Complex* (1981), Colette Dowling blamed women for passively relying on men to rescue them from responsibility and for sacrificing achievement and self-confidence in the quest for security. To Dowling, "dependency—the deep wish to be taken care of by others—is the chief force holding women down today"(31).

Such arguments ignore three facts (apart from the obvious one that there are more forces holding women down than women's own presumed psychological deficiencies). First, every relationship is a mosaic of interlocking dependencies that shift and change over time. Second, *both* sexes, especially in times of trouble, long "to be taken care of by others." In exchange for economic security, both men and women have been known to forfeit independence: traditionally, women have done so in their marriages, but men have done so in their work. Third, men are just as dependent on their partners as women, but often they are neither as aware of it nor as willing to admit it. Thus men have a much more difficult time than women do adjusting to the loss of a spouse through divorce* or death; single men have a higher rate of mental and physical illness than married men. It is as if men are unaware of how dependent they become on their wives for everyday caretaking and emotional support—until they are alone. So striking are the statistics on the frailty of unmarried men that some observers, such as Luise Eichenbaum and Susie Orbach, believe that men are the "dependent sex": their apparent autonomy is based on the confidence that they will be cared for. Although women seem dependent and helpless, in this view, they learn from childhood to rely on themselves, to be the caretakers of their children, husbands, friends, and eventually their parents.

In either gender, both extreme dependence and extreme independence carry psychological costs. The excessively dependent person stakes everything on continued support from the partner; if the relationship fails, the individual lacks resources and self-esteem. The excessively independent person risks nothing by trying to remain invulnerable to hurt and rejection; but he or she becomes sealed off from the pleasures and intimacies of close relationships. According to social psychologist Sharon Brehm, both extremes seek the same goal: absolute security. The dependent individual seeks the security of total protection and care; the independent person seeks the security of emotional invulnerability.

But most people do not fall at either extreme. Most men and women continue to depend on their friends, relatives, and lovers throughout their lives for love, moral support, financial aid, and good times.

Further References. J. Bernard, *The Future of Marriage* (New York, 1972). S. Brehm, *Intimate Relationships* (New York, 1985). L. Eichenbaum and S. Orbach, *What Do Women Want? Exploding the Myth of Dependency* (New York, 1983).

CAROL TAVRIS

DEPRESSION, in mental health usage, is a mood or affective disorder characterized predominantly by pervasive feelings of sadness, hopelessness, and despondency, negative self-image, decrease in ability to experience pleasure, and, in some cases, recurrent thoughts of death or suicide. A depressed person may also report loss of interest in work, decline in productivity, low energy level, lack of interest in sex, social withdrawal, and sleep and appetite disturbances.

It is important to distinguish depressive illness from normal mood fluctuations. Feelings of sadness, disappointment, and unhappiness are common reactions to the vicissitudes of life experienced by most people at one time or another. Indeed, it is normal to feel depressed in the face of a major loss, such as death of a loved one, or to feel "down" or "blue" when things go wrong in the primary arenas of love and work. The fact that the symptoms of depressive illness are common sometimes makes it difficult to discern when a person has crossed the line into mental illness. The difference lies in the intensity and severity of the symptoms and in the extent to which they interfere with the person's functioning.

Theories of Causation. Several theories of the causes of depressive illness have been proposed, implicating biological, psychological, social, and environmental factors.

Biologically based theories implicate genetic transmission and brain neurochemical activity. Family studies show that depression occurs more often among the close relatives of depressed patients than in the general population. Twin studies have found that identical twins have a higher concordance rate for depressive illness than nonidentical twins have.

Experimental studies have shown that reduced levels of certain brain chemicals are associated with depression, while enhanced levels produce euphoria or even mania. Such chemical interactions are very complex, however, and the causes of fluctuations sufficient to cause mood swings in some people are not known.

Some theories relate depression to personality needs, such as an overly punitive superego, resulting in anger and aggression being turned against the self, taking the form of self-blame and guilt. Such needs could be rooted in early childhood experiences with dominating and rigid parents who, by being too judgmental and critical, prevented the child from developing a positive self-concept and feelings of mastery in meeting life's challenges.

Other theories relate the onset of depression to the stress engendered by loss of or separation from a love object. Researchers such as Rene Spitz and John Bowlby studied depression in young children who were separated from their mothers for long periods. Comparative animal studies of monkeys deprived of their mothers indicate that the human capacity for depression as a reaction to loss is part of our evolutionary heritage.

Depression has been related to the thoughts and belief patterns that the depressed person has. Such persons hold pervasive negative views of themselves, environmental events, and the future. Given the mind-set, they then misinterpret or distort the meanings of events to fit with or to confirm their worldview, which is basically that life is beset with misfortune and unhappiness, and that nothing good has happened or ever will happen to them. An example is a young woman who developed herpes after having sex with a man she met in a bar. On relating what has happened she said, "Every time I try to do something good for myself [i.e., having sex] I get slapped down." For such persons, their depression is a self-fulfilling prophecy* in that every negative event, important or trivial, is interpreted as a confirmation of their basic belief that they are singled out for an unhappy life.

Animal experiments have created a condition of "learned helplessness"* that is quite similar to depression in humans. Dogs subjected to trials of inescapable shock began to accept the shock passively, having learned that no response of theirs would be effective in eliminating the discomfort. The analogy to depression in humans is that a person who feels unable to control environmental reinforcements may develop a profound pessimism because of her inability to effect positive change in her life. One thinks, for instance, of the battered wife who has learned the futility of any action of hers to protect herself or to remove herself from the situation.

Treatment for depression consists mainly of drugs and some form of psychotherapy, often used together. Certain drugs are effective in alleviating depressions related to brain chemistry. Because depressed persons usually have psychological problems such as negative self-image and feelings of futility and helplessness, psychotherapy is indicated along with drug therapy.

Women and Depression. Many studies have found women to have higher rates of depressive disorders than men have, regardless of the type of disorder. For example, in one study women using out-patient psychiatric facilities had about three times the rate of depressive disorders compared to men in the 25 to 44 age group. Several explanations for this gender-related disparity have been put forth. It has been proposed that the differences in men's and women's lives make women more vulnerable to stress. For example, men may have two major sources of life gratification, their work and their families. Women, by contrast, have traditionally been restricted to only one role, that of the family, thus reducing for them the possibilities for rewards and achievements. Even when women are employed outside the home, most work in low-paying, dead-end jobs that are secondary to their husbands' work role as primary provider. Too, the dependency* of women on men, coupled with their relative lack of resources, could induce in vulnerable women the "learned helplessness" syndrome wherein the woman feels helpless to take action to change an unrewarding situation.

Whereas earlier theories of psychopathology leaned toward locating the source of mental health problems in the afflicted person's psyche, it is now clear that many problems are generated by situational stress, that is, by features of the society and of the person's life over which the individual may have little or no control. Our society, as well as others, has a long history of discrimination* against women and of the relegation of women to second-class status. The incidence of depression is high among oppressed people who feel powerless to alter their situation. While women today have more control over their destinies than did our foremothers, the residuals of the oppressive effects of poverty*, lack of opportunity, and sexual and racial discrimination are still formidable barriers to many. For example, low-income mothers in single-headed households with young children have the highest rate of depression of any demographic group. It is not difficult to appreciate the relationship between environmental stress and depression when we contemplate the difference between the life of such a woman and that of one more affluent with plenty of support and a sense of personal strength and control over her life.

It has been suggested that the preponderance of women over men who are treated for depressive disorders is an artifact reflective of other gender differences. In our society women are freer to express distress than men are and tend to report more symptoms. Women visit doctors more often and get more prescriptions for mood-altering drugs. Also, it may be easier for women to enter the "patient" role because of socialization pressures that foster dependency and reliance on authority for women, but not so easy for men, who are encouraged to be strong and stoic.

Another explanation relies on the different coping styles of women and men under stressful conditions. It is possible that, given the same subjective levels of stress, women are more likely to become depressed while men may handle their distress in other ways, such as substance abuse or acting-out of anger* and frustration. Men do in fact have much higher rates of the latter symptoms than women have.

Finally, there is the possibility that some women are more vulnerable to depression because of biological factors. For example, it has been observed that for some women depression tends to be associated with changing hormonal levels of reproductive events, such as menstruation, the postpartum period, and menopause*. Yet most women experience all these events without developing symptoms. Also, mild depressions during the premenstrual or postpartum periods should not be confused with clinical depression, which is usually more severe and longer lasting.

Like most other psychological phenomena, depressive illness in most cases has no single cause. People vary greatly in their resistance to stress, in their vulnerability to the development of mental disorder, and in the circumstances of their lives. Some people develop a clinical depression after exposure to relatively moderate stress; others never do, in spite of extreme emotional and physical pressures.

Further References. D. D. Burns, *Feeling Good: The New Mood Therapy* (New York, 1980). M. Scarf, *Unfinished Business: Pressure Points in the Lives of Women* (Garden City, N.Y., 1980)

JUANITA H. WILLIAMS

DIFFERENTIAL SOCIALIZATION. That lifelong process based on social interaction by which individuals develop those attitudes and behaviors considered appropriate to their gender roles*. Every society assigns females and males to differing roles; therefore, every society must include structures and processes to ensure that males and females develop those characteristics assigned to each sex.

The predominant agencies of differential socialization include family*, schools, peer groups, the mass media, the public opinion.

Sex roles and stereotyped expectations begin shaping people's lives even before they are born. When asked whether they had a preference for the sex of their firstborn child, two-thirds of the adults questioned in a survey expressed a preference; 92 percent of those with a preference wanted a boy. The influence of sex roles becomes more apparent after the babies are born: studies show that parents tend to have different expectations for sons and daughters from birth. In a classic study (J. Rubin, F. Provenzano, and Z. Luria, "The Eye of the Beholder: Parents' Views on Sex of Newborns," *American Journal of Orthopsychiatry* 44 [1974]: 512–519), 30 pairs of parents of newborns were interviewed within 24 hours of their infant's birth. No objective differences between the babies in birth weight, length, nor any other physical or neurological characteristics were evident. Fathers were especially influenced by the sex of their child; they described their daughters as more inattentive, delicate, and weak than did the mothers, while the fathers rated their sons as stronger, better coordinated, and more alert than did the mothers. Both parents of girls described their infants as little, beautiful, pretty, and cute more often than did parents of boys; parents of boys, on the other hand, were more likely to describe their infants as big. We find then that early sex-role expectations set in motion a complex pattern that creates in individuals the characteristics expected. As a classic statement of social psychology states, we become what we are called; the labels attached to us create what they describe.

The differential treatment of male and female infants is closely connected to parents' sex-role expectations. For example, mothers of females have been observed to touch their infants more often than mothers of males. They also talked to and played with their daughters more often. By 13 months, the girls, in turn, talked to and touched their mothers more often than did the boys. This difference in treatment by parents of their sons and daughters can be further seen in children's bedroom furnishings: girls' rooms contain more floral furnishings and more dolls, while boys' rooms contain more animal furnishings, more educational toys, more athletic equipment, more art materials, and more vehicles (see K. F. Schaffer, *Sex Roles and Human Behavior* [Cambridge, Mass., 1981]).

Most researchers agree that male and female infants show more similarities than differences during infancy and early childhood and that females and males follow similar developmental paths. Despite these developmental similarities, however, young children are being provided the basic information on how girls and boys, women and men, should behave.

During adolescence major differences in sex-role behavior become much stronger, laying the groundwork for adult roles. Socialization pressures become more pronounced, and social reinforcement encourages different behavior from girls and boys. Boys are encouraged to be competitive, assertive, and goal seeking, being strongly supported in identifying and pursuing career goals and in developing fully their interpersonal, intellectual, and physical skills and abilities. Girls, on the other hand, often find themselves in a "double-bind"* situation: a conflict between achievement and "femininity"* (M. Horner, "Toward an Understanding of Achievement Related Conflict in Women," *Journal of Social Issues* 28 [1972]: 157–175). Sex-role prescriptions frequently reward popularity and social ability for girls more than academic and intellectual achievement. Girls are often discouraged from in-depth preparation for a specific career, being urged rather to maintain a flexible identity that will be compatible with their anticipated future roles as wife and mother, while boys are told that they must be successful in a job or career as the way to prepare for shouldering family responsibilities. While parents and family continue to play an important role in differential socialization, during the adolescent years the most important influences are school and peer groups.

While teachers and other school personnel are becoming more sensitive to the detrimental effects of sex-role stereotypes both on boys and girls, the schools continue as powerful agents of differential socialization. Teachers often directly influence sex roles by conveying feelings about appropriate or inappropriate behavior. Throughout their school experience, girls and boys are treated differently. Lisa A. Serbin and K. Daniel O'Leary, for example, report a study of teacher-student classroom interaction where teachers reinforced boys' aggressiveness by responding immediately to boys who misbehaved and by giving them a great deal of attention. All the teachers observed gave the boys more attention and twice as much individual instruction on tasks than they gave girls. Boys were rewarded more for academic achievement while girls were rewarded for staying close to the teachers and for dependency. Boys were encouraged to take risks, to be creative, to be independent, while teachers were more likely to take over girls' tasks, finishing them for the girls (L. Serbin and K. O'Leary, "How Nursery Schools Teach Girls to Shut Up," *Psychology Today* 9 [1975]: 56–58). Numerous studies show that these differential expectations and different patterns of interaction continue through students' academic careers, including college, and have considerable effects on students' sex-role identity as well as on academic pursuits. In addition to teachers' expectations and actions, the school curricula and textbooks themselves offer powerful but stereotyped portraits of appropriate sex-role behavior. Boys and men are far more likely to be characters in school literature, to be used as examples in textbook illustrations and exercises, and to be shown in active, assertive roles, while girls and women are absent, are in supportive roles, or act as a passive audience for boys' exploits (see, e.g., R. Best, *We've All Got Scars: What Boys and Girls Learn in Elementary School* [Bloomington, Ind., 1983]).

Especially during adolescence, peer groups are particularly powerful in socializing girls and boys into sex roles. Peer groups typically encourage activities that are greatly influenced by sex role stereotypes. Acceptance by peer groups entails conforming and subscribing to the values, norms, and goals of the group. Deviance is punished by the threat of withdrawal of support and friendship. The stigmatizing of deviants and the avoidance of them set clear, although unidi-

mensional, standards of what is acceptable. The forces for conformity are probably more intense during adolescence than at any other time during the life cycle.

The mass media, and most particularly television, are potent agencies of
differential socialization, especially in their provision of largely stereotyped
images of appropriate female and male roles. TV is especially important since
nearly everyone in America watches TV; for preschool children, viewing TV
consumes more time than any other activity except sleeping. Studies continue
to find marked differences in the portrayal of female and male characters. There
are far more male characters on TV; further, male characters are shown as
aggressive, constructive, helpful, and more likely to be rewarded for their behavior, while female characters are usually portrayed as passive, deferent, and
often punished if they were too aggressive or active. This characterization is
even more true of TV's commercial advertisements (see, e.g., I. Ang, *Watching
"Dallas": Soap Opera and the Melodramatic Imagination* [London, 1985]; A.
Courtney and T. Whipple, *Sex Stereotyping in Advertising* [Lexington, Mass.,
1983]).

The effects of differential socialization are to produce adults with the knowledge, skills, motivation, and emotional tendencies to perform the sex roles
appropriate to their status. Humans are not, of course, automatons, but socialization acts powerfully to produce in us not only the ability but the desire to
take on and enact our gender roles. Socialization is a lifelong process. Traditional
family structures and expectations, schools organized along sexist lines offering
stereotyped curricula, peer groups operating as intensifiers and transmitters of
traditional culture, and the media and public opinion reinforcing sexist images
work to produce humans limited to sex-linked repertoires of acts and feelings.
But socialization is also a human process, one that can be restructured to expand
rather than limit the human repertoire.

                                                                ALLEN SCARBORO

DISCRIMINATION occurs in the context of employment when employers
assign similarly qualified men and women to different kinds of jobs, give women
lower promotion opportunities than men, or allot women salaries and fringe
benefits inferior to those given to similarly qualified men. Discrimination also
arises in other economic contexts—women, on account of their sex, are sometimes refused the right to borrow money or buy on credit, the right to purchase
insurance on the same basis as men, to buy or rent a house or apartment, or to
try out an automobile that is for sale. Women are sometimes excluded from
educational opportunities on account of their gender. They suffer many social
snubs, which are damaging in the context of work. Males commonly display a
lack of interest in women colleagues' opinions and suggestions. Experiments
conducted by psychologists have shown that writing or artwork attributed to a
woman is rated as of lower quality than identical work attributed to a man.
Sometimes discrimination takes the form of sexual harassment*, in which a
woman in a typically male job is hazed by coworkers who annoy her with sexual

questions, suggestions, and mock invitations. The "social" forms of discrimination all serve directly or indirectly to impair women's economic opportunities.

Discrimination reduces women's direct access to economic means of self-support, reinforcing the economic disadvantage that women suffer on account of childbirth*, childrearing, and socialization to fit into female roles. Discrimination thus has intensified women's need to form relationships with men in order to gain access to economic goods. For this reason it has been a major cause of women's subordination to men in the family and in society generally.

Full-time women workers in the United States in the 1980s earn 20 to 25 percent less than men of similar education and length of experience. In Japan and Ireland, the gap between men's and women's pay is greater than it is in the United States, but in most of the other developed countries the gap is lower. However, there is no country in which women have parity with men in earnings.

There has been considerable controversy among economists as to how much of the difference in pay between women and men is due to discrimination. Some economists have argued that discrimination against capable women employees in favor of less capable male employees would go counter to the interests of employers. They go on to deduce that discrimination must therefore be rare or nonexistent. These economists attribute women's lower wages not to employer discrimination but to women's own choices. Women's vocational choices are limited, these economists argue, by their willing acceptance of the burden of child care* and housework*. On the other side of the argument is case study material derived from lawsuits, containing testimony to grossly discriminatory practices. Also favoring the hypothesis of pervasive discrimination is the bulk of statistical studies, whose authors have looked for evidence that the entire salary gap between the sexes might be explained away innocently, but have failed to find it.

Occupational segregation* is the leading symptom of discrimination in employment. Women have been welcomed only in a narrow range of occupations: clerical worker, retail sales worker, nurse, librarian, teacher of young children, and low-level factory and service worker. In the United States in 1985, about half the women workers were employed in those occupations in which the workers were more than three-quarters female. Research that has focused on placement within individual workplaces shows that the isolation of women from men doing the same work is even more extreme than suggested by the occupational statistics. For example, about 20 percent of the workers in the occupation "waiters and waitresses" are men. But the colleagues of the typical waitress are not 20 percent male; on the contrary, restaurants that hire men to wait on tables typically hire no women at all, and those hiring women hire no men.

Discrimination in employment derives from a number of sources. Males have tended to behave in ways that contribute to the maintenance of male superiority. Women are denied the opportunity to have jobs in which they would exercise authority, have high pay, and interact with men as equals. Employers appear to have beliefs about women's incapacity for certain work; as an example, women have been excluded in many instances from jobs in which operating a vehicle, even a passenger car, is part of the duties. Employers have also reasoned that family duties (from which men have been able to keep themselves aloof) make women less desirable employees in certain roles. Employers have not been willing to commit resources to training women, on the grounds, now shown to be false, that women are more likely to quit than men.

In the United States, an Equal Pay Act was passed in 1963. It required an individual employer to pay women and men the same wage if they had virtually identical jobs. The following year, the Civil Rights Act was passed, containing far broader provisions barring discrimination in employment on account of sex, as well as on account of race, religion, or national origin. The Civil Rights Act makes it unlawful for employers to discriminate in hiring, job assignment, promotion, pay, or fringe benefits. It forbids employers to limit, segregate, or classify employees or applicants by sex in any way that might adversely affect them. The courts have interpreted the Civil Rights Act as forbidding employers to bar women as candidates for any job, even in cases where a considerably smaller proportion of women than men are capable of performing it. Tests given to job candidates that pass a smaller proportion of women than men, unless such tests can be shown to be job-related, also violate the act. The United States has also enacted laws that forbid discrimination in awarding credit and that bar federal support of school programs in which male and female students are treated differently. Through the mid–1980s, complaints to enforcement agencies or court suits brought under these laws have had only a small result in reducing the economic disparities between women and men. More vigorous attacks on job segregation might be mounted through affirmative action plans mandating employers to achieve numerical goals for the hiring of women in all occupations on specific timetables. Such goals and timetables have been a part of the U.S. government program to require firms that sell to it to achieve better representation of workers by race and sex. However, enforcement of the program has been slack.

"Pay equity," or "comparable worth"*, offers a second possibility of accelerating progress against discrimination and its effects. The idea of pay equity is that employers should be required to adjust upward the wages of workers in the traditionally female occupations so as to make them commensurate with the pay of traditionally male occupations requiring similar levels of skill, mental ability, and responsibility. In Australia and England, pay equity adjustments have had considerable success in raising wages of women workers with little discernible adverse affect. In the United States, pay equity campaigns have for the most part been targeted against state and local governments in their role as employers.

Further References. B. R. Bergmann, *The Economic Emergence of Women* (New York, 1986). D. J. Treiman and H. I. Hartmann, *Women, Work and Wages: Equal Pay for Jobs of Equal Value* (Washington, D.C., 1981).

BARBARA R. BERGMANN

DISPLACED HOMEMAKER is a woman whose principal job has been that of unpaid homemaker and who has lost her main source of support because of the dissolution of her marriage or the cessation of income from other sources.

(Definitions vary; the above is based on the definition in *Displaced Homemakers: Programs and Policy—An Interim Report* [Washington, D.C., 1985].) The woman is usually in the 35 to 60 year age span and either has not been in the paid labor force or has earnings below the subsistence level. She either has no marketable skills or has rusty or outdated skills. Usually she is too young (under 60) for social security* and in many cases her youngest child has become too old for public assistance.

Estimates of the number of displaced homemakers in 1983 varied, largely according to definition, from about 2 to 4 million. The Office of Technical Assessment estimate of displaced homemakers between 35 and 64 years of age was 2.2 million. More than 60 percent were over age 45, and over 60 percent still had children living at home.

Many displaced homemakers just recently have had the wrenching emotional experience of the death of a loved one or a divorce. Many are facing poverty* for the first time in their lives. Feelings of depression* and inadequacy are likely to be heightened as they try to cope with their new life circumstances.

To prepare to support themselves and their families, displaced homemakers need a variety of services, including counseling; training, to refresh and/or update skills, learn marketable skills, or acquire basic education; and job placement. Many need financial support, for transportation, child care*, or living expenses, and emotional support. Personal counseling is at least as important as vocational counseling, and support groups are important in the transition.

The first displaced homemaker center opened in California in 1975. Since then, with state, very modest federal (until 1985 federal support was not over $10 million at its height), and private funds, the number of centers increased. In 1984, there were at least 425 centers, located in almost every state and the District of Columbia, some independent, but most connected with educational institutions, women's centers, organizations such as the YMCA. They served anywhere from a handful to several thousand clients a year and offered services from counseling and referral only to a full range of counseling and support service through training* to job placement and follow-up (*Displaced Homemakers*, 15).

DIVORCE is the complete dissolution of a marriage, with the right to remarry. The term is sometimes used broadly to include separation (divorce from bed and board) and annulment as well.

Every society establishes methods, formal or informal, for ending marital unions and decides how easily they can be ended, by whom, and whether or not the parties can remarry. In general, it tends to be much easier for marriages to be dissolved at will by either the wife or husband in matrilineal (as ancient Egyptian) and matrilocal (as ancient Japanese) societies. In preindustrial patriarchal societies the husband might have the sole right of repudiation (as in Israel, early Rome, China), he might be able to divorce easily and at will and the wife only through a legal procedure and for cause (as ancient Babylonia and Greece,

Islam). Or, as in Rome by the Late Republic, husband, emancipated wife, or father of an unemancipated daughter, even against her wishes, might initiate divorce.

Because until recent times marriage was the only socially acceptable state for a woman (with the rare exception of some priesthoods such as the Vestal Virgins of Rome and, later, the cloister), even where women had a liberal right to divorce, they would rarely initiate it without the backing of their natal families. In patriarchal society another deterrent was that they would lose custody of the children. With few exceptions, all children belonged to the father, although sometimes, as in Muslim countries, the child would remain with the mother up to the age of seven. In Western society it was not until the latter nineteenth century that it became customary to award custody of the children to the mother.

Where men could divorce without cause, the economic arrangements acted as a brake. If a women was repudiated, her dowry* had to be returned. Since the dowry often was mixed with other possessions, mortgaged, or even wrong-fully depleted, its return might be difficult. Where the marital payment was brideprice or bridegift*, it would not be returned, and in some cases, additional compensation had to be given to the wife. This might prevent the man from remarrying.

Religious and social ideology determined the ways a society relieved marital tensions. Major social and economic developments, such as industrialization and urbanization or the introduction of Western ideas and institutions into Eastern society, modified old ideologies or created new ones, bringing, among many others, changes in divorce law and practices. Such changes occurred in Western Europe and North America during the early sixteenth century, the latter nineteenth century, and the 1970s and early 1980s. In Eastern societies most radical changes occurred in the first half of the twentieth century.

In the West in the latter nineteenth century, with the exception of some Catholic countries (e.g., Italy, which accepted divorce in 1961, and Ireland, where a referendum to allow divorce was voted down in 1986), divorce was permitted, usually on very narrow grounds. During the period, as part of the social reforms aimed at alleviating some of the problems of the new industrial society, England, most of the states in the United States, and much of Protestant Europe made changes in divorce laws. Even though it was not the intention of the reformers, and even though divorce was still considered scandalous, there was a great rise in the number of divorces, and especially in the divorces gotten by women. It was also during this period that women began to gain custody of the children of the marriage.

The great upsurge of industrial production after World War II also culminated in a reform movement, including divorce reform. No-fault divorce*, which marks a radical departure from past thinking, was widely adopted. Reformed divorce laws in Europe, North America, Australia, and New Zealand were again followed by a great rise in the divorce rate. They also signaled that divorce is now recognized by a large segment of the population, not as a drastic and shameful concession of failure, but as the accepted solution to an unhappy marriage. It is estimated that half of all marriages will end in divorce.

For divorce in the United States, see below.

DIVORCE (U.S.). Colonial divorce laws and procedures were fundamentally sexist. The laws of the Northern colonies, although more expansive than those of England, worked in ways that discriminated against women; for example, both men and women could receive divorces on the grounds of adultery*, but men were the chief beneficiaries of this law, evidence suggesting the depth of the sexual double standard*. In the South, absolute divorce was proscribed, thereby leaving women at the mercy of their more powerful husbands. This is not to say that the double standard and legal restrictions left colonial women with no recourse. Although only a few hundred colonial women legally dissolved their marriages, several thousand more simply deserted their husbands. These "self-divorces" reveal a higher level of marital incompatibility than the low divorce rate of the period would suggest: they also prove that thousands of women found the risks of independence more inviting than continued residence with husbands they despised.

During and after the American Revolution, women's situation regarding divorce improved. Wives increasingly included allegations of adultery among their complaints; moreover, most state legislatures expanded the grounds of divorce. Although a variety of new grounds were added to statutory laws, the inclusion of cruelty as a just cause played a key role in fueling the surge of female divorce complaints in the nineteenth century. By 1900, approximately two-thirds of all divorces went to women, and by 1929, 44 percent of all divorces granted to women came on the grounds of cruelty. What is more, judges continually expanded the interpretation of cruelty until some late nineteenth-century jurists began recognizing "mental cruelty" as a sufficient reason for divorce, a development that allowed husbands, but especially wives, to break free of spouses who threatened no violence but who made life miserable nevertheless. The thousands of women who received divorces on the grounds of cruelty and desertion—the two most common late nineteenth-century complaints—rarely received alimony* or child support but most always received custody of the children. Thus, divorce for women brought some independence but also the advent of new obligations, dependencies, and financial difficulties.

As the divorce rate continued to rise in the late nineteenth and early twentieth centuries, supporters and opponents of divorce engaged in a protracted debate. On one side stood a handful of feminists and a more numerous group of liberals who supported access to divorce. For feminists like Elizabeth Cady Stanton, women needed divorce to free themselves from fools and tyrants; for liberals, divorce was a remedy in line with their commitments to freedom and happiness. On the other side stood conservatives who viewed divorce as a sign of female selfishness and wider social breakdown: to their mind, tougher laws, an end to divorce havens, and a reinvigoration of traditional morality were needed to stop this fearful erosion of traditional morality were needed to stop this fearful erosion of traditional morality and social stability.

Although conservatives had no luck with their hope for a uniform divorce code, they did manage to abolish catchall omnibus clauses, restrict the rights of remarriage, and impose stricter residency requirements on those seeking a divorce, but such reforms could not stand against the small army of petitioners seeking an end to marriage. Fed by rising romantic and sexual expectations within marriage, increased leisure time* and consumption wants, growing female opportunities for economic self-support, and expansive judicial interpretations of statutory laws, the divorce rate continued to rise in the early twentieth century. By 1920 there were 3.41 divorces per 1,000 married population, up from 0.81 in 1870. Almost 150,000 divorces were granted in 1920: the figure a half century earlier was scarcely more than 11,000.

Divorce continued to be a major social issue in the first half of the twentieth century. Progressive reformers shifted the focus away from individual moral failure and toward an emphasis upon the social, economic, political, and demographic changes that produced rising rates of divorce. Progressives believed only fundamental changes could reduce the frequency of divorce; in the meantime, reformers proposed stricter access to marriage, education about marriage* and family life, and even trial marriages to stem the rate of divorce.

Environmental interpretations soon gave way to clinical conceptions of divorce, and from 1910 to 1940, the divorce question was couched in the language of psychopathology and medicine: rejecting earlier moral or environmental explanations, divorce reformers now used psychological and medical terminology to brand divorce seekers as neurotic, infantile, and abnormal. The solution to the divorce problem, reformers now believed, lay in curing the neuroses that produced divorce, but the agent of cure was to be a therapeutic, patriarchal legal system singularly ill-equipped for the task. All too easily legal therapy in the form of family courts, social work investigations, reconciliation sessions, and counseling services simply degenerated into a form of patriarchal state control. Moreover, reformers often found it difficult to implement these reforms in the face of legislative conservatism, splits within the reform camp, and a continued emphasis on divorce as an adversarial rather than a therapeutic procedure.

The post–World War II story is one of sharply rising divorce rates, the emergence of no-fault divorce*, and the growing recognition that no-fault laws have been a disaster for women and children. Beginning with California's no-fault law of 1969, all but two states had some kind of no-fault law in place by the mid-1980s. Promising an end to the fraud, collusion, and acrimony that accompanied the adversarial system of divorce, no-fault was initially hailed as a significant and progressive achievement in the history of divorce litigation. The consequences, however, have left women and their dependents worse off than they were before the change; the reason is that no-fault presupposes an equality between husbands and wives that has no basis in reality. Instead, men's standard of living rises sharply in the first year following divorce whereas women's and children's declines by over 70 percent, a situation brought on by men "cashing out" on home sales and by inadequate alimony awards and child support payments. No-fault reflects the erroneous assumption that women—often out of the job market for years and ill-equipped by training* or education for today's job market—can readily become self-supporting, independent household heads. Only spousal and child support awards founded on an attempt to achieve parity in standards of living can bring justice to women and their dependents. Until that happens, the divorce revolution of no-fault will be a revolution that made losers of women and children.

Further References. R. L. Griswold, *Family and Divorce in California, 1850–1890: Victorian Illusions and Everyday Realities* (Albany, 1982). L. Halem, *Divorce Reform: Changing Legal and Social Perspectives* (New York, 1980). E. T. May, *Great Expectations: Marriage and Divorce in Post Victorian America* (Chicago, 1980). W. O'Neill, *Divorce in the Progressive Era* (New Haven, Conn., 1967). L. Weitzman, *The Divorce Revolution: The Unexpected Social and Economic Consequences for Women and Children in America* (New York, 1985).

ROBERT L. GRISWOLD

DOMESTIC SERVICE is an occupation involving such tasks as cooking, cleaning, washing, ironing, sewing, and child care*, traditionally done by unpaid female family members. In the nineteenth century it emerged as the primary form of gainful employment for women in countries undergoing industrialization. The term *domestic servant* usually referred to someone employed full-time and living on the premises of a private household. By the mid–1800s, in such countries as the United States, France, and England, most domestic servants were women, and in the United States by 1870 over half of all women workers and over two-thirds of all women working in non–farm-related occupations were servants.

The growth of industrial capitalism, urbanization, and a large and increasingly status-conscious urban middle class, with economic changes in rural areas, explain the emergence of domestic service as the primary occupation for women. During the period 1790–1830, these changes began to undermine the household economy throughout England, the United States, and certain regions of Europe, depriving many women of such traditional domestic responsibilities as spinning, while at the same time creating a need for additional family income. These rural and working-class women provided a fairly inexpensive supply of labor just as the growing number of middle-class families began to predicate their status and identities on being able to release their own wives and daughters from all the more onerous aspects of household labor.

Although domestic service was not a new occupation, by the mid-nineteenth century the nature of the job had been transformed. Previously, most domestic servants worked for the nobility of Europe and the wealthiest families of America where large, complex staffs of servants had been the standard, and male servants usually outnumbered females. This pattern began to change dramatically in the eighteenth century as the commercial and industrial revolutions provided a wide range of jobs outside domestic service for men and as women became available for service at much lower wages. By 1851, less than a third of the servants in France, and no more than 10 percent in the United States and England, were male. In addition, while it had not been uncommon for less wealthy rural households to hire females to perform domestic chores, prior to the late eighteenth century most of these women were considered "hired help" rather than servants. They were often daughters of neighboring farmers, usually employed for intermittent periods of time, and informally incorporated into the family* (sitting down with the family for meals, etc.).

In contrast, the typical domestic servant of the nineteenth century was unlikely to be either a male member of a large domestic staff or a friend of the family acting as temporary "hired help." Instead, she was most likely to be a young, unmarried female who lived and worked alongside at most one other servant in a small, middle-class urban household. Although, as was true previously, most domestic servants in England, Europe, and rural America were native born, in the large northern cities of America where the bulk of domestic service jobs were found, immigrant women and their daughters predominated, with Irish and Scandinavians more likely than any other group to work as servants.

Although domestic service jobs varied, the majority of servants were "maids-of-all-work" and the only live-in staff. They were responsible for cooking, waiting on tables, washing the dishes, all cleaning and bed-making, laundry and ironing, mending, and child care. If a second live-in domestic was hired it was usually as cook or child's nurse. For all live-in servants the hours were long, on average 11 to 12 a day, seven days a week, and a domestic servant was "on call" 24 hours a day. Domestic servants traditionally got one or two afternoons a week off, but they were expected to have accomplished most of the daily chores, which meant working at least seven hours before leaving. Wages including room and board (which varied considerably in quality) were the same as or higher than wages of other unskilled or semiskilled occupations available to women but generally lower than professional or clerical wages.

Wages, however, did not usually determine whether or not a woman chose domestic service employment. Although some women preferred it, particularly newly arrived immigrants who found the assurance of room and board a distinct advantage, most women took the job because lack of education, limited job opportunities in the area, or discrimination* made other jobs inaccessible. Long hours, hard physical labor, cramped living quarters, and bad food made domestic service undesirable; but tense employee-employer relations and the job's low status seem to have represented its major drawbacks. Class, ethnic, and religious differences strained the working relationships of employers and servants. Servants bitterly resented the control their employers exercised over their dress, speech, use of leisure time*, and contact with family and friends.

Just as the early stages of industrialization prompted the emergence of domestic service as the primary form of employment for women, the maturation of industrialization played an important role in its decreasing significance. Between 1890 and 1920, although the demand for domestic servants persisted, the importance of the job for women diminished. Child labor laws and compulsory education that kept the very young out of the workforce, combined with immigration restrictions that cut off the flow of immigrant labor, depleted two of the traditional sources of domestic labor. In addition, as the industrial economies matured, a much wider array of jobs for women became available, and greater proportions of women chose offices, stores, and factories as their place of employment. As a result, in the United States the proportion of working women in domestic service fell from over half in 1870 to less than a fifth in 1920.

The women in and the nature of the job changed as well during this period. Women doing household labor were older, less likely to be single, and less likely to be white or foreign born. The percentage of black domestic servants rose from 24 percent in 1890 to 40 percent in 1920. To a degree, because of these changes, domestic service ceased to be done by women who lived in. A growing proportion of the women in domestic service, like the black women who were denied access to alternative forms of female employment, were married and unwilling to live apart from their own families.

In conclusion, throughout the twentieth century domestic service has become an increasingly marginal job for women in industrialized nations, held by a small percentage of women who generally for reasons of race, ethnicity, or marital status can not obtain other form of employment. However, for those women still engaged in household employment the disadvantages of long hours, relatively low wages, difficult personal relations with employers, and lack of status have persisted to the modern period.

Further References. F. E. Dudden, *Serving Women: Household Service in Nineteenth-Century America* (Middletown, Conn., 1983). D. M. Katzman, *Seven Days a Week: Domestic Service in Industrializing America* (New York, 1978). T. McBride, *The Domestic Revolution: The Modernization of Household Service in England and France, 1820–1920* (New York, 1976).

MARY LOU LOCKE

DOMESTIC SPHERE comprises the family* and household, and all the duties, activities, and concerns associated with their functioning. In traditional society the domestic sphere has been woman's primary concern. In the sexual segregation of labor, she has usually been responsible for the primary care and rearing of small children, the tasks necessary in cleaning the house, clothing and feeding members of the household, and production for household consumption. On the other hand, the man's primary concern was the public sphere*: production for the market, buying and selling in the market, defense of the home, and relations with the world outside the home.

The duties and concerns of women and men were never exclusive to one sphere, and the spheres themselves overlapped (e.g., what is woman's work in one society might be man's work in another, surpluses from production for household consumption were sold, men purchased items for household use, women influenced public policy, directly or indirectly). However, at the end of the eighteenth and in the early nineteenth century, as men's productive activities left the home and as it became cheaper to buy than to produce more and more items for household consumption, there was a physical separation of production activity from the household. The gap between the public and private spheres appeared so wide that they came to be thought of as "separate spheres." The domestic sphere was "woman's sphere." The ideology of domesticity was developed out of this apparent dichotomy between the home as woman's sphere and the world as man's.

DOMESTIC VIOLENCE. The crime of intimidation and physical abuse of one family or household member by another with whom they may or may not reside. The term *domestic violence* is often used interchangeably with *family violence* or *spouse abuse*. It is a broad term encompassing child abuse, spouse abuse, sibling abuse, abuse of a parent by a child, and abuse of the elderly or handicapped. It includes sexual abuse and incest*.

Domestic violence occurs in all socioeconomic and racial groups. Its victims may be of any age or sex. The family*, which is seen as the place of love and nurturance, is the scene of emotional and physical pain for many people. Domestic violence has been condoned historically because it has taken place in the sacred confines of the family. It has been protected by the right of privacy, but abuse impinges on the community-at-large. The highest number of assaults upon police officers, some resulting in death, occur while responding to domestic disturbance calls. Perpetrators may have learned the violent expression of anger* in order to control, or their violent behavior may be rooted in low stress tolerance. Frequently they have been abused, or have witnessed abuse, in their families of origin. Cultural factors such as violence in defense, advertising, entertainment, and sports reinforce permissible use of violence to control others. Loss of such control may arouse emotions of fear, hurt, anger, jealousy, frustration, and vulnerability, emotions closely linked with violence toward others. The violence continues while no one in authority prohibits it.

Child abuse refers to acts of neglect or violence committed on children by adults. Violence has been a fundamental part of the American way of childrearing. It is epitomized by the expression, "Spare the rod and spoil the child." Many parents of both sexes believe it is permissible and necessary to physically hurt children as a means of discipline. Children are also an available target for the expression of violence-linked feelings. Child abuse many range from deprivation of necessities through emotional maltreatment, minor physical injuries, sexual abuse, and major injuries to murder. The Child Abuse Prevention Act of 1974 focused attention on the problem. Its severity has been denied by many, yet a 1976 study revealed a high incidence of physical abuse of children. That study estimated that from one to two million children had been kicked, bitten, or punched by parents or caretakers during the previous year. Another study estimated that from 275,000 to 750,000 children were "beaten up" during the year (M. A. Straus, R. J. Gelles, and S. K. Steinmetz, *Behind Closed Doors: Violence in the American Family* [New York, 1980], 60–62).

One-half million children are sexually abused each year. The majority of these children are molested by a family member or someone that they know. Incest and sexual abuse refer to the manual, oral, or genital sexual contact that an adult imposes on a child. Children are unable to stop or understand this adult behavior because of their powerlessness in the family and infantile level of personality development. Children who survive such abuse lose their sense of trust in adults and carry this loss into adult relationships. Statutes require the reporting of child abuse to the state authority vested with the responsibility of protecting children.

The term *spouse abuse* refers to acts of violence between sexual partners who may or may not be married or living together at the time of the abuse. ("Wife-beating" and "woman battering" are popular terms for spouse abuse.) In the 1970s interest expressed by the women's movement gave rise to local, state, and national efforts to end spouse abuse. In the mid–1980s there were some 900 crisis intervention and shelter programs in the United States. These programs emphasize advocacy and self-determination. Out of domestic violence research and the shelter experience a body of knowledge about spouse abuse has grown. It is estimated that one in 26 American wives, or 1.8 million women, are beaten by their husbands each year. Statistics (Straus et al., 40) indicate that men commit 95 percent of reported assaults on spouses. In spouse abuse there is an identifiable cycle of violence that repeats over time. Battered women* grow to believe they are deserving of their mates' treatment. Women feel a responsibility to keep the relationship intact and may be vulnerable to the third phase of the cycle, when men may promise an end to the violence (Lenore Walker, *The Battered Woman* [New York, 1979], 55–77).

Violence between siblings may be the most common form of domestic violence. One study indicates that sibling violence occurs more frequently than parent-child or husband-wife violence. Since boys of every age are more violent than girls, the highest frequency of violence occurs in families that have only boys. While many violent acts are pushing, shoving, and hitting, significant numbers of beatings take place (Straus et al., 80–94).

Abuse of parents by children is the least-studied form of domestic violence. Parents frequently hit their children in retaliation. Serious injuries are inflicted by children on parents (Straus et al., 119–122). Adult children may continue to abuse parents.

In the 1980s there is a growing awareness of the incidence of elder abuse. The first National Conference on Abuse of Elder Persons was held in 1981. Elder abuse, like other forms of domestic violence, occurs in a repeating pattern. Frail elderly victims are dependent upon others to provide for their living and health needs. The abuser is usually a member of the immediate family responsible for the care of the elderly person and frequently lives in the same house as the victim. Abuse ranges from exploitation of resources through neglect and threat of physical abuse to gross physical injury and murder. Victims cluster between ages 75 and 85, with female victims predominating. The victim usually suffers from debilitating physical illness or mental impairment. As with all domestic violence the secrets are kept while the abuse is denied by victims through fear and resignation or through unwillingness to expose a loved one as an abuser.

Mentally retarded, mentally ill, and physically handicapped individuals are also vulnerable as victims of domestic violence. The abusers are again family members or guardians with responsibility for their care. These caretakers may be emotionally, physically, or financially unable or unwilling to care for their elderly or handicapped family members. Medical and social service professionals are taught to recognize the indicators of psychological and physical abuse. They are charged with intervening and offering alternatives. By statute many states now require mandatory reporting of abuse of elderly and incapacitated adults and provide protective services for this population.

Further References. *Attorney General's Task Force on Family Violence: Final Report* (Washington, D.C., 1984). *Adult Abuse and Neglect: Handbook for Medical Personnel* (Tulsa, 1984).

SYLVIA ROBERTSON

DOUBLE BIND. Any situation in which a person is subject to mutually incompatible directives, such that to fulfill one of those directives is ipso facto to have failed to fulfill the other. Thus, no matter what a person does, she or he "cannot win." When first formulated in 1956 by Gregory Bateson et al. ("Toward a Theory of Schizophrenia," in M. Berger [ed.], *Beyond the Double Bind* [New York, 1978]), the concept was a lynchpin of the then newly emerging communications and "family systems" approaches to schizophrenia. Such approaches, which viewed schizophrenia as a strategy of accommodation to intolerably paradoxical expectations within the network of family relationships, in many ways represented a distinct advance over prevailing organic and psychodynamic models.

Double bind theory, however, like most therapeutic models of the post–World War II period, was unable to transcend the gender ideology of the time, which placed the "good" or "bad" mother at the center of family function and dysfunction. Both in theory and practice maternal scapegoating and victim-blaming become ubiquitous. The starring role in the family drama nearly always fell to the "schizophrenogenic mother"—typically described as both hostile and emotionally needy, withholding and "engulfing." (The "classic example" of the double bind, cited frequently in textbooks and articles, describes the mother who, visiting her son in his hospital room, stiffens when he embraces her, and then, when he withdraws his arm, chides him for not loving her.) Very rarely do paternal "mixed messages" figure in the literature; rather, the father is typically represented as passive bystander to his wife's more actively destructive manipulations. No significance is attached to the social milieu outside the family.

The intensification of feminist consciousness* in the late 1960s and early 1970s generated a good deal of criticism of these early psychiatric uses of the "double bind" concept. At the same time, feminists were able to discern the valuable uses to which Bateson's original insights might be put in describing key conflicts within women's experiences. The "double bind" concept—by now part of our common cultural vocabulary—was pressed into the service of a newly emerging clinical focus on the feminine "role," and the paradoxes and contradictions embedded in it.

At the very center of this theoretical turn was the perception that the prevailing ideology of successful "femininity" was utterly at variance with our high cultural emphasis on self-realization, achievement, and self-reliance. A classic 1970 study of therapeutic attitudes painted the first stroke. In Inge Broverman et al., "Sex Roles Stereotypes and Clinical Judgments of Mental Health" (*Journal of Consulting and Clinical Psychology* 34 [1970]: 1–7), it was found that most therapists equated mature femininity—much as Freud had—with passivity, vulnerability, helplessness, and submissiveness. At the same time, mature, health *adulthood* (sex unspecified) was defined in terms of qualities such as competence, independence, ambitiousness, adventurousness—qualities also strongly associated, by the therapists, with mature masculinity. Thus, not only did there appear to be a gendered double standard* with respect to criteria for mental health, but a painful double bind for women clients: to be a healthy, mature woman, in the dominant therapeutic mentality (and certainly in the reigning popular mentality as well), required truncating one's development "as a person"; to be an accomplished, independent adult was ipso facto to have failed to achieve healthy adjustment to the prevailing construction of the feminine role.

Other studies—focusing on sexuality*, the psychology of battered women*, career-related issues, etc.—articulated other binds resulting from the constraints of "femininity." Perhaps the most influential and controversial among them was Martina Horner's 1970 study of "achievement anxiety" (popularly known as "fear of success"*), "Femininity and Successful Achievement: A Basic Inconsistency" (in J. Bardwick et al. [eds.], *Feminine Personality and Conflict* [Belmont, Calif., 1970]). It suggested that such anxiety, which Horner found to be prominent among the college women she interviewed, was the result of historically long-standing notions that to succeed in the public, male world is to become less of a woman, is to "lose one's femininity."

Horner's studies, while initially celebrated, drew criticisms in the late 1970s and early 1980s. The ethnocentrism of the study was pointed out; if black women had a "fear of success" (which studies did not show very strongly), *their* "double bind," it was argued, involved anxiety over conflicts between the goals of feminism and the struggle against racism, rather than concern for a white ideal of "femininity." Later criticism, inspired by Carol Gilligan's influential work on gender and moral values, *In a Different Voice* (Cambridge, Mass., 1982), reinterpreted the "fear" of achievement as a rejection of the competitive values associated with achievement in our culture. Attempts in the early 1980s to duplicate Horner's study found little if any success anxiety among college women. These, however, cannot be considered to be "refutations" of Horner's findings, since 12 years and a good deal of cultural transformation might well account for the difference in results.

At mid-point in the 1980s, one of the most coercive images spawned from the current gender ideology is that of the "Superwoman." The glamor and appeal of the Superwoman is precisely that she appears to have escaped the demoralizing double binds presented to past generations of women. Rather, she can "have it all"—professional success *and* "femininity," public accomplishment *and* domestic satisfaction. Have the demands of "femininity" and the values of "personhood" in our culture come to be reconciled?

Catherine Steiner Adair's study ("The Body-Politic: Normal Female Adolescent Development and the Development of Eating Disorders," doctoral dissertation, Harvard University, 1984) suggests not. On the basis of a series of interviews, high-school women were classified into two groups, one which expressed skepticism over the attainability of the Superwoman ideal, the other which thoroughly aspired to it. Later administration of diagnostic tests revealed that 94 percent of the "superwomen" group fell into the eating-disordered range of the scale; 100 percent of the other group fell into the non–eating-disordered range. Media images notwithstanding, young women today appear to sense the impossibility of simultaneously meeting the demands of two spheres whose values have been historically defined in utter opposition to each other. Those who do not, it seems, may wind up enacting the tension through the female pathologies of our time. The traditional domestic construction of femininity insists, both literally and metaphorically, that women should learn to feed others, not the self. In her debilitating obsession with diet and self-denial, the eating-disordered woman fulfills this injunction most obediently. Yet with the very same gesture, she rigorously strives to embody those culturally overesteemed values previously reserved for men: control, autonomy, will, and the exercise of power. Far from escaping the double bind of gender, young women in the second half of the twentieth century, it could be argued, have inscribed it on their bodies.

Further References. S. Brownmiller, *Femininity* (New York, 1984). E. Howell and M. Bayes (eds.), *Women and Mental Health* (New York, 1981). S. Ohrbach, *Hunger Strike* (New York, 1986). R. Unger, *Female and Male: Psychological Perspectives* (New York, 1979).

SUSAN BORDO

DOUBLE JEOPARDY is the identification of women of color's subordination within societies as the product of the dual discriminations of sexism* and racism. *Racism* refers to the ideological, structural, and behavioral systems in society which deny and limit opportunities for some groups because of their racial identity in order to create and maintain a racial hierarchy. *Sexism* refers to a system of control which maintains and legitimates a sexual hierarchy in which males are dominant. Both racism and sexism operate in various spheres of society—economic, political, cultural, educational, religious—and both are perpetuated by organizations and individuals in subtle and explicit ways. Individuals who are doubly disadvantaged because of their membership in both the subordinate sexual and racial groups are the victims of double jeopardy. Double jeopardy, then, recognizes the simultaneity of racial and sexual oppressions and the compound consequences of dual discriminations. Frances Beale, in "Double Jeopardy: To Be Black and Female" (in T. Cade [ed.], *The Black Woman: An Anthology* [New York, 1970], 90–100), initially applied the concept to African-American women, but it has become generally applicable to all women of color*, including Native Americans, Latinas, and Asian-Americans.

As the complexity of various women's circumstances in society has become more fully understood, this notion of multiple discriminations has been further elaborated. In her initial explication of the term, Beale extensively discussed the negative economic ramifications of double jeopardy. Most black women, and many women of color, are unemployed or underemployed in jobs with low pay, minimal authority, limited opportunities for mobility, and low prestige. Because educational deprivation and economic marginality circumscribe the lives of many women of color, "class," or socioeconomic status, is the most frequent augmentation, expanding the concept to triple jeopardy. In this case, maleness, whiteness, and wealth are independently and collectively advantageous.

The recognition of two major oppressions confounding and intensifying sexism has been a critical development in the comprehension of women's subordination. However, there are certain limitations in its conceptualization. The first and most problematic issue is the continual addition of oppressions. The concept, both theoretically and practically, loses its potency the more broadly and arbitrarily it is applied. Other prejudices and discriminations based on sexual preferences, religion, age, or nationality are substituted or added. Such variations in the components of double or triple jeopardy create confusion and conceptual fussiness. Would quadruple jeopardy refer to "sexism, racism, hetrosexism, and ageism" or to "sexism, racism, classism, and heterosexism"?

Second, the approach has led to misguided attempts at ranking the components in terms of their severity and pervasiveness. This has occurred because early discussions of double and triple jeopardy assumed that the relationships among the variables are additive. Increasingly, it appears more useful to conceive of these relationships as dialectical: that is, as multiplicative interactions, with the relative importance of any determined by specific sociohistorical conditions. Thus linkages among systems of oppression are viewed as dynamically interrelated and varied for those distinct groups of women subject to the double or triple jeopardy of racism, sexism, and class oppression.

Further References. E. M. Almquist, "Race and Ethnicity in the Lives of Minority Women," in J. Freeman (ed.), *Women: A Feminist Perspective* (Palo Alto, Calif., 1984).

A. Davis, *Women, Race and Class* (New York, 1981). B. T. Dill, "Dialectics of Black Womanhood," *Signs* 4 (1979): 543–555.

DEBORAH KING

DOUBLE STANDARD. Two different sets of acceptable behavior, one for females and one for males. In patriarchal societies women are allowed less freedom to express their sexuality* than are men and are judged more harshly, not just for sexual activity that, if engaged in by a man, is condoned or even considered normal or desirable, but for any conduct, or even speech, that is considered unsuitable to women's sex role as the caretaker of children.

Women's liability for actions for which men are not punished at all, and their harsher punishment for committing some of the same acts that men commit, are found in law codes from the second millennium B.C. to the twentieth century A.D. But the chief means of enforcing the double standard has always been through sex-role socialization*.

DOWER is the widow's portion of, or interest in, her deceased husband's real property.

From the ninth century in much of Europe the bridegift* was gradually transformed from property given to a wife at the time of marriage to a promise of the use and profits of a portion, usually a third, of the husband's patrimony. This dower right, the right of a widow to the use of a part of her husband's property, in time became a recognized part of English law.

Under common-law property division, as reformed in the early twentieth century, if a husband dies intestate the widow receives the dower portion, commonly one-third, sometimes one-half, of her husband's property; or if, by her deceased husband's will she would receive less than the amount of the dower, she may be able to elect the dower portion. (Of the common-law property states, only Georgia has no statutory provision for dower.) Feminists are working to replace the dower right with the concept of marital property*.

DOWRY is a marriage payment made by the bride's family. It goes with the bride on her marriage* and is administered by her husband for the duration of the marriage. The dowry represents the contribution of the wife's family toward her support and the profits may be used to that end, but the principal is supposed to be kept intact. After the wife's death it passes to her children or, if there are none, reverts to her family. Upon divorce* the dowry is returned to the wife or her family. In some societies, if there are children, not all the dowry may be returned; or if the wife is guilty of adultery*, she may lose a part or all of it.

The dowry is often considered a form of premarital inheritance. In societies in which the daughters do not inherit except in default of sons, if a man dies before his daughters are married, his sons are expected, although not usually required, to dower their sisters.

Dowry as a system of marriage payment is associated with patrilocal and monogamous marriages, and with hypergamy* (the woman's "marrying up") in stratified societies.

DUAL-CAREER COUPLES. Partners in a relationship in which both members pursue jobs which require commitment and training and have advancement potential. Such couples can be married or cohabiting, heterosexual or homosexual.

Two-thirds of all married women work outside the home. In nine out of ten such marriages, the husband has the major career interest and the wife views her employment as secondary to her family responsibilities. However, the percentage of couples in dual-career marriages (a term coined by Rhona Rapoport and Robert Rapoport, *Dual-Career Families* [Hardmondsworth, England, 1971]) is rising. Couples most likely to be in dual-career relationships are college educated, with strong needs for achievement and self-esteem, and a belief in egalitarian gender roles*. Women are more likely to desire such relationships than are men.

Dual-career relationships are difficult, especially if children are involved, since child care responsibilities traditionally have fallen on the mother, and most careers are patterned for individuals without such concerns (traditionally, men). Societal attitudes also cause stress since most people believe a woman should put her husband and children ahead of her career. However, dual-career relationships seem to have clear economic, intellectual, and psychological benefits, particularly for women. Wives in dual-career marriages tend to have higher self-esteem, a greater sense of competence, and greater relationship satisfaction than wives in the labor force solely out of economic necessity or wives not in the labor force.

SUSAN A. BASOW

DUAL ROLE is the double job of the woman who is employed full-time and also has the complete or major responsibility for the care of home and children. A growing number of women who head single-parent households must not only provide all, or the major share of, income for the family* but must, after finishing a full day's work, assume all the duties and responsibilities of a homemaker.

In marriages in which both husband and wife work an equal length of time producing income, the husband rarely spends an equal, or anywhere nearly equal, time in doing housework*. Since the wife usually earns less than the husband, her job tends to be considered less important and so does not entitle her to more than minimum assistance in the home—helping to clear the table and emptying the dishwasher, perhaps. Even when the wife and husband earn comparable salaries, or the wife earns more than the husband, she may still have the major responsibility for homemaking, although in such marriages the husband is more likely to share more of the housework than in marriages in which he is the primary breadwinner.

E

ECTOPIC PREGNANCY is a pregnancy outside the uterus, most usually in the Fallopian tube, but also possible in other locations, such as the ovary, abdominal cavity, or cervix. Untreated ectopic pregnancies are the major cause of maternal deaths in early pregnancy.

In an ectopic pregnancy the fertilized egg does not complete its normal passage down the Fallopian tube to the uterus, but attaches itself to tissue outside the uterus. In most cases, the journey is stopped by an obstruction in the tube, such as scar tissue or a malformation. Unable to proceed, it implants itself on the tube wall. Failure of the egg to reach the uterus can also be caused by impairment of the muscle activity of the tube, inhibiting the contractions necessary to move the egg, or the fertilized egg may have implanted on endometrial tissue (the tissue lining the uterine cavity) in the tube wall (endometriosis*). In some cases a fertilized egg may have passed into the pelvic cavity instead of entering the tube, or a tubal pregnancy may have aborted and traveled back up the tube into the pelvic cavity, to replant on the abdominal wall. In all cases the site and tissue are not suited for the development of a fetus.

All ectopic pregnancies are life threatening and need to be discovered and treated surgically as early as possible. In tubal pregnancies, if not aborted early or removed surgically, the fetus will rupture the tube, usually within 8 to 12 weeks. Modern technologies have greatly increased early diagnosis and treatment. Before the mid–1970s over three-quarters of tubal pregnancies ruptured before being discovered; by the mid–1980s, around three-quarters were being treated before rupture. If the pregnancy is discovered before it ruptures the tube, the tube can be saved. An incision is made in the tube and the conceptus is removed, or possibly it can be "milked out" without incision. A ruptured tube must be removed. There have been instances of pregnancies in other locations going near to term, but the delivery of a normal infant is rare.

The number of ectopic pregnancies has been rising. The use of contraceptive intrauterine devices and the increasing occurrence of pelvic inflammatory disease are thought to be responsible for much of the increase. Older estimates put the incidence at about 1 in 300 pregnancies. Some estimates in the early 1980s have run as high as 1 in 40. After an ectopic pregnancy, about 60 percent of women retain the ability to reproduce, but they are at risk for a recurrence of ectopic pregnancy or for miscarriage. (See L. Madaras and J. Patterson with P. Shick, *WomanCare: A Gynecological Guide to Your Body*, 2nd ed. [New York, 1984], 683–692.)

EDUCATION, ECONOMICS OF WOMEN'S. Education is an important determinant of the nature of and rewards to women's work* both in the market and in the home. Women's probability of being in the labor force, continuity of participation over the life-cycle, earnings, occupational attainment, fertility, and allocation of time across household tasks all vary with educational attainment. Highly educated women have been offered employment opportunities in the growing white-collar occupations and have been able to take advantage of the breakdown in occupational segregation* in the professions since 1970.

If one simply looks at school attendance, educational experience will be seen to have varied much more by race and class than it has by gender, at least since the early nineteenth century. Earlier there had been substantial gender differences among whites. While both girls and boys were taught to read the Bible, only about half as many girls as boys were taught to write. Colleges and universities barred all women no matter what their scholastic abilities, thirst for knowledge, wealth, or social standing.

The spread of academies and the growth of the common schools in the early nineteenth century, however, greatly expanded educational opportunities for white women and tended to equalize the educational attainment of women and men. By 1850 the attendance rate of white girls in primary schools nearly equaled that of boys. By the turn of the century girls outnumbered boys in the high schools. Higher education became available to women in the 1830s, and by the turn of the century white women accounted for 20 percent of all college students. The proportion of female high school graduates attending college grew steadily through the twentieth century so that by 1983 women accounted for over half (51.7 percent) of degree credit enrollment.

Black women shared the educational discrimination facing black men. Under slavery, education was prohibited. After emancipation, poverty and discriminatory school boards kept black women's and men's educational attainment far below that of whites. Within these limitations, black girls were far more likely than boys to attend school. In 1900, 216 black women graduated from high school for every 100 black men who did so. Among whites the gender imbalance was not so great: 139 white women graduated for every 100 white men (S. B. Carter and M. Prus, "The Labor Market and the American High School Girl 1890–1928," *Journal of Economic History* 47 [1982]: 163–171). Relative improvement in educational opportunities for black women did not occur until segregated schools were outlawed and antidiscrimination legislation brought about by the civil rights movement implemented. In 1960 median educational attainment of blacks was only 73 percent of that of whites. By 1982 it had risen to 97 percent.

Class continues to have an important influence on the attendance patterns of both women and men. A study of the high school class of 1972 revealed that among high school graduates whose fathers had received at least some college education, 60.4 percent of white males and 57.6 percent of white females enrolled in college. Among those whose fathers did not complete high school the enrollment rates were 24.6 percent and 20.1 percent respectively. Similar differentials exist for blacks. These differences appear to be due to the influence of family status on the quality of elementary and high school educational attainment and the importance of family income in financing college attendance (G. E. Thomas, K. L. Alexander, and B. K. Eckland, "Access to Higher Education: The Importance of Race, Sex, Social Class, and Academic Credentials," *School Review* [February 1979]: 133–156).

The relative equality between women and men in enrollment rates, however, conceals tremendous differences within and across institutions, in motivation for and constraints inhibiting attendance. While scholastically able women from well-to-do families are about as likely to attend college as similarly situated men, able women from poorer families are much less likely than their brothers to do so. In one sample the college enrollment rate for academically able men from upper-income families was 98 percent as compared with 89 percent for those from lower-income families. Among women, however, the enrollment rates are 95 percent and 65 percent respectively. The greater effect of family income on daughters' attendance rates may be due to women's low wages in the labor market, which make it more difficult for women to repay college loans and put themselves through school and/or to less willingness of families to finance daughters' education (A. E. Blakemore and S. A. Low, "Scholarship Policy and Race-Sex Differences in the Demand for Higher Education," *Economic Inquiry* 21 [1983]: 504–519).

Among those who attend, women are more likely to enroll in two-year colleges. In 1983 women accounted for 55 percent of those enrolled in two-year colleges as compared with 52 percent of all degree credit enrollment. Women's share of enrollments falls progressively as one moves to four-year colleges, research universities, and graduate programs. It took federal legislation to enable women to gain access to education for particularly prestigious and lucrative fields like medicine and law (M. L. Radour, G. L. Strasburg, and J. Lipman-Blumen, "Women in Higher Education: Trends in Enrollments and Degrees Earned," *Harvard Educational Review* 52 [1982]: 189–202).

Within institutions women are concentrated in traditionally female fields. As late as 1970 over half of the female undergraduates received their degrees in the fields of education, English, languages, and fine arts. However, in the 1970s large numbers of women began moving into formerly male fields so that by 1980 the four traditionally female fields listed above accounted for only 30 percent of women's bachelor's degrees. Even in the same classroom, however, women and men often have very different educational experiences. Attitudes of teachers and classmates may discourage women from class participation, result in less feedback on their work, and cause them to lower their career aspirations and lose self-confidence in the process. The curriculum may make it difficult for women to learn to think for themselves and develop a consciousness of themselves as independent intellects.

There are a number of theoretical perspectives on these issues. Neo-classical economic theorists have focused on the differences in attendance patterns between women and men. The decision to go to school, or the demand for education, is modeled as an investment undertaken on the expectation of monetary and non-monetary returns. The payoff to education is greater the greater the earnings differential between educated and uneducated labor, the longer the expected time in the labor force, the greater the benefits of education in nonmarket activities, and the lower the educational costs.

According to this approach women would be expected to take less education than men to the extent that expected lifetime labor force participation* was less. As women's expected labor force participation has risen, so has their optimal level of education. In this view changing patterns in the educational attainment of women result from women's choices in the context of changing conditions.

Feminists tend to view changes in women's school attendance rates as the outcome of political and social struggles. Women would generally be expected to have preferred far more education than they in fact were able to obtain. Rising educational attainment, the institution of women's studies, and the mainstreaming of feminist scholarship are evidence of success in wresting control over access to educational institutions and programs from patriarchal forces. Such victories, however, are not permanent as evidenced by the backlash against coeducation around the turn of the century, the fall in women's share of graduate students in the 1930s, and the efforts to restrict the impact of Title IX* in the *Grove City College* v. *Bell* decision.

Reproduction of labor power theorists tend to focus on the curriculum and to view schools as institutions for maintaining gender inequalities over time. By portraying the gender-based division of labor as natural, training women for their traditional roles, and failing to develop women's capacity to view these patterns critically, the schools have reinforced women's subordinate position in the larger society. In this view, schools will help liberate women only if critical feminist scholarship is developed and taught.

Further References. G. J. Clifford, " 'Shaking Dangerous Questions from the Crease': Gender and American Higher Education," *Feminist Issues* 3 (1983): 3–62. C. B. Lloyd and B. T. Neimi, *The Economics of Sex Differentials* (New York, 1979). B. M. Solomon, *In the Company of Educated Women: A History of Women and Higher Education* *in America* (New Haven, Conn., 1985). P. J. Perum (ed.), *The Undergraduate Woman: Issues in Educational Equity* (Lexington, Mass., 1982).

SUSAN B. CARTER

EDUCATION AMENDMENTS OF 1972. See TITLE IX

EMBRYO, in human development, is the term for the developing human organism during its early stage of differentiation and growth, the stage during which the organ system and the basic body structure is established. By about the end of the eighth week after conception, at which time the body structure becomes recognizably human, the embryonic stage is completed and gestation has entered the fetal stage.

EMPTY NEST SYNDROME is the name given to feelings of depression caused by the loss of the mother role when a woman's children leave home. Its prevalence among women has been greatly exaggerated. A woman whose identity is dependent upon her role as mother and who has lived her life through her children often feels that her life is purposeless when she loses her role. However, most women whose children have left home find that they are happier than they have been in years (E. Hall, "Motherhood," in C. Tavris [ed.], *EveryWoman's Emotional Well-Being* [Garden City, N.Y., 1986]).

ENDOGAMY/EXOGAMY. Endogamy is a term for marriage* within a defined group. Marriage within the group may be preferred or may be required by custom or law. The group may be defined by kinship or fictive kinship ties, as, for instance, a clan or tribe, or might be based on some other social division, such as village, socioeconomic class, ethnic, racial, or religious group.

Exogamy is the opposite of endogamy: marriage outside the defined group. Marriage within the defined group may be discouraged, or it may be prohibited by law or custom.

ENDOMETRIAL CYCLE is the monthly renewal of the lining of the uterus (endometrium) in order to support a developing fetus*, and the subsequent breakdown and shedding of the lining when no conception takes place.

The regenerative phase of the cycle begins about the fifth day of menstruation and lasts until after ovulation. Under the stimulus of estrogen new glandular cell tissue covers the base layer of the endometrium (which remains unchanged throughout the cycle). The progestational or secretory phase begins after ovulation when progesterone stimulates glandular secretion of nutrients. The lining doubles in thickness, becoming rich and soft. If no fertilization takes place, after about 12 days estrogen and progesterone decline. Without hormonal stimulus, the lining begins to break down. As blood circulation slows, blood vessels constrict; without blood, tissue dies. As the weakened blood vessels dilate again, some blood escapes. Blood, glandular secretions, and dead tissue flow from the uterus into the vagina and menstruation begins.

ENDOMETRIOSIS is a condition in which endometrial tissue (the tissue that lines the uterus) grows in locations outside the uterus: usually on surfaces within the pelvic cavity, especially on the ovaries but also on other areas, as the Fallopian tubes, intestines, etc.; occasionally even outside the pelvic cavity, as on lung, thigh, or upper arm. When the endometrial tissue bleeds during menstruation, blood trapped in the pelvic cavity can cause internal bleeding, cysts, inflammation, and, subsequently, scar tissue, obstructions, adhesions, and, often, intense, chronic pain.

Endometriosis can affect women from menarche* to menopause*, but the most severely affected are aged 25 to 45. The bits of "misplaced endometrium" vary in size and extent; they may be confined to one area or be found in different areas. Some women have no symptoms; others have a great deal of pain, before or during menstruation and during sexual intercourse—and the severity (or absence) of pain is not related to the extent of the endometriosis. It may be related to the size of cysts, the frequency of cyst breakage, and the amount of scar tissue.

Endometriosis is one of the major causes of infertility* in women. Why is not always clear. Nor are the causes of endometriosis known. Various theories have been proposed to explain how it could be spread from the uterus. It has also been suggested that some cells in the tissue of other organs in the pelvic cavity may, under hormonal stimulus, undergo modification, resulting in bits of endometrium among other tissue. There is also support for a genetic explanation (it may run in families).

The type of treatment, or whether there should be treatment, will depend upon whether the woman wishes to have children, the severity of the symptoms, and the woman's age. When there is no or little pain, a woman nearing menopause has little to gain by treatment. Oral contraceptives will relieve symptoms but are not a satisfactory solution for a woman who wishes to have children or for someone at risk from oral contraceptives. A synthetic steroid, Danazol, is effective in arresting and reducing the condition and has had some success in allowing fertility, but the condition is likely to recur after its use is discontinued. It is also quite expensive and has side effects, possibly including cardiovascular risk. Surgery is sometimes used, usually cutting the tissue out, scraping, or cauterizing it. Hysterectomy, with or without removal of ovaries and Fallopian tubes, is usually resorted to only when the condition is widespread and the pain acute and debilitating. (Ovaries should be removed only when recommended by two independent physicians. Also, removal without hormone replacement increases cardiovascular risk.)

The Endometrius Association (PO Box 92181, Milwaukee 53202) was formed in 1980 as a self-help group and clearinghouse for information, support, and help.

Further Reference. Julia Older, *Endometriosis* (New York, 1985).

EQUAL EMPLOYMENT OPPORTUNITY LAWS: REGULATION AND ENFORCEMENT.

Since 1978, the responsibilities for developing regulations for and enforcing equal employment opportunity laws and orders have been consolidated with the Equal Employment Opportunity Commission (EEOC), which is appointed by the president, the Office of Federal Contract Compliance Programs (OFCCP) of the U.S. Department of Labor, the Justice Department, and the Department of Education. EEOC's authority covers all public and private employers and unions, as well as the federal government as an employer. In addition, EEOC enforces the Equal Pay Act and the Age Discrimination Act. OFCCP enforces Executive Order 11246* as amended and deals with all federal contractors. The Justice Department is responsible for litigation against state and local governments under Title VII* of the Civil Rights Act of 1964 and represents the federal government when suits are brought against federal contractors. Title IX* of the Education Amendments of 1972 is enforced by the Department of Education. In 1978, EEOC, the Labor Department, and the Justice Department jointly issued the *Uniform Guidelines on Employee Selection Procedures*.

Further References. E. Kirby, *Yes You Can: The Working Woman's Guide to Her Legal Rights, Fair Employment, and Equal Pay* (Englewood Cliffs, N.J., 1984). U.S. Department of Labor Women's Bureau, *A Working Woman's Guide to Her Job Rights (Leaflet 55)* (Washington, D.C., 1984).

DAYLE MANDELSON

EQUAL RIGHTS AMENDMENT (ERA) is a proposed amendment to the U.S. Constitution, originally introduced into Congress in 1923. Proposed by Alice Paul, suffragist and founder of the National Women's party, the ERA stated, "Equality of rights under the law shall not be denied or abridged by the United States of by any State on account of sex." It received congressional approval in March 1972 but failed to secure ratification before its extended deadline, March 22, 1982.

Legal Impact. The ERA would be one of a series of measures, including congressional acts, executive orders, and judicial decisions, which seek to clarify the legal standing of sex in law and to prohibit sex discrimination*. The ERA would most probably establish sex as a category like race, subject in judicial review to the rarely used standard of strict scrutiny. Under this exacting standard, differential sex classifications or consequences would be permissible only if they further a compelling state purpose.

While there is a measure of uncertainty in the eventual interpretation of any amendment, much of the legal scholarship on the subject of impact suggests that ERA's passage would ensure the elimination of laws, governmental regulations, and practices that treat females and males unequally. These would include inequality in admissions, financial aid, and facilities in public education; the sentencing and correctional treatment of convicts; compensation and benefits in public employment; and obligations and privileges of domestic relations. This elimination of discrimination might entail the extension of traditionally male prerogatives and obligations to women (e.g., payment of alimony), as well as the extension of traditionally female protections to men (e.g., survivor's benefits). However, passage would not require any violation of fundamental rights of privacy, such as same sex restrooms, sleeping quarters, or dressing rooms; nor would it necessarily sanction homosexual marriages or prohibit unisex schools. In one of the most controversial areas, military service*, Congress would retain its power to establish eligibility for conscription and combat.

The Politics of ERA. The campaign for an equal rights amendment grew from the success in gaining a suffrage amendment in 1920. Forty-nine years elapsed between its initial introduction, December 10, 1923, and approval by the Senate, March 22, 1972. For decades, the amendment languished in committees, was periodically modified, and on rare occasions was presented and voted down. The Republican and Democratic parties began to include the ERA in party platforms in 1940 and 1944 respectively, but many influential groups, including major women's organizations and labor unions, opposed it until the late 1960s or early 1970s.

Debates on the amendment were based primarily on two divergent views of women's equality. The first perspective, that females and males are so constitutionally and socially distinct that women must be treated differently in order to be equal, is associated with social or relational feminism, as well as with more traditional views of gender relations. For example, the League of Women Voters, the National Consumers League, and the National Women's Trade Union League long opposed the ERA because it would nullify the protective labor legislation for which they had worked. This view's disapproval of conscription and combat for women because such roles are antithetical to female qualities also led to opposition of the ERA. Individual or egalitarian feminism, on the other hand, insists that females and males must be treated the same, that gender neutrality must hold in all public matters. Thus, women should be equally subject to the draft and combat, just as they should be equally compensated economically and empowered politically. The National Women's party and the National Federation of Business and Professional Women's Clubs supported the amendment.

The watershed was the Equal Pay Act of 1963 and the Civil Rights Act of 1964, which prohibited employment discrimination on the basis of sex. Finally persuaded by the Equal Employment Opportunity Commission's invalidation of protective legislation* and the Department of Labor's endorsement, the decades-old opposition of labor unions withered. As the women's movement increased in strength throughout the late 1960s, women's organizations began to advocate the amendment, with the League of Women Voters finally reversing its long opposition. Congressional support built. In 1971, after numerous failed attempts to defeat the bill, the House of Representatives approved it 354 to 23. On March

22, 1972, the ERA passed the Senate 84 to 8. The amendment was then ready for state ratification.

Within 12 months, 30 states had ratified the amendment. However, during the next four years, only five additional states approved. Then, until the expiration date in June 1982 (an unprecedented three-year extension of the original seven-year time limit) no other state voted favorably, and several sought to rescind their ratification. The ERA was three states short of the three-fourths necessary to amend the Constitution. Alabama, Arizona, Arkansas, Florida, Georgia, Illinois, Louisiana, Mississippi, Missouri, Nevada, North Carolina, Oklahoma, South Carolina, Utah, and Virginia comprise the nonratifying states.

Given its many early and swift victories and public opinion polls showing that a majority supported the ERA, why did it fail? A number of reasons have been suggested for its defeat. (1) Amending the Constitution is a deliberately difficult process, and historically amendments that propose substantive changes have had a low rate of success. Opponents needed to concentrate their efforts in a mere 13 states to block ratification (M. F. Berry, *Why E.R.A. Failed: Politics, Women's Rights and the Amending of the Constitution* [Bloomington, Ind. 1986]).

(2) Support for ERA was not evenly distributed over all states. The nonratifying states were primarily southern or southwestern and the bedrock of religious fundamentalism and the New Right. Given its conservative ideology, the New Right tended to see the ERA as a threat to traditional values and institutions, most importantly gender roles* and the family*. In 1980 the Republican party failed to endorse the ERA in its national platform, and the nation elected a president who opposed the amendment.

(3) As Jane J. Mansbridge (*Why We Lost the E.R.A.* [Chicago, 1986]) has argued, the abstract notion of equal rights was not the problem. Rather it was the rhetorical debates over the substantive impact of the amendment on abortion* homosexuality*, alimony*, unisex facilities, and military service. Specific events, including the reinstitution of draft registration and the 1972 *Roe* v. *Wade* abortion decision, heightened concerns about these issues.

(4) The strategy of the opposition was more effective than that of ERA's supporters. (See ANTIFEMINIST MOVEMENTS.) The opponents, led by Phyllis Schlafly's STOP ERA, persuasively manipulated cultural fears regarding gender roles and ERA's substantive impact. Even though they mobilized late, opponents concentrated their resources on the more conservative states while the proponents, unsuspecting and overconfident, were unprepared for opposition.

Despite its failure, the ratification campaign had some successes. During the ten-year campaign the revitalized women's movement gained some legislative and judicial actions supporting and strengthening women's rights. Some states passed their own equal rights amendment or revised state laws. More members and funds were attracted to feminist organizations, especially the National Organization for Women, coalitions among numerous traditional women's and feminist organizations were formed, and more women ran for public office. By

March 1982, more than 450 organizations with memberships totaling over 50 million were on record in support of ERA.

Further References. S. D. Becker, *The Origins of the Equal Rights Amendment* (Westport, Conn., 1981). J. K. Boles, *The Politics of the Equal Rights Amendment: Conflict and the Decision Process* (New York, 1979). J. Hoff-Wilson (ed.), *Rights of Passage: The Past and Future of the ERA* (Bloomington, Ind., 1986). G. Y. Steiner, *Constitutional Inequality: The Political Fortunes of the Equal Rights Amendment* (Washington, D.C., 1985).

DEBORAH KING

EVALUATION BIAS is discrimination* based on gender when judging an individual's competence.

Women are less likely than men to attain high levels of achievement in our society despite the fact that there appear to be few if any substantive differences between the sexes in intelligence or competence in a wide variety of situations. One explanation for the difference in achievement is that females often are evaluated as less competent than males with identical or equal accomplishments and qualifications.

In Philip Goldberg's landmark study ("Are Some Women Prejudiced against Women?" *Transaction* 5, no. 5 [April 5, 1968]: 28–30), female college students evaluated journal articles from either traditionally masculine, feminine, or neutral fields. For half the subjects, a given article was said to have a female author; for the other half, a male author. Male-authored articles received more favorable ratings than female-authored ones, especially in masculine fields.

Since 1968, many studies have shown that both female and male evaluators, children as well as adults, show similar antifemale bias when judging the quality of articles, essays, paintings, and applicants for managerial, scientific, academic, and semiskilled positions. In addition to bias regarding performance or qualifications, studies reveal that devaluation may extend to personal and social traits as well. Competent women have been judged to be less likable and less preferred as coworkers than equally competent men. Competent women also have been judged less "feminine" and more "masculine" than less competent women.

Not all studies find evaluation bias, however, and in some cases the bias is profemale. Factors other than gender influence evaluation bias in complex ways. These include the gender association of the field or task, characteristics of those being rated, and characteristics of the raters. Devaluation of women is more likely to occur in fields traditionally dominated by men, whereas women are often evaluated more favorably than men in tasks or jobs typically associated with females.

The level of competence of the person being rated may influence the nature of evaluation bias as well. When there is external evidence that an individual possesses outstanding credentials or achievements, antifemale bias diminishes or disappears. Moreover, some studies have found that women who are portrayed as being highly successful in traditionally male occupations are judged more competent than males in the same occupation. This has been called the "talking platypus phenomenon": i.e., it makes little difference what the platypus says; the amazing thing is that it can talk at all. But even when the competence of a successful woman is recognized, the explanations offered for her success may differ markedly from those offered to explain a man's success. His successful performance generally is attributed to the stable, internal attribute of skill, while the same performance by a woman is attributed to such unstable or external factors as luck, effort, or ease of task.

At the other end of the competency continuum, males of low competence often are evaluated more poorly than females of low competence. In the middle range of average competence, which includes most people, antifemale bias is the rule, however,

In general, the more relevant the information that raters are provided about those being judged, the less likely they are to devalue women. For example, women are likely to be rated as competent as men when performance is judged on the basis of clear, explicit criteria. Moreover, anti-female bias is least likely when raters are evaluating someone they know well or with whom they have worked and interacted.

Other characteristics that affect evaluation bias include sex, sex-role attitudes, and the nature of the sample (e.g., college students versus employers). Males are more likely than females to show antifemale bias. Males with traditional attitudes toward women, in particular, are apt to devalue women.

Studies which ask college students to evaluate hypothetical persons are less likely to find consistent evidence of evaluation bias against women than are studies in which actual employers, managers, or recruiters are asked to judge prospective employees in hypothetical or actual decision-making situations. It has been suggested that employers, unlike students, are making their judgments in a more realistic context in which they have a potential stake in the outcome.

To sum up, evaluation bias is a complex phenomenon that depends not only upon the gender of the person being judged but also upon other characteristics of the individual, the social context, and characteristics of the evaluator.

Further References. S. A. Basow, *Gender Stereotypes: Traditions and Alternatives*, 2nd ed. (Belmont, Calif., 1986), Chapter 11. B. Lott, "The Devaluation of Women's Competence," *Journal of Social Issues* 41 (1985): 43–60. B. S. Wallston and V. E. O'Leary, "Sex Makes a Difference: Differential Perceptions of Women and Men," in L. Wheeler (ed.), *Review of Personality and Social Psychology* (Beverly Hills, Calif., 1981), 2: 9–41.

CLAIRE ETAUGH

EXECUTIVE ORDER 11246 was issued by President Johnson in 1965. It prohibits discrimination* on the basis of race, color, sex, religion, or national origin in all terms and conditions of employment and requires affirmative action* for women and minorities by agencies and institutions with federal contracts. In 1971, Revised Order Number 4, applying to firms with contracts over $50,000 and with 50 or more employees, mandated the development and implementation of written affirmative action plans including goals and timetables and requiring "good faith" effort in order to "remedy the effects of past discrimination" and to eliminate present discrimination. In 1985 and 1986, President Reagan considered the repeal or substantial revision of Executive Order 11246, including the elimination of goals and timetables, but, although the administration did little to enforce the order, it was not substantially changed. Authority for the enforcement of Executive Order 11246, as amended by Executive Orders 12086 and 11375, is held by the Office of Federal Contract Compliance Programs of the U.S. Department of Labor.

DAYLE MANDELSON

F

FAMILY is "a married couple or other group of adult kinfolk who cooperate economically and in the upbringing of children, and all or most of whom share a common dwelling" (K. Gough, "The Origin of the Family," *Journal of Marriage and the Family* 33 [1971]: 760–771). Gough's definition is one of many attempts to identify essential, universal components and functions of the family, a social form and cultural construction that varies considerably through time and space. Much controversy exists over whether the family is universal, what functions it must or should perform, what structural components are essential, whether it should be understood as culturally constructed (i.e., from an emic perspective) or cross culturally, and how and why it varies and changes.

Anthropological definitions of the family are devised to develop specific argumentation about these controversies. For example, the debate over whether the family is universal is bound up with the question of how to define it. Melford Spiro ("Is the Family Universal?," *American Anthropologist* 56 [1954]: 839–846) argued that the family does not exist within the Israeli kibbutz because parents and children do not share a common residence and husband and wife do not form a basic economic unit, two essential characteristics of the family as defined by George Murdock's now classic definition: "a social group characterized by common residence, economic cooperation, and reproduction. It includes adults of both sexes, at least two of whom maintain a socially approved sexual relationship, and one or more children, own or adopted, of the sexually cohabitating adults" (*Social Structure* [New York, 1949], 1). However, Spiro later reformulated his argument to suggest that Murdock's definition be revised to reflect the existence of the family within the kibbutz where it performs essential psychological functions.

The commonly accepted view among anthropologists today is that the family is universal and that definitions of "the" family should reflect its universality. This concurrence is based, in part, upon arguments by early twentieth-century anthropologists, principally Bronislaw Malinowski, against those nineteenth-century social evolutionary theorists who questioned the existence of marriage* and the family in primitive societies (e.g., Friedrich Engels, *The Origin of the Family, Private Property, and the State* [New York, 1970]). By distinguishing between sexual and conjugal relationships and conceptualizing "social fatherhood" (where the husband of the mother is considered to be the father of the child), anthropologists rejected the idea that group marriage and promiscuity characterize primitive, non-Western societies.

Within this consensus about the universality of the family, general agreement exists that its functions are economic cooperation as well as reproduction and socialization of children and that its structural components include the incest taboo, kinship, marriage, the nuclear family, common residence, and a gender-based division of labor.

It is largely from the last characteristic—a gender-based division of labor—that feminist anthropologists have derived a renewed critique of the universality of the family. In mid–twentieth-century America it was popularly assumed that the family was a natural institution and that women's place within it was naturally fixed—that the nurturing and expressive functions of the family were best performed by women who by their nature were suited for it. Placing women's primary functions and identity within the family meant a lesser role for women in public life and, concomitantly, a universally subordinate position relative to men.

The feminist critique is that "family" is best understood as a culturally constructed concept as opposed to a cross-cultural imperative and concrete institution. For example, Jane Collier, Michelle Rosaldo, and Sylvia Yanagisako ("Is There a Family? New Anthropological Views," in B. Thorne [ed.], *Rethinking the Family, Some Feminist Questions* [New York, 1982]: 25–39) examine American ideas of "The Family" from this perspective and conclude that "The Family is not a concrete 'thing' that fulfills concrete 'needs' but an ideological construct with moral implications . . . " (37). They propose that analyzing the family as a cultural construct rather than as a functional imperative will lead to better understanding and explanation of the moral and symbolic weight placed upon the concept of family in America today and its symbolic significance in other cultures.

Historians of the family have also challenged the usefulness of universal definitions of the family for analyzing changes in family forms, relationships, and attitudes.

To account for such critiques and obvious cultural variations while proposing cross-cultural generalizations, anthropologists have developed an extensive vocabulary of terms related to family, marriage, and kinship. With the proviso that the definitions of these terms are also debatable, some of the more important ones are the following:

Nuclear Family (or *Conjugal Family*): A married couple and their dependent children.

Extended Family: Three or more generations of kin (a *stem family*) or two or more adult siblings, their spouses, and dependent children (a *joint family*), all of whom share a common dwelling and cooperate economically.

Compound Family (or *Polygamous Family*): A person and his/her spouses (two or more) and their dependent children.

Family of Orientation: The family in which one is born and raised, including one's parents and siblings.

Family of Procreation: The family one forms at marriage, including one's spouse and children.

Household (or *Domestic Group*): A group of people who share a common dwelling and cooperate economically.

LYNN WALTER

FAMILY (AS A SOCIOECONOMIC UNIT). The social institution that exerts profound influence on the construction of gender, the socialization of children into gender roles*, and the organization of sexuality. Although the family shapes relationships of power and dominance, as well as cooperation and affection, in all societies, there are great differences across societies in the ways in which the family is connected to social and economic life. For example, some societies make a sharp distinction between economic life and domestic life; in other societies, the family is the location where productive labor takes place. In some cultures large families and complex households are encouraged; in other cultures, the norm is small families and simple households. Women are expected to manage the work of running the household in most societies, yet some societies encourage all members of the family to share household tasks. To understand the position of women in a society at any historical period, it is important to analyze the structure of the household and family and the way the family relates to the social, economic, political, and legal systems of that society. These factors reveal a great deal about how gender roles and sexual stratification function in a particular society.

Feminist scholarship has profoundly reshaped the analysis of the family as a socioeconomic unit. This reshaping has occurred in several ways. First, feminist research has raised the possibility of understanding the family as an *ideology*, rather than as a social unit. In most societies, norms of who should live together, share resources, form affectional ties, and engage in sexual relationships are used to define the family unit. Such normative definitions then serve to justify restrictions on the social access and privileges of women, children, and the aged and to restrict alternative forms of family and household arrangements. The ideology of family in modern life in the Western industrial world emphasizes a division between public and private life in which women's place is defined as the private sphere of home and family and men's place is defined as the public sphere* of economic and political life. Such an ideology of family is consistent with a sex/gender system in which gender is constructed so that the aspirations, personalities, opportunities, and emotional makeup of women are seen as being greatly different from those of men. As an ideology, the family also has been a potent political issue. Historically, calls to "save the family" have been used both to justify the restriction of rights and protections for women and children and to motivate labor, community, and personal struggles against oppressive conditions.

Second, feminists have challenged the assumption that the family is a monolithic social unit and that there is a harmony of interests within the family. Feminists have argued that different members of the family experience life within the family in different ways. Although members of the family may share common interests or work toward common goals, such commonality cannot be assumed. Often, perceived harmony disguises intense differences of power and resources within the family and the monopolization of control and decision-making by the most powerful member(s). This is most apparent in the exercise of power and violence within the family. Women, children, and the elderly have been the most common victims of family violence, reflecting their relative lack of power and resources in the home and in the larger society. The divergent interests of family members, often separating along lines of sex and age, are reflected in many other areas of family life as well. Decisions about employment of family members, childbearing, residential location, and ties to extended family members are examples of areas in which family members may have different interests and goals.

Third, feminist scholarship suggests that the family is intimately connected to a variety of other structures of society. Although the family sometimes is portrayed as a "haven" from the heartless, impersonal world of work and commercialized relationships, feminists argue that family life, too, is permeated by judgments of worth and value from the larger society and economy. In societies divided by social class distinctions, the family acts to perpetuate these distinctions over time by socializing children and by preparing its members to assume a class-proscribed place in the economic, social, and legal systems. Moreover, the family contributes directly to the economic system through the invisible, unpaid work of women within the family and home. New research on the labor of housework* indicates the enormous economic contribution of household labor to the functioning of the economic system. Moreover, feminist research has affirmed the inseparability of production (work) and reproduction (family/home) in modern life. Understanding the lives of women—or the lives of men—requires attention to both the paid labor of public economic life and the unpaid labor of life within the household. In modern societies, the family is the social unit that bridges production and reproduction since it is within the family that consumption of goods and services is organized. Thus the family affects, and is affected by, many aspects of the economy and society.

Fourth, feminist scholarship has affirmed the importance of understanding the structure of the family and household in an historical perspective. A central interest in this area has been the nature of nurturance, especially female mothering in Western, industrial societies. Research on the "reproduction of mothering" indicates that the predominance of female nurturance of young children in modern Western society has long-term consequences for adult personality development and sex/gender relationships. In societies in which the primary social bond of infants and children is developed mainly through adult female mothering, gender begins to be shaped at a very early age. Girls, with whom mothers identify closely, tend to develop facility with emotional life and relationships but may have difficulty establishing a sense of autonomy and personal boundaries in adulthood. Boys, for whom separateness from female mothers is easier, tend to possess a sense of independence and autonomy but often have difficulty with emotional relationships. This divergence of gender is reinforced through so-cialization processes in the family that encourage boys to specialize in skills for a future work life and girls to specialize in skills for a future family life. The success of sex-defined mothering and sex-role socialization* pressures is evident in the strength of gender roles within and outside the family. Despite a great deal of publicity about changes in the male sex role, the participation of adult men in housework and child care* has changed very little over time in Western societies. In modern industrial societies, women continue to be the primary caretakers of children and men continue to predominate in the world of work.

Fifth, feminist historians have pointed to the impact of changes in household and family composition upon the lives and opportunities of women and men in the family. In modern Western societies, households typically have been nuclear in composition (i.e., consisting of an adult couple and their children) although it is not uncommon for households to stretch to accommodate additional members during times of economic or personal crisis. Yet the size of the household and family has changed significantly over time. For the most part, family size (es-pecially the number of children born) has declined in Western industrial societies. This has freed women for activities other than childrearing for a greater period of their lives. Moreover, the functions of the family have changed. Productive activities that used to be centered in the household are now usually found outside the home, creating a dichotomy between the public world of work and the private world of home and family, but ultimately freeing women for labor in the public sphere. Other functions that the family performed in earlier times, such as training and educating children, increasingly have become the province of the state, with mixed results for the lives and power of women within the family.

Finally, feminist analysis points to the wide variety of forms, functions, and processes of family life over time, across cultures, and within any society. Although general patterns in family structure and family relations can be dis-cerned within specific historical societies, differences across racial, ethnic, re-ligious, cultural, and geographic boundaries are complex and numerous. Indeed, a major contribution of feminist scholarship is to make clear that the family is not a monolithic entity. The forms that the family takes (nuclear, extended, childless, or other) and the relationships that underlie family life (monogamous or polygamous; heterosexual or homosexual; privatized or communal) are neither "natural" nor inevitable. Families, like other relationships of intimacy, are the product of constant negotiation and change in every society.

Further References. N. Chodorow, *The Reproduction of Mothering* (Berkeley, 1978). B. Thorne with M. Yalom, *Rethinking the Family: Some Feminist Questions* (New York, 1982). L. Tilly and J. Scott, *Women and Family* (New York, 1978).

KATHLEEN M. BLEE

FEAR OF SUCCESS (FOS) is a concept invoked to explain the vicissitudes of women's achievement. Originally proposed by Martina Horner (see "Femininity and Successful Achievement: A Basic Inconsistency" in J. Bardwick et al., *Feminine Personality and Conflict* [Belmont, Calif., 1970]), it is defined as the fear that the attainment of success can have negative consequences. An avoidance motive, learned in early childhood in conjunction with sex-role identity, it is most salient for bright, competent women who are highly motivated to achieve. As Margaret Mead noted many years before Horner, "Men are unsexed by failure, while women are unsexed by success."

Horner was working within a dominant paradigm in psychology, the Atkinson-McClelland theory of achievement motivation, one that had defined and studied achievement as a masculine characteristic. In the measure that Horner devised, college women wrote stories about Anne, a women who was first in her class in medical school. Anne was described by college women in very negative terms, as currently, or ultimately, suffering negative consequences (e.g., loss of friend) or as having attained her success unfairly (e.g., by cheating or in cutthroat competition).

The introduction of FOS helped trigger a new look in the study of women's achievement motivation and behavior. It was a stimulus, very much in tune with the Zeitgeist of the late 1960s and early 1970s, for a surge of research on social-psychological underpinnings of women's achievement behavior. Since its introduction, the concept has received great attention from researchers, clinicians, and general observers of the social scene. The scientific context and definition have been frequently overlooked, particularly in lay discussions about the question of whether women, in general, have or do not have fear of success. The term took on a life of its own and was for some time a media event, a much-touted explanation for why women don't achieve.

Hundreds of studies have examined the reliability and validity of the concept and its measures. Arguments center on the questions of how to assess the construct (e.g., thematic imagery versus questionnaire) and on whether there are sex differences. Researchers have asked whether FOS reflects an accurate observation by all people of a cultural attitude (i.e., a stereotype), or whether it is a motive, an *intrapsychic* disposition to certain kinds of behavior, or a logical response to specific situations (e.g., stress of competition, or intellectual evaluation).

While early studies upheld the validity of the idea and the measure, recent ones have not. Questionnaire and imagery methods have both met with mixed success and inconsistent results. These may be due in part to changes in social perceptions that affected the meaning of the measures. For example, Anne, the successful medical student, is certainly no longer a deviant. The inconsistencies may also reflect researchers' expectation that FOS involves *all* women rather than only the high-ability achievement strivers whom Horner talked about, as well as real changes in the cohorts being studied (at least by the 1980s).

Studies have included men as well as women and have varied class, age, ethnicity, and race. A recent review summarized 20 studies of black women done between 1970 and 1982. Also examined have been personality characteristics such as identity stage, self-esteem, Type A, locus of control*, and psychological femininity*. FOS has been looked at in relation to competition, causal attribution, task sex-typing, level of aspiration, peer or public acceptance or rejection, and a host of achievement-related behavioral variables. While interest has abated, it has not ceased; a search of the 1980s literature uncovered about 40 new references.

In conclusion, FOS has a heuristic value: it sparked an area of research and forced within psychology a new look at women's achievement strivings. As a scientific concept, its status is now shaky. This is due, in part, to inadequate attention to the complexity of the causes of women's achievement behavior.

Clinicians' reports indicate a perception of usefulness of these ideas in their work with women. For example, a clinician writes "I . . . know it exists . . . [it is] linked to the female sex role . . . women brought up in traditional homes never even imagined it possible that they might have positions of high status. . . . Such possibilities pose for women the [anticipation of] pain of negotiating these matters in a hetrosexual relationship . . . [such conflicts] lead to . . . self-defeating behavior . . . fear of success and imposter phenomena arise when the individual's script . . . does not include success" (quote from J. Sherman, talk at APA convention, 1986).

By 1986, FOS was an idea not so much in the public eye, yet with a persistent appeal. Work on women's achievement has progressed to a consideration of multiple causation, with success concerns as one of a myriad of factors. Further, the status of the concept may reflect cultural change as much as scientific verity.

Further References M.T.S. Mednick, S. S. Tangri, and L. W. Hoffman, *Women and Achievement* (Washington, D.C., 1975). D. Tresemen, *Fear of Success* (New York, 1977).

MARTHA T. MEDNICK

FEMALE DEVELOPMENT: A LIFE SPAN APPROACH. Contemporary theories of female development consider how the personality and various roles evolve over the entire life span. Throughout the course of life there is change

as well as continuity and an expanding array of alternative life-styles and pathways to be forged by individual women. To make sense of such diversity, the
following description of each stage of development will focus on the accomplishment of certain tasks that are relevant to the experience of being female.

Infancy and Childhood. During the early years of development the major
tasks involve the construction of a gender identity and knowledge of gender
roles*. The process of socialization into a feminine role begins even before birth
with parental attitudes and expectations. Parents of newborn females tend to
view their offspring as more delicate and sensitive than male babies and are
more gentle with them. There are few behavioral differences between males and
females at birth, although the greater maturity and resiliency of females may
have implications for emerging sex differences*. For example, because females
are more sensitive and cognitively aware of changing and novel events at an
earlier age than boys, they may be more wary of their environment than are
boys. By the time a girl is three years old, she may manifest different preferences
for activities and toys than her male peers. She has learned to label herself as a
girl and is very much aware of many of the gender-role stereotypes of her culture.

Girls, as well as boys, develop their concepts and gender-related behaviors
from a variety of sources. According to Lawrence Kohlberg, the acquisition of
gender identity is assumed to partially reflect an active intellectual process
whereby the child learns to label herself as a "girl" and then to seek out behaviors
and ideas that help to define the gender label. In the formation of gender identity
the girl essentially comes to believe that "I am a girl, therefore, I will do girl-
type things." Furthermore, she learns to recognize that her gender is immutable
through time and superficial changes in appearance. A girl also learns about
gender-typed behavior through imitation of same-sex peers, and significant adults
such as parents and teachers. Mimicry of gender-typed behavior will particularly
occur if there is reward in doing so.

Two important extrafamilial influences in early gender development are television and school. Television has consistently depicted women in stereotyped
roles. Women typically are portrayed in a romantic, married, or family role—
rarely as achievers or leaders. Unfortunately, there is a strong relationship between heavy televiewing among children and gender-role stereotyping. As for
schooling, the evidence suggests that girls and boys are treated differently.
School, during the elementary years, generally is a positive experience for females because they usually are rewarded for such feminine behaviors as neatness
and compliance. Achievement, prior to adolescence, is not viewed as a negative
attribute for girls. However, research also shows that teachers prefer the intellectual challenge and stimulation provided by boys, and they reward them more
for their competence while girls are praised for their cooperation. Girls are rarely
criticized by their teachers, but when they are, it typically is not for the intellectual
quality of their work. Thus, early on, expectations that differentiate boy from
girl are apparent to the child.

Adolescence. A central task of adolescence involves the crystalization of identity. Identity issues are intertwined with the dramatic changes of puberty, such as the growth spurt, onset of menstruation, development of secondary sex characteristics, and heightened sexual arousal. Thus, self-conception partially is defined in terms of becoming a mature male or female. For adolescent males, identity is often focused upon future career goals; however, female identity typically is confounded by both personal goals and anticipatory intimacy needs, i.e., "who will I become" is determined by "who will I marry." Beginning with adolescence, achievement and femininity* are essentially viewed as incompatible. Academic achievement begins to spiral downward for many adolescent girls while dating and heterosexual activities assume great significance. The interpersonal focus of adolescent female identity formation is also manifested in many dimensions of her life. For example, the friendships that girls form in their adolescent years are exclusive and intimate. As in the adult years, these friendships capitalize on the willingness to self-disclose and to be mutually supportive. Dating also becomes a means of expressing the intermingling of identity and intimacy needs. The rituals of dating serve to solidify the vested identity that the adolescent girl anticipates from her future marriage and provides an opportunity for her to play out some of the gender-role stereotypes.

Early and Middle Adulthood. The stereotyped view of feminine development during adulthood places women squarely within the role of housewife and mother. David Guttman, drawing upon the work of Carl Jung, believes that women's behaviors are guided by the *parental imperative*. During adulthood, women become more "passive-accommodative" and emotionally supportive as part of the division of labor involved in the rearing of children. Thus, the traditional role for a woman during adulthood channels her into gender-typed behaviors.

While the centrality of motherhood is indisputable, the reality of contemporary female adulthood is best characterized more by a number of variations on the family and work theme. In addition to the traditional mode, many women are opting to combine careers and family, to remain child-free, to be divorced with or without children, or to pursue a career within a single life-style. Unfortunately, women deviating from the traditional role often continue to use the increasingly rare traditional housewife-mother model as a yardstick to gauge their behavior. Despite the conflicts created by these options, the task of adulthood for many women is to find a rapprochement between their interpersonal needs and their needs for identity achievement. The return to college by increasing numbers of adult women reflects an active reversal of the adolescent aversion to educational and intellectual achievement.

For many women, the themes of intimacy and work continue to be central from the young adult period through the midlife years. Now, however, the content of the issues changes to a consideration of the impact of the "empty nest" and the climacteric*. According to the parental imperative notion, once children have outgrown their need for emotional and physical security, women are free to reclaim the repressed masculine side of their personalities. With the launching of their children from the home, women often express delight in the rediscovery of talents and abilities that may have been neglected during the years of child-rearing. Also supporting this finding are the positive attitudes that many post-menopausal women express toward their menopause. Women who have made the housewife-mother role the core of their adulthood experience may have a greater sense of loss over children leaving and in reduction of reproductive capability than those who have maintained a more diversified life-style. Even in the former case, most women are effective in reorganizing their lives in assuming new roles through work, education, or volunteer work.

Later Life. There are a number of issues that are particularly salient for elderly women. Over half of all women aged 65 or older are widowed. When their husbands die, such women lose not only their friends and companions but their financial providers and sources of identity. The loss of income for elderly women has contributed to the "feminization of poverty*." Many widows, however, derive psychological comfort and support from a well-established network of intimate friendships.

Susan Sontag has suggested that women experience a "double standard* of aging*." Women are appreciated for their sexual, reproductive, and nurturing functions—all of which are valued within the context of youth. An aging man becomes more handsome and dignified, but an aging woman is a "has been" as a mother and sexual partner. Thus, concludes Sontag, ageism and sexism* are intertwined during a women's elderly years.

Finally, the impact of retirement* upon the aging woman is a psychological event that will warrant increasing attention as women continue to enter the workforce. Will the issues they face be the same as those for retired men, or will the unique mosaic of work and family lead to a different set of concerns for women as they face the loss of their worker status? For example, women who began working once their children were of school age may be at the height of their career just when they are expected to retire. Unfortunately, relatively little is known at present about how women experience their retirement, primarily because of the failure to separate research findings by sex.

In summary of the above overview, it is evident that female development involves the tensions between personal identity, family relations, adaptability to social constraints, and the flexibility of alternative life-styles. Such issues become significant at the beginning of adolescence and underscore the theme that the life stages of women reflect an ongoing process of change and development.

Further Reference. J. H. Williams, *Psychology of Women: Behavior in a Biosocial Context*, 2nd ed. (New York, 1983).

ILLENE NOPPE

FEMININITY. The characteristics claimed to constitute femaleness. Femaleness and maleness, those traits that differentiate males and females, have received increasing attention in Western culture over the last 300 years. During the nineteenth century these traits were examined primarily through three genres: char-

acterization in fiction (women's sensibilities), prescriptions for appropriate social
and moral arrangements (the idea of separate spheres), and research on the
biological bases of such characteristics (sex differences* in cranial size, special
functions of the reproductive organs).

These genres of knowing contributed to refined conceptions of male and female
and particularly to a discursive sense of the attributes of masculinity and femininity. By the end of the century interest in these special sexual attributes shifted
toward the psychological realm, and eventually the primary locus of examining
sexual difference became an *intrapsychic* one. The terms *femininity* and *masculinity* came to signify the mental characteristics, often unconscious traits, that
differentiated females and males. Sex differences came to be equated more often
than not with psychological properties. Although not available to ready observation and measurement in the same way that cranial and physical strength are,
such mental differences nevertheless were taken as *real*. In other words, they
were fundamental, enduring, and essential properties.

These essential psychological properties of masculinity and femininity came
under scrutiny through psychoanalysis and scientific psychology. With psychoanalysis, Sigmund Freud set the tone for a universal, although sometimes ambiguous, conception of the feminine psyche. While Freud maintained that the
libido is the same in males and females, he believed it to be basically masculine.
Feminine sexuality is a specific variant of masculine libido: it results from the
girl's realization that she has no penis and her consequential repression of masculine (active) desires for feminine (passive) ones of penis substitution. Other
analysts have amended Freud's interpretation of the origins of the feminine
psyche. Some argue that libido itself is sex-specific. That is, males and females
have fundamentally different psychological experiences due to physical differences—males' experiences being phallic or outward-oriented and female's being
concentric or inward-oriented. Taking this perspective Erik Erikson developed
notions of the feminine sense of "inner space" (and masculine sense of "outer
space"). Taking another approach, analysts of an object relations perspective
attribute essential sex-specific characteristics to the earliest relations between
mother and infant. For instance, Nancy Chodorow has suggested that the girl's
interior world reflects her earliest environmental experiences: psychosexual traits
arise when the mother continues to promote a sense of unity or connectedness
with female infants while promoting separation or independence with male infants. By internalizing a world of connectedness with others, girls acquire psychological traits of attachment, dependence, and passivity.

Scientific psychology has rejected psychoanalytic models, but nevertheless
has developed conceptualizations of femininity and masculinity that are strikingly
congruent with psychoanalytic theory. During the early twentieth century psychologists began experimental investigations into the nature of sex differences.
The initial findings were equivocal: differences in various psychological abilities
were variable and often not found at all. The search continued with construction
of psychometeric tests that purportedly measured more essential mental functions,

those of femininity and masculinity. The first such masculinity-femininity test was published in 1936 by Lewis Terman and Catherine Cox Miles. By the 1960s dozens of scales had been created to assess these supposedly deeply embedded, frequently concealed traits. The tests also were used to identify abnormal deviations that were thought to be predictors of psychopathology, notably latent homosexuality* or poor adult adjustment. Like the psychoanalytic models, these conceptualizations associated femininity with passivity, emotionality, dependence, and involvement in personal relationships while masculinity was associated with activity, independence, rationality, and interest in objects.

These ideal types hardly differed from their nineteenth-century counterparts. They are held to be universal, fixed, essential, and intrapsychic features of men and women. They are features that are ascribed according to biological sex rather than achieved by performance or activities. In most theories, the types also are prescribed as characteristics of healthy functioning in adults, and they have fitted well with the structure of existing social relations. On one level, this duality of personality types matches the occupational roles accorded to the sexes in society. The feminine personality complements the role demands intimated in the nineteenth-century conception of "expressive" roles (as opposed to "instrumental" or task-oriented ones): mothering, caregiving, attending to social and environmental "housekeeping," etc.

Feminist theorists have identified another level at which the duality of masculinity and femininity relates to societal forms. Masculinity is the ideal that is represented in cultural forms generally: the masculine personality corresponds to the enshrined rationality, disinterestedness, the objectivity (distance) of scientific epistemology; the autonomy and individualism of liberal political doctrines; and the object orientation and aggressiveness of the modern technological workplace. Femininity represents the "other," that category that is not achievement, that is not representative of cultural progress. Yet femininity remains absolutely essential to maintaining social and emotional relations. From this perspective many feminist theorists see femininity as a cultural construction that is constitutive in maintaining social relations in societies where differential status and options are accorded to men and women.

The concepts of femininity and the feminine personality type, therefore, are themselves cultural contradictions. While femininity represents the "other," or the absence of traits valued in postindustrial conceptions of personhood, it also contains qualities (passion, caring, intuition) that are sometimes recognized as virtues. Those feminists who advocate women-centered models as correctives to patriarchal conditions face this contradiction. Other feminist theorists have attempted to resolve the cultural contradiction by advocating "androgyny*," for the androgynous personality encompasses desirable traits of both femininity and masculinity. The androgynous being can be independent, assertive, and rationally motivated in one situation and caring, receptive, and emotional in another. The androgynous person has a psychological repertoire that allows him or her to respond to a wide range of situational demands. However, the androgynous being is too often presented as to protean *man*, a disarmingly transient personality that manifests primarily masculine virtues or at least is accorded stature and power for displaying masculine attributes.

Recent feminist scholarship has moved toward revealing the feminine personality as a social construction: femininity can be seen as a manufactured status or state that serves maintenance of particular social systems. However, this move only challenges existing social discourse and practice. Further transformations are needed to establish the future possibilities regarding femininity, for until such time, femininity will be attributed to fixed, intrapsychic characteristics, and the recognition of feminine behavior will be restricted in its social value and power.

Further References. N. Chodorow, *The Reproduction of Mothering* (Berkeley, 1978). J. G. Morawski, "The Troubled Quest for Masculinity, Femininity and Androgyny," in P. Shaver (ed.), *Review of Personality and Social Psychology* 7 (Beverly Hills, 1987). C. Smith-Rosenberg, *Disorderly Conduct: Visions of Gender in Victorian America* (New York, 1985). R. Steele, "Paradigm Lost: Psychoanalysis after Freud," in C. Buxton (ed.), *Points of View in the History of Modern Psychology* (Orlando, 1985).

JILL G. MORAWSKI

FEMINISM refers to a belief in and commitment to equal rights and opportunities for women. Feminists of differing theoretical perspectives differ in their beliefs about the causes and foundations of patriarchy, the methods to be pursued, and the nature and extent of the changes that must be made, but all agree that biological sex is not a justification for domination or subordination.

For discussions of feminist theory, see CULTURAL FEMINISM, FEMINIST THEORY, LIBERAL FEMINISM, MARXIST FEMINISM, and SOCIALIST FEMINISM. For feminism and women of color*, see CHICANA FEMINISM and BLACK WOMEN AND FEMINISM.

FEMINIST CONSCIOUSNESS is an awareness that the individual woman is part of a larger social group and that her personal problems, as a woman, are problems that affect all women, and hence are political problems—that the personal is political.

Feminist consciousness is an awareness that women's experiences must be examined and interpreted, the nature of women's oppression understood, as a necessary precondition for social change.

FEMINIST THEORY. The philosophical analysis of the concept of gender and the meaning of sexual difference. Feminist theory critically evaluates the claim that gender is determined directly by biology. Generally, feminist analysis depends on the premise that gender is a socially constructed, historically changing reality.

The central project of feminist theory is fourfold: (1) to evaluate critically the claim that gender is determined directly by biology; (2) to explore the ways that sexist assumptions have distorted the meaning of gender so that women's experiences either have been rendered invisible or have been undervalued; (3) to challenge the claims to truth of science and the humanities on the grounds that their metatheoretical foundations are sexist, and (4) to propose an alternative, more inclusive epistemological framework.

Feminist theory claims that to acknowledge the gender bias of traditional theory is to transform radically the structure of our knowledge of reality. Since thinking is a human activity engaged in by sex-gendered beings, whose specific historical identity influences their perceptual capacity, then knowledge—the product of that activity—is always bounded by this fact. Feminist theorists differ both in the extent to which they accept the idea of a unique, gender-determined knowledge and in their recommendations for the reconstruction of scientific and non-scientific discourses. To some, the assertion of "female" ways of knowing is the reproduction of sexist thinking, while to others "female" discourse is the epitome of undistorted communication. Earlier feminist theory tended to subscribe to the former point of view. More recent theorists, especially those influenced by French feminist writings and contemporary philosophies of deconstruction* and hermeneutics, tend to endorse the latter position.

Contemporary feminist theory has developed through several stages of inquiry. It began with the project of exploring the *origins* of women's oppression. Early work during this stage concentrated on considering the ways that women's reproductive biology and women's roles in the family* were used throughout history to segregate women as a group (class) and to isolate them from the full range of human activity. The concept of patriarchy* was introduced to this debate about the root causes of the exploitation of women and became a central category of analysis. For example, early work in anthropology demonstrated how the development of surplus production contributed to the institutionalization of patriarchal property systems. Since kinship and property systems were structured through male lines, women's position in these exchange systems became defined by their position in relation to the male-dominated family/property nexus. Although women's activity was important to the daily life of the community, both economically and socially, women appeared to wield little official power, being absent from most positions of recognized leadership. Theorists in anthropology and other fields continue to debate the question of women's relative powerlessness. Some contend that anthropological fieldwork focuses on male experience and interprets social reality from a masculinist perspective, thus obscuring or distorting the significance of women's roles.

During this earlier stage of theory building, major disputes developed among liberal, socialist, radical, and lesbian feminists, with each school claiming to have identified the basic cause of patriarchy. For liberals, it was the lack of equal rights and opportunities to participate in mainstream activities that led to the exploitation of women. Socialists saw relations of property under capitalism as the motor of patriarchal ideas and practices in the modern era. Radical feminists argued that women's biology was the root cause of patriarchy. Lesbian feminists challenged compulsory heterosexuality* as the mainstay of patriarchal relations.

Later, feminist theorists attempted to treat the concept of patriarchy with greater historical rigor, claiming that patriarchy was not a universal, unchanging phenomenon, but had a history and a material foundation that empirical analysis could uncover. This stage of theory shifted debate away from the question of origins to the question of how patriarchy was maintained. Feminist historians researched women's multifarious activities in different epochs. They challenged the extent to which history had provided an accurate picture of either the pattern of development of civilization or the relative value of women's contributions to that development. Contending that most historical models had been based on unfounded assumptions about the ways that women's biology had impaired their participation in state or economy building, feminist historians reviewed existing records and discovered new archival materials to substantiate their argument that women had made important political and economic contributions. Since women had been "hidden from history" by distorted models of social change that privileged male-dominated activities, these theorists contended that reinserting women into the historical record altered substantially both the way that history would be written and the image of women as a silent and inactive oppressed group.

Most recently, feminist theorists have been reassessing the concept of patriarchy and debating the relevance of the "oppressed group" model for describing women's experiences. Once again, the nature of sexual differences and the role they play in defining gender has become central to the debate. But the emphasis on difference is different. Some theorists argue that gender differences need to be emphasized, so that the uniqueness of female experiences and values can be recognized and appreciated. For example, scholars like Adrienne Rich and Sara Ruddick redefine mothering as a culturally progressive and potentially subversive institution whose values and practices could challenge the male system of power and hierarchy if it were structured along gynocentric lines. Artists and literary critics claim that women's visions and voices are unique because of the historical segregation of male and female activities. Rather than attempt to imitate male styles, women's creativity should flourish in different ways. Other theorists react strongly against this reasoning because they contend that it defines women as ontologically distinguishable from men. To these theorists any renewed emphasis on differences, especially by feminists, is politically dangerous because it contributes to the re-establishment of sociopolitical hierarchies that disadvantage or oppress women. Eradication of differences is the goal for this group.

The issue behind all of these debates is the epistemological challenge that feminist theory represents by its endeavor to create a theory of knowledge that is more inclusive of the full range of human experience. Regardless of their divergent political ideologies, feminist theorists share this project. By critically evaluating and redefining the basic methods of science and interpretation, and by developing new categories of analysis, feminist theory has made seminal contributions to the philosophy of science and the humanities.

KATHLEEN B. JONES

FEMINIST THERAPY emerged in the mid–1970s as a reflection of feminist criticism of psychiatry, of efforts to rid psychiatry of sexist biases, such as its double standard and the hierarchical relation between practitioner and client which too often replicates the source of the client's problem, and of new research and new insights into women's psychology. Feminist therapists have no one technique, but share common underlying principles and common goals. These are incorporated in the ethical code of the Feminist Therapist Institute, Inc., adopted in 1987 as guidelines for feminist therapists and to indicate to the public the accountability of Feminist Therapy Institute members.

FEMINIST THERAPY ETHICAL CODE. *Preamble.* Feminist therapy evolves from feminist philosophy, psychological theory and practice, and political theory. In particular feminists recognize the impact of society in creatirg and maintaining the problems and issues brought into therapy. Briefly, feminists believe the personal is political. Basic tenets of feminism* include a belief in the equal worth of all human beings, a recognition that each individual's personal experiences and situations are reflective of and an influence on society's institutionalized attitudes and values, and a commitment to political and social change that equalizes power among people. Feminism strives to create equal valuing of all people by recognizing and reducing the pervasive influences and insidious effects of patriarchy on people's lives. Thus, a feminist analysis addresses the effects of sexism* on the development of females and males, and the relationship of sexism to other forms of oppression, including but not limited to, racism, classism, homophobia, agism, and antiSemitism. Feminists also live in and are subject to those same influences and effects, and continually monitor their beliefs and behaviors as a result of these influences.

Feminist therapists adhere to and integrate feminist analysis into all spheres of their work as therapists, educators, consultants, administrators, and/or researchers. Feminist therapists recognize that their values influence the therapeutic process and clarify with clients the nature and effect of those values. Feminist therapists are accountable for the management of the power differential within the therapist/client relationship. Because of the limitations of a purely intrapsychic model of human functioning, feminist therapists facilitate the understanding of interactive effects of the client's internal and external worlds. Feminist therapists possess knowledge about the psychology of women and utilize feminist scholarship to revise theories and practices, incorporating new knowledge as it is generated.

Feminist therapists assume a proactive stance toward the eradication of oppression in their lives and work toward empowering women. They are respectful of individual differences, challenging oppressive aspects of both their own and the clients' value systems. Feminist therapists engage in social change activities, broadly defined, outside of and apart from their work in their professions. Such activities may vary in scope and content but are an essential aspect of a feminist perspective.

Feminist therapists are trained in a variety of disciplines, theoretical orientations, and degrees of structure. They come from different cultural, ethnic, and racial backgrounds. They work in many types of settings with a diversity of clients and practice different modalities of therapy, training and research. Amid this diversity, feminist therapists are joined together by their feminist analyses and perspectives.

Feminist therapy theory integrates feminist principles into other theories of human development and change. As a result, the following ethical principles are additive to, rather than a replacement for, the ethical principles of the profession in which a feminist therapist practices. Feminist therapists also will work toward incorporating feminist principles into existing standards when appropriate.

The code is a series of positive statements which provide guidelines for feminist therapy practice, training and research. Feminist therapists who are members of other professional organizations adhere to the codes of those organizations. Feminist therapists who are not members of such organizations are guided by the ethical standards of the organization closest to their mode of practice. These statements provide more specific guidelines within the context of and as an extension of most ethical codes. When ethical guidelines are in conflict, the feminist therapist is accountable for how she prioritizes her choices.

These ethical guidelines, then, are focused on the issues feminist therapists, educators, and researchers have found especially important in their professional settings. As with any code of therapy ethics, the well-being of clients is the guiding principle underlying this code. The feminist therapy issues which relate directly to the client's well-being include cultural diversities and oppressions, power differentials, overlapping relationships, therapist accountability, and social change. Even though the principles are stated separately, each interfaces with the others for form an interdependent whole. In addition, the code is a living document and thus is continually in the process of change.

I. Cultural Diversities and Oppressions
  A. A feminist therapist increases her accessibility to and for a wide range of clients from her own and other identified groups through flexible delivery of services. When appropriate, the feminist therapist assists clients in accessing other services.
  B. A feminist therapist is aware of the meaning and impact of her own ethnic and cultural background, gender, class, and sexual orientation, and actively attempts to become knowledgeable about alternatives from sources other than her clients. The therapist's goal is to uncover and respect cultural and experiential differences.

C. A feminist therapist evaluates her ongoing interactions with her clientele for any evidence of the therapist's biases or discriminatory attitudes and practice. The feminist therapist accepts responsibility for taking action to confront and change any interfering or oppressing biases she has.

II. Power Differentials

A. A feminist therapist acknowledges the inherent power differentials between client and therapist, and models effective use of personal power. In using the power differential to the benefit of the client, she does not take control or power which rightfully belongs to her client.

B. A feminist therapist discloses information to the client which facilitates the therapeutic process. The therapist is responsible for using self-disclosure with purpose and discretion in the interests of the client.

C. A feminist therapist negotiates and renegotiates formal and/or informal contacts with clients in an on-going mutual process.

D. A feminist therapist educates her clients regarding their rights as consumers of therapy, including procedures for resolving differences and filing grievances.

III. Overlapping Relationships

A. A feminist therapist recognizes the complexity and conflicting priorities inherent in multiple or overlapping relationships. The therapist accepts responsibility for monitoring such relationships to prevent potential abuse of or harm to the client.

B. A feminist therapist is actively involved in her community. As a result, she is especially sensitive about confidentiality. Recognizing that her clients' concerns and general well-being are primary, she self-monitors both public and private statements and comments.

C. A feminist therapist does not engage in sexual intimacies nor any overtly or covertly sexualized behaviors with a client or former client.

IV. Therapist Accountability

A. A feminist therapist works only with those issues and clients within the realm of her competencies.

B. A feminist therapist recognizes her personal and professional needs, and utilizes ongoing self-evaluation, peer support, consultation, supervision, continuing education, and/or personal therapy to evaluate, maintain, and improve her work with clients, her competencies, and her emotional well-being.

C. A feminist therapist continually reevaluates her training, theoretical background, and research to include developments in feminist knowledge. She integrates feminism into psychological theory, receives on-going therapy training, and acknowledges the limits of her competencies.

D. A feminist therapist engages in self-care activities in an on-going manner. She acknowledges her own vulnerabilities and seeks to care for herself outside of the therapy setting. She models the ability and willingness to self-nurture in appropriate and self-empowering ways.

V. Social Change

A. A feminist therapist actively questions other therapeutic practices in her community that appear abusive to clients or therapists, and when possible, intervenes as early as appropriate or feasible, or assists clients in intervening when it is facilitative to their growth.

B. A feminist therapist seeks multiple avenues for impacting change, including
   public education and advocacy within professional organizations, lobbying for
   legislative actions, and other appropriate activities.

Reprinted with permission of the Feminist Therapy Institute, Inc., 50 South
Steele Street, Suite 850, Denver, CO 80209.

FEMINIZATION OF POVERTY. Since the 1960s in the United States the
poor have been more likely to be single females, members of female-headed
households, and elderly females than to be single men, members of male-headed
households, and elderly men. There has been a great increase in female-headed
families, and over 40 percent of those living in female-headed families are poor.
Less than 10 percent of persons living in male-headed households live in poverty*.

Higher female poverty has long been a fact of life of colonial capitalism,
especially in Africa. As men were coerced to work in mines or on settler farms,
women, children, and the elderly were left to eke out a living on infertile
reservation lands. Migrant workers are paid on the basis that they are single.

FEMINOLOGY. Literally, the science of women, *feminology* is an alternative
term used to signify women's studies in some countries, notably the Scandinavian. Used at the Royal Library in Copenhagen since 1971, this word was
invented by librarian Nynne Koch for the ease with which it would be adapted
to numerous languages and used in both substantive and adjectival forms as well
as for its neutral, scientific connotations and its ability to project "a new image
of the scientific landscape." The term is not, however, altogether new, for it
was used decades earlier to designate a prototypical women's studies course
offered at the *Collège libre des sciences sociales* (Free College of Social Sciences)
in Paris between 1900 and 1905. Taught by a French woman of letters, Mme.
Marguerite Souley-Darqué, this "course on feminology" resembled contemporary women's studies courses in its content, institutional innovativeness, and
diversity of student audience. Cross-disciplinary, it combined philosophical,
sociological, and historical approaches to understanding the "nature," experience, and perceptions of women. Similar to the early women's studies courses
offered in community-based "free schools," it was housed in an institution
established in 1895 to foster innovative research and teaching, especially for the
new "social scientists" who sought to apply scientific methods to the solution
of social problems. Also like many of the first women's studies courses, instruc-
tors taught and students attended voluntarily, without recompense other than the
intrinsic value of educational experimentation. Feminology then as now attracted
students of both sexes and diverse ages and conditions. It was likewise placed
under a rubric of "feminist education." Influenced by Darwinism, Mme. Souley-
Darqué was concerned primarily to demonstrate that women's social inferiority

was explicable as a response to past environmental conditions that industrial capitalism made obsolete. Her course, which disappeared with the decline of the *Collège libre* (and the increasing acceptance of social sciences in established universities), demonstrates the continuity of feminist effort to revise definitions of femininity grounded in bias or ignorance.

Further References. S. G. Bell and M. S. Rosenhan, "A Problem in Naming: Women Studies—Women's Studies?" *Signs* 6 (1981): 540–542. M. J. Boxer, "For and About Women: The Theory and Practice of Women's Studies in the United States," *Signs* 7 (1982): 660–695, esp. 664–665, n. 11. M. J. Boxer, "Women's Studies in France circa 1902: A Course on Feminology," *International Supplement to the Women's Studies Quarterly* 1 (1982): 25–27.

MARILYN J. BOXER

FETUS, the term for an unborn vertebrate, is sometimes used to refer to the human organism during the entire period of its development from conception to birth. It is also used more specifically of the second, or fetal, stage of development, beginning around the ninth week, after the body structure has become recognizably human. The preceding stage of development is the embryonic.

FOOD AND EATING DISORDERS. Responsibility for food preparation continues to be a central part of women's lives. A North American study has shown that even though one-fifth of household work is now "shared" by family members, the woman carries out 88 percent of meal preparation tasks and 86 percent of the chores related to cleaning up after food preparation. Even in "progressive" families, men and children "help" while the woman manages what is seen to be her responsibility.

Food preparation is distinctly different from other domestic responsibilities. Unlike child care*, which is a building process with each day's work adding to a growing product, food preparation is a process that constantly starts from the beginning. Responsibilities for child care gradually diminish as society assumes some role through nurseries and schools and as the child can take care of itself. In contrast, work required for feeding the family* increases as children grow and make individual demands. Housework* is different from food preparation in that it can be delayed or organized into times that fit into a busy schedule. Meal times impose constant deadlines. No one will die if windows are not cleaned regularly, but feeding the family is literally a life or death responsibility.

Industrialization has changed the work women do as food producers. Unlike our sisters in the Third World, the North American woman's role has changed from producing food on the land to buying food. A shift has occurred from time spent cooking food to time spent shopping for food. A woman's identity has become increasingly connected to her role as consumer.

Technology in the home may *increase* women's workload. Rather than reducing work, appliances seem to raise the standards of domestic labor. Studies have shown a direct correlation between the number of appliances owned and the time spent in housework. In the urban US, time spent per week in housework increased from 51 hours in 1929 to 77 hours in 1971. Appliances are also used as a substitute for a more equal division of household chores, i.e., men and children are more likely to do the dishes if a home does *not* have a dishwasher.

Women have ambivalent feelings about their roles as food producers. Many women get great satisfaction from cooking and find it more rewarding than other household tasks. For many women, food production is their principal source of identity, a prime way to express creativity, an ideal way to show love and caring for others, and their major source of power and control in the world. Food then takes on an enormous significance. Food becomes symbolic of a woman's love for her family. She is unable to let down high standards of meal preparation, perpetuated by advertising and the media, without feeling she is reneging on her expected caring role. Rejecting or accepting mother's food is seen as rejecting or accepting mother. Food becomes the channel through which power struggles in the family are fought. In violent homes, battering is often connected to food preparation duties. Men punish women when buying, cooking, or serving food is not done according to their wishes.

Fear of Fat. Women's responsibility for food preparation is an important part of the domestic division of labor which restricts women from making their maximum contribution to society and to changing that society. But, on a day-to-day basis, most women are far more aware of the conflict between their role as producer/consumer and the pressure on women to be thin.

An abundance of food, particularly low fiber, high fat, high sugar foods, means that many people are plump. Plumpness is common, so slimness is valued and there is extreme prejudice against fat people. Obesity is the most stigmatized, by all age groups, physical feature except skin color. The prejudice against fat people is exaggerated because obesity is thought to be a voluntary choice even though metabolic factors and physical exercise have more to do with body weight than eating habits.

The fear of getting fat or staying fat is much more a concern for women than for men. Women's roles as food producers mean that they can never get away from thinking about and dealing with food. Women need relatively fewer calories (an average of 1,600 to 2,400 calories needed per day compared to 2,300 to 3,100 for men), and hormonal changes make them more susceptible to weight gain. Women are judged by their appearance far more than men and live with constant reminders of the narrow range of body images acceptable for the "ideal woman." There is less pressure on men to diet, but when men decide to lose weight, they do so more easily, partly because of the support they get from women.

Eating Disorders. Anorexia nervosa*, bulimia*, compulsive eating, and dieting are all women's issues symbolic of contradictions in women's relationship to food as preparers and consumers.

Anorexia = self-starvation, a loss of weight of 20 to 25 percent of initial body weight. Ninety-five percent of anorexics are women. Anorexia is common only in societies where there is an abundance of food and where thinness is valued. Health professionals are most aware of anorexia in white, middle-class young women, labeled as "overachievers," though this may be more a reflection of who calls upon the mental health services than an accurate picture of the occurrence of anorexia. Although anorexia is predominantly a mental health issue, there are serious physical consequences of the extreme weight loss. There is an absence of menstruation, the risk of sterility, and extreme susceptibility to infection, and a wasting away of vital muscle (including heart) tissue. It is estimated that 15 to 20 percent of anorexics die because of their eating disorders.

Bulimia = a cycle of binging and purging. Bulimics get rid of food by vomiting, fasting, or using diuretics, laxatives, or amphetamines. Eighty-five percent of bulimics are women, and studies indicate that 15 to 20 percent of college women are bulimic. Many bulimics do not seek professional help and are of "normal" weight without weight fluctuations, so the incidence may be even more common. Physical health problems include rotting teeth (from stomach acids), dehydration causing long-term mineral imbalances, and increased infections.

Compulsive eating is usually defined as having an addiction to food, feeling out of control about one's eating habits, or eating without regard for the physical body signals of hunger and satiety.

What Is Ordered Eating? The above conditions are usually labeled as eating disorders. Instead of viewing them as extreme conditions, it is probably more useful to view them as extensions of a continuum of problematic relationships women have with eating habits, weight control, and their role in this society. Sophisticated psychological tests (used for diagnosis and treatment of anorexia) find little difference between ordinary weight-preoccupied women and anorexics. Indeed, the goal of treatment for anorexia is that the person is "no more neurotic about food than anyone else."

NANCY WORCESTER

G

GATHERING/HUNTING THEORIES OF EVOLUTION. Anthropologists have put forward several theories of human evolution based on the assumption that females gathered and males hunted. These theories seek to understand how our early ancestors developed into modern humans. Although physical evolution is often confused with cultural evolution, it is important to keep the two concepts distinct. Physical evolution is the actual morphological changes that led to the development of modern Homo sapiens. Humans have gone through virtually no physical changes in the past 40,000 years. Cultural evolution, however, which follows the development of human society, is in a constant state of flux, and is also much more difficult to analyze than physical evolution is.

Early anthropologists had little information on the physical development of humans and concentrated instead on the evolution of human society. One of the first comprehensive evolutionary theories was that of Lewis Henry Morgan, who introduced the idea that early societies were ''matrilineal,'' that is, they traced descent through the mother's rather than the father's line (*Ancient Societies*, 1877). He speculated that women would have higher status in such a society, but he never seriously considered that women would wield any real power. Later work by Friedrich Engels (*The Origin of the Family, Private Property, and the State*, 1884) and archaeologists like V. Gordon Childe echoed these ideas, which assumed an early, male-dominated culture of hunters. This gave way to a more egalitarian and peaceful era of plant gathering and incipient horticulture. All these evolutionary theories take for granted that the later phases of civilization are not only the most highly evolved but are those in which the males dominate.

Most recent theories of evolution seem unable to escape from the early assumptions that differentiate between peaceful female gatherers and violent male hunters. When anthropologists began to unearth real evidence of physical evolution, a debate began on the question of innate human aggression, a debate that continues today. Findings of hominid (prehuman) bones with large numbers of animal fossils were supposed to indicate that those hominids killed large numbers of animals and even their own kind for food, giving rise to a man-the-killer theory. The subsequent discovery that the entire assemblage of bones, the hominid bones included, were the remains of hyena meals has not erased the popular notion that we became human through violent behavior and that the female's only duty was to raise the children and prepare the meat brought home by the successful hunter.

In response, a number of experts have been reconsidering the evolution of human society. Nancy Tanner is among those who have constructed an alternative to the man-the-hunter evolutionary model. The early human female, says Tanner, having the greater investment in reproduction and child care*, would have more influence in mating procedures. Therefore, the male would have to be more attractive in terms of sociability and willingness to share food and time with the children, rather than resorting to aggression and coercion.

Tool making is the first archaeological indication we have of early human culture, and this may well have emerged out of a gathering rather than hunting tradition. A container for gathered foods or a baby carrier would have been an early necessity, as would digging sticks for gathering root vegetables. This does not mean that there was an early division of labor between the sexes, however. Big game hunting was a late evolutionary development, which did not necessarily exclude females from participation. Additionally, human physical evolution shows a trend away from sexual dimorphism*. The most probable evolutionary model for early hominids was nonspecialized hunting, gathering, and collecting activities that stressed flexibility in food choices and cooperation among all band members. It is this emphasis on flexibility and cooperation, rather than on dominance, that may have led to the survival and success of Homo sapiens as a species.

Further References. S. B. Hrdy, *The Woman That Never Evolved* (Cambridge, Mass., 1981). N. M. Tanner, *On Becoming Human* (Cambridge, Mass., 1981).

WENDY R. EISNER

GATHERING AND HUNTING SOCIETIES include all cultural groups, past and present, that subsist exclusively on noncultivated foodstuffs. They do not raise animals nor practice agriculture, but depend on collecting wild plants, fishing, hunting, and a variety of intermediate food-procuring activities. Because the terms *hunting* and *gathering* do not fully describe the variety of food-collecting activities that these groups engage in, and because of the cultural bias that associates hunting with males and gathering with females, some anthropologists have suggested the term *forager* as a more accurate label for this type of society.

Both prehistoric and modern foraging bands have several characteristics in common, although there are exceptions to these generalizations. Most are small, with a maximum of fifty individuals. They are generally nomadic and move within a prescribed territory in order to exploit the area's resources. They are considered to be egalitarian, meaning that there is no ranking of individuals within the band, and no band member, male or female, can dominate another. This last feature is a behavior observed in several modern foraging societies; therefore, we cannot be sure that prehistoric peoples were also egalitarian.

The assumption in most traditional studies of foraging bands has been that women are inferior to men. Males were seen as the major protagonists in humanity's past, with women having a secondary or incidental role. This bias led anthropologists and archaeologists alike to focus on the hunting activities of band societies as exclusively a male activity, while underestimating the importance of gathering, which is generally assumed to be a female activity. Women were thought to have little power within the group, based on their low status as gatherers and mothers.

Feminist anthropologists saw the danger of the man-the-hunter myth in its underlying support of the "natural" inferiority of women. Their studies, and a move toward a more objective viewpoint in ethnographic studies, led to a shift away from the male orientation to a more balanced view of gender roles. A new picture of band societies, which is beginning to emerge, includes a realization of the importance of plant collection in the subsistence strategies of many past and present societies. However, it is also important to understand the enormous variation in gender roles* that is possible among foraging peoples. Many cultures may not assign hunting and gathering tasks based on gender, nor need these tasks be an indication of status.

Prehistoric Gatherer-Hunters. For most of human history, people have practiced a foraging way of life. Our earliest ancestors, who lived two million years ago, during the Lower Paleolithic (Old Stone Age), collected wild plants, insects, and small animals. They left no evidence of large-scale hunting activity and probably scavenged meat from the remains of larger carnivores' meals. Because there is so little evidence of variation in tools and in food-procuring techniques, it seems reasonable to assume that hunting and gathering were not specialized activities until later in human evolution. Females and males probably took part in all these activities, with little regard to gender-assigned roles.

With the emergence of the first member of the human species, the Neanderthal, 125,000 years ago, there is growing evidence that human society was becoming more complex. Neanderthals made more sophisticated tools and buried their dead. There is still no evidence that anyone had higher status within the group, however, nor that men dominated women.

The beginning of the Upper Paleolithic, about 35,000 years ago, marks the appearance of modern humans: homo sapiens sapiens. This period coincided with the drier, colder climatic conditions of the late Pleistocene. Vast areas of Europe were covered with grasslands, upon which roamed reindeer, mammoth, bison, horse, and woolly rhino. Archaelogical research reveals that the number of sites increased dramatically at this time, as did the complexity of society. There were more specialized tools for working wood and bone and for making clothing.

Spectacular cave paintings and carvings appear during this period, including the first representations of the human figure, often called the "Venus" figurines. It was traditionally assumed that these figures were fertility or sexual symbols and were made by men, but it is equally possible that they were made by women. Interestingly, they appear when, for the first time in human history, there was a rapid rise in population. Women were having more children and may have encouraged fecundity by weaning their children at an increasingly earlier age.

The late Paleolithic people of Eurasia were dependent to a great degree on hunting, but this is no reason to assume that women did not enjoy equal status. The usual technique for hunting the grazing herds was to organize animal drives, in which animals were driven into ravines or into artificial enclosures to be killed. These drives required the entire community's cooperation, and ethnographic studies indicate that women and men could have had similar roles in this operation.

Archaeologists have held on firmly to their conception that all prehistoric people were hunters. This must be seen as an intrinsic problem in the nature of the archaeological record. Animal food leaves a greater amount of waste in the form of bone, which is well preserved in most soils. Plant foods leave less waste and are poorly preserved. Stone tools may be interpreted as hunting and butchering implements, although they may actually have been used for plant harvesting and preparation. Also, many tools may have been made of wood or other perishable substances, and hence not survive as well as stone, which would also skew the bias toward hunting. There is even speculation that the most indispensable tool of a foraging culture would have been the carrying pouch, used to carry foodstuffs and children. These, too, being made of skins or plant fibers, would have perished long ago.

The hunters of the Eurasian plains were only one type of society during the Late Paleolithic, albeit the most intensively studied. Other groups, in Africa, Asia, and in the Middle East, were practicing more intensive food-collecting techniques that would eventually lead to the emergence of plant and animal domestication and the growth of stratified society.

Modern Gathering and Hunting Societies. There is no culture group living today that has not been deeply affected by modern Western society. However, there are small bands of people who still practice a "stone age" economy, getting most of their food by foraging. These groups have been investigated in an effort to understand our human ancestors. Modern foragers, however, have had as long a history as any present-day society and therefore cannot be considered to behave like prehistoric people.

Women's status in these societies is extremely variable, and anthropologists have had a difficult time interpreting gender roles objectively. Most anthropologists have been male and have tended to bias their studies toward male activities, interviewing only the men of the band. Anthropological research is now focusing on the entire experience of the community of women, men, children, and the elderly. The outcome of such research shows that women's status in these groups often cannot be described in our culture's terms and that our ideas of power and aggression may be inadequate to understanding the experiences of people in other societies.

The !Kung of the Kalihari Desert in Botswana are often used as an example of a typical hunting and gathering community. The men traditionally hunt with poisoned arrows, while the women collect nuts, roots, and fruits. Eighty percent of the !Kung diet is provided by the women. Females and males enjoy equivalent status within the group structure. Their economy is based on sharing and cooperation, and anthropologists have postulated that prehistoric humans were similar to the !Kung. Although this is a simplistic approach to understanding prehistoric behavior, the !Kung do offer an alternative to Western society's biased attitude toward male/female roles.

The Agta Negritos of the Philippines, a present-day tribal people, are an example of a culture whose women and men share all subsistence activities. Most interestingly, the women of a number of Agta tribes hunt large game with bows, arrows, and hunting dogs. The women are prevented from hunting only during late pregnancy and the first few months after giving birth. Teenagers and women with older children are the most frequent hunters. The women space their children to allow for maximum mobility. They maintain that they keep their birthrate down through the use of herbal contraceptives.

By studying these ethnographic examples and by questioning the assumptions that have been made about female and male roles in prehistory, it becomes possible to understand that Western society's traditionally low view of women's status is by no means universal. If the study of human culture has one thing to teach us, it is that human behavior and culture allow for adaptation and that gender roles are not determined by biological laws, but can be changed.

Further References. M. Conkey and J. Spector, "Archaeology and the Study of Gender," in M. Schiffer (ed.), *Advances in Archaeological Method and Theory* (New York, 1984), 7: 1–38. F. Dahlberg, *Woman the Gatherer* (New Haven, 1981).

WENDY R. EISNER

GENDER/SEX. *Gender* is a cultural construct: the distinction in roles, behaviors, and mental and emotional characteristics between females and males developed by a society. *Gender* is sometimes used as a synonym for *sex*, but feminists draw a clear distinction. *Sex* is a term that encompasses the morphological and physiological differences on the basis of which humans (and other life forms) are categorized as male or female. It should be used only in relation to characteristics and behaviors that arise directly from biological differences between men and women.

GENDER AND SCIENCE. A subject that is a relative latecomer in the recent history of feminist scholarship and that, even today, continues to invite quite different interpretations among feminists (as well as others). To some (perhaps surprisingly many), it is understood as a subject about women in science; to others, as the science of sex differences*; and to yet others (this author included), as the study of the mutual interactions between ideologies of gender and science in the social construction of gender and science as we actually encounter them. These differences in interpretation reflect deep differences in understandings of the meanings both of gender and of science—in particular, the extent to which each category is, on the one hand, given to us by nature, and, on the other hand, subject to the influence of (perhaps even constructed by) social forces. An examination of how these conceptions have varied, among people and over time, will in fact help us to explain the relatively late emergence of this subject as part of feminist theory* proper. Simultaneously, it will enable us to identify the critical intellectual problems with which students of this subject must now deal.

In the extreme case, both science and gender are seen as purely natural categories, subject to immutable laws of development. From this perspective (which actually describes most traditional views of both science and gender), the mere juxtaposition of the terms *gender* and *science* is a reminder of the most conspicuously gender-specific fact about science—the historical absence of women from science. But although the "natural" character of science has in general appeared to be self-evident and uncontroversial, the same cannot be said, for any historical period, about the actual "nature" of women. Thus, to some, the absence of women from science bespeaks in inherent opposition between women's nature and the nature of science, while, to others, it is seen merely as the consequence of a residual social prejudice that bears no relation to the true nature of either women or science. In other words, depending on one's assumptions about "woman's nature," the subject of gender and science invites two readings even within this extreme case: first, as a natural opposition between women and science that warrants respect, and second, as a regrettable, and remediable, throwback to manifestly unscientific prejudices about women.

As feminists have become more conscious of the extent to which women are "made" rather than "born," and, accordingly, of the need to distinguish gender, a social category, from the biological category of sex, attention has turned to the social forces that have mediated the construction of women. It soon became evident that certain (mis)uses of science itself had to be counted among these social forces. With this shift in perspective, feminist scientists began to reread the subject of gender and science as an inquiry into the ways in which "biology constructs the female"—more specifically, as an inquiry into the failure of proper scientific standards in research on sex differences.

Only with a parallel shift in perspective about the nature of science did it become possible for feminists to include in their inquiry an examination of the mutual influences of ideologies of both gender and science in the construction of science itself—not only in its departure from proper standards but in its very normative values. In other words, it is only with the advent of an effective challenge to the traditional view of science as determined solely by exigencies of logic and experiment, a challenge that has come from recent developments in the history, philosophy, and sociology of science, that feminists have been able to study the influence of gender norms on the actual historical construction of standards of "good" science. Accordingly, the subject of gender and science has now enlarged to a study of the mutually reinforcing dynamics that operate on the making of men, women, and science. A growing body of work on the historical, psychological, and scientific dimensions of these dynamics has focused attention on the deep interpenetration of the language of gender in scientific discourse and, simultaneously, of the language of science in normative psychological discourse. In this effort, the historic conjunction between masculinity, objectivity, and autonomy ceases to be construed as a "natural" given but comes to be seen as a product of and contributor to social norms simultaneously dividing masculine from feminine and scientific from nonscientific. Of perhaps the greatest interest are the consequences, for science, of the exclusion from scientific norms of all those values that have been *culturally* labeled as feminine. Scholars have begun to explore three levels on which such consequences might be seen: first, in the selection of scientific problems; second, in the designation of "legitimate" methodology; and third, in the role of tacit explanatory preferences in choices of "best" theory.

Perhaps the most critical problems facing scholars currently working in this area derive from continuing uncertainty and confusion about the nature of both gender and science. To many, gender continues to be read as synonymous with sex. To such readers, any discussion of "masculine" values in science automatically invites the supposition that women should do science differently. Not only are such readings not in accord with the intent of a scholarship aimed at the deconstruction* of the categories of masculine and feminine rather than at their reinstitution, but they are also experienced as direct threats to the political aims of women scientists who have struggled heroically to transcend such stereotypes. Alternatively, to other readers who see gender and science as purely cultural artifacts, gender appears as only one of a series of demarcators, including race, class, and ethnicity, invoked by the institution of science (one of many such social institutions) for the purposes of political domination. The most pressing questions for the subject of gender and science today are therefore twofold: What are the actual relations between gender and sex, on the one hand, and between science and nature on the other? If gender is not to be equated with sex, might it nonetheless be seen as partially rooted in nature—different from, but not entirely independent of, sex? And, analogously, if science can no longer be relied upon to mirror nature, can we nonetheless recognize its difference from other social institutions—deriving precisely from the ways in which science remains constrained, albeit not contained, by nature? The importance of these questions is not, however, limited to the subject of gender and science, nor does responsibility to address them lie exclusively in the domain of scholars working in this area. Rather, the relation between sex and gender has become the central question for contemporary feminist theory as a whole, just as the question about the relation between science and nature has come to reside at the center of current work in the history, philosophy, and sociology of science.

Further References. R. Blier, *Science and Gender* (New York, 1984). A. Fausto-Sterling, *Myths of Gender* (New York, 1986). S. Harding, *The Science Question in Feminism* (Ithaca, 1986). R. Hubbard, M. S. Henifin, and B. Fried (eds.), *Biological Woman: The Convenient Myth* (Cambridge, Mass, 1982). E. F. Keller, *Reflections on Gender and Science* (New Haven, 1985).

EVELYN FOX KELLER

GENDER ROLES. Behaviors and attributes expected of individuals on the basis on being born either female or male. Whereas *sex* is a biological term based on an individual's reproductive organs and genes, *gender* is a psychological and cultural term.

The gender role for females is quite distinct from the gender role for males. In Western society, to be "feminine" is to be nurturant, expressive, cooperative, and sensitive to the needs of others. To be "masculine" is to be active, aggressive, dominant, and ambitious. The distinctions have been characterized as the difference between a people orientation and an action orientation. Although "masculinity" and "femininity"* and their related traits are regarded as opposites, research clearly indicates that people possess both sets of traits in varying degrees, regardless of their biological sex. Furthermore, individual differences are far greater than gender differences with respect to all personality traits and human abilities. For example, people differ with regard to how competitive they are, but they do not differ primarily on the basis of gender.

Current gender roles probably had their origin in the division of labor prevalent in all societies. In cultures where birth control is primitive, tasks assigned to women generally have to be compatible with frequent childbirth* and nursing activities. The actual tasks assigned to women and men depend on the subsistence base of the particular society and the supply of and demand for labor. In industrialized societies, traditional gender roles have women concerned about the domestic sphere* and men concerned about the public sphere*. In all societies, the male role is more highly valued.

Personality traits assigned to each gender role generally stem from these traditional divisions in labor. Because of their maternal possibilities, women are supposed to develop qualities that would enhance the maternal role, such as empathy and nurturance. Because of their role as hunters, warriors, and breadwinners, men are supposed to develop qualities that would enhance performance in those roles, such as aggressiveness and competitiveness.

Gender roles are socially constructed, not biologically given. All human behavior is shaped primarily by cultural factors, in some cases in interaction with physiological predispositions. From the moment the sex of a newborn is announced, girls and boys are perceived and treated differently. As children age, parents tend to pay increasing attention to gender roles, dressing boys and girls differently, assigning different household tasks, and providing different toys. Teachers, peers, and the mass media also tend to discourage children, especially boys, from doing things viewed as more appropriate for the other sex.

The male gender role appears to be particularly rigid. During childhood and adolescence, being "masculine" involves rejecting all "feminine" behaviors and traits. Girls appear to have more leeway in their gender role, at least until puberty. At that time, however, they are supposed to concentrate on their expected role—to find a mate who will be "a good provider" and have children. For many girls, this means focusing on what males find attractive rather than on developing their own talents.

Strong conformity to traditional gender roles affects individuals on personal, relationship, and societal levels. On the personal level, traditional gender roles may be hazardous to one's health. Men have a shorter life expectancy, more accidents, and more serious illnesses than do women. Most of these gender differences can be attributed to such role-linked behaviors as risk-taking, aggression, type-A (compulsive, impatient) behavior, emotional nonexpression, and smoking. In contrast, women appear to suffer more from some mental health problems than do men. In particular, they are more likely to suffer from depression*, anxiety, and eating disorders than are men, and these may be related to a gender role that emphasizes appearance and inculcates a sense of helplessness in many women.

On a relationship level, women and men who conform to traditional gender roles may have difficulty relating. Since men may not have developed skills conducive to intimate interpersonal communication, the quality of their relationships with their friends, partners, and children may be poor.

The activities traditionally assigned to members of each sex may no longer be appropriate. The smaller families and longer life expectancies in modern societies, combined with the fact that many child care* responsibilities previously borne by the family* alone are now borne by society, means that the traditional division of labor by biological sex no longer is necessary. Most women, including most mothers of young children, now are employed. However, as a result of traditional gender-role socialization of females with its lack of emphasis on career decision-making, women are in the lowest-paying, lowest-status jobs. Furthermore, since our society values paid employment so much more than unpaid work, women who spend their lives, or parts of their lives, engaged in homemaking and child care activities often suffer from low self-esteem and self-confidence in comparison with their employed counterparts.

The traditional gender role for males also prepares men for a world that no longer exists. Men no longer are the sole breadwinners in most families, and their traditional place of dominance in society no longer is assured. Many are unprepared for the demands placed upon them by dual-worker marriages and by a changing work environment in which a woman may be their coworker or supervisor. The values underlying our major societal institutions, such as law, politics, and business, that reflect a "masculine" emphasis on competitiveness and dominance currently are being challenged.

For these reasons, change is slowly occurring in the definition of gender roles for both women and men. The modern gender role for women involves expectations for both children and a career and the development of assertive qualities along with the more traditional expressive ones. The modern gender role for men involves expectations of greater sensitivity to feelings and stronger communication skills along with traditional instrumental traits. Thus the two gender roles have moved closer together. However, to the extent to which these roles are rigidly assigned to individuals solely on the basis of their biological sex, they may prove as restrictive as the traditional roles. The relationship between sex and gender is a problematic one, but a way must be found to recognize the reproductive differences between women and men without structuring an individual's entire personality and life around them.

Further Reference. S. Basow, *Gender Stereotypes: Traditions and Alternatives*, 2nd ed. (Monterey, Calif., 1986).

SUSAN A. BASOW

GENDER ROLES, PRESCHOOL. Gender consciousness, as all social learning, is enhanced and intensified in a school setting. Given the opportunity to create fantasy worlds in the company of their peers, preschool boys and girls begin playing in similar ways but are attracted to distinct and separate play roles by the time they enter kindergarten. In the course of acting out a wide variety of make-believe characters, the children seek dramatic and social definitions for "boy" and "girl" with the same curiosity that governs other investigations into social and personal identity. The doll corner and block area are good places to observe the unfolding of gender roles.

In the beginning, domestic play looks remarkably alike for both sexes. Costumes representing male and female roles are casually exchanged in a flurry of cooking, eating, telephoning, and bedding down. Mother, Father, and Baby are the primary actors, but policemen, kittens, and even robbers often perform the same tasks. If asked, a boy will likely say he is the father, but if he were to say mother it would cause no concern.

Behavioral differences become more apparent in the block area, where the momentum of movement and sound begins to produce a noticeable gap between the sexes. The boys zoom about, colliding and exploding in ways that have little appeal for the girls, who continue their doll corner rituals wherever they go. Both sexes build structures together, but the girls soon disperse to the art tables while the boys remain until the buildings are toppled. We see here the first self-selected separation by sex in the classroom.

At four, gender specialization receives closer attention. Girls and boys still share roles, mainly in the guise of unisex pets, baby bears, and medical personnel, and continue to cook and make beds together. However, the list of he-roles and she-roles grows longer, each class developing its own inventory. In particular, the boys have begun to band together in superhero cliques whose large-scale maneuvers suit the banging-running impulses of young boys. As images of power and intrigue dominate the boys' play, the girls turn to dramatic plots that focus on female characters, adding more sisters and princesses to the mother-baby story. It is this continuing re-enactment of family dramas that most distinguishes the girls' play. Four- and five-year-old boys and girls act out similar issues—jealousy and rivalry, friendship and contentment, fear and loneliness—but the disguises are different and the boys prefer outer space to hearth and home.

Since the early 1970s, the causes and effects of stereotyped play among the young have been debated and cataloged. As direct connections are traced to adult mores, to biological differences, and to psychosexual stages, attempts have been made to create a school environment in which masculine and feminine roles are nearly indistinguishable. Yet the children continue, in their fantasy play, to visualize differences and act them out in stories of their own making. The persistence with which young boys and girls create separate roles in fantasy play may represent as primitive a need as the play itself.

Further References. V. G. Paley, *Wally's Stories* (Cambridge, Mass., 1981). V. G. Paley, *Boys and Girls* (Chicago, 1984). V. G. Paley, *Mollie Is Three* (Chicago, 1986).
VIVIAN GUSSIN PALEY

GENDER STEREOTYPES are structured sets of beliefs about the personal attributes of women and of men. (The terms *sex stereotypes* and *sex-role stereotypes* are often used interchangeably with *gender stereotypes*.) Gender stereotypes are beliefs held by individuals (personal gender stereotypes) and are also shared patterns of thinking within a particular society (cultural gender stereotypes). Cultural gender stereotypes are reflected in cultural forms (e.g., television) and practices (e.g., legal system).

Gender stereotypes has been an active area of social science research for two decades. Early work on the content of stereotypic conceptions focused on the superordinate gender categories *men* and *women* and the personality traits associated with these broad groupings. More recently, researchers have taken a broader view of how people think about the sexes. Gender-stereotype targets include not only the two overarching categories *women* and *men* but also gender subtypes (e.g., "career women," "jocks"). In addition to personality traits (e.g., "Women are emotional"), the elements of stereotypic conceptions include abilities (e.g., "Men are good at math"), physical appearance (e.g., " 'Artistic' males have relatively slight builds and wear bulky sweaters"), behaviors, including role behaviors (e.g., "Women are more likely than men to care for children"), and occupations (e.g., "Most nurses are female").

Although men and women are not "opposite sexes" in terms of actual personality and behavior, gender stereotypes are "bipolar," i.e., women and men are perceived to have opposing personal qualities. The content of beliefs about what men and women are like has most often been summarized by the terms *instrumental* (for the male stereotype) and *expressive* (for the female stereotype). Some researchers, however, feel that the core meaning of stereotypic beliefs about the sexes is best captured by the distinctions "hard-soft," "active-passive," or "agency-communion." This difference of opinion may be resolved in the near future as workers increasingly treat gender stereotypes as multidimensional. Historically, the male stereotype in American culture has comprised more positive and fewer negative attributes than the female stereotype. There is recent evidence, however, that this imbalance in the social desirability of gender stereotypes is declining.

Stereotypic conceptions of the sexes are acquired by three primary means. First, and perhaps most important, is exposure to and participation in mainstream culture. For example, American children watch a considerable amount of television, which portrays men and women quite differently (e.g., men are depicted as powerful, women as peaceful). A second significant input to thinking about the sexes is contact and interaction with specific women and men. Given the general state of male dominance in American society, more men than women occupy positions of power and prestige; this means that most people have contact with men who, on average, have higher status than women. Third, the development of personal gender stereotypes is fostered by basic mental processes such as the need to form categories and the tendency to accentuate between-group differences and underestimate within-category variation.

Gender stereotypes influence information processing and overt behavior. They provide a cognitive frame of reference for the development of self-concept. That is, stereotypic conceptions of what men and women are like serve a prescriptive function by suggesting to individual women and men what they should be like. Thus, for example, the stereotypic belief that ''women are not good at math'' may lead individual women to avoid mathematics courses in school and to not consider careers that involve math.

Gender stereotypes also influence how we form impressions of others. Beliefs about the sexes create expectancies about specific others. These expectancies shape what is noticed about the other, how the target's behavior is interpreted, and what is remembered about the person. Although there are exceptions, the tendency is for stereotype-consistent actions to be more attended to and better remembered and for ambiguous behaviors to be interpreted in stereotype-consistent terms.

Stereotypic conceptions not only influence how we think about others but also shape how we treat other people. Thus, for example, since men are stereotyped as ''having leadership ability,'' males are more likely to be given leadership positions and have their orders complied with. Two important areas where gender stereotypes have particularly pernicious impact are the workplace (where gender stereotypes create the expectancy that men are better suited for managerial positions, while women are ''naturally'' good secretaries) and therapeutic encounters (in which stereotypic male attributes are often regarded as more ''healthy'' than characteristics thought to be more typical of women).

Gender stereotypes are resistant to change. Beliefs about the sexes create strong forces toward their own fulfillment. At the societal level, gender stereotypes are pervasive in the major mediators of culture (e.g., magazines, popular music), and they tacitly influence how social institutions such as schools and the judicial system treat men and women. In interpersonal relations, our expectations that others fit our stereotypic conceptions lead us to treat them in accord with these beliefs, making it more difficult for them to exhibit stereotype-disconfirming actions. At the level of the individual, if individuals feel that they should possess traits and abilities typical of their gender, then they are likely to develop stereotype-consistent qualities.

The foregoing does not mean that gender stereotypes are unchanging or un-changeable. As noted above, there has been an increase in the social desirability of the female stereotype. Also, specific interventions such as exposing children to nontraditional models have been shown to be effective in reducing gender stereotypes.

Further References. R. D. Ashmore, F. K. Del Boca, and A. J. Wohlers, "Gender Stereotypes," in R. D. Ashmore and F. K. Del Boca (eds.), *The Social Psychology of Female-Male Relations: A Critical Analysis of Central Concepts* (New York, 1986). K. Deaux and M. E. Kite, "Gender and Cognition," in B. B. Hess and M. M. Ferree (eds.), *Analyzing Gender: A Handbook of Social Science Research* (New York, 1987). D. N. Ruble and T. L. Ruble, "Sex Stereotypes," in A. G. Miller (ed.), *In the Eye of the Beholder: Contemporary Issues in Stereotyping* (New York, 1982).

RICHARD D. ASHMORE AND FRANCES K. DEL BOCA

GENITAL WARTS (*Condylomata Acuminata*) are caused by a sexually trans-mitted virus called human papillomavirus (HPV). They are particularly relevant for women because of an association with increased risk of cervical cancer*. Warts enlarge during pregnancy, become more vascular, and may even obstruct the birth canal.

Genital warts appear as small cauliflower-like bumps on the external genitals. After exposure to the virus it may be six weeks to eight months before initial bumps appear, during which time a person may be spreading the virus. Using condoms in sexual contacts with men helps to reduce the risk of infection.

Treatment involves the use of podophyllin applied topically to the affected tissue only. Podophyllin may not be used during pregnancy or for warts in the vagina, urethra, or rectum. Alternative treatments include use of liquid nitrogen, laser surgery, or topical 5-Fluorouracil. Weekly or biweekly treatment may be needed. Partners must be examined for the presence of warts.

ELAINE WHEELER

GESTATION (PREGNANCY). The development of the fetus* in the uterus. The period of gestation takes about 38 weeks and is divided into trimesters of three months each. The first trimester is most critical for development. The fetus is more subject to spontaneous abortion and anomalous development during this time than it is later.

During the first eight weeks the fertilized ovum is implanted in the lining of the uterus, and through tremendous cell proliferation and diversification, the embryo develops. By the end of the embryonic stage, the rudiments of the basic organ and cardiovascular systems and body structures are established. From about the ninth week, the conceptus, which now has a recognizably human shape, enters the fetal stage. By the end of the trimester, the major organ systems are developed.

During the second and third trimesters the organ systems continue their development and diversification. The fetus, which is usually from three to less than four inches in length and one to one and a half ounces in weight at the beginning of the second trimester, averages around seven and a half pounds and 20–22 inches at birth. During the second trimester, as the fetus grows, the womb begins to swell noticeably. By around the fourth to fifth month the fetus is large enough for the mother to feel its movement ("quickening"). At about the same time, the breasts have become capable of producing milk, although they will not do so until after the birth.

By the third trimester, the uterus is quite large and feels hard to the touch. Late in the seventh month, the fetus begins to add subcutaneous fat, fleshing out the face and filling in the wrinkled skin. Braxton-Hicks contractions (painless) begin pulling and stretching the uterus, preparing it for labor and delivery. As the period of gestation nears its end, the contractions will become more frequent and intense. In the last month, two to four weeks before delivery, the fetus should assume its birth position, which normally means that its head settles into the pelvis so that the crown will be presented to the cervical opening. The action is known as "lightening" or "dropping." The period of gestation ends with parturition, or birth.

GONORRHEA, caused by the bacteria *Neisseria gonorrhea*, is a highly contagious sexually transmitted disease*. Women rarely have symptoms because the organism first affects the cervix. Therefore, women are largely dependent on their male partners, who are much more likely to have symptoms, to inform them that they have been treated for gonorrhea. If untreated, gonorrhea will spread to the internal organs, causing pelvic inflammatory disease and infertility and affecting the heart and the joints (arthritis). Women are much more likely to suffer the complication of joint involvement (arthritis) than men, at least in part because men are more likely to get treated before complications arise. Gonorrhea is the number one cause of persistent joint pain in persons under 45 years of age.

Gonorrhea is a disease of the mucus membranes; that is, it thrives in the cervix, urethra, rectum, and even in the throat. Women who have had oral or anal sex with a partner whom they suspect of having gonorrhea should tell the examiner to test the throat and/or anal area for the presence of the organism.

It is estimated that a woman who has had one exposure to an infected man has a 30 to 50 percent chance of developing gonorrhea. After two or three contacts, the risk increases to 95 percent. The extremely high risk illustrates the importance of using condoms as barriers.

Gonorrhea increases the chance of premature labor and stillbirth. Newborns may develop serious eye infections and may also suffer upper respiratory infections, pneumonia, and rectal infections. It is even more important for women to ensure condom use by male sexual partners during pregnancy.

Even though gonorrhea is a disease of the mucus membranes, it does not appear to spread between women. However, lesbians should take care to avoid oral sex with a woman known or suspected to have gonorrhea.

Gonorrhea can occur with other sexually transmitted diseases such as chlamydia* or even syphilis. If a woman tests positive for gonorrhea, she should be tested for other sexually transmitted diseases as well. It is vital that when antibiotics are prescribed, they be taken exactly as directed. It is also important to get a test of cure to determine that the medication in fact killed the organism. A person can have gonorrhea many times. Partners must be treated to avoid reinfection or spreading the infection further.

Further Reference. R. Platt et al., "Risk of Acquiring Gonorrhea and Prevalence of Abnormal Adnexal Findings among Women Recently Exposed to Gonorrhea," *Journal of the American Medical Association* 250 (1953): 3205–3209.

ELAINE WHEELER

GYNECOLOGY/OBSTETRICS (OB/GYN). *Gynecology*, from the Greek words for woman (*gyn*) and reason or discourse (*logos*), is the branch of medicine that deals with the health and proper functioning of the female reproductive system*. *Obstetrics*, from the Latin word for midwife (*obstetric*), is the branch of gynecology that deals with pregnancy and childbirth*. To become board certified in gynecology and obstetrics (certified by a board of gynecologists that certain standards for knowledge and competence have been met), physicians must complete a residency and pass a written examination, then, after two years of practice, have all of their hospital cases reviewed and pass an oral examination.

H

HEALERS. See HEALTH CARE PROVIDERS

HEALTH, ECONOMICS OF. Women use more medical care on an average than men even after accounting for use of gynecological and obstetrical care. Women have about 25 percent more visits to the physician, spend 50 percent more on prescription drugs, are more likely to see a psychiatrist, and are admitted to a hospital more often. Men use more health care when they are admitted to the hospital: they stay longer. Only under the age of five do females use less care than males.

Women's Health Status. Do women use more medical care because they are sicker than men, or do women live longer because they use more care? Measures of women's health status as compared to men's provide a confusing answer when both physical and emotional health are examined. Women live on average eight years longer than men, and their life expectancy has been growing at a faster rate. Women have better health statuses when clinically measured, but worse health status when self-reported.

A greater percentage of women report themselves to have stress and anxiety, and a smaller proportion report feelings of positive well-being than do men. Although women are more likely to attempt suicide, more men actually take their own lives. Historically, women were reported to have more psychiatric problems, although now that new measures of psychiatric conditions include alcohol and drug abuse, the percentages of psychiatric problems are more equal across the sexes.

Medical Problems and Health Habits. Women suffer from different medical problems than men, and this may account for, or be caused by, differential use of medical care. For example, women die two to six times less often than men of behavioral-related diseases: lung cancer, emphysema, motor vehicle accidents, other accidents, suicide, and cirrhosis of the liver. An open question is, as women become more like men in their professional and pleasure pursuits and in their health habits, will women's health suffer like men's? For example, women's increased smoking and job stress may negatively affect their health.

Role in the Family. Part of the difference in the use of medical care and in health status across gender may be attributed to traditional differences in family roles by gender. An obvious and inescapable difference is that women bear the children. Additional medical expenses are incurred for women in childbearing, even in uncomplicated cases. The traditional division of labor in the home can also account for part of women's greater use of health care. If the mother does more of the child care*, then she has more exposure to the contagious diseases of children. As the traditional person in charge of the family's health, she may also seek medical care, in part, for the informational content of a visit. She can then use this information to produce the health of the rest of her family.

Women's greater use of medical care may be attributable in part to the fact that the wife is more likely to give care to her husband than to receive care from him. The man may substitute home care while the woman must seek market care. The difference in the provision of home health by gender shows up in differences in the effect of marital status on health. Being married is associated with greater health for men but not for women. This is seen most vividly in elderly couples. When an elderly man's wife dies, his health declines rapidly and he is likely to die sooner. However, the loss of an elderly woman's spouse has little effect on her health.

Insurance Coverage. Only about 10 percent of the total population is without health insurance coverage. However, women are slightly less likely to have health insurance coverage and often have less extensive coverage. This occurs because women are less likely to be employed, more likely to have jobs that do not offer insurance coverage (or provide less comprehensive coverage), and because women sometimes lose their coverage with divorce* or the death of their spouse. The "feminization of poverty"* leads to increased reliance on the public provision of coverage. Health insurance coverage increases the use of medical care. Thus with women's slightly lower coverage it is even more dramatic to find that women use more medical care in general.

Health insurance is more costly to provide for women because women use more care. If a woman buys health insurance coverage as an individual, i.e., not through a group plan, she typically must pay more for her coverage than would a man. Often the employer charges both men and women the same premium although it costs more to cover the woman. The pricing of health insurance by sex is part of the broader policy controversy on unisex pricing of insurance policies.

One of the reasons that women are more expensive to cover is the possibly high expenses of pregnancy. Coverage for pregnancy was often confined to married women with a family health insurance plan. However, relatively recent federal legislation mandates that the expense of pregnancy be covered without regard to marital status: it is covered as a "disability."

Special Needs of Women and Public Programs. *Maternal and Child Health.* In the enduring controversy about whether preventive care can actually be cost-effective, the case of maternal and child health seems to be a clearcut cost-effective investment for the family and society. Timely provision of medical care, proper nutrition, and guidance on health habits can help both the child and the mother and prevent future, more expensive problems. Private insurance programs typically provide coverage for prenatal care and well child care. For the poor, Medicaid and Aid to Families with Dependent Children often cover pregnancy-related medical expenses. It is important to note that health depends on many more things than just the use of medical care. Other factors can be vitally important, e.g., health habits, sanitation, education, and nutrition. Many public programs unrelated to medical care have an important impact on health. The federally supported Women, Infant and Child (WIC) program, for example, provides important foods for eligible women and children.

Old Age. Because women live longer than men and are less likely to be married in the older ages, women are often living alone and in poor health in their old age. This can present a problem; in old age medical expenses increase, health declines, income can decline, and the ability to care for oneself decreases. This often leaves women with large expenses for medical care including either home health care or nursing home care. The Medicare program is designed to help the elderly population meet additional medical expenses; however, it does not meet all of the expenses. Medicare covers little home health care and does not cover extended nursing home care. Thus, women with husbands in nursing homes often spend the family wealth on the husbands' care and then live in poverty*. If driven to poverty by the expenses of their dying husbands and/or their own expenses, they become eligible for Medicaid, which covers nursing home care.

Coverage for nursing home and long-term care is an increasingly important policy issue as the population ages, home care is no longer provided by the extended family, there are more single elderly women, and the costs of nursing home care rise. It is an issue of critical importance to women. Most residents of nursing homes are women. Long-term care presents a real policy problem; to cover it is extremely costly but without it the elderly face large expenses or inadequate care. Currently, private coverage is not widely available and public programs are inadequate.

Further Reference. *Women's Health: Report of the Public Health Service Task Force on Women's Health Issues*, vol. 2 (Washington, D.C., May 1985): esp. 1–32.

JODI SINDELAR

HEALTH CARE PROVIDERS. Women have always practiced medicine. Often, though, their contributions have been overlooked because women typically practiced within the domestic setting; mothers, friends, neighbors, and even slaves provided important health care. Women also have a long tradition of practicing medicine outside their private domestic sphere* as priestesses, doctors, nurses, medicine women, wise women, midwives, and herbalists. For example, Egyptian tomb pictures from c.2500 B.C. show women lancing boils, circumcising babies, and operating on feet. Not surprisingly, many of the healing deities of ancient societies have feminine attributes. For example, in Egypt, Isis was the goddess of medicine; in Greece, Artemis, the goddess of childbirth. Legends tell of Hygeia and Panacea, daughters of the god of medicine Aesculapius, highly respected healers eventually worshipped as deities. Homeric and other classical literature, as well as biblical and Talmudic writings, attest to the prevalence and acceptance of women as healers, though few names were recorded.

Inscriptions on gravestones, particularly from the Roman period, describe women healers of later centuries. Many Greek women, both physicians and midwives, were brought to Rome as slaves in the second century B.C.. Previously, Romans had relied on the domestic medicine of female relatives and friends. Over the next four centuries Greek medicine, frequently practiced by women, came to dominate Roman health care. By the third and fourth centuries A.D., other women found a commitment to healing in their Christian belief. In time much of their practice was centered in convents where women could study medicine, nursing, and herbs. After the fall of the Roman Empire, formal medical and nursing training died out in the Christianized West, except in the monasteries and convents where monks and nuns laborriously copied and preserved ancient texts and cared for the sick. This monastic tradition continued for many centuries; some women who founded nursing orders, such as Catherine of Bologna, were even elevated to sainthood.

In the middle of the eleventh century, organized medical education was established at Salerno, Italy. Reputedly, women as well as men attended this school and taught there; more usually, women were excluded from universities, which were the seats of medical education in the medieval and early modern periods. Women did care for the sick in hospitals, especially those established along the crusaders' routes and later in growing urban centers such as Paris. However, with few trained physicians and few hospitals, the majority of the populace undoubtedly still relied on traditional domestic medicine, particularly midwifery*, which had served them in the past.

By the seventeenth and eighteenth centuries, formal medical certification, such as university degrees and government licenses, increasingly inhibited women's involvement in organized medicine, since women were barred from attending the classes necessary to be certified. On the other hand, many people who could not afford or did not trust expensive university-educated physicians still called in women healers. Midwifery typically remained women's work. Furthermore, in the American colonies the marked shortage of formally trained doctors required that people employ alternative, often women, healers, midwives, and apothecaries.

While these women practiced medicine, they were outside the "profession" of medicine. With the drive for professionalization and the gradual proliferation of schools, hospitals, and medical societies in the late eighteenth and nineteenth centuries, women practitioners were denied access to these institutions and were pushed more to the periphery. This is seen clearly in the medicalization of parturition*. Childbirth* was redefined as pathologic rather than natural; physician-managed labor equated with safety and progress; midwives labeled ill-trained; and, later in the twentieth century, hospitals accepted as havens for parturient women. In the eighteenth century midwives attended almost all births in this country; by 1910 they attended about 50 percent; over the next several decades midwives practically disappeared.

At the same time, two significant nineteenth-century movements—the push for women's rights and for health reform—coupled with developments in medical science and practice, helped open up other medical careers to women. Reformers blamed women's supposed poor health on female modesty before male physicians and insisted that the health of the nation would improve if more women became doctors. Feminists also supported women entering medicine. Following the graduation of Elizabeth Blackwell from Geneva Medical College in 1849, hundreds of women sought medical training. By the 1880s a few previously all-male institutions admitted female students, but many continued to reject women. To provide more opportunities, all-female medical colleges were founded. When women graduates were denied internships and residencies, they founded hospitals and hired female graduates. As more schools and hospitals accepted women, the call for separate institutions diminished; many women's schools and hospitals closed or merged with men's. By the end of the century, women accounted for between 4 percent and 5 percent of U.S. physicians, a proportion that stayed fairly constant until the 1960s.

Women entered other health care occupations, most particularly nursing, in greater numbers. Before the late nineteenth century the United States had few hospitals and no nurse-training schools. By the 1870s, however, partly influenced by the successes of Florence Nightingale's trained nurses in improving hospital conditions, some hospitals began to establish schools of nursing to train their workers. By 1880, 15 schools enrolled 323 and had graduated 157; by 1900, 432 schools enrolled more than 11,000 students and had graduated almost 3,500 nurses.

Today, as in centuries past, women practice medicine. According to census figures published in 1985, they comprise over 75 percent of health care workers. More than 95 percent of the registered nurses are women, over 98 percent of the dental hygienists, and 97 percent of licensed practical nurses. But, despite these figures, women do not dominate the field; in the more prestigious, influential, and lucrative occupations their numbers are much fewer. Women account for less than 16 percent of the physicians and under 7 percent of the dentists in this country. During the past several decades many health occupations have apparently begun to readjust such sex imbalances. For instance, more men are attending nursing schools, though male graduates are frequently directed away from patient care and toward administration. Moreover, women are graduating from medical school in increasing numbers; from about 5 percent of the graduating class in 1960 to over 25 percent in 1983. The trend is clear. We shall see whether the health care system can replace its sex-stratified occupational structure in the future.

Further References. K. C. Hurd-Mead, *A History of Women in Medicine: From the Earliest Times to the Beginnings of the Nineteenth Century* (Haddam, Conn., 1938). Out of date but still the only single source on the topic, this book must be used cautiously. P. A. Kalisch and B. J. Kalisch, *The Advance of American Nursing* (Boston, 1978). J. W. Leavitt (ed.), *Women and Health in America: Historical Readings* (Madison, Wisc., 1984).

RIMA D. APPLE

HEALTH MOVEMENT, WOMEN'S. Women cannot have control over their lives until they have control over their bodies and their health, so understanding their own bodies and gaining a voice in health care and medical policy have been central to the women's movement.

Women call upon the health services more than men do, and health issues are a fundamental part of women's lives for a number of reasons. (1) Women live longer than men (an average of 78.2 years compared to 70.8 years), so, as elderly members of society, have more need for medical care. (2) Normal, healthy women call upon the health services for birth control, pregnancy, childbirth*, and other services related to their reproductive organs and functions. (3) Women are hospitalized (even excluding deliveries) more often than men. Sixty-three percent of all surgeries are done on women. Women aged 15 to 44 experience 2.5 times more surgery than men of those ages. Much of this surgery is not necessary. For example, studies have found that 30 to 40 percent of performed hysterectomies were not necessary. (4) The sexual division of labor means that as unpaid workers, women are responsible for the health care of children, elderly parents, the chronically sick, and disabled. (5) The health services treat men and women differently even if they present the same symptoms. Men are more likely to be given physical exams and tests. Women are more likely to be labeled as "neurotic" and given drugs. Mood-altering drugs are prescribed to women more than twice as often as to men. (6) Although men have the power in medicine and are in the decision-making positions, 75 percent of health care workers are women. In hospitals, 85 percent of health care workers are women.

The women's health movement has been made up of a wide range of individuals and groups involved in different activities and campaigns. Working for a more appropriate health care system has been a unifying issue even for women who have not consciously identified themselves as a part of the women's movement. Activities have ranged from single-issue campaigns for better local health services, to self-help groups, setting up women's health information libraries, building alliances and coalitions around women's health issues, teaching women's health courses, producing leaflets and books, and providing women-controlled health centers.

A central theme has been the recognition that much of the power of the medical profession comes from their possession and use of knowledge and information to which consumers do not have access. A primary goal of health activists has been to collect, produce, and distribute information that is accessible to women and relevant to their needs, so that women can themselves make decisions about their bodies, their health care, and their lives.

Our Bodies, Ourselves by the Boston Women's Health Collective (Simon and Schuster, 1984) is the classic of the women's health movement. Originally (1969) a set of notes for a women's health course, it is now a 600-page book available in many languages, adapted for many different health systems.

The *National Women's Health Network* (224 7th Street S.E., Washington, D.C. 20003) is a national consumer/provider membership organization that monitors and influences policies, as well as providing consumer information.

NANCY WORCESTER

HERPES GENITALIS is a sexually transmitted disease* caused by a virus from the same family of viruses that causes chicken pox. Herpes, which received extensive exposure in the popular press until AIDS took over the limelight, is of particular importance for women because infection with herpes genitalis increases the risk of cervical cancer*. Infants born to women who are experiencing a first (primary) infection with herpes may develop only mild, localized infection, but could develop a systemic infection that, in 90 percent of cases, results in neurological damage or death of the infant. The health of the infant is preserved by cesarean birth in those mothers who have a primary infection.

Herpes is characterized by a fluid-filled blister that appears on the external genitals, in the vagina, or on the cervix. The lesion breaks open and eventually disappears without treatment. Thirty percent of people experience only one episode. The remainder, however, have recurrent episodes. Primary infections are treated with an antiviral drug, Acylovir, which is of minimal effectiveness in recurrent infections. Studies to develop a vaccine for herpes are promising.

Likelihood of transmission of the virus is greatest when the blister (vesicle) breaks, shedding virus in the fluid. However, the virus may be present and communicable when vesicles are not evident. Use of condoms is recommended for sexual contacts with men when one partner has herpes. Herpes is not as easily transmittable between women, but very little is known about herpes transmission in women.

In order to detect precancerous changes in cervical cells, women affected with herpes should have Pap smears at least every year, or perhaps oftener, according to the advice of a physician.

ELAINE WHEELER

HETEROSEXUALITY is a sexual orientation* that manifests itself in preference for sexual partners of the opposite sex. It is considered the "norm" by Western society in general, and in most areas open deviation from that norm may be met with legal discrimination*.

HOME ECONOMICS (also DOMESTIC SCIENCE). A profession devoted to the development and application of scientific rules for home management, consumerism, child development, and nutrition, as well as cooking and sewing.

Formal instruction in the domestic arts began in the early nineteenth century when private seminaries for girls were anxious to prove that education would enhance, rather than threaten, female domesticity. Catherine Beecher, Lydia Maria Child, and others reinforced that message through domestic self-help books for American housewives. Beecher's *Treatise on Domestic Economy* (1841) argued that homemaking was a demanding profession, requiring skill, efficiency, and precise training.

Domestic education remained in the home or in private schools until land-grant colleges in Iowa, Kansas, and Illinois established home economics programs for women students. They were regarded as practical companions to the agricultural programs for men.

The period 1880–1910 saw growth and self-definition for "home economics." A number of social concerns, coinciding at the turn of the century, made Americans particularly receptive to the claims of home economics advocates. The first was concern that industrialization and urbanization were destroying traditional home life. Alongside that worry was nativist concern that the millions of immigrants pouring into America were insufficiently educated in sanitation, consumer protection, and household management to establish stable, healthy homes. Also, consciousness of the new "germ theory" and a new enthusiasm for science, medicine, and technology meant that Americans sought to preserve the traditional family in a highly sanitized, modernized context. Finally, underlying all of these concerns was a deep anxiety about the place of American women and the effect of education on women's role in society. Many worried that the declining marriage and birth rates among educated women and the increasing employment opportunities for women in the cities meant that women were defying the laws of nature in refusing to assume their biologically destined roles as wives and homemakers.

All of these concerns were addressed and appeased by the home economics movement that came to prominence between 1880 and 1910. Ellen Swallow Richards (Massachusetts Institute of Technology), Marion Talbot (University of Chicago), Helen Kinne (Columbia University), and Caroline Hunt and Abby Marlatt (University of Wisconsin) were in the vanguard of the academic forces that joined with the American Household Economics Association and the General Federation of Women's Clubs to promote the synthesis of scientific research and household management for improved health, efficiency, and economy. Leaders of the movement expressed confidence that cities could be civilized, immigrants Americanized, and educated women domesticated with systematic exposure to the principles of home economics. For all its modern, scientific thrust, then, the early home economics movement was quite conservative in its social goals and its attitude toward gender roles*.

The first efforts at national coordination were the Lake Placid Conferences, 1899–1909. The first conference agreed on the name "home economics," in preference to "domestic arts," "domestic science," or even "euthenics." Subsequent conferences dealt with school curricula, teacher training, and community service. In 1909, the conferees decided to affiliate more formally as the American Home Economics Association (AHEA).

In its first 75 years, the membership of the AHEA grew steadily from just over 800 in 1909 to over 9,000 in 1935 to over 50,000 by the early 1980s. Paralleling that growth has been steady growth in home economics education in the United States, from elementary schools to universities. Throughout these years, the American home economics movement has had to deal with two fundamental conflicts over goals and strategies: whether to offer narrow training in specific skills or a broad education in the science and philosophy of home management and whether to train women for the traditional role of wife and mother or for a professional career as a home economist. Attitudes have ebbed and flowed with general currents in American society. In the 1920s and 1930s, for example, collegiate home economics focused on job opportunities for women as home economics teachers, nutritionists, and textile experts. Later, in the 1940s and 1950s, there was greater focus on courses in marriage, family relations, child development, and consumer science on the assumption that students would soon marry and become managers of their households. Since the 1960s, there has been a switch back to preparation for professional jobs as social changes and women's increased desire, and need, for economic independence increased demand for consumer advocates, child care specialists, nutritionists, and family relations experts.

Contemporary home economics has abandoned its original hostility to feminism* and has sought to adapt its goals to those of modern American women. Though the field is still stigmatized by its historical advocacy of female domesticity, the fact remains that home economics has been an important avenue of economic and professional mobility for many American women.

Further References. M. N. Carver, *Home Economics as an Academic Discipline* (Tucson, 1979). B. Ehrenreich and D. English, *For Her Own Good: 150 Years of the Experts' Advice to Women* (New York, 1978). H. Pundt, *AHEA: A History of Excellence* (Washington, D.C., 1980).

VICTORIA BROWN

HOMELESSNESS in the United States in the 1980s reached its greatest extent since the Depression. And for the first time women and children were visible among the homeless. To the old picture of the homeless white male alcoholic was added the picture of the bag lady, the teenage runaway or throwaway soliciting on the streets of major cities, and the family group eating in a soup kitchen. Another new element was the rising minority population among the homeless.

The homeless and the number of women and children among them cannot be estimated with any accuracy—for 1984, estimates of the homeless ranged from a quarter million to three million. Estimates of single women and of those in family groups in New York City were put at 17 percent and 21 percent respectively of a total homeless population of 40 to 50 thousand. Many homeless families are headed by women. A Boston study estimated that 84 percent of the homeless families in that city were female-headed. (Statistics in this article are taken from the Committee on Government Operations, *Federal Response to the Homeless Crisis* [Washington, D.C., 1985] and *Families: A Neglected Crisis* [Washington, D.C., 1986].)

Causes of homelessness include unemployment*, lack of affordable housing, cuts in public welfare, and personal crises. A major cause, which some argue may account for 50 percent or more of the homeless, was the "reform" of the mental health system: the switch from warehousing to dumping

A steady decline in unemployment after it reached 10.8 percent in 1982 did not bring a proportional decline in homelessness, especially among women. Most homeless women capable of holding jobs lack the skills required by the changing needs of industry. The wages they can earn in low-skill service sector jobs are too low to pay the rent in most cities. A continuing decline in rental housing through conversions to condominiums, decreased new construction, inner-city renovation, arson, abandonment, demolition, and lack of federal funding for low-income housing has meant a steady decline of single-room occupancy (SRO) units, an even more serious shortage of family units, and consequent rent inflation.

Personal crises such as divorce*, desertion, other disruptions of living arrangements, family violence, and health problems may lead to temporary or permanent homelessness. Alcoholism or other chemical substance abuse also accounts for a sizable part of the homeless.

A leading cause of homelessness, especially among single women, is mental illness*. From 1955 to 1980, the number of mental patients in state institutions fell from 559,000 to 138,000 as legal reforms mandated the release of patients whose illness could be controlled by psychotropic drugs and tightened requirements for admission to mental institutions. Community mental health centers were to care for all except the few who were a danger to themselves or to others. Unfortunately, only the first half of the reform was really carried out. Far fewer centers were built than are needed; there is no mechanism to assure that, once released from the hospital, the patient will go to a center, should one be available, for continued treatment; there is little or no effort to train and place former patients in jobs so that they can function in society; and very little possibility of channeling those in the community in need of it into treatment if they do not seek it themselves. Those who voluntarily commit themselves to hospitals are released as soon as possible. A woman with mental health problems who does not have a strong support network is at risk of joining the ranks of the homeless.

The homeless, except for those in SRO "welfare hotels" and transition houses, spend their days on the streets, looking for work, scavenging, panhandling, or just constantly moving. They spend their nights in emergency shelters, in public parks, streets, and alleys, in subways and bus and train terminals, under bridges, under stairwells or in other hidden niches of public buildings to which they can gain access, in abandoned buildings, or in their own cars.

There are insufficient shelters; in some areas, none. In cities all over the country people are regularly turned away. The shelters that do exist are often overcrowded and/or unsafe. Some are in large, open areas offering no privacy. Many are in dangerous neighborhoods or in unsafe buildings, or are so lacking in facilities as to be inhumane (e.g., in one case, one toilet to 150 beds). "Welfare hotels," used by social services to house families in some cities, are often crime-, drug-, and prostitution-infested slums, without cooking and refrigeration facilities for families, or even beds and cribs.

Not all shelters are overcrowded. Some are so unsafe that people prefer to remain on the street. Those shelters that require delousing, attendance at religious services, or pay in the form of chores tend to be avoided if possible. The homeless who sleep the streets are prey to the weather and to crime. Deaths related to exposure to weather in New York City are put at 25 to 50 a month during the winter.

Until the 1980s almost all the homeless were single. Since then the number of homeless families has grown more rapidly than the number of homeless single persons. Many, perhaps most, of these families are headed by women. The women are likely to have been victims of child abuse and/or battering as adults. Most have little education and no work skills. When they can find work, it is unskilled, with pay insufficient to support a family. Without a support network, homelessness is almost inevitable. The children are likely to lack food and are probably not attending school. About half have developmental disorders or suffer depression.

Most homeless receive no public assistance. Under the Reagan administration (1981–1989), there were cutbacks in federal funding of all social programs and tightening of eligibility of many. Also, once a person becomes homeless, it is very difficult to receive federal benefits. Many eligible for Social Security Disability Insurance (SSDI) and veteran's benefits do not receive them, and in some areas food stamps are not given to those without an address. Applying for Aid for Dependent Children (AFDC), especially in California, can result in the children being taken by social services, then, since there are no children, denial of aid. The attitude of the Reagan administration has been that homelessness is a problem that must be dealt with locally by public and philanthropic sources.

The elimination of homelessness involves policy issues in the care and treatment of the mentally ill and the chemically addicted and requires federal and state support of affordable housing and social programs for counseling, aid, health care, and the education and training of the homeless.

HOMEWORK (INDUSTRIAL HOMEWORK). Also known as home industry, domestic industry, cottage industry, the putting-out system, and protoindustry, *homework* refers to gainful employment at home in the manufacture of articles for the market. Originally, artisans, or craftsworkers, of both sexes typically performed their labor in a home workshop, with the aid of family members, servants, apprentices, and other helpers. Only a small percentage of people, who lived in urban centers, engaged exclusively in artisanal labor. More commonly, industrial homework served to supplement agricultural labor and allowed the rural working classes to make productive use of time not allocated to outdoor work. Typically, raw materials were brought to the workers' homes by distributors, or "middlemen," employed by distant manufacturers; and sometime later finished articles were collected and wages paid based on piecework. Articles commonly produced in the home included pins, nails, scythes, clogs, chains, furniture, household linen, lace, garments, and various clothing accessories. With the growth of national and international markets during the early modern period (the sixteenth through the eighteenth centuries), opportunities for homework expanded. Men, women, and children participated; increasingly such earnings allowed young people to gain economic independence and thereby to marry at earlier ages than before.

By the late eighteenth and early nineteenth centuries, changes in the location and organization of manufacturing and distribution, the introduction of new sources of power, the invention of new tools and machines, and the development of improved transportation systems combined to shift production in some industries (led by textiles) from home to factory. With notable exceptions, such as weaving in parts of Germany, cabinetmaking in France, and cigarrolling in the United States, by the mid-nineteenth century men began to work away from home and homework became gender-specific, that is, women's work*. An increasingly refined division of labor followed the breakdown of manufacturing processes into smaller and smaller tasks that took less and less skill. Fewer skilled workers and more "little hands" could be employed, for lower wages. Men employed in workshops and factories often organized against competitors, including female, unskilled, and homeworkers (whose lower overhead and unrestricted hours allowed them to undercut workshop labor prices). Children increasingly fell under compulsory education laws that limited their service as homeworkers. Women working at home, however, continued to provide a major source of labor. Whether bound to home by responsibility for dependent children or for ill or aged relations, by reasons of their own health, or by social norms that required "respectable" married women to remain at home, most working-class and significant numbers of middle-class women still had to make financial contributions to family subsistence. They constituted a ready labor supply for manufacturers in seasonal industries, especially for garmentmakers in expanding ready-to-wear industries. Homeworkers could be employed, at minimal overhead cost, for long hours in times of press and let go in "dead seasons." Some women, often daughters of artisanal workers, served apprenticeships or worked in shops for years to learn skills that enabled them to earn good wages at home; the artificial flower makers of Paris constitute one example. By the early twentieth century, however, most homeworkers in garmentmaking, jewelry assembly, and other home industries were women of little skill or training forced to take whatever work they could find.

Isolated from each other, homeworkers rarely attempted to organize for higher wages or better working conditions and continued to labor for less than subsistence wages, often in conditions that shocked social reformers; they dominated the labor force of the "sweatshops" that raised social consciences and led to international conferences and some regulation by legislation (often poorly enforced) in the early twentieth century. "Protective" labor legislation, instituted in many industrial countries between the 1880s and 1930s, usually bypassed homeworkers; indeed, by restricting the employment of women in factories, it often intensified the sexual division of labor whereby highly organized, largely male, factory workers improved their wages and working conditions, while unorganized, largely female, workers continued to constitute a marginal workforce with minimal benefits. In many urban centers today, including London, Los Angeles, Paris, and Toronto, large numbers of women continue to do homework in the garment and other industries. (See PROTECTIVE LEGISLATION.)

Further References. M. J. Boxer, "Women in Industrial Homework: The Flowermakers of Paris in the Belle Epoque," *French Historical Studies* 12 (1982): 401–423. E. Hope, M. Kennedy, and A. de Winter, "Homeworkers in North London," in D. L. Barker and S. Allen (eds.), *Dependence and Exploitation in Work and Marriage* (London, 1976), 88–108. J. H. Quataert, "Combining Agrarian and Industrial Livelihood: Rural Households in the Saxon Oberlausitz in the Nineteenth Century," *Journal of Family History* 10 (1985): 145–162. J. W. Scott, "Men and Women in the Parisian Garment Trades: Discussions of Family and Work in the 1830s and 1840s," in P. Thane, G. Crossick, and R. Floud (eds.), *The Power of the Past: Essays for Eric Hobsbawm* (Cambridge, England, 1984), 67–93.

MARILYN J. BOXER

HOMOPHOBIA. Fear of homosexuality*. This term, given prominence in 1972 by George Weinberg (*Society and the Healthy Homosexual* [New York]), and has since been used to refer to a wide range of negative attitudes, feelings, and behaviors toward homosexuals and homosexual activity evidenced on both individual and societal levels.

On the societal level, homophobia is a component of heterosexism, the belief that heterosexual activity is superior to homosexual activity. Like sexism, racism, and ethnocentrism, heterosexism is a form of social prejudice based mostly on misconceptions and stereotypes. Unlike discrimination* based on race, sex, or national origin, discrimination based on sexual orientation is not specifically prohibited by federal civil rights laws. Thus in most states, homosexuals can be fired from their jobs, not hired for certain positions, discharged from the military, denied housing and custody of children, and arrested for engaging in private consensual sexual activity between adults, solely on the basis of their sexual orientation*.

Whereas nearly all cultures are heterosexist, cultures vary in the degree to which homosexuals and homosexuality are feared. In a number of cultures, male homosexuality during youth or adolescence is socially acceptable or even encouraged (e.g., among a number of African tribes and the Mohave Indians); in the United States, homosexuals are nearly totally rejected and stigmatized. Male homosexuality is more often culturally proscribed or sanctioned than female homosexuality in part because female homosexuals are less frequently thought of as sexual and partly because a female still can become pregnant even if not sexually attracted to men. Another reason for the greater stigma attached to male homosexuality is that rejection of the male heterosexual role can be viewed as a rejection of status privileges, whereas rejection of the female heterosexual role can be viewed as a rejection of a subordinate status. It is also the case that in the United States males are socialized more rigidly than females and define their role by denying all qualities and behaviors that are vaguely feminine. Thus, sexual relations with another man threaten the rigid gender lines drawn by the culture.

On an individual level, homophobia is related to a range of personality characteristics typical of prejudiced individuals: authoritarianism, conservative support of the status quo, and rigidity of gender roles* and gender-role attitudes. These attitudes appear to be acquired particularly easily by men as part of their gender-role socialization that produces a generalized fear of femininity*. More men than women think homosexual relations should be prohibited, but this may relate to the fact that most people think of males when they hear the word "homosexual." It also may relate to the rigidity of male socialization and to the higher status males have in the culture.

Homophobia and heterosexism operate as social control mechanisms for both women and men to keep them in "their place." Heterosexuality is "compulsory" is our society, and rebels are punished (A. Rich, "Compulsory Heterosexuality and Lesbian Existence," *Signs* 5 [1980]: 631–660). If one deviates from traditional gender-role behavior, one runs the risk of being labeled a "dyke" or lesbian, if one is female, or a "queer" or "faggot," if one is male. Such labeling can cause one to lose credibility, friends, jobs, housing, and advancement opportunities. It can also subject one to harassment and physical violence, as in "queer baiting" and "queer bashing." Since homosexuals are so stigmatized, many people cling to traditional gender-stereotyped behaviors in order to avoid giving anyone the opportunity to suspect their sexual orientation. Such social control was evident in the women's movement in the 1970s when there was much concern about lesbians* being "too" visible and vocal in the movement, thereby "threatening" the success of the movement's objectives. Lesbianism, in particular, threatens traditional social arrangements since it belies the patriarchal belief that women need men for their happiness and protection. Consequently, nearly all feminists who are vocal are subject to accusations of lesbianism.

Such is the power of homophobia in our society that many homosexuals have internalized these attitudes and act them out in self-denying and frequently self-defeating ways. As long as societal homophobia exists, and being thought a homosexual is a major stigma, many people, both gay and straight, will restrict their behavior and their lives to try to ensure societal acceptance.

SUSAN A. BASOW

HOMOSEXUALITY. A term coined in 1869 to refer to sexual relationships among persons of the same sex.

Though women have loved and lived with women, and men with men, in societies around the world and in ancient and modern times, the ways in which these relationships have been recognized (or suppressed) have varied immensely by time and place. In societies as widely separated as Melanesia, Amazonia, central Africa, and western Egypt, it has been common for many (sometimes all) males to have homosexual relations for at least a part of their lives. In these societies, sexual relations between older and younger males are thought to be part of the experiences of parenting and growing up. Best known to Western society is the classical heritage from Greece and Rome, where adolescence was a time when young men left their biological families to becomes lovers of adult men. Sexuality was but one element of an affectional and educational relationship.

With women's experiences so often left out of the historical record by patriarchal societies, less is known about female bonding, but the writings of Sappho from ancient Greece did give the name of the island of Lesbos to love between women. (See LESBIANS.)

Anthropological research shows, as well, the existence of gender-mixed persons among many of the native peoples of North and South America, Polynesia, Indonesia, and eastern Siberia. The *berdache* of North America and *mahu* of Polynesia included men who took on aspects of women's dress and work, and it is known that female *berdaches* sometimes married women, and male *berdaches*, men.

In societies where homosexuality is both universal and obligatory, it makes little sense to talk of homosexual persons, but in Western societies there has been a strong tradition of sharply differentiating between "homosexual" and "heterosexual." At least as early as the seventeenth century (and probably before) there is evidence of a homosexual underground in the European capitals, where men could meet, court, and make sexual contact with one another. From these origins has emerged the modern gay world, which is organized not unlike an ethnic group with its own bars and neighborhoods, newspapers and churches, recreational and political groups.

For women, the development of lesbian networks is more recent. Lacking the financial independence and public mobility of men, some women formed "romantic friendships'' without abandoning family participation. Only with the growing independence of women in the twentieth century could some choose to create women-only households and public places of their own and thus form a lesbian subculture.

The process has not been easy, and lesbians and gay men have suffered centuries of persecution at the hands of church and state through banishment, imprisonment, torture, and even execution. Periodic governmental campaigns have resulted in the murder of dozens, sometimes thousands, of homosexual people, as in fifteenth-century Venice, eighteenth-century Holland, early nineteenth-century England, and in Nazi Germany. Today homosexual acts between consenting adults are legal in most jurisdictions around the world with the notable exception of the USSR and half of the states of the United States and Australia, as well as in theocratic nations such as Iran, Israel, and Ireland. Romania and Cuba have also conducted active campaigns of persecution in recent history. On the other hand, places that have actively moved to prohibit discrimination* on the grounds of sexual orientation include Norway, France, Ontario, Quebec, Wisconsin, and New South Wales, as well as a number of cities in the United States and Canada.

In the 1970s and 1980s, research on gay and lesbian people has emerged from the grip of moralistic and pathological frameworks to explore the dynamics of apparently gender-free relationships in comparison with heterosexual arrangements. Recent scholarly work shows that lesbians tend toward egalitarian bonding and value sexual fidelity, while gay men often successfully combine a primary love relationship with sexual pluralism. Studies by Karla Jay and Allen Young and by William Masters and Virginia Johnson have pointed toward high levels of versatility in sexual roles and techniques and of mutual sexual understanding among same-sex couples.

Despite some easing of homophobic attitudes in recent times, the decision to express homoerotic feelings and carry them through to loving and living with same-sex persons continues to be experienced as an important status passage. Called ''coming out,'' the affirmation of one's own emotional life still entails, for most gay people, a willingness to brave the incomprehension or censure of families, coworkers, neighbors, employers, and friends. Though homosexuality is often experienced as a crisis of adolescence when peers are dating and marrying, many homosexuals come out later in life, sometimes after years of heterosexual marriage and denial. Recent studies have punctured the myth that growing old gay leads to inevitable loneliness. There is no lack of evidence of happy and productive lives among older gay people who tend to have developed extended circles of supportive friends.

Today there is some organized gay presence in almost every city of Western Europe, North America, and Australia, which can be reached simply by looking up ''gay'' in the local telephone directory. A perusal of any gay/lesbian newspaper reveals a wealth of activities centering around sports, education, politics, religion, and self-help. Larger cities offer such gay-oriented professions and services as law, medicine, travel, accommodation, and restaurants. Gay and women's bookstores are bursting with novels, plays, and recordings that have flowed from the gay cultural renaissance of the modern era.

In 1981, the hitherto unknown disease of Acquired Immune Deficiency Syndrome (AIDS)* became known, claiming, in its first five years, more than 12,000 deaths, the majority of which occurred among gay men. Though some sought to exploit the disease to attack the civil liberties of gay people and governments were slow to respond, organizations have sprung up in gay communities to offer support to those afflicted by the epidemic, to push for research funding, and to counsel everyone to practice "safe sex" to stop the epidemic.

Today lesbians and gay men have succeeded in carving out a limited social space where they can "be themselves" but remain vulnerable to the depredation of heterosexist forces.

Further References. E. Blackwood, *Anthropology and Homosexual Behavior* (New York, 1986). P. Blumstein and P. Schwartz, *American Couples* (New York, 1983). J. Weeks, *Coming Out* (London, 1977).

BARRY D. ADAM

HORMONES. See REPRODUCTIVE SYSTEM

HOUSEWIFE (HOMEMAKER). A married woman who works within her own home serving the needs of her own family* and who is not a member of the paid labor force. Because the work she does is not legally an occupation and is not waged, it tends to be discounted. Although her work differs in many respects from work in the paid labor force, it is of economic value to the family. The standard of living that can be achieved from the income of a one-earner family that includes a housewife can go considerably beyond that attained by the same income earned by the combined efforts of husband and wife.

The housewife's work is recompensed, not in money, but in sharing whatever level of economic support her husband's earnings makes possible and in sharing in her husband's status. The level of the housewife's "pay," then, has no necessary relation to the kind, amount, or quality of the work she does. With the availability of technology and the unavailability of paid domestic workers, except for the very wealthy, housewives of all socioeconomic levels perform much the same basic duties. The "pay" may very well vary in inverse proportion to the amount of work done. Housewives whose husbands earn less, or who have more children, will usually have to work harder and enjoy fewer luxuries than those with few children or whose husbands earn more. Further, the quality of the housewife's work is irrelevant to her status. The best housewife and the worst get their status from their husband, not from their own accomplishments.

The housewife has no set hours of work but is on call 24 hours a day, seven days a week. She has no job description; the work consists of whatever needs to be done. There is no necessary order for doing housework, and most jobs can be postponed or put off. Housework is almost always done in isolation from other adults. Loneliness and lack of adult companionship are two drawbacks that encourage many women to consider a return to the paid workforce.

A considerable part of the housewife's time and energy is spend shopping for goods for household consumption and in further preparing the purchases for family use. Personal services to family members also constitute a significant part of the housewife's tasks. A large number of her chores are low-skill, monotonous, and repetitive and for immediate consumption. Her work tends to be taken for granted and is more likely to be noticed when it isn't done than when it is.

The housewife's access to economic support for the services she performs does not depend entirely on the husband's income, but also depends on the economic arrangements of the individual household. In some cases, the housewife is the fiscal agent for the family, managing all family finances. Or she may have a household allowance, set with more or less collaboration between husband and wife, from which she supplies personal and household needs, or she may have the use of charge accounts and joint bank accounts. In other cases, the housewife may be put in the demeaning position of having to ask her husband for all monies needed, even inconsiderable sums.

Emotional and sexual services are a regular, legitimate part of the job. It is on the emotional satisfaction derived from the marriage that its success or failure, and its continuation or dissolution, are most likely to depend. However, in an era in which divorce* is easy and acceptable, a marriage may be ended, not because of dissatisfaction with the housekeeping, nurturing, or sexual services preformed, but because the affection of one of the partners has shifted. Although it might be either party, the husband has much more opportunity to find new sources of affection and sexual gratification than does the housewife.

When there are preschool children in the home, the work of the housewife fills her days and sometimes her nights. But after the youngest child reaches school age, the time needed for housework begins to decline. The job of the housewife ceases to be a full-time occupation. Many housewives turn to volunteer work, but increasingly, more of them enter, or re-enter, the workforce. In 1988, the number of married women in the United States who were housewives was still almost 50 percent of the total, but fewer of them, and fewer in the future, will be housewives for their entire married lives.

The occupation of housewife carries high economic and physical risks. The housewife is vulnerable to impoverishment upon the death of her husband or as a result of divorce. Feminist efforts to obtain social security payments for divorced housewives who were married less than 20 years and mandatory survivor benefits in pension plans met with success. Social security credit independent of the husband's account and provision of equitable economic support for displaced homemakers are among issues of continuing concern. The housewife's dependent position in relation to a husband who is the sole earner of the family makes her liable, not just to economic risk at the dissolution of the marriage, but to economic, emotional, and physical risks during the marriage. Police response to family violence and the establishment of crisis centers, safe houses, and support groups for battered women are also feminist concerns.

Further References. B. R. Bergmann, *The Economic Emergence of Women* (New York, 1986), Chapter 9. A. Oakley, *The Sociology of Housework* (New York, 1974).

HOUSEWORK is work done for the care and maintenance of a home and its occupants. This service may include child care* as well as the provisioning of food, clothing, and household items, doing laundry, and cleaning and maintaining the home. The duties are traditionally "women's work,"* and except for very wealthy families, most or all of them are done as unpaid labor by family members, primarily by the wife/mother of the family.

The multitude of tasks involved in housework cover the entire range from low-skill to high-skill work. However, most of the essential services are monotonous and repetitive, the product of the labor being almost immediately consumed (prepared food, made-up beds, cleaned dishes, etc.). The work is not counted as part of the gross national product and, since it is unpaid, is not as highly valued as paid labor. When it is paid, the personal services required and the working conditions make it a low-paying, low-status job.

Technology took much of the production for household consumption and the heavy manual labor out of housework. By increasing standards for all classes and putting some work back into the duties of the middle-class wife/mother (e.g., laundry), it has largely erased differences in the general nature of housework done by middle- and working-class wives/mothers and has increased the monotonous and repetitive nature of much of that work.

Reformers interested in maintaining the patriarchal family system have tried at various times to give housework a different name in an attempt to raise its status. In the early twentieth century the terms *domestic science* and *home economics* were tried. In the period after World War II *homemaking* became the preferred term. The status was unaffected. Utopian and feminist theorists have proposed various schemes for making housework, including child care, communal or completely professional. The utopian communities of the nineteenth century generally made the work communal, but it was still done by the women.

Women who prize traditional feminine values and enjoy cooking, sewing, and other skills involved in housekeeping prefer housework to work in the paid labor force. There are, however, many women who do not enjoy or have an interest in those skills. The assumption that women have a "natural" inclination for housework and "are good at it" is deeply embedded in the patriarchal system of gender-role segregation. Since destroying that myth threatens the work roles of men in the home, it is not a myth that will be easily demolished.

HUMAN CAPITAL THEORY first appeared in a special issue of the *Journal of Political Economy* in 1962 on "Investment in Human Beings." It was preceded by Jacob Mincer's "Investment in Human Capital and Personal Income Distributions" (*Journal of Political Economy* 66 [1958]: 281–302) and Theodore W.

Schultz's *The Economic Value of Education* (New York, 1961) and was followed by Gary S. Becker's *Human Capital* (1964, 2nd ed., New York, 1975). Human capital theory has flourished ever since, at the University of Chicago and elsewhere. If its success is to be judged by the impact it has had on scholarly work, not only in economics but in the other social sciences as well, it has been quite spectacular. A vast empirical literature, testing its predictions and implications, has succeeded in confirming many of both. Its very success, however, has caused some of its more enthusiastic proponents to go beyond taking credit for contributing to our knowledge of human behavior, and come perilously close to claiming that they can explain all of it. These extreme claims are particularly misplaced when it comes to differences in the economic status of women and men.

As its very name suggests, human capital theory is essentially an extension of the idea of physical capital. Just as business people spend on new plants and equipment today in order to increase productive capacity and obtain greater returns later, so people spend on themselves in ways that do not result in present satisfaction, but in future returns, pecuniary and otherwise. Examples are expenditures, of time as well as money, on education and training*, job search, migration, better health, more and higher quality children. Such items had earlier, for the most part, been treated as "consumption goods." They were viewed primarily as influencing well-being directly, not as a means of raising future income. Thus the new approach was genuinely innovative and provided the foundation for a massive and successful research program.

Both the strengths and the weakness of the human capital approach are well illustrated by the way it has been used to explain the male-female earnings gap. Beginning with the premise that individuals and their families decide to invest in themselves today in order to achieve higher returns later, it is reasonable to assume that both the quantity and the type of human capital accumulated will be influenced by the amount of time the person expects to spend in the labor force.

As Jacob Mincer and Solomon W. Polachek ("Family Investments in Human Capital: Earnings of Women," *Journal of Political Economy* 82 [1974]: S76–S108) argue, men who normally work for pay all of their adult lives will tend to make greater investments in human capital than women who are likely to be in the labor force intermittently. Hence men are more inclined to become physicians, while women are likely to become nurses. Similarly, women will be more reluctant than men to acquire skills that atrophy rapidly when not used. Hence, women are more inclined to become social workers, while men may become physicists. Further, time spent out of the labor force directly reduces the amount of work experience women have in general, and with a given employer in particular. An extensive survey of studies of the earnings gap that take such factors into account shows that the most thorough ones explain almost half of this differential (Donald J. Treiman and Heidi I. Hartmann [eds.], *Women, Work, and Wages: Equal Pay for Jobs of Equal Value* [Washington, D.C.:

1981]). It is, however, equally important to note that this leaves at least half of the differential unexplained, and raises the possibility that some of that might be caused by discrimination*.

Thus, human capital theory helps us to understand why women earn less than men. It also has useful policy implications, for it suggests that women can improve their situation by acquiring more and different kinds of education, training, and experience. At the same time, there is no justification for ignoring a variety of other factors that stand in the way of economic equality for women that call for other remedies.

More generally, there is reason to question the single-minded focus of the most dogmatic adherents of human capital theory on economic rationality, which suggests that all persons in full knowledge of available alternatives and outcomes make choices so as to maximize satisfaction. It is also assumed that these choices are always freely made. Hence differences in occupations, earnings, marital status, fertility, and even health are viewed as the result of voluntary decisions.

Similarly, the contention that all "widespread and/or persistent human behavior can be explained by a generalized calculus of utility-maximizing behavior" (George J. Stigler and Gary S. Becker, "De Gustibus Non Est Disputandum," *American Economic Review* 67 [1977]: 76–90) needs to be critically examined. It represents a very narrow view of a complex world, ignoring the potential importance of traditional attitudes, social pressures, and institutions in influencing human behavior. All these may themselves have been shaped by economic conditions in an earlier time, but they tend to last long after they have outlived their relevance. They can constitute significant constraints on the choices individuals make. The emphasis on voluntary choices particularly tends to underestimate the extent to which persons confronted by less favorable options, say because of their race, sex, or social background, are likely to be caught up in a circle of unfavorable feedback effects.

A well-balanced view, fully recognizing that the extent to which people are willing to use resources to enhance their own productivity has much to do with their earnings potential, also acknowledges that in a world where all individuals are not born equal, where markets are imperfect, and where uncertainty abounds, many other factors influence the outcome. Thus, for instance, it is important to recognize that, in large part because of lingering traditional values, boys and girls are socialized differently, and, according to much available evidence, face substantially different opportunities in the labor market. It is equally important to recognize that labor market discrimination—when two equally qualified individuals are treated differently solely because of a personal characteristic such as sex, race, religion, or disability—may help to explain occupational segregation* and male-female earnings differentials. Further, the expectation of discrimination would be likely in turn to influence decisions on how much human capital to accumulate.

The issue whether or not to accept the broadest claims of human capital theory is an important one from a practical point of view. The theory lends itself all too readily to explaining inequality in a way that amounts to blaming the victim. Poverty* is the result of insufficient investment. Women earn less in the labor market because they tend to specialize in homemaking—never mind that they supposedly specialize in homemaking, in large part, because they earn less in the labor market.

Such premises naturally encourage complacency and comfortable acceptance of the status quo. There is no reason, however, to reject the valuable insights the theory has to offer, or the increased knowledge the related active research program continues to provide. The basic idea that persons can and do invest in themselves in ways that enhance their earning power need not be combined with acceptance of the implications suggested by the most extreme proponents of human capital theory. It can, in fact, be used to support policies that would more nearly equalize the opportunity to make such investments, and the rewards for making them, once the unrealistic assumption that equal opportunity already exists in discarded.

MARIANNE A. FERBER

HYPERGAMY/HYPOGAMY. Hypergamy is a marriage system in which the woman "marries up." The preferred marriage is one in which the woman marries a man of a higher social class. The man should not marry a woman of higher status nor a woman marry below her status. This system is found in conjunction with hierarchical societies and with the dowry* as the only form of marital payment, as among the higher castes in India and in Renaissance Italy. The wife's family*, by giving a dowry that tends to become extravagantly high, may hope to improve its rank and social position or to make politically advantageous connections. The upward movement of women from lower social strata means that there will be an excess of women at the top. The high costs of dowries also means that families will be not able to, or will be very reluctant to, dower more than one daughter. Female infanticide, forcing daughters into the cloister, and polygamy are among the methods used to decrease marriageable women at the top. In the lower social classes there may be a scarcity of marriageable women.

Hypogamy is the opposite of hypergamy. In this system the desired marriage is one in which the man marries up. Such hypogamous marriages appear frequently among the heroes of the Greek legends. In modern hypogamous marital systems high marital payment in the form of bridewealth benefits the maternal lineage, as hypergamy benefits the paternal.

I

IMPOSTOR PHENOMENON is an internal experience of intellectual phoniness that seems to be prevalent among high-achieving persons, with particularly deleterious effects on women. The term was first used by Pauline Rose Clance and Suzanne Imes in a 1978 paper describing their clinical findings among high-achieving women. It is an emotionally debilitating condition characterized by persistent and unwarranted anxiety about achievement, dread of evaluation, fear of failure and exposure, inability to internalize success, and lack of enjoyment of accomplishment and achievement. Research using Clance and Imes's, original construct, as well as a scale to measure Impostor Phenomenon behavior, which Clance developed in 1985, is ongoing. Results at this point indicate that the Impostor Phenomenon is more prevalent among women whose educational or other achievements surpass expectations based on their family or cultural milieu. In most studies, men are found to identify themselves as suffering from Impostor feelings as readily as do women. Clance has recently suggested that, although men may acknowledge the presence of Impostor Phenomenon characteristics at rates comparable to their acknowledgment by women, women's achievements may be affected more, and affected more adversely, by these feelings than are men's. This is due in part, she hypothesizes, to sex-role stereotyping in child-rearing and other cultural practices, which leads women to denigrate their achievement needs and to become hyperresponsible in meeting the nurturance needs of others.

Further Reference. P. R. Clance, *The Impostor Phenomenon: Overcoming the Fear That Haunts Your Success* (Atlanta, 1985).

PAULINE ROSE CLANCE AND MAUREEN O'TOOLE

INCEST is prohibited by law in all states of the United States, with the exception of New Jersey. Although legal definitions of incest vary considerably, in most states incest statutes prohibit marriage* or sexual intercourse between blood relatives, regardless of age (American Bar Association, *Child Sexual Abuse and the Law* [Washington, D.C., 1981], 52). Because of the narrowness of the legal definition, many cases of incestuous abuse are prosecuted under the broader child sexual abuse laws. Sexual activity between children and adults—including genital touching as well as sexual intercourse—is a crime in every state. While states differ in their definitions of a child, most use 16 or 18 years as the criterion.

Incest researchers and clinicians generally consider sexual abuse by nonblood relatives such as stepfathers, stepgrandfathers, or uncles by marriage as cases of incestuous abuse, as well as sexual abuse by blood relatives. However, there is no consensus among professionals on what sex acts constitute incestuous abuse. Some include noncontact experiences such as verbal propositions or genital exhibition, while others limit their definition to offenses involving sexual contact.

The percentage of women who have ever been incestuously abused in this country is unknown. The best estimate comes from a study based on face-to-face interviews with a probability sample of 930 adult female residents of San Francisco in 1978 (D. E. H. Russell, *The Secret Trauma* [New York, 1986]). Defining incestuous abuse as any sexually exploitative contact or attempted contact between relatives, 16 percent of these respondents reported at least one experience of incestuous abuse before the age of 18. Only four cases (2 percent) were ever reported to the police, and only one case resulted in a conviction. However, with the mandatory reporting laws now in effect, the percentage of cases that are reported today is likely to be much higher than 2 percent. (Every state now requires certain people such as doctors, psychologists, teachers, and others who work closely with children to report all suspected cases of child sexual abuse to child protective services or to law enforcement agencies.)

Four and a half percent of the 930 women disclosed having been sexually abused by a father, 4.9 percent by an uncle, 2.0 percent by a brother, and 1.2 percent by a grandfather. The prevalence rates for incestuous abuse by female relatives were strikingly low: only 0.1 percent of the sample had been abused by a mother, 0.3 percent by a sister, and 0.3 percent by some other female relative. Female perpetrators constituted only 5 percent of all the incest perpetrators combined.

The fact that the overwhelming majority of incest perpetrators are male suggests that male sexual and sex-role socialization* likely plays a key role in the causation of incestuous abuse. For example, in contrast to women, men are reared to prefer partners who are younger, smaller, innocent, vulnerable, and relatively powerless. It follows that children would be more sexually attractive to men than to women. In general, predatory behavior by males toward females is embedded in the culture. Males are expected not only to take the initiative but also to overcome resistance. In addition, Judith Herman found that the traditional patriarchal family in which the father is boss and perceives his wife and children as there to serve him is a family at risk of father-daughter incest (*Father-Daughter Incest* [Cambridge, Mass., 1981]).

Most knowledge about the psychological characteristics of incest perpetrators is still based on the very small percentage of reported cases. These cannot be considered representative of the many undetected perpetrators.

It is only in the last decade that the magnitude and seriousness of this problem have begun to be recognized. As well as much suffering at the time of the incestuous abuse, such victimization can cause very severe long-term effects. Children are being taught how to deal with abusive adults in school prevention programs in many states. And appropriate treatment techniques are being developed, including self-help groups for the many adult survivors of incest.

Further References. W. Maltz and B. Holman, *Incest and Sexuality: A Guide to Understanding and Healing* (Lexington, Mass., 1987). F. Rush, *The Best Kept Secret* (Englewood Cliffs, N.J., 1980).

DIANA E. H. RUSSELL

INFANTICIDE is the killing of an infant under one year of age. Infanticide has been, at least for some infants, tolerated, condoned, or even encouraged from the Stone Age to the present by peoples in every stage of cultural sophistication.

In many societies there is a period after birth before the newborn is considered fully human. During this period of a day (before nursing begins), a week or two (before the child is named or publicly recognized by the father), or even as long as three years (as among the Amahuaca of Peru), destruction would not be considered the killing of a person.

For infanticide to be condoned or tolerated, it must be committed for reasons and by means that are acceptable to the community. Poverty*, real or relative, of the family* or the community is the leading cause of infanticide. Killing newborns has been a widely accepted way of limiting family size in societies without safe and proven methods of contraception. In some cases families are not to exceed what the community decides is "normal size."

Killing infants whose presence will overburden the mother, hence jeopardizing other family members or the entire community, is sometimes mandatory. Among migrating people, the death of a child born too late in the season to stand the rigors of a migration or born before an older sibling is out of its mother's arms may be required. Infants are also killed to increase spacing between children, allowing the others more chance of survival. One or both pairs of twins or an infant whose mother dies as a result of childbirth* may be murdered.

Mentally or physically defective infants may be killed out of fear that the deformity is hereditary, that the child is a "changeling" or the work of the devil, that the mother will be blamed, or out of the need not to "waste" food and care on poor risks for survival. The killing of neonates in modern maternity hospitals may stem from the belief that the "quality of life" in store for the child makes life not worth living. The ethical and legal problems involved in decisions on anomalous infants are enormous and, as neonatal medicine improves, will become even more so. (See REPRODUCTION, ETHICS OF.)

Infants are also killed for political reasons, such as infant sacrifice for the good of the community or elimination of possible rivals, and for reasons not usually condoned by society, such as killing the children of rival wives or concubines or killing one's own offspring because they are not wanted by a new sexual partner or because they are illegitimate. The legalizing of abortion may have reduced, but has not eliminated, the murder of newborns by unwed mothers.

Historical and anthropological evidence indicates that where infanticide is condoned or tolerated, it is often directed against female infants more than male infants. "Ideal" sex ratios favor males. In Rome an early law is supposed to have required citizens to keep all sons and the firstborn daughter. In China the ideal ratio of boys to girls was 5 to 2. In patrilineal societies, where poverty or relative poverty is a cause of infanticide, females do not add to the patriliny*, but take wealth from it for dowries. Especially where hypergamous marriages (in which women marry up) are common and dowries tend to become excessive, female infanticide is likely to be practiced.

Although Buddhism and Taoism opposed infanticide, it was widely practiced in poorer districts of Imperial China, directed against girls. The efforts of the People's Republic to limit families to one child have again brought reports of female infanticide. In India female baby killing was tolerated into the nineteenth century. Daughters were so devalued that they were sometimes accepted as punishment for sins of the past life. No longer condoned, female infanticide has been replaced in some parts of India by "underinvestment" (deliberate under-nourishment and insufficient care), leading to excessive female mortality. Female infanticide, sometimes required by tribal custom in ancient Arabia, was condemned by Mohammed but continued to be practiced among bedouins until modern times. In some areas of the Middle East, too, it has been replaced by "underinvestment."

In Europe, infanticide was tolerated until the advent of Christianity. Thereafter, the level of frequency and of toleration varied according to area, time period, and status of the perpetrators. Evidence of infanticide directed primarily against females is so scattered for the ancient and medieval periods that some scholars deny that there was more killing of female than of male infants. Although there is too little evidence to conclusively prove the case, the little demographic evidence from Greece and Rome and the few registers from medieval villages that show evidence of badly skewed sex ratios *all* show an unnaturally large number of boys in comparison to girls (see E. Coleman, "Infanticide in the Early Middle Ages," in S. M. Stroud [ed.], *Women in Medieval Society* [Philadelphia, 1976], 47–70). In Renaissance Florence, where dowries were high and demographic records more plentiful, a higher incidence of female infant deaths can be documented (R. C. Trexler, "Infanticide in Florence: New Sources and First Results," *History of Children Quarterly* 1 [1973]: 98–116).

Except when done by public agents, most deaths, overt and covert, are by passive means, chiefly abandonment. So in Sparta state officials threw anomalous infants over a cliff; elsewhere in Greece unwanted infants were usually abandoned in the wild to starve or be killed by wild animals. In the Amazon infants are left under a tree in the rain forest; in the desert, buried in the sand; in the Arctic, left on the ice; in the neonatal intensive care unit, put in a room in an out-of-the-way corridor. Sometimes they are left where there might be hope for their survival, as at hospitals and churches. ''Overlaying'' is thought often to have been a covert form of infanticide. (But many cases of ''overlaying'' may actually have been crib deaths—see M. P. Johnson, ''Smothered Slave Infants: Were Slave Mothers at Fault?'' *Journal of Southern History* 47 [1981]: 493–520). In different areas of Europe from the sixteenth through the eighteenth centuries, parents could murder their infants by sending them to wet nurses. Infants are also killed by intentional neglect. Leaving the infant in dangerous situations, to be killed by ''accident,'' was especially common in the nineteenth century. Today most infanticide has been replaced by ''underinvestment,'' greatly increasing the child's chance of death in early childhood.

Almost all murder of infants is done by parents (or surrogate parents), alone or through accomplices. The mother is the most likely agent. Abject poverty or overwhelming stress may prevent her from relating to her baby. Fear of blame because of the child's deformity or its sex and fear of shame and stigma because of the child's illegitimacy are frequent causes for a mother's getting rid of her newborn.

During the Middle Ages infanticide usually came under the jurisdiction of the church courts, which could not dispense capital punishment. It was not until the early modern period that civil governments began to take an interest in prosecuting cases of infant deaths, for which the death penalty was given into the nineteenth century. Prosecution of offenders was marked by biases regarding sex, class, and marital status: only certain types of people were ever tried or punished. Fathers of murdered infants were never tried; married mothers, seldom. Wet nurses were not tried—unless the child lived. In Florence returning the child before it was 30 months old could result in a fine or a whipping. It was the unwed mother and the poor and the old (accused as witches) who were tried and convicted. The unwed mother had little chance of acquittal unless she could show evidence, such as the preparation of clothing, that she was planning to raise the child.

In patriarchal society infanticide has been directed against female infants, committed primarily by women, and until the late twentieth century, only women, almost always marginal women, were punished for it.

Further References. G. Hausfater and S. B. Hrdy (eds.), *Infanticide: Comparative and Evolutionary Perspectives* (New York, 1984). W. A. Langer, ''Infanticide: A Historical Survey,'' *History of Childhood Quarterly* 1 (1974): 353–365.

INFERTILITY affects between 10 and 15 percent of women. In addition, about 20 percent of pregnancies end in miscarriage. In the past the major solution to childlessness was adoption, but since the number of babies available for adoption has dropped substantially, the only real solution to infertility is now a medical one. Women's experience with medical procedures and personnel has become an important part of their experience of infertility.

Infertility has many causes. Genetic factors, environmental hazards, infections, and hormonal imbalances can all make women and men infertile, although it is usually impossible to pinpoint a cause for an individual. Each of three kinds of infertility accounts for about one-third of problems: male infertility (low sperm count, antibodies); female problems (failure to ovulate, blocked tubes, endometriosis* [i.e., the accumulation in the pelvic cavity of tissue from the uterine lining]); and incompatability between sperm and the woman's reproductive system (hostile mucus). Much of our knowledge about reproductive problems is a by-product of contraceptive research. Because contraception interferes with women's rather than men's bodies, more is known about women's reproduction and more tests of their fertility are available.

Men's fertility is examined using one major test, the semen test. And the only treatment commonly available (and the only reasonably successful one) is artificial insemination by donor (AID) which treats male infertility by bypassing it. With AID a woman is given semen from a (usually anonymous) donor.

Treatments for women range from antibiotics for infections, basal temperature charts and hormone therapy to induce and check ovulation, to microsurgery and the well-publicized in vitro fertilization (IVF) for damaged tubes. IVF is used infrequently compared with other techniques and has a low success rate. It has, however, made infertility visible generally and ensured that it is a major issue for the women's movement.

By making it difficult to become mothers, infertility creates a crisis. Women are encouraged to see themselves through their relationships with children, and for many motherhood is a powerful source of identity, giving them a sense of purpose and belonging. The great majority of women become mothers, as they have always done, although they have fewer children than their grandmothers. Motherhood is no longer linked to economic survival for women in the developed world, but there are still strong links between fertility and women's social position and status. Childlessness (whether by choice or not) is a deviation from a powerful norm, and childless women are stigmatized and marginalized.

Infertile women have to adjust to their disappointment and come to terms with the failure of their bodies (or the men's). Often they feel isolated and bereft as they go through a process akin to grief and mourning. Eventually women create identities for themselves and ways of caring and being cared for which allow their needs to be met in ways that are not dependent on a relationship with a child. This is an agenda for all women, those with children as much as those without.

Further References. N. Pfeffer and A. Woollett, *The Experience of Infertility* (London, 1983). P. Singer and D. Wells, *The Reproductive Revolution: New Ways of Making Babies* (Oxford, 1984).

ANNE WOOLLETT

INTELLIGENCE QUOTIENT (IQ) is a measure of intelligence derived from performance on one of several available standardized tests. Originally, IQ scores were computed by dividing an individual's mental age by his or her chronological age and multiplying by 100. (Mental age refers to one's mental development relative to others'; thus a child with a mental age of nine performs on an intelligence test at the level of the average nine-year-old.) Today scores on most tests are based on their deviation from (distance above or below) the average score of a normative group, with this average usually set by convention at 100. Psychological opinion is divided on the extent to which these scores reflect genetic versus environmental influences on mental ability.

Critics of IQ tests have argued that test items tend to be biased in favor of white, urban, middle-class individuals. They have also observed that cultural values can affect attitudes toward taking the test, motivation, comfort in the testing situation, and rapport with the test giver. Efforts have been made to construct reliable and valid culture-fair tests that eliminate group differences in performance, but on the whole they have been disappointing.

On the most widely used intelligence tests, average female and male scores do not differ, but this is by design. On early versions of the Stanford-Binet Intelligence Scale, the first standardized IQ test in the United States, girls scored higher than boys at every age up to 14. Psychologists were reluctant to conclude that girls were intellectually superior to boys. Instead, in the 1937 revision of the test, psychologist Lewis Terman eliminated sex differences once and for all by simply deleting items that favored one sex or adding items favoring males. Other tests have followed similar procedures.

Although the sexes do not differ in average performance, over the years several writers have proposed that males as a group are more *variable* than females in intellectual ability, i.e., are overrepresented at both the low and high ends of the scale. (See VARIABILITY HYPOTHESIS.) Historically, this notion has sometimes been used to argue that training females for intellectually challenging professions is a waste of educational resources. It is true that a somewhat greater proportion of males than females score at the lower end of the IQ scale, possibly because boys are more vulnerable than girls to congenital defects and early illness and head injury. However, evidence for a *general* difference in variability, or for a greater proportion of males at the high end of the spectrum, has been plagued by methodological problems and is considered weak by most feminist and mainstream psychologists.

The original purpose of IQ tests was to predict school achievement, and for both sexes, modern tests do this fairly well, especially when supplemented by others sorts of information. However, IQ scores are less than accurate in predicting achievement outside the classroom, where educational preparation, motivation, and opportunity are critical determinants of occupational success. Even intellectual giftedness does not ensure such success if other factors conspire to limit it. In 1921, Stanford University researchers began to study a cohort of children in the top 1 percent of the IQ score distribution. Most of the boys grew up to achieve prominence in professional or managerial fields. In accord with social expectations of the time, most of the girls grew up to be homemakers. Those employed outside the home overwhelmingly went into lower-status occupations.

Related research finds that females are more likely than males to show a decline in IQ after grade school. Traits traditionally defined as "masculine," such as assertiveness and independence, seem to promote intellectual development in both sexes. It is not yet clear whether sex-role changes during the 1970s and 1980s have reduced or eliminated sex differences* in patterns of intellectual development as measured by IQ tests.

Currently, static descriptions of how well individuals or groups do on IQ tests are giving way to analyses of the problem-solving strategies used by high and low scorers. This shift in emphasis may eventually lead to insights about why the sexes, although they do not differ in average IQ test performance, do sometimes differ slightly on tests of specific skills, such as verbal or mathematical ones. It should be noted, however, that such differences account for only a small proportion of the overall variance in test scores and cannot explain existing occupational disparities.

Further References. E. E. Maccoby and C. N. Jacklin, *The Psychology of Sex Differences* (Stanford, 1974). P. Sears and A. H. Barbee, "Career and Life Satisfactions among Terman's Gifted Women," in J. C. Stanley, W. C. George, and C. H. Solano (eds.), *The Gifted and the Creative: A Fifty-year Perspective* (Baltimore, 1977).

CAROLE WADE

INTERNAL LABOR MARKET is a unit within a large organization to which a specific set of rules and procedures relative to wage rates and promotion paths is applied. Men have been found concentrated in internal labor markets with opportunities for promotion and high pay while women's internal labor markets are characterized by dead-end jobs paying low wages. Even when they enter the same internal labor market, job tracking may be very different for men and women with similar credentials.

J

JURORS. Women jurors were almost unknown until well into the twentieth century. Under common law, adopted by the American colonies, jury service was restricted to males. In 1879, the U.S. Supreme Court sanctioned this practice saying that while states could no longer restrict jury service to whites due to the passage of the Fourteenth Amendment, they could continue to restrict it to males (*Strauder* v. *West Virginia*, 100 U.S. 303 1879).

During the nineteenth century efforts to include women on juries were sparse and short-lived. In 1870 Wyoming became the first state or territory to permit women to serve as jurors. It did so because transient male jurors were unwilling to convict lawbreakers. This experiment ended after three court terms when the judge who had initiated it resigned in 1871 and was replaced by a judge opposed to woman suffrage. Washington Territory assumed that the obligation to serve on juries followed from suffrage. This assumption and the resulting practice of mixed juries survived a court challenge in 1884, but three years later the territorial court reversed its position and excluded women from territorial juries. In 1896 Utah became the first state to include women on juries. Of the 15 states that extended full suffrage to women prior to the passage of the Nineteenth Amendment, only 5 also permitted women to serve as jurors.

Even after the Nineteenth Amendment in 1920 extended the right to vote to women, many states continued the practice of all-male juries. Opposition to women jurors centered around the following arguments: (1) jury service would cause women to neglect their homes and families, (2) women would be embarrassed or upset by the material that they would encounter in courtrooms, (3) jury service would unsex women, (4) women jurors would have difficulty comprehending complex legal arguments, and (5) sequestering female jurors would be difficult. By 1942 only 28 states permitted women jurors. Fifteen of these allowed women to claim exemptions not available to men. The 1957 Civil Rights Act required that women be included on federal jury lists; however, it did not affect state practices. In 1961 the U.S. Supreme Court upheld a Florida statute that required women to register with the clerk of court if they wished to be included in jury lists (*Hoyt* v. *Florida*, 368 U.S. 57 1961). The Court's rationale was that women's family responsibilities would make jury service a hardship. Since most women could be expected to take advantage of an automatic exemption, the state was justified in requiring those who wished to serve to register.

By 1973 all 50 states permitted women jurors, but 19 provided them exemptions not available to men. As a result, jury lists tended to underrepresent women severely. In 1975 the U.S. Supreme Court held that the practice of excluding women who did not specifically indicate their willingness to serve on juries was unconstitutional because it deprived the accused of a jury drawn from a cross section of the community (*Taylor* v. *Louisiana*, 419 U.S. 552 1975). In 1979 the Supreme Court overturned an automatic exemption for women jurors, but indicated that a gender-neutral child care exemption would be permissible (*Duncan* v. *Missouri*, 439 U.S. 357 1979).

The inclusion of women on jury lists does not necessarily result in their representation on jury panels. During their *voir dire* (an examination of prospective jurors to ascertain that they are competent and objective) attorneys have an opportunity to question prospective jurors and challenge those they believe biased. During this process women are often asked questions about their spouses, their spouses' occupations, and their family life that are not posed to men. In addition, trial practice books frequently provide advice based on sex-role stereotypes. For example, lawyers are advised to avoid women jurors if their clients are women because female jurors tend to be harsher on members of their own sex, but to seek women jurors if their clients are attractive young men. Female jurors are also portrayed as unpredictable and tenderhearted, thus good jurors for the defense in criminal cases and for the plaintiff in civil cases. However, since housewives are unaccustomed to handling large sums of money, lawyers should avoid women jurors if their clients are seeking large damage awards.

Research on the relationship between gender and juror performance is limited and somewhat mixed. Nevertheless, it yields a few generalizations. Both male and female jurors tend to favor litigants of their own sex. There appears to be no support for the notion that women jurors are acquittal prone; in fact, women jurors seem more likely to convict. Finally, female jurors have been found to participate less in deliberations, to be selected to serve as foreman less frequently, and to be less likely to be judged influential by other jurors.

Further Reference. A. R. Mahoney, "Women Jurors: Sexism in Jury Selection," in L. Crites and W. Hepperle (eds.), *Women, the Courts, and Equality* (Beverly Hills, Calif., 1989).

JILDA M. ALIOTTA

L

LABOR FORCE PARTICIPATION. Active employment or actively seeking employment in the paid labor market. Any individual 16 years of age or older who is currently employed (i.e., working for pay at least one hour in the last week) or who is currently unemployed (i.e., actively seeking employment in the last four weeks) is classified as "in the labor force." Labor force participation (LFP) is usually expressed as a rate:

$$\text{Labor Force}$$

$$\frac{\text{Employed} \quad + \quad \text{Unemployed}}{\text{Employed} + \text{Unemployed} + \text{Out of the Labor force}} \times 100$$

This rate is the percentage of the population engaged in paid labor market activities. The formula has been changed twice, in 1940 and in 1983. Prior to January 1, 1983, the denominator was the civilian noninstitutional population (i.e., military workers were not included). Before 1940, the concept of labor force was not used. Instead individuals were classified as "gainfully employed" according to their "usual occupation." Statistics have been adjusted to make them comparable over time.

Women uniformly have lower labor force participation rates than men (in 1983, 52.9 percent and 76.4 percent respectively); however, there are vast differences in rates among different subgroups of women. Black women always have had higher LFP rates than white women (in 1983, 54.2 and 52.7 percent respectively) and married women have lower LFP rates (51.8 percent) than separated (58.7 percent), divorced (74.6 percent), or single (62.6 percent) women. Married women with children under five have the lowest rates. Women with some college education are more actively engaged in the labor force than women with less education.

Although data prior to 1940 are not strictly comparable to today's estimates, a consistent picture has emerged. Female LFP has been increasing since the turn of the century, both overall and in every sociodemographic category. While popular belief holds that the labor shortages created by World War II served as a catalyst for bringing women into the labor market, this dramatic influx of women into the paid labor market had antecedents at the beginning of this century. In fact, much of the rising LFP in the last two decades represents a return to pre–World War II patterns. The long-term growth trend in female LFP was temporarily interrupted by the high fertility years following World War II (creating the baby boom) when LFP rates were far below historic trends.

The century-long upward trend of women's LFP is explained by changes in the pre–1900 labor market that had inhibited females from paid employment. In 1900, 17 percent of white and 42 percent of black women were in the labor force; however, only 2 percent of white married women were in the labor market, at least in part as a response to very low wages, 30 percent less than those of single white women.

One reason for low levels of female LFP was that few jobs were available since women were confined to employment in only a few occupations and industries. Usually, this employment resembled the tasks women performed in household production. Before the large demand for women clerical/secretarial workers, a large proportion of women were employed as domestic servants or in the clothing industry.

Fertility and household production were other factors that inhibited labor force participation. In 1900, a woman averaged about four children in her lifetime; today the average is 1.8. (See CHILDREN: THEIR EFFECT ON LABOR SUPPLY.) Also, in 1900 over one-third of all women lived on farms in homes resembling "small cottage firms." Most women's production was here rather than in the paid labor force. Thus, during this period, the working woman was not the "average woman." In contrast to today, working women* at the turn of the century tended to have less education, to be married to men with low or nonexistent incomes, or to be immigrants.

Between 1900 and 1920, the picture began to change. There were increases in womens' wages, opportunities for employment, and levels of educational attainment. This period also saw rapid increases in urbanization, as well as in the long-term decline in women's fertility.

Women's wages increased 16 percent faster than men's during this period. Much of this economic change, and the increase in school completions, can be attributed to the emergence of clerical employment, for which increased education was necessary.

The decline in fertility decreased the time spent in childrearing, enabling women to substitute paid employment for home production. At the same time, the movement of our economy into a more urban industrial base facilitated women's entrance into the paid labor market by moving them from the rural and "cottage firm" environment into the industrial centers where paid employment was available.

While changing socioeconomic factors facilitated women's increasing labor force participation, the increase varied throughout this century and among sociodemographic groups. Labor force participation rates increased 10 percent (18.7 to 29.4) during the first *40* years of this century, 11 percent (29.4 to 40.7) during the next *20* years, and about 12 percent (40.7 to 52.9) since 1960. These aggregate patterns mask dramatically different subgroup patterns. Between 1920 and 1940 participation rates of young females aged 25 to 34 rose from 16.5 to 33.3 percent (a 17 percent increase). At the same time participation rates for women aged 45 to 54 increased by only 10 percent (from 12.5 to 22.5 percent). For the next 20 years (during the years of high fertility) this age pattern reversed, and labor force participation for women under 35 actually declined while participation rates for women over 35 increased dramatically. After 1960, the earlier age patterning resumed but on a much larger scale. In 1983, over 70 percent of the women aged 25 to 34 were employed (a 75 percent increase over 1960). While participation rates increased for older women, they did so much more slowly: only 14.4 percent for women aged 45 to 54.

Educational and occupational patterns also have shifted over time. Although female LFP rises with education, between 1940 and 1970 the largest influx of women into the labor force occurred among less educated women. This trend then reversed itself, with the more highly educated increasing their participation more rapidly. Women are still primarily employed as administrative support (30.6 percent); however, an increasing number are professionals or managers (20.8 percent today compared to 16 percent in 1970).

In recent years, there has been an increased awareness of discrimination against women in society and in the labor market. Although legislation of the 1960s and 1970s attempted to rectify past injustices, its effect on current LFP is probably small, and it did little to raise women's wages relative to men's. However, changed social attitudes have facilitated women's increased LFP and may have created an increased awareness of how much time females spend in the labor force. In the past, young women underestimated the overall time spent in labor market activities and did not prepare adequately for continuous employment. Increased awareness can only improve this.

The trend of increased female labor force participation contrasts with the trend of declining male labor force participation (due to earlier retirement and decreases in black male participation). Thus, while the aggregate differential between male and female participation today is 23.5 percentage points, the trend is toward equalization, with a projected differential for 1995 of only 15.8 percentage points.

Further References. C. Lloyd and B. Niemi, *The Economics of Sex Differentials* (New York, 1979). J. P. Smith and M. P. Ward, *Women's Wages and Work in the*

Twentieth Century (Santa Monica, 1984). R. E. Smith (ed.), *The Subtle Revolution: Women at Work* (Washington, D.C., 1979).

NAN L. MAXWELL

LANGUAGE. See SEMIOTICS AND FEMINISM

LEARNED HELPLESSNESS. A number of psychologists have speculated about the role of helplessness and hopelessness in depression*, but it was Martin Seligman (L. Y. Abramson, M.E.P. Seligman, and J. D. Teasdale, "Learned Helplessness in Humans: Critique and Reformulation," *Journal of Abnormal Psychology* 87 [1987]: 40–74) who formulated the learned helplessness theory of depression. The concept of learned helplessness evolved out of a series of experiments with dogs on the effects of prior Pavlovian conditioning on later learning. Dogs subjected to inescapable shock later demonstrated a failure to initiate voluntary attempts to escape. The theory was tested with humans, and it was postulated that depressed persons believe they have little control over important outcomes in their lives and, thus, do not attempt to exercise control. Learned helplessness theory contends that the basic cause of all the deficits observed in helpless animals and humans after uncontrollable events occur is the expectation that in the future they will not be able to control outcomes.

This theory of depression has affected psychotherapeutic treatment of women, since women are more frequently diagnosed as depressed than men and since this theory has influenced treatment approaches for depression. The learned helplessness theory recognizes the importance of a sense of powerlessness and its possible impact on mood, and it also concedes that helplessness can be learned in response to certain environmental contingencies. However, the "problem" of learned helplessness is still viewed as residing within the individual, and, by implication, the solution lies in treating the individual.

Theorists make several recommendations for therapeutic interventions based on the learned helplessness theory. For instance, therapeutic strategies that undermine the expectation that goals are uncontrollable and unattainable should be effective in reversing the depressive feelings (S.R.H. Beach, L. Y. Abramson, and F. M. Levine, "Attributional Reformulation of Learned Helplessness and Depression: Therapeutic Implications," in J. F. Clarkin and H. I. Glazier [eds.], *Depression: Behavorial and Directive Intervention Strategies* [New York, 1981]. A number of specific strategies have been presented: reversing an individual's expectations of no control; facilitating a change from unrealistic to more realistic goals; decreasing the importance of unattainable goals; and reversing an individual's expectations that other people have control over his/her goals. Basically, if the cause of learned helplessness and depression is hypothesized to be the expectation that responding will be ineffective in controlling future events, then the basic therapeutic effort should be to change this belief to one in which the individual believes that responding will be effective and that anticipated bad events will be avoided. The focus of these treatment models is thus on altering the depressed individual's *expectations* or *goals*.

What is missing from these perspectives, however, is a recognition of the individual's circumstances. For women and other disfranchised persons, ignoring these circumstances can be tantamount to prescribing acceptance of limited control or institutionalized powerlessness. For example, if a single mother of three children reports depression and a sense of helplessness, her depression may be the result of a realistic sense of powerlessness resulting from, for instance, limited occupational opportunities and inadequate facilities for child care. To attempt to modify her expectations or goals without recognizing the actual limitations under which she is operating may lead to a minimization of the difficulties she is facing. That is, treatments derived from the learned helplessness theory of depression focus on the expectations or beliefs of the individual, for the most part ignoring situational factors.

If the learned helplessness model recognizes that environmental contingencies can influence one's beliefs about future expectations, it seems appropriate to also understand that these contingencies may be stable elements of an individual's circumstances and thus may have a pervasive influence on an individual's outlook. An individual's attributions that outcomes are stable may not be an indication of a cognitive aberration, but rather may be an accurate appraisal of his/her circumstances. It is essential that mental health professionals recognize and take into consideration the multiplicity of factors that may be contributing to an individual's distress.

The learned helplessness theory has made some valuable contributions toward the understanding of depression: it explains some of the beliefs and behaviors of depressed persons and even provides experimental evidence as to how beliefs about helplessness are acquired. In this respect it furthers our recognition of factors that may contribute to depression in women. However, it is important, especially when women and disfranchised persons are being treated, not to neglect the role that situational factors may play in supporting a sense of helplessness.

MARY KAY BIAGGIO

LEISURE TIME (U.S.). Women's use of leisure time has been historically defined in relation to household and work obligations, prevailing ideologies about women's appropriate sphere of action, and the expansion of the leisure and entertainment industries.

In the premodern American colonies, leisure was understood not as a separate sphere of activity but as intertwined with the rhythms of the day and seasons. Quilting bees, huskings, and barn raisings were among the activities in which work, recreation, and sociability were mingled. Leisure was not sex-segregated ideologically, but grew out of the work roles of women and men. In villages and towns, shared labor such as spinning, laundering, berrying, and attending at childbirth* were occasions for women's sociability. Depending on the degree of settlement, visiting was a primary form of leisure, reinforced by women's customary practices of borrowing and bartering. In the larger towns and cities of the late eighteenth and early nineteenth centuries, commercial entertainment such as taverns and theaters were part of an informal, heterogeneous public life with relatively little segregation by sex and class.

Urbanization and the changes wrought by capitalism, especially the rationalization of the workday and increased separation of home and workplace, profoundly altered the sexual division of leisure in the nineteenth century. Leisure became increasingly stratified by sex, class, and race. Men's recreation, based in commercial and voluntary organizations such as saloons, militias, and fraternal orders, excluded women from many forms of social life. Victorian notions of respectability and purity also proscribed female participation in public recreation. At the same time, the household, and women within it, became culturally identified with leisure and rest, a realm apart from the competitive market and workplace. Despite the widespread mythology of the leisured woman, in reality only a small elite could employ enough servants to free women of child care and household duties. Women's leisure continued to be intertwined with household labor and kinship relations, but it was increasingly homosocial in character, particularly among middle-class wives. For working-class and black women, the pressing demands of survival left relatively little time or opportunity for leisure.

By the 1890s, new ideas about women's roles and the growth of the entertainment industry expanded women's leisure activities. The "New Woman" not only represented the movement of women into education, employment, and political activity, but symbolized an expanded social life. Active sports such as bicycling and tennis became popular among young middle-class women, while working-class adolescents sought pleasure and autonomy in dance halls. Leisure entrepreneurs tamed and refined formerly male-oriented entertainment, such as music halls and variety theaters, for the new female audience. In the early twentieth century, new forms of mixed-sex leisure, including dance palaces, motion pictures, and amusement parks, expressed and legitimated an emergent ideology of companionate social relations between the sexes. The image of the "family that plays together" was later reinforced by the advent of radio and television.

Still, gender divisions remain one of the most salient characteristics of leisure. Women more often report leisure activities that involve socializing and are located at home, church, and clubs. Moreover, women do not experience leisure as a sphere separate from "obligatory" time as men do; housework* and child care* overlap with the family's leisure hours. Most significant is women's loss of leisure time with the expansion of female labor force participation* since World War II and the consequent legitimation of the "double day" for working wives. Since the 1920s, men's overall working hours, in employment and at home, have risen only one-half hour per week, while women's have increased five hours. Ironically, while women's housework produces goods and services used in the family's leisure, their employment has enabled many men to labor fewer hours in support of their families and has given them increased leisure time.

Further References. R. A. Berk and S. F. Berk, *Labor and Leisure at Home* (Beverly Hills, Calif., 1979). K. Peiss, *Cheap Amusements: Working Women and Leisure in Turn-of-the-Century New York* (Philadelphia, 1986).

KATHY PEISS

LESBIAN MOTHERHOOD is the condition or institution of being a mother when the woman defines herself or is labeled as a lesbian. Because homosexuality* is stigmatized behavior, it is difficult to estimate the number of lesbian mothers in the population, though researchers have agreed that there are at least several hundred thousand and possibly as many as two or three million in the United States. Lesbian mothers include women who have become mothers through widely varying circumstances: in heterosexual marriages; by means of adoption; and outside of marriage by means of heterosexual intercourse or artificial insemination by donor.

While some lesbian mothers remain legally married to the fathers of their children, the majority are probably divorced or never-married; from a legal point of view, most are "single" despite the fact that they may be involved in long-term relationships with women partners. This means that they share many problems also experienced by other "single" mothers and female heads of household. These include low income (often linked to difficulties collecting child support payments), housing discrimination, problems locating adequate, affordable child care*, and stress derived from performing parental roles without assistance from another adult.

At the same time, lesbian mothers are especially vulnerable to some problems less frequently faced by heterosexual mothers. Most significant among these are legal challenges to child custody. Lesbian mothers are likely to be viewed as "unfit" by judges solely because of their sexual orientation* and therefore try to avoid custody litigation whenever possible. In many cases, this leads them to compromise with former husbands about child support and other paternal obligations, thereby exposing themselves and their families to more severe financial problems than they might otherwise encounter. Cases have been documented in which former husbands have explicitly demanded such compromises in exchange for agreements not to challenge custody. Some recent research also indicates that fear of custody disputes may be a major source of anxiety for many lesbian mothers, even when such disputes have not occurred.

Probably the majority of lesbian mothers had their children during marriages, in many instances before recognizing their sexual orientation. For self-defined lesbians who wish to become mothers, both pregnancy and adoption may be difficult to achieve. An increasingly visible group of lesbian mothers are those who become pregnant through artificial insemination, either using semen donated by a friend or a person contacted through an intermediary, or using semen obtained from a sperm bank or similar service. If a known donor is used, there is some risk that he may later seek visitation or even custody rights. Artificial insemination by donor, on the other hand, entails no legal obligations for the donor and is entirely anonymous. It may be expensive, however, and some physicians may be unwilling to provide the service for unmarried women or for lesbians. For similar reasons, lesbians usually encounter difficulties qualifying as adoptive parents.

Another issue of concern to lesbian mothers is the effect of their stigmatized sexual orientation on their children. Some women, sharing the values of the wider culture, prefer that their children develop a heterosexual orientation and take measures that they feel will encourage their children in that direction. For others, concern centers around the reactions of other children and the possibility that they will tease or harass children whose mothers are known to be lesbian. Both of these concerns, as well as anxiety about custody litigation, may lead mothers to be secretive about their lesbianism.

Much of the literature on lesbian mothers has concerned psychological outcomes for children, particularly the impact of lesbianism on sexual orientation. Virtually all research has shown that maternal homosexuality has no effect on children's later sexual proclivities. Rather, a substantial body of research indicates that children of lesbian mothers fare no differently than children of other single mothers.

There is also a growing literature on lesbian mothers themselves. This has included personal accounts by lesbian mothers, especially of experiences with custody litigation, and a number of practical guides to becoming mothers or to dealing with the legal complexities of lesbian motherhood. A significant legal literature, aimed both at attorneys representing lesbian mothers and at judicial audiences, also has emerged. More work remains to be done in a number of key areas, including the long-term experience of children conceived through artificial insemination and the implications of changing mores on the legal problems faced by lesbian mothers.

Further References. N. D. Hunter and N. D. Polikoff, "Custody Rights of Lesbian Mother: Legal Theory and Litigation Strategy," *Buffalo Law Review* 25 (1976): 691–733. J. Jullion, *Long Way Home: The Odyssey of a Lesbian Mother and Her Children* (San Francisco, 1985). E. Lewin, "Lesbianism and Motherhood: Implications for Child Custody," *Human Organization* 40 (1981): 6–14. C. Pies, *Considering Parenthood: A Workbook for Lesbians* (San Francisco, 1985).

ELLEN LEWIN

LESBIANS are women who choose other women as affectional and sexual partners and who identify themselves as lesbians. In doing so, they break with deepseated cultural assumptions about heterosexuality*, suffer the social consequences of this identification, and create through this sense of difference a community with a distinctive approach to everyday life.

While lesbians are usually defined (and define themselves) in relation to an erotic response or choice, many understand their lesbianism as a specific political commitment centered in their interests in woman-identification and women's political challenge to patriarchal institutions and mythology.

The word *lesbian* itself derives from the Greek Isle of Lesbos and a colony of female homosexuals associated with Sappho of Lesbos, c.600 B.C. The term *lesbian* was redefined positively with the advent of the feminist and gay liberation movements of the 1960s and 1970s. Some lesbians now describe themselves as gay, female homosexuals, or dykes. The author Alice Walker has coined the term *womanist** to describe female bonding among black women.

Lesbian identity derives from social definitions and categorizations that are grounded in specific historical and cultural conditions. "Coming out" is a process of recognition and self-awareness of oneself as a lesbian. This process is not linear, but includes most, if not all, of the following: the realization of erotic interest in women, sexual experiences with women, strong emotional attachments to women, involvement and membership in a lesbian subculture, and transformation of identity. Many women on the route to a lesbian identity deny and repress their desires, interests, and connections to women.

There are lesbians of every race, economic background, age, religious, and political affiliation. Yet lesbians are often invisible. Lesbian invisibility results both from others' denial of the possibility and existence of women-identified relationships and women-centered sexuality as well as from deliberate efforts on the part of lesbians to keep their sexual identity unknown. Lesbians who are members of ethnic communities and racial minorities in the United States often keep their identity unknown to maintain important ties with those communities despite homophobia*.

Lesbians suffer problems similar to those of other women with regard to economic and legal discrimination*, the lack of control over reproduction, limited representation in the major social institutions, violence against women, and ideologies prescribing "proper womanhood" promulgated by religion, the psychological profession, and the media.

But lesbians, as a consequence of their sexual identity, have additional problems as well. They are excluded from legal protection in housing, employment, military service, adoptions, and child custody. Their relationships do not have the economic and social supports of heterosexual married couples. Lack of legal protections and negative cultural attitudes often result in lesbians' denial of their identity to coworkers, friends, or family members. For example, though the vast majority of lesbians are self-supporting and must rely on their own labors for survival, they anticipate discrimination at work; some portion do lose their jobs; and very often these fears and experiences force lesbians to limit their workplace contacts with colleagues and to keep their identity secret.

Crucial to lesbians' survival are their extended family* of friends. These friendship networks support lesbians through major and minor life events, provide the context for kin-like rituals at holiday times, and serve as the source of new lover relationships. Lesbian relationships hold the potential for a unique pairing of equals; however, they, too, must grapple with issues of autonomy and dependence and disparities in couples of age, income, religion, or class.

Many lesbians are mothers of children from heterosexual marriages. Lesbian mothers share with other single women the problems of low income, limited housing, and child care* options. Lesbian mothers, however, also fear child custody battles in which their sexual identity might be used to declare them "unfit mothers." In the 1980s, other lesbians are able to choose to have children through artificial insemination by using formal sperm banks or informal networks of friends willing to donate sperm.

The development of explicitly public and feminist-identified lesbian communities has occurred recently. Between the 1920s and World War II, most lesbians were either isolated or participated in the "homosexual underground" of bars and social clubs in urban bohemian quarters. World War II altered the lives of lesbians who joined the military by advancing their economic independence and fostering the development of urban meeting grounds at which other lesbians could be found. The cultural milieu of the 1950s exercised considerable pressure on lesbians to marry, and the political persecution of the cold war/McCarthy era resulted in serious repression of sexual minorities and political dissidents. Nevertheless, Daughters of Bilitis was formed in 1955 as an organization focused on providing support for lesbians and educating the general public about the "normality" of these women. Most lesbians in the 1950s chose to survive either by being "obvious dykes" who appeared manly to others and worked in jobs traditionally defined as masculine or by being "super ladies" who chose to "pass" as heterosexual women.

The black civil rights movement of the 1960s was the prototype for the early women's and gay liberation movements. The new movements emphasized lesbian and gay pride, the importance of "coming out" and not being invisible, and the positive assertion of rights to end sexual and political oppression. Lesbians have complicated relationships to both the feminist movement and the gay liberation movement.

The 1970s lesbian communities were motivated by feminist politics. Lesbianism was seen as a choice for women in a sexist world. Women's independence from men and the importance of female identification, bonding, and loyalty to other women was encouraged. Lesbian separatism, the repudiation of and withdrawal from male society, was a particular organizational and political strategy that emerged in the early years of lesbian community development. Though not embraced by most lesbians, it was a necessary ingredient in the formation of an alternative feminist culture. The issue of separatism caused conflict within the women's movement and among lesbians themselves. More recently, serious conflict has emerged concerning class and race among lesbians and the extent to which the primarily white and middle-class lesbian communities attend to racism and economic difference. The 1980s saw considerable controversy among lesbians about sexual practice and sexual pleasure.

Some of the most enduring features of lesbian communities are cultural: the creation of presses, publications, and music that assert the distinctiveness of lesbian experience and offer a portrayal of lesbians' lives that makés sense to them. Books about lesbian sexuality, written by lesbians, were published in the early 1980s. Lesbians have also created for themselves and other women coffeehouses, bookstores, and self-help health and other projects in most small and large cities across the country.

Further References. T. Darty and S. Potter (eds.), *Women-Identified Women* (Beverly Hills, Calif., 1984). C. Moraga and G. Anzaldua (eds.), *This Bridge Called My Back: Writings by Radical Women of Color* (Watertown, Mass., 1981). J. P. Stanley and S. J. Wolfe (eds.), *The Coming Out Stories* (Watertown, Mass., 1980). C. Pies, *Considering Parenthood: A Workbook for Lesbians* (San Francisco, 1985).

BETH SCHNEIDER

LEVIRATE is a marriage law or custom by which the widow and a brother (or failing a brother, the nearest male kin) of the deceased husband may or must marry. The dead husband is presumed to continue his duties to his wife and children, and any progeny by the brother are considered to be the children of the deceased.

The custom existed widely in ancient Western Asia (e.g., among the Israelites, Hittites, Assyrians) and is found in Polynesia, Central Africa, the Americas, and elsewhere. In some societies (e.g., Israelites, Malagasy), the law prescribed brother-widow marriage only if the deceased husband had no sons. In Deuteronomy (25: 5–10) only the first son was considered the son of the deceased.

Interpretations vary. Some see the practice as an aspect of patrilineal inheritance, although not all societies with the custom are patriline. Others point to its social utility in providing a system for the maintenance of widows and orphans or to its significance in providing heirs to perform rites and sacrifices for the deceased.

LIBERAL FEMINISM (also Mainstream Feminism) is the bedrock of the women's movement. Most people are probably unaware that there is any other kind of feminism.

Liberal feminism has its roots in eighteenth-century rationalism and the doctrine of natural rights, but because women's position in the home subjected to the arbitrary authority of men was not completely analogous to men's position in society subjected to the arbitrary authority of absolute monarchy, liberal feminism has never fit completely within the restricted framework of political liberalism. However, the basic foundation of liberal feminism was, and remains, that women are "persons" and therefore must be entitled to the same rights and subject to the same responsibilities as men.

The founder of modern feminism, Mary Wollstonecraft, in her *Vindication of the Rights of Women* uses the natural rights rhetoric of the French Revolution to advocate reform of the treatment of women. The thought of Elizabeth Cady

Stanton and Susan B. Anthony was grounded in the doctrine of equal rights, the basis of the American republic and of Jacksonian democracy. And John Stuart Mill's *The Subjection of Women* applies the nineteenth-century liberal ideas of individual liberty, equal civil and political rights, and equal opportunity to women. Mill gave liberal feminist theory its classic formulation, which has been little developed since. As liberal democracy became the preferred political system in the West, liberalism ceased to be thought of as an ideology; it became a normal, accepted political value. Liberal feminism, then, is to the majority of Americans "feminism," a course of action more than a theoretical construct.

Modern liberal feminists tend to be pragmatists, not theorists. In the resurgence of the feminist movement in the 1960s and 1970s liberal feminists tended to be older, often professional women, associated with the "women's rights" wing of the movement in contrast to younger, more radical women associated with the "women's liberation" wing. As professionals who had a stake in the existing system they were interested in working within the system to change conditions: to end legal, economic, political, and social discrimination*, to bring about legal equality, equality of opportunity, freedom of choice, and to destroy or change female stereotypes in education and the media. They created feminist organizations such as the National Organization of Women, Women's Equity Action League, and Women's Political Caucus, which pursue feminist goals through legal action, legislation, lobbying, coalitions, and political action groups.

Liberal feminists believe that sex differences* are confined to reproductive organs and secondary sexual characteristics* and do not extend to mental ability—they dismiss all varieties of biological determinism as biased and unsound scientifically. They are opposed to differential treatment of men and women; therefore, they opposed protective legislation* as essentially denying women equal opportunity. They support an equal rights amendment*, freedom of choice in abortion*, and equal opportunity in education and employment. Many are aware of, and troubled by, the contradiction between affirmative action*, which treats women differentially, and equality, but, as pragmatists, see it as a remedial measure necessary to reform conditions. Their support of women in the military is based on women's right to enter any occupation for which they are qualified, without regard to sex.

Most liberal feminists continue to be, as they have been from the beginning, white middle-class women. But they have been energized, made to examine their ideas and priorities, by more radical feminists. They have achieved a better awareness of the poor, women of color*, and lesbians*. But the major goal of mainstream feminism remains the promotion of the ideals of equal rights and equal treatment for women.

LIBRARIANSHIP. Although the existence of libraries can be traced as far back as the ancient cultures of Sumer and Egypt, modern American library service derived a great deal from England. Probably the first university library was established in 1638, when John Harvard left 400 volumes to the college that was renamed after him. Social libraries (libraries in which members bought stock) and circulating libraries (libraries that charged users rental fees) began in the 1700s. Public libraries came into existence in the nineteenth century, with the Boston Public Library (opened in 1845) being one of the earliest large public libraries.

It appears that the earliest librarians were men. In fact, because some of the social and circulating libraries catered to popular taste (not necessarily literary quality), "[t]he use of these libraries by women went so far as to raise serious doubts about the propriety of teaching the feminine sex to read" (J. H. Shera, *Introduction to Library Science* [Littleton, Colo., 1976], 37). In 1853, the first convention of librarians was held in New York. It was attended by 82 *men* ("librarians, educators, authors, and clergy") (J. K. Gates, *Introduction to Librarianship* [New York, 1968], 87).

Women soon entered the field of librarianship, however. When Melvil Dewey established the first library school in 1887, the majority of students were women. Dewey recruited women into the profession, partially because of economics. Since library resources and funds were limited, Dewey and other leaders in the library movement saw the employment of women as a way to save money. Well-educated women could be employed for less money than men, and since librarianship was one of the few professions open to them, women were content to settle for this inequity (A. R. Schiller, "Sex and Library Careers," in M. Myers and M. Scarborough [eds.], *Women in Librarianship: Melvil's Rib Symposium* [New Brunswick, N.J., 1975], 11–20).

For years the occupation of librarianship has continued to be dominated by women. For example, in 1972 the number of women librarians, archivists, and curators was 129,000 compared to 29,000 men (*A Statistical Portrait of Women in the United States: 1978* [Washington, D.C., 1978], 63). This trend continues to the present day. Of the 3,538 students reported to have graduated from accredited library schools in 1986, 2,585 were reported to be women, and 733 men. (The gender of 220 graduates was not reported.) Of these, 1,840 women and 502 men began careers in library positions. (See C. Learmont and S. Van Houten, "Placement and Salaries 1986: An Upswing," *Library Journal* 112, no. 17 [October 1987]: 27–34.)

The prevalence of women in the library field does not carry over into the top positions, however. The average beginning salary of the 1986 graduates mentioned above was $20,718 for women, while it was $21,498 for men. Another study shows the national median salary for male public library directors is $48,026, while for female public library directors it is $42,486 (K. F. Jones, "Sex, Salaries, and Library Support," *Library Journal* 112, no. 17 [October, 1987]: 35–41). Jones's study does show that this trend may be turning around: in 1985–1987, the percentage of public library directorships held by men decreased, while the percentage of women directorships *increased*. The percentage of male public library directors (58.6 percent) is still greater, however.

CHERYL BECKER

LOCUS OF CONTROL is a theory of individual differences in expectancies for control. The theory states that people learn, through rewards and punishments, to hold certain expectations as to control over the events of their lives. Persons holding internal locus of control beliefs expect personal control over their lives. Those holding external locus of control beliefs place the expectancy for control outside themselves, on luck, fate, chance, or powerful others (J. Rotter, "Generalized Expectancies for Internal-External Control of Reinforcement," *Psychological Monographs* 80 [1966]: 1–28).

Early work with the locus of control construct tended to overgeneralize the concept by labeling people "internals" or "externals," and a great deal of research demonstrated the social, emotional, and psychological superiority of "internals." Hanna Levenson ("Multidimensional Locus of Control in Psychiatric Patients," *Journal of Consulting and Clinical Psychology* 41 [1937]: 397–404), among others, questioned this either/or conceptualization of locus of control. She thought it possible to believe both in the power of luck and in individual effort. Levenson further pointed out that many people believe that not only luck and fate but also powerful other people control their lives. She developed a scale to measure the internal and two external dimensions (chance and powerful others) of the locus of control concept.

P. Gurin et al. (P. Gurin, G. Gurin, R. Lao, and M. Beattie, "Internal-External Control in the Motivational Dynamics of Negro Youth," *Journal of Social Issues* 25 [1969]: 29–53) also objected to the mental health assumptions attached to an internal locus of control. They argued that when outcomes are positive, feelings of internal or personal control are more likely to result in positive mental health. However, when outcomes are negative an internal locus of control can result in self-blame and self-hatred. Gurin et al. also pointed out that for some groups an external locus of control may be more healthy, especially if that external view acknowledges the role of society in determining personal outcomes. Among their sample of low-income blacks, they asserted, it is probably more realistic to acknowledge the societal constraints on individual behavior; racial and economic discrimination* limit personal control. Gurin et al. thus introduced an additional external dimension of locus of control, "system's blame," and demonstrated the healthy consequences of such external beliefs for the politically and economically disadvantaged.

A similar process has been demonstrated with feminists. Feminists were found to be internal on personal control but external on ideological measures and more critical of the system as responsible for women's inferior status in society. Externality for this group was shown to be related to involvement in the feminist movement, a result similar to that found for blacks: involvement in social and collective action for blacks was positively related to a belief in system's blame. Thus, an awareness of systematic factors controlling one's outcomes, especially when coupled with internality on the personal control dimension, seems to motivate one to try to change the system.

A number of studies have found women in general to be more external in their locus of control than men. Self-esteem and sex-role socialization* are cited as possible determinants of the extent of internal-external locus of control. Women with higher self-esteem and less rigid sex-role socialization tend to be more internal in their locus of control. This difference is important in that women with a more internal locus of control are also found to be higher achievers and are probably more assertive. Among recent college student samples, however, there tend to be fewer sex differences in locus of control beliefs.

The locus of control concept has generated a rich body of literature and many questionnaire-format instruments with which to assess locus of control beliefs. In addition to the several general assessment instruments, specialized instruments have been developed to assess locus of control with regard to health, achievement, affiliation, and so on. Current theorists point out the need to include a measure of the value of the reinforcement. Presumably, the extent to which one values health, for example, the more internal or personal will be the expectancy to control health-related behaviors.

PATRICIA ROZEE-KOKER

M

MAMMARY GLANDS (BREASTS) are modified sweat glands present in both males and females. Under the influence of estrogen and progesterone, the glands in young girls begin to grow and develop during puberty. (See PUBERTAL PROCESSES.) Further development takes place during pregnancy under the influence of the hormone prolactin from the anterior pituitary gland as well as increasing levels of estrogen and progesterone. The association of the breasts with the reproductive system is indirect and functional. They secrete milk for the nourishment of the infant. Each mammary gland is a skin-covered elevation positioned over the chest muscles usually over the second to sixth rib. Just below the center of each mammary gland is a pigmented protruding *nipple* surrounded by a pigmented circular *areola*. Smooth muscles within the areola and nipple cause the nipple to become erect when stimulated.

Internally each gland consists of 15 to 20 lobes of glandular tissue arranged radially around the nipple. Each lobe terminates in a single *lactiferous duct* that opens onto the nipple. The lobes are separated and surrounded by adipose tissue. The amount of adipose tissue determines the size and shape of the breast. There is considerable variation due to genetic differences, age, percentage of body fat, or pregnancy. Size of mammary gland has nothing to do with the ability of a woman to nurse an infant or with the amount of milk produced.

FRANCES GARB

MAMMOGRAPHY. See CANCER

MANAGEMENT. Women in management are a phenomenon of the times. The ascendancy of women executives into positions of power in corporate suites of American business and in the service sectors has been one of the most important developments of recent years. Although they have made progress into and throughout the lower- and middle-management ranks, there are barriers and differences between men and women in similar positions. To understand those barriers and differences we look at demographics, attitudes, and beliefs that affect women's progress and performance.

Demographics. Participation rates of women in the labor force continue to grow. In the 1970s women's labor force participation rate was 43 percent. This rate grew to 53 percent in 1983, and is projected to reach 60 percent in 1995. In the period between 1972 and 1983 the number of women in executive ranks in U.S. business more than doubled from 1.4 million to 3.5 million.

Although the number of women, both in the workforce and in management positions, has grown, there are wide gaps in the salaries earned by male and female executives. Weekly earnings of wage and salary workers who usually work full-time in occupations employing 50,000 and more in the census classification of executive, administrative, and management in 1983 showed a total of 8,117,000 employed. Men in these categories numbered 5,344,000 and received $530 average weekly earnings. Women numbered 2,772,000 with average weekly earnings of $340. The ratio of females employed in these categories was 35 percent of the total. Their average salary was 36 percent less than the average male salary (*Monthly Labor Review* 101, no. 1 [January 1985]: 54–59).

Education levels continue to climb for workforce members. One-fourth of the adult labor force between ages 25 and 64 have attended college. This figure shows that numbers of college-educated participants have risen for three consecutive years. Population increase and a higher participation rate for females contribute to this rise. Thirty-eight percent of all employed persons with four years of college are female. The majority of workers in the professional specialist and executive, administrative, and management classification (52 percent of the males and 35 percent of the females) have a college degree. The younger workers are more likely to have at least a bachelor's degree. It is expected that the requirement for managers to complete advanced studies will increase as more technical expertise and specific knowledges are needed by managers.

Occupational employment projections for the period 1984–1995 predict that three major occupational groups will have the largest proportion of college-educated workers with postsecondary technical training*. Executive, administrative, and managerial workers are one of those groups and are predicted to increase by 22 percent during that period. A continued demand for increased numbers of salaried managers is projected as firms continually depend on trained management specialists. Projections show that women will account for 60 percent of labor force growth during that period. Since women are earning more than one-half of all bachelor's degrees, it would seem that opportunities for women at managerial levels will continue to grow.

Attitudes and Beliefs. Both men's and women's attitudes are changing. Young women are facing the fact that if they marry, they still will work at least 25 years. They also know that with a high divorce rate they are likely to find themselves as head of a household. This knowledge encourages them to take career preparation seriously and to think in long-range terms rather than in discrete time intervals. They are setting goals beyond the immediate. At the same time, role socialization for males is changing too. Men are beginning to deal with their feelings. They are better able to relate to women and are becoming more supportive of changes in female roles. Men are expressing a greater willingness to work with and for women. Women are taking positions of authority and are treating those roles seriously. Women are continuing to gain in the traits and skills needed to succeed in management. Both sexes are becoming more aware of the potential for women and more supportive of women in their efforts to succeed. Surprisingly, men seem to have moved further along the acceptance and supportive scale for women than many women have. There are still pockets of resistance toward women executives from other women.

Competitiveness, assertiveness, and decisiveness traits are associated with success in management. In a study by Anne Harlan and Carol Weiss ("Sex Differences in Factors Affecting Managerial Career Advancement," in P. A. Wallace [ed.], *Women in the Workplace* [Boston, 1982]) men and women were found to have basically the same attitudes and motivations. Women are expressing positive attitudes toward success, are concerned about results, and continue to express a desire for responsibility. Persistence, ambition, integrity, and a concern for effective resource utilization are traits shared by both successful men and women managers. The elements for success are becoming more favorable for females as attitudes change. However, as more women achieve middle management, very few have broken through what is popularly known as the "glass ceiling" to the top. Rosabeth Kanter (*Men and Women of the Corporation* [New York, 1977] in her classic study discusses some of the structural barriers that inhibit women's progress. One of these is lack of power. Howard Smith and Mary Grenier advise women to analyze the organization to determine the informal power structure and to seek out those departments and positions that are central to the organization and that control resources and uncertainty ("Sources of Organizational Power for Women: Overcoming Structural Obstacles," *Sex Roles* 8 [1982]: 733–746).

Summary. Greater numbers of women continue to enter the workforce. Their rise in the ranks of management will continue. There are several things that women can do to help themselves and other women succeed.

They need to continue to develop their competencies through college preparation and experience. These may be technical and knowledge competencies, as formal education. Women must continue to improve their competencies in resource utilization. The resources may be money, material, or human resources. To be effective managers women must learn how to attract and use all resources well; and they must continue to develop their administrative competencies.

As competencies increase, women will become more confident. They are more confident of their own ability and willingness to use their competencies. As they become more confident of their own competencies, they are freed up to be more confident of the ability and willingness of other women to use their competencies. Increased competence and confidence will result in women's ability to gain acceptance, respect, and a portable credibility in the eyes of others. The barriers related to position, authority, and salary will erode as attitudes and beliefs change. The future for women in management continues to improve.

Further References. "Is a New Male Manager Emerging?" *Fortune* 113 (February 3, 1986): 135–136. Korn/Ferry International, *Profile of Women Senior Executives* (New York, 1982 and 1985). *Monthly Labor Review* 108, nos. 1, 2, 5, and 11 (1985) for census data. "More and More, She's the Boss," in "Economy and Business," *Time* 126 (December 2, 1985): 64-66. C. D. Sutton and K. K. Moore, "Executive Women—20 Years Later," *Harvard Business Review* 63, no. 5 (September-October 1985): 42–66.

MARGARET FENN

MARITAL PROPERTY. Property acquired during marriage. To achieve a more equitable distribution of property at divorce, all common-law property states except Mississippi classify certain property acquired during marriage, regardless of title ownership, as spousal or marital property, subject to division at divorce. Like community property* in community property states, traditionally marital property includes all earned income, savings, interest, dividends, all returns on investments, and property purchased with that income (e.g., home, automobile). Traditionally, it does not include property brought to the marriage or property acquired through inheritance or certain gifts received after marriage. Today divorcing couples are likely to have relatively little of their wealth invested in the traditional forms of property and more in "new property" such as pensions, insurance, professional degrees, and intangibles such as goodwill built up in a business or future earning capacity. States vary widely in their acceptance of this "new property" as marital property. As yet very few include intangible assets.

The advantages of the marital property concept and the growing awareness that marriage is an economic partnership to which both parties contribute led to the idea of extending the concept to the entire marriage, not just to divorce settlement. The Uniform Marital Property Act (1983), a model law that states may adopt, establishes marital property within the common-law property system. It recognizes marriage as a partnership to which each spouse makes an equal contribution and in which each has an equal share. Its marital property laws are based on laws in community property states, but common-law features are also incorporated. The spouses share ownership of marital property throughout the duration of marriage. Management, however, is by whichever spouse holds the title. In 1984 Wisconsin became the first state to adopt a marital property system based on the Uniform Marital Property Act.

MARKEDNESS, in linguistics, is a characteristic of two categories that appear, on one level, as a pair of complementary opposites, but that are, on a higher level, in a hierarchical relationship. Gender categories are so characterized. On one level the categories masculine and feminine appear as opposites (man, woman); on a different level, the feminine is contained within the masculine (woman as part of Man). The member of the pair with the broader, more inclusive meaning is "unmarked." The more narrowly defined term is "marked."

MARRIAGE is a legally and socially sanctioned institution that has existed in every society but under widely different forms. It is, generally speaking, an approved sexual relationship, in almost all cases between one or more women and one or more men. There are instances of legally approved same-sex marriages but they are rare.

Marriage provides the basic unit for the procreation and rearing of offspring, the sexual division of labor, production and consumption, and fulfilling personal needs of affection and companionship. Through a legally sanctioned marriage offspring acquire legitimacy and the rights that go with legitimacy, including inheritance rights.

The relationships within marriage are, to a large extent, governed by the laws, customs, and mores of the community. Choice of partner, work roles, rights to children, division of authority, dissolution of marriage, remarriage, and division of inheritance are all regulated, at least to some degree. Incest taboo is universal, but the proscribed degrees of kindred differ. Only parent-child sexual relations are universally condemned. Sexual division of labor is also universal, but "men's work" and "women's work" are not everywhere the same. Authority in patriarchal societies (in which the vast majority of people have lived for at least the last 5,000 to 6,000 years) resides ultimately in the male, although the extent of subordination of females has varied widely over time and place.

The condition of subordination in America and Europe in the nineteenth century was such that marriage reform was a priority of the feminist movement that began in mid-century. Some gains were made, but marriage reform remains a major concern of second-wave feminism. Some feminists think that the abolition of marriage and the family is the only solution to women's subordination. Others think that reforms in education, institutions, and attitudes can turn marriage into an egalitarian relationship. (See also FAMILY and FAMILY AS A SOCIO-ECONOMIC UNIT.)

MARRIAGE PENALTY (MARRIAGE TAX). A married couple, both of whom are employed, pay more income tax than an unmarried couple, both of whom are employed. Under U.S. income tax law, married couples must pay tax on the sum of their income. Since the income tax is progressive, the tax will be higher on the combined income of two people than it would be if the incomes were taxed separately. The difference is called the marriage penalty or marriage tax.

A two-earner couple, however, pays less tax than a single person would pay on an income equal to the couple's combined income. Also penalized are single parents. Households headed by currently unmarried mothers (or fathers) are not taxed as leniently as households headed by a couple, only one of whom receives income. The tax rate for single heads of household is between the single person and the two-earner married couple rates. The marriage penalty has the effect of encouraging unmarried employed couples to remain unmarried and unwaged housewives to remain out of the labor market.

MARXIST FEMINISM. A materialist analysis of the social relations of gender. Marxist feminist theory claims that social relationships of capitalist production determine the ideology and organization of social relationships of reproduction which, in turn, reinforce the exploitation of women in nonsocialist systems. Elimination of the oppression of women depends on the dual transformation of capitalist relations of production and patriarchal relations of reproduction.

Marxist feminists argue that Marx's own theories provide an inadequate analysis of the oppression of women, but that Marxism can be amended and broadened to include the analysis of patriarchy*. Nevertheless, priority is given to economic factors.

Early Marxist feminist work relied heavily on the writings of Charles Fourier and Friedrich Engels as well as the fragmentary comments of Marx on the "woman question." Tracing the roots of patriarchy back to the origins of private property, as Engels had, theorists assumed that women's exploitation would be ended when they were integrated more fully into the workforce, with the structure and organization of work democratically controlled without class or sex distinctions. But when women's status in Soviet-styled socialist systems provided evidence to challenge that assumption, theorists looked to the structure and nature of women's work within the domestic sphere*, and contended that exploitation of women within "the family" would not end automatically with increased female participation in the paid labor force. Instead, women's paid labor would be added to their labor at home, creating a "double burden" of exploitation.

The demand for "wages for housework" reflected the analysis of the hidden exploitation of women. This exploitation, theorists contended, was hidden by measuring exploitation by the amount of labor time appropriated beyond that necessary to reproduce the worker. The "costs" of reproducing the worker included the costs, measured in time, of the "free" labor of the worker's spouse, whose domestic chores included a wide range of manual, emotional, and intellectual activities to maintain the home and family* deemed essential to the worker's survival. Reminiscent of the late nineteenth-century demands for a "family wage," Marxist feminists demands for "wages for housework" are concerns for the economic autonomy of women.

Consideration of how patriarchal gender hierarchies reinforced, and were reinforced by, class relations under capitalism required detailed analyses of the ideology and structure of the bourgeois familial ideal. Marxist feminists explored the economics and psychology of women's work* within the family*, and the ways that this work was structured to maintain patriarchal power relations within the home, the economy, and the state against the logic of capitalist rationalization of the productive process. By transforming the family itself into a "market" for capitalist goods and by redefining the nature of women's mothering responsibilities, the capitalist system worked to sustain patriarchy despite the fact that its productive requirements seemed to contribute to the development of more sex-neutral definitions of labor power.

There was considerable debate about the dynamics of this process. Some claimed that treating capitalism and patriarchy as discrete systems of social control begged the question of accounting for the centrality of the sexual division of labor* under capitalism. If the development of capitalism required the construction of a private domain within which to satisfy the laborer's needs for human comfort in ways that would reinforce capitalist production, the reasons why this necessitated the labor of women in the home required explanation. Some argued that more rigorous historical documentation was needed before accounting for the sexual division of labor through the ideology of patriarchy. Later theorists contributed to the development of this archival record. They documented how the effects of the ideological redefinition of women's reproductive and childrearing roles; the actions of employers to reduce women's wages to accord with the bourgeois ideal of womanhood; and the exclusion of women from certain trades by unionists to avoid the depression of wages, along with the interpretation of protective labor legislation by legislatures and courts, combined to reinforce the segmentation of the labor market along sex lines.

Other Marxist feminists, influenced by psychoanalytic feminists, turned to the analysis of the way that the female monopoly over early child care* affected the development of the ideology of male superiority as well as submission to the requirements of capitalist production. Mothering in the context of the nuclear household, these theorists argued, created a sexual division of psychic organization and development that perpetuated the social organization of gender along traditional patriarchal lines. This psychoanalytic turn in theory allowed for consideration of how the internalization of cultural norms, developing different relational needs and capacities in men and women and contributing to the psychological reproduction of women as mothers, perpetuated and reinforced patriarchal relations in the home and at work outside the home. The insights of this theory were connected to the demand for "equal parenting."

Most recently, Marxist feminists have turned their attention to analysis of the ways that the development of the modern welfare state have further contributed to the maintenance of patriarchal relations in society, even as it has buffered the effects of economic hardship for single-parent families headed by females. Women's economic dependence on individual males has been replaced by their dependence on mostly male-oriented state bureaucracies, according to these theorists. They have attempted to develop a theory that would account for the situation of women in terms of their often conflicting roles as persons, citizens, mothers, workers, and welfare recipients.

KATHLEEN B. JONES

MASCULINITY. See FEMININITY

MASOCHISM. Term introduced by ethologist/sexologist Richard von Krafft-Ebing (c.1901) in reference to sexual "perversions" detailed in the novellas of Leopold von Sacher-Masoch (b.1836). The writings of Sacher-Masoch regularly featured the sexual subordination of men to women. Krafft-Ebing used the term to describe the phenomenon wherein the individual derives sexual gratification by being completely and unconditionally subjected to the will of a person of the opposite sex, deriving sexual gratification from enslavement, humiliation, and abuse.

Krafft-Ebing introduced the term to the sexology literature, but it was left to Sigmund Freud and his followers, specifically Helene Deutsch and Marie Bonaparte, to make it a permanent feature of psychological discourse on women. They transformed the theme of Sacher-Masoch's novellas (subordination of men to women) into a metaphor for male neurosis, but an innate feature of psychological femininity*. Freud located masochism in his larger theory of *thanatos*, and *eros*, death and life drives. His theory outlined three types of masochism, *moral*, *erotogenic*, and *feminine*. In his paper "The Economic Problem of Masochism" Freud distinguished the three: the first was a norm of behavior, the second a condition imposed on sexual excitation, but the final, feminine masochism, was "an expression of feminine nature." For males, masochism is linked in part to unresolved feelings of guilt that only pain can alleviate. Part of the source of this guilt, Freud theorized, was the wish to be beaten by the father, a wish to have a "passive female relation to him." For women, however, masochism was a natural extension of their biological experience of coitus and childbirth. Freud's disciple, Helene Deutsch, concluded that women are naturally masochistic. She noted that much of what is pleasurable to women (sex and motherhood) is, indeed, painful. The distinction between the tolerance for pain and the enjoyment of it was not addressed in these theories.

It was left to psychoanalysts interested in sociocultural factors of personality to connect women's social subjugation to their "desire" to be dominated by men, to their "innate" masochism. In the early 1930s, psychoanalysts Clara Thompson and Karen Horney each located instances of so-called masochism in the structural constraints on female sexuality and behavior. Thompson called it "an adaptation to a circumscribed life," and noted that Freud based much of his theory of feminine masochism on his therapy with passive male homosexuals. Horney saw the cultural influences on women as so powerful that some degree of masochism was seemingly inevitable.

It is interesting to note how Sacher-Masoch's erotic vision of male subordination has become so completely subsumed into a theory of feminine psychology. Both the professional and the public mythology that women secretly, manipulatively, or unconsciously enjoy abuse remains—to the extent that the concept of masochism has become a foundation of clinical theories about female personality and, specifically, about abused women. The enjoyment/endurance argument persists to this day.

Current research into woman abuse, female personality development, and mental illness* continue the controversy. It has been researchers in woman abuse and victimization, such as Lenore Walker and Paula Caplan, who have sought to counter the myth of women's masochism. Walker traces women's endurance of physical abuse to both social conditioning and the cumulative effects of defenselessness and emotional exhaustion. Caplan has traced women's endurance of victimization to its roots in the female role in society and the institutionalized right of men to abuse women. The very question "why does she stay?" tends to presuppose that a woman chooses to endure abuse, that she, indeed, has *real* choice.

The vast body of recent empirical research on woman abuse finds no evidence for unconscious masochism. The last study to seriously entertain the masochism hypothesis as an explanation was published in the early 1960s. Since the 1970s, the majority of writers in the field have devoted their energies to refuting the masochism hypothesis, and empirical evidence provides little support for the assumption that masochism has any role in women's endurance of abusive relationships.

In modern psychiatry, the word has evolved from a description of a sexual perversion to a categorization of a persistent pattern of self-defeating behavior. Still, however, it has remained a "feminine" characteristic and has come to be applied to self-sacrifice, even to altruistic behaviors, particularly as they are practiced by women. In 1985, the American Psychiatric Association (ApA) proposed a new category for its manual of clinical diagnosis (DSM III): "Masochistic female personality disorder." Assailed by feminists and therapists for being sexist in name and victim-blaming in spirit, the ApA revised the name to "Self-defeating personality disorder." Although feminists, therapists, and researchers remain uncomfortable with its implications, the category has been added to the revised appendix of the new manual, and "self-defeating" behavior has become the newest metaphor for enduring domination and the newest way to imagine that women enjoy it.

Further References. P. Caplan, *The Myth of Women's Masochism* (New York, 1985). K. Horney, *Feminine Psychology* (New York, 1967). C. Thompson, *On Women* (New York, 1964). L. Walker, *The Battered Woman* (New York, 1979).

ALYSON L. BURNS

MATERNAL INSTINCT. A presumed biological readiness, desire, or ability to mother. Speculations about such an instinct go back to ancient times and have figured predominantly in scientific theories since the time of Charles Darwin. In the late nineteenth and early twentieth centuries, such leading psychologists as William James, William McDougall, and G. Stanley Hall argued that women have a special need and ability to protect and care for the young. Theorists linked this maternal "instinct" to women's purported emotionality and tendency to focus on the immediate and concrete. Even in the behaviorist era that followed, when the idea of instinct fell into disrepute, many psychologists continued to refer to innate motherly feelings or abilities.

In recent years, formal instinct theories have not found wide acceptance in academic psychology. However, the assumption of a biological basis for maternal behavior has figured in psychological speculations on the importance of perinatal "bonding" between mother and child (for which there is no empirical support) and in the evolutionary theories of ethologists and sociobiologists. Sociobiologists consider a human maternal instinct to be a predictable response to the facts of procreation: since males can impregnate many females but females can transmit their genes to only a limited number of offspring, females are assumed to be more willing to protect their genetic investment in any given child.

In traditional conceptualizations, an instinct is an adaptive, complex, genetically programmed behavior pattern performed without learning by all appropriate members of a species in the presence of a specific stimulus. Such fixed patterns are well documented in many nonhuman animal species. Thus a spider will spin an intricate web without being taught to do so, and a wolf will howl in a certain way even if it has never heard the howl of another wolf. However, contemporary scientists generally agree that fixed, automatic patterns of complex behavior do not exist in human beings. Certainly none of the hundreds of behaviors that go into infant and child care emerge automatically in all women.

More recent approaches to instinctive behavior emphasize biological *predispositions* to engage in certain behaviors under given conditions rather than fixed behavior patterns. Again, ethological work has established the existence of such predispositions in nonhuman species, including, in many, a maternal predisposition to nurture the young. The clearest examples are in lower animals. For example, after female rats give birth, they ordinarily respond to their young by nursing, building a nest, and retrieving pups that wander off. In contrast, male rats typically have nothing to do with newborns and may even attack them. After a few days of contact, males will lick and retrieve the young, but they still do not feed them or build nests. Virgin female rats also take longer than new mothers to show parental behavior. Hormones may influence maternal behavior in female rats postpartum; when virgin females are injected with blood plasma from rats that have recently given birth, their maternal behavior reportedly begins sooner than it otherwise would.

Evidence from higher animals, however, is far less clear. Moreover, many biologists and social scientists question the common practice among ethologists of generalizing from animal to human behavior. They observe, too, that not all animals are alike. Ethologists looking for a maternal instinct have tended to concentrate on species in which parental sex differences* are obvious and follow human stereotypes, e.g., baboons and rhesus monkeys. But in many other species males play an active part in infant care. Male mice help care for their young, some male birds take turns sitting on eggs and feeding new hatchlings, and male wolves aid in feeding by regurgitating food. Male owl monkeys, titi monkeys, and marmosets carry infants around, handing them over to their mothers only for nursing.

Other problems plague theories of maternal instinct. For example, equating an instinct with a predisposition or with readiness makes the concept difficult if not impossible to evaluate scientifically, since then it is not susceptible to disconfirmation. If the predicted behavior occurs, one can argue that conditions were right for its emergence. If it does not, one can argue ad hoc that conditions must have been wrong; the instinct exists but has not been activated. In addition, arguments for a maternal instinct have difficulty explaining the many examples of neglectful, cruel, and even murderous behavior by human mothers toward their children. In tribal cultures that practice or condone infanticide*, it is often the mothers who kill their infants. In the eighteenth century, middle- and upper-class European women commonly sent their offspring to live with wet nurses under conditions that almost ensured an early death. During the Victorian era many women abandoned or killed their illegitimate children rather than face scandal.

Historically, reliance on instinct as an explanation of parental behavior has discouraged empirical investigation of fathering and of male responses to children. However, researchers have begun to fill the gaps. They find that in the United States, fathers of newborns are as likely as mothers to hold their babies, rock them, talk to them, smile at them, and look directly at them. They are also as competent as mothers in handling them. Women do tend to react more enthusiastically than men to unfamiliar infants, but there is evidence that males suppress their responses in public in accordance with social norms. While it is likely that unlearned responses to the young do exist in both sexes, the specific conditions under which such responses emerge or fail to emerge remain to be determined.

In the meantime, popular belief in a maternal instinct continues to have far-ranging social and personal consequences, including pressure on women to procreate, feelings of guilt in women who wish to or must remain childless, feelings of inadequacy in women who mother, acceptance by both men and women of women's greater responsibility for children, and lack of social and economic supports for childrearing.

Further References. S. Shields, "To Pet, Coddle, and 'Do For': Caretaking and the Concept of Maternal Instinct," in Miriam Lewin (ed.), *In the Shadow of the Past: Psychology Portrays the Sexes* (New York, 1984). C. Tavris and C. Wade, *The Longest War: Sex Differences in Perspective*, 2nd ed. (San Diego, 1984) [see esp. pp. 68–71 and 159–163].

CAROLE WADE

MATH ANXIETY. A fear of mathematics and a conviction that one does not understand math, has never understood it, and never will understand it. Both women and men have math anxiety, but more women seem to have it than men and women avoid mathematics more than men. From high school, females take relatively fewer math courses than males, and girls consistently score lower than boys on standardized mathematics tests from about the age of 14.

In the mid–1970s, at the same time that women students were being urged to enter nontraditional fields such as the physical sciences and engineering, there was growing concern about the overall decline of interest in mathematics

(13, 723 fewer bachelor's degrees in mathematics were awarded in 1981 than in 1971) and particularly about the decline in test scores on nationally used standardized tests.

John Ernest's "Mathematics and Sex" (*American Mathematics Monthly* 83 [1976]: 595–614) was preprinted by the Ford Foundation and sent to educators all over the country. Research mounted and workshops and special programs for the "math anxious" were started. Special programs geared specifically toward women were sponsored by women's colleges, women's centers, affirmative action offices, and university mathematics and engineering departments.

Some researchers concluded that the major problem for women is not math anxiety but math avoidance, and that if four years of mathematics were required of all high school students, the drop in girls' test scores would be eliminated. However, the National Mathematics Assessment tests in 1978 and 1982 distinguished scores on the basis of the amount of mathematics taken, and the results continued to show that girls outperform boys by a slight margin until age 14, then boys outperform girls by about three percentage points (National Assessment of Educational Progress, *Third National Mathematical Assessment: Results, Trends and Issues* [Washington, D.C., 1983]).

Sociobiologists, talking about visual spatial perception and brain lateralization, credit the differences in ability to genetic differences in men and women. Feminist mathematicians, sociologists, and psychologists found abundant environmental evidence to explain the differences. From birth, girls are protected, encouraged to be less independent, less adventurous than boys. Gender-specific toys and games encourage passivity in girls; movement, interest in speed, and eye-hand coordination in boys. Girls are not encouraged to take toys apart, but it is expected of boys—taking dolls apart is just not the same as dismantling trucks anyway. Parents often accept poor performances from girls that they would not tolerate in boys. Some parents deliberately discourage their daughters from taking advanced math programs.

The attitudes of teachers also discourage mathematical achievement in girls. It was found that girls are called upon less than boys, are not encouraged as much to perform well, and are treated more leniently when they fail. Textbooks used in mathematics classes were found to be highly sexist. When they did not completely ignore girls and women, they presented the worst possible stereotypes, insulting and denigrating to women.

Researchers found that a major difference between boys and girls who do not like math is that girls give up much more easily than boys. Once they pass the minimum requirements, girls are free to avoid math, boys aren't—they know that math is needed for their careers. Among girls, math avoidance is a greater problem than math anxiety.

Another factor cited was the pressure on girls, once they reached adolescence (the time that their math scores drop), to not compete with boys academically and to pay more attention to being popular than to getting good grades. Peer pressure may make a girl decide not to get good grades in math or not to take any math beyond tenth grade geometry.

By the mid–1980s women still took less mathematics in high school and college than men, more women disliked mathematics more than men disliked mathematics, and girls still scored lower in mathematics on national tests such as the college boards and SATs. Nevertheless, there was improvement. Sexism* is less pervasive in textbooks, more parents and teachers are encouraging girls to perform well in math, and more women are taking more math courses in high school and college. The rise in the number and the percentage of women graduates in engineering and the physical sciences has been conspicuous. The percentage of women graduates in engineering rose from 0.8 percent in 1970 to 12.5 percent in 1985. In the physical sciences, women's share of earned doctorates rose from 5.6 percent in 1970 to 16.2 percent in 1985. Of the degrees given in mathematics, in 1970 women earned 37.4 percent of the bachelor's degrees and 8.4 percent of the doctor's; in 1985 their share had increased to 46.1 percent and 15.6 percent respectively (Center for Education Statistics, *Digest of Education Statistics, 1987* [Washington, D.C., 1987]).

The number of women in fields that require competence in calculus or advanced mathematics is still very low when compared with the numbers in traditional fields that require little or no mathematics, but if present trends continue, as more high school girls realize that mathematics is vital to their futures the gap in test scores should gradually close.

MATING AND DATING GRADIENT, an informal process for defining an appropriate field of marriage-eligibles, helps to ensure that higher-status females are more likely to date, and therefore to marry, higher-status males than lower-status males. The dating and mating gradient was first described by Williard Waller, then a sociologist at the Pennsylvania State University, in an article published in 1937.

In the United States, marriage* is a more important determinant of the social position of women than of men; women tend to take on the social status of their husbands, while the husband's social status is more determined by his occupation, income, or wealth. Marriage, and the dating process that leads to marriage, thus tends to be more important for women (and their parents) than for men. Cultural norms prescribe that women should strive to move up the status hierarchy (or at least to remain stable) through their mate selection.

Waller and other family sociologists argue that dating as a process for mate selection first emerged alongside modernization, especially after World War I, in the United States. The institution of dating weakens the traditional family control of its children's mate selection. The dating and mating gradient developed to limit children's choices of dating partners and thus to increase the likelihood that children would choose an "appropriate" (from the family's perspective) mate.

As Waller first described it at the Pennsylvania State University, the dating and mating gradient operated within the Greek fraternity and sorority system. Each fraternity and sorority had a prestige ranking on campus. Students dated in accord with the ranking: members of high-prestige sororities dated only members of high-prestige fraternities. A key object in dating was to reassert one's status by showing off the high ranking of one's date. Waller argued that this "dating gradient" operated primarily in casual dating rather than in marriage-oriented dating. Later research found that serious, marriage oriented dating followed the same patterns Waller had described for casual dating.

Ira Reiss, in further explorations of the gradient, argued that the dating patterns of a group follow the social-class origins of the group so that dating facilitates endogamous marriage (people marry people of similar social characteristics). That is, young people date in accordance with their parental social class, race, religious, and ethnic backgrounds. A series of studies supported this argument. Parents usually want their children to marry someone of a similar (or higher) social class; campus dating systems unintentionally achieve this because of the ways in which they reflect parental social class. Little work has been done with noncampus dating patterns, but sociologists argue that the concern for endogamy is widely distributed among American families.

The dating and mating gradient is a primary method used by middle-class American families to get their daughters married to the "right" man. Operating primarily on college campuses, it is an institutionalized way for preserving class endogamy* by narrowing dating choices to a field of eligibles composed of persons of the same class, ethnic, religious, and economic stratum.

Further References. I. L. Reiss, *Family Systems in America*, 3rd ed. (New York, 1980). J. F. Scott, "Sororities and the Husband Game," *Trans-Action* 2 (1965): 10–14. W. Waller, "Rating and Dating Complex," *American Sociological Review* 2 (1937): 727–737.

ALLEN SCARBORO

MATRIARCHY is a system in which women rule. J. J. Bachofen (*Das Mutterrecht*, 1861), John McLennon (*Primitive Marriage*, 1865), and Lewis Henry Morgan (*Ancient Society*, 1877) theorized that all societies passed through a matriarchal period before the development of herding and agriculture (as opposed to hoe culture). Morgan (followed by Friedrich Engels in *Origin of the Family, Private Property, and the State*, 1884) believed that herding and agriculture, by enabling men to accumulate property, brought about patriarchy* and the subjection of women. Other evolutionary anthropologists denied that there had ever been a matriarchal period.

By the early twentieth century anthropologists began to distinguish between matrilineal descent, matrilocal residence patterns, and rule by women. In the general movement of British and American anthropologists away from general evolutionary theories toward functionalism, matriarchal theories were no longer considered viable.

The idea of matriarchy has been revived by some feminist anthropologists and by some cultural and socialist feminists. They do not, however, see matriarchy as a female version of patriarchy, but as an egalitarian society in harmony with nature. They cite the newly recognized importance of gathering in the economy of foraging societies, the widespread worship of mother goddesses, and evidence from female burials as indications that women occupied a different and higher place in prehistoric society. Other feminists believe male dominance has been universal and dismiss matriarchy as wishful thinking. Even as wishful thinking, however, matriarchy has served as an important symbol. Women utopian writers, philosophers, and poets have used the concept to construct their vision of the future.

MATRIFOCALITY is a term usually applied to a culture system in which the mother has the major responsibility for the economic and social well-being of the family. The father is often absent or, if present, plays a weak role in domestic life. Black Caribbean family groups and the separate units of compound poly- gamous families in some areas of Africa are cited as examples of matrifocality. In the United States matrifocality is associated with poverty*. The term has also been used to describe British working-class family life, in which there is a strong division between the domestic sphere*, where the mother is the dominant figure, and the public sphere*, where the male has authority.

MATRILINY is a lineage system in which kinship and descent are traced through the female. Although there are many variations among matrilineal societies, in general, women are responsible for the care of the children and adult males have authority over women and children; however, that authority is divided: the father- husband having authority over the nuclear family and a male of the mother's family, most likely the brother or oldest son, having authority over the lineage.

Although matrilocality* is thought to have been a necessary, but not deter- mining, precondition for the original appearance of matriliny, matrilineal soci- eties are not necessarily matrilocal. Either can exist without the other. (The Hopi are both matrilineal and matrilocal; the Trobrianders of the South Pacific are matrilineal and patrilocal.) Today less than half of the matrilineal societies are also matrilocal.

Survivals of matriliny in later patriarchal-patrilineal societies (as the Hebrew and the Bronze Age Greeks) have been found. At present, matrilineal societies are scattered over the world with concentrations in Africa, the Pacific, and North America. They are most common in the Pacific Islands and among American Indians of the eastern grasslands and the arid southwest.

Further Reference. D. M. Schneider and K. Gough (eds.), *Matrilineal Kinship* (Berkeley, 1961).

MATRILOCALITY. A residence pattern in which a married couple settles with or near the wife's family. Matrilocality may have been a precondition for the development of matrilineal descent, but each can exist without the other (e.g., matrilocal residence in patrilineal neo-Babylonia). The Hopi and the Apache are examples of matrilocal societies.

MEDICALIZATION OF MOTHERHOOD. See SCIENTIFIC MOTHER-HOOD

MEDICINE, WOMEN IN. See HEALTH CARE PROVIDERS

MENARCHE, the first menstrual bleeding, results from multiple and complex neuroendocrine processes that occur throughout puberty. Menarche usually occurs late in the four- to five-year span needed for observable pubertal changes, such as breast development, growth spurt, and pubic hair growth.

There are tremendous variations in the age of onset of menarche. Generally, the mean age of menarche in American girls is reported to be 12.5 to 13 years of age, with 95 percent of girls reaching menarche between 10.5 and 14.5 years. However, age of menarche is dependent upon cultural and environmental differences as well as individual differences related to genetic characteristics. Thus, menarche can be reached anywhere between 9 and 16 years and, with few exceptions, still be considered within the normal range of development.

Over the past century, the mean age of menarche has gradually declined by two to four months with each passing decade. This decline, referred to as the secular trend in the age at menarche, is attributed to improved nutritional standards and an increased opportunity for health care. With health and nutrition at higher levels in American girls, it is generally concluded that the age of menarche has plateaued.

Menarche has both biological and psychological significance. Biologically, menarche signals one's "becoming" reproductively capable. Regular cyclicity of the hormonal patterns important for initiating and maintaining a pregnancy do not usually occur simultaneously with menarche. In addition, the majority of menstrual cycles remain anovulatory (i.e., without releasing an egg) throughout the early menarcheal years. Even though regularity in hormones and ovulation is not usually attained immediately at menarche, it is possible to become pregnant shortly after menarche or in rare instances even prior to menarche, if the very first egg is fertilized.

Psychologically, menarche may bring with it mixed feelings and emotions. Some girls may feel proud or grown up at the onset of menarche while simultaneously having negative feelings or anxiety. In general, however, girls today view menarche as less traumatic than was reported in the past. Parents may also experience ambivalent feelings when their adolescent reaches menarche; this is a sign of the daughter's impending adulthood and growing up, and a sign of the parents' aging. Research on changes in parent-adolescent interactions suggests that around the midpoint of the pubertal process, adolescents begin to press for greater voice in family decision-making, especially pertaining to themselves;

parents may resist and cause greater conflict or suppress the adolescent's attempts, or they may accommodate a relationship with more autonomy and responsibility for the adolescent. The role which menarche plays in parent-adolescent relations continues to be explored.

Further References. D. Apter and R. Vihko, "Hormonal Patterns of the First Menstrual Cycles," in S. Venturolz, C. Flamigni, and J. R. Givens (eds.), *Adolescence in Females* (Chicago, 1985), 215–238. S. Golub (ed.), *Menarche* (Lexington, Mass., 1983).

LORAH DORN AND ANNE C. PETERSEN

MENOPAUSE (Physiological). The ending of menstruation, considered complete when a woman has not had a period for one year. Menopause can happen anytime from age 35 to 60 but most commonly occurs around the ages of 45 to 50.

During menopause, the ovaries gradually decrease estrogen production, but postmenopausal women still have estrogens in their bodies primarily because androgens produced by the adrenal glands and ovaries are converted to estrogens. Estrone, the form of estrogen predominant in postmenopausal women, is biologically less active than estradiol, the major estrogen in premenopausal women. Factors that seem to cause greater production of estrone include higher body fat levels, increasing age, and exercise.

Symptoms associated with menopause are different from one culture to another. In our society, approximately 20 percent of women experience no menopausal symptoms, about 15 percent suffer severe problems, while most women notice changes but manage to live with these fairly comfortably. Only two of the symptoms associated with menopause are known to be related to the drop in estrogen. These are hot flashes (caused by blood vessels dilating and constricting irregularly and unpredictably) and changes in the vagina (thinning of walls, losses of elasticity, less lubrication). (See OSTEOPOROSIS, also.) Although estrogen replacement therapy (ERT) does relieve these symptoms, it is controversial. ERT has been strongly implicated in increasing the risk of endometrial (uterus lining) cancer*, and there are suspected links with heart disease and breast cancer. Safer, more enjoyable ways to minimize vaginal changes include arousing sexual activities and Kegal exercises (contracting pelvic floor muscles).

Many of the symptoms associated with menopause have more to do with social than biological changes. For example, menopause may coincide with the stage when children are leaving home, and for the woman who has never had children, menopause clarifies that now she never will. The average age of widowhood is 56, so many women face widowhood and menopause simultaneously, and this is also an age at which people commonly lose or have lost their parents.

Menopause can be a difficult time for a woman in a society that values women primarily for their youthful beauty or reproductive capacity. Menopause is easier for women in a society that values the experience and wisdom of the older woman and gives them a definite role in the community.

NANCY WORCESTER

MENOPAUSE (Psychological). The physiological changes of menopause are universal: it has been suggested that it is the only maturational event in adulthood comparable to maturational changes in childhood. The psychological significance of menopause to the individual, however, may also derive from the cultural context as it shapes her psychosexual history and the social framework of reproduction—and thus in turn shapes her response to the termination of fertility.

Like most organic changes of middle and old age, climacterium (a gradual involution of the ovaries and concomitant biological processes) is a biological loss. Its most salient consequences, however, are the cessation of fertility and menstruation; these changes may function to protect the aging woman from biological demands she has become less able to meet. Thus, as a physiological change, menopause may have both positive and negative implications.

Organ systems mature and age at differing rates: the reproductive system is mature at adolescence and senescent at menopause, many years before a woman is "old." Thus, menopause may be viewed as the "premature" aging of the ovaries, though it should also be noted that only comparatively recently has life expectancy increased to the point where women outlived their reproductive capacities by a substantial period.

A duality of psychological meaning—the loss of, together with freedom from, the vital and demanding function of reproduction—may be inferred from the physiological changes at menopause. A parallel ambiguity is found in psychoanalytic discussions of the significance of menopause. Helene Deutsch viewed menopause as involution and loss and claimed that women perceive the cessation of fertility primarily as an omen of aging and death. Those women who have experienced gratification in earlier phases of psychosexual development, according to Deutsch, adapt to the losses of menopause with relative ease, while women who have been unfulfilled at earlier life stages will experience menopause as the final "closing of the gates" on a potentiality that will be forever unfulfilled (*Psychology of Women*, vol. 2, 1945).

Therese Benedek offered an opposing interpretation, stressing freedom rather than loss as the primary significance of menopause. She viewed menopause as a development phase in which psychic energy, previously bound up in the fluctuations of the menstrual cycle*, is now freed for new purposes. Moreover, the capacity for adaptation that evolved in response to the demands of female physiology now becomes available as a psychic resource. Thus Benedek saw menopause as a time of potential psychic expansion (*Psychosexual Functions in Women*, 1952).

Developmental psychologists offer a more complex picture. Robert Havighurst termed menopause a developmental task—that is, a crisis precipitated by the confluence of maturational and social events, for which there exists an optimal solution. The potential freedom created by the loss of fertility and departure of children from the home is optimally utilized for emotional and intellectual growth (*Human Development and Education*, 1953).

A refinement of this view was provided by B. L. Neugarten, who conducted the first study of attitudes toward menopause among 100 normal, nonclinical middle-class women (B. L. Neugarten, V. Wood, and R. J. Kraines, "Women's Attitudes toward the Menopause," *Vita Humana* 6 (1963): 140–151). These women did not view the biological change as a crisis, but as a comparatively trivial event within the larger and more important context of family life cycle changes.

The question thus arises: how do culture and biology interact? How is the loss of fertility viewed by women with different childbearing histories? It might be expected, as Else Frenkel-Brunswich has suggested, that the extent of separation between the biological and biographical becomes greater as biography becomes increasingly independent of vital functions, and this separation will increase with increasing age, as generally, research in adult development and aging has shown that individual differences increase over the life span with the cumulative effect of varied experience ("Adjustments and Reorientation in the Course of the Lifespan," in R. G. Kuhlen and G. G. Thompson [eds.], *Psychological Studies of Human Development* [New York, 1963]).

However, a broad-scale cross-cultural study of the responses of normal, middle-aged women from traditional, transitional, and modern cultures to the changes of menopause and middle age showed just the opposite to be the case. Women across five widely varying ethnic groups universally welcomed the loss of fertility at menopause, despite dramatic differences in childbearing history, ranging, at the traditional extreme, from women who had been pregnant, child-bearing, and nursing almost without interruption since marriage*, and who entered middle age with small children still at home, to the modern extreme, women who bore no more than one or two children, and indeed often expressed regret that they had not had more—but did not now want to become pregnant.

It would seem, then, that menopause is indeed a universal developmental event that may have universal meaning, and that the biological gains and losses, which translate into conflicting psychoanalytic interpretations, are experienced by normal women as a welcome end to an ambiguous stimulus: the promise implicit in the potentiality of biological fertility, together with the burden of childrearing.

Further Reference. N. Datan, A. Antonovsky, and B. Maoz, *A Time to Reap: The Middle Age of Women in Five Israeli Sub-Cultures* (Baltimore, 1981).

NANCY DATAN

MENSTRUAL CYCLE.

Biology. The menstrual cycle is governed by the hypothalmus, a part of the brain, and results from systematic fluctuations of the ovarian hormones—estrogens and progesterone. During the menstrual flow, estrogen and progesterone are at a low level. Estrogen peaks about midcycle, and progesterone reaches a peak a few days later as a result of ovulation (the releasing of the egg from the ovary). Menstrual bleeding results from the decline in estrogen level (which is also accompanied by a decline in progesterone). The normal duration from one menstruation to the next ranges from 20 to 40 days. The usual bleeding phase lasts about 4 to 5 days. Ovulation generally occurs about 12 to 13 days before menstruation, although there is a great deal of variability in its timing. Menstruation in the absence of ovulation is very common. Women differ with respect to the amount and patterning of hormonal production. Other hormones from the pituitary and thyroid glands also fluctuate with the menstrual cycle.

The average age of menarche* (first menstruation) is leveling off at about age 12.5. Evidence suggests that reaching a particular body weight (about 105 lbs.) is associated with its onset, and an extensive loss in body fat can suppress menstruation. Menopause* (cessation of menstrual periods) occurs around age 52. There does not seem to be any connection between age at menarche and age at menopause, but similarities in age of menarche and menopause between mothers and daughters suggest that genetic factors influence their timing. Nutrition also plays a role.

There is no currently known analogous cycle in males; the cycling center, located in the hypothalmus, is suppressed prior to birth. Testosterone in males fluctuates predictably from morning to evening hours. All animals, including humans, are subject to a variety of cycles, which may be 24-hours, monthly, seasonal, etc. The menstrual cycle is one of the more obvious of these biological rhythms.

Behavior. A number of studies have been made concerning mood changes and task performance over the menstrual cycle. Some studies used self-reports on questionnaires, while others studied actual performance of women at different times in their cycle. There is no support for a premenstrual or menstrual decline in such skills as judgment, learning, thinking, and related mental activities. There may be some individual exceptions, but properly designed studies of random samples of women show no such effect. It is not uncommon for women to believe they are impaired, even when their actual performance doesn't show it. Changes in mood are more often reported, but the findings are not consistent. When there is a mood change across the cycle, negative moods are more likely to be reported before or during menstruation. While factors associated with the menstrual cycle may affect mood, they seem less influential than environmental ones.

Pathological States. There are two general forms of menstrual distress, *dysmennorhea* and *premenstrual symptoms*. It is difficult to gauge the incidence of menstrual distress because the numbers depend upon how questions are asked. "Do you ever experience discomfort with menstruation?" might produce an affirmative response rate of 90 percent. If the question is "during your last period, did you experience discomfort?" the affirmative answers are likely to be less than 10 percent. Although there have been no large-scale surveys on the topic, at a rough estimate, fewer than one-fourth of menstruating women have symptoms severe enough to induce them to stay home from work or school, stay in bed, or see a physician.

Dysmennorhea refers to pain and discomfort accompanying menstrual flow, and usually occurs only on the first day or two. The most common symptoms are uterine cramps and nausea. The source of the symptoms is believed to be an excessive amount of prostaglandin (a hormone-like substance) in the uterus. The prostaglandin level is linked with ovulation. Thus, cycles in which ovulation does not occur may be symptom free. Psychological factors as well as general health may play a role in symptoms. The interpretation of pain and discomfort of any sort is subject to learning. Some people ignore discomfort, others emphasize it. Symptoms also may carry a symbolic meaning. For example, dysmennorhea may be a threat to feelings of control, or considered a sign of weakness or inferiority.

Premenstrual symptoms refer to changes that occur in the days immediately preceding menstruation. Women do not automatically become depressed, irritable, hostile, or weepy before or during their periods. Some women do report consistent and predictable symptoms and mood changes. Many others do not. The more common complaints are water retention, breast tenderness, mood change, and general physical discomfort. The mood change tends to be negative. On the most positive side an increase in activity level is frequently reported, as is increased sexual arousal.

Premenstrual changes stem from biological, social, and psychological factors. There is a cultural expectation that menstruation produces negative mood and behavior. Both boys and girls of junior high age have learned stereotypic attitudes about women and menstruation. There are considerable cross-cultural differences in the reporting of menstrual cycle symptoms. Because discomfort and mood change are private and subjective experiences, it is virtually impossible to know whether individual and cultural differences are true differences in symptoms or whether they reflect differences in reporting.

While many women report mild to moderate premenstrual symptoms of one type or another, only a few show marked behavioral change or physical impairment. The term Premenstrual Syndrome (PMS) has been applied to those cases where symptoms are so severe as to interfere with normal functioning. The use of "syndrome" has been controversial because of the wide range of symptoms to which it applies. However, PMS is currently undergoing a more strict definition by the medical and psychiatric communities, and will be labeled Late Luteal Phase Dysphoric Disorder when it appears in the appendix of the next revision of the *Diagnostic and Statistical Manual* (DSM-III-R) of the American Psychiatric Association. Other terms that have been used are *premenstrual tension*, *premenstrual tension syndrome* (*PMT*), and *premenstrual molimina*.

In contrast with dysmenorrhea, which can be treated with antiprostaglandins, a variety of therapies have been used for premenstrual symptoms, including nutritional and fitness improvement, psychoanalysis, vitamin and mineral supplements, and hormone therapy. Each treatment has worked for some women; no one therapy has been consistently successful.

Other pathological states associated with the menstrual cycle are amenorrhea, oligomenorrhea, and menorrhagia. *Primary amenorrhea* refers to the absence of menstruation at puberty. *Secondary amenorrhea* refers to the cessation of menstruation after it has been established at puberty. A marked weight loss (or failure to gain weight around the age of puberty) will produce amenorrhea. Hypothalamic control of estrogen production by the ovaries is probably involved in its occurrence. It is a common symptom of anorexia nervosa* and in women who recently have stopped using oral contraceptives.

Menorrhagia refers to excessive menstrual bleeding, either heavier than usual or of longer duration. *Oligomenorrhea* refers to scanty or irregular menstrual periods. The psychological aspects of menorrhagia and oligomenorrhea have not been studied, and they tend to be treated as strictly medical disorders.

Further References. D. Asso, *The Real Menstrual Cycle* (Somerset, N.J., 1984). S. Golub (ed.), *Lifting the Curse of Menstruation; A Feminist Appraisal of the Influence of Menstruation on Women's Lives* (New York, 1983).

BARBARA SOMMER

MENTAL ILLNESS. The belief that women have a higher rate of mental illness than men is based on the way the label "mental illness" is used. Women have higher rates of neuroses and functional nonorganic psychoses, men have higher rates of "personality disorders," organic disorders, and chemical addiction. More men are admitted to mental hospitals and psychiatric wards than are women, but women tend to be hospitalized for longer periods. For instance, in 1980, 51.7 percent of admissions to state and county mental hospitals, private psychiatric hospitals, and nonfederal general hospitals were male; and 97 percent of admissions to Veterans Administration Mental Hospitals were male. The average stay in a psychiatric hospital or unit for women was longer than for men in every age category (R. W. Manderscheid and S. A. Barrett [eds.], *Mental Health, United States, 1987* [Washington, D.C.; National Institute of Mental Health, 1987]).

Schizophrenia, one of the most disabling illnesses, shows no gender preference. Depression*, which like schizophrenia is highly disabling, occurs about twice as often in women as in men. Other leading disorders more common to women than men are agoraphobia* and anorexia nervosa*, overwhelmingly (95 percent) a young woman's disorder.

The higher incidence of neuroses and nonorganic psychoses among women has been attributed to women's traditional role of dependence, which may produce frustrations and stress that lead to psychological problems. It has also been attributed to women's being more likely to admit to loss of control and to seek help. Damage caused by rape, violence, and child sexual abuse that may not surface in mental health problems until years later also needs to be given serious consideration.

Women and men seeking treatment from mental health professionals may receive differential treatment. Labeling of mental health and mental illness have been largely at the hands of male professionals, and their interpretations have been applied by male therapists who necessarily bring their own cultural values with them into treatment. What is "mentally healthy" for a woman may be judged quite differently from what is "mentally healthy" for a man. When treating women, a male therapist (or a female therapist who has been conditioned by male ideologies) may be less likely to listen to what a woman is actually saying, more likely to be guided by his own interpretation of the situation than by her feelings about it than would be the case were he dealing with a man. Therapists are also more likely to advise women to adjust to the situation that has caused the problem than they are to advise adjustment for men.

In 1972 Phyllis Chesler (*Women and Madness* [Garden City, N.Y.]) called the unequal psychiatrist-patient relationship into question. The dominant position of the male in the male psychiatrist, female patient relationship re-creates the same subordinate position for the patient that in many cases is a major source of her problem. Chesler also charged that psychiatrists frequently exploit their position by having sexual relationships with female patients. Professional associations, while of course denying that the practice was frequent, developed ethical codes for their membership.

Reform movements of the 1970s, including mental health care reform, the women's health movement*, the movement to reform health care delivery, and feminist criticism of psychiatry have all affected mental health care. There has been a growing diversity of theoretical approaches and alternative therapies. Feminist therapies building on consciousness-raising techniques eschew power relations. Reforms and rethinking of basic concepts have brought some improvements, but much of the old thinking remains.

A major reform that had unexpected consequences was the de-institutionalizing of mental health care. Those suffering from mental disorders are now hospitalized for as short a time as possible, then discharged to be taken care of by the local community. But few communities have adequate facilities to care for the mentally ill. It is estimated that in 1980 there were from 1.7 to 2.4 million chronically mentally ill, of whom 900,000 were in hospitals, 750,000 in nursing homes, and the rest in the local community: in their own homes, under community care, which may be adequate but is often a single room in an unsafe and unhealthy welfare hotel, or on the streets (*Mental Health, United States, 1987*). Single women are especially likely to be among the homeless on the streets where they are targets for violence. Those chronically ill who have homes to return to will usually be cared for by a female relative.

MENTOR is an individual who acts as a career advisor or sponsor to a particular person, the latter sometimes referred to as a protégé or mentee. In the usual case, the mentor is older and more established than the protégé and is in a more powerful position from which to help the mentee by providing access to inside information and important people. Mentors also provide mentees assistance, support, advice, encouragement, and example. Though similar in some respects to "role models," mentors also have features that set them apart. A mentoring relationship is usually more intense, exclusive, and mutually recognized than one involving a role model. Even though both mentors and role models are transitional figures in a person's personal and professional development, the termination of a mentoring relationship is also thought to be more emotional and conflictful.

"Mentor" is first heard of in Homer's *Odyssey* as the name adopted by the goddess Athena when she assumed the form of a man charged with converting a naive and meek boy (Telemachus) into a mature and accomplished adult. Despite the "feminine" origins of the term *mentor*, the history of traditional mentoring has been more a history of relationships between men. In fact, mentoring first gained attention with the publication of the book *The Seasons of a Man's Life* in 1978. Numerous subsequent social science and business articles have testified to the importance of mentoring for career success and have ventured the debatable hypothesis that women's lack of advancement might be substantially attributed to the absence of mentoring in their lives.

Research does indicate that women are less involved in mentoring relationships than men. A number of factors are thought to account for this: (a) there are fewer women than men in top positions and hence few women available to be mentors; (b) male mentors are more likely to select male mentees; (c) informal organizational networks exclude women; (d) high-ranking women are under tremendous demands and hence have little time to devote to mentoring; (e) women are less positively disposed to the hierarchical influence typical of mentoring; and (f) mixed-sex mentoring relationships can be problematic in ways not characteristic of same-sex pairings, including issues of sexuality and expected patterns of male dominance–female submission.

Mentoring has been hailed as an important but underused resource for the advancement of women. While there are benefits to the recipients, there can also be drawbacks. Mentoring relationships can be exploitative and restrictive, may lead to peer rejection, can produce real or perceived dependency, or may disintegrate or disappear, leaving the mentee without a base of support. Mentors can provide significant resources for women, but questions remain about the extent and exclusiveness of these benefits.

Further References. R. Hall and B. Sandler, "Academic Mentoring for Women Students and Faculty: A New Look at an Old Way to Get Ahead" (Washington, D.C., 1983). M. P. Rowe, "Building Mentorship Frameworks as Part of an Effective Equal Opportunity Ecology," in J. Farley (ed.), *Sex Discrimination in Higher Education: Strategies for Equality* (Ithaca, 1981). J. Speizer, "Role Models, Mentors and Sponsors: The Elusive Concepts," *Signs* 12 (1981): 692–712.

MARIANNE LAFRANCE

MIDWIFERY in the past encompassed a female community's knowledge, beliefs, and techniques for the care of women and newborns. Female traditions, cultural restrictions, and modesty reinforced the midwife's important but unspecified role. In time the expansion of medical knowledge modified these factors. Women's continuing search for a safer and less painful birth experience also challenged the traditional role of the midwife and brought men into the birthing chamber for routine deliveries for the first time. Formalization of medical knowledge, professionalization of medicine, and other social changes further altered the perception of the birth experience and the practice of midwifery.

In ancient Greece and Rome some women studied with male physicians to become obstetricians, gaining both a theoretical and practical understanding of childbirth, anatomy, and gynecology* consistent with the knowledge of the time. But most midwives did not have this theoretical training.

The transmission of the Graeco-Roman heritage to the West was an uneven process characterized more by the loss of knowledge than its preservation. In medieval and early modern Europe, many midwives had no formal training. Whenever possible, a woman apprenticed herself informally to an experienced midwife. Although custom ordained that a midwife be a woman at least 45 years of age who had children of her own, sometimes mothers taught their unmarried daughters the required skills as a matter of tradition. There are indications that a midwife was usually of the artisanal classes and often worked as a midwife part-time out of economic necessity.

The roles and tasks of a midwife were varied. Besides psychologically supporting the laboring woman through her delivery and cutting the cord of the newborn, a midwife might advise a pregnant woman on health matters before the birth of a child. After birth she brought the newborn to church for its baptism or, for a dying newborn, performed an emergency baptism and after the baby died, prepared the body for burial.

Birth was a lesson in patience. Many midwives believed in letting nature take its course. On the other hand, birth manuals suggest that to ease a delivery and fortify the mother, midwives oiled the stomach, prepared special drinks, herbal remedies, and food. Many midwives stayed to help the mother after the birth as well, cooking, cleaning, and caring for mother and newborn. The fee was nominal and usually in kind.

Sometime during the Middle Ages, the Catholic church required that midwives be recognized officially by a group of their peers and the local bishop. The basis for a midwife's acceptance was her respectability and religiosity, not her medical expertise. The church wanted to ensure that she would not perform an abortion*, commit infanticide*, or conceal the name of an unknown father, if the mother revealed it during labor. She was also required to know the correct prayers for use in emergency baptism.

Midwives also played a medico-legal role in their communities. City governments had them perform physical examinations of women in cases of alleged rape*, claimed virginity, pregnancy, etc. In the sixteenth century, male practioners began to supervise midwives who performed this function.

The midwife's close association with birth and death as well as her knowledge of abortifacients and other medicaments made her vulnerable to witchcraft accusations. The extent of the midwife's involvement in witchcraft has not been well documented, nor is there a good record of the extent to which she was actually accused of witchcraft during the late sixteenth- and seventeenth-century witchcraze.

The first written regulations for midwives were those of Regensburg (Bavaria) in 1452. Candidates were required to be examined publicly by "honorable, sworn women." Unlike other artisans, midwives did not have an independent guild structure. Some urban regulations put them under the tutelage of "honorable women" as in Regensburg, but more commonly midwives were supervised by a group of physicians, surgeons, and sworn midwives. These urban regulations marked the official beginning of secular control over a domain that was perceived "natural" to women. As a result male practitioners became increasingly interested in this traditionally female domain. At the same time the midwives became more conscious of their own work identity.

During the sixteenth and seventeenth centuries the development of anatomical science and new obstetrical knowledge challenged the traditional lore and practice of midwives. Barber-surgeons used the new knowledge to advance themselves professionally. Low in the medical hierarchy, barber-surgeons promoted themselves claiming their presence at a delivery would make it safer and easier for all women. They reintroduced the ancient technique of version, a method of grasping a child lying sideways in the uterus so that it could be delivered feet first. After 1728, forceps were used. Although invented in the seventeenth century, the instrument had been kept a proprietary secret by the Chamberlain family until that time.

By the mid-eighteenth century men had established a firm niche in what had once been almost exclusively women's territory. Many royal, noble, and wealthy women sought the services of male midwives or "accoucheurs." Safer and more comfortable deliveries as well as fashion seem to have been the motivating factors. Midwives, however, continued to deliver most babies. The accoucheurs' fees were high, and a male presence at a birth was still perceived as a possible compromise of female virtue (unless a surgical intervention was required).

The mid-eighteenth century was a crucial moment in the history of midwifery. The English Dr. William Smellie's innovative techniques allowed forceps deliveries without mutilation of the newborns. The appearance of maternity hospitals for poor women allowed more practitioners to observe and learn about the birthing process firsthand. Not having equal access to educational institutions and hospitals, female midwives did not benefit from the growth of the new knowledge to the same degree as men. Men were also reluctant to allow women to use the forceps, and custom made many midwives equally reluctant to use them.

Midwifery in the American colonies followed English and West European traditions. As in Western Europe, the colonial midwife played a key role in the birthing chamber. Women depended upon the presence of their midwife, friends, and neighbors to help them through what was usually a painful and frequently risky experience. The fear of death accompanied most women's thoughts about childbearing well into the twentieth century. The few professional and legal regulations appeared to control morality rather than promote expertise. Some colonies, such as New York, appointed official midwives. In southern colonies many plantations had their own midwife, often a slave.

Few women in America or England were able to learn the new midwifery techniques developed by Smellie and others. The lack of government support explains, in part, the paucity of female midwifery students in these countries. In contrast, pronatalist governments in Denmark, Russia, and France, for example, raised the standards of midwife practice and improved midwife services to the poor by means of training and regulation.

In America, 1890–1930 was a transitional period. Increasing numbers of upper- and middle-class women chose physicians to tend them in childbirth*. Women's demands for a painless childbirth, for example, brought physicians ever more often to the birthing room and women to the hospital. "Twilight Sleep," as this type of delivery was popularly called, required the presence of an obstetrician trained to administer various drugs in a hospital setting.

Still, at the turn of the century approximately 50 percent of all recorded births in the United States were overseen by midwives. Among those attendants were the newly arrived immigrant midwives who were well-trained and the southern black "granny" midwife, often empirically trained. In the early decades of the twentieth century, infant and maternal mortality rates in this country soared above those in European countries. These statistics compelled physicians and other health officials to look for causes and possible solutions. This led to the "midwife debate" of the period between 1910 and 1930.

The findings of the White House Conference on Child Health and Protection (1930) and the New York Academy of Medicine were more critical of physicians than midwives. However, the more popular view was that midwives contributed more to the high mortality rates of mothers and infants than did physicians. The solutions offered varied. Many obstetric specialists wished to see the midwife completely eliminated; some wished to increase and regularize her training and licensing; others saw her as a "necessary evil" to be eliminated gradually. While some physicians such as Josephine Baker and Abraham Jacobi spoke strongly in the midwife's favor, their efforts were not very productive. The midwives themselves, isolated, often foreign born, and without a local or national organization, were unable to respond adequately on their own behalf.

Between 1921 and 1929 American midwives enjoyed a brief-lived period of government support under the Sheppard-Towner Maternity and Infancy Protection Act. Midwife training and maternal education programs were launched. The programs were not adequately funded and, because of opposition by the American Medical Association, were discontinued after 1929. The number of midwives also greatly declined. By 1930 midwives attended only 15 percent of all recorded births in the United States.

As traditional midwifery with all of its foibles and strengths declined, the needs of the urban and rural poor helped to bring about the foundation of the

Frontier Nursing Service in Kentucky, the Maternity Center Association in New York, and a center for training and regulation of midwives in New Jersey. These institutions trained nurses to become midwives for the indigent. Thus, the concept and reality of the "nurse-midwife" was born.

In 1955 the American College of Nurse-Midwifes (ACNM) organized nurse-midwives on a national level. By 1984 certified nurse-midwives had established a legal basis for practice in all but two jurisdictions in the United States. Today, the nurse-midwife is a registered nurse with a postgraduate education in midwifery. Most practice in hospitals and birthing centers with physician backup. At the present time, the nurse-midwife's practice is limited by the reluctance of many physicians to collaborate with her and by the recent rise in malpractice insurance rates. The ACNM is implementing innovative strategies to deal with rising insurance rates.

The lay midwife and home-birth movement of the 1970s reflect discontent with the psychological and financial costs of medicalized, hospitalized birth. In contrast to those who see birth as a potentially dangerous and pathological situation, home-birth advocates believe that birth is a natural, usually uncomplicated event to be experienced with one's loved ones at home. Lay midwives learn their craft by apprenticeship to other midwives. Their legal status, varying from state to state and year to year, is less clear than that of the certified nurse-midwife. Only seven states recognize lay midwives by law. In some of the other states where their status is shaky or clearly illegal, lay midwives have been prosecuted for practicing medicine without a license.

The advent of anatomical science, modern obstetrics, the obstetrical profession, and women's search for a safer, painless childbirth lent themselves to altering the traditional role of female midwives. We have observed a variety of transitions in beliefs and practices. None has completely disappeared. Myths, religious sanctions, territoriality, power struggles, economic limits, and political and legal interventions and interdictions are still present. In contemporary Western culture, male obstetricians are the dominant attendants. Nurse-midwives and trained European midwives are not autonomous. Their training and regulations are geared so that they may handle all types of low-risk births in and out of hospitals with the same expertise as physicians. A major debate still exists: that of the licensure of the lay midwife.

Further References. J. Donnison, *Midwives and Medical Men* (London, 1977). J. W. Leavitt, *Brought to Bed* (New York, 1986). J. B. Litoff, *The American Midwife Debate: A Sourcebook on Its Modern Origins* (Westport, Conn., 1986) and *American Midwives: 1860 to the Present* (Westport, Conn., 1978). D. C. Wertz and R. W. Wertz, *Lying-in: A History of Childbirth in America* (New York, 1977).

ALISON KLAIRMONT LINGO

MILITARY SERVICE. Throughout history women have been a part, in one way or another, of the military establishment. As camp followers (wives, daughters, widows, prostitutes) they served as a support service, doing cooking, sewing, nursing, laundry, sexual servicing, acting as sutlers and "molly pitchers" (women who cooled off cannon between firings); as rulers and charismatic leaders they took troops into battle; and they fought, mostly by enlisting disguised as men but occasionally in female units. It was not, however, until the late nineteenth and early twentieth centuries that Western countries formed permanent, legally recognized women's auxiliary units and not until World War II that they became a permanent part of the regular professional military service.

The first women's unit in the U.S. military was the Army Nurse Corps, founded in 1901 as an auxiliary service. The women held no rank and did not receive equal pay or benefits. The Navy Nurse Corps was established in 1908 along the same lines. In 1920 nurses were given officer status and "relative rank" (up to major) but not relative pay or benefits. It was not until 1944 that the nursing corps attained full military status and 1947 that they became permanent staff corps.

Women served briefly as enlisted reserves in the navy during World War I. Office work had been feminized around the turn of the century, and the secretary of the navy used a loophole—the navy's authorization to enlist did not include the word "male"—to enlist women to do clerical work. As soon as the war ended women sailors (and marines, enlisted in 1918) were demobilized. In 1925 the word "male" was added to the naval authorization to enlist civilians.

All the services enlisted women in World War II. The army moved first, reluctantly establishing the Women's Army Auxiliary Corps (WAAC) in 1941. Its auxiliary status, unequal pay, and lack of benefits hurt recruiting and morale, especially after the other services gave women reserve status. In 1943 the army changed the WAAC to the Women's Army Corps (WAC). In addition to the four military programs were the WASPS, 1,000 women pilots who served for three years under civil service status. Congress granted veteran status to survivors in 1977.

Service women were employed in "suitable jobs." Any job that might suggest a form of control over men was not "suitable." And there were problems. The services paid little attention to the real needs of its women—the clothing issued to women was often unsuited to the conditions they were sent into, for instance. Condescension and sexual harassment* were problems. Women had to constantly prove themselves and to face resentment because they were women in "this man's army" or because the men resented being replaced from safe jobs to go into combat. Slanderous attacks were a particularly ugly problem. A widespread and vicious slander campaign against the WACs in 1943 damaged the reputation of all service women with the public and hurt recruiting. Nevertheless, morale and performance remained generally high.

The women's programs, originally scheduled to disband at the end of the war, proved so valuable that they were made permanent. The Women's Armed Services Integration Act of 1948 established a permanent place for women in the military outside the health services. The WAC alone retained its separate organization. The number of women in the peacetime service was to be kept under

2 percent, a small nucleus that would be used as a base for mobilization in case of need. From the end of the Korean War until the late 1960s the number of women did not even approach the 2 percent ceiling. The peacetime service was not a great career for women.

More and more jobs were classified as "unsuitable" for women; 90 percent of the women did clerical work. Dissatisfaction and turnover were high. Discrimination* permeated the services. Officer promotions were limited: the highest rank was colonel (navy captain) and each service had only one, who was limited to a four-year term. Some of the few who reached that rank had to take a demotion after their four-year term in order to stay in the service long enough to earn retirement. Promotions to lieutenant colonel (or commander) were limited to 10 percent. Mandatory retirement was earlier for female than for male officers.

There was a double standard for enlistment: women's age and intelligence requirements were higher; women with children were not accepted. Most resented was the "special rule": the secretary of defense could dismiss any woman at any time "under circumstances and in accordance with regulations prescribed by the President." The rule existed to dismiss any women who became pregnant, adopted a child, or acquired a child by marriage. Dependency rules differed. A woman who had a dependent child living with her for more than 30 days was dismissed from service. She could claim her husband only if she could prove that he depended on her for over half his support. Service couples could not claim each other. They were classed as single, not eligible for base housing or housing allowances. Marriage between officer and enlisted ended the careers of both.

In the early 1960s women in the military reached their lowest level. With the draft the services had more men than they needed and enlisted very few women. For those few, femininity and physical appearance took on major importance. The marines were looking for "a few good-looking women." Physical appearance was a leading criterion for air force recruits.

In the late 1960s and the 1970s enormous changes in the position of women in the military, unthinkable ten years before, were brought about by the confluence of different movements: the rising draft resistance, the Vietnam War, the civil rights and feminist movements, congressional passage of the Equal Rights Amendment (ERA), the end of the draft, and the all-volunteer force (AVF). Change began modestly in 1967, then gained momentum. The period 1973–1977 was the time of greatest change, as the draft ended and the services adjusted to the AVF. By the 1980s most of the institutional discrimination had been eliminated and the U.S. military forces had the largest number and largest percentage of women of any army in the world.

The major changes were the result of the ERA, the AVF, and the rising determination of women in the services to fight the institutional discrimination that surrounded them. In the course of ERA's passage through Congress much attention was paid to the effects ERA would have on the draft and on women in the military, and to discrimination against women in the services. The Defense

Department, having to concern itself with the effect of ERA on personnel policies and with an army of volunteers, by 1972 realized that to maintain a large AVF would require increased use of women and that to attract more women institutional discrimination would have to be eliminated.

In 1972 women made up 1.6 percent of the military. By 1977, there were 110,000 women, an increase of 20 percent a year. The annual increase was then slowed to 5 percent, to reach a total of 7 percent women in the services by 1982. Job classifications were studied; by 1982, 805 occupations had been opened to women.

The Carter administration moved to integrate women into every facet of the military. Enlistment criteria were equalized, and most procurement and training programs for males and females were combined. The remains of the women's support systems in the services were abolished. Women were assigned to most noncombat units and to some combat units on an interchangeable basis.

Family policy was slowly reversed, much of it from the pressure of class action suits that worked their way through the courts during this period. Although many of the early suits were unsuccessful, the litigation helped spur the services to make changes. The services had accepted married women since 1964; in the 1970s those with minor children were granted exemptions by individual waivers that became automatic, but dependency allowances were fought all the way to the Supreme Court. The major battle was over pregnancy. Faced with litigation the navy finally gave in, but the army held out until the Supreme Court declared the practice a violation of women's rights in 1975.

Integration of officer training began in the late 1960s on a small scale and proceeded quietly during the 1970s in ROTC, officer training, and officer candidate schools before public attention was drawn to the integration of the service academies, which began in 1976. The attrition rate of women in the first class, of 1980, was 34 percent, not very different from the 30 percent rate of men students.

Some integration was not as successful, such as the 1978 attempt to completely integrate basic training. The services had to pull back. Affirmative action quotas were used to bring more women into nontraditional occupations, but in some cases women were placed in occupations beyond their physical ability, and there was some movement out of nontraditional occupations back toward clerical work, which is preferred by many of the women recruits.

The 1948 Women's Armed Forces Integration Act restricted women from combat and from service on some kinds of ships and aircraft. It did not restrict them from serving in combat positions. Gradually, they began to be trained as pilots for aircraft and helicopters; in 1978 they began serving on ships; and in the 1980s were assigned to combat arms branches such as the field artillery, combat engineers, and to missile launching crews.

By the end of 1986, there were almost 223,000 women in the armed forces, 10 percent of the entire service. They were in all officer grades up to brigadier general (rear admiral). Over 4,500 women had served on 42 ships. Women were in the armed forces in the 1983 invasion of Grenada, were on planes on the raid on Libya in 1986, and served on the destroyer tender sent to repair the *Stark*, damaged by a missile in the Persian Gulf in 1987. Most institutional discrimination against heterosexual women had been eliminated (discrimination against homosexuals remains a policy), but attitudes are harder to change. Sexist behaviors and sexual harassment remain serious problems.

Under current law women do not register for the draft and are forbidden from taking part in combat. But the law against taking part in combat is meaningless in the context of modern weaponry and military strategy, which does not determine prime targets on the basis of front and rear positions. The armed services have become so integrated that it would be virtually impossible to separate women out of units likely to be in combat situations and still maintain an effective fighting force.

MISOGYNY means woman-hating. The use of the term *misogyny* or *misogynist* dates back to the seventeenth century in literature. The word *misogynist* can be used to refer to an individual who is a woman-hater, but more recently the concept has been broadened to include certain social traditions (e.g., sexism*) thought to both underlie and perpetuate woman-hating. Contemporary usage has so broadened the term that it is now often used synonymously with the terms *sexism*, *sex discrimination**, *patriarchy**, or *male dominance*.

The first recorded instance of the use of the word misogynist was in 1620, in the treatise *Swetnam Arraigned*, referring to the misogynist character who was its subject. However, the history of literature is so replete with misogyny as to be the topic of an entire book, *The Troublesome Helpmate: A History of Misogyny in Literature*, by Katherine M. Rogers (Seattle, 1966). According to Rogers, there are strong misogynous themes in ancient, medieval, and Renaissance literature in the West. Misogyny is also evident in Eastern literature, most notably in the writings of Confucius.

Misogynist literature, according to Kate Millett in *Sexual Politics* (Garden City, N.Y., 1970), is a primary repository of male hostility and is a major instrument of patriarchal propaganda. Its goal is to reinforce the unequal statuses of the sexes. In this way, misogynist literature is related to the so-called battle of the sexes, acting in some sense as ammunition for the imposition of male authority.

Scholarly discourse of a misogynous nature is not, however, limited to literary fields. For example, many feminist writers cite the psychological theories of Sigmund Freud as among the most misogynous. His theory of female sexuality, especially, is based on the male-as-norm assumption that females are incomplete or imperfect males. Freud's ideas about the female "castration complex" revolve around the assumption that females develop penis envy as a result of having discovered their own castration (as evidenced by the missing penis). The "inferior" female organs and the desire to have a penis have lasting affects on female psychology, according to Freud.

Contemporary feminist theorists note the connection between misogyny and gender-role socialization, male dominance, and sexism. Gender-role socialization is thought by some feminist theorists to instill misogynist attitudes early in little boys. The making of a man requires the repudiation of all things feminine, both in himself and in others. The rejection of girlish or "sissy" behaviors is the first expression of the misogynist attitudes soon to be fairly embedded in his adult male gender role.

Misogyny is related to male dominance, according to Judith Long Laws, in *The Second X* (New York, 1979). In our society males are the dominant class and women are the deviant class. Males and maleness are the norm while females and femaleness are a deviation from that norm. Thus, woman's experience has been described and interpreted for her through a male filter. Rarely has she been allowed to express her experience, as the means to such expression, in media, literature, and scientific publication, are male-controlled.

The concept of misogyny is also important to feminist theory* because of its close association with sexism (see Andrea Dworkin's book, *Woman Hating* [New York, 1974]). The general misogynist character of our society, according to feminist theorists, is evidenced by the prevalence of pornographic images of women; the implicit acceptability of rape* and other forms of violence against women; the stigma and secrecy surrounding the natural functions of the female body, such as menstruation, pregnancy, and lactation; the devaluation of women's work, whether paid or unpaid; the inherent sexism within our social institutions (e.g., marriage*, medicine, law enforcement, religion, education); and so on.

In summary, most feminist theorists would agree with Jessie Bernard (*The Female World* [New York, 1981]), that while individual men may deeply love individual women, the male world as a whole does not. The term misogyny has come to represent the broader implications of hatred and hostility toward women as a class by men as class. Among feminist theorists, misogyny has become a catchall term used to describe the fundamental relationship of gender and power in contemporary society.

PATRICIA ROZEE-KOKER

MODE OF PRODUCTION, in Marxist economics, includes the material forces and the social relations of production. Material forces include not only factories, equipment, and tools, but education, skills, techniques, and labor power necessary for production. The social relations of production arise from the acquisition, ownership, and control of the material forces of production. The most important social relation is the one between the classes that is formed on the basis of ownership and control of the forces of production. Housework* contributes to the reproduction of labor power* but not directly to production, so that women's labor power in caring for the home and its members is not included in the material forces of production.

MULTIPLE REGRESSION ANALYSIS is a statistical method for predicting the value of a dependent variable from the known values of independent variables. It is one of the most successful methods for investigating salaries within an organization or unit of an organization for evidence of discrimination*. When salaries of women and/or minorities as a group fall below their predicted values, there is thus prima facie evidence of discrimination.

N

NEOLITHIC. An archaeological stage of human development usually implying the presence of either food production or pottery. The term was coined with reference to prehistoric sites containing stone tools finished by grinding and polishing (neolithic = new stone). In the preceding Paleolithic and Mesolithic periods stone tools were made by flaking while the Neolithic was followed by the use of metals for tools. An interesting feature of many neolithic sites is an abundance of female figurines.

The term *neolithic* is somewhat out of currency in archaeology and prehistory, but no acceptable general term has arisen to take its place. In Europe and Southwest Asia *neolithic* minimally implies food production, while in South and East Asia the term usually is applied to sites with pottery but without metals, having no necessary implication of plant or animal domestication. In the Americas an equivalent stage is called Formative.

The minimal meaning of *neolithic* is often expanded to refer to a complex of traits, including permanent villages, pottery containers, weaving, and domesticated plants and animals. These attributes of the extended definition of neolithic were at one time believed to have appeared more or less simultaneously as a decisive step in human cultural evolution. This event was dubbed the Neolithic Revolution (V. G. Childe, *Man Makes Himself* [New York, 1951], 59–86). However, subsequent research, especially the application of radiocarbon dating, has unraveled this concept, for the traits are first found singly and in widely separate locations. For example, the earliest pottery containers have been found in Japan dated around 10,000 B.C. unaccompanied by evidence of plant or animal domestication for several thousand years; the earliest settled villages appear in the Upper Paleolithic; advanced weaving is found on the coast of Peru long before the advent of pottery, domestication, or settled villages; and even ground and polished stone appears in the Hoabinhian (early postglacial) tradition of Southeast Asia without being accompanied by any other neolithic traits. One can only conclude that from a worldwide perspective there was no neolithic revolution.

Although the term *neolithic* is one coined by archaeologists, it is sometimes extended to apply to ethnographic groups that do not produce metal tools but do practice horticulture. In this sense, the neolithic began independently in many places as the glaciers of the last Ice Age melted, and it continues in a few places into the present or recent past.

It is interesting to note that all of the neolithic accomplishments, with the exception of polished stone tools, are designated more often as women's work than men's work in cultures around the world. Women are more frequently potters, weavers, gardeners, and even house builders. This does not mean women have necessarily been given credit for these inventions, nor that scholars have accorded them respect for these purported accomplishments. For example, Childe speculated, ''Probably at first cultivation was an incidental activity of the women while their lords were engaged in the really serious business of the chase'' (71). Partly because of the association of women with early domestication, one school of nineteenth-century thinkers postulated a matriarchal stage in human evolution. The work of Lewis Henry Morgan (*Ancient Society*, 1881) also assumed an early stage of matrilineality based on kinship terminology, which he called ''barbarian.'' Appropriated by Friedrich Engels (*The Origin of the Family, Private Property, and the State*, 1884), Morgan's stages became part of Marxist doctrine, accounting for the almost universal assertion of a matriarchal society for neolithic sites in the USSR and the People's Republic of China.

Another proposed trait of the neolithic is the worship of the Goddess, based on the existence of female figurines, which are common but not ubiquitous in the neolithic. They are not the earliest portrayals of the human body, for about 200 statuettes of women have been found on the Eurasian continent dating from the Upper Paleolithic, and Mesolithic rock art depicts the activities of both women and men. Interpretations of the uses of neolithic figurines and the meanings of the cultures in which they are found tend to focus on fertility rites for agriculture, although it seems unlikely that one explanation will suffice for the function of all neolithic figurines. There are marked differences in the contexts of the finds, as well as in the figurines themselves. Some examples that illustrate these contrasts are from Japan, Mesoamerica, Eastern Europe, and Turkey.

The first figurines of Japan belong to the stage known as Earliest Jomon. These are rare, very crude, and little is known of their context. However, by Middle Jomon (3600–2500 B.C.) the figurines are found in large numbers, with sometimes more than 100 at a single site. Although clearly human in their stance and clearly female with breasts well delineated, these figurines were not intended to depict real people. They are highly ornamented and often grotesque. Even when broken the figurines were sometimes given deliberate burial, encircled by stones and covered by stone slabs. More often they are found in pits, jars, and house floors, or simply in the trash. J. E. Kidder (*The Birth of Japanese Art* [London, 1965]) argued for the presence of food production in the Middle Jomon on the basis of these figurines, which he believed to represent a cult with "a direct bearing on the fertility of the land." To him this "would represent the material form of cults surrounding an embryonic form of cultivation . . . from the Middle Jomon period onward" (5). In recent years more direct evidence of plant cultivation in these sites has been accumulating, adding considerable weight to this suggestion. M. Nagamine ("Clay Figurines and Jomon Society," in J. R. Pearson [ed.], *Windows on the Japanese Past: Studies in Archaeology and Prehistory* [Ann Arbor, 1986], 255–266), while asserting that subsistence was still based on foraging, proposes that "women may have been raising very young wild animals for ritualistic sacrifice" (261).

More realistic female figurines are found in Mesoamerican Formative sites (1500–1000 B.C.), especially in the valleys of Mexico, Oaxaca, and Tehuacan. Depicted with wasp waists and large thighs, they wear a variety of headdresses and jewelry and appear in many poses. Although some figurines are male, the bulk are female, sometimes thousands of them in a single site. Most often they are found fragmented in the trash deposits—along with postherds in a ratio of about 4:1,000 in one site where they are quantified. Therefore, it is assumed that all households participated in whatever ritual event involved the figurines and that it occurred with some frequency. One group of four figurines found buried together included three women standing with folded arms and one sitting with crossed legs. There is no question that these sites were inhabited by food producers who lived in sedentary villages (R. Drennan, "Religion and Social Evolution in Formative Mesoamerica," in K. V. Flannery [ed.], *The Early Mesoamerican Village* [Orlando, Fla., 1976], 345–368).

Figurines from the neolithic of Eastern Europe (7000–5000 B.C.) are more realistic than those of Japan but more stylized than the "pretty ladies" of the Valley of Mexico. They are often shown sitting, and the poses are naturalistic. Again male representations exist, but the figurines are preponderantly female. Often they were found in oversized buildings or in conjunction with shrines, implying village-wide rather than household use. Marija Gimbutas (*The Goddesses and Gods of Old Europe* [London, 1982], 9) interprets these sites as "characterized by a dominance of woman in society and worship of a Goddess incarnating the creative principle as Source and Giver of All."

Çatal Hüyük in Turkey has produced not only a profusion of female figurines but solid evidence for the centrality of women's place in that society. Many figurines are of corpulent women, often associated with wild animals. They are usually found in shrines with other evidence of goddess worship, including wall paintings. Human remains indicate differential treatment of women and men at death. Graves more commonly contain women than men. All the burials with obsidian mirrors are female, as are all those which were sprinkled with red ocher. The excavator of the site concluded, "The position of women was obviously an important one in an agricultural society with a fertility cult in which a goddess was the principal deity" (James Mellaart, *Çatal Hüyük, a Neolithic Town in*

Anatolia [New York, 1967], 181). It appears that an interpretation of the neolithic as a period when women were at least not unequal is a valid one.

SARAH M. NELSON

NO-FAULT DIVORCE is the term used for divorce* granted on the basis of "irreconcilable differences" without consideration of fault. California in 1970 instituted the first nonadversarial divorce procedure as a reform to eliminate the hostility and fraud prevalent in adversarial divorce proceedings. The reform quickly swept the country, so that by 1987 only South Dakota had no form of no-fault divorce.

Under the California reform, either party can unilaterally decide that the marriage should end. Gender-neutral rules are then applied to the division of property, with equal division required.

Roughly half the states have done away with fault-based divorce in favor of some form of no-fault divorce, but less than half have adopted California's unilateral divorce system and only a few have followed California in requiring equal division of property. Twenty-two states have added no-fault, but have kept fault-based divorce as well. Retaining both systems allows for economic negotiations between the parties, with resort to the adversarial system as a threat. Several states have simplified divorce proceedings to the point that "mail order" divorce is permitted. It is usually limited to childless couples, who can get a divorce without a court appearance. The decree is sent through the mail.

Although no-fault divorce has been a reform in that it has reduced some of the acrimony surrounding adversarial divorce, it has also had disastrous economic effects on women. The result has been a serious decline in income for most women after divorce, a considerable increase in income for most men. The groups hit hardest are older full-time homemakers and mothers of young children. (See DIVORCE [U.S.].)

NONVERBAL COMMUNICATION is an area of social psychology examining behaviors that allow both the sending and receiving of information which may be redundant to spoken language but often provides information additional to it. Nonverbal behaviors serve a number of functions. They may either supplement or negate verbal messages and also provide insight into the emotional states of and/or relationships between interactants. Nonverbal behaviors are sufficiently subtle and occur in ways that may be out of the awareness of either the encoder who sends the message or the decoder who receives it. Researchers have concentrated on five major channels of nonverbal behaviors: *paralanguage*, *kinesics*, *proxemics*, *facial expression*, and *visual behavior*.

Paralanguage includes vocal nonverbal aspects of speech and vocal sounds: nonlanguage sounds (yawns, sighs, etc.), nonwords ("er," "humm," etc.), and spoken variables such as intensity, pitch, tempo, regional accents, and speech disturbances, all the information that is conveyed by a spoken message less the semantic meaning of the words. The 1974 U.S. Supreme Court decision that the transcripts of President Nixon's Watergate-related conversations were less informative than the audio tapes pointed out the importance of paralanguage. How something is said may be more meaningful than simply what is said.

Kinesics refers to all discernible bodily movements except facial expressions and eye movements. A distinction is often made between two classes of gestures. *Emphasis gestures*, which supplement verbal messages, are usually directed away from the body. They may be emblematic, may be directly translatable into words such as a wave good-bye, or may illustrate and/or regulate the flow of an ongoing conversation. *Comfort gestures*, directed toward one's body, are, on the other hand, usually indicative of the behaver's emotional state. Scratching, rubbing, or twirling one's hair are examples. Kinesics also includes posture, postural adjustments, and movements through space. Consider the very real difference between the graceful leap of the dancer and the clumsy stagger of the drunk.

Proxemics refers to how people structure, use, and are affected by space and spatial considerations in their interaction with others. The amount of space around and between bodies is an important variable; different social functions are served by various interactional distances. Generally, the space directly around our bodies is reserved for others who by invitation or relationship are allowed intimate proximity. Occasionally, we may have little or no control over this variable, as in a crowded subway or elevator. When this happens, we avoid eye contact, position objects, and decrease communication in an attempt to minimize the impact of the invasion of our personal space. In other settings, the use of furniture and seating arrangements may also mediate spatial usage. Evidence indicates that different amounts of space are culturally appropriate for different types of interaction, based on relationships and the task at hand. Studies of personal space protection and invasion have documented the use of defenses and retreats. How people use and are affected by space varies by culture as well as by sex, age, and personality differences. There is strong evidence that men tend to spread their bodies out and take up more space than do women, even after relative body size is controlled for. Included in proxemics is research of the most proximal of behaviors: touching. Touching signals and demands involvement such as aggression, affiliation, or sexual interest. Research into female-male differences indicates that women and men evaluate and respond to the touch of another person in different ways. North American women not only touch same-sex others more often than men do, they evaluate the touch of others based on their relationship with the toucher and the situation in which touch occurs. Men seem predisposed to evaluate the touch of a woman as sexual in nature. Men also touch women more than women touch men; one might speculate that this is a masculine power-ploy since touching, as opposed to being touched, signals power and status in same-sex interactions such as between employer and employee.

Facial expressions may be the most important channel for nonverbal communication. It is the face more than any other bodily part to which others attend. Historically, research on facial expression has addressed the universality and classification of various displays and the use of facial display in the sending and attribution of emotion or mood. The intricate muscles of the human face allow for a variety of expressions, which researchers have examined in cross-cultural and even cross-species contexts.

Arising out of the facial display literature, *visual behavior* has become a separate area of research. Based on the fundamental significance that interpersonal gaze plays in human interaction, this is not surprising. Visual interaction signals involvement with another. It is also an important moderator in the giving and taking of the floor inherent in normal conversation. The eyes are used to signal attention, understanding, puzzlement, and provide feedback. Visual behavior has been shown to be an important variable in social encounters such as aggression, attraction, self-defense, and in situations involving power and dominance. The stare may be interpreted as a threat or flirtation depending on the situation and the relationship between interactants. Higher ratios of looking while speaking to looking while listening (*visual dominance behavior*) have been shown to affect both the encoding and decoding of power in an interpersonal context. Research has shown that when women and men interact in a setting of equal power, men visually behave as if they are in high power position while women show normal visual behavior. When men interact with men in similar settings, they do not exhibit such visual dominance behavior. Other important areas of gaze research have focused on sex, cultural, and personality differences. Lastly, there is also speculative research into the role of pupilary dilation as an unconscious indicator of interest in what is being viewed.

Probably the most important factor with regard to all nonverbal behaviors and their meaning, singly and in combination, is the social context in which they occur. Behaviors "mean" different things in different situations. In some settings, touching, staring, being close, whispering, and smiling are likely to be signs of intimacy, maybe even part of courtship. In another setting, they may indicate a fight is imminent. On a broader level, there is good evidence that nonverbal behaviors are, for the most part, learned behaviors that differ from culture to culture. Interacting with someone of a different culture may lead to "language problems" of a nonverbal nature.

Many differences between women and men in their use of and response to nonverbal behaviors parallel differences associated with interpersonal power and status. It is unclear whether these are diffuse status characteristics, merely reflecting existing power inequity, or are evidence of a strategy of dominance covertly employed by males to perpetuate such differences. One conclusion from the literature argues that women are more sensitive to nonverbal behaviors than are men, perhaps because that information and its monitoring are more important to those who have traditionally been subjected to socially disadvantaged positions, or it may also be based on the traditional feminine gender role of intuitiveness, self-disclosure, and social sensitivity.

Lastly, nonverbal behavior has been cited as having potential for those seeking to explore more unbiased or comfortable personal styles (i.e., nonsexist and/or assertive). Because nonverbal behaviors are "low in profile" and one is generally held less accountable for their display, they may be a fruitful "testing ground" for someone attempting to effect personal change. However, there is a potential disadvantage, from a feminist perspective, in that men may misinterpret such behavior. The possibility for perpetuation of sexual inequality (predominantly, but not exclusively, by males) through subtle and not so subtle means may be both a strategy and a result of the use of nonverbal behaviors.

Further References. S. L. Ellyson and J. F. Dovidio, *Power, Dominance, and Nonverbal Behavior* (New York, 1985). N. M. Henley, *Body Politics* (Englewood Cliffs, N. J., 1977).

STEVEN L. ELLYSON

NURSING. See HEALTH CARE PROVIDERS

O

OBSTETRICS. See GYNECOLOGY/OBSTETRICS (OB/GYN)

OCCUPATIONAL SEGREGATION refers to the pronounced tendency of women and men in the labor market to work in different occupations. For example, in 1980, women comprised over 90 percent of child care workers, registered nurses, secretaries, kindergarten teachers, and telephone operators, while over 90 percent of engineers, dentists, tool and die makers, workers in the construction trades, and truck drivers were men. Overall, almost half of all employed women worked in occupations that were at least 80 percent female.

The extent of occupational segregation may be measured using an index of segregation that gives the proportion of women (or men) in the work force who would have to change jobs in order for the occupational distribution of the two groups to be the same. In 1981, the index was 62 percent. While the extent of occupational segregation by sex is substantial, since 1960 there has been some modest progress in reducing segregation. The pace of change accelerated during the 1970s when the index fell by nearly 7 percentage points. The gains have been concentrated in professional and managerial jobs where there have been remarkable increases in the representation of women in some traditionally male occupations. However, little progress has been made in integrating male blue-collar jobs. The decrease in segregation was larger for younger women, probably because they have the most flexibility in responding to greater opportunities for women in nontraditional pursuits.

Explanations for occupational segregation tend to emphasize either differences in the choices that women and men themselves make (supply-side factors) or differences in employer treatment of women and men (demand-side factors). Both sets of factors most likely play a role in producing the observed gender differences in occupational distribution.

On the supply side, the human capital explanation (see HUMAN CAPITAL THEORY) has received the most attention. Human capital theorists argue that women who adhere to traditional roles in the family will anticipate a shorter and more discontinuous pattern of labor market experience than men. They will have fewer incentives to invest in work-related education and on-the-job training* and will thus select occupations where such human capital investments are less important. In this view, female jobs pay less than male jobs because of their lower skills.

The human capital model emphasizes the impact of rational decision-making and the voluntary choices of men and women. However, women's decisions about the role of work in their lives and about what occupations to pursue may also be a response to societal discrimination*. This refers to the situation in which the influences of family, friends, school, and the media adversely affect women's choices.

On the demand side, labor market discrimination may also constrain the occupational opportunities of women. This occurs when employers discriminate against equally qualified women in hiring, placement, access to training programs, and promotion for traditionally male jobs. Employers may be motivated to discriminate against women by their own prejudices or because the prejudices of their male employees or customers make it less profitable for them to hire women than men. They may also believe, perhaps incorrectly, that on average, women would be less desirable employees—for example, because they would be more likely to quit their jobs. It is also the case that the anticipation of such labor market discrimination may lower women's incentives to aspire to or train for what are perceived to be "male" jobs.

One reason that occupational segregation is a cause for concern is that many economists believe it lowers the earnings of women relative to men. It has indeed been found that women and men workers in predominantly female jobs earn less than equally qualified workers in predominantly male jobs. This is believed to occur because of "crowding." That is, due to the concentration of women in such female occupations, the supply of labor in those jobs tends to be large relative to the demand, depressing wages in the female sector.

Further References. A. H. Beller, "Changes in the Sex Composition of U.S. Occupations, 1960–1981," *Journal of Human Resources* 20 (1985): 235–250. F. D. Blau and M. A. Ferber, *The Economics of Women, Men and Work* (Englewood Cliffs, N.J., 1986). B. F. Reskin and H. I. Hartmann (eds.), *Women's Work, Men's Work: Sex Segregation on the Job* (Washington, D.C., 1986).

FRANCINE D. BLAU

OFFENDER. The definition, presence, characteristics, and disposition of the woman offender can be viewed as representing in microcosm women's political and legal status crosscut by realities of class and race. The very definition of who is a woman offender is complex. It may include any woman who has violated the range of federal and state criminal statutes (some of which are themselves gender-specific), a population unknown and, with the exception of self-report data, unknowable; women who have been arrested and are therefore identifiable as a group by offense, race, and age but who are not indentifiable as individuals; and finally, women in jails and prisons whose personal backgrounds and characteristics have been recorded.

Most self-report data involves juveniles. Young males consistently report more serious and repeated illegal activities than young women, but young women appear in all offense categories. However, race and class differences appear to play minimal roles. Almost equal percentages of males and females report drug, alcohol, and petty theft violations, but significantly lower numbers of young women engage in acts of violence or vandalism. A higher percentage of young men than women report involvement in prostitution,* but juvenile women's arrests for prostitution are double those for males.

Despite the media coverage of Freda Adler's description of an increasingly violent and aggressive "new female criminal" in *Sisters in Crime* (1975), attributed to the 1970s women's movement, later research found no real change in arrest rates for women in male-dominated violent crimes. An increase in arrests has occurred for larceny-theft, fraud, forgery, and embezzlement, the same small property offenses which consistently have been the focus of women's criminal behavior and more reflective of a "feminization of poverty"* than liberation. As an example, based on U.S. Bureau of Justice Statistics, in 1983, 20 percent of all women's arrests were for larceny-theft, as opposed to 10 percent of male arrests. Prostitution, often associated in people's minds with the woman offender, only accounted for 5 percent of female arrests. Of the 10 million arrests that year, 16.6 percent were of women. At the same time, 7.7 percent of the jail inmates were women, while women made up only 4.5 percent of the prison population. On any given day, males are almost 26 times more likely to be in prison than females, a ratio that has been decreasing in the last decade, however.

Explanations for these differential figures have remained remarkably stable through time. Francis Lieber's exposition, in Gustave de Beaumont and Alexis de Tocqueville's *On the Penitentiary System in the United States*, of why only 9 percent of the prisoners were women in 1833 is similar to Dale Hoffman-Bustamente's exploration in "The Nature of Female Criminality" (*Issues in Criminality* 8 [1973]: 117–132), 140 years later. Both attribute the levels and patterns of women's offenses to their position in "civil society," which results in differing role expectations and socialization, differential social control and opportunity to commit offenses, limited access to criminal subcultures and careers, and statutory sexual specification of some offenses. The "chivalry factor" in arrest and disposition of women offenders remains a question for research, but there is evidence of differential sentencing and sentence-length linked to paternalism, assumptions regarding the degree of women's naïveté and dangerousness, and their responsibility for children. However, these differentials become less clear when the factors of class and race are examined. Recent statistical analyses by the U.S. Department of Justice (1985), indicate that a black woman is six to eight times more likely to be imprisoned in her lifetime than a white woman, a ratio greater than black to white males.

When we examine the characteristics of women offenders who are in prison, the dynamics of the criminal justice system and the status of women are more clearly revealed. The study by Josephina Figueira-McDonough (*Females in Prison in Michigan, 1968–1978* [Ann Arbor, 1981]) of the background of women imprisoned in Michigan from 1968 to 1978 provides insight. Although women are found in prison from every background and for all offenses, the highest percentage were there for larceny and forgery. Approximately 90 percent came from working or marginally poor backgrounds, about half were unemployed or with unskilled jobs, while most had no male companion when incarcerated. Nearly half were caring for dependents. Almost 70 percent had not finished high school. Seventy-three percent were nonwhite. The study concludes that the women were "disadvantaged losers" in a complex and competitive society.

Further References. J .R. Chapman, *Economic Realities and the Female Offender* (Boston, 1980). C. R. Mann, *Female Crime and Delinquency* (University, Ala., 1984).

ESTHER HEFFERNAN

OFFICIALS, WOMEN ELECTED AND APPOINTED have attained several major breakthroughs in the United States following the emergence of the contemporary feminist movement. In 1968 the first black woman, Shirley Chisholm (Democrat, New York), was elected to Congress. In 1974, Ella Grasso (Democrat, Connecticut) became the first woman elected as governor of a state in her own right, rather than in her capacity as wife of a major political figure. In 1978, Nancy Kassebaum became the first woman elected to the U.S. Senate without having first reached Congress by filling the unexpired term of a congressman. In 1981, Sandra Day O'Connor was appointed to the U.S. Supreme Court by President Ronald Reagan and became the first woman justice to serve on that body. In 1984, Arlene Violet (Republican, Rhode Island) became the first woman elected as attorney general of any state, and Geraldine Ferraro (Democrat, New York) became the first woman nominated for vice president by a major political party.

Despite these major breakthroughs and despite substantial increases in the number of women elected and appointed officials in the 1970s and 1980s, the proportion of elective and appointive governmental positions held by women remains low. By the mid–1980s, women held no more than 16 percent of elective positions (except school boards) in the United States at any level of government, and they were about equally as underrepresented in appointive offices.

At the beginning of the 100th Congress, 1987–1988, women held only 23 of the 435 positions in the U.S. House of Representatives and 2 of the 100 seats in the U.S. Senate. By early 1987, a total of 123 women had served in Congress during its 200-year history. The first was Representative Jeannette Rankin (Republican, Montana), best known because she was the only member of the U.S. House to vote against the entry of the United States into both world wars. Rankin served from 1917 to 1919 and again from 1941 to 1943. The first woman U.S. Senator was Rebecca Latimer Felton (Democrat, Georgia). She was appointed in 1922 to complete the term of a senator who died in office. However, Felton served as a member of the Senate for only one day before giving up her seat to a man who was elected to fill the vacancy. Felton's path into office was not atypical for those women pioneers who served in Congress prior to the contemporary women's movement. In fact, a majority of pre–1970 congresswomen first came to Congress to fill midterm vacancies, often created by the deaths of their husbands. However, the "widow's succession" is no longer a common means for women to gain entry into Congress; most of the women who served in Congress during the 1980s were elected in their own right.

Historically, women have been as absent from high-level, federal appointive offices as they have been from elective congressional offices. The first woman cabinet member was Frances Perkins, who served as secretary of labor from 1933 to 1945 under President Franklin Delano Roosevelt. Only two women in addition to Perkins served in presidential cabinets prior to the administration of President Jimmy Carter. Presidents Carter and Reagan each appointed three women to cabinet-level positions in their administrations, thereby easily surpassing the records of their predecessors. Women also fared better in receiving subcabinet appointments under Presidents Carter and Reagan than under their predecessors. Women were appointed to 13.5 percent of full-time, Senate-confirmed positions in the Carter administration and to 9.0 percent of all such positions in the first term of the Reagan administration.

Women have made slightly larger gains in most state and local offices than they have at the national level. Progress is perhaps most noticeable at the state legislative level, where the proportion of women among state legislators more than tripled between 1969 and 1987, from 4.0 percent to 15.5 percent. By 1986 women also held 17.9 percent of appointed positions in governors' cabinets and 14.2 percent of top statewide elective offices across the 50 states. By the mid–1980s, about 8 percent of all county governing board members and 14 percent of municipal governing boards and mayoral positions were occupied by women. While by 1987 only 8 women had ever served as governors of states, 3 women occupied gubernatorial mansions in that year.

A number of explanations have been put forth to account for women's continued underrepresentation in elective and appointive office. Three sets of factors seem most important.

First, people traditionally have been socialized to believe that men are better suited to politics and that political officeholding is an inappropriate activity for women. These beliefs have limited women's political aspirations and have led men in positions of political power who control access to public office to doubt women's capabilities.

Second, the sexual division of labor* in both the family* and the paid labor force has constrained women's political participation. The fact that women have had primary responsibility for childrearing and household maintenance has meant that most women, particularly those who also work outside the home, have not had the time and flexibility necessary to pursue an activity as demanding as political officeholding. Women who seek elective office often wait to do so until their children are grown; this places them at a disadvantage relative to men of the same age, who often have accumulated political experience while their children were young and are thus better positioned to run for higher-level offices. Women who hold high-level appointive offices in state and federal government are much less likely to be married or to have children than their male counterparts, suggesting that they have had to make a choice between career or family while men have been able to pursue both.

The sexual division of labor in the paid labor force also affects women's ability to compete for political office on an equal basis with men. Political officeholders have most often come from the fields of law and business where the numbers of women have traditionally been low. Women who seek political office, like women in the population more generally, are concentrated in the fields of nursing, social work, teaching, and clerical work. These female-dominated occupations less often than law or business allow for the leaves of absence and flexible work hours that are necessary for officeholding, less often provide credentials that will be viewed as demonstrating competence for officeholding, and less often serve as inroads into networks that can provide the money necessary for financing political campaigns and the contacts necessary for obtaining political appointments.

The third explanation for women's underrepresentation in public office focuses on basic biases in the way Western democratic political systems operate. These political systems, structured so as to ensure stability, promote the continued tenure of groups and individuals who are in positions of power. Political parties want to win and party leaders are reluctant to back women's candidacies if they view them as high risk. Women candidates in the United States more often than not must challenge incumbents who have huge advantages in terms of visibility and fund-raising. The high costs of campaigning in the United States and the absence of public financing of campaigns for most offices ensure that the have-nots, including most women, will not be able to seek political office. Those who control appointments to high-level executive offices demand loyalty among those they appoint and consequently rely on networks of close friends and associates— networks that are mostly male and very elite—in seeking potential appointees.

Although the barriers to women's election and appointment are considerable, the presence of women in public office has important consequences both for politics and for women's lives. Despite some visible exceptions, most women officeholders do seem to have perspectives and priorities different from those of most men. In the aggregate, women in elective and appointive office are more liberal than their male counterparts on a variety of public policy issues, are more concerned with the effects that various public policy issues will have on women's lives, show higher levels of support for issues like the ERA and abortion* that have been closely associated with the feminist movement, and encourage and assist other women to follow in their footsteps.

Further References. J. A. Flammang, *Political Women: Current Roles in State and Local Government* (Beverly Hills, 1984). K. A. Stanwick and K. E. Kleeman, *Women Make a Difference* (New Brunswick, N.J., 1983).

SUSAN J. CARROLL

ORGASM is a psychophysiological experience, and recently it has become a symbol of sexual equality and female sexual entitlement. Although, as Margaret Mead pointed out (*Male and Female: A Study of the Sexes in a Changing World* [1955; orig. publ. 1949]), female orgasm is unknown and apparently unmissed in many societies, it is presented in most contemporary Western texts as an important, innate, universally pleasurable biofunction, a simple somatic response consisting of involuntary pelvic muscle contractions that occur in reaction to a neurovascular buildup of tension in the genitalia. The immense societal attention paid in the West to this little physical event, however, and its absence from sexual practice in some cultures, indicate that whatever the physical value of orgasm as pleasurable reliever of vascular congestion, its symbolic value has been and continues to vary and require study.

Until the writings of feminists and sexologists in the late 1960s and 1970s, orgasm was said to occur during vaginal intercourse if a woman was well adjusted and could just let herself go (''surrender'') in a sexual encounter. Any woman not so capable was considered to have a problem that required professional treatment. At that point, however, feminists began to criticize those norms and the ways that Freudian theory, traditional heterosexual technique, and gender socialization all prevented women from experiencing orgasm. Sexologists stressed that women's anatomy made orgasm during vaginal intercourse far less likely than with an act that stimulated the sensitive clitoris directly, and that with ''proper'' stimulation and sexual assertiveness women were actually more orgasmically capable than men, even having ''multiple'' orgasms. Sexual liberation for women became, for a while, focused on asserting a political right to orgasm justified by the biological equality of male and female sexual response presumably demonstrated by the scientific research of Alfred Kinsey (A. C. Kinsey, W. B. Pomeroy, C. E. Martin, and P. H. Gebhard, *Sexual Behavior in the Human Female* [1953]) and, later, of William Masters and Virginia Johnson (*Human Sexual Response* [1966]). Women in consciousness-raising* and other groups recommended masturbation and the use of vibrators to learn orgasm.

As a result of the writings of this period and the social changes they fostered, orgasm was said to occur during any sexual act if a woman was well adjusted and had knowledge of her own body and the ability and opportunity for communication and assertion. Ironically, the importance given to orgasm as a symbol for female sexual equality has resulted, for some, in a technical, goal-oriented focus for sexual relations that may or may not have improved women's overall sexual satisfaction, sexual freedom, or sexual self-knowledge. Orgasm is still considered, by most, the centerpiece and goal of a sexual encounter, and women not having that experience are still considered to have a problem that requires professional treatment. It will take, it seems, further research and further revolution before women achieve true sexual self-determination.

Further Reference. B. Ehrenreich, E. Hess, and G. Jacobs, *Remaking Love: The Feminization of Sex* (Garden City, N.Y., 1986).

LEONORE TIEFER

OSTEOPOROSIS is a condition of increased porosity of the bones that results in their increased fragility. It is more common in women than men and is most common in postmenopausal women.

It is a biological condition with immense social ramifications, too often turning a lively, independent woman into a dependent "little old lady." Women may lose as much as eight inches in height, as one or more vertebrae collapse. Fractures from falls (falls may actually be the result of weakened bones) often have serious complications. More than half of women with hip fractures never regain normal functioning; nearly one-third die within a year of the fracture.

Bone remodeling (constant process of breaking down and reforming) is a complex interaction of hormonal, dietary, and physical activity factors. Estrogen replacement therapy (ERT) probably does slow down bone loss in the years immediately after menopause. However, ERT is effective only for as long as it is used. As the safety of ERT is questionable (see MENOPAUSE), emphasis should be placed on other preventive measures. Regular weight-bearing exercise (such as walking) is an excellent preventive measure. Calcium intake, in the diet or as supplements, also needs to be stressed as a prophylactic measure because while women's calcium requirements increase with age, calcium absorption decreases with age, and many women do not take in sufficient calcium. (Recommendation: 800–1000 mg. calcium per day before menopause, 1200–1400 mg. calcium during and after menopause.) Vitamin D and fluoride are also important. Factors known to have an adverse effect on bone restructuring include high intakes of alcohol, caffeine, phosphorus, protein, and salt.

Although osteoporosis is probably preventable in most women, some women have more natural protection than others. Black women, for example, are less likely to develop osteoporosis than light-skinned women. Fat women are less prone to the condition than thin women. Osteoporosis is an issue for women of all ages because while the fastest changes take place at menopause and its consequences are felt many years later, it can best be prevented in early midlife.

Medical facilities are increasingly responding to women's fears of osteoporosis by marketing a range of bone density measurement services. Two points must be clarified for potential consumers. Bone density measurements cannot predict whether or not a person will develop osteoporosis; measurements can only detect signs of osteoporosis as they occur. Bone measurements at one site do not necessarily predict the presence or absence of osteoporosis at another site.

NANCY WORCESTER

P

PAP SMEAR is a method developed by the American scientist Dr. George Papanicolaou for detecting changes in cells. Its principal use is in detecting cancerous and precancerous cells in the cervix. It can also detect inflammatory cell changes and the presence of viruses (e.g., herpes) and can be used to test cell changes in areas other than the cervix. Cells are collected from the surface of the cervix (or other area) and spread thinly on a slide. The slide is sent to a laboratory where it is stained and examined microscopically.

The Pap smear is not completely accurate. Mistakes in collecting cells and handling the slide are sometimes made. It is also possible, without anyone being at fault, that the test may not detect cancer when it is present or may suggest the presence of malignancy when none is present. The most common inaccuracy lies in the pathologist's classification of the degree of abnormality, if abnormality is detected. Any finding of abnormality needs to be followed up by a biopsy*. All women over 20, or younger if they are sexually active, should have periodic Pap smears.

PARTURITION is the process of giving birth. The first of the three stages of parturition, or childbirth*, begins with labor, involuntary rhythmic contractions that strengthen in intensity and discomfort as they continue. The contractions shorten and dilate (open) the cervix and break the fetal membrane. When the cervix is fully dilated, it will be large enough for the baby to pass through.

In the second stage, after the dilation of the cervix, labor contractions begin to push the baby through the birth canal. In 95 percent of the cases, the baby is in the optimal position, with the top of the head presented first. Following the appearance of the head, there is usually a quarter turn, then the shoulders come out one at a time, followed by the body. In other cases the head may appear first, but with the face or brow presented. In breech births, the buttocks or the feet appear first; in a transverse birth, one of the shoulders comes first.

The baby may nurse right away or may not. Suckling helps to bring about the third and final stage, which should follow within a half hour of delivery. There is a return of uterine contractions, which expel the afterbirth (the placenta and fetal membrane).

PASTORAL SOCIETIES. In pastoral societies women occupy a pivotal position in the organization of production. Among the nomadic groups who specialize in raising sheep and goats in the mountainous regions of the Middle East, a woman's labor and decision-making input are prodigious. (1) She performs nearly all daily chores including milking and processing of the milk into yoghurt, cheese curds, butter, or ghee (clarified butter) for domestic consumption and exchange. (2) She bears enormous, though not exclusive, responsibility for the maintenance of the flock and the newborns while in the camp. (3) She has a prominent role in hiring shepherds and dairymaids who are recruited from kinsmen with surplus labor. (4) Although men do assist in shearing the animals, she alone does the carding and spinning of wool and goat hair. Woven pile rugs, blankets, kilims (flat-woven rugs), tent-cloth, saddlebags, horse-covers, grain sacks and ropes are among a large number of utilitarian and ornamental objects crafted by women. These items constitute the savings of a family and can be readily converted into cash to meet economic and social obligations. (5) She takes an active part in the allocation of all products for market, local barter, and ceremonial occasions. In this respect men and women share similar power. (6) Her intimate knowledge of the flock and concern for its continual growth perforce give her a strong voice in decisions with respect to the sale of animals to raise cash or to repay debts to urban creditors. (7) Her routine managerial duties become even more onerous during the annual migrations between the summer and winter pastures. In this labor-intensive period she carries out such seemingly masculine activities as loading and unloading baggage animals. These demanding tasks, however, free the men to devote full attention to the security of the herd while en route. As an adult member of the camping community (comprising several tent-households of close kinsmen), she participates in deliberations about departure time, the distance of daily moves and the relative advantage of the various stops along the migration route.

Typically the tent-households that make up a camping unit share a corporate interest in all aspects of herding. Matters regarding pasture, water, seasonal migration and movements, selection of camping sites, the safety of the migration routes, all require collective decision-making that transcends the private sphere. Put differently, concern for the well-being, care, and growth of the family herd bridges the private and public domains.

Although the majority of pastoral nomads engage in some subsidiary farming, it is the optimal herd of about 30 head that forms the economic underpinning of the family. To illustrate, pastoral products are of crucial importance for obtaining credit from the urban trade partners. Meat, though conspicuously absent from the daily diet, is consumed ceremonially as an integral part of the collective

observance of all life crises. The generational continuity of the nomadic life-
style itself is dependent on the herd; the son's brideprice as well as the nucleus
of his productive capital (considered his patrimony) after marriage is allocated
from the main herd. The daughter, however, does not receive an analogous
anticipatory inheritance upon marriage even though Islam prescribes a share
equal to one-half of the male's.

Similarly, in these intensely patrilineal societies women do not inherit political
office and play no part in the formal leadership structure. Nevertheless, they
wield considerable influence in the public arena. Women among the ruling elite
in particular have historically achieved a legendary reputation for their ability
to exercise informal power in favor of male relatives.

The foregoing discussion may permit at least two generalizations: first, that
among the transhumant groups women enjoy an extraordinary decision-making
power by virtue of their dominant role in the economy. Second, the community's
overarching interests seem to preclude a clearcut division between the private
and public spheres; the two dimensions of power are interdependent and insep-
arable, and the public emanates from the private as a necessary and logical
extension.

In the past few decades nomadic pastoral societies in nearly every country in
the Middle East have increasingly been undergoing change in response to both
internal and external pressures. While the causes are manifold and vary from
one country to another, a confluence of demographic and ecological factors have
had significant effects. Modern medicine, for instance, has been responsible for
an unprecedented rate of human population growth and a parallel rise in animal
population. The result is often widespread overgrazing and severe animal epi-
demics occurring with an alarming frequency.

Setbacks in the pastoral economy, on the other hand, are almost predictably
accompanied by a shift to full-time subsistence farming and an attendant reduction
in female-dominated economic activities. Though women customarily assist with
the harvesting of crops, the main agricultural tasks are performed by the men.
One important corollary of a male-dominated production is generally an increase
in the men's control over the recruitment and deployment of labor and the
allocation of resources. In sum, to the extent that nomadic herding is replaced
by settled farming, women will experience a decline in their economic role and
social status.

REZA FAZEL

PATRIARCHY is the system of male dominance by which men as a group
acquire and maintain power over women as a group.

Literally, patriarchy means "rule of the father." Prior to its use by radical
feminists, it was employed primarily by students of anthropology and history to
designate the structure of pastoral and nomadic societies. The early seventeenth-
century English writer Robert Filmer used the model of the patriarchal family
as the basis of his vision of government, one in which rulers act toward their

subjects as men act toward their wives and children. Responding to Filmer, political theorist John Locke rejected the parallel between family and state without rejecting the legitimacy of father rule within families. Late nineteenth-century writers such as Lewis Morgan (*Systems of Consanquinity and Affinity of the Human Family* [1871]) and Johann J. Bachofen (*Mother Right* [1861]) used the term to debate whether the earliest human societies were male- or female-dominated.

Contemporary feminists have inherited some of these debates and have also tried to go beyond them. Disputes among feminists about the origins of patriarchy, the historical status of matriarchy*, and the wisdom of using the term *patriarchy* at all make generalizations difficult. Feminists such as Michele Rosaldo ("The Use and Abuse of Anthropology: Reflections on Feminism and Cross-Cultural Understanding," *Signs* 5 [1980]: 389–417) and Allison Jaggar (*Feminist Politics and Human Nature* [Totowa, N.J., 1983]) have objected to such a blanket term because it implies a lack of attention to the historical particularities of different systems of male dominance, while others, such as Mary Daly (*Gyn/Ecology: The Metaethics of Radical Feminism* [Boston, 1978]), have insisted on the importance of naming the common patterns of women's subordination and men's power across historical circumstances. While many radical feminists speak of patriarchy as universal, feminist anthropologist Peggy Sanday (*Female Power and Male Dominance* [New York, 1981]) argues that many early societies had substantially egalitarian relations between the sexes and that patriarchy develops out of particular environmental and social circumstances. In some ways patriarchy is most important to feminism* not for what it *is*, but for what it *is not*: it signifies the systemic conditions of female subordination which feminism opposes. It also makes possible the conditions through which feminism arises as a movement for social change.

Patriarchy refers both to institutions and to discursive accounts of the world within which institutions are embedded. On the institutional level feminists have pointed to male dominance within family, state, religion, capitalism, education, and other social structures and have analyzed the practices by which male dominance is established and maintained. Further, feminist analyses of conventional relations between women and men show how male power insinuates itself into the psyches of women, teaching them to collaborate in defining themselves as subordinate to and dependent upon men. Yet the experiences women have within patriarchy, especially those binding them to other women in recognition of their common plight, can be the source of feminist resistance.

On the level of discourse, feminists have condemned patriarchy for creating and reflecting an exclusively masculine view of the world and for rendering women's experiences and women's perspectives invisible. Patriarchal thought is characterized by the imposition of dualisms and oppositions onto the disparate flow of experience: reason versus emotions; mind versus body; subject versus object. Patriarchy then favors one side of each pair over the other, establishing a hierarchy of classifications in which that which is associated with the male is given priority to that which represents the female. Thus patriarchy establishes male dominance in its basic accounts of the world, its standards of knowledge and judgment, as well as in its concrete institutions and practices. But once again women's experiences as marginalized within patriarchy can spur a more determined articulation of their points of view, thus evoking a set of feminist discourses that arise to challenge the dominant patriarchal view.

Despite differences over proper usage of the term, most feminists would agree that patriarchy entails efforts by men to control women's bodies. Patriarchal discourse defines women as uniquely, sometimes solely, suited for bearing and raising children. Through patriarchal institutions men in power attempt to control women's fertility by restricting or imposing contraception and abortion. Through direct violence against women, through rape* and the threat of rape, men exercise control over the activities and choices of women. Through the reduction of women to objects of male sexual desire, men turn women's bodies into possessions and reward women for successful competition with one another for the attention, approval, and protection of men. Yet once again patriarchy can be turned on itself, and the controls imposed on women's bodies can be transformed into vehicles for their liberation: thus some feminists have embraced the values and practices of mothering as the source of alternatives to patriarchal institutions, and others have looked to knowledge residing in the body to confront patriarchal discourse.

Different conceptualizations of patriarchy imply distinct strategies of analysis. Feminists who emphasize the universal or nearly universal character of male dominance tend to see patriarchy as a single thing and to stress the search for its origins. Feminists who take a more historically specific approach tend to advocate the investigation of particular institutions and processes within concrete settings.

Differing conceptualizations of patriarchy also lead to different strategies of resistance and change. Those who conceive of it as a nearly universal web of male dominance tend to embrace a strategy of cultural change, whereby women are encouraged to establish a separate women's culture with a woman-centered set of rituals, symbols and languages. Those who emphasize the historical particularity of male power tend to look to its operation within particular institutions and practices and to stress resistance to these structures. Some emphasize marriage as the crucial institution to be resisted, while others point to compulsory heterosexuality*, or to the control of women's productive and reproductive labor by men.

Further References. G. Lerner, *The Creation of Patriarchy* (New York, 1986). L. Nicholson, *Gender and History: The Limits of Social Theory in the Age of the Family* (New York, 1986).

KATHY E. FERGUSON

PATRILINY, descent through the male line, is the lineage system that has prevailed in Western society. Descent cannot be passed through a woman, although women are accounted as patrilineal kin. The need of men to be assured of the continuation of their lineage, for the performance of rites and the inheritance of property, has been cited as a primary factor in the subjection of women.

PATTERN AND PRACTICE APPROACH TO DISCRIMINATION is the approach used when plant-wide evidence that women and/or minorities are concentrated in low-paying jobs is used to argue that discriminatory policies (even though not necessarily discriminatory intent) are in operation. It is to be contrasted to an approach where complaints by individuals are dealt with on a case-by-case basis or with "small" class action suits where each member of the affected class is specifically named.

SUSAN B. CARTER

PAY EQUITY. See COMPARABLE WORTH

PEASANT SOCIETIES are primary producers who convert the natural resources of their environment into subsistence goods, typically through agricultural and home craft production within complex societies. The basic production and consumption unit is the household, usually composed of family members only, but in some cases, of servants as well. While the products of peasant labor are primarily for their own consumption, a portion (either in kind or cash) is directed to market exchange and to ceremonial exchange within the local community. Also, some of the peasant's product is siphoned out of the peasant household and community through taxes and rent to support state-level functions and functionaries (e.g., armies, bureaucrats, the aristocracy, the church). In addition to its products, peasant labor may be directly extracted in imperative labor services to the landlord, the state, the church, and the local community. As an ideal type, peasants are distinguished from primitive, village-level horticulturists by being economically and politically bound to towns and state and a subordinate rural class within a stratified society. Peasants differ from capitalist farmers in that peasant production is primarily for subsistence rather than for the market and profit, and from landless agricultural laborers in that peasants control the means of production (especially land) and, typically, do not view labor as a commodity to be bought and sold. For a more comprehensive analysis of the peasantry from an anthropological perspective, see Eric Wolf's definitive study (*Peasants* [Englewood Cliffs, N.J., 1966]).

Peasant, as an ideal type, encompasses enormous cross-cultural variety, from the villages of feudal Europe to the present Mexican campesino and the worker in a Chinese communist agricultural commune. Given the depth and breadth of variation between peasantries, few generalizations can be made about the position of women in peasant society. However, a significant one derives from Michelle Rosaldo's distinction between the domestic and public spheres of life ("A Theoretical Overview," in M. Rosaldo and L. Lamphere [eds.], *Women, Culture, and Society* [Stanford, 1974]: 17–42). In social evolutionary terms, the distinction between domestic and public life is more significant in peasant societies than it is in simpler (and earlier) societies where kinship organizes economics and politics. In every society in which the peasantry are an important sector of the population, power is more centralized and more public and the centers of power more remote from the local community. Therefore, women's close association with domestic life (especially childrearing) places an additional handicap on their participation in public decision-making and public power. Second, peasants, as opposed to primitives, live in class-stratified societies. Since stratification is a central organizing principle, patriarchy may be reinforced and reinforcing, as, for example, in ancient Chinese and Indian empires.

In general, then, the development of peasant societies with status and class stratification meant less involvement by women in public life and less public power. However, at the level of the local community, where public power is less significant, women's position within the peasantry varies considerably. It varies with inheritance patterns, the gender-based division of labor, and the weakness or strength of the patrilineal descent principle. Peasant women's status relative to men's is highest when women inherit productive resources equally with men, where women and men contribute equally to agricultural labor, and where patrilineal descent systems are either absent or weak. An example of this is the Otavalo Indian women of highland Ecuador, who enjoy relative equality of power with their men within the local village and ethnic group. An example of the opposite—where only men inherit land and perform the agricultural labor and where the patrilineal descent system is strong—is rural, upper-caste women in India, whose status is relatively low even at the local village level.

One of the important debates related to the question of the status of women in peasant societies is whether the change from peasant to capitalist farmer or wage laborer (a process often labeled "economic development" or "modernization") improves or degrades the status of women relative to men. Prior to recent questioning by feminist anthropologists, it was generally assumed that economic development would improve women's position in society; absolutely, through a rise in the general standard of living, and, relative to men, through the adoption of liberal, democratic ideals. Laurel Bossen ("Women in Modernizing Societies," *American Ethnologist* 2 [1975]: 587–601), in an examination of several peasant societies, found no case in which this assumption was unambiguously true. Further, the job segregation and wage differentials that contribute to the feminization of poverty* in the United States are also found in developing societies with more devastating consequences, given their lower standard of living and higher unemployment levels.

LYNN WALTER

PHYSICAL ATTRACTIVENESS. The degree to which one's appearance conforms to a prevailing ideal standard of beauty and therefore is perceived as pleasing to the eye. It is derived from the expectations of the beholder interacting with the physical characteristics of the beheld. Like gender and race, physical attractiveness is an easily observable trait that serves as an information cue. It strongly influences how a person is perceived by others and consequently becomes a source of stereotyping. Although beauty standards are in constant flux, a high level of agreement in ratings of physical attractiveness prevails within a culture at a given time. Measures of attractiveness based on general consensus are quite reliable. Preschool children can accurately judge the appearance of their playmates and have already begun to stereotype others according to looks. The relative level of a person's physical attractiveness generally remains fairly stable over the life span.

There is a strong tendency for people to believe that what is beautiful is also desirable in other ways. Highly attractive people of both sexes are assumed to be happier, kinder, socially competent, and more successful than less attractive people. They also receive preferential treatment from friends, parents, teachers, and employers in a wide variety of situations. Beauty bias or "looksism" is real and is applied differently to members of each sex.

There is considerable evidence that physical attractiveness is emphasized and valued more highly in females than in males. Parents rate newborn daughters as pretty and cute, but they see infant sons as strong and active. The cuter the baby, the more likely it is to be judged a girl. People recognize and remember female faces more readily than male faces and possess better defined concepts of ideal attractiveness for women than for men. Ratings of physical attractiveness correlate more highly with ratings of femininity* than with those of masculinity. As they grow older women are judged to be not only less attractive but also less feminine. In contrast, men are seen as less attractive but not less masculine as they age. Males consistently place greater emphasis on good looks when choosing dates and mates than do females.

Appearance also influences psychological adjustment. When clinicians were asked to rate the characteristics of mentally healthy adults, they indicated that a healthy female would be more concerned with her appearance than a well-adjusted male would be. Preoccupation with physical attractiveness promotes both insecurity and excessive narcissism. Yet this pathology is frequently overlooked because it remains a culturally sanctioned requirement for "healthy" adjustment to the feminine role.

Belief in one's own attractiveness can be as difficult to achieve as physical beauty itself. Body image is as much a function of subjective self-perception as of objective attractiveness. Self-ratings do not correlate highly with evaluations made by others. Women tend to distort their own body image in the negative direction, just as depressed people of both sexes do. In contrast, men tend to distort body image in a more positive direction, just as nondepressed people do. Adolescent girls express increasing concern about their appearance in comparison to their peers than do boys. Poor body image is frequently reported among women who may distort their mental image of a particular body part and then generalize this distortion to their whole appearance. Negative body image in females is unrelated to actual levels of physical attractiveness. Women are less satisfied than men are with their appearance and are much more concerned about their weight.

The relationship between physical attractiveness and self-concept is especially salient for people whose appearance is in some way either unusual or incongruent with the current vogue. Low self-esteem can result from an underlying body loathing or can lead to it. Men derive self-esteem from a variety of sources including achievement, economic strength, and fitness, while women's sense of self-esteem is more highly correlated with self-ratings of attractiveness.

Good looks can be a liability as well as an asset. Pretty women are more vulnerable to sexual exploitation and to harassment on the street or on the job. They complain of not being taken seriously and suffer anxiety when their beauty begins to fade with age. As compared to men, middle-aged women are more threatened by the loss of attractiveness with age, and they make greater cosmetic efforts to preserve a youthful appearance.

In the occupational sphere, good-looking people are more readily hired and promoted for positions that are deemed traditionally appropriate for a candidate of that sex. However, attractiveness can also be a professional hindrance. Exceptionally pretty women are disadvantaged when aspiring to top management jobs because their beauty is seen as incompatible with the traits of leadership and authority that such jobs require. For many females, a conflict persists between cultivating beauty or brains, between pursuing attractiveness or pursuing achievement. Adolescent girls still report that they hide their accomplishments in order to enhance their social acceptance.

Body beautification is a universal social gesture. Rituals of adornment are used by both males and females to display themselves, to accentuate greater contrast between the sexes, and to signal social conformity. Cosmetics, hairstyles, fashion, all create gender differences that are culturally contrived rather than naturally acquired. In most societies males and females decorate differently but to an equal extent. However, for the past two centuries in Western culture, body adornment and cosmetic rituals have been highly associated with feminine vanity. Females are referred to as "the fair sex" (as well as the weaker sex) and are encouraged to use physical attractiveness as an important source of social power. Consequently, appearance has become a major arena of competition between women and a key factor in their economic and social survival.

Feminists have been concerned with a variety of issues related to physical attractiveness including health, mobility, and sexual and commercial exploitation. A century ago, fashion reformers advised women to remove corsets, put on bloomers, and ride bikes to achieve a healthy glow. A new phase of the women's liberation movement was ushered in when demonstrators picketed the 1968 Miss America contest, protesting the exploitation of women as beauty objects. Feminists of the 1970s were sometimes stereotyped as "homely libbers" or "bra burners," just as the suffragettes a century earlier were described as "unsexed women devoid of physical attractiveness."

Further References. S. Brownmiller, *Femininity* (New York, 1984). R. Freedman, *Beauty Bound* (Lexington, Mass., 1986). R. T. Lakoff and R. L. Sheer, *Face Value* (Boston, Mass., 1984).

RITA JACKAWAY FREEDMAN

PHYSICIANS. See HEALTH CARE PROVIDERS

POLITICAL OFFICE (U.S.). See OFFICIALS, WOMEN ELECTED AND APPOINTED

POLITICAL PARTICIPATION BY WOMEN (EUROPEAN) reflects diverse political and cultural traditions. Women were enfranchised at widely different times. The Scandinavian nations first gave women the vote, beginning with Finland in 1906. Immediately after World War I nine North and Central European nations followed suit: Great Britain, Ireland, Luxembourg, the Netherlands, Germany, Austria, and the three Baltic republics. Women's suffrage was also included in the constitutions of various Soviet republics. The interwar period saw the extension of women's suffrage (generally short-lived) south and east, to Poland, Czechoslovakia, Hungary, Greece, Spain, and Turkey. Then, after World War II women won the vote in the remaining European nations, the last holdout, the Principality of Liechtenstein, succumbing in 1984. Thus, while women in Scandinavia have been voting for several generations, women in some other countries have had only limited experience with the franchise. Swiss women were enfranchised for national elections only in 1971; Spanish and Portuguese women are just beginning to vote again with the reinstatement of democratic elections.

These different histories of enfranchisement affect the turnout rates of women. In the early enfranchising nations of Northern and Central Europe, women and men today vote at nearly identical rates; sex differences are less than 1 percent. In contrast, in late-enfranchising countries women may still lag behind men unless voting is mandatory or quasi-mandatory, as in Italy, Greece, and, of course, Eastern Europe. For example, in Switzerland recent sex differences* in turnout are the largest known in present-day Europe: the 1975 Samuel Barnes and Max Kaase survey found an 18 percent difference, with 50 percent of women and 68 percent of men claiming to have voted in the general election (S. Barnes and M. Kaase, "Political Action—An Eight-Nation Study" [Survey available from the Inter-University Consortium for Political and Social Research, University of Michigan]). However, these remaining differences in voting rates should narrow, as they did in early enfranchising nations. Note that wherever differences have disappeared, women constitute the majority of the electorate because of their predominance in the adult population.

In every West European country where data are available, women once were more likely to vote for the parties of the right. This "gender gap" was greatest, over 10 percent, in Italy and France during the 1950s. There women particularly favored the religious parties of the right, while men especially supported the Communist parties. The presence of a politically powerful Catholic church combined with women's greater religious practice accentuate this gender gap. (Note that women tended to favor Protestant religious parties as well. For example, Norwegian women voted slightly more for the traditional Christian People's party.)

Secularization and other factors are currently eliminating this gender gap in voting, however. In fact, a new type of gender gap may be emerging; survey data indicate that women slightly favored the parties of the left in Norwegian and British elections of the early 1980s.

Sex differences still persist in other types of political participation. Everywhere women profess less interest in politics and are less exposed to political information via the mass media* and interpersonal communications. A 1983 survey of the ten European Economic Community countries showed that attitudes toward women's political activity can still be quite restrictive. When asked if politics should be left to men, two-fifths of the West Germans and one-third of the Luxembourgers, Irish, and Belgians agreed. The Danish were most egalitarian, with only one-tenth agreeing with the statement. Besides culture, women's homemaking and childrearing roles constrain their political activity; sex differences tend to be smallest in those types of participation that are most compatible with traditional female roles such as ad hoc and local community activities.

Political parties, essential gateways to political office in Europe, rarely represent women equally to men. In only a few known instances do women make up half or more of the membership: Great Britain's Conservative party, the small religious parties of Norway, Denmark, and Sweden, and a few other small conservative or moderate Scandinavian parties. The parties of the left usually have lower percentages of female members because they recruit more through unions, where women are scarcer. However, these parties' greater commitment to equality often leads to special efforts to increase women's representation in party office and parliamentary parties. Nevertheless, the ratio of male to female party members can be quite large, for example, three-to-one (or more) in the Italian and East European Communist parties and both major parties of West Germany.

Representation in political office also varies enormously across Europe. Data from the early 1980s show Scandinavia with the largest proportion of women in national legislatures. Except for Iceland, one-quarter to one-third of the delegates are women. Eastern Europe also ranks high, with between one-sixth to one-third of the delegates being female. In these latter countries elite decisions to increase women's representation can produce strikingly rapid changes, as in Romania and Bulgaria. In contrast, change occurred more gradually in Scandinavia, with the rate of increase accelerating after the mid-to-late 1960s. Iceland and the Netherlands also rank relatively high, with 15 and 19 percent female legislators respectively.

For the remaining European nations women's representation in the lower house ranges between 4 and 11 percent. Women fare better in countries where voters choose between party lists of candidates, for parties are less reluctant to nominate a woman when several candidates run as a group. In contrast, single-member districts and plurality election systems lessen women's representation. Great Britain, one of the few European nations with this electoral system, has one of the lowest proportions of women.

The Law of Increasing Disproportion operates in Europe, as elsewhere. That is, the proportion of women shrinks as the power of the position increases. Thus women are not as common in cabinets and government ministries and on the sometimes quite influential consultative committees representing powerful economic interests. Likewise, East European women are scarcer in the governing organs of the Communist party, the Central Committee, and the Politburo. Moreover, higher proportions of women usually are found at the local, compared to the national, levels of government. Nevertheless, Western Europe's parliamentary system tends to facilitate women's access to the highest office. Europe has had two female prime ministers: Margaret Thatcher of Great Britain (Conservative party) and Gro Harlem Brundtland of Norway (Labor party).

Further References. C. A. Christy, *Sex Differences in Political Participation* (New York, 1987). J. Lovenduski, *Women and European Politics* (Amherst, Mass., 1986).

CAROL A. CHRISTY

POLITICAL PARTICIPATION BY WOMEN (U.S.) has a history as long as America's. Abigail Adams admonished her husband John and the founders of the new nation to "remember the ladies." But even before the American Revolution, colonial women were politically active in behalf of literacy, general education, and religious tolerance.

The first political action organized by women was the Seneca Falls, New York, conference, in 1848, called by Elizabeth Cady Stanton and Lucretia Mott. There, over 100 women and some men signed a Declaration of Sentiments including the resolution "that it is the duty of the women of this country to secure to themselves their sacred right to the elected franchise." From that moment until the Nineteenth Amendment was ratified in August 1920, three generations of women used every political means available in order to secure what is now regarded as a fundamental right. Thus, the protest and demonstration tactics of present-day feminists can be seen as part of a long heritage of political activism by women.

Kansas became an early scene of controversy over woman suffrage, and is the first state in which a constitutional amendment granting suffrage to women was introduced. In 1867, two suffrage amendments emerged from the state legislature, one enfranchising black men and the other enfranchising women. The state received nationwide attention, and the fight was fierce. Susan B. Anthony made her famous trek across the state, spending many nights camped out under the stars. Other noted feminists, such as Stanton, Lucy Stone and her husband Dr. Henry Blackwell, and the Reverend Olympia Brown, the first woman ordained as a minister of the Universalist church, blazed campaign trails with her. Their efforts were not enough. The woman suffrage amendment failed in popular referendum, by a vote of 9,070 for to 19,857 against.

But by the 1880s, Kansas, like other western territories, enfranchised women for local elections, and women quickly used that power to virtually seize control of many town governments. Wyoming became the first state to enter the union with woman suffrage in 1890. Next came Colorado, in 1893, and Utah and Idaho followed in 1896. Some attribute the West's relatively quick move to grant women political rights to the necessity for cooperation between men and women as they pioneered together, although others emphasize that women's "traditional" concerns about public schooling and community affairs were motives for gaining the vote.

Nationally, though, the progress of this early women's movement was not so steady. The movement seemed to slow and falter in the late nineteenth century. New desire for reforms in labor, public health, and social conditions, however, galvanized the movement once more, as reformers thought that a "woman's vote" would help to bring about social change. From about 1908 the struggle intensified, and 12 years later women were enfranchised. All women were first eligible to vote in 1920, and by 1924 their turnout ranged from around 20 percent in the South to a high of 40 percent in Illinois.

For much of this century, women trailed men in their voting turnout rates. Other forms of women's participation, the protesting, petitioning, and marching, in which suffrage activists had engaged, also temporarily disappeared from the scene. Generations of gender-role socialization, teaching women *not* to be politically active, had to be overcome. The World War II years offer an exception: women dominated at the polls in the presidential election of 1944, with so many male voters overseas. But women's war work, as, for example, Red Cross volunteer or Rosie the Riverter, marked an entry of women into public spheres that persisted and grew.

In 1970, on the 50th anniversary of the ratification of the Nineteenth Amendment, a new generation of feminists staged a Women's Strike for Equality. Despite doubts about response, thousands and thousands of women participated, making it one of the first of many mass events of the most recent wave of feminism*. Since then, women have used every political tactic available to them in the quest for equal rights. Women's voting rates also have caught up with, and in some cases passed, men's. By 1980, the gap between men's and women's turnout had completely closed, with 59 percent of each sex voting. Older women and women who have little education, who are blue-collar workers, or who are housewives, continue to vote with less frequency than men. This is more than compensated for by well-educated women, and women in sales, managerial, and professional occupations, who participate more than do their male counterparts. Since women outnumber men in the population, the identical turnout rates by sex actually means that the majority of voters are women.

Whether this numerical majority would mean a change in the way votes are cast has interested contemporary observers, and evidence suggests that the "gender gap," the phenomenon of men and women preferring different candidates and different public policies, is real. Since 1980, women and men have cast their votes differently. While 61 percent of men voted for Ronald Reagan in 1984, only 57 percent of women did so. More striking are the findings that gender gaps in several states have been great enough to determine election outcomes. Mark White of Texas, for example, believed that he owed his 1982 election to the governorship to women. In 1986, women voters provided the margin of victory for Democratic Senate candidates in Louisiana, North Carolina, Washington, and Colorado. Not all women are alike by any means. But public opinion polling in the 1980s has shown repeatedly that women tend to prefer some policies more than most men do. It may be that the hope of the early activists, that a "woman's vote" would be used for reform and change, will be vindicated.

Women's voting has always been tied to women's participation in other, less traditional kinds of political participation. Women demonstrated, protested, and agitated to *get* the vote, and with each successive wave of feminism, these forms of political participation have gone hand in hand with ever-growing numbers of women at the polls.

Further References. S. Baxter and M. Lansing, *Women and Politics: The Visible Majority* (Ann Arbor, 1983). E. Flexner, *Century of Struggle* (Cambridge, Mass., 1959). E. Klein, *Gender Politics* (Cambridge, Mass., 1984).

SUE TOLLESON RINEHART

POLITICAL PARTIES are a source of political influence for women and an increasingly significant outlet for their political ambition.

The two major U.S. political parties seek to win elections to influence the policy-making process. Women's integration into the major parties has occurred across the twentieth century; the parties' contexts have worked to encourage and maintain the extent and direction of women's participation. As the policy-making process is the government's central focus, women's participation in political parties is a significant source of influence for them.

Partisan influence is affected by the nonprogrammatic nature of the major parties. Rather than determine what their candidates' policy stands will be, these parties label candidates Democrat or Republican for voters. The two parties are not strikingly different in ideology; and candidates set their own issue positions.

Partisan participation occurs in a heterogeneous setting. The two major parties are made up of a series of formal organizations; become effectual in several government settings; and are characterized by citizens' strong, moderate, weak, and, for some, nonexistent identification with them.

An early nineteenth-century traveler in the United States, Alexis de Tocqueville, noted that "even the women often go to public meetings and forget household cares while they listen to political speeches. For them clubs to some extent take the place of theaters.'' Before U.S. women had universal suffrage, they had auxiliaries to the Democratic and Republican parties. Women also were active in third parties, which operate as pressure valves in the U.S. political system and may lead to changes in the major parties. Third-party activists have included women such as Mary Ellen Lease, who organized and worked in Farmers Alliances and the resulting Populist party; near the nineteenth century's end the Populist party set off a realignment of groups underlying the Democratic and Republican parties. Although the names of the two major parties may stay the same, a realignment changes the two-party system.

Women have run for public office on third-party tickets. In 1872 on the Equal Rights line, Victoria Claffin Woodhull ran for president. In the 1890s women began to be elected to state legislatures on major party lines, and in 1916 on the Republican ticket, Jeannette Rankin (Montana) was elected to the U.S. House. In 1918 she ran unsuccessfully for the U.S. Senate on the National party line, not having received the Republican nomination. In 1940, as a Republican, she won a second term in the House.

In 1920 the Nineteenth Amendment to the U.S. Constitution gave women universal suffrage. Officeholders who led the major parties expected women to vote as a bloc and feared for their own incumbencies. Using quotas, party leaders began integrating women into national, state, and local party committees. These committees administer party business. National American Woman Suffrage Association (NAWSA) president Carrie Chapman Catt expected women to inform "the whole field of public life with woman spirit" and urged them to join a major political party.

Bypassed by Catt was the National Woman's party (NWP), a militant offshoot of the NAWSA that advocated a responsible parties system. In this system parties take responsibility for their candidates not only by labeling but also by offering distinctive policy programs and requiring candidates to adopt both label and program. After 1923, the NWP basically offered a "one-plank platform," a constitutional equal rights amendment. Major women's organizations opposed the amendment because it would nullify protective labor legislation, a policy concern of theirs. Neither major party responded to the NWP's sectarian influence; and its "woman for Congress" action did not catch on.

A bloc of women voters did not emerge until 1928 and 1932, because newly enfranchised groups need socialization into the electorate. Republicans ceased to court women so ardently. But women such as Mary (Molly) Willliams Dewson achieved sex-typed posts as Democratic party regulars and, along with public officials such as Frances Perkins and volunteers like Eleanor Roosevelt, made inroads through the Women's Division of the Democratic National Committee (WDDNC). Entry into the electorate by women, immigrants, and young people and change to Democratic party labels of black, Jewish, and working-class people contributed substantially to President Franklin Roosevelt's election and led to another major party realignment. Because of the importance in the New Deal's evolution of women activists working through women's clubs, until World War II the WDDNC was so prominent it maintained year-round headquarters with a paid director; among its functions was patronage distribution to key Democratic women.

The presidential nominating conventions first emerged in 1832. Convention delegates operate as a social force in their own right and compose a pool of potential candidates for office. Women convention delegates' history is less known than that of women as party regulars and volunteers. At least since 1912, the major parties have differed proportionately in their integration of women delegates; but women have achieved greater representation as delegates, regardless of party, than as congresspeople or state legislators. Republicans have had fewer women delegates than Democrats, who since 1932 have relied for support on a coalition of disadvantaged social groups. In context the Democratic party may offer women more political "pleasure" and opportunities than the Republican. In 1972 the Democratic party's McGovern-Fraser Commission upgraded requirements of proportionate representation among delegations of women, young people, and minorities; Republicans introduced similar changes. Women now constitute 35 to 45 percent of delegations. Like men, these women delegates are socialized to internal party standards and are similarly professional.

Where gender roles* influence women's partisan roles, they influence ambition and type of activism. The context of formal party organization can reinforce or stimulate change in women's ambition and activism. Women and men delegates to the 1972 conventions felt equally ambitious about their party careers, but women showed less ambition than men for public office. Republican women were most likely to shun public office seeking for continued party activism. They did not, however, lack ambition. Differences in the foci of Republican and Democratic women's ambition related to differences in their family-work roles. Among party regulars at Atlanta, Georgia, the ambition levels of Democratic and Republican women stemmed from early learning experiences that varied by party identification; Democratic and Republican men were not so affected. Among white women ambition depended upon countersocialization to unconventional gender roles. Black women party regulars' ambition related to politicization in their parental families and also to what they made of their current activities.

A person's party identification is a self-identification likely learned in childhood in the family setting. If there are two parents at home and the two do not have the same identification, because of her often greater proximity to childrearing the mother may most influence a child's development of an identification. Single parent homes with children most often are headed by women, increasing opportunity for a mother to influence a child's identification. No distinction by sex is made among children in this transmission. In adulthood, certain situational factors may mitigate or supersede childhood learning. The party identification of women in the paid workforce and of single women especially is least influenced by factors external to them.

Women are said to be "more partisan than men" because women will most likely have a party identification. Women and men with an identification do not tend to differ, though, in desire to see their party prevail in a presidential election; education and an election's circumstances account for any differences. Women and men also do not differ in degree of party loyalty.

Women running on major party tickets in congressional, state legislative, and municipal general elections are as likely as men to win their contests. Democratic women candidates for Congress are more likely than Republican women to win, because Democratic women run in urban districts where most voters are Democrats. Republican women's opportunities to run tend to come in districts not as friendly to their party. Women running on third-party lines lose because third parties lose; more women run on these lines than as Democrats or Republicans. Barriers to women's achievement of public office on a major party line are found in the educational and occupational status of many women; in certain electoral district factors, which also may interact with a candidate's race; and in voters' tendencies to re-elect incumbents, who are mostly men.

Further References. R. Darcy and S. S. Schramm, "When Women Run against Men," *Public Opinion Quarterly* 41 (1977): 1–12. D. L. Fowlkes, J. Perkins, and S. T. Rinehart, "Gender Roles and Party Roles," *American Political Science Review* 73 (1979): 722–780. J. S. Lemons, *The Woman Citizen: Social Feminism in the 1920s* (Urbana, Ill., 1973). V. Sapiro and B. G. Farah, "New Pride and Old Prejudice: Political Ambition and Role Orientations among Female Partisan Elites," *Women and Politics* 1 (1980): 13–36.

SARAH SLAVIN

PORNOGRAPHY was originally used to refer to various descriptions of the lives of prostitutes. The term is derived from the Greek *pornographos*, which means "writing of harlots." Within and outside the legal community, the terms *pornography* and *obscenity* have often been confused. The term *obscenity* has mainly referred to filthy and disgusting acts or depictions that offended people's sense of decency. Pornography was traditionally not viewed as obscene in the sense of shame and filth. Catholic canon law initiated a confusion of the two terms. For the most part, Victorian morality reinforced the confusion, and the Supreme Court of the United States has maintained it. It seems unlikely that in the near future the two terms will become untangled although various attempts have been made.

Unfortunately, even today the term *pornography* has been loosely applied to many forms of explicit (and even nonexplicit) depictions of sexual activity. What depictions are considered pornographic depend to a large extent on the political and religious orientation of those who use the term. For some, pornography is defined as depictions that elicit or are intended to elicit sexual arousal. Others have suggested that the label apply only to materials that include degrading and dehumanizing images of women, not simply those that are sexually arousing. And for others the term refers only to those depictions that are violent in nature.

Feminist Gloria Steinem, for example, stresses the idea that the dehumanizing aspect of pornography distinguishes it from material that may be termed "erotic." According to Steinem, the message in pornography is one of violence, dominance, and conquest in which sex is used to create an inequality between men and women. Pornography also suggests that pain and humiliation are to be seen as pleasurable for women. On the other hand, erotica depicts sexual expression between people that is mutually pleasurable and does not require the viewer to identify with a conqueror or victim.

One definition which has received considerable support within the feminist community is that which was offered by Catherine MacKinnon and Andrea Dworkin as part of a Pornography Ordinance in the city of Minneapolis. This ordinance defined pornography as: The sexually explicit subordination of women, graphically depicted whether in pictures or in words, that also includes one or more of the following (a) Women are presented dehumanized as sexual objects, things or commodities; (b) Women are presented as sexual objects who enjoy pain or humiliation; (c) Women are presented as sexual objects who experience sexual pleasure in being raped; (d) Women are presented as sexual objects tied up or cut up or mutilated or bruised or physically hurt; (e) Women are presented in postures of sexual submission or sexual servility, including by inviting penetration; (f) Women's body parts, including but not limited to vaginas, breasts, and buttocks, are exhibited, such that women are reduced to those parts; (g) Women are presented as whores by nature; (h) Women are presented being penetrated by objects or animals; (i) Women are presented in scenarios of degradation, injury, or torture, shown as filthy or inferior, bleeding, bruised, or hurt in a context that makes these conditions sexual.

The material in question must meet each part of the definition—it must be sexually explicit *and* graphically depicted in pictures or words and must contain at least one of the listed characteristics—to be considered pornography.

When the research community has discussed the effects of pornography upon the viewer, these definitional problems have also surfaced. As an aid in understanding the large amount of research in this area, researchers have recently grouped the variety of materials used in their research into six categories. Rather than employing the term *pornography*, the research community tends to use the following categories in their discussions:

1. Nonviolent, low-degradation sexually explicit stimuli: This material is most consistent with Steinem's definition of erotica (e.g., nonviolent, noncoercive, and nondegrading, but sexually explicit). This material would usually be X-rated.

2. Nonviolent, high-degradation sexually explicit stimuli: These materials are considered demeaning and degrading to women. What they have in common is the debasing depiction of women as willing recipients of any male sexual urge (excluding rape) or as oversexed, highly promiscuous individuals with insatiable sexual urges.

3. Violent pornography: This material depicts sexual coercion in a sexually explicit context. Usually, a man uses force against a woman in order to obtain sexual gratification. A common theme of many of these depictions is to portray "positive victim

outcomes." Rape* and other forms of sexual assault are depicted as pleasurable, sexually arousing, and beneficial to the female victim. This theme contrasts with other forms of media violence.

4. Nonexplicit sexual aggression against women: This category includes depictions of sexual violence against women that are similar to violent pornography but are less sexually explicit (i.e., are not X-rated).

5. Sexualized explicit violence against women: The materials in this category are R-rated and, while less sexually explicit than X-rated materials, are far more graphic in terms of violence. These materials do not depict positive victim outcomes, and the violence is not sexual violence (rape) but contains images of torture, murder, and mutilation. The unique feature of this material is the sexual context in which this violence occurs.

6. Negative-outcome rape depictions: These materials depict graphic and brutal rapes, but unlike most forms of violent pornography there is no indication that the victim enjoys being raped. The materials may or may not involve explicit depictions of sexual activity.

It is important to note that this typology includes materials that would not be considered obscene or pornographic in a legal sense. Likewise, the six categories do not completely classify the materials into mutually exclusive categories. They have, however, allowed researchers to better understand the influence that pornography has upon the viewer.

For those attempting to answer the question "does pornography have any positive or negative effects on individuals?" the conclusion is as straightforward as the definition of pornography—confusing. The 1970 *Commission on Obscenity and Pornography* basically concluded that pornography was not harmful to individuals. More recently, the 1986 *Attorney General's Commission on Pornography* declared that most forms of pornography are directly related to crimes of sexual violence. It is important to note that both commissions were criticized for their findings, methodology, and recommendations.

The resolution to this conflict of whether pornography is or is not harmful may never be resolved, as both the term *pornography* and its potential effects are tied up in moral, ethical, emotional, and political debates. The public discussion of the issue, however, should go a long way to resolving many of the issues.

Further References. E. Donnerstein, D. Linz, and S. Penrod, *The Question of Pornography: Research Findings and Policy Implications* (New York, 1987). A. Dworkin, *Pornography: Men Possessing Women* (New York, 1981). L. Lederer, *Take Back the Night: Women on Pornography* (New York, 1980).

ED DONNERSTEIN

POSTPARTUM DEPRESSION. After giving birth, some women experience feelings that can vary from a day or two of the "baby-blues" to a long period of severe depression. During pregnancy, physiological changes give the mother a sense of well-being. After childbirth, a rapid drop in estrogen and progesterone levels are combined with the reality of incessant demands from a completely dependent infant present 24 hours a day, every day. A first-time mother especially may have difficulty in adapting to the new demands on her life. The severity of postpartum depression has been found to relate to the individual mother's tolerance of stress, the condition of her surroundings, her attitude toward her pregnancy and motherhood, and her relationship with the child's father and others with whom she is closely associated as well as to changes in her hormone levels.

POVERTY still characterizes a large segment of the American population. Between 1959 and 1973, the number of poor fell from 39.5 to just under 23 million; the poverty rate was cut in half, from 22.4 to 11.1 percent. But, between 1973 and 1983, both the numbers in poverty and the poverty rate began to rise; by 1983, these numbers were the highest since 1964.

The composition of the poor has changed as well over the last 25 years. The female share of the overall poverty population was the same in 1983 as in 1966 (the earliest available data). The poor today, though, are more likely to be single females, members of female-headed households, elderly females, or members of minority groups.

The growth of female-headed families and their greater representation among the poor has been a particularly noticeable trend over the last quarter century. Between 1959 and 1983, female-headed families in the United States grew from 4.3 to 10.4 million, from 9.8 to 14.3 percent of all families. These families are more than four times as likely to be poor as male-headed families.

In 1983, 35.4 percent of all poor people lived in households headed by women, up from 17.8 percent in 1959, while the percent of the poor living in families headed by men had declined from 69.8 to 45.1 percent. Currently, 40.5 percent of all persons in female-headed households live in poverty, versus 9.3 percent of those in male-headed households.

The increase in female-headed families has been particularly disastrous for the children in these households. In 1983, there were 13.8 million children under the age of 18 in households in poverty. Over 55 percent of all children living in female-headed households were in poverty, compared to 13.4 percent of the children living in other types of households.

For black families, these trends were even more exaggerated. The number of poor blacks remained nearly constant between 1959 and 1983 (about 9.9 million). But the percent of poor blacks living in female-headed households rose from 29.3 to 53.8 percent of all poor blacks in those same years. This means that 75 percent of the black children in poverty lived in female-headed households.

Poor women share many characteristics with poor men. The poor, compared to the nonpoor, have less education, lack market-relevant job skills, and are located in relatively job-poor locations. But the greater rates of poverty among women can be traced to three distinctly gender-related causes.

First, women in poverty are more likely than other women to be unmarried, and thus to depend on only one adult as income producer. In 1983, female-headed households had only 43 percent of the income of married-couple households ($11,790 vs. $27,290 for married-couple families). This disparity increases when female-headed households are compared to married-couple households with wives in the paid labor force ($32,110—almost three times the income for female-headed households). Further, while between 1972 and 1982, married-couple families managed an increase in median family income, the median income for families maintained by women declined almost 5 percent when adjusted for inflation. Thus, not only did female householders have greatly less purchasing power than did male-headed households, but their relative position has been deteriorating over the last 15 years.

Second, women who head their families often bear most or all of the economic costs of rearing their children. Married women share substantially in the resources obtained by their husbands. The woman's share declines sharply if the husband is absent. For example, in 1975, only 25 percent of the women eligible actually received child support. Roughly one-third of the fathers required by the courts to pay child support never make a payment. Only 5 percent of never-married fathers provide child support.

The number of poor female-headed households is increased by the growing numbers of unwed mothers. Between 1960 and 1980, the proportion of unmarried women aged 15 to 19 who were mothers increased from 15 to 28 of every 1,000. Further, 57 percent of births to black women in 1982 were out of wedlock, compared to 12 percent of white births. Approximately 60 percent of unwed mothers had incomes under the poverty threshold; three-fourths of the unwed mothers aged 15 to 19 were receiving Aid to Families with Dependent Children (AFDC) in 1980.

Third, sex discrimination* and occupational segregation* in a segmented labor market increase women's representation among the poor. While most women today expect to work or have worked, sex-role socialization* in general and vocational preparation in particular do not prepare women to be primary breadwinners. Further, women are concentrated in what are called secondary sector jobs (marginal, seasonal, sporadic, low-paying positions).

Although many new jobs have been added to the American economy in the last quarter century, these have offered workers little likelihood of moving out of poverty. The vast majority of these new jobs have been in the service sector, which pays much less than primary sector jobs. The wage differential between manufacturing jobs and jobs in retail trade illustrates this point. In 1970, for every dollar earned in manufacturing wages, retail trades workers earned 62¢. By 1980, this differential had increased: for every dollar earned in manufacturing, the retail trades worker earned only 51¢. Women have increased their participation in the labor force, but that increase has gone mostly to service jobs so that women's relative share of the national income does not reflect their share of the jobs.

Even when women enter primary sector jobs, they continue to suffer the effects of sex discrimination. Thus, women who worked full-time year-round in 1986 earned only 64¢ on the dollar earned by male full-time year-round workers.

Recent changes in women's occupational choices, and in litigation and legislation, have moderated this disparity somewhat, but the differential remains.
Mary Corcoran et al. assert that two-thirds of the wage gap* between white men
and white women, and three-quarters of the wage gap between white men and
black women, "cannot be accounted for by sex differences* [between women
and men] in skills, work participation, or labor-force attachment." Thus women
income-earners have significantly less money to support themselves and their
families than do men income-earners.

The "culture of poverty" thesis argues that a significant component of the
people in poverty constitutes a distinctive subsociety that passes poverty on across
the generations. This "permanent underclass," the argument asserts, shares a
set of values, norms, attitudes, expectations, and structural arrangements that
socialize its members into a pattern that malequips them for participation in the
larger social and economic structures of American society. Recent data do not
support such a thesis. Rather, it appears that there is a continual movement across
the poverty threshold, with a sizable number of "floating poor," or individuals
and families who remain suspended above the poverty line until illness, rent
increases, unemployment, additional children, or family dissolution leads them
into the ranks of those officially defined as poor.

Changes in household composition are a better predictor of changes in economic status than variables usually proffered, such as education or achievement
orientation. That is, decisions about marriage, divorce*, or additional children
have a strong impact on the resources available to members of a family*. These
factors tend to have a greater impact on women than on men.

Marriage*, or a woman's relationship to a man, continues to have the most
profound impact on a woman's economic well-being. Entering a marriage typically has an immediate positive effect on a woman's income, while divorce,
separation, desertion, and widowhood* tend to have an immediate negative
effect. Marriage tends to have the opposite effects for men.

Entering marriage thus tends to promote women to an enhanced economic
status, while leaving marriage tends to demote them. Likewise, remarriage leads
to greater income gains for women than for men. Since the great majority of
divorced women, especially younger women, do remarry, their tenure in poverty
is usually temporary. Black women tend to marry or remarry at lower rates than
white women, and they tend to stay single longer if they do remarry. Thus the
dip into poverty for black women tends to be of longer duration than that for
white women.

Hence, rather than a large cadre of permanent poor female-headed families
characterized by a "culture of poverty" transmitted over the generations, most
poor should be seen as transients in poverty. This is illustrated by the tenure of
people on welfare rolls. For example, contrary to popular belief, over half of
all AFDC families have been on the welfare rolls for under three years; only 7
percent have been recipients for ten years or more.

While poor adult females share many characteristics with poor adult males, they are distinguished by three specific marks. Poor adult females are more likely to depend on one adult as income producer for the family. Further, female householders bear the economic burdens of childrearing. This is particularly acute for never-married mothers. Finally, females continue to suffer the effects of differential sex-role socialization and of sex discrimination in the occupational structure of our society.

Nevertheless, the majority of female poor do not exist in a transgenerational "culture of poverty." Rather, they should be characterized as transient poor, moving into and out of poverty in response to changes in family composition, in the economy, and in demands on the family budget. Women's marital relationships continue to have a profound impact on women's economic status, so that, for females, the unmarried state increases their likelihood of being poor. Sexual stratification in America continues to exert a primary influence on women's economic status.

Further References. M. Corcoran, G. J. Duncan, and M. S. Hill, "The Economic Fortunes of Women and Children: Lessons from the Panel Study of Income Dynamics," *Signs* 10 (1984): 232–249. W. P. O'Hare, "Poverty in America: Trends and New Patterns," *Population Bulletin* 40, no. 3 (June 1985): 2–43. U.S. Bureau of the Census, *Current Population Reports*, Series P–60, 146 and 147 (1983) (Washington, D.C., 1985).

ALLEN SCARBORO

PREGNANCY. See GESTATION

PREMENSTRUAL SYNDROME (also Premenstrual Molimina, Pre-Menstrual Tension Syndrome) is a combination of usually minor but sometimes serious psychological and physical symptoms experienced during the week preceding menstruation. These symptoms may include irritability, weight gain, tension, restlessness, depression, swelling, especially of the breasts, headaches, and other discomforts. Observable for most women but not very often incapacitating, these premenstrual problems are popularly called "PMS." In the medical profession, however, the term *premenstrual syndrome* is generally reserved for severe physical or psychiatric cases, like unbearable headaches, suicidal tendencies, or acute depression. (See MENSTRUAL CYCLE.)

A number of studies show that the premenstrual syndrome is most intense in women between the ages of 30 and 40; others find that it intensifies after each pregnancy. Some medical researchers say that as few as 20 percent of all women suffer from PMS, whereas others claim that PMS is universal, affecting all women to some degree or another.

The consensus today is that PMS has a physiological origin, but that it is accompanied by certain psychological symptoms, and that it is not one "disorder" but many. Yet with the overwhelming evidence that the premenstrual syndrome has real physical symptoms, physicians are still not sure how to treat it. Often the theories and experiments of one researcher are not borne out by the work of another.

For nonprofessional treatment of the problems of PMS it is best to watch one's diet, to get plenty of exercise, to restrict salt, to be observant about the effects of tranquilizers or oral contraceptives, and to use a diuretic (although the use of caffeine as a diuretic may possibly exacerbate breast tenderness and hypoglycemic-type symptoms).

Professional treatment varies. According to its leading advocates the most effective is progesterone therapy, developed by a British doctor, Katharina Dalton. There are no known significant adverse side effects to long-term progesterone use (perhaps mainly because no conclusive studies of long-term progesterone users have yet been published). Antiprostaglandins, along with thyroid treatment and prolactin suppression, are among other medical therapies for PMS relief.

Information for this article is based on *The Curse: A Cultural History of Menstruation*, by Janice Delaney, Mary Jane Lupton, and Emily Toth (New York: E. P. Dutton, 1976) and on an updated edition (Champaign: University of Illinois Press, 1987).

MARY JANE LUPTON (WITH JANICE DELANEY)

PRISON, MOTHERS IN. At midyear 1985 there were 22,646 women in state and federal prisons nationwide, an increase of about 180 percent since year end 1974. Roughly 67 percent of the women in prisons had one or more children under age 18; more than 30,000 children were affected by their mothers' incarceration. Studies indicate one of the greatest concerns of incarcerated mothers is their children. Several studies describe the characteristics of these women, their general feelings about the separation, and the problems confronting agencies in meeting their needs and the needs of their children.

Incarcerated mothers tend to be black more often than white, under 35 years old, usually divorced or never married, and, like most incarcerated women, poorly educated and poorly skilled. With few skills and little education, they have a limited selection of job options. In 1979, those women who had held jobs prior to incarceration usually worked in traditional female positions (i.e., waitress, cook, or secretary), and earned average wages of $2 to $3 per hour, the equivalent of about $6,000 to $9,000 a year.

Most incarcerated mothers have two or three children, and many have children under 13 years old. More than half of them lived with their children prior to arrest, and many had not been separated from their children in the past by incarceration. Although little is known about the quality of the mother-child relationship before the mother's arrest, most inmate-mothers plan to reunite with their children following release; thus, they perceive the separation by incarceration as only temporary.

During the mother's incarceration, relatives, usually the woman's own mother, care for children. If relatives are unavailable or unsuitable to care for children, they may be put up for adoption or, less frequently, placed in foster homes.

Inmate-mothers feel a great deal of conflict, guilt, and shame that their behavior has resulted in the separation. Moreover, many fear that after their release they will be inadequate in disciplining their children. Some mothers fear their children will not know or respect them, or may outright reject them because they have been in prison.

Except for very small children, many children apparently understand that their mothers are in prison, or as some women put it, "in jail" or "a place to be punished." Moreover, mothers frequently tell children themselves that they are in prison; often mothers explain at the time of their arrest or prior to imprisonment that they are going away because they did something bad. Inmate-mothers explain their absence realistically because they fear that their children will lose respect for them if they find out the truth from someone else.

Many mothers retain legal custody of children during incarceration; those who voluntarily relinquish custody do so because they feel that caregivers in the community will be better able to obtain services and meet the needs of their children. Although most of the women who gave up custody plan to regain it upon release, they fear their felony conviction will make this process more difficult.

Institutional visitation policies determine the extent of mother-child contact during incarceration. Women's prisons in several states including California, Florida, Georgia, Iowa, Kentucky, Missouri, New Jersey, Texas, Minnesota, Nebraska, New York, Tennessee, and Washington provide parenting programs, extended daylong visits, or overnight visitation with mothers. The federal women's reformatories at Alderson, West Virginia, and at Pleasanton, California, also provide parenting and extended visitation opportunities. The women's prison at Bedford Hills, New York, has the only nursery in this country where infants born to inmate-mothers after their incarceration may stay with their mothers for up to a year after birth.

However, prisons are security-oriented and foster a sense of dependence, while alternative programs, perhaps in the community, that house inmate-mothers and children together can encourage independence. An important component of this approach is voluntary involvement of inmate-mothers in the development, implementation, and operations of these programs. In order to develop a vested interest in the program and a sense of responsibility, inmate-mothers must participate in determining the selection criteria and process, the nature and directions of the program, rules and disciplinary procedures, and for themselves, whether they want to participate. A less security-oriented environment that encourages independence and personal growth and that provides access to community resources enables inmate-mothers to develop a better sense of responsibilty for themselves and for their children and to plan realistically for their transition into the community after their release.

Further References. P. J. Baunach, *Mothers in Prison* (New Brunswick, N.J., 1985). B. McGowen and K. Blumenthal, *Why Punish the Children?: A Study of Children of*

Women Prisoners (Hackensack, N.J., 1978). A. Stanton, *When Mothers Go to Jail* (Lexington, Mass., 1980).

_____

The views in this article are those of the author and do not reflect the views or policies of the Bureau of Justice Statistics or the U.S. Department of Justice.

PHYLLIS JO BAUNACH

PRISON, WOMEN INMATES IN. Women currently comprise only 4 percent of the state and federal prison population and 7 percent of the population of local jails. Historically, too, women's numbers have been low relative to those of male prisoners. While these differences may be partly due to "chivalry"— judicial reluctance to commit women (or at least white women) to penal institutions—a better explanation lies with women's much lower crime rates, especially for serious offenses. Socialized to give rather than take, to be nurturant rather than aggressive, women of the past and present have been far less involved than men in crime. Ironically, their low rates of offending and commitment have worked to put women at a disadvantage within jails and prisons.

Through the mid-nineteenth century, women were incarcerated alongside men in predominantly male institutions. Supervised by men, they were subjected to various crimes of sexual exploitation. When scandals ensued, officials tended to blame the women. To minimize contact between male and female inmates, officials gradually isolated the latter into separate cellblocks or small buildings of their own off in a corner of the prison compound. Although isolation improved protection, now women were cut off from whatever services were available. Chaplains, physicians, and teachers found it bothersome to visit the women's quarters and often ignored them entirely. In any case, these officials were male and hence less attuned to the needs of female inmates. Today, their much smaller numbers continue to create similar problems for women who are held in sections of mainly male jails and prisons.

About 1870, officials began to establish separate penal institutions for women, a policy still favored though it has not been put into practice by jurisdictions whose female populations seem too small to justify the expense of a separate institution. Even when women were given institutions of their own, however, the problem of low numbers continued to pose barriers to equal treatment. The current situation of women held in state institutions provides an example. Most states operate only one prison for women. Whereas the more numerous men's prisons can specialize by security level and type of treatment (drug cases, work-camps for those nearing release, a separate institution for the mentally ill, and so on), the state's sole prison for women must attempt to provide the full range of treatment. Usually it fails; states have found it too expensive to deliver, in one small women's prison, the many options available to men. Thus women have far fewer programs and much more limited access to medical and legal resources. In addition, having but one possible placement, women are more likely to be incarcerated at a considerable distance from family, friends, and community resources.

The numbers problem is not the only source of the inferior conditions of women inmates. Gender, too, has placed them at a disadvantage. Since the prison system began, women have been assigned to sex-stereotyped jobs—cooking, cleaning, and sewing uniforms for male inmates. These jobs have paid less well than those available to men, and they have put women at an employment disadvantage after release. Even today, most women's institutions offer few programs other than cosmetology, typing, and institutional chores. Further, these institutions continue to stress conformity to a narrow definition of the "good woman," pure and passive, as a requirement of early release. Gender has thus combined with low numbers to create the situation in which women experience discrimination on the basis of sex.

For the first time in U.S. history, women inmates recently have begun to challenge discriminatory treatment through the courts. Increasingly, judges are ruling in their favor and requiring jurisdictions to provide equal treatment—not identical but comparable care—for incarcerated women and men. Although to date women have won only a handful of these cases and it is not at all clear how satisfactorily jails and prisons will respond to court orders, this type of litigation has the potential for dramatically improving the lot of female prisoners.

The profile of the woman inmate has not changed greatly since the early nineteenth century. Most female prisoners are young adults, in their twenties. About 50 percent are women of color. Most are poor and poorly educated— currently, 60 percent have not completed high school. Over 40 percent of women incarcerated today were charged with a violent crime, 36 percent with a property crime, 13 percent with substance abuse, and the rest with other types of offenses.

Within institutions, many women join "pseudo-families," make-believe kinship networks in which an inmate may act as a sibling to some family members, as mother, child, aunt, or uncle to others, and as husband or wife to yet another. As studies since the turn of the century have indicated, black and white women are particularly likely to pair off in couples (this is one reason why there is much less racial tension in women's than men's institutions). Sexual activity is less important in the formation and maintenance of pseudo-families than their ability to provide goods and services, relief from boredom, and substitutes for actual family relationships.

The majority of female inmates have children who, at the time of incarceration, were dependent solely on them. In this respect, too, women differ considerably from male inmates. A man, if living with children at the time of imprisonment, usually leaves them with his partner; women seldom have this option. Finding means to provide for dependent children forms a central anxiety of incarcerated women. Throughout the country, the most successful efforts to help women inmates are being organized around means to relieve this anxiety and maintain ties between the prisoners and their children.

Further References. N. H. Rafter, *Partial Justice: Women in State Prisons, 1800–1935* (Boston, 1985). T. A. Ryan, *State of the Art Analysis of Adult Female Offenders and Institutional Programs* (Washington, D.C., 1984).

NICOLE HAHN RAFTER

PROSTITUTION is a form of nonmarital sexual activity characterized by financial reward and absence of long-term fidelity between the parties. This definition includes neither promiscuity without material gain nor concubinage*, in which a couple lives together as husband or wife or, in some legal systems, in an inferior form of marriage in which the man does not convey his rank or quality to the woman, although many discussions of prostitution will include one or both of these.

Early History. Whatever its origins, prostitution was well established by the time of the Babylonian Empire. Its most famous epic, *Gilgamesh*, features a prostitute sent to entrap and weaken an innocent hero. In fact, the only occupations for women mentioned in the Babylonian law codes (c.2000 B.C.) are priestess, tavern worker, and prostitute.

These prostitutes of the Tigris-Euphrates Valley were ranked in a hierarchy similar to that found in many parts of the world. First were the temple prostitutes, mistresses of the gods who sometimes took the form of priests or rulers; whether they should be defined as prostitutes is questionable, since their sexual intercourse was a sacred enactment of the annual rebirth of vegetation, not a commercial enterprise. Second were courtesans, entertainers as well as sexual partners. Third were women who worked in taverns or houses of prostitution, and last were slaves of individuals or temples, whose earnings belonged to their owners.

The Old Testament mentions prostitution frequently. Moses forbade fathers to prostitute their daughters, but the law allowed a father to sell his daughter as a concubine. Daughters of priests were forbidden to become harlots, nor could priests marry harlots, but these strictures did not apply to other Israelites. This separation between prostitution and the priesthood may have been a reaction to the sacred prostitution practiced among Israel's neighbors, in which the prostitute herself was regarded as a priestess or sacred person.

The prostitute played a particularly prominent role in the life and literature of classical Greece where proper women did not participate in public or social life. Prostitution was so accepted that many states levied a tax on it; tradition ascribed the Athenian tax to the legislator Solon, who reputedly filled the brothels with female slaves and used the tax revenue to build a temple to Aphrodite, goddess of love. Brothel prostitutes were lowest in status and price, below streetwalkers and women who worked in inns. Musicians, singers, dancers, acrobats, and other entertainers often added to their income by prostitution. Most respected of the prostitutes were the hetaerae, whose superior education, training, and charm enabled them to win the affections of the most prominent and powerful men of their time. Claiming the patronage of Aphrodite, hetaerae used their skills in dress, makeup, sexual techniques, male psychology, and conversation to amass fortunes and influence the powerful, often establishing long-lasting relationships and winning respect, although not respectability. When Pericles divorced his wife and lived openly with Aspasia, the poets and politicians who had celebrated her wit, wisdom, and beauty when she was his mistress turned on her when she tried to assume a more conventional status; she was insulted openly in the streets and was brought to court on a charge of treasonable impiety.

Roman prostitutes never achieved the influence or status of Greek hetaerae, perhaps because Roman matrons played a larger part in social, commercial, and political affairs than did their Greek counterparts. Since a wife could supply intellectual and social companionship, relationships with prostitutes were purely sexual, which undoubtedly contributed to their low status. No woman of the knight class was allowed to register as a prostitute; prostitutes were not allowed to approach the temple of Juno (patroness of married women) lest they pollute it, and they were often required to dress in styles that distinguished them from proper matrons. Prostitution was tolerated as an evil necessitated by the importance of chastity for respectable women and the fact that many men could not afford to marry at all or until late in life; soldiers, for example, were not allowed to marry during their 20 years of military service. Continence for such men was seen as desirable, but probably biologically impossible. These attitudes permitted prostitution to exist but did not lead to the celebration of the courtesan found among the Greeks.

Although most Romans considered sex a biological necessity, at least for males, neo-Platonist and neo-Pythagorean philosophers considered celibacy an attainable ideal for both sexes. This attitude was adopted and elaborated upon by the early Christians, who combined hostility toward sex with compassion for the prostitute, an attitude encouraged by the tradition of Mary Magdalene, the converted prostitute who was the first witness to the reappearance of Jesus. Although the church fathers imposed a stricter sexual morality than that found in the Old Testament and treated women as sources of temptation to men, they saw the prostitute as a woman who had been led astray and could be saved: Mary the Harlot, Mary the Egyptian, Afra, Pelagia, Thais, and Theodota were all redeemed prostitutes who achieved sainthood.

Islam. Islam regards sex as a gift from Allah, to be thoroughly enjoyed within marriage, but women were seen as the source of male sexual pleasure, not as partners or companions. This attitude produced a special class of high-priced courtesans as well as a larger number of less-skilled prostitutes. Unique to Islam is the *mut'a*, a form of temporary marriage contract lasting from a fraction of a day to several years. The man supports the woman only for the duration of the contract, and any offspring of the union are considered legitimate.

India and China. Hindu women were portrayed as highly sexual beings in need of protection by early marriage. With secluded, uneducated wives, men might seek the company of courtesans well versed in dancing, music, and literature. Their presence was expected during formal visits and required when the king performed certain state ceremonies. Young girls could be donated to temples where they learned singing and dancing and earned money for the temple through prostitution; there were also secular prostitutes who were allowed to own property.

In China, commercial brothels, located in a special quarter of the city and taxed by the state, reputedly date from the seventh century B.C., and prostitutes who could amuse with songs, dances, and conversation were an indispensable feature of upper-class entertainment. Courtesans skilled in poetry and the arts might become independent and wealthy. Lower-class prostitutes were owned by their brothel keepers and lived under strict supervision, having no choice of customers. Since Taoism and Tantric Buddhism taught that regular intercourse was essential to male well-being, there was a lively market for prostitutes of all classes.

The Middle Ages. The legal basis of medieval prostitution is found in the Emperor Justinian's codification of Roman law (c.A.D. 500), which followed earlier practice: toleration of prostitution while trying to curb its worst abuses. The forced prostitution of daughters and slaves was forbidden, and the distinction between prostitution and concubinage was legalized, the latter classified as an informal type of marriage characterized by ''marital affection.'' In the thirteenth century Thomas Aquinas summed up much of medieval thinking when he compared prostitution to a sewer in a palace. If the sewer were removed, the palace would be filled with pollution. Similarly, if prostitution were abolished, the world would be filled with rape and other sexual crimes.

The later Middle Ages brought systematic attempts to segregate prostitutes by confinement to specified sections of cities and by distinctive dress. In Paris, prostitutes lived in the quarter known as the Clapier, which gave the name *clap* to the venereal disease gonorrhea*. Contemporary observers, however, repeatedly noted that prostitutes could be found in all parts of the city, openly soliciting customers. The end of the Middle Ages and beginning of the Renaissance saw the reemergence of the courtesan, the woman whose virtues attracted love as well as lust. Codifiers of courtly love made it clear that such virtues were to be found only in upper-class women; ordinary prostitutes were not worthy of the courtesies and attentions merited by the courtesan.

The Reformation and the Pox. ''Renaissance morality'' collided with the Prostestant Reformation. Both Martin Luther and John Calvin rejected the toleration of prostitution as a means of avoiding greater sins. They preached premarital virginity and marital fidelity for both sexes; Calvin went further, teaching that the primary function of marriage was social, that the wife was the lifelong associate of the husband.

In the sixteenth century, religious hostility toward prostitution was joined by a powerful ally—a particularly virulent outbreak of syphilis. In 1536 the Imperial Diet of the Holy Roman Empire prohibited all extramarital relations including prostitution. A series of edicts closing brothels and enacting harsh punishments for both prostitutes and customers followed. By the end of the century, however, the fear of the disease and the energy of the reformers both declined. Prostitution resurfaced and, in the seventeenth and eighteenth centuries, blossomed with the elaborate brothels that characterized the London and Paris of that time. Then, at the end of the century, mass mobilization of men for the Napoleonic Wars spread gonorrhea, and renewed concern about prostitution, throughout Europe. The authorities tried to confine prostitutes to certain areas, register them, and enforce regular medical inspection, often with compulsory hospitalization for those found to have the disease. Given the medical expertise of the time, it proved impossible in most cases to trace the source of contagion, only the most obvious cases could be detected, and the lack of aseptic techniques probably meant that the inspections themselves spread the infection. Nevertheless, variants of this system were to be found all over Europe. England, however, repealed similar regulations in 1886, after a campaign waged largely by women demonstrated not only that the measures virtually legalized prostitution but also that they were ineffective, discriminated against poor and working-class women, and allowed police officers to blackmail and intimidate both prostitutes and innocent women. Prostitution was again practiced openly and without regulation, although Victorian morality of the later nineteenth century dictated greater discretion, at least among the upper classes.

American attitudes toward prostitution tended to reflect those of Europe, modified by the fact that migration and the settlement of the frontier often brought about a dramatic imbalance of men over women. Although many American cities considered regulatory systems, most just tried to confine prostitution to "red light" districts, allegedly named for the lights trainmen left outside of the brothels they were visiting. A 1917 survey, however, found that relatively few cities had been able to maintain such "tolerated" districts.

Twentieth Century. In Britain, prostitution itself has been decriminalized, although solicitation on the streets is illegal. Some European countries license prostitutes and restrict them to certain areas of the city, while others have decriminalized prostitution entirely. Communist countries claim to have eradicated prostitution entirely, but visitors question these claims. In the United States prostitution remains illegal in 49 of the 50 states, although enforcement of the laws is often erratic. Some prostitutes have banded together into organizations like COYOTE (Call Off Your Old Tired Ethics) in an attempt to have prostitution decriminalized.

The decline of the double standard*, the recognition of women as sexual beings, and increased economic opportunities for women have contributed to the decline, although not the disappearance, of prostitutes, who are still sought by men who want sex with no other obligations, men with unusual sexual proclivities, those who find prostitution sexually exciting, and those who believe that they are unable to attract other women. There is some speculation that the liberation of women is producing a group of male prostitutes to service women with the same needs.

Further Reference. V. Bullough and B. Bullough, *Prostitution: An Illustrated Social History* (New York, 1978).

DOROTHY H. BRACEY

PROTECTIVE LEGISLATION is a term used to designate labor laws enacted to give exceptional or preferential status to selected categories of workers, notably women and children. Originating in England in the first decades of the nineteenth century, laws were passed initially to limit the working day of young children and apprentices to 12 hours. By the 1830s the increasing employment of children and women in English factories gave rise to demands for more extensive action by the state for "protection." Descriptions of physical hardships in factories, textile mills, and coal mines led to official investigations by parliamentary committees. As a result of an industrial survey undertaken by a British Royal Commission, the famous Sadler Report of 1832 documented the "degradation" of factory workers and, despite the opposition of laissez-faire liberals who opposed all governmental intervention in economic activities, a landmark bill of 1833 forbade employment of children under nine and limited the working day of those under 13 to eight hours. The Factory Acts of 1842 and 1844 extended the legislation to women, outlawing their labor in mines, prescribing a maximum 12-hour day, and prohibiting nightwork (between 8:30 P.M. and 5:30 A.M.). Critics of conservative right- and left-wing views agreed that the effects of the factory system were often deleterious for all workers but assumed that their potential to corrupt the health and, especially, the morals of women was worse; furthermore, they assumed that women were by "nature" less able than men to protect themselves. Continental countries followed the British lead. In the 1830s the prestigious Academy of Moral and Political Sciences in Paris commissioned the famous study by Dr. Louis Villermé, which exposed the terrible working conditions of women and children and focused on the resulting "demoralization" of the working classes and consequent "degeneration" of the French nation. Villermé also linked the employment of women in factories with prostitution*, which he labeled the "fifth quarter" of the working woman's day. Aristocratic Catholic political leaders, socialists, and even some liberal economists called for "English legislation." However, legislation specifically addressing the condition of working women* was adopted only in 1874, when their employment underground was prohibited, leading to a decline in women's share of employment in mining and metallurgy from 9 to 2 percent. Laws comparable to the British legislation of the 1840s waited until the 1880s and early 1890s in Germany and France, respectively, and until the early twentieth century in the United States. In many cases, effective enforcement lagged long behind.

Political leaders, journalists, and social reformers of many persuasions, often opposed on other issues, united in the interest of "safeguarding the reproductive forces" of their nations by limiting women's access to factory labor, and thus their potential for exploitation under unhealthy or unsafe working conditions.

Working-class men often supported restrictions on female labor as a means of limiting competition for jobs, especially in artisanal industries threatened by the reorganization of work processes and the introduction of machinery that reduced the demand for skilled craftsworkers. By conflating the problems of female industrial labor (outside the home) with other aspects of the woman question, many reformers as well as workers came to accept the passage of protective legislation as a solution to broader, more fundamental issues related to women's changing social roles. Thus it served to deflate pressures for reform of gender inequalities and, indeed, inaugurated a new form of institutional inequality, for protective legislation, by restricting female factory work, increased the pressures on women, especially those who were married, mothers of young children, older, or in poor health, to work longer hours for lower pay in industrial homework. (See HOMEWORK.) Specific injunctions, such as limits on lifting heavy objects or working at night, came to be used as justifications for denying women access to job opportunities; and the general assumption that women were weaker and in greater need of protection than men workers continued to contribute to the denial of equal access to employment even after protection laws were extended to both sexes. Protective legislation also helped channel women into newer white-collar and low-paid service jobs. It also served to create dissension between groups of women reformers, separating "social feminists" (usually educated middle-class women concerned with social reform and supportive of exceptional legislation to "protect" working-class women) against "equal rights feminists" (usually educated middle-class women concerned primarily with reducing gender inequalities). Working-class women themselves sometimes opposed protective legislation out of concern for maximizing their earnings; nightwork often carried premium wages and longer hours increased total pay. Professional women viewed protective legislation as further discrimination* against women that "add[ed] another inferiority to all those from which they suffer[ed] already." Conflict over protective legislation has been credited with accelerating the decline of feminist activity in the second quarter of the twentieth century. For the perspective of an American social worker, see Mary Anderson, *Woman at Work* (Minneapolis, 1951), esp. Chapter 19, "The So-Called Equal Rights Amendment" (159–172). For an opposing point of view of a French feminist, see the excerpt by Maria Pognon in *La Fronde* (December 20, 1899) (trans. K. M. Offen, in S. G. Bell and K. M. Offen (eds.), *Women, the Family, and Freedom*, vol. 2: *1880–1950* (Stanford, 1983), 211–213.

Further References. E. F. Baker, *Protective Labor Legislation* (New York, 1925), esp. Chapter 7, "The Controversy," 429–456. M. J. Boxer, "Protection Legislation and Home Industry: The Marginalization of Women Workers in Late-Nineteenth, Twentieth-Century France," *Journal of Social History* 20 (1986): 45–65. A. Kessler-Harris, *Out to Work: A History of Wage-Earning Women in the United States* (New York, 1982), esp. Chapter 7, "Protective Labor Legislation," 180–214. M. L. McDougall, "The Meaning of Reform: The Ban on Women's Night Work, 1892–1914," in J. F. Sweets

(ed.), *Proceedings of the Tenth Annual Meeting of the Western Society for French History,
14–16 October 1982* (Lawrence, Kans., 1984), 404–417.

MARILYN J. BOXER

PSYCHOANALYTIC CONCEPTIONS OF WOMEN represent a family of
theories that are derived from and related to the works of Sigmund Freud (1856–
1939). The psychoanalytic approach originated in Freud's scheme of the dynamics, structure, and development of the human psyche. Behavior is motivated
by sexual energy (the *libido*) that is directed toward areas sensitive to pleasurable
stimulation. With development, these zones of pleasure (erogenous zones) change
their locus in a series of successive developmental stages known as the oral,
anal, phallic, latency, and genital stages. Structurally, the human psyche is
divided into the id (present at birth), the ego, and superego (emerging during
later psychosexual stages). Freud also proposed that one's level of awareness
could either be preconscious (accessible to awareness with small effort), conscious, or unconscious (memories and ideas that cannot voluntarily be brought
to awareness).

Freud's original ideas on sexual development appeared in *Three Essays on
the Theory of Sexuality* (1905). In this work the evolution of male and female
sexuality is presented as parallel processes. For males, this means that the original
love and attachment for mother during the first two stages of life develops into
a "love triangle" during the phallic stage. Now, as the genitals become the
primary area of libidinal gratification, the child's attachment to the mother takes
on sexual overtones, while at the same time the little boy's father is viewed as
a dangerous (i.e., bigger and more powerful) rival. The child's anxiety over this
state of affairs is exacerbated by the "realization" that women are castrated and
that he too might be so punished if his father learns of his desires for his mother.
As a result of such fears, claimed Freud, the Oedipus complex is "smashed to
bits" when the male child gives up his libidinal attitudes toward his mother and
seeks out his father as a source of identification. One important consequence of
the Oedipus complex is the development of a superego that leads to a strong
sense of justice and morality in men.

While acknowledging that female development was somewhat of a mystery,
Freud originally supposed that the above Oedipal drama was similar for the
female. However, in later papers on the subject (e.g., *Some Psychical Consequences of the Anatomical Distinction between the Sexes* [1925] and *Female
Sexuality* [1931]), Freud clearly proposed a different and more complicated
evolution of female sexuality. According to Freud, pre-Oedipal girls, like pre-
Oedipal boys, are strongly attached to their mothers. During the phallic stage,
females find the major locus of libidinal gratification to be the clitoris (an "inferior" form of the penis) and their masturbation therefore takes on an active
(i.e., masculine) character. The Oedipus complex for the female involves a
change in the direction of sexual attachment from the mother to the father and
an abandonment of the clitoris for the vagina as the major autoerotic zone. The

substitution of the vagina for the clitoris is considered to be essential for the establishment of a feminine (i.e., passive) attitude. Perhaps the major impetus for these significant changes in female sexuality during the phallic period is the girls' observation that they, as well as their mothers, do not have a penis. Freud believed that the female must learn to accept the "fact of castration." But the desire for male genitalia leads to "envy for the penis" and great anger and hostility toward the mother for not having one. The little girl's incestuous feelings toward her father are provoked by the desire to obtain a penis through sexual relations with him. It is also such penis envy that leads to the rejection of the "inferior" clitoris. Indeed, the Oedipus complex is only truly resolved when the female symbolically obtains a penis through the birth of a child, preferably a male. Thus, the female personality is born out of envy, a sense of inferiority, a change from active to passive modes of sexual expression, and the despair of castration. Women, according to Freud, were narcissistic as a compensation for their sexual deficiencies, as well as vain, frigid, and underdeveloped with respect to their sense of morality.

A number of students of psychoanalytic theory have refined or reformulated Freud's original conception of female psychosexual development. Representative of those who have remained most faithful to Freud's assumption that biology directs psychology is Helene Deutsch (1884–1982) whose work on female sexuality appears in the *Psychology of Women* (1944). Deutsch emphasized that a full understanding of female sexuality must include a consideration of post-Oedipal events, particularly menstruation, pregnancy, birth, and lactation. The core elements of the female personality, narcissism, passivity, and masochism* stem primarily from the female anatomy and reproductive functions that direct her toward a passive mode of receptivity and waiting, and attract her to pain and suffering (masochism). Failure to switch to the passive feminine mode of sexuality could lead to a conflict-laden "masculinity complex." A significant extension of Freud's theory involved Deutsch's consideration of the importance of the anticipation and experience of motherhood. Deutsch also recognized that the pre-Oedipal girl had a most significant and complex relationship with her mother that must be acknowledged in its own right.

Erik Erikson (b.1902) is also a psychoanalyst who has remained close to Freudian theory. However, he does acknowledge the role of culture and historical context in human development and therefore presents female development in a more sympathetic light. The core of Erikson's theory is the negotiation of eight turning points (nuclear conflicts) throughout the course of development. The task before the individual is to seek a positive resolution to each of the successive developmental tasks. Erikson did not specifically address the question of female development until relatively late in his career. The catalyst for his theory of female development was observations of the play constructions of 10-, 11-, and 12-year-old boys and girls. Boys tended to build erect towers and buildings with elaborate cones and cylinders, and busy street scenes of animals and cars. Girls constructed enclosed spaces that housed peaceful scenes and static figures. From such spatial representations, Erikson saw parallels to male and female genitalia and ways in which they influenced the experiences of biological and social roles. According to Erikson, the essence of a woman's identity development involves her "inner space," which matches the biological ground plan of womb and vagina and its reproductive potential. Identity is centered on the anticipation and realization of motherhood, not the lack of the male organ as proposed by Freud. Problems for women ensue when their potential for fulfillment of this innerspace is not met. In addition, women's psychological interpretation of the inner space leads to a unique constellation of personality characteristics such as warmth, tenderness, nurturance, and compassion.

Representative of psychoanalytic theorists who have significantly departed from Freudian orthodoxy in the accounts of feminine development are Karen Horney (1885–1952) and Clara Thompson (1893–1985). A number of points made by Horney also appear in contemporary criticisms of Freudian theory. For example, Horney emphasizes that psychoanalytic theory presents feminine development from a masculine vantage point. In her revision, Freud's ideas of penis envy, the masculinity complex, female inferiority, and masochism are considered not to be characteristics particular only to women. Horney also refuted the contention that such traits are primarily of biological origin or are significant to female personality development. Rather, such behaviors appear to be culturally related, particularly in cultures where women are denied opportunities to be creative and independent. Horney also objected to the idea that penis envy played a central role in female psychosexuality, pointing out that men can also manifest envy of the anatomical and reproductivity functions of the female. The notion that males may experience "womb envy" or manifest a "femininity complex" was developed further in cross-cultural investigations of male puberty rites and male mimicry of birth (couvade*) by Bruno Bettelheim.

Clara Thompson also believed that cultural factors, in terms of whether they impede or promote the need for growth and competence, were more significant to human development than were biological factors. Thus, women's personalities were not a result of their so-called biological inferiority, but rather due to the ascription of an inferior status to women in a patriarchal society. Thompson reasoned, for example, that what women envied and desired was not the penis but the position of power and privilege attained by those who had one. Thompson did not deny that many women exhibited feelings of inferiority, a poorly developed superego, rigidity, or, in some cases, masculine behaviors. However, such behaviors were a cultural creation, not of biological origin. While Freud claimed that such traits stemmed from a psychological interpretation of one's biological structures (i.e., "anatomy is destiny"), Clara Thompson pointed to the inferior status of women in society, their dependency* on men, and the goals of marriage* and motherhood as the only pathways of achievement possible.

A number of critiques of the psychoanalytic approach to female development refer to its biological and phallocentric emphases. Freud certainly cast women as psychologically subordinate to men and did not offer any hope for their ability to change and develop. Much of this is probably due to the Zeitgeist within which Freud lived and worked. In contemporary psychoanalytic versions of female development, the fusion of the psychoanalytic fundamentals with the acknowledgment of cultural factors has led to a more forgiving and/or positive view of the psychology of the female.

Further Reference. J. Strouse (ed.), *Women and Analysis: Dialogues on Psychoanalytic Views of Femininity* (New York, 1974).

ILLENE NOPPE

PSYCHOANALYTIC DEVELOPMENT THEORY (CONTEMPORARY).

Personality development theories derived from and related to the works of Sigmund Freud (1856–1939). Freud's instinct or drive theory is a conflict theory: mental life develops from the conflict of asocial impulses (id) with socially enlightened defenses against them (ego). All motivational, developmental, and structural phenomena can be explained in terms of drive derivatives and defenses against drive derivatives. All relations with others are directly or indirectly linked to their use in and relevance to drive gratification. Thus, the individual seeks others because they may result in tension reduction.

Psychoanalytic theory can no longer be equated with classical Freudian theory. There are two major revisions of classical theory: (1) ego psychology, represented by the works of Heinz Hartmann (1894–1970) and Margaret Mahler (1897–1985); and (2) object relations theory, represented by the works of W.R.D. Fairbairn (1889–1965) and D. W. Winnicott (1896–1971). Within traditional psychoanalytic theory, Freud's notion that all behavior and all psychic functions are derived from and secondary to instincts was first seriously questioned with respect to ego functions. While attempting to preserve the basic id-ego structural model and the basic assumptions of traditional theory, ego psychologists reworked its structural components. They focused on the development of adaptive (rather than defensive) ego abilities.

Object relations theorists emphasize human connections, a focus that was largely undeveloped in classic Freudian theory. Their work calls into question the relationship between object relations and the underlying conceptual foundations of drive. Within this broad theoretical framework, two major strategies have been used for dealing with relations with others. One involves abandoning the drive model completely. Theorists such as Fairbairn deal with object relations by replacing drive theory with a different conceptual framework in which relations with others determine mental life and replace drive discharge as the force motivating human behavior. Thus, people seek objects (persons) as an end rather than as a means to achieve tension reduction. In the other approach, loyalty to classical drive theory is maintained. The classical model is adapted to recognize the importance of object relations and of self. One adaptation involves utilizing the concept of diagnosis. Otto Kernberg (b.1928), for example, holds that classical theory is apppropriate for neurosis while a model focused on object relations is required for more severe disorders such as borderlines, narcissistic personality disorders, and developmental arrests. Within a second adaptation, sequence is considered in order to encompass relational processes and issues. Winnicott, for example, maintains allegiance to the drive model by keeping instinctual and relational issues temporarily separate, with relational issues at an earlier developmental time. Thus, these theorists start with relational assumptions and move to the traditional version of the Oedipus complex. A third revision of classical theory is self psychology, represented by the works of Heinz Kohut (1913–1981). Self psychology stresses the strivings of people to become and remain cohesive and to fulfill a creative/productive potential. This approach questions the centrality of drive theory.

Contemporary psychoanalytic theorizing on female psychology has been influenced by theoretical psychoanalytic formulations that emphasize object relations and the concept of self rather than instinct as well as cultural changes, findings from research on infant observation and academic psychology, and feminist criticism of Freudian theory. While some formulation of women's development is based on the drive model, most contemporary reappraisals are based on object relations theory.

Freud's theory on female sexuality, derived from his theory about male sexuality, emphasized organs, bodily sensations, reactions to the discovery of anatomical differences between the sexes that lead to penis envy, feelings of inferiority, and the Oedipus complex. Girls blame mother for their castration; turn to father; relinquish masturbation; and become passive, masochistic, and narcissistic. Within this theory, girls' desire to be mother is seen as a conversion of penis envy and desire to be masculine. The girl's task in the Oedipal period is to become heterosexual, which, according to Freud, involves a change of object, a change from activity to passivity, and the shift of primary organ of sex gratification from clitoris to vagina.

Representative of reformulations based on drive theory is the work of Irene Fast (b.1928), who indicates that masculinity and femininity* are parallel constructs. Young children are not attuned to sex differences* or aware of the limitations in belonging to a particular sex. Thus, while Freud pointed to girls' lack and envy, Fast points to the envy of both sexes. Fast draws implication for the Oedipal process resulting from boys' and girls' overinclusive perspective.

Much of contemporary psychoanalytic theorizing on female psychology is based on object relations theory. An important work is that of Nancy Chodorow (b.1944), a sociologist who uses object relations theory to account for gender-related aspects of personality development. Chodorow considers psychodynamic processes within their social and political context. She considers and accounts for the psychological dissimilarities between men and women by pointing to differential effects of the mother's gender on males and females during pre-Oedipal years. Men have a more impersonal and autonomous orientation. Women have an interpersonal orientation in which their attachments to others is central in their lives. These differences result from infants having their first social relationship with women. Boys must develop a masculine role without the continuous presence of a father. As mothers experience their sons as different, mothers treat sons as separate persons. The identity of boys, therefore, is more diffuse. Since girls are parented by a person of the same gender, they experience themselves as more continuous with and related to the external world. Mothers experience their daughters as extensions of themselves and unconsciously communicate this sense of connection and identification. Girls, in turn, have more difficulty separating and individuating from their mothers than boys do. The Oedipal conflict has been reformulated based on the revised pre-Oedipal relationship. While the boy's Oedipal attachment to his mother is perceived as an extension of his pre-Oedipal attachment, the girl's Oedipal attachment to her father is seen as an attempt to free herself from mother and experience a sense of self. Engagement with father is important as it fosters separation and individuation.

Contemporary views on female development stress the pre-Oedipal mother: the differential impact of mother on the gender of boys and girls; the role of learning in gender role identity; and the centrality of separation-individuation. Presently masculinity and femininity are seen as parallel constructs. It is no longer believed, as did Freud, that all children are originally masculine or that girls' desire to be mothers develops other than as a conversion of penis envy and the desire to be masculine. The earliest gender differentiation is believed to be the result of sex assignment, and the behavior of infant males and females differs before sexual distinctions are known, contrary to Freud's belief. Further, gender identity or the knowledge that one biologically belongs to one or the other gender is firmly and irreversibly established by age three for both sexes, rather than as a consequence of the Oedipal conflict. Contemporary thinking is that penis envy, while a phase-specific developmental phenomena, undergoes reworking in subsequent stages, and is not an inevitable outcome of the anatomical differences between the sexes as Freud held.

Further Reference. J. L. Alpert (ed.), *Psychoanalysis and Women: Contemporary Reappraisals* (Hillsdale, N.J., 1986).

JUDITH L. ALPERT

PSYCHOSEXUAL STAGES OF DEVELOPMENT is a five-stage model of the normal development of personality proposed by Sigmund Freud. Freud posited that the major determinants of personality in later life were the result of an invariant sequence of stages occurring, for the most part, very early in life. He believed that the newborn is a sexually charged entity seeking sexual gratification through a predictable sequence concentrating on specific parts of the body termed "erogenous zones." Movement within and between stages is important for satisfactory and healthy adult sexual functioning. There were, however, numerous pitfalls and conflicts to be resolved at each stage. Successful transition through stages allowed enjoying, but not becoming obsessed with, the expression of personal sexual energy. His five stages are:

Oral Stage (approximately the first year of life). Innate sexual energy is focused on oral behaviors. Pleasure is derived from one's lips and oral cavity associated with the taking of sustenance and exploring the environment through oral means. Later in this stage, oral activity also involves biting, a form of aggression. Weaning presents a crisis for the child, who must forsake the breast or bottle even though it provides intense sexual pleasure.

Anal stage (approximately the second year and part of the third). Sexual energy is concentrated on the abilities to "hold on" and to "let go" associated with toilet training. The ability to control one's eliminative functions is seen by Freud as a source of pleasure. As in the oral stage, there is a conflict between satisfying parental demands and the release of sexual tension.

Phallic stage (approximately the third through the fifth years). During this period children become aware of the sexual pleasure associated with the touching of their genitals. Conflict with parental concerns over masturbation is important in this stage. Freud believed this the most critical stage because of the Oedipus and Electra complexes.

Males experience the Oedipus complex—unconscious desires to kill their fathers and sexually have their mothers. The boy resents father, his rival for mother, but hides his sexual interest because he fears paternal retaliation in the form of castration. The normal resolution of this crisis is sexual identification with father, in particular, and males, in general.

Females are assumed to go through a similar but separate process called the Electra complex. Generally, Freud expended little time and less empathy on women. Girls, like boys, start out loving mother and resenting father because he is a rival for mother's attention. In this stage, however, the girl discovers that she has no penis and feels incomplete and inferior to males, perhaps blaming mother for her shortcoming. "Penis envy" is the outcome and the girl is seen as growing into womanhood still stricken by this lack of an organ. She eventually expresses her desire for her father as she sexually identifies with her mother and females in general, but only with the birth of her first male child does this crisis of her incompleteness become totally resolved.

Latency period (from approximately 6 to 12 years of age). Sexuality "goes underground" in this period only to reawaken with puberty. Females continue to feel inferior based on their nonresolution of penis envy.

Genital stage (from late teens until senility). In this final stage of psychosexual development, normal mature healthy sexual functioning is the ideal. Personal sexual pleasure is finally channeled outward as sexual expression and love for another person merge. Women without a male child may be aggressive and hostile to men in an unsuccessful attempt to compensate for their anatomical deficiency.

One could become fixated (stuck) in a stage or regress (revert to an earlier stage)—outcomes by definition abnormal. Crucial to Freudian thought is the premise that the foundations of personality are laid down by the age of five and little can be done to change afterward.

Freudian rebuttal to criticisms of this theory is to point out that these conflicts are powerful and threatening to the individual and hence are driven into the unconscious. Freud believed that "anatomy is destiny," and the demeaning nature of his theory toward women has been the focus of much feminist interest both in and out of the psychiatric profession. Vestiges of these sexist notions still pervade the male-dominated domain of Freudian psychoanalysis.

Further References. A. A. Brill (ed.), *The Basic Writings of Sigmund Freud* (New York, 1938). C. S. Hall and G. Lindzey, *Theories of Personality*, 3rd ed. (New York, 1978).

STEVEN L. ELLYSON

PUBERTAL PROCESSES. Secondary sexual characteristics develop during puberty, when the young girl's body is transformed into that of a woman. This development involves the most rapid growth that the human experiences, with the exception of fetal and neonatal growth. The changes that occur at this time have psychological meaning to the young girl and sociocultural meaning to others, over and above their physical characteristics.

Bodily changes leading to reproductive maturation are preceded by dramatic changes in the endocrine system (glands that secrete internally). Endocrine levels are high in the first months of fetal life, at about two to four months of age, and in late childhood/early adolescence. After infancy, a negative feedback cycle keeps endocrine levels low until age eight or nine, when increases in the amplitude and frequency of hormonal releases initiate alterations in body shape and size. In girls, breast buds typically mark the beginning of secondary sexual development, followed by the appearance of pubic hair. Additionally, height and weight increase; auxiliary hair growth begins; the uterus, labia, and vagina are transformed; and sweat glands begin operating. Body fat rises dramatically, with the distribution resulting in broader hips and proportionately more body fat in hips, buttocks, and thighs in females than males. In boys, one of the first developments is testis enlargement, with penile and body hair growth occurring shortly thereafter. Weight increases are in the form of muscular development. Breaking of the voice and spontaneous ejaculation of seminal fluid are additional male-specific changes.

In order to chart the progression of secondary sexual development, J. M. Tanner devised a system for rating the amount of growth in breasts for girls, the penis for boys, and pubic hair for both (*Growth at Adolescence* [Springfield, Ill., 1962]). This system superimposes five stages upon the continuous process of growth. The growth spurt typically occurs for girls between the prepubertal stage and the midpoint of development (Tanner Stages 1–3) and from the last stage of development to postpuberty (Stages 4 and 5) for boys. The peak of the spurt occurs on the average two years earlier for girls than boys. Menarche*, or the onset of menstruation, occurs late in the process (Stage 4). Increases in weight occur throughout pubertal growth, with a weight spurt around the time of peak height velocity. Rapid weight gain is associated with an accumulation of body fat in girls and increased muscle mass in boys. The most rapid rises in body fat occur during the final stage of development and the postpubertal stage (Stages 4 and 5).

While it takes four to five years to complete the pubertal process, interindividual differences in its onset (and offset) abound; for example, breast development may be initiated anywhere between 8 and 13 years of age and be complete as soon as age 12 or as late as age 18, and still be within normal ranges. Also, intraindividual variability is common; for example, while breast buds supposedly appear before pubic hair, the opposite is seen in one-quarter of all girls. The same is true for the timing and sequencing of other pubertal events. Variability is due in part to the fact that different hormones are associated with different characteristics (i.e., menarche and breast growth are more estrogen-dependent, and pubic hair growth more dependent on androgen), different genetic timetables for various processes, and different cell-receptivity to hormonal effects. Secondary sexual development is typically measured by physical examinations. However, pubertal girls (even their mothers) are able to use the Tanner stages schematics to characterize their growth.

The psychological significance of menarche has been studied quite extensively. In general, menarche heralds increases in social maturity, peer prestige, self-esteem, heightened self-awareness of one's body, and self-consciousness. However, somewhat ambivalent reactions to menarche are reported. Girls who are early and girls who are unprepared for menarche report more negative experiences at menarche than on-time or prepared girls. In addition, not being prepared seems to have long-term effects, as adult and late adolescent females who remember being unprepared report more severe menstrual symptoms, more negative attitudes about menstruation, and more self-consciousness.

Like menarche, breast development is linked culturally to childbearing, as well as to sexuality. Unlike menarche, it is observed by others (no matter how private the girl might wish to be) and may be an event which is frequently commented upon. Little information is available on the meaning of breast development. In one study (J. Brooks-Gunn, "The Psychological Significance of Different Pubertal Events to Young Girls," *Journal of Early Adolescence* 4 [1984]: 315–327), elementary school girls with more advanced breast growth had better adjustment, higher body image, and more positive peer relationships and rated marriage* and children as more important than less advanced girls. Whether such effects are due to the meaning of breast development to girls themselves, the reactions of others, to a press for more grown-up behavior, or some combination of these is not known. The same girls were asked a series of questions about direct comments made to them about their breast development. The one-third who were teased were more physically developed. The most frequent teasers were parents and female peers. Girls were most likely to be embarrassed or angry by others' comments.

Another pubertal event that is not as easily observed is body hair growth. Where it is private like menarche, it does not carry the sexual and reproductive meaning that menarche does. No associations with behavior and adjustment have been found.

In general, girls in whom secondary sexual characteristics appear early may be at more risk for poor body images, negative self-esteem, dieting behavior, earlier dating, and smoking (J. Brooks-Gunn, "Antecedents and Consequences of Variations in Girls' Maturational Timing," *Journal of Adolescent Health Care* 9 [1988]): 365–373. However, these effects are small, and they are often influenced by contextual factors. Perhaps the unique feature of this period of growth is that the young adolescent is able to reflect upon, and in some cases, to affect these changes; to integrate them into her self-identity; and to incorporate others' responses to her changing body and role status into that identity.

Further References. J. Brooks-Gunn and A. C. Petersen (eds.), *Girls at Puberty: Biological and Psychological Persepctives* (New York, 1983). J. Brooks-Gunn, A. C. Petersen, and D. Eichorn (eds.), "Time of Maturation and Psychosocial Functioning in Adolescence," *Journal of Youth and Adolescence* 14, nos. 3 and 4 (1985): 149–372. M. R. Gunner and W. A. Collins (eds.), *Development During the Transition to Adolescence* (Minnesota Symposia on Child Psychology Ser. Vol. 21, Hillsdale, N. J., 1988). R. M. Lerner and T. T. Foch (eds.), *Biological-Psychological Interactions in Early Adolescence: A Life-Span Perspective* (Hillsdale, N.J., 1987).

J. BROOKS-GUNN

PUBLIC SPHERE is the sphere of activity outside the home. Relationships with nonfamily members and business other than that related directly to the consumption needs of the family* are carried out in the public sphere. Employment outside the home, political activity, and economic activity beyond consumer buying of retail purchases for the home are part of the public sphere that, in patriarchal societies, has generally been monopolized by men. Especially during the nineteenth-century "Cult of True Womanhood" the public sphere and domestic sphere* were looked upon as, ideally, mutually exclusive domains, the public sphere under man's control; the domestic sphere, under woman's.

Q

"QUEEN BEE SYNDROME" describes a pattern of antifeminist attitudes held by some women who are professionally and socially successful in male spheres that typically exclude women. Having "made it" on their own, such women identify with men and oppose organized efforts on the part of women to improve their opportunities as a class. For example, the writer Helen Lawrenson described the resurgence of the women's movement in the early 1970s as "a phony issue and a phony movement. . . . These are not normal women. I think they are freaks"("The Feminine Mistake," *Esquire* [January 1971]: 83); and Midge Decter, in her book *The New Chastity and Other Arguments against Women's Liberation* (1973), argued that feminists are neurotic whiners who are incapable of handling freedom.

Although the term *Queen Bee* has been around for decades to describe various species of successful women, the "Queen Bee Syndrome" was defined in 1974 by social psychologists who were analyzing a survey of attitudes toward women and women's liberation for *Psychology Today* magazine. In this survey, highly successful, married professional women were indeed more likely than other groups to believe that "women have only themselves to blame for not doing better in life" and that women can best overcome discrimination* by "working individually to prove their abilities." The Queen Bees were also more likely to be doing most or all of the housework* and child care*, and to believe that it should be that way. They seemed to be grateful to be "allowed" to have careers, and in exchange were prepared to do all the housework and to accommodate their careers to their husbands' work.

Queen Bees always draw media attention out of proportion to their numbers, as has been true at the start of every new phase of the women's movement in this century. For example, after World War II, several prominent female physicians warned other women of the physical and mental "dangers" of having careers. However, the "Queen Bee Syndrome" is actually a tiny blip in the larger picture of women's attitudes toward feminism*. As women enter the workforce and formerly male jobs in larger numbers, and especially as female tokens are joined by others of their gender, the social and economic bolsters of Queen Bee-ness are shattered.

Further Reference. G. Staines, C. Tavris, and T. Jayaratne, "The Queen Bee Syndrome," *Psychology Today* 7 (1974): 55–60.

CAROL TAVRIS

R

RADICAL FEMINISMS. Catharine MacKinnon, the ovular radical feminist, or, as she would say, feminist, wrote me, "Liberal Feminism is liberalism applied to women, socialist feminism* is socialism applied to women and radical feminism is feminism*, hence feminism unmodified." Radical feminism looks Medusa in the eye, and puts women first. To put it more academically, radical feminists believe that gender is the variable that explains more of the variance in women's oppressed condition than any other factor. If a good enough mother and a good enough father were fighting over child custody, liberal feminists, committed to gender neutrality and the ideology of equality as sameness, would be in a quandary (see MacKinnon's *Feminism Unmodified* [1987] for a discussion of equality as an end to subordination rather than treating differently situated people, i.e., women and men, the same). Radical feminists would support the mother (see P. Chesler, *Mothers on Trial* [1987] and *Sacred Bond: The Legacy of Baby M* [1988]).

Because of the emphasis on women as women we have been criticized for ignoring race and class. That statement is either libel or slander depending on whether it is written or spoken. Almost all radical feminists and radical feminist publications such as *Off Our Backs* devote substantial effort, operationally defined as space, to issues of poverty* and its feminization, to women in prison*, and to racism, but we are more likely than liberals and socialists to focus on the effects of race and class on *women*.

It is primarily radical feminism that addresses the pervasive nature of violence in women's lives, including that the violence is *by men*, although Canadian Marxist feminists such as Dorothy Smith and Mary O'Brien speak of such violence and address the failure of Marxists to deal with the problem. We do not say "spouse abuse." We say woman abuse. In contrast, a syllabus for a ten-week graduate course "Feminist Perspectives in the Social Sciences" prepared by a socialist feminist at a midwestern university had *no* topic dealing with violence against women. A syllabus on women and work prepared by another socialist feminist had no reference to sexual harassment.

If we look at particular feminist issues we can see how radical feminists differ from other kinds of feminists. We do not consider rape*, battery, sexual harassment*, incest*, and child sexual assault crimes perpetrated by sick men or the results of sex stereotypes, as liberal feminists do. Neither do we consider such injuries the results of unemployment* or the oppression of working- and lower-class men, as many socialist feminists do. We consider such behavior perpetrated by normal men, statistically speaking, who do it because it feels good and because they have a sense of entitlement to goods and services from women as a class, including infants and the frail elderly in their definition of women. Thus MacKinnon writes, "If you do not see the bloody footprints tracking across your desk you are not writing about women" (*Feminism Unmodified*, 5). And I wrote that an analysis of women's condition without using the concept of misogyny* is not worth killing a tree for (in a review of *Mothers on Trial*, 1988).

We do not consider "surrogate motherhood" and other reproductive technologies an example of women's freedom of choice, as do many liberal feminists. In fact, we consider "women's freedom of choice" an oxymoron, a liberal ideology masking our *lack* of choice. We do not consider pornography an expansion of women's sexual freedom, or speech protected by the First Amendment. Rather we consider it pro-rape propaganda making subordination sexy. Most of us support the MacKinnon Dworkin anti-pornography civil rights model law, although most of us are opposed to obscenity law, a criminal rather than a civil remedy. Civil law empowers the injured party; criminal law empowers the state. It is not censorship, i.e., prior restraint, but sex discrimination.

We are not afraid to say, as MacKinnon has often maintained, that seeing women's victimization as not socially exceptional marks the feminist argument, although "victim" is now a taboo word among many feminists. While we understand the therapeutic value of telling women who have been raped, battered, etc., that they are survivors, not victims, we do not confuse political analysis with therapy. Besides, as MacKinnon noted, why is not telling women the truth about our condition, about the endemic nature of violence against women, a feminist act? Haven't we been lied to enough by men?

Not only are feminists not supposed to speak of women's victimization, but we must not express our anger*. Women say, "I used to be angry." These omissions facilitate coalition politics. In my experience feminist coalition politics makes for much politics but little feminism. Radical feminists are still angry, do use the V word, and are wary of coalitions.

Although we have been called "cultural feminists," allegedly believing in a female and male essence, for the most part we believe that our experience, including our sexuality*, is socially constructed. We agree with Adrienne Rich that we must always ask, "What is it like for the women?" and that heterosexuality is compulsory; that is, there are sanctions for not being heterosexual.

Radical feminists differ on the issue of motherhood; some believe it paradigmatic for relationships in a future good society, while others, such as early radical feminist Shulamith Firestone, consider it the source of our oppression.

We agree with Audre Lorde that we cannot use the master's tools (traditional, i.e., male, methodology) to tear down the master's house. Thus this article is not written in standard (read Male) academic style. And we agree with Mary Daly in considering traditional education "mindbindings" a noun comparable to Chinese footbindings (*Webster's First New Intergalactic Wickedary of the English Language* [1987], 210).

We disagree with the fashionable theory put forth by Dorothy Dinnerstein and Nancy Chodorow that misogyny would wither away as the state after the revolution were children socialized by fathers as well as mothers. We take women's accounts of rape by their fathers too seriously to turn over our children to them. Radical feminists Judith Arcana and Rich say that the solution to motherhood as a institution lies in mothers' bonding with other women, rather than with men. Some radical feminists, such as Jeffner Allen, Monique Wittig, and Christine Delphi, think that women should not be mothers at this time. Other radical feminists think that the mother-child relationship is paradigmatic for relationships in a future good society. Some early radical feminists such as Firestone believed that women's ability to reproduce is a cause of our oppression; others consider our capacity for motherhood a strength.

While there was not a focus on strategy and tactics in the 1970s, radical feminists have become more action oriented in the 1980s, particularly on the issue of pornography and the organizing of poorly paid women. The latter is also a socialist feminist goal. According to Ann Douglas (unpublished manuscript), both radical and lesbian feminism are political theories "linked historically and epistemologically" since they both "assume that men form a class or caste separate from women in all societies," and "that the class or caste of men oppresses women." Both radical and lesbian feminists believe that the personal is the political. This belief system led to organizing collectively rather than hierarchically.

Historically, radical feminist theory was developed by Boston and New York women who realized while struggling for the freedom of subordinated racial groups that they themselves were subordinated sexually and in their work by their macho co-strugglers (see M. Rothschild, *A Case of Black and White* [1982] for data on the systematic rape of the white women who went South for Freedom Summer). They came to understand that male-domination was the root of women's oppression, and that apparently economic issues, such as colonialism, were "developed as an extension of male dominance over women" (J. Donovan, *Feminist Theory: The Intellectual Traditions of American Feminism* [1985], 142, citing Roxanne Dunbar). Radical feminists urged women not to work in groups with men; Dana Densmore pointed out that the sexual revolution was but another ploy to subordinate women. The New York Radical Feminists, started in 1979, believed that women's oppression was rooted in psychological factors, namely, the male need to establish his manhood by subordinating women. Kate Millet's *Sexual Politics* (1970), Susan Brownmiller's *Against Our Will* (1975), and Phyllis Chesler's *Women and Madness* (1972) were early radical feminist classics showing the institutionalization of male privilege in literature, rape law, and psychotherapy.

A useful way to distinguish radical feminist analysts from socialist and liberal feminist analysts is that the former describe the world as it is and draw inferences from that analysis. The latter, having the goal of a humanistic, classless, nonracist, nonsexist society, focus their analysis on how to obtain that goal. In so doing, they soft-pedal the horrors of life for women now and in the past, notably the endemic misogyny and violence against women *by men*.

Would that the radical feminist analysis were wrong. Would that gang rape were not a spectator sport. Would that incest and child sexual assault were exceptional as we once thought. Would that battered women were able to obtain justice in the courts. Would that poverty were not being feminized. Would that all we needed was a piece of the pie and that the pie were not ptomaine. Would that the liberals were right and more legislation were the answer. Would that the socialists were right and socialist revolution were the answer. Would that the feminist spiritualists were right and that feminist ritual and Goddess worship would solve our material problems and the Pentagon were stilled by being surrounded by circles of women.

I agree with MacKinnon that even though our analysis shows the crushing totality of our subordination, as feminists we dedicate ourselves to resistance; "how sisterhood became powerful while women were powerless will take its place among the classic alchemies of political history" (*Feminism Unmodified*, 3).

PAULINE B. BART

RAPE. According to Susan Brownmiller, "If a woman chooses not to have intercourse with a specific man and that man chooses to proceed against her will, that is a criminal act of rape" (*Against Our Will* [New York, 1975], 18). She goes on to point out that "this is not and never has been the legal definition."

The law distinguishes between *forcible rape* and *statutory rape*. *Forcible rape* is defined by the Federal Bureau of Investigation (FBI) as "the carnal knowledge of a female forcibly and against her will." Attempts to commit rape by force or threat of force are also included in this definition. In some states "carnal knowledge" is limited to acts of penile-vaginal intercourse or attempts at such acts, but an increasing number of states are recognizing forced oral or anal sex as rape, as well as the rape of men. Some states also include penetration by an object in their definitions. *Statutory rape* refers to intercourse with a female who is below the age of consent. This age varies from a low of 12 years in some states to a high of 18 years in others.

It was only in the late 1970s that a few states began to recognize and criminalize rape in marriage. More than half the states have now dropped the so-called marital rape exemption, with more states following their lead every year. The rationale behind this exemption was that "marriage, with the promise to obey, implied the right to sexual intercourse with the wife upon all occasions" (H. Feild and L. Bienen, *Jurors and Rape* [Lexington, Mass., 1980], 163).

There are no accurate statistics on the yearly incidence of rape in the United States. In 1986 the FBI reported that 87,340 cases of forcible rape or attempted rape (hereafter referred to as rape unless otherwise stated) had occurred in the previous year. However, these figures do not include the much larger number of unreported rapes. Estimates of reporting range from 1 in 3 (FBI) to 1 in 12 rapes (D.E.H. Russell, *Sexual Exploitation* [Beverly Hills, Calif., 1984], 35). Many rape victims are unwilling to report their experiences to the police because they fear being blamed for their own victimizaton. The FBI figures also exclude from 15 to 19 percent of the rapes that are reported to them each year because the police consider the evidence too weak to stand up in court or because they believe the report is false. Rape is the only crime subject to such high rates of what is referred to as "unfounding." There is a long-standing myth that women often "cry rape" falsely out of vengeance.

According to the FBI, the number of rapes reported to the police in 1985 (excluding the unfounded cases) increased by 6 percent since 1984, and the rate rose from 69 to 71 per 100,000 females. This compares with a rate of 51 per 100,000 females in 1975, indicating a 39 percent increase in the rate of reported rape over this ten-year period. Rape has the lowest apprehension and conviction rate of any violent crime.

International statistics suggest that rape is considerably more prevalent in this country than in other Western nations. Arthur Schiff reported in a 1971 article that while the rate per 100,000 females was 35 in the United States, it was only 1.9 in France, 1.2 in Holland, and 0.8 in Belgium ("Rape in Other Countries," *Medicine, Science and the Law* 11, no. 3 [1971]: 139–143). John MacDonald agrees that "available statistics, despite their deficiencies, suggest that the United States has an unusually high rape rate" (*Rape Offenders and Their Victims*, [Springfield, Ill., 1971], 25). He contrasts his figure of 30 per 100,000 in the United States (year unspecified) with less than 1 per 100,000 in Norway, 3 in England, and 7 in Poland.

In a comparison of 186 tribal societies, Peggy Sanday concluded that rape is not a frequent occurrence in most of them. However, she found high rape rates in societies that were both highly dominated by males and in which considerable violence occurred (*Female Power and Male Dominance* [New York, 1981]). Rates of murder, aggravated assault, and robbery with violence certainly qualify the United States as a very violent society. Whether or not it is more male dominated than other Western nations is, however, a more controversial question.

In recognition of the gross underestimation of the prevalence of rape in the United States conveyed by the FBI figures, a major federally funded study of rape based on in-person interviews with a probability sample of 930 adult female residents of San Francisco was undertaken in 1978. Applying the legal definition of rape in California and most other states at that time, 24 percent of these women disclosed at least one experience of completed rape at some time in their lives, and 44 percent disclosed an experience of attempted or complete rape (Russell, *Sexual Exploitation*). Half (22 percent) of the women who disclosed an experience of rape or attempted rape in this survey had been raped more than once by different perpetrators.

When tracing the rape rates reported by five different cohorts of woman— i.e., women of roughly the same age—survey researchers found that the rape for those San Francisco women became significantly higher for each younger cohort: 22 percent of the women who were 60 or older had been victimized by rape or attempted rape at some time in their lives compared with 34 percent of the women in their 50s, 46 percent of the women in their 40s, 59 percent of the women in their 30s, and 53 percent of the women aged 18 to 29 (Russell, 1984). Since the youngest cohort still had the most years when they would be at risk of rape, their rape rate was the highest per number of years at risk.

Thirty-five percent of the 930 women surveyed by Russell had been the victims of rape or attempted rape by an acquaintance, friend, date, boyfriend, unrelated authority figure, lover, or ex-lover—over 3 times more than had been victimized by a stranger (11 percent). Twelve percent of married women had been the victims of rape or attempted rape by a husband.

Other studies conducted on student populations also report very high rates of rape or attempted rape. In several studies, Eugene Kanin and his colleagues found that from 20 to 24 percent of female college students and senior high school students disclosed at least one experience of forceful intercourse or attempted intercourse in the year prior to the studies (for example, see E. Kanin and S. Parcell, "Sexual Aggression: A Second Look at the Offended Female," *Archives of Sexual Behavior* 6, no. 1 [1977]: 67–76). In a major national sample survey of 3,187 women students at 32 institutions across the United States, Mary Koss and her colleagues found that 27.5 percent reported an experience of rape or attempted rape ("The Scope of Rape: Incidence and Prevalence of Sexual Aggression and Victimization in a National Sample of Higher Education Students," *Journal of Consulting and Clinical Psychology* 55 [1987]: 162–170). While this figure is significantly lower than Russell's 44 percent prevalence figure or Kanin's 20 to 24 percent (which applies only to a one-year period rather than the woman's entire life), it is still 10 to 15 times greater than the rates based on the National Crime Surveys (Koss et al.).

It is widely believed that Afro-American women are far more subject to rape than white women. This was not the case according to Russell's probability sample; 55 percent of the Native American women disclosed an experience of rape or attempted rape, 46 percent of white women, 44 percent of Afro-American women, 30 percent of Latina women, 17 percent of Asian women, and 17 percent of the Filipino women. Whether or not these differences are due to differential willingness by women in some ethnic groups to disclose experiences of rape requires further research. Also contrary to prior studies, women from upper-middle-class backgrounds were more likely to become rape victims (47 percent) than women from middle-class or lower-class backgrounds (35 percent and 36 percent, respectively) (Russell, *Sexual Exploitation*, 86).

Difficult as it is to estimate the prevalence of rape victimization, it is more difficult still to estimate the percentage of men in the population who perpetrate rape. However, in one random sample survey of 400 male college students, Eugene Kanin found that 26 percent admitted to having attempted to force a woman to have intercourse at least once since entering college ("Male Sex Aggression and Three Psychiatric Hypotheses,"*Journal of Sex Research* 1 [1965]: 222). Only attempts where the victim responded by crying, fighting, screaming, or pleading were included. Numerous other studies reveal high percentages of male students with rape-supportive attitudes or self-reported interest in raping women. For example, Neil Malamuth found that on average 35 percent of several groups of male college students admitted there was some likelihood that they would rape a woman if they could be sure of getting away with it (Rape Proclivity among Men," *Journal of Social Issues* 37 [1981]: 138–157). In another study, 60 percent of 356 male students indicated there was some likelihood that they would rape or force a sex act on a woman if they could be assured they would not be punished for it (J. Briere and N. Malamuth, "Self-Reported Likelihood of Sexually Aggressive Behavior," *Journal of Research in Personality* 17 [1983]: 315–323). And half of the 432 high school males interviewed in another study believed it was acceptable "for a guy to hold a girl down and force her to have sexual intercourse" in situations such as when "she gets him sexually excited" or "she says she's going to have sex with him and then changes her mind" (J. Goodchilds and G. Zillman, "Sexual Signaling and \Sexual Aggression in Adolescent Relationships," in N. Malamuth and E. Donnerstein [eds.], *Pornography and Sexual Aggression* [New York, 1984]).

The high prevalence of rape and rape-supportive attitudes suggests the inadequacy of theories that stress psychopathology as the major causative factor in rape. A multicausal theory must be developed that can explain (1) why such a high percentage of men harbor a desire to rape; and (2) what factors counteract some men's personal and social inhibitions against acting out this desire.

Feminist theorists, pointing to the fact that the vast majority of rapists are male, consider male sex-role and sexual socialization as crucial to understanding why rape occurs. Lorenne Clark and Debra Lewis, for example, argue that rape is a consequence of the coercive sexual and nonsexual power males have over females in patriarchal cultures and believe that rape cannot be eradicated without changing this power relationship *(The Power of Coercive Sexuality* [Toronto, 1977]). Brownmiller and others have also stressed that men as a gender benefit from rape because it keeps women fearful and dependent.

Before females started writing about rape in the early 1970s, most scholars and clinicians blamed the victims for their victimization. By recognizing the connections between sexism and rape, feminists have transformed contemporary thinking about this traumatic form of male aggression, as well as the treatment of rape victims. Rape crisis centers, first started by feminists (also in the early 1970s), have been set up throughout the country to assist victims. But while rape victims often receive better treatment today than they did 15 years ago, the problem of rape is far from being solved. In addition, rape by intimates—a far more prevalent crime than stranger rape—still gets insufficient attention, both by theorists and by those who are trying to ameliorate the rape problem.

Further References. P. Bart, *Stopping Rape* (New York, 1985). S. Estrich, *Real Rape* (Cambridge, Mass., 1987). D.E.H. Russell, *The Politics of Rape* (New York, 1975). D.E.H. Russell, *Rape in Marriage* (New York, 1982).

DIANA E. H. RUSSELL

REPRODUCTION, ETHICS OF. The material in this article was abstracted from Marilyn L. Poland, "Reproductive Technology and Responsibility," *International Journal of Moral and Social Studies* 1 (1986): 63–76, with permission of the author and journal.

Advances in reproductive technologies are influencing pregnant women's roles and responsibilities and raising major ethical and legal questions about the rights of the fetus and the rights and responsibilities of the gestating woman, the physician, and society.

Genetic counseling can inform parents of the probabilities of genetic diseases or conditions in their offspring. By use of sonography, amniocentesis*, and chorionic villi biopsy, the presence of fetal diseases, genetic anomalies, and birth defects can be more precisely estimated. Parents, with this information, can make an informed decision to prepare for the birth of their child or to abort.

Prenatal diagnosis and treatment has raised questions about the long-term consequences for gene pool variation. The possibility over time of decreasing human genetic variation that might perhaps make future generations less able to adapt to environmental change must be balanced against the moral and ethical obligation to relieve human suffering by diagnosing, treating, and preventing genetic disorders.

Most debate has concerned the rights of fetuses; the rights and responsibilities of parents, physicians, and society; and women's control over their own reproduction. Some responsibility has been established through court cases finding physicians and counselors negligent for failure to inform prospective parents of the availability of testing for diagnoses and treatment of fetal defects, of the possible consequences to the fetus* of certain maternal disorders and drugs, and of possible genetic causes of anomalies in elder siblings. Some would hold women liable if they fail or refuse to get counseling and/or treatment.

In the United States, except in cases in which the life or health of the mother is at stake, a viable fetus (one with the potential of separate existence outside the uterus) has a legal right not to be aborted. Some would make women responsible for any behavior that might affect the health and well-being of the fetus from viability—or even earlier if there was no intention to abort. Such a development could seriously abrogate the woman's rights as well as raise the possibility of mandating procedures without benefit to mother or fetus. The woman's rights might also be abused by genetic manipulation. As knowledge of the human chromosome increases, in the name of fetal well-being intervention to produce the "perfect child" (in IQ, body build, etc.) could assume importance.

As diagnostic technologies become more reliable, prenatal testing will become more widely accepted and practiced. If it becomes the norm, an accepted maternal responsibility, those unable or unwilling to undergo testing could be labeled "irresponsible" and legal sanctions could be imposed on them. State-ordered testing raises a host of problems. Since it cannot guarantee that treatment will be available for any problem uncovered, a woman tested against her will might be forced to receive information that would add to her distress. It is also conceivable that the possibility of a wrongful life suit could cause undue pressure on a mother to abort a fetus with an untreatable defect. And can tests that must be performed early in pregnancy be ordered on a woman who still has the right to abort?

Fetuses can now be treated by medication and surgery. Medication (orally to the mother or by injection) is relatively noninvasive and of little objective risk to the mother. Treating a malformation surgically, however, carries more risk. Successful fetal surgery can significantly benefit the fetus by preventing handicapping conditions and later suffering. But assessment of benefit over risk may be hard to ascertain. Risks include the possibility of surgery in the presence of other undetected anomalies not amenable to surgery, the chances that the fetus will not survive the surgery or that the surgery might result in a chronic condition after birth, the possibility that the mother will be subjected to major surgery that is unsuccessful or that could bring on premature labor. In cases of twins, the affect on the health of one twin must be measured against the benefits of surgery to the other.

The new techniques are costly. As reliable techniques are developed and new procedures are deemed a necessary part of prenatal care, there must be assurance that they will be available to all women.

When a mother refuses surgery, the rights of the mother and fetus may conflict. If surgery is ordered against the mother's will, it is a violation of her body and her personal autonomy. It may represent a significant risk from which she receives no benefit. Generally, the decision of an adult to receive or refuse surgery is respected. To place legal restrictions on a pregnant woman's right to decide to accept or refuse surgery would be a dangerous precedent. The personal rights of women against their responsibilities to the fetus, and the physician's ability to act in the best interests of both mother and fetus, will assume more importance as fetal surgery becomes a more accepted medical practice.

Forced cesarean sections have highlighted the conflict between maternal and fetal risk. In three cases in 1981 and 1982, courts in Georgia, Colorado, and Michigan ordered mothers to undergo cesarean sections after they had refused consent to surgery. In only one case was a cesarean actually performed, but in all three cases, decided in from a few hours to a few days and on the basis of faulty medical technology, healthy babies were born. In all three the mother's right was denied in favor of the fetus's right. The legal precedent for fetal over maternal right could be established for other intrusive programs as well as fetal surgery. As viability is pushed back, women could lose personal rights even earlier.

Traditionally, the decision of rational adults to accept or refuse surgery has been respected. Court decisions giving preference to the authority of medical judgment over the personal rights of women places women with nonconsenting children and incompetents. They lose their status as rational adults.

The treatment of women as nonadults can be associated with the general patronizing attitude of physicians, who tend to label nonconformity with medical notions of proper health behavior as "uncooperative" or "ignorant." When a woman refuses a cesarean section, a surgical procedure involving some risk to her, the fetal "patient" is jeopardized. Obstetricians are divided in response to this conflict, from accusing women of a felony to respecting their rights. The popularity among women of nontraditional and self-help services has grown in response to medical attitudes. The increasing resort to the courts to enforce physician control of reproduction may increase this popularity.

Court-ordered surgery raises questions of woman-physician relationships in maternal-fetal conflict. Two patients, whose interests may conflict, are under the care of the same physician. The questions of who is the primary patient and what are the responsibilities of the physician to each have been raised in forced cesarean cases. Court-ordered surgery also raises the issue of professional responsibility. If a physician operates on a nonconsenting adult, can she sue for assault? If the physician doesn't intercede, can the family sue him for damages? How safe is it to operate on a struggling adult? Should the concern for institutional liability, more than concern for the survival of the fetus or health of the mother, decide medical procedure?

All societies apply some restrictions to pregnancy and childbearing. The behavior of pregnant women is often monitored closely—because of their vulnerability to harm and because society has a stake in the healthy outcome of pregnancy. Medical experts believe new understanding will further reduce fetal harm, and as techniques of diagnosis and treatment become more reliable, women will accept them as their responsibility even if it means surgery on the woman to reach the fetus. Women vary, from accepting all of the new technology, to a collaborative relationship, to partial or complete rejection. Recent court-ordered cesarean sections and laws of the United States mandating maternal duties run counter to the expressed belief in personal rights and informed consent.

The growing body of scientific knowledge about fetal abnormalities and prevention are forcing re-examination of maternal prenatal responsibilities. They indicate a conflict of rights of the fetus against the rights of the woman. The medical response has been to resort to the judiciary. A broader approach, including professional self-examination, is needed to ensure a fairer hearing.

REPRODUCTION OF LABOR POWER is the maintenance of the workers and the producing and rearing of future workers who supply labor power for production. Although Marx does not include the reproduction of labor power within the sphere of surplus value production, feminist theorists, by assigning value to the reproduction of labor power, apply Marx's theory of value to the position of women under patriarchal social relations and the capitalist mode of production and to the relationships and contradictions between patriarchy and capitalism.

REPRODUCTIVE SYSTEM. Those organs which are adapted to produce and unite sex cells in order to produce offspring. In human reproduction the organs, called *genitalia*, include (1) *gonads*, ovaries and testes, which produce ova and sperm cells, respectively; (2) *ducts*, which transport, receive, and store gametes (sex cells); and (3) *accessory glands*, which produce materials that support gametes. In addition, organs of the female system are adapted to support a developing offspring and to transport it to the outside of the female's body.

Despite a common embryological origin and structure, the anatomy and physiology of the reproductive organs are the major differences between male and female. The reproductive system becomes functional when it is acted upon by hormones produced in the pituitary glands during puberty.

The male reproductive system is specialized to produce sperm and to deposit the sperm within the female reproductive tract. The system consists of the paired testes, contained in the external *scrotum*. Within the testes sperm are produced in *seminiferous tubules*. Between the seminiferous tubules are *interstitial cells (Cells of Leydig)*, which produce and secrete male sex hormones, predominately testosterone. The duct system, which stores and transports sperm, includes the *epididymis, ductus deferens (vas deferens), ejaculatory ducts*, and *urethra*. Accessory glands include seminal vesticles, prostate gland, and bulbourethral glands. The *penis*, which surrounds the urethra, contains masses of erectile tissue and serves as the copulatory organ.

The female reproductive system is specialized for internal fertilization, implantation, fetal development, and parturition (labor and delivery). Although not actually a part of the reproductive system, the *mammary glands*, located in the *breasts*, are functionally associated since they secrete milk for the nourishment of the young.

The female reproductive system includes

1. **Ovaries.** The female gonads, a pair of glands resembling an unshelled almond, 3.5cm long, 2cm wide, and 1cm thick, located in the upper pelvic cavity, one on each side of the uterus. The ovaries produce ova and secrete the sex hormones estrogen and progesterone under the control of hormones LH (luteinizing hormone) and FSH (follicle stimulating hormone) produced and secreted by the pituitary gland.

Oogenesis is the process of cell division (meiosis) by which ova are formed. Prior to birth several million *primary follicles* develop in each ovary. These consist of a single large cell, the *primary oocyte*, and surrounding *follicular cells*. Many of the oocytes degenerate through a process called atresia and at birth about 2 million are present. Continuing atresia reduces this number to about 400,000 at puberty. Beginning at puberty, in response to pituitary hormones LH and FSH, some of the primary follicles are stimulated to grow and develop into *secondary follicles* each month. Only one normally completes the process and releases its ovum. The oocyte completes the first meiotic division into a large *secondary oocyte*, a future egg, and a small *polar body* that will eventually fragment and disappear. The surrounding follicular cells also divide. Some of these cells secrete increasing amounts of *estrogen* as the follicle grows.

Ovulation, stimulated by pituitary hormones, is the release from the ovary of the secondary oocyte and its surrounding cells. The secondary oocyte will complete the second meiotic division, to form an ovum and second polar body, only following fertilization by a sperm.

The *corpus luteum* is a structure formed as a result of structural and biochemical changes in the empty follicle left in the ovary following ovulation. The corpus luteum secretes both estrogen and progesterone. If fertilization of the ovum does not occur, the corpus luteum regresses about 12 to 14 days after ovulation.

Estrogen is a class of steroid hormones secreted primarily by the adult ovary. It is also secreted in small amounts by the adrenal cortex and in increasing amounts by the placenta during pregnancy. The functions of estrogen include development and maintenance of the female reproductive structures and the development and maintenance of the female secondary sex characteristics.

Progesterone, a steroid hormone, is secreted primarily from the corpus luteum of the adult ovary. It is also secreted in increasing amounts by the placenta during pregnancy. Progesterone promotes the changes that occur in the uterus to prepare it for implantation. It also affects the mammary glands and causes the mucus at the cervix of the uterus to become very thick and sticky.

The *ovarian cycle* is the cycle of events: maturation of a follicle, ovulation, formation of a corpus luteum, regression of the corpus luteum, with its accompanying cycle of estrogen, then estrogen and progesterone, release.

2. **Uterine (Fallopian) Tubes, also called Oviducts.** Extend laterally from the uterus and open into the abdominal cavity near the ovaries. Each muscular tube is about 10cm long and 0.7cm in diameter and is positioned between the folds of the broad ligament of the uterus. The open funnel-shaped end, called the infundibulum, lies close to the ovary, and a number of fingerlike projections, the *fimbriae*, surround the ovary. Following ovulation the ovum is swept into the tube by ciliary action of the cells lining the infundibulum. Fertilization normally occurs within the uterine tubes.

3. **Uterus.** A hollow, thick-walled muscular organ, shaped like an inverted pear (7.5cm long, 5cm wide, 2.5cm thick) which is the site of menstruation, implantation of the fertilized ovum, development of the fetus during pregnancy and labor. It is located in the pelvic cavity between the urinary bladder and the rectum. Anatomical subdivisions include the *fundus*, a dome-shaped portion

above the entrance of the uterine tubes; the *body*, the major tapering portion surrounding the uterine cavity; and the *cervix*, a tubular, narrow portion which opens into the vagina. Normally the body of the uterus is bent forward over the urinary bladder and the cervix enters the anterior wall of the vagina at nearly a right angle.

Support of the uterus is both by muscles and by a series of ligaments including *broad ligaments*, a pair of folds of the membrane that lines the abdomino-pelvic cavity (peritoneum) and attaches the uterus to the sides of the pelvic cavity; *uterosacral ligaments*, which attach the uterus to bone at the base of the vertebral column (sacrum); *cardinal ligaments*, which extend laterally from cervix and vagina to the wall of the pelvis to maintain the position of the uterus and keep it from dropping down into the vagina; and the *round ligaments*, which extend from upperlateral wall to pelvic wall.

The *wall of the uterus* consists of three layers of tissue; the *serosa*, outer layer, is continuous with the broad ligament; *myometrium*, the middle layer, consists of three layers of smooth muscle fibers; and *endometrium*, the mucus membrane lining that consists of a layer closer to the uterine cavity (stratum functionalis) that is shed as menses during menstruation and a permanent layer (stratum basalis) that produces a new functionalis following menstruation.

4. **Vagina.** A muscular tubular organ, about 9 cm long, extending from cervix to vestibule. It serves as the receptacle for the sperm released from the urethra of an erect penis during coitus, the passageway for menses, and the birth canal. The wall of the vagina is very distensible due to the presence of a series of transverse folds, the *rugae*, and layers of smooth muscles that can stretch considerably. The lining, or mucosal tissue, consists of several layers that are maintained by estrogen. They form a tough protective lining. The normally acidic environment (ph 3.5 to 5.5) protects against microbial growth.

The *hymen* is a thin fold of mucus membrane that may form a border around the lower end of the vaginal opening (vaginal orifice), partially closing it. The hymen is the subject of folklore, misconception, and nonsense. It is a highly variable structure. It may be very thick or thin; vascular or avascular; cover all or only a very small portion of the vaginal orifice; may be very pliable or may rupture easily during physical exercise, sports, play, or coitus. An intact hymen is not proof of virginity; a ruptured hymen is not evidence that sexual intercourse has occurred. An *imperforate hymen* (very rare) covers the vaginal orifice completely and will impede menstrual flow and coitus. This condition is corrected by a small surgical incision.

5. **Vulva (Pudendum).** The external genitalia of the female. It includes the following components:

Mons pubis (veneris): an elevation of adipose (fat) tissue that covers the anterior pelvic bones (symphysis pubis). At puberty it becomes covered with coarse pubic hair usually in a triangular pattern with a horizontal upper border.

Labia majora, two thick longitudinal folds of skin, fat, and muscle that extend from the mons pubis. They are covered with hair and contain sebaceous (oil) and sweat glands. The labia majora are the female homologue of the scrotum and function to enclose and protect other organs of the vulva. Toward the posterior end the labia are tapered and merge into the perineum near the anus.

Labia minora, flattened longitudinal folds of tissue located between the labia majora. They are hairless, do not contain fat, but do contain sebaceous glands. At the anterior end, the two labia minora unite and form a covering (prepuce) over the clitoris.

Clitoris, a small cylindrical mass of erectile tissue and nerves (2cm long and 0.5cm in diameter) that is the female homologue of the glans penis of the male. The exposed portion of the clitoris is the *glans*. The unexposed portion is composed of erectile tissue that engorges during sexual excitement. The clitoris is richly supplied with the sensory nerve fibers that initiate the female sexual response cycle.

Vestibule, the cleft between the labia minora. Within the vestibule are the hymen, opening of the vagina, opening of the urethra (tube that transports urine from urinary bladder to outside) and openings of several ducts from:

(a) Paraurethral (Skene's) glands that are embedded in the wall of the urethra and secrete mucus. These are homologous to the male prostate gland.

(b) Greater vestibular (Bartholin's) glands that open by ducts into the vestibule near the lateral margin of the vaginal orifice. These correspond to the bulbourethral glands of the male and produce a mucoid secretion that supplements lubrication during sexual intercourse.

6. **Perineum (clinical perineum).** The area between the vagina and anus. A small incision, episiotomy, is sometimes made in the perineal skin and underlying tissues just prior to delivery of an infant to prevent its tearing.

FRANCES GARB

RESERVE ARMY OF LABOR. Women have been called a reserve army of labor, a pool of surplus workers who are drawn into the labor force in times of economic expansion or scarcity of male labor, and are drawn back out of the paid labor force when male labor is plentiful. Although there is considerable evidence for the entry of women into the labor market in times of expansion (e.g., the world wars), as Ruth Milkman ("Women's Work and the Economic Crisis," in N. F. Cott and E. H. Pleck (eds.), *A Heritage of Her Own: Toward a New Social History of American Women* [New York, 1979], 507–541) points out, the "reserve army" theory is too mechanistic to satisfactorily explain the situation of women in a highly sex-segregated labor market in times of recession.

RETIREMENT is a stepping-down from previous levels of labor market activity. The decline may be abrupt, involving a one-time transition from full- or part-time employment to complete retirement, or may be a gradual move from full-time employment, for example, to part-time work ("partial retirement") and eventually to full retirement. The latter process may involve a number of transitions among retirement "states," some of which may be moves stepping up the level of market activity. This pattern of retirement has become more widespread among women (and men as well) as pressures for early retirement from career jobs have continued at the same time that medical advances have prolonged the working life. Among unmarried women (including widows and divorced women), for example, a higher proportion spend time in the intermediate stage of partial retirement than retire in the "classic" one-step move from full- or part-time employment to full retirement (based on a sample from the Retirement History Survey, 1969–1979, of the Social Security Administration).

Among older unmarried women, a large proportion remain in the labor force. In the United States in 1982, 61 percent of unmarried women aged 55–61 had income from earnings, 45 percent of those aged 62–64, and 25 percent of those 65–67. In contrast to younger workers, the majority of older women workers are not married. Among those aged 62–64, 49 percent of women with income from earnings were unmarried in 1982, and among those aged 65 and above, 61 percent were unmarried.

The retirement behavior of unmarried women is very similar to that of men, the primary differences arising from the relative unimportance of self-employment among older women and the greater reliance among women on Social Security* rather than private pension income. The primary factors determining the timing and pattern of retirement of unmarried women are age, health, earnings, labor force experience, and Social Security benefits. Women in poor health tend to retire earlier, as do those with larger Social Security benefits or other nonwork income. Higher levels of education and longer experience in the labor force are associated with delayed retirement. Private pensions do not appear to influence the retirement decisions of unmarried women, possibly because of relatively low coverage (38 percent of women in the Retirement History Survey, compared to 66 percent of men).

Among married women, retirement behavior appears to be strongly conditioned on the retirement decisions of husbands. Roughly two-thirds of wives retire prior to or simultaneously with their husbands (based on a Retirement History Survey sample). Wives' own economic opportunities, in the form of potential earnings or pension income, appear to be relatively unimportant. Interestingly, wives are more likely to continue working if their husbands are in poor health. They are also more likely to work if their husbands' income is relatively high, the latter providing some evidence for marital selection in tastes for work. In 1982, 45 percent of married women aged 55–61 had income from earnings, 31 percent aged 62–64, and 10 percent aged 65 and above.

Recent changes in Social Security are likely to affect the retirement behavior of women. The 1983 Amendments to the Social Security Act raised the age of eligibility for full retirement benefits from 65 to 67, beginning in 1999, which effectively reduces benefits for those retiring before age 67. The reduction in benefits is especially critical for women because they have relatively less pension income and savings. Women who do not increase their labor market activity will experience reduced retirement income. Research findings to date suggest that, while the behavior of married women may not change significantly, unmarried women are likely to delay retirement in response to these changes.

Further References. J. C. Henrietta and A. M. O'Rand, "Joint Retirement in the Dual Worker Family," *Social Forces* 62 (1983): 504–520. M. Honig, "Partial Retirement among Women," *Journal of Human Resources* 20 (1985): 613–621. S. Pozzebon and O. S. Mitchell, "Married Women's Retirement Behavior," Department of Labor Economics Discussion Paper, Cornell University, 1986.

MARJORIE HONIG

S

SCIENTIFIC MOTHERHOOD, an ideology that developed in the nineteenth century, gives mothers the central role in childrearing while promoting scientific and medical expertise as the chief guides in fulfilling women's familial responsibility.

In the nineteenth century, science promised to solve all society's problems; so mothers, concerned over high rates of infant mortality, turned to scientific experts for advice.

Rapidly expanding print media, emerging governmental health agencies, the developing medical specialty of pediatrics, and the increasing institutionalization of childbirth* all spread the new ideology. The most well-known example of scientific motherhood literature was *Infant Care*, first published in 1914 by the U.S. Children's Bureau, which distributed 59 million copies by the 1970s. The original author, Mrs. Max West, a mother of five and graduate of the University of Minnesota, complemented the works of leading physicians with her experience. Advertisements for child care products also promoted scientific motherhood with testimonials from physicians acclaiming their medical validity.

These sources grew in importance as old information systems broke down or became less feasible or less attractive. In an increasingly mobile society, women who found themselves without supportive relatives and friends to answer questions and give suggestions instead used available resources, often publications and physicians. Immigrants and their daughters, partly influenced by public health personnel and educators, wanted to raise their children the "American way." This Americanization process discouraged reliance on family and tradition, replacing them with professional expertise.

Physicians concerned with high infant mortality rates echoed sentiments of lay authors: mothercraft education could prevent many infant deaths. Some doctors also recognized the economic potential of the emerging specialty of pediatrics. Moreover, physicians expected that educated mothers would better appreciate the physicians's advice in child care*. But women received advice from other sources, which in essence supplanted the physician's authority. Believing mothers should look to medical experts for direction, professional medical organizations attempted to limit information available from nonmedical sources and to encourage mothers to visit physicians. For example, in the late 1910s, an Advisory Committee, composed of representatives from the leading medical an pediatric societies, proposed that it review all Children's Bureau publications dealing with child care techniques. By the late 1920s the compilers of *Infant Care* were physicians.

In time, more and more women birthed in hospitals, accelerating the medicalization of motherhood, the modern form of scientific motherhood. In 1920 under 20 percent of American women delivered their babies in hospitals; by 1950 the number had grown to over 80 percent. The hospital, cloaked in the aura of medical authority, provided a fertile ground for scientific motherhood training. New mothers were taught child care practices in hospital classrooms; they also learned from hospital routines that suggested mothers needed the expertise of medical personnel in handling their infants.

Nineteenth-century scientific motherhood stressed self-education: mothers were responsible for childrearing and for using science to shape their mothering practices. Dr. Benjamin Spock's "Trust your own instincts, and follow the directions that your doctor gives you" *(The Common Sense Book of Baby and Child Care* [New York, 1945, 1946 and subsequent editions]) exemplifies the mid-twentieth-century version. Today women still bear the major burdens of child care, but at the same time, many mothers are denied decision-making power.

Further References. N. P. Weiss, "Mother, the Invention of Necessity: Dr. Benjamin Spock's *Baby and Child Care,*" *American Quarterly* 29 (1977): 519–546. R. D. Apple, " 'To Be Used Only under the Direction of a Physician': Commercial Infant Feeding and Medical Practice, 1870–1940," *Bulletin of the History of Medicine* 54 (1980): 402–417. K. Jones, "Sentiment and Science: The Late Nineteenth-Century Pediatrician as Mother's Advisor," *Journal of Social History* 17 (1983): 79–96. K. M. Reiger, *The Disechantment of the Home: Modernizing the Australian Family, 1880–1940* (Melbourne, 1985).

RIMA D. APPLE

SECONDARY SEX CHARACTERISTICS. Anatomical differences between men and women, resulting from the action of testosterone and related androgen hormones (male characteristics) and estrogen and related estrogenic hormones (female characteristics) on nonreproductive tissues. These differences vary widely among individuals. It should be noted that these hormones are not gender-exclusive. The testes are a major source of androgen, predominantly testosterone, in males, and the ovaries are a major source of estrogen in females. In both sexes, the adrenal cortex also secretes small amounts of androgens and lesser amounts of estrogen.

Androgen hormones, by stimulating protein synthesis, effect muscle and bone growth. Hence, male secondary sex characteristics include muscular and skeletal development resulting in wide shoulders and narrow hips and a generally larger and more muscular body. The larynx (voice box) grows and enlarges in response to testosterone resulting in a deep voice. Hair growth is stimulated on the face, along the midline of the abdomen, on the pubis and on the chest and axillary region. In those individuals with a genetic predisposition to baldness, testosterone causes hair loss. Androgens promote activity in oil and sweat glands which may lead to acne, particularly around puberty. There is also evidence of behavioral effects of androgens. In both males and females androgens appear to be related to libido.

Estrogen causes cellular proliferation in many areas: glandular tissue in the breast grows and fat is deposited in the breast; and increase in adipose tissue in the hips, buttocks, thighs, and subcutaneous areas results in rounded body contours; the pelvic bone structure grows and widens so the general body shape is narrow shoulders and broad hips. Although development of axial and pubic hair seems to be a response to adrenal androgens, the pattern of hair growth is estrogen dependent. It cannot be overemphasized that within these general responses there is tremendous individual variation, and for all secondary sex characteristics there is more variation among same-sex individuals then there is difference in the average values between the sexes. (See also PUBERTAL PROCESSES.)

FRANCES GARB

SELF-FULFILLING PROPHECY is a concept of the social and behavioral sciences referring to the idea that one person's expectations for the behavior of others can help to bring about the expected behavior.

Social scientists have discussed the phenomenon at least since 1885 and a landmark exposition of the concept appeared in 1948, written by the sociologist Robert K. Merton under the title "The Self-Fulfilling Prophecy" *(Antioch Review* 8 [1948]: 193–210). Experimental evidence for the operation of this phenomenon, however, did not begin to appear until more than a decade later.

The earliest such research was conducted in laboratory situations. Psychological experimenters were given arbitrary expectations about the future behavior of their research subjects who then tended to behave as their experimenters expected them to behave. For example, in one series of studies, some experimenters were told that their research subjects would tend to see photographs of other people as being of relatively successful people while other experimenters were told that their research subjects would tend to see photographs of other people as being of relatively unsuccessful people. Results of these studies showed that the degree of success attributed to photographs of others was significantly affected by the expectations arbitrarily given the psychological experimenters who had shown the photographs to the research subjects. Further research implicated the role of nonverbal cues in the mediation of these interpersonal self-fulfilling prophecies; experimenters tended to obtain the responses they expected to obtain even when their verbal communications to their research subjects were carefully constrained.

An important incidental finding from these studies was that male and female research subjects were treated quite differently by their experimenters. For example, experimenters were much more likely to smile at their female subjects than at their male subjects, and it seemed likely that this differential treatment of female and male subjects might have affected subjects' performance. This finding was quite troubling methodologically since it suggested the possibility that some of the sex differences* obtained in psychological research might be caused not by genetic, constitutional, or socializational differences between the sexes but simply by the fact that they were treated differently during the course of the data collection.

Subsequent experiments on the self-fulfilling prophecy showed that these effects could be obtained even if the subjects were animals. For example, in one series of experiments, half the experimenters were told that the rats assigned to them had been specially bred to be "maze-bright" while the remaining experimenters were told that the rats assigned to them had been specially bred to be "maze-dull." In fact, of course all rats had been bred normally and were neither maze-bright nor maze-dull. Nevertheless, after only a few hours the rats that had been arbitrarily labeled maze-bright had become better maze-learners than had the rats arbitrarily labeled maze-dull.

If rats became brighter when expected to by their experimenter, it seemed possible that students might become brighter when expected to by their teacher. Accordingly, the Pygmalion experiment was conducted in which teachers were led to believe that certain children in their classroom would show unusual intellectual development. The names of these children (who did not really differ from their fellow students) were then given to their teachers. Subsequent intelligence testing revealed that those children whose teachers had been led to expect greater intellectual gains in fact showed greater intellectual gains than did the children of the control group for whom no special expectations were created.

Subsequent research suggested that there were two major factors contributing to the mediation of teacher's expectation effects. (1) *Climate*. Teachers tended to create a warmer socioemotional climate for those students for whom they held more favorable expectations. (2) *Input*. Teachers tended to teach more material and more difficult material to those students for whom they held more favorable expectations.

Current research is investigating the extent to which male and female teachers teach different subject matters to their female and male students in overtly or covertly different ways. The goal is to learn more about the ways in which differences in teacher behaviors toward male and female students in the teaching of sex-typed materials (e.g., verbal vs. quantitative) might contribute to sex differences in the performance of different intellectual tasks.

More generally, research is underway that is designed to show the degree to which sex differences of many kinds are increased or decreased by the differential treatment of male and female members of our society. This differential treatment may sometimes be quite overt, even blatant; often, however, this differential treatment may be quite covert, subtle, and unintended.

Further References. R. Rosenthal, *Experimenter Effects in Behavioral Research* (New York, 1966; enlarged ed. New York, 1976). R. Rosenthal, "From Unconscious Experimenter Bias to Teacher Expectancy Effects," in J. B. Dusek (ed.), *Teacher Expectations* (Hillsdale, N.J., 1985): 37–65. R. Rosenthal and L. Jacobson, *Pygmalion in the Classroom* (New York, 1968).

ROBERT ROSENTHAL

SEMIOTICS AND FEMINISM.

Semiological Theory. Semiotics began with the early twentieth-century work of American philosopher Charles Sanders Peirce and Swiss linguist Ferdinand de Saussure. In Peirce's theory of reality, though we have direct experience of a world of things, we have only indirect knowledge of them through their representations in our thoughts. Peirce called these mental representations *signifiers*, and the objects of the world of things he called the *signified*. He acknowledged that language is related to conceptual objects more often than not only by convention, and that therefore reality might not be truly represented by the signs, but he also believed that the true relationship between the signified and the sign could, over time, be established by that which the "community" or culture continues to reaffirm.

Saussure's *Course in General Linquistics* (1916) proposed a science called semiology (from a Greek word meaning "sign") that studies the life of signs within society. According to Saussure, semiology "would show what constitutes signs and what laws govern them," and would be a general science with importance to many fields of study, such as psychology and anthropology. Central to his thought, however, was the argument that language is the most important and the most characteristic or ideal of all the sign systems because it is the most arbitrary. Like Peirce, Saussure designated two parts of any sign: the "signifier" and the "signified." Unlike Peirce, he did not believe that a true relationship between the signifier and signified could be established in reality or in the community's continued reaffirmation, but only in the study of language as a system of signs that established differences among the signifiers.

Saussure focused on several distinctions within linguistics: (1) between paradigmatic relationships (the similarities of signs at the level of signifier and signified) and syntagmatic relationships (the connections between and among signs used in a particular speech act or utterance); (2) between *langue* (the language system) and *parole* (manipulation of the language system within a concrete utterance); and (3) between synchronic, relational, and diachronic (historical) linguistic analysis. Working toward establishing a rigorous science of linguistic analysis that would yield structural rules, Saussure's insistence that signs can only be understood within a system began the structural approach to the study of language and gave the methodological foundation to structural linguistics, which maintains that language structures the mind.

Building on Saussure's linguistics, Roman Jakobson demonstrated that the smallest units of meaningful language, phonemes, necessarily operate as systematically binary oppositions which produce structural patterns through the gradation and mediation of the phonemes, e.g., voiced and voiceless consonants. The anthropologist Claude Lévi-Strauss, assuming that Jakobson's structural linguistics had established structural rules that governed all language and that all of human culture was an extension of language, used this linguistic theory to interpret his cultural data. Lévi-Strauss used the linguistic principles of polarity and homology to show what he thought were universal laws of signification. He was ambivalent about why he thought language rules would be universal.

Roland Barthes continued Saussure's and Lévi-Strauss's ambition to use the principles of linguistic structuralism to interpret culture itself. To Barthes, all cultural complexes, lingusitic and otherwise, are systems of signs. The general conventions governing a cultural complex are considered to be the equivalent of Saussure's *langue*; the individual instance is *parole*. Moving beyond the work of Saussure, Barthes says that the signifier and the signified have indicative levels that begin a suggestive or associative process. To Barthes, the associative level was the same as myth, the surreptitious expression of the dominant values of the dominant class. Barthes shows that in all kinds of cultural products, such as advertisements, the signifiers are related to one another, and express one or many myths. Such displays of myth control people without obvious coercion.

Jacques Lacan uses semiotics to develop his theories of psychological structuralism. Deeply indebted to Freud, Lacan studies the unconscious as a sign system. Saussure's belief in the primacy of language meant that reality was differentiated and structured by language. Freud had shown that the unconscious was highly structured and usually made known through language. Lacan theorizes that the unconscious is constructed as language develops in the child and that the child's mass of instinctual drives becomes differentiated by language. The desires do not go away, but become the unconscious which "speaks" through dreams and complexes in rhetorical ways. Among Lacan's suppositions is that the father figure becomes the "reality principle" that says a child must not be the same as its instinctual desires, that is, cannot have the mother. The father makes the child repress desire and identify with the father. The subject is radically split into its imaginary and symbolic selves.

Feminism and Semiological Theory. The political implications of language have made linguistic study imperative for feminists. Feminist language theory has sought to study possible sex differences in the language of men and women, sexism embedded in language, and the mechanism of women's oppression through language. The use of semiotic theory has been every important in these investigations through the use and examination of structural linguistics, psychological linguistics, and the cross-disciplinary nature of signs.

Feminists have used semiotics in the same two ways linguists in general have, that is, by stressing either methodology or theory. Structuralism, Saussure's tool for analyzing sign systems, has been a dominant method of linguistic study even by those feminists who were less accepting of Saussure's insistence that the signified and signifier are arbitrarily related. For the feminist who is more concerned with Saussurean theory, meanings are made possible by language and language structures, rather than by the expression of an individual's experience. Experience and the individual are products of the institutionalized system of signs, and both function accordingly.

Feminists have intensively researched the differences in the language used by men and women. Much time and effort have gone into the description of the differences in order to see if women have their own language and if the power of men is related to the language men use. This purpose often necessitates the use of Saussure's concepts of *langue* and *parole* and shows women's speech as *parole* or variation from the norm, *langue*, which white males speak. Critics, often feminists themselves, point out that researchers within the language are not value-free, and they perpetuate stereotypes as well as skew the evidence. To these critics, only painstaking empirical research to establish paradigmatic and syntagmatic differences based on what women actually say will reveal the truer structures of the language sign-system and possibly gender differences in use of the language.

Feminists have not only been involved in collecting and interpreting the descriptive data of difference between related language structures, but they have also employed Saussure's use of contrast as a principle of linguistic structure. Many feminists have made use of binary oppositions in their linguistic analyses, assuming as do most nonfeminist linguists that binary opposition as an ordering device is universal and possibly innate. Other feminists have looked hard at this assumption. Some, like Dale Spender, say the feminine opposite often doesn't really exist. Other feminists, such as Luce Irigaray and Hélène Cixous, say that paradigmatic and syntagmatic analyses do not show that antonyms form a persistent logical structure in the language sign-system. The duality, they say, lies outside linguistics, but is in no way shown to be innate. Feminist criticism of the linguistic structuralists' assumptions about the necessity for polarity wishes to show that sexual dichotomy is not necessary.

Feminists find that sexist language becomes very noticeable in linguistic structural analysis when some paradigms become unbalanced by too many or too few relational words for one sex. Furthermore, as feminists have pointed out, linguistic structures involving negative relationships are often heavy in words related to women. Mary Daly, Dale Spender, Kate Millet, and Kate Swift are a few of the better-known feminists who specialize in investigating sexist language. Although feminist linguists use the methods of Saussure, they usually reject Saussure and semiology's point of stress that the signified and signifier are arbitrary relationships that have meaning only within the sign-system, not in reality. They focus occasionally on changing reality and therefore language, and changing the sign-system, which must be a very long and difficult task.

Feminists who stay close to semiotic theory as well as to semiotic methodology are almost all French as opposed to the British-American school of feminists that have adopted much of Saussure's methodology and only some of his theory. In general, French feminists insist on the arbitrary nature of signs and have found that Lacan's psychological structuralism elucidates semiotics. Feminists point out that his theories demonstrate how male and female children enter into language differently. Although feminists have been concerned about the patriarchal basis of his theory, he does not claim that the formation of the unconscious is outside the sign-system of language, a sign-system which is based in arbitrary connections. On the other hand, Lacanian theory believes that there can be no language until the mother/child relationship is broken and absence is felt. The phallus or penis represents the loss of the mother's body; therefore, symbol making is dominated by the penis.

As is true of most French feminist critics, Julia Kristeva both admires and criticizes Lacan's theories. Kristeva's work builds upon Lacan's, by discussing its importance and implications for women, but she rejects his "anatomy is destiny" principle, which he inherited from Freud. Kristeva's contributions to feminist semiological criticism are very important. Luce Irigaray is probably Lacan's most adamant critic. She challenges his idea of the language sign-system as incorrect because women have a language of their own which is not acknowledged by patriarchy. Moreover, she challenges Saussure's idea that the signified and signifier have a one-to-one meaning instead of multiple ones. These are challenges to structuralism and Lacanian theory at their base.

Feminism has shown continuing interest in semiotic theory as it extends beyond the language sign-system to other sign-systems. Applying the concept of sign-system to cultural analysis as Lévi-Strauss does, or to myth viewed and written about in cultural products, as Barthes does, has proved a fertile area for feminists. The exposure of the myths that those in power perpetuate so that their values become the values of all the people has brought every cultural ritual and product under the scrutiny of feminists. Barthes illustrates his ideas with visual cultural products. This helped direct feminist theory toward the whole area of cinema as a sign-system. Semiological theory can be applied to all areas of study, as Saussure envisioned it would be, and feminists have not hesitated to do so.

GLORIA STEPHENSON

SEX DIFFERENCES (Gender Differences, Sex-, Gender-Related Differences, Sexual Dimorphisms) refer to physical, behavioral, and personality characteristics which differ for females and males. The term *sex* is used for biologically based categories, and *gender* is more appropriate when referring to psychological and behavioral differences.

A topic of concern of Western philosophers throughout the ages, the formal study of sex differences by behavioral scientists received its theoretical impetus from Darwinian theory and its greatest empirical boost from the psychological testing movement. The issue has been heavily politicized throughout its history, with "facts" and theory often being fashioned to alternately support or challenge dominant social attitudes about acceptable gender roles*. Recent advances have made the biases in this work more explicit.

The two major points of controversy have been the existence (and magnitude) of sex differences and their cause(s). A related issue has been the relevance (or irrelevance) of this research to social policy and attitudes regarding the appropriate roles of women and men.

Research on the existence of sex differences has been marred by definitional problems associated with using broad, heterogeneous, and culturally biased categories of behavior, and with numerous methodological problems, including flawed experimental designs, biased observational techniques, inadequate data analysis and distortions in the reporting of results. A more subtle but important issue has been the way a sex difference is defined. Most research compares average scores for males and females to determine whether a statistically significant difference exists. Few such differences account for more than 1 to 5 percent of the total variance. There is always considerable overlap between the female and male distribution. Thus "significant" differences may not reflect large differences between the sexes. Little attention has been given to testing interactive models in which gender differences could occur under some conditions but not others, or in which the impact of environmental extremes are more variable for one sex than for the other.

Physically, *Homo sapiens* are moderately sexually dimorphic. Boys are approximately 4 percent heavier and 1 percent taller at birth. Other differences that emerge during development include greater male muscular strength, lung capacity, metabolic rate, and ratio of lean body mass to overall weight, and greater female tactile and olfactory sensitivity. Many of these differences increase with sexual maturity, which is approached more rapidly by girls than by boys, are maximum in adulthood, and decline with old age. Although biologically based, the expression of many physical sex differences is environmentally dependent. For example, differences in body size are maximum in plentiful environments but are reduced in populations under chronic nutritional stress.

Females have lower morbidity and mortality rates throughout the mid to late prenatal and early postnatal periods. With the exception of the higher incidence among females of some nervous system malformations and autoimmune disorders, males are more frequently afflicted with virtually every neurologic, psychiatric, and developmental disorder of early childhood. Some of these are mental retardation, autism, hyperactivity, dyslexia, epilepsy, cerebral palsy, learning and adjustment disorders, and schizophrenia. However, when females are affected, it is frequently with greater severity. The development of females also appears to be less adversely affected by environmental hazards. Non–mutually exclusive hypotheses that have been proposed to account for these differences include (1) X chromosome-linked disorders for which males are more susceptible,

(2) hormone differences during gestation, (3) the female's greater physical maturity at critical developmental stages such as birth, and (4) immunological incompatibility between mother and male fetus which might lead to fetal damage. Some of these causal factors also have been proposed to explain other sex differences which appear in older children and in adults.

Lower female morbidity and mortality continue into adulthood. Some differences also reflect biological factors, such as the relative protection against coronary heart disease afforded women by ovarian hormones. But historical changes in differential life expectancy and even reversals to higher female mortality in some less industrialized societies point to important interactions with cultural factors. These include sanitation, nutrition, and the level and availability of health care, particularly as it applies to dangers associated with pregnancy and childbirth*. They also include the relative contribution to overall mortality made by high-risk behavior such as smoking, alcohol consumption, accidents, homicides, and suicides, for which males show a greater excess in some cultures than in others.

Psychological differences between women and men are less clearcut and are strongly influenced by cultural and social factors. Regarding abilities, there is some evidence that girls develop verbal skills earlier and that women on the average score higher than men on tests of verbal abilities, although the differences are small. Male scores on certain tests of spatial ability are higher, as are scores on mathematical achievement. However, recent evidence suggests that these differences must be qualified by the type of test used and, particularly in the case of mathematical achievement, whether the comparison is made between those scoring at the extremes (highest and lowest achievement) or between overall average scores. Differences in interests and prior experience also affect these scores.

Analysis of gender differences in personality variables suggests an even greater role for cultural and social learning factors. Men are more aggressive, although this must be qualified by the type of aggression being considered, as well as by the nature of the target and the perceived consequences. The clearest difference is for physical aggression that produces pain or physical injury, which is more likely to occur between men than between women. While biological factors such as circulating hormone levels may contribute to sex differences in aggression, the complexity of these differences suggests that learned aspects of gender roles play a critical role in their development. Other personality differences are not as large. Generally, women are more influenced by group pressures for conformity and are more susceptible to social influence. Related to this is a continuing finding that women are more sensitive to the nonverbal behavior of others and are more able to interpret nonverbal displays of others' emotions. All of these differences have been more clearly associated with traditional gender role enactment than with biological factors. Other personality characteristics that are stereotypically associated with women such as sociability and nurturance have received mixed empirical support at best.

In adulthood, women show a higher incidence of disorders such as depression*, anxiety, and eating disorders (anorexia, bulimia, and obesity). Men exhibit a higher frequency of personality disorders and of psychosexual disorders such as paraphilias (e.g., fetishism), sexual dysfunction, and disorders related to gender identity (e.g., transsexualism). Men are also more likely to be alcoholic or take illegal drugs such as heroin, although women take more medically prescribed mind-altering drugs such as tranquilizers. Men have much higher rates of criminal behavior, including assault, rape, and property crimes. For both teenage and adult populations more males commit suicide.

Overall, data on physical and psychological characteristics of women and men demonstrate many similarities and some differences. Past attempts to explain the differences that do exist focused on either biological or cultural determinants, but most researchers now argue for an interaction of biological, environmental, and socialization factors.

Further References. K. Deaux, "Sex and Gender," *Annual Review of Psychology* 36 (1985): 49–81. A. H. Eagly and V. J. Steffen, "Gender and Aggressive Behavior: A Meta-analytic Review of the Social Psychological Literature," *Psychological Bulletin* 100 (1986): 309–330.

ANTHONY R. CAGGIULA AND IRENE H. FRIEZE

SEXISM is discrimination* or bias against people because of their sex, particularly used to denote discrimination against women. The perceptions people have about men and women are organizing principles upon which sex-related behaviors are based. A considerable amount of research has been devoted to the influence of individuals' sex-related perceptions on (1) evaluations of performance, (2) achievement, (3) responses and interactions to infants, and (4) conceptualizations of mental health. Results from research in these areas have generally indicated that part of the definition of gender roles* in Western culture involves assumptions about the types of occupations, life-styles, and abilities that are held to be appropriate for males and females. Distinctions have been in agreement with traditional stereotypes about personality traits. For example, men have typically been described by a series of characteristics that reflect rationality, assertiveness, and competency (i.e., objectivity, self-confidence, independence). Occupations sterotyped as "male-appropriate" that are associated with these personality characteristics include attorney, police officer, physician, and office manager. Traits such as submissive, subjective, emotional, and gentle have been used to describe women. Traditional "female-appropriate" occupations include elementary school teacher, typist, librarian, and nurse. Both masculine personality characteristics and occupations are rated by men and women as more desirable, important, and prestigious.

Consistent with stereotypes, both men and women have been found to value the professional work of men more highly than the identical performance of a woman. Men have been rated superior to women (by both men and women) as authors, artists, applicants for employment, and medical school students. Women are likely to be evaluated as being as competent as men when their performance is (a) acknowledged by an authoritative individual, (b) judged on explicit criteria, or (c) successful in male-dominated occupations or activities. The possibility that equivalent performances by men and women are evaluated differently because they are ascribed to different causes has been well documented. A man's successful performance is attributed to skill, while a woman's identical performance is attributed to luck and/or effort. A man's failure is more likely to be explained by unfair allegation of cheating, while a woman's failure is attributed to lack of ability. Furthermore, this overall discrimination has been found to be greater in men, who maintain more stereotypic values than women.

Sensitivity to the sex of the protagonist in achievement research serves to prejudice men and women against the success of a woman and the failure of a man. There exists a tendency to positively evaluate successful men in relation to unsuccessful men and downgrade successful women in relation to unsuccessful women. Negative imagery in the form of socially undesirable personality characteristics (e.g., unpleasant, overly emotional) and anticipation of future failure and social ostracism has been projected onto fictitious successful women by both adult men and women. In addition, success at an occupation is more highly valued when the success is consistent with societal conceptions about the gender role than when it is inconsistent. Thus, behavior in achievement situations is differentially perceived and evaluated according to the sex label assigned to the protagonist. In laboratory and real-world studies, when women and men in the same occupation are compared, women make a lower wage than men, women are less likely to be accepted into postgraduate programs than men, and are less likely to receive financial support for their education. Thus, there has been a pervasive devaluation of women in relation to men, suggesting a general belief in male superiority and female inferiority.

This argument certainly can be applied to another research area in which sexism has been found to play a prominent role: adults' evaluations and expectations of infant and child development. Experimenters requiring adults to play with infants have generally found that parents and nonparents interact and treat infants and children differently on the basis of the perceived or actual sex of the infant. Girls, for example, receive more distal stimulation (i.e., touch and holding). Parents describe their newborn girls (within the first 24 hours after birth) as soft, fragile, and petite, while they describe newborn boys as strong, firm, and muscular despite no differences in babies' birth length, weight, or neonatal assessment! These differences in adults' responses to infants are not attributable to the infants' behavior. Rather, the results are directly related to the adult responsivity as a function of the infants' sex.

It is interesting to note that the use of different criteria, less favorable to girls and women, is also practiced by clinicians. Male and female mental health workers typically have described a mature, healthy, and socially competent man or adult (sex unspecified) similarly, and significantly different from a woman.

A healthy woman was considered less independent, less adventurous, less aggressive, and less objective, while more easily influenced, more excitable in a minor crisis, and more conceited about her appearance than either a healthy man or a healthy, sex-unspecified adult.

It appears from this review of research in a variety of areas that the male, and by extension, "masculine" activities, occupations, and personality characteristics are perceived as normative; the female and the "feminine" is a deviation from the norm. The male is seen as the important person, the "healthy" one, and the female is a variation on him. Simone de Beauvoir expressed it as man is the Subject, woman is the Other. Perhaps the best example of the male as normative theme is the sex bias in the psychological research process, implicit in the above discussion. The hypotheses tested by a researcher are shaped by a theoretical model but also by gender-role stereotypes. Stereotypes about women have influenced the kinds of questions researchers have investigated scientifically. In addition, there appears to be good evidence that sexism exists in selecting participants for research. Boys and men are used more frequently as participants than girls and women are. In fact, some entire areas of research have been conducted using males only (e.g., moral development, achievement motivation). Thus, sexism has typically existed in the field of psychology inasmuch as that it has led to a psychology of male behavior, not human behavior. Furthermore, there may be a tendency for research conducted by women scholars to be considered less authoritative than reports by men. In recent years, a constructive alternative to sexist research methodology had been offered, namely, feminist methodology. The feminist alternative suggests that researchers avoid thinking in terms of simple causal statements and focus on interactive relationships. Feminists also devote specific research attention to the special concerns of women. Feminists do not assume that political activism and scientific research are contradictory to each other. Feminist methodology and feminism in general have changed the way psychology and other disciplines in the academy have thought about a variety of important issues: politics, children, pay equity, psychopathology, achievement, and morality. Feminist methodolgy has provided answers to a set of research questions that were not asked, let alone answered, in the sexist paradigm, e.g., androgyny*, rape*, sexism in psychotherapy. Thus, feminist researchers have counteracted the neglect and misrepresentations of women in psychology and other disciplines. Feminist scholarship has helped shift viewing the world as revolving around men to viewing it as revolving around men and women jointly.

Further Reference. V. O'Leary, R. Unger, and B. Wallston, *Women, Gender, and Social Psychology* (Hillsdale, N.J., 1985).

MICHELE A. PALUDI

SEX-ROLE SOCIALIZATION refers to the process whereby an individual's behavior, attitudes, and perceptions come to resemble those prescribed by society for persons of his or her gender. Several different theories have been proposed to explain this process.

The first theorist to write extensively, and influentially, on this topic was Sigmund Freud. Freud believed that children discover the anatomical differences between boys and girls at around four to six years of age and that this event has profound implications for their differential development. Girls are supposed to envy boys for having a penis (penis envy) and turn toward the hope of having a child as a substitute. Boys are supposed to feel both proud of possessing a penis and fearful of losing it (castration anxiety). They also perceive a rivalry with their father for the love of their mother and fear him because he has the power to castrate them. Boys must, in the resolution of this conflict, shift their primary identification from mother to father. Freud's theory of socialization is not widely accepted by most contemporary psychologists. Because of the un-conscious nature of the processes he described, it is extremely difficult to test any of the basic propositions.

Social learning theorists propose that general principles of learning can explain the process of sex-role socialization. If boys and girls receive different rewards and punishments for various behaviors based on their gender, then they would be expected to come to behave differently. Such differential rewards and pun-ishments would include those administered by parents, teachers, and other adults, as well as by other children. Empirical research confirms that in a number of ways parents consciously and unconsciously respond differently to the behavior of boys and girls.

According to social learning theory, observational learning also plays a major role in sex-role socialization. By observing the behaviors of others, in real life and in the media, children learn that some behaviors are rewarded in males but not in females, that some behaviors are considered more appropriate for one sex than the other. It is assumed that girls learn it is more advantageous for them to imitate their mothers and other females, whereas boys learn to imitate their fathers and other males.

A third perspective on sex-role socialization derives from the cognitive-developmental theory of Lawrence Kohlberg ("A Cognitive-Developmental Analysis of Children's Sex-Role Concepts and Attitudes," in Eleanor E. Mac-coby [ed.], *The Development of Sex Differences* [Stanford, Calif., 1966], 82–173). Kohlberg proposes that a key ingredient in the process of sex-role social-ization is that children acquire the concept of gender constancy, the idea that gender is an aspect of a person that does not change with time or situation. Prior to age five children will not consistently give correct answers or explanations to questions such as "When a boy grows up can he become a mommy?" or "If a girl plays football is she a boy or a girl?" According to Kohlberg, when a child acquires an understanding of gender constancy, he or she then tries to model his or her behavior to the way society defines masculinity or femininity*, as shown in the behavior of others, on television, or in books. That is, the child is intrinsically motivated to become competent, and becoming competent is equated with conforming to society's sex-role expectations.

Support for Kohlberg's theory comes from research showing that children who have a thorough understanding of gender constancy are more sex-typed than those who do not. However, a major limitation of Kohlberg's theory is that differentiation of behaviors according to gender appears much earlier than age five or six when gender constancy is typically attained. Boys will play more with cars and trucks and girls with dolls as early as age two.

The most recent theory of sex-role socialization is that proposed by Sandra L. Bem ("Gender Schema Theory and Its Implications for Child Development: Raising Gender-Aschematic Children in a Gender-Schematic Society," *Signs* 8 [1983]: 598–616). It is also the only theory which evolves from a feminist perspective on sex roles and on development. According to Bem, the process by which children become socialized to society's sex-role expectations involves gender-schematic processing, which she defines as "a generalized readiness on the part of the child to encode and to organize information—including information about the self—according to the culture's definition of maleness and femaleness" (603). Gender-schematic processing is a direct result of society's emphasis on the importance of distinctions based on gender, distinctions consistently enforced, but unrelated to the biological characteristics that define men and women. Thus gender comes to be a primary way of reorganizing input from the world.

Some support for Bem's theory comes from studies showing that children remember pictures that are sex-consistent better than those that are sex-inconsistent. She has also developed her theory so that it includes a framework for planning and implementing approaches to rearing children who are not limited by traditional sex-role stereotypes. For these reasons Bem's theory represents a major contribution to the field. Like Kohlberg's theory, it cannot explain sex differences in the behavior of very young children who are unlikely to have developed gender schemas.

In conclusion, Freudian theory of sex-role socialization is not held in high regard by most academic and research psychologists, although it probably continues to have substantial influence outside of these disciplines. Social learning theory is a very broad-based theory that has great explanatory power. The cognitive-developmental theory of Kohlberg remains somewhat influential because of its emphasis on the influence of cognitive factors, and on the child as an actor on his or her environment, not merely a passive recipient of its influences of others. Bem's theory is important because of the introduction of concepts from contemporary cognitive psychology, and especially because of the integration of theory about sex-role socialization with feminist contributions to psychological thinking.

Further References. For a sociological perspective, see DIFFERENTIAL SOCIALIZATION. C. Travis and C. Wade, *The Longest War: Sex Differences in Perspective* (Orlando, Fla., 1984).

JANE M. CONNOR

SEX-ROLE STEREOTYPES. See GENDER STEREOTYPES

SEXUAL AMBIGUITY. Those rare cases in which babies are born whose sexual gender is ambiguous or indeterminate offer an instructive illustration of the power of socialization on gender identity. Sexually ambiguous infants, who may either appear to be female but be biologically male or appear to be male but be biologically female, are sometimes called pseudohermaphrodites. When this condition is recognized early, gender is usually assigned by parents or the physician, on the basis of chromosomal sex. Hormonal treatments or surgical treatment may be performed in order to enhance the chromosomal gender. In extensive investigations, J. Money and A. Ehrhardt *(Man and Woman, Boy and Girl* [Baltimore: 1972]) conclude that gender assigned and accepted can have greater impact on self-image and self-identity than does biological gender. In virtually all the cases they studied, sex of assignment and rearing proved dominant even if the individual remained biologically the other sex. Biological males raised as females on the basis of physical characteristics developed female attitudes and sex-role identifications. Apparently, gender identity can be acquired independently of genes and hormones. Further, when chromosomes and hormones are incongruent with the sex of assignment and rearing, the cultural and social influences will prevail.

ALLEN SCARBORO

SEXUAL DIMORPHISM refers to differences in form between males and females of a species. The obvious and biologically significant difference in humans is in the development of the reproductive system. The male develops testes, epididymis, vas deferens, seminal vesicles, prostate gland, bulbourethral gland, urethra, and penis. The female develops ovaries, uterine tubes, uterus, vagina, and clitoris. The sex of an individual is ultimately determined by a single pair of chromosomes (1 of 23 pairs in humans), the "sex chromosomes," designated X (a large chromosome) and Y (a small chromosome). A mature ovum always contains an X chromosome. A sperm may contain an X also, in which case the fertilized ovum, i.e., zygote, will be XX and develop female. A sperm may contain a Y chromosome, in which case the zygote will be XY and develop male. All other chromosomes are identical in males and females. The reproductive structures in both sexes arise from identical embryological tissue. If a zygote is XY, genes are present which lead to the production of testosterone by the embryo. In the presence of testosterone, male internal and external genitals develop. In the absence of testosterone, i.e., in XX embryo, the female internal and external genitals form. The development, then, is in response to the hormone environment.

Additional anatomical differences between males and females develop at puberty. These secondary sex characteristics* are extragenital and include such traits as size, body shape, breast development, body hair, fat deposition, size of larynx, and pitch of voice. All of these characteristics are tissue responses to differing amounts of various sex hormones produced by the primary sex organs (testes and ovaries) and, in smaller amounts, by the adrenal cortex in both sexes. There is great individual variation in all these characteristics.

There is also an important physiological sexual dimorphism in the human brain. The hormones LH (luteinizing hormone) and FSH (follicle stimulating hormone), which regulate the reproductive systems in adults, are released from the anterior pituitary gland under the control of releasing hormones from an area of the brain called the hypothalamus. (This is a tremendous simplification: the regulation is a complex interaction between levels of various hormones, and numerous physiological and psychological factors.) In the female this control is a cyclic phenomenon, underlying the ovarian and menstrual cycles. In the male this control is a steady-state pheomenon. Studies on nonhuman species indicate the male or female pattern of release of hypothalamic hormones depends on the prenatal hormone environment.

Sexual dimorphism is widely reported or assumed to exist in a wide variety of behaviors (aggression, compliance, emotional response), skills (dexterity, tactile sensitivity), and abilities (verbal, mathematical, visual-spatial). Some of these reported differences simply do not exist at all. In other cases, there may be small differences in average score between males and females, differences that are much smaller and less significant than those between same-sex individuals. There are not sex-exclusive behaviors, skills, talents, or achievements. In these areas where differences do exist, the complex interaction of biology, early experience, socialization, etc., makes it impossible to conclude that there is an exclusively biological explanation.

FRANCES GARB

SEXUAL DIVISION OF LABOR is traditionally seen as a natural arrangement which forms the basis of all economic specialization and social structuralization leading to the formation of kinship groups and the family. Scholars have focused their attention essentially on the consequences rather than the causes of the division of labor. Actually, its origins and causes are not known, though various hypotheses have been developed using factual and assumed biological differences between the sexes as the basis for an explanation. Thus, greater physical strength of males, female involvement in biological and social reproduction—usually perceived of as a handicap rather than a contribution—and differences in moral and intellectual development have been understood to be causal factors with regard to the division of labor by sex. Based on these assumptions, the most prominent of all hypotheses is the male-the-hunter thesis which identifies the male as the first and main provider in human history who became the center of all economic and social development. This position, however, fails to acknowledge the significance of women's contributions as gatherers in early human history and thus their role in economic and social development.

This traditional approach likewise fails to explain (1) the variations of gender-specific task assignments cross-culturally (example: spinning is a female task among the Guajiro from Colombia, but a male task among the Kogi, also from Colombia); (2) the distribution of same-task assignments between women and men in the same culture (example: among the Jivaro from Ecuador women are the horticulturists, but maize planting and harvesting is an exclusively male task); and (3) the flexibility of gender-specific task assignments (example: among the Mazahua from Central Mexico, women and men have interchanged tasks traditionally defined as gender specific for prolonged periods of time during national and cultural crises). Thus the variations in the division of labor by sex and the flexibility exercised in certain situations indicate clearly that it is not biologically determined but strongly affected by the ideological concepts of a social system. This is important since it is not the performance of an activity but the evaluation of a task's significance which determines the cultural meaning of the sexual division of labor.

Certain areas of scholarship are especially important to help us gain a better understanding of this phenomenon. *Prehistory* provides data on the first work arrangements of humans, and, indeed, the gathering and hunting complex of our early ancestors represents one of the core issues in the discussion. *Mythology* gives data on people's rationalizations, justifications, and explanations of how and why they do what they do. Mythical materials contain rich documentation on the question of gender-specific task assignments that allows us to understand the "sex-role plans" of societies and thus their explanations of their system of a division of labor between women and men. *Cross-cultural studies of socialization* are crucial in helping us to understand the goals and ideas of a society since they provide data on how a people prepare the next generation for its roles. Socialization patterns clearly express the gender concepts of a society and the significance attributed to them.

As a result of the interest in consequences rather than causes, the focus on the present, and the strong male-oriented bias in research, traditional scholarship has produced a one-sided picture of the division of labor between the sexes. As a result, hunting has been overestimated in its significance as compared to gathering. Instead of interpreting the early patterns of labor division in their own historical context, scholars have applied contemporary Western patterns of gender conceptualization to the beginning of human history. Roles of females in the mythic traditions as creators, initiators, and agents have been downplayed, and cross-cultural socialization studies have focused, with few exceptions, on males only. Traditional research on the sexual division of labor has essentially ignored female activities related to pregnancy and childrearing as well as male involvement in this sphere. Because of this, terminology, methodology, and theories reflect a male-oriented understanding of labor and its role in the evaluation of people's contribution to society.

Because Western nations assume a universal meaning of gender-specific task assignment and assessment, which in reality ignores the wide variation cross-culturally, the existing hypotheses on the sexual division of labor have gained global significance affecting national policies and international programs.

Further References. G. P. Murdock and C. Provost, "Factors in the Division of Labor by Sex: A Cross-Cultural Analysis," *Ethnology* 12 (1973): 203–225. P. R. Sunday, *Female Power and Male Dominance: On the Origins of Sexual Inequality* (London, 1981).

MARIA-BARBARA WATSON-FRANKE

SEXUAL HARASSMENT has been ruled by the federal courts as a form of sexual discrimination that is outlawed by Title VII* of the Civil Rights Act of 1964. The law was extended to the field of education by Title IX* of the Education Amendments of 1972. Unwelcome sexual advances, requests for sexual favors, and other verbal or physical conduct of a sexual nature constitute sexual harassment when (1) submission to such conduct is made either explicitly or implicitly a term or condition of an individual's employment or academic advancement, (2) submission to or rejection of such conduct by an individual is used as the basis for employment decisions or academic decisions affecting such individual, or (3) such conduct has the purpose or effect of unreasonably interfering with an individual's work or academic performance or creating an intimidating, hostile, or offensive working or academic environment (Policy statement, University of Minnesota).

Though sexual harassment is not a new phenomenon, it wasn't until the rise of the women's movement in the 1970s and 1980s that this issue became an important item on the public agenda. While codified in the 1964 act, it was in 1976 that, for the first time, a federal court ruled that job retaliation toward a female employee who turned down sexual advances constituted sexual discrimination (*Williams* v. *Saxbe*, 413 F. Supp. 654, 66 D [DDC 1976]).

In 1980 the federal Equal Employment Opportunity Commission (EEOC) published its definition of sexual harassment as an amendment to its *Guidelines on Discrimination Because of Sex*. This definition covered the aforementioned areas of sexual submission as an explicit or implicit condition of employment and specifically included mention of an intimidating or offensive working environment. Court rulings and EEOC guidelines have further held that an employer is liable when sexual harassment takes place, "regardless of whether the acts were authorized, and whether they are known or should have been known of by the employer."

Despite clear guidelines in federal rulings, issues of sexual harassment remain sensitive and difficult. Myths of the victim "inviting the relationship" are so pervasive that women tend to expect a skeptical reaction to their complaints. This, when added to the fact that sexual harassment often occurs in a situation of an unequal power relationship, creates an environment in which many victims are reluctant to file charges. However, in the face of growing public sensitivity to these issues, this environment appears to be changing.

Sexual harassment is an issue that our society has long swept under the rug. As an increasing number of victims are refusing to remain quiet, and as an increasing number of men and women in our society are defining acts of harassment as an ethical as well as legal violation, procedures are being adopted to inform and protect potential or real victims. Professionals who work in this field, however, warn that the problems are more persistent and widespread than is generally acknowledged.

Further References. B. W. Dziech and L. Weiner, *The Lecherous Professor* (Boston, 1984). C. A. MacKinnon, *Sexual Harassment of Working Women* (New Haven, 1979).

BETTY A. NESVOLD

SEXUAL ORIENTATION in Western cultures refers to an enduring erotic, affectional, or romantic attraction to individuals of a particular gender. Sometimes *sexual preference* is used as a synonym, although this term can be misleading because it suggests a degree of conscious choice in sexuality that most people do not experience, and implies that those with a stigmatized sexuality could choose (or be compelled) to change it.

Sexual orientation is usually characterized as either *homosexual* (a primary or exclusive attraction to individuals of one's own gender) or *heterosexual* (a primary or exclusive attraction to individuals not of one's own gender). The term *bisexual* is used to describe persons with attractions to both men and women.

Discussions of sexual orientation have been rife with controversy. Prior to the 1970s, most scholars and professionals presumed the inevitability and desirability of a heterosexual orientation and sought to explain the "etiology" of homosexuality, though never with great success. In 1973, the American Psychiatric Association (later endorsed by the American Psychological Association) declared that a homosexual orientation is not inherently associated with psychopathology. This recognition helped to broaden inquiry from the "problem" of homosexuality* to the question of how sexual orientation develops generally. More recently, the question has been raised whether the very notion of "sexual orientation" is culture-bound, historically recent in origin and confined to specific societies.

Current discussions of sexual orientation are dominated by two opposing perspectives. Social constructionists view homosexuality and heterosexuality* as categories that have developed over time in particular cultures; the most radical proponents of this view argue that all sexuality is completely determined by social influences. Essentialists, in contrast, view homosexuality and heterosexuality as universal categories that describe a core part of human nature; some essentialists go so far as to explain sexuality entirely in biological terms, emphasizing genetic and prenatal hormonal factors. Choosing sides in the constructionist-essentialist dispute may be unnecessary, however, since the two camps generally focus on different components of sexuality.

Sexual orientation includes at least four components. First, *sexual behavior* refers to specific acts that are defined as sexual by the individual or society. As primates, humans are born with a highly plastic behavioral repertoire and are capable of a wide variety of sexual behaviors. Sexual behavior is not synonymous with sexual orientation. People with homosexual orientation can engage in heterosexual behavior and yet remain homosexual (e.g., lesbians* and gay men who marry heterosexually), and heterosexual persons can engage in homosexual acts without changing their sexual orientation (e.g., in a gender-segregated institution).

A second component of sexual orientation is *psychological attraction*. Whereas sexual behavior is what a person actually does, psychological attraction refers to what a person would like to do if the environment permitted. A homosexual person's attractions are to members of her or his own gender, and may or may not be expressed behaviorally. The same is true for heterosexual persons with members of the other gender. Heterosexual attractions are more likely to be acted upon than are homosexual attractions because no societal sanctions prohibit the former (although cultural norms prescribe appropriate settings and practices). The Kinsey studies (*Sexual Behavior in the Human Male* [1948], *Sexual Behavior in the Human Female* [1953]) demonstrated that significant numbers of U.S. citizens have consciously experienced both homosexual and heterosexual attractions and behaviors during their adult lives.

The sexual essentialists have focused primarily upon sexual behavior and psychological attraction in their discussions of sexual orientation. This perspective permits them to generalize across cultures and historical periods (and even across species), since sexual behaviors (and, most likely, attractions) of all varieties are ubiquitous among humans.

Because constructionists assume that sexual behaviors and attractions are endowed with meaning by one's social group, they emphasize two additional components of sexual orientation: *social roles* that attach cultural meanings and expectations to various behaviors and attractions, and *psychological identities*, or ways in which individuals define themselves in terms of their sexual behaviors and attractions and their associated social roles. Defined in terms of socioerotic identities and roles, sexual orientation clearly is not a universal phenomenon; it is a way of categorizing human sexuality that has developed in Western societies relatively recently.

A cross-cultural example is illustrative. In many societies of Papua New Guinea, male sexual behavior appears to be shaped largely by situational variables. Adolescent males are expected to engage exclusively in homosexual behavior for several years. Later, they are expected to marry a female and engage in heterosexual behavior with her. Sometimes married adult males participate in the homosexual initiation of adolescents. Although many individual males in these cultures appear to develop preferences for particular behaviors and attractions to particular types of partners, no social role or psychological identity exists comparable to Western notions of "the homosexual" or "the heterosexual." In the constructionist sense, therefore, sexual orientation is not a meaningful term for describing these societies. From the essentialist perspective, however, males in these cultures can be said to have a sexual orientation to the extent that they have an enduring preference for partners of one gender over the other (which can vary over their life span).

Failure to recognize the differing emphases of the essentialist and constructionist schools has clouded consideration of the individual origins of sexual orientation within Western cultures. From a constructionist perspective, individual sexual orientation clearly has a sociocultural basis, since the very concept is viewed as a cultural construction. Nevertheless, constructionists have not yet adequately explained how behaviors and attractions (from which individual identities are constructed) initially develop. The essentialists have focused on prenatal factors and early experiences that shape individual behaviors and attractions; they have paid less attention to sociocultural roles. Empirical research on the contributions made by these variables to adults' sexual orientation remains inconclusive, however. Despite recurring arguments for the primacy of genetic or hormonal determinants, neither has been shown to be sufficient or necessary for the emergence of a heterosexual or homosexual orientation in humans. Nor have retrospective accounts revealed clear differences in the life experiences of homosexual and heterosexual persons. Future research is needed to illuminate how patterns of behavior and attraction are shaped by prenatal and experiential variables and how they come to be manifested as socioerotic identities within a particular culture.

Further References. A. P. Bell, M. S. Weinberg, and S. K. Hammersmith, *Sexual Preference: Its Development in Men and Women* (Bloomington, Ind., 1981). J. Boswell, "Revolutions, Universals, and Sexual Categories," *Salmagundi* 58–59 (1983): 89–113. G. Herdt, *Guardians of the Flutes: Idioms of Masculinity* (New York, 1981). J. Money, "Sin, Sickness, or Status? Gender Identity and Psychoneuroendocrinology," *American Psychologist* 42 (1987): 384–399.

GREGORY M. HEREK

SEXUALITY (FEMALE) is a social construct mixing sensuality, reproductive life, eroticism, and gender-role performance, diffused throughout all social and personal life in activities, feelings, and attitudes. The social construct, and thus the values, experiences, and behaviors, differ widely over time and across cultures, and they deserve our closest analysis and attention once we understand that ideas of "proper" and "normal" sexuality have served everywhere to socialize and control women's behavior.

A major impact of contemporary feminism* has been to shatter old beliefs about what sexuality was, could be, or should be. New feminist research in history, psychology, anthropology, and political science has altered earlier, more biologically based ideas and definitions regarding female sexuality. Although it would be patently false to claim unanimity in women's studies on the subject of sexuality, much current thinking rejects transhistorical ideas, and sees biological sexuality only as a precondition which is never unmediated by social and individual experience.

Women's sexual freedom and women's sexual victimization have been both more closely analyzed and more visible in recent years than ever before. At first, feminists wrote at length about the need for transformation. Women were to reclaim and redefine their sexual identity, rechoreograph their sexual acts, and develop a sense of themselves as agents of their own sexual expression and satisfaction. Feminists called for more and better sexuality education, focusing not just on the facts of reproduction and plumbing but on the politics of pleasure, the potential of relationships and of fantasy. For a while there was a thrilling sense of new possibilities. But in more recent years, the pendulum within feminist writings has swung away from an emphasis on the power of self-definition to an emphasis on how women are victimized by coercive sexual acts and dehumanizing sexual images. The central metaphor for female sexuality seems to have moved from masturbation and vibrators to rape*.

The female body has always been contested terrain in patriarchal society, and we should expect that controversies over female sexuality will rage among feminists as well as in the wider society. Controversy can enrich feminist theory* and practice if the debate is creative and not destructive. Several issues concerning sexuality can be identified as especially important in current feminist writings:

1. The relationship of women's sexual opportunities and experiences to their political and economic status. Sociological research within societies, anthropological studies of disparate societies, and even microanalyses of status relations within couple relationships show that sexual freedom and satisfaction for women are intimately connected to women's self-respect, self-knowledge, and the sense of having options in life, which are in turn directly related to women's socioeconomic opportunities.

2. Meanings of lesbianism. Women's love for and bonding with other women take a wide variety of forms in different historical eras, cultures, and subcultures. Herstorians are frustrated by the paucity of materials with which to illuminate the nature and extent of sexual expressions between women, but have determined that the concept and category of "lesbian" was established within the past 150 years, during a time of great emphasis on sex-role identity and on the medical development of categories of sexual normality and abnormality. Our current ideas about sexual preference seem inextricably related to rigid gender categories which are themselves social constructions.

3. Roles of medicine and psychology in shaping definitions of sexuality, and through the definitions, society's and women's sexual expectations and experiences. Much feminist writing has properly criticized the Freudian disparagement of clitoral pleasure, the sexologist's selection of certain acts as "foreplay" and others as "the real thing," the ready classification of women who are not "adjusted" to current norms as having various forms of pathology, etc. Whereas feminists at first celebrated the scientific evidence recognizing physiological similarity between male and female bodily sexual response (including the equivalence of male and female orgasm), later writers underscored the danger of a biological hegemony that might result from valorizing allegedly "objective" research. Instead of promoting respect for diversity, such research seems to establish new norms and new abnormalities. Moreover, all medical research seems inattentive to relationship issues and the social contexts of such relationships, and pursues a definition of sexuality that is excessively privatized and apolitical.

4. Changing priorities within feminist discourse for different aspects of female sexuality such as imaginal fantasy, relational intimacy, and physical pleasure.

Because sexuality has not typically been seen as a social construction with psychological, sociological, biological, linguistic, legal, etc., meanings, writers have competed to identify *the prime aspect* of sexuality, as if such a thing existed in the material world just awaiting empirical discovery. This has led to some destructive name-calling, with feminists who might emphasize one aspect of sexuality or another being labeled "male-identified" or "separatist" by others.

5. The impact on personal and social experience of female sexuality in a world where women's control over their own bodies is limited by real and threatened violence. Feminist writings have tried to assess the impact of patriarchal society on women's sexuality. As a strategy of adjustment, for example, have women learned to eroticize subordination and objectification? What are the differences between societies that criminalize aspects of women's choice (e.g., regarding abortion*, prostitution*, homosexual activities) and those where women's rights to freedom of choice and expression are better protected and longer established?

6. The relationship of sexuality to reproductive function (e.g., interconnections of sexuality and menstrual cycling, the effects of pregnancy or having birthed or nursed children on psychological and physiological sexual experience, life span shifts in sexual meanings and needs). Some feminists have claimed that female menstrual rhythmicity has special consequences for women in terms of sexual desire and experience. Others argue that the embodied aspect of female sexuality is a social construct from stem to stern, and that menstrual rhythmicity is on the same subliminal and trivial level as circadian rhythms in enzyme production. This type of probiological and antibiological standoff denies individual differences, and seems less likely to be resolved than to continue vacillating in tune with political emphases within the movement at large.

7. The role of learning. Although we experience our sexuality as immediate (even instinctive!) and are usually unaware of acquiring and changing psychological meanings and valences, we know that learning must be involved from the evidence of cultural diversity and our own changes over the life span. How and when are bodily meanings and pleasures learned? Some contemporary feminists have turned toward psychoanalysis with its focus on unconcious meanings, preverbal learning, and the symbolism that adheres to actions and attractions. Others use the ideas of social learning and reinforcement theory to show how what society teaches women to value and rewards them for choosing is what gets internalized and practiced.

8. Male sexuality. Feminists are agreed that, in a patriarchy*, male sexuality sets the frame and the norm for women and that female sexuality is constructed to serve men's interests. But other than casual, usually pejorative, references to male sexuality as "genitally dominated" or "inherently aggressive," feminists have chosen to write very little on the subject. Men's preoccupation with correct sexual equipment and its performance at the expense of emotional communication or enjoyment of their sensual potential needs to be understood as a function of their desperate need to establish and maintain proof of their masculinity. Because

of the power relations in patriarchy, such masculinity is actually more directed toward establishing men's status with other men than with women.

These are issues of interest to one feminist, but their listing only serves to point to the complex and syncretic nature of the subject and to the idiosyncratic perspective of any analysis. Each of us has her own list, her own definitions, her own experience. Female sexuality is the totality, no less.

Further References. M. Valverde, *Sex, Power and Pleasure* (Toronto: Women's Press, 1987). C. S. Vance (ed.), *Pleasure and Danger: Exploring Female Sexuality* (Boston, 1984).

LEONORE TIEFER

SEXUALLY TRANSMITTED DISEASE (STD) discriminates against women (John Hatcher et al., *Contraceptive Technology* [New York, 1981], 37). Because women are less likely to have early symptoms, or any symptoms at all, STD is harder to recognize, diagnose, and treat in women. Late diagnosis and absent or inadequate treatment increase the likelihood of complications such as a pelvic inflammatory disease which can be life threatening or result in infertility*. It is estimated that 40 percent of women with untreated gonorrhea* will develop pelvic inflammatory disease (R. Platt et al., "Risk of Acquiring Gonorrhea and Prevalence of Abnormal Adnexal Findings among Women Recently Exposed to Gonorrhea," *Journal of the American Medical Association* 250 [1983]: 3206–3207). Because of women's potential reproductive role, the health implications of negative influences on pregnancy, labor and delivery, and offspring health status are of grave concern to women and to society at large. Finally, certain sexually transmitted diseases such as herpes* and genital warts* increase the risk of cervical cancer.

Public attention focused on Acquired Immune Deficiency Syndrome (AIDS)* has dominated concern and overshadowed potential risks of other sexually transmitted diseases. Fear and panic about AIDS have brought into the foreground misconceptions people hold about women's role in the spread of STDs. Women—especially prostitutes—are regarded as a reservoir of disease when, as in the case of AIDS, women are actually more likely to contract the virus from men than men are from women. Women in the sex industry have been leaders in education about the practice of safe sex ("Prostitutes: Forced Testing," *Off Our Backs* 18 [1988]: 5). Men are rarely admonished to utilize recognition of early symptoms of STD as a means to protect partners—often women—against the risk of sexually shared infections. A number of articles in the popular media have proposed the nineteenth-century view that women as the moral respository are responsible for halting the spread of AIDS by curtailing their sexuality, being monogamous, and insisting that men use condoms.

A major problem in dealing with STDs is the rapidly changing information about them and their proper treatment. For example, only recently has chlamydia* been recognized as a clinical entity. Before this it was included in a collective term: nongonococcal infections, being described by what it isn't instead of what it is. As a result of rapidly changing information, large numbers of women are not being screened appropriately or tested accurately when testing is indicated. Even when conditions such as chlamydia are diagnosed, proper treatment is sometimes not administered. Standardization of screening indications and treatment guidelines is sorely needed.

Currently, two conditions called ureaplasma and mycoplasma are little known, rarely tested, and the implications unknown even though observers have noted that these conditions may be related to chronic cystitis*, inflammation of the cervix (which could precipitate precancerous changes) and even spontaneous abortion* (miscarriage) and premature labor. These conditions are successfully treated with an antibiotic, erythromycin, but confusion exists about the necessity to treat women at all. Little research has been published even though a diagnostic test is available.

There needs to be concern about the currently evolving sexually transmitted diseases such as ureaplasma and mycoplasma as well as the threats of old standard diseases such as gonorrhea and syphilis to women's health.

Prevention of Sexually Transmitted Diseases and Promotion of Vaginal Health. The single most important preventive measure to use with male partners is the condom. Other barrier methods such as the diaphram with the spermicide nonoxly–9 or other products containing this spermicide are also effective in preventing the spread of sexually transmitted diseases. Establishing a rapport with sexual partners that allows for the exchange of information about a history of STD is critical. Looking at sexual partners and avoiding sex with persons who have inflammation, discharge from the penis and vagina, or bumps or sores on the genitals will avoid exposure.

Women must avoid experiences which abuse the vagina and genital area. Products such as deodorant tampons, perfumed douches and soaps, restrictive clothing made of synthetic fibers, a diaphram left in place longer than eight hours without adequate lubrication jeopardize the health and natural resistance of the vagina.

Promoting vaginal health should be an active process of maintaining nutritional balance, including cultured yogurt and adequate fluids in the diet, avoiding excessive refined sugar intake, and avoiding the use of antibiotics that are not absolutely necessary since vaginitis* is often a side effect of antibiotic therapy. Regular sexual response and exercising the muscles surrounding the vagina help to build resilience. Bathing before and after interactions reduces the chances of getting and giving STD. Care needs to be taken during anal sexual interactions that bacteria from the anal area is not spread to the vagina or urethra or that damage to the delicate tissue does not provide an entry point for bacteria.

Being cognizant of vaginal sensations and genital comfort helps women to detect early signs of imbalance. If modification of diet and health behavior does not alleviate the problem, a health professional should be consulted.

Further References. P. Andersen, "Behavioral and Clinical Indicators of Chlamydia Trachomatis in Women," unpublished master's thesis, University of Wisconsin–La

Crosse, 1987. Federation of Feminist Women's Health Centers, *A New View of a Woman's Body* (New York, 1981). J. Loulan, *Lesbian Sex* (San Francisco, 1984).

ELAINE WHEELER

SHADOW PRICE is a measure for valuing services, such as household production, that are not sold on the market and that therefore do not receive a market price. This concept is used in economic analyses of women's labor force participation.

SUSAN B. CARTER

SOCIALIST FEMINISM. A mode of analysis of women's oppression and a strategy for change. As an analytical approach to women's situation, socialist feminism argues that neither feminism* nor Marxism alone can explain women's experience. Women are the victims of class inequality and conflict. Yet even when they are members of an economic elite, women suffer the negative consequences of male domination. The liberation of women means freedom from both sexism* and classism.

The nexus of class and sexual oppression has been the subject of debate in feminist and socialist movements for decades. Early Marxists and socialists saw women's position as an extension of their husbands' or fathers': the wife of a male worker was herself a proletarian; that of a capitalist, a member of the bourgeoisie. Socialists thus thought women's interests were best served by political alliance with males to destroy economic hierarchy.

Feminists have objected to the classic socialist framework for failing to account for several dimensions of women's experience. First, women's work* in the home is often unrewarded by male kin, whether rich or poor. Throughout modern history males have treated women as property, subject to physical, sexual, and emotional abuse. Second, women increasingly participate in the marketplace, as traders, entrepreneurs, and paid laborers, and thus hold a different position in the capitalist system than their spouses. Finally, women in precapitalist societies have frequently had substantial economic power, unmediated by fathers, brothers, or spouses, an indication that capitalism may have increased women's subordination to men.

Early twentieth-century socialist feminist Emma Goldman argued that capitalism distorts sexuality and sex roles. Contemporary theorists synthesize the feminist perspective on the material origins of male dominance with the socialist critique of capitalism. It is now generally agreed that patriarchy*, the control of women's labor by adult males, was linked to agrarian society. As capitalism developed it "articulated," or merged with, patriarchy. Capitalist wage relations permit the equality of males and females, but patriarchal relations endure at home and shape the workplace as well. Capitalist relations of production may eventually supersede patriarchy, it is argued, with males and females equally able to gain or lose social resources through the capitalist system.

Socialist feminist political strategies diverge on questions about the tenacity of patriarchy in modern capitalist society. Some argue that sexism is pervasive and institutionalized: it must be fought at every stage of the battle against capitalism. Indeed, socialism coexists with patriarchy in many contemporary societies. Others contend that women's issues are among many minority concerns on the socialist agenda. This position is closer to classic Marxism in its suggestion that sexism is tractable, a by-product of capitalism that will disappear with the advent of a socialist economy.

Further References. F. Engels, *Origin of the Family, Private Property and the State,* ed. with intro. by E. B. Leacock (New York, 1972). H. I. Hartmann, "The Unhappy Marriage of Marxism and Feminism: Towards a More Progressive Union," in L. Sargent (ed.), *Women and Revolution* (Boston, 1981), 1–41. A. K. Shulman (ed.), *Red Emma Speaks: Selected Writings and Speeches by Emma Goldman* (New York, 1972).

MARIETTA MORRISSEY

SOCIAL POWER. The ability of one person to intentionally influence another person's behavior, opinions, or emotions using one or more resources as the source of influence. The concept of social power received little systematic attention until the women's movement, when feminist scholars (R. K. Unger, "Male Is Greater Than Female: The Socialization of Status Inequality," *Counseling Psychologist* 6 [1976]: 2–9) noted that many differences between women and men reflected differences in power and status rather than gender. Since then, the concept of power has figured prominently in women's studies.

For example, Paula Johnson ("Women and Power: Toward a Theory of Effectiveness," *Journal of Social Issues* 32 [1976]: 99–110) suggested that traditional gender stereotypes* led to the expectation of different styles and bases of power for the two sexes. She posited three dimensions of gender differences in power styles—indirect (e.g., manipulation) vs. direct power, personal (e.g., affection, sexuality) vs. concrete (e.g., money, knowledge) power, and helplessness vs. competence—with the first of each pair being the female style of power and the second, the male style. According to Johnson, female styles of power are less effective than male ones, and their use by women serves to sustain their less powerful position in society. She advocates that women adopt male power styles to increase their access to power; however, doing so may have interpersonal costs (e.g., less liking and less perceived competence).

The Power Motive. Individuals differ in their desire for power and the satisfaction they derive from exercising power over others. Contrary to traditional gender stereotypes, there are no consistent sex differences in the strength of the power motive. Members of both sexes respond similarly to conditions designed to arouse power motivation. Women and men with strong power motives express this need similarly in some regards: pursuing and entering occupations allowing them influence or control over others (e.g., psychology, business, teaching) and being more involved and successful in organizations. In other regards, power-motivated women and men differ. The tendency for men high in need of power to indulge more in "profligate" behaviors, such as drinking, gambling, and interest in vicarious sex, than those with weak power motivation is not apparent among women with different levels of power motivation. This link between power motivation and "profligacy," however, is now believed to be due, not to gender per se, but to differences in the socialization of responsibility. For both women and men, the socialization of responsibility channels strong needs for power into socially constructive directions (D. G. Winter and Nicole B. Barenbaum, "Responsibility and the Power Motive in Women and Men," *Journal of Personality* 53 [1985]: 335–355). Other differences in the way women and men express power motivation may well reflect genuine differences in gender roles and gender socialization. For example, power-motivated men are more prone than their female counterparts to treat their intimate, heterosexual relationships as a forum to exercise power and to choose as spouses individuals over whom they can do so.

Sex differences in power motivation among business managers have also been recently explored. According to one study, personnel officers of both sexes believe female managers possess lower needs for power than their male counterparts. Another view sometimes expressed is that when women do seek power, it is for personal, selfish ends. Both stereotypes are fallacious. In recent studies of full-time managers, women scored higher than men in needs for power and achievement. Moreover, the sex difference in need for power was largely due to women's superiority to men in "socialized" power oriented mainly to the good of others. As well, since high achievement motivation and high power motivation together predict managerial success and effectiveness, the motive profile of female managers fits the "successful manger" images better than male managers. Women today may offer more management potential (L. H. Chusmir, "Motivation of Managers: Is Gender a Factor?" *Psychology of Women Quarterly* 9 [1985]: 153–159).

Power in Intimate Relationships. Power is an important aspect of close or intimate relationships, especially when partners try to coordinate their preferences, goals, and/or means of attaining them. Toni Falbo and Letitia Anne Peplau ("Power Strategies in Intimate Relationships," *Journal of Personality and Social Psychology* 38 [1980]: 618–628) proposed a two-dimensional model of power in intimate relationships, which categorizes the strategies partners use to influence one another according to their directness and bilaterality (i.e., how interactive the power strategy is). To test the model, partners in homosexual and heterosexual couples indicated how they felt they got their partner to do what they want. Sex differences occurred only in heterosexual couples: males reported more reliance upon direct and bilateral strategies in their intimate heterosexual relationships, whereas females said they made greater use of indirect and unilateral power strategies. These findings were interpreted as due to power differences between the sexes. Presumably, since women expect less compliance from an intimate, heterosexual partner than men, they must depend more upon power strategies that do not require the partner's cooperativeness to get their way. More recent research, however, suggests that reliance upon indirect and unilateral power strategies in intimate relationships is not tied to femaleness per se, but rather reflects other factors, such as one's level of androgyny* and especially one's status relative to a potential target of influence.

Other studies of heterosexual dating relationships also indicate that bases of power differ for the two sexes. Controlling the partner's reciprocation of love, contributing less to the relationship than one's partner, and having high educational and career goals help to give women the balance of power in a dating relationship. In contrast, men's power is determined by being able to attract alternative dating partners.

Power is also obviously important to marital happiness. Research on power and satisfaction in marriage* has yielded two consistent findings: (1) the use of coercive power tactics is associated with, and may well cause, marital unhappiness and dissatisfaction, and (2) marriages in which the wife dominates the husband yield the least satisfaction, with egalitarian couples having the greatest satisfaction (B. Gray-Little and N. Burks, "Power and Satisfaction in Marriage," *Psychological Bulletin* 93 [1983]: 513–538). Why wife-dominant marital relationships are least satisfactory remains unclear, though two factors probably working together have been proposed as most likely: (1) a role congruency explanation emphasizing the departure of the wife-dominant marriage type from more usual, traditional, or modern forms of marriage, and (2) a role-incapacity explanation stressing the husband's abdication of marital role responsibilities.

As the preceding illustrates, power is an important explanatory concept in women's studies.

KENNETH L. DION

SOCIAL SECURITY. Old Age and Survivors Insurance (OASI), generally called social security, was established in the United States by the Social Security Act of 1934. Since the 1930s social security has expanded to include disability insurance (it is now OADSI) and to the vast majority of Americans.

Earnings subject to social security tax are credited to each person's separate account, but since the program was intended to provide a basic minimum income for retired workers, benefits are not proportional to the monies paid into each account. As earnings rise, the proportional return of the benefits is reduced. Lower paid workers, who are expected to have fewer savings, receive payments covering a larger portion of their preretirement income than more highly paid workers receive.

Social security pays extra benefits to married workers. At the time social security was instituted, most wives did not work after marriage. To give some support to housewives, since 1939 benefits to married couples include a spousal benefit of 50 percent of the worker's benefit. Working wives can elect to use their own retirement benefits or the spousal benefit, whichever is greater. If the husband predeceases the wife, which normally happens, the widow receives her husband's benefit, if she is of retirement age. Until reforms were made in the

1970s, however, a widow who remarried lost her widow's benefits, and a divorced woman who was married for less than 20 years received no spousal benefits at all. In 1978 the time was cut to 10 years.

Feminists have been especially concerned with the way social security policy affects divorced women and housewives. One concern is to allow the divorced wife to collect benefits as soon as she reaches minimum retirement age, whether or not her ex-husband has retired. This is part of the broader issue of separate accounts for housewives. Various methods have been proposed for crediting a housewife's account (e.g., having 50 percent of the husband's earnings credited to his wife's separate account). Some recommend more comprehensive changes, such as giving all persons of retirement age an across-the-board sum as the principal part of their benefit, with a smaller sum, based on earnings, added.

SOCIOBIOLOGY, a subfield of biology, first appeared in 1975 with the publication of E. O. Wilson's book, *Sociobiology: The New Synthesis* (Cambridge, Mass.). It is defined by its practitioners as the systematic study of the biological basis of all social behavior, from social insects to humans. The importance of sociobiology derives from its role as a theory of human nature. Using the "New Synthesis" or "Modern Synthesis," sociobiologists mean to transform the study of society. As Wilson says, "One of the functions of sociobiology, then, is to reformulate the foundations of the social sciences in a way that draws these subjects into the Modern Synthesis" (4).

Biologists and anthropologists adopted sociobiology very quickly and books, articles, and journals proliferated. It is now widely accepted as a field, positions have been created for sociobiologists, and courses in the subject are taught at many universities. Sociobiological arguments have made their way into other fields such as economics and political science and are widespread enough that they appear in high school and even grade school material. Opposition to sociobiology has also been widespread, however. Critics have pointed to the flaws in assumptions and methodology that result in conclusions about human behavior that do nothing more than reflect the cultural biases of the sociobiologists. These critics have also drawn attention to the relationship of sociobiology to earlier, discredited theories of biological determinism. (See R. C. Lewontin, S. Rose, and L. J. Kamin, *Not in Our Genes* [New York, 1984]; R. Hubbard and M. Lowe [eds.], *Genes and Gender II* [New York, 1979].)

When applying the theory to humans, sociobiologists assert that human social behavior and social institutions are the result of the action of genes. They argue that these genes have been selected during evolution because they give rise to behaviors that increase the reproductive success of individuals. At times the sociobiologists do not claim complete genetic determination, but speak of propensities or say that genes promoting flexibility in social behavior are strongly selected. However, these qualifying statements have little force, since the body of the theory is based on the assumption that the details both of the structure of

human society and of the social behavior of individuals are genetically determined.

Sociobiologists have claimed biological control for a large part of human
social behavior, such as warfare and aggression, religion, rape, xenophobia,
territoriality, conformity, competition, cooperation, altruism, entrepreneurial
ability, a hierarchical structure of society, differing birth rates of the rich and
poor, women marrying rich men, and children not liking spinach. In particular,
a number of sex differences in behavior are claimed to exist and to be genetically
determined; for example, differences in aggression, in nurturing and parenting,
in representation in male-dominated professions such as business, politics, and
science, and in philandering.

When theorizing about an observed human behavior, sociobiologists do not
prove genetic control, but instead assert that it exists, at best trying to make the
assertion plausible. The heart of sociobiological argument is the attempt to show
that given behaviors are adaptive; that is, that natural selection results in that
particular behavior. For example, in dealing with the sexual division of labor in
our society, sociobiologists have argued that since females certainly share half
of their genes with their children, while males cannot be completely sure of their
paternal contribution, it is adaptive for females "to invest heavily in the well-
being of the children" but not for males. This "suggests why women have
almost universally found themselves relegated to the nursery while men derive
their greatest satisfaction from their jobs" (D. P. Barash, *Sociobiology and
Behavior* [Amsterdam, 1977]). A genetic basis is assumed, not demonstrated,
and then an evolutionary story is developed to explain what is observed. Furthermore, since behavior is said to be shared so as to be adaptive, the sociobiological explanation carries the suggestion that the end result is the optimal
one.

Sociobiological explanations require that behavior be under genetic control,
at least to some extent. Since no one has yet identified any social behavior in
humans that is controlled by a specific gene or genes, sociobiologists resort to
several arguments to try to demonstrate genetic determination of behavior. The
first is the proposal that traits observed universally in human cultures are genetically based. No one, however, has demonstrated convincingly that any traits,
including often-cited sex differences in behavior, are universal. There are fundamental problems with the methods sociobiologists have used to try to demonstrate universality given the wide variation in behavior shown both within and
across cultures. Furthermore, even if a trait were to be identified as universal,
this in itself would not be evidence of a genetic underpinning except in the most
trivial sense.

A second, related line of argument points to social behaviors that are said to
be similar in both humans and other primates, such as aggressive dominance
systems. However, there are the same basic problems in identifying such behaviors across species as within. A more fundamental objection is that even if

similar behaviors could be identified, similarity alone does not allow one to draw the conclusion that the traits share the same evolutionary or genetic basis.

A final claim is that some traits, such as schizophrenia, IQ, and dominance, have been directly shown to be somewhat heritable and that this is indirect evidence that others may be as well. This argument is no stronger than the previous ones, however, since no reliable evidence exists to show that any human behavioral trait is heritable. Furthermore, the ground of the argument has shifted here, since heritability measures the degree to which differences in behavior are due to genetic factors.

Since there is thus no evidence that human social behavior is under genetic control, the evolutionary stories are pure speculation. Furthermore, if a given behavior is not known to be genetically determined, then one can in general just as well explain its appearance through cultural development or adaptation. There are no criteria for choosing either the biological or the cultural explanation or some particular combination of the two. The wide cross-cultural variations in behavior make it clear that environment plays at least some role in behavioral development. However, despite the claims of the biological determinists, one cannot say more than this about the origins of human social behavior.

Sociobiology is neither a new phenomenon nor an isolated one. In the nineteenth century, theories claiming to have scientifically demonstrated a relationship between biology and behavior were very prevalent and widely accepted. (See, e.g., R. Hofstadter, *Social Darwinism in American Thought* [New York, 1959]; E. Fee, "Science and the Woman Problem: Historical Perspectives," in M. S. Teitelbaum [ed.], *Sex Differences: Social and Biological Perspectives* [New York, 1976].) These nineteenth-century theories of biological determinism, collectively known as Social Darwinism, were eventually discredited, but they have now reappeared in modernized forms. The revival began in the late 1960s and there has been a increasing interest in them since. Sociobiology is only one of a wide variety of theories purporting to show that biology determines human social behavior. Most of the other theories, however, are not evolutionary models but attempts to find direct biological underpinnings of behavior by looking at such things as brain function or hormones. (See, e.g., A. Fausto-Sterling, *Myths of Gender* [New York, 1985]; Lewontin et al., *Not in Our Genes.*) The current theories are often direct descendants of their nineteenth-century predecessors and rest on arguments and scientific underpinnings that are no firmer than those of the Social Darwinists.

The wide acceptance of sociobiology and other theories of biological determinism may well be due to their political implications. Such theories offer support for the status quo, since our social organization is said to be due to nature. Sociobiology particularly suggests that we live in the best of all possible worlds, since behavior is held to have evolved adaptively. The sociobiologist Barash, for example, has said that "there should be a sweetness to life when it accords with the adaptive wisdom of evolution" (310). Sociobiological theories claim to give us the limits of possible change, or at least of desirable change. They are also, at bottom, theories not about the origins of human society but about the origins of inequalities in human society. They are works which are used to justify social inequities such as sexism* and racism. Starting from the very questionable assumption of meritocracy, that is, that ability is the primary determinant of social position, they add that abilities are largely determined by biology. It then follows that if people are in positions of privilege, it is not because of unfairness but because their genes are better. The importance of differing and inequitable sex roles in our society is reflected in the fact that sex differences play a large part in all the theories of biological determinism. It is also not surprising that much media attention has been directed to theories of the origins of sex differences.

A disturbing trend is the appearance of a number of feminist versions of biodeterministic theories in response to sociobiology and other works. Alternative evolutionary and hormonal theories have been suggested by A. S. Rossi ("A Biological Perspective on Parenting," *Daedalus* 106 [1977]; E. Morgan, *The Descent of Women* [New York, 1972]; and S. B. Hrdy, *The Woman that Never Evolved* [Cambridge, Mass., 1981]). In addition, results from works on brain lateralization have been widely adopted, with a left brain vs. right brain dichotomy identified with male vs. female thinking. These ideas attempt to counter the stories of mainstream biological determinists that accept the male stereotype as the norm and devalue women. They attempt instead to assert the legitimacy of the cultures and values that are typical of women's worlds. These theories, however, have no better basis than any of the others. The search for understanding human societies lies elsewhere than in studying our biology.

Further References. R. Bleier, *Science and Gender* (New York, 1983). R. Dawkins, *The Selfish Gene* (Oxford, 1976). S. Mosdale, "Science Corrupted: Victorian Biologists Consider the Woman Question," *Journal of the History of Biology* 11 (1978): 1–55. J. Sayers, *Biological Politics: Feminist and Anti-Feminist Perspectives* (London, 1982).

MARIAN LOWE

SPORTS. Women's participation in public sporting events in Western society has been limited to Bronze Age Crete, Classical Sparta, and the twentieth century. Although women's participation is still much more limited than men's, within the last 50 years the track and field, winter, and aquatic events and the team sports in which women publicly engage have grown enormously.

In 1896, the modern Olympic Games began in Athens, Greece. In the early years of this competition, almost all of the events were considered "men-only affairs." Not until the 1900 games did women officially enter the Olympics and then only in two events, golf and tennis. Next to be added were archery and ice skating, with swimming following in 1912. Although women began applying for the inclusion of track and field events to the Olympics in 1919, it was not until the 1928 games that any women's track and field was offered, and even then participants were allowed only five events in a provisional program.

Besides their late entrance into sports participation, women in the United States have faced additional restrictions in their athletic involvement. First, only white women were initially allowed to participate in sporting events, and only upper-class women could generally afford to. Second, individual sports were socially acceptable much earlier than team sports, which might involve physical contact. Third, women's involvement in sports was considered acceptable only if the women had "feminine" motivations: e.g., weight control, sociability (in high schools and colleges "competition" was "unfeminine" but noncompetitive "play days" with other schools might be allowed). Finally, even today, many women with interest and ability in athletics lack the opportunity to participate. Scholarships, facilities, and adequate training and coaching needed to participate in athletics are not available to women on a level comparable to their availability to men.

Despite the fact that women were latecomers in sports participation and that they continued to face additional restrictions once in the sports arena, women have made dramatic improvements in their level of performance. In fact, when comparing women's with men's times in speed events over a 50-year period, the statistics show not only that women have improved their times but also that their improvement has proceeded more rapidly than men's. These female athletes' improvements have been so great that K. F. Dyer suggests that women will "catch up" with men in the near future (*Challenging the Men* [New York, 1982]; see this work also for more detailed comparisons of women's and men's times).

Of the many factors involved in this greater improvement in women's athletic accomplishments, one is the increase in medical knowledge of the female body. Social factors include greater societal acceptance of female participation, changes in female socialization toward sports, and the emergence of positive female role models for younger female and male athletes. There have also been political and legal factors such as the women's liberation movement, the drive to ratify the Equal Rights Amendment (ERA)*, and Title IX* of the Educational Amendments of 1972.

Women have made impressive advances in performance level over the last 50 years. But the future of women's sports in the United States was suddenly jeopardized in 1984 when the Supreme Court, in its *Grove City College* v. *Bell* decision, determined that Title IX applied only to those specific programs receiving federal funds. Since athletic programs in the nation's schools do not normally receive federal funding, it was feared that the *Grove City* decision might send women's athletic programs back to their pre–Title IX condition. However, after several failed attempts, in 1988 Congress passed a law undoing the *Grove City* decision and overrode President Reagan's veto. The future of women's sports in the United States again looks hopeful, but the lesson of the *Grove City* decision needs to be remembered. Constant pressure is still needed to see that all educational institutions offer girls and women athletic opportunities comparable to those they offer boys and men.

Further References. M. A. Boutilier and L. SanGiovanni, *The Sporting Woman* (Chicago, 1983). R. Howell, *Her Story in Sport: A Historical Anthology of Women in*

Sports (New York, 1982). E. McGrath, "Let's Put Muscle Where It Really Counts," *Women's Sports and Fitness* 8 (December 1986): 59.

MELISSA LATIMER

STATISTICAL DISCRIMINATION. Theory developed as a way to explain why employers whose goal is to maximize profits might nonetheless have a preference for one worker over another equally qualified worker. Given imperfect information about an individual's productivity, but known differences among groups, say women and men, a person's sex may be assumed to provide relevant information. Hence men may be hired in preference to or paid more than women because they are, on the average, more productive or, for that matter, because their productivity varies less.

It has been argued that such behavior does not constitute economic discrimination if the employer's perception of the differences between the groups is correct (D. J. Agner and G. G. Cain, "Statistical Theories of Discrimination in Labor Markets," *Industrial and Labor Relations Review* 30 [1977]: 175–187). In such a situation, however, a woman may be less likely to be hired and may be paid less than equally qualified men, because each is judged as a member of a group rather than on individual merit (G. J. Borjas and M. S. Goldberg, "Biased Screening and Discrimination in the Labor Market," *American Economic Review* 65 [1978]: 918–922).

There are two additional reasons why statistical discrimination is a matter for concern. One is that information about groups may also be imperfect and that the employer's perception about them is not necessarily correct. This might happen because real differences existed in the past and are erroneously projected to the present and even into the future. A second and equally serious problem is that unequal treatment of equals is likely itself to result in unequal outcomes. Assume, say, that a man and a woman are both looking for a job, fully intending to remain in the labor force until they reach retirement age. The man is offered a better job, promoted more rapidly and paid more. If the woman then decides to drop out of the labor force, this is likely to be a case of self-fulfilling prophecy*.

It is clear therefore that statistical discrimination, like other forms of discrimination, must be expected to lead to both unfair treatment of workers, and inefficient allocation of resources.

Further References. K. Arrow, "Models of Job Discrimination," in A. H. Pacal (ed.), *Racial Discrimination in Economic Life* (Lexington, Mass., 1972), 83–102. K. Arrow, "The Theory of Discrimination," in O. Ashenfelter and A. Rees (eds.), *Discrimination in Labor Markets* (Princeton, 1973), 3–33. E. S. Phelps, "The Statistical Theory of Racism and Sexism," *American Economic Review* 62 (1972): 659–661.

MARIANNE A. FERBER

T

TEACHING as a profession opened its doors to women in the 1830s. The nation's growing systems of common schools needed teachers, and economic and social factors combined to produce a new philosophy that regarded women as the *natural* teachers of the young, extending into the public sphere the female domestic role of nurturing the young.

Public school teachers were needed to educate the children to become useful members of the democracy, and the nation recruited its young womanhood to answer this call to duty. The status of teaching was low when women first entered the arena. Men who stayed in education left the classrooom for higher paying, more prestigious administrative positions. By default the classroom became woman's domain, elementary school teaching her territory.

After the Civil War, the crucial need for schoolteachers became even more pressing, and questions of the propriety of women working outside the domestic sphere became irrelevant. Black and white women went into the South with the zeal of missionaries to teach recently emancipated blacks; immigration into the urban areas of the East and settlement of the West contributed further to the expanding need for teachers. Through the 1870s and 1880s the proportion of women teachers rose in secondary education and administration as well as in elementary teaching. Concern seems to have developed only as people realized that women were monopolizing public secondary schools as they had already monopolized the elementary schools.

The need was so great that college-educated women and normal school graduates could fill only a small portion of the teaching positions available. Teacher training characteristically was included as part of secondary education curriculum in industrial institutes and high schools.

Teaching became a respectable stopgap for women before marriage* or a respectable career for the unmarried. After World War I, it became the democratic road to social mobility for daughters of the working class. Although women's salaries made it possible to be self-supporting, they were not sufficient to support a family or even a high standard of living for one. From the start women were hired because they worked cheap. The taxpayers wanted, and got, a bargain. Men always were paid higher salaries because it was assumed they had families to support, but in fact the majority of female teachers historically supported other family members even though they themselves were unmarried. Not until the 1970s did teacher organizations gain bargaining strength to bring salaries into parity.

Why were schoolteachers unmarried? Public opinion, more often than law, prohibited the hiring and retention of married teachers. School boards demanded that only single women be teachers, citing the argument that a working married woman deprived a theoretical male head of household of a potential job. Only in large city districts where teachers were granted tenure was it safe for a woman to marry. Married teachers were hired after World War I as an emergency measure, and fired during the Great Depression. Until the post–World War II era, few teachers were married.

As a rule, city school districts pay better salaries, offer better chances for promotion, more attractive living conditions, and greater personal freedom than small towns and rural areas where, traditionally, the teacher turnover rate is high as teachers move on to better pay and professional advancement or, in the past, to marriage.

Black women, like their white counterparts, have considered the vocation of teaching to be the logical public extension of their domestic roles as caretakers and teachers of children in the home. More to the point, because sexism* as well as racism limited employment opportunities of educated black women, teaching became the primary occupation for black as well as for white women, no matter what their professional training.

Further Reference: S. N. Kersey, *Classics in the Education of Girls and Women* (Metuchen, N.J., 1981).

CAROL O. PERKINS

TITLE VII is that portion of the Civil Rights Act of 1964, as amended, that prohibits discrimination on the basis of race, color, sex, religion, or national origin. It covers *all* terms, conditions, and privileges of employment such as hiring, discharge, training, promotion, compensation, and fringe benefits. Sexual harassment* is considered to be a form of discrimination*. The law applies to virtually all public and private employers, including educational institutions and state and local governments, whether or not they receive any federal financial assistance. The law also states that the courts may "order such affirmative action as may be appropriate" in particular cases. This has included court-imposed quotas to correct the effects of past discrimination. Enforcement of Title VII has been influenced by the 1971 Supreme Court decision in the case of *Griggs* v. *Duke Power Company* which determined that the existence of discrimination could be inferred not only through a demonstrated *intent* to discriminate but also through a review of the *consequences* of employment practices. The responsibility for enforcing Title VII rests with the Equal Employment Opportunity Commission (EEOC), which was created for that purpose.

DAYLE MANDELSON

TITLE IX, part of the Educational Amendments of 1972, prohibits sex discrimination* against students and employees in any educational program or activity receiving federal financial assistance. It affects virtually all public school systems and postsecondary educational institutions and has had its greatest impact on athletic programs. Title IX's employment provisions deal with employment criteria, recruitment and hiring, compensation, job classification and structure, leaves of absence and fringe benefits, and sex as a bona fide occupational qualification*. Other provisions affect admissions, financial aid, and academic programs. The law is enforced by the Department of Education. In 1984, the Supreme Court decision in the case of *Grove City College* v. *Bell* greatly narrowed the scope of Title IX by reducing its coverage from the whole educational institution receiving federal funds to the specific program or activity that has received the assistance. Congress's attempts to reinstate the original intent of Title IX finally succeeded in 1988 when legislation was passed and then a presidential veto overridden.

DAYLE MANDELSON

TOXIC SHOCK SYNDROME (TSS), named in 1978 by Dr. James K. Todd, is a disease believed to involve a bacterium, Staphylococcus aureus. Current researchers have connected it with a protein (TSST-1) and possibly with an enzyme capable of breaking down the tissue during an infection. It has also been, since 1980, associated with the tampon by researchers at the Centers for Disease Control (CDC).

The CDC reported a total of 2,814 cases between 1979, when reporting began, and June 1, 1985. Of these, 122 were fatal. The symptoms of the disease are by now household words, required by federal law in 1982 to be inserted in all tampon boxes: sudden fever, vomiting, dizziness, diarrhea, a severe rash, peeling skin, and paralysis.

Scientists from the Harvard Medical School announced in June 1985 that they had discovered how tampons "caused" toxic shock: the major ingredients in the super absorbent tampons are polyacrylate rayon and polyester magnesium, which, in concentrated forms, can enhance the production of the bacterial toxin that leads to TSS. Nonetheless, it is crucial to stress that TSS has no exclusive claim on tampon users. It also afflicts children, men, and postmenopausal women. Although the risk is still greatest for menstruating women, the disease can affect people having surgery, using diaphrams, or being bitten by insects.

But many women are concerned about the frequently publicized connections between TSS and the tampon; many believe that the industry should play a far larger part than it has in improving the safety of its product and protecting the health of its customers.

Since 1979 representatives from the Food and Drug Administration (FDA), women's health and other public interest groups, and the sanitary products manufacturers have been meeting regularly. Warnings have been instituted. Potentially more useful to women than warnings, however, has been the attempt to establish an industry-wide standard of absorbency, so that a woman could use the least absorbent product necessary to prevent vaginal dryness. Because of different methods of testing for absorbency, however, a uniform system of labeling has yet to be established and put into effect.

Since the appearance of toxic shock syndrome many women, fearing the tampon, have reverted to the sanitary napkin for at least part of the menstrual period. Yet many of these napkins are constructed from the same superabsorbent materials found in certain tampons, and many contain unspecified deodorants. In this climate of uncertainty it is important that scientists, feminist consumer groups, and the FDA seek further facts on toxic shock syndrome and further accountability from the menstrual products industry.

All information in this article is from the "Afterword" to Chapter 14, *The Curse: A Cultural History of Menstruation* (Champaign: University of Illinois Press, 1987). *The Curse*, by Janice Delaney, Mary Jane Lupton, and Emily Toth, was originally published by E. P. Dutton (1976) and New American Library (1977).

MARY JANE LUPTON (WITH JANICE DELANEY)

TRAINING. *General Training* is training in skills such as literacy, mathematics, typing, computer programming, etc., that enhance productivity in a wide variety of occupations. Because of its wide applicability, employers are reluctant to pay for it. Women's labor market skills tend to derive from general training.

Specific Training is training that provides skills needed for work in a particular firm only, for example an introduction to a firm's idiosyncratic bookkeeping system. Employers tend to pay for this, but offer it only to those employees they expect to stay with the firm for a long time. Women tend to be excluded from this type of training, and from the advancement within the firm that such training can promote.

SUSAN B. CARTER

TRANSSEXUALISM (also called sex reassignment) is actually the culmination of a series of professional procedures, both psychological and medical, designed to change the "gender identity," sex role, and anatomy of transsexuals to conform to the opposite sex. The word *transsexualism* did not become part of the English language until the 1950s when it was used to define persons who had an overwhelming desire to change their sexual anatomy because they asserted that they were members of the opposite sex. Thus the popular definition of a transsexual is that of, for example, "a woman trapped in a man's body." The popular definition also highlights that more men desire and undergo sex reassignment than women. Although the exact ratios are disputed in the professional literature, the generally accepted ratio is 4:1.

Transsexual surgery has been possible since the early 1930s. The hormonal and surgical techniques, however, were not refined and made public until the 1950s when Christine (formerly George) Jorgensen was transsexed in Denmark, and the event gained international publicity in 1953.

In the United States, Dr. Harry Benjamin is responsible for the initiation of transsexual surgery and research. A major expansion of this research and surgery took place in 1967 with the formal opening of the Johns Hopkins Gender Identity Clinic in Baltimore, Maryland. That a major medical institution with the prestige of Johns Hopkins had undertaken such controversial treatment and surgery catapulted transsexualism into the public and professional eye as a legitimate medical problem. However, as Johns Hopkins was the first major medical institution to perform the surgery in the United States, it was also the first to terminate its program in 1979—12 years later.

Reports conflict about the actual number of transsexual operations that are performed in this country, as well as how many persons seek the surgery. In the absence of any national directory of transsexual applicants, data on patients for surgery are inconclusive. It is estimated that there are over 3,000 transsexuals in the United States who have undergone surgery (postoperative transsexuals) and 10,000 more who actively seek the surgery (preoperative transsexuals).

For the male-to-constructed female transsexual, primary surgery entails castration, penectomy, and vulvo-vaginal construction. Surgery for the female-to-constructed male transsexual consists of bilateral mammectomy, hysterectomy, and salpingo-oophorectomy. These procedures may be followed by phalloplasty and the insertion of testicular prostheses. Because the technology of phallus construction is still quite primitive, most female-to-constructed male transsexuals undergo only mammectomy and hysterectomy. Secondary surgery often follows any primary procedures and is sought by the transsexual for aesthetic reasons and/or to correct real or felt complications. Such surgery can range from limb, eye, chin, to ear surgery, scar revision, and/or reduction to the Adam's apple. Many transsexuals, especially male-to-constructed females, go to great lengths to adapt to the culturally prescribed body type of the opposite sex.

The medical odyssey of the transsexual does not begin or end with primary or secondary surgery. It starts with the administration of hormones that decrease certain existing sex characteristics such as body hair and augments, for example, the development of breasts in men. The treatment of male transsexual candidates is almost totally dependent on estrogen to induce hormonal castration and feminization. Such treatment is long-term—in most cases, lifelong.

The causes of transsexualism have been debated. Most etiological theories fall into two camps—organic and psychogenic. Organic theories have emphasized neuroendocrine factors while psychogenic etiologies have focused on imprinting, family conditioning (with an emphasis upon mother-son symbiosis), and/or separation anxiety. While organic and psychogenic explanations seek different causes, both locate the cause of transsexualism within the individual and/or interpersonal matrix. In these etiological theories, social, political, and cultural causes tend to be relegated to a subsidiary or nonexistent role. For example, psychogenic theories measure a transsexual's adjustment or nonadjustment to the cultural identity and role of masculinity or femininity*. They seldom locate the origins of a transsexualism in a gender-defined society whose norms of masculinity or femininity generated the desire to be transsexed in the first place.

The diagnosis of transsexualism is problematic from many points of view. That it is subject to diagnosis is in itself an issue that follows upon its designation as legitimate medical territory. If transsexualism is a disease, then does desire qualify as disease? As Thomas Szasz has asked, does the old person who wants to be young suffer from the "disease" of being a "transchronological," or does the poor person who wants to be rich suffer from the "disease" of being a "transeconomical"? Transsexualism is a self-diagnosis by definition. But it is a self-diagnosis that has become colonized by the medical model.

In the last century, more and more areas of life have come to be defined as medical and technical problems. Feminist critics contend that accepting transsexualism as a medical and therapeutic problem encourages persons to view other persons (especially children) who do not live out proper and appropriate sex-role behavior as potential transsexuals. Thus, for example, for the boy who likes to play with dolls or the girl who wants to be a truck driver, these behaviors can be interpreted as transsexual behavior instead of as nonstereotypical behavior that reflects a protest against, or a discomfort with, sex roles.

The treatments for transsexualism are also problematic from many points of view. Specifically, feminist critics question the political and social shaping of masculine and feminine behavior that is an integral part of the treatment process. Persons wishing to change sex come to so-called gender identity clinics, as well as private therapists, to receive counseling and ultimately to be referred for treatment and surgery. It is a primary requirement of these centers that men who wish to be transsexed must prove that they can "pass" as "true women" in order to qualify for treatment and surgery. "Passing" requirements evaluate everything from an individual's style of feminine dress, to feminine body language to so-called feminine positions in intercourse. Most clinics require candidates for surgery to live out opposite-sex-roles and rigidly defined opposite-sex-behavior for periods of six months to two years. Thus the role of these clinics and clinicians in reinforcing sex-role stereotypes is significant.

Transsexual surgery for persons wishing to change sex is controversial. There is a lack of well-controlled follow-up studies documenting the safety and effectiveness of the surgery itself. Furthermore, transsexual surgery cannot change a person's chromosomal sex, nor can it change the person's past history of being born male or female. Surgery may confer the artifacts of outer and inner female organs, and it may alter the anatomical and hormonal sex of a person. On the fundamental levels of chromosomes and history, however, it is impossible to change one's sex. George Burou, a Casablancan physician who has operated on over 700 American men who wanted to be women, has given this summary of his work: "I don't change men into women. I transform male genitals into genitals that have a female aspect. All the rest is in the patient's mind."

Further References. R. Green and J. Money, *Transsexualism and Sex Reassignment* (Baltimore, 1969). T. Kando, *Sex Change: The Achievement of Gender Identity among Feminized Transsexuals* (Springfield, Ill., 1973). J. Raymond, *The Transsexual Empire: The Making of the She-Male* (Boston, 1979). NCHCT (National Center for Health Care Technology) Assessment Report Series, "Transsexual Surgery," vol. 4, no. 4, Office of Health Research Statistics and Technology, U.S. Department of Health and Human Services, 1981.

JANICE G. RAYMOND

U

UNEMPLOYMENT of women is a relatively new concern with serious implications for equity and feminist goals.

According to the official definition, a person is *unemployed* if he or she is looking for work but is unable to find a job. The official *unemployment rate*, based on a survey that is published monthly by the Bureau of Labor Statistics, is the total number of unemployed persons during a survey week relative to the entire labor force of employed and unemployed persons. For instance, if 95 people are employed and 5 arc unemployed, the labor force consists of 100 people and the unemployment rate is 5 percent. Unemployment rates are computed for various demographic groups, and it is possible to examine gender differences in unemployment.

It is important to recognize that the official concept of unemployment in the United States, as well as in virtually every other country, applies only to work in *paid* employment. "Employment" refers to paid work, and "unemployed" persons are seeking paid work. People who perform unpaid work at home or volunteer work and who are not seeking paid employment are neither "employed" nor "unemployed." Despite the fact that unpaid activities are both useful and time-consuming, for all practical purposes, they are ignored in our economic statistics. Like many other aspects of our economic life and social relations, unemployment has been defined from a male perspective. Until quite recently, work in paid employment has been predominantly a male activity, while women, especially married women, worked at home, and were neglected in the official unemployment statistics.

The increasing participation of women in paid employment has raised questions regarding the interpretation of women's unemployment. Should women who formerly "worked" as full-time homemakers be counted as unemployed just because they now declare themselves "looking for work"? During the 1970s, as homemakers began entering the labor force in increasing numbers, many observers alleged that the attendant rise in the unemployment rate was an illusion. Had these women continued in their former roles as homemakers, they would not be included in the unemployment count, and hence the national unemployment rate would not be so high. Some people suggested that women's unemployment should not be included in the official figure, and press releases began to emphasize the unemployment rate for married men as well as the overall rate, the rate for married men being considerably lower. Others suggested a "weighted rate" in which women's unemployment should receive a lesser weight than men's. By the mid–1970s, the whole question of how to treat women's unemployment in a period of rapid transition in women's work roles became a major national controversy in which policy-makers took advantage of the issue to divert attention from the deflationary economic policies that were the major cause of high unemployment in those years. A distinguished national commission was established to consider the issue, and after lengthy hearings and debates, disbanded with no major recommendations.

One reason that women's unemployment was controversial during the 1970s was that women experienced higher unemployment rates than men, and this in turn increased the national rate above historic levels as more women entered the labor force. During the 1970s the unemployment rate for adult women averaged 6.0 percent, compared with 4.5 percent for adult men. The higher rate for women was partly related to their new entry into the work force, but it also resulted from the fact that they received less on-the-job training* than men and were often the last hired and first fired.

During the 1980s, however, this picture changed dramatically. Between 1980 and 1984, the average unemployment rates for adult women and men were identical at 7.3 percent. Although unemployment rates for both groups increased substantially as a result of deflationary economic policies, the rate for men increased disproportionately due to a major shift in the composition of employment away from sectors traditionally dominated by men. Between 1980 and 1984, 5.8 million new jobs were created in the female-dominated sectors of wholesale and retail trade and service occupations, while 1.5 million jobs were lost in the male-dominated sectors of manufacturing, mining, construction, and transportation. In fact, since 1981, the unemployment rate for adult women has been below the male rate in every year, a phenomenon that had never previously occurred.

Another, and perhaps more fundamental, reason why women's unemployment is controversial is the belief that women do not need jobs or that they are not serious jobseekers. High unemployment, in general, is viewed as problematic for two reasons. First, it represents a loss in potential output that could be remedied by more expansionary economic policies. However, if women are not really interested in work, then expansionary policies would just add to inflation, as these alleged jobseekers would not take the jobs that became available. Some critics argue that women's unemployment is illusory, as there are always "job opportunities" in the home. Of course, this is an extreme antifeminist position, but reflects the continuing controversy about women's economic roles, and stems, of course, from the fact that the unemployment concept does not extend to the home economy where women have traditionally worked.

The second problematic aspect of unemployment is its link with poverty*. The unemployed person lacks the financial resources that come with a paying job. Moreover, in our work-oriented society, the unemployed person lacks an important source of social status and upward mobility. In the past, many women relied on their husbands for both financial support and social status. Today this is no longer the case. Most women work or are seeking work because they need the money. Roughly two-thirds of all women in the labor force are either single, widowed, or divorced, or are married to husbands with incomes below $15,000 per year. Moreover, with the current high divorce rate, a paid job becomes a kind of "divorce insurance" for those women who are married to relatively affluent husbands. Paradoxically, women who maintain families and who presumably have the greatest financial need, have much higher unemployment rates than other women, while married men have much lower rates than other men. This suggests that family responsibilities are viewed by employers as desirable for their male workers but as a negative for women workers.

Regardless of financial considerations, a paid job provides an independent source of social status for women. For those women in our society trying to achieve independence along many lines—economic, social, psychological, emotional—a job in the paid labor market is an important first step. To be unemployed is to be seeking this opportunity. Certainly the ramifications of women's unemployment are different from men's in this regard—men are not newly seeking economic independence, and men's unemployment is a threat to their established dominance. Yet as an equity issue, women's unemployment has serious consequences and conflicts most fundamentally with feminist goals. Like most issues relating to women, the debate over women's unemployment is largely a debate over feminist goals. Those who wish to minimize the significance of women's unemployment are simply reflecting the view that "women's place is in the home."

Further Reference. R. E. Smith (ed.), *The Subtle Revolution: Women at Work* (Washington, D.C., 1979).

NANCY S. BARRETT

UTERINE PROLAPSIS is a condition in which the uterus drops out of its normal position. The ligaments that hold the uterus in place may be weakened during childbirth by lacerations or "overstretching." It will not be until years later, however, when estrogen levels have dropped after menopause*, that the weakened supports will shrink or atrophy, causing the uterus to fall.

In some cases the uterus falls backward into the vaginal canal (retrodisplacement). In other cases, the uterus goes partially or wholly through the vaginal canal, bringing the vagina in upon itself. In second-degree prolapse, the cervix will extend partially or completely through the vaginal opening. In a complete prolapse, the uterus itself will extend outside the vagina. Prolapse of the bladder, urethra, and rectum often accompany the more severe degrees of prolapse. Retrodisplacement may not need treatment. Second-degree prolapse may be corrected by surgery, but hysterectomy is usual for complete prolapse, and is often chosen in second-degree prolapse as well.

V

VAGINITIS, inflammation of the vagina, is so common that it is said that every woman has the irritation at some time in her life. Problems with vaginitis are most likely to occur, however, in women who are sexually active with men, who have multiple (three or more) partners, who are pregnant or using oral contraceptives, or whose vaginas respond with symptoms to stress and nutritional imbalance. After menopause* women who do not respond sexually on a regular basis either by masturbating or interacting with others are at greater risk of vaginal symptoms resulting from diminished estrogen.

Vaginitis in women who are premenopausal is most likely caused by Candida albicans (yeast), bacteria (often Gardnerella vaginalis or associated anaerobic bacteria), or Trichomonal vaginitis (trich), a one-celled organism. Distinguishing among the causes of vaginitis is only possible by microscopic examination of vaginal secretions and is not always definitive. Treatment with over-the-counter or nonprescription medications is not usually helpful (such medication may merely suppress symptoms temporarily). Treatment with herbal remedies may better control early symptoms. If these fail, medical treatment may be sought.

Difficulties with vaginal irritation may begin with an increase in vaginal secretions and a change in color from clear or white to yellowish, greenish, brownish, or clear with shreds of mucus. The secretions may cause inflammation and irritation of the vaginal opening, labia, and perineal area as well as the urethra, where passage of urine will sometimes be painful. (It is helpful to differentiate this irritation of the external genitals by the passage of urine from the internal irritation of the urethra or even the bladder, which is likely due to a urinary problem.)

Other changes in vaginal health indicators may include a stronger scent, which may result from an increase in quantity of secretions or may be characteristically "fishy," a sign not found in yeast overgrowths. Itching of the vaginal area may range from vague uneasiness to intense misery. Sexual interactions, especially vaginal sex, may be uncomfortable or painful.

Yeast "infections" (actually an overgrowth of a fungus that is commonly present in the vagina) are most commonly characterized by vaginal secretions which clump and are therefore described as "cottage cheese-like" with an earthy scent. Yeast is most amenable to changes in life-style such as reducing refined sugar intake, increasing intake of lactobacillus (in milk and yogurt), soothing baths, and nonirritating sexual response that increases circulation to the genital area. Yeast overgrowth that does not respond to these interventions can be treated with an antifungal preparation such as Nystatin.

Yeast overgrowth can cause irritation of the penis in male sexual partners, and the male may need treatment if the woman continues to have yeast infections. Women may transmit yeast to female sexual partners. This may or may not result in symptoms in the partner. Yeast may cause a condition of the mouth and throat called thrush; therefore, oral sex should be avoided while yeast or other vaginal symptoms persist. Infants may develop thrush (which is also treatable with an antifungal preparation) if the mother has an active yeast infection during birthing. Yeast is more commonly transmitted from affected mother to infant due to poor handwashing. To prevent recurrence, medication must be used for its full course of treatment, not just until symptoms subside.

Bacteria is a common cause of vaginitis and is treatable with oral antibiotics. When a woman is diagnosed with a bacterial vaginal infection, sexual interactions should be modified to minimize transmission, and oral sex avoided until antibiotic therapy is completed. Condoms should be used in sexual interactions with men during the course of treatment. The man should be tested for the presence of a bacterial infection and treated if indicated. Bacteria can be transmitted to female sex partners and may or may not cause infection.

Trichomonal infections are less common but may be persistent and be harbored by a male sex partner who has no symptoms. Trich is usually treated with metronidazole (Flagyl), a controversial drug which cannot be used in pregnancy. Home remedies are less effective but are a possible alternative. One folk remedy is the use of a garlic suppository.

Some aspects of a woman's life-style may inadvertently promote the likelihood of developing vaginitis. Eating a diet high in refined sugar, using antibiotics such as tetracycline, wearing nylon underwear or tight-fitting restrictive clothing, and using tampons or toilet tissue infused with perfume inhibit the body's ability to maintain a balance in the vagina and to resist infection.

General health measures such as a balanced diet, adequate sleep, exercise, and avoidance of debilitating stress levels help to reduce problems with vaginitis.

ELAINE WHEELER

VARIABILITY HYPOTHESIS. Developed in the late nineteenth century, the hypothesis asserts that males are more likely than females to vary from the norm in both physical and mental traits. Variability was defined most often in terms of range of ability or incidence of abnormality. The variability hypothesis provided a way of explaining sex-related differences in social and intellectual achievements after the doctrine of generalized female inferiority was no longer tenable.

The variability hypothesis is noteworthy for three reasons. (1) It gained popularity among scientists largely because of an overextension of Darwinian theory by a zealous popularizer, Havelock Ellis. (2) It became an issue as much because of personal interests of scientists as because of its compatibility with the Zeitgeist. (3) Early feminist researchers were largely responsible for its eventual decline.

The idea that the sexes might differ in their tendency to vary was introduced by Charles Darwin in 1868. Darwin invoked the idea of greater male variability in an attempt to explain the elaborate nature of male secondary sex characteristics in many species. Like most other nineteenth-century scientists, Darwin considered female mental inferiority a fact of nature.

Evolutionary theorists considered variation the driving force of evolution. Greatness, whether of an individual or a society, was achieved through deviation from the norm.

Havelock Ellis suggested that sex differences in physical variation might be accompanied by sex differences in mental variation. In the first edition of *Man and Woman* (London, 1894), he devoted an entire chapter to the variability hypothesis. He argued that both physical and mental abnormalities are indicators of variability and that both are more frequently observed in males. As regards mental abilities he asserted that both retardation and genius are more frequent among males than females.

Ellis used as proof of male mental variability statistics from homes for the "mentally defective," which housed many more males than females. His evidence of the greater frequency of male genius was the overwhelming preponderance of men of eminence. He reasoned that men are more likely to achieve fame, fortune, and professional prestige, and that an innate difference in variability must therefore exist.

His major critic was the biometrician Karl Pearson who himself regarded male intellectual superiority a kind of male secondary sex characteristic.

Ellis's ideas had a major impact on the generation of male psychologists then developing the first tests of mental ability. By 1903 one of them (J. McK. Cattell) asserted the sex difference a truism: "The distribution of women is represented by a narrower bell-shaped curve." That is, the population of males is described by a broader range of ability; the population of females clusters more about the average. For some scientists, the idea that females would be unlikely to excel suggested that it was unnecessary to provide them with opportunities to do so.

At about the same time the first wave of female Ph.D. psychologists were commencing their careers. Helen B. Thompson (Wolley) published her doctoral dissertation, *The Mental Traits of Sex* (Chicago, 1903), and reported finding no differences in variability. Mary Whiton Calkins (later the first female president of the American Psychological Association) carried on a lively debate in the journals with one of the more vociferous proponents of the hypothesis, Joseph Jastrow. The most active feminist critic and the one who ultimately had the greatest impact was Leta Stetter Hollingworth, the doctoral student of a nationally known and respected educational psychologist who was also a prominent advocate of the variability hypothesis (E. L. Thorndike).

Hollingworth approached the question of variability from several different research angles. She demonstrated the inconsistency among the various statistical techniques purporting to demonstrate a sex difference. Then, in an effort to isolate innate variations she examined the length and weight of a large group of newborns and found no sex difference in physical variability. As for variations in intellect, Hollingworth argued that low IQ women would be more capable of finding work or support outside an institutional setting (via housework* or prostitution* for example) and so should be underrepresented among the institutionalized. She further argued that the limitations circumscribing women's social role accounted for the rarity of women's public achievement ("Variability as Related to Sex Differences in Achievement," *American Journal of Sociology* 19 [1914]: 510–530). Because women's role was defined in terms of housekeeping and childrearing, "channels where eminence is impossible," and because of the constraints that the female role placed on women's education and employment, there was simply no valid way to compare the ability of women with that of men, who "have followed the greatest possible range of occupations, and have at the same time procreated unhindered" (526 and 524).

During World War I, the mental testing movement rapidly became more technically sophisticated. The issue of sex differences* in variability became just one of many dimensions on which the sexes were contrasted and probably would have faded into obscurity except for the work of psychologist Lewis Terman. He began a longitudinal study of children with very high IQ in the 1920s. The highest-scoring child in his sample was female, but the ratio greatly favored males. Terman concluded that there was merit in the variability hypothesis after all, and a new round of scientific debate was initiated. Later in his career Terman reversed himself and attributed the apparent rarity of female genius to "motivational causes and limited opportunity" rather than inherent intellectual limitations.

Even in the past two decades one finds occasional scholarly speculation as to the merits of the hypothesis. Notably absent is the notion of complementarity of the sexes, which provided the framework and justification for the hypothesis originally. The variability hypothesis is treated today as a statistical question rather than a justification for limiting opportunities for girls and women.

Further References. S. A. Shields, "The Variability Hypothesis: The History of a Biological Model of Sex Differences in Intelligence," *Signs* 7 (1982): 769–797. S. A. Shields, "Ms. Pilgrim's Progress: The Contributions of Leta Stetter Hollingworth to the Psychology of Women," *American Psychologist* 30 (1975): 854–857.

STEPHANIE A. SHIELDS

VICTIMIZATION OF WOMEN is the practice of visiting abuse—physical, psychological, and/or sexual—upon women and then blaming the women for being abused. Women have come to internalize the blame. A typical reaction of a man to an unprovoked attack might be: "Why did he do that to me?" The typical reaction of a woman: "What did I do that he did that to me?"

VICTIMS OF CRIME. An important source of information on the victimization of women*, the National Crime Survey (NCS) has been collecting data on victimization since 1973. The NCS gathers data for victims 12 years of age and older, by sex of victim for four interpersonal crimes—rape, robbery, assault, and personal larceny. In this data base seven important sex differences emerge.

The male rate of victimization is generally higher than the female rate, with differences most pronounced for violent crime. In 1984 the male rate for theft victimization was 76 per 1,000 and for females, 68 per 1,000. For the three violent crimes the male rate of victimization was 39 and the female rate 23. Over the 12-year span covered by the data, the female portion of the total increased slightly, causing a convergence of the rates by sex. For theft, the female rate as a proportion of the male rate increased from 77 percent to 89 percent and for violent crime from 50 percent to 58.7 percent.

For all violent crime in 1984 the sex difference was 16.3 (39.5 male rate–23.2 female rate), but the sex difference for violent crimes by nonstrangers was only 1.5 (14.6 male–13.1 female).

Employment status affects men and women differently. For women the category "housewife*" is safest of all (with the exception of "retired," a category confounded by age). Employed females are two to three times as vulnerable as housewives; unemployed women have a victimization rate almost three times that of the employed. Unemployed males, too, have much higher rates that those employed. If we think of work broadly, as including both unpaid housework and labor market work, it is clear that employment as a housewife provides the most protection from crime, and that this option is not nearly so viable for men. (In some years the "househusband" category is too small to be even statistically significant.)

The types of crime to which the sexes are subject present provocative differences. Men's and women's vulnerability are most similar in theft, where the female rate is 90 percent of the male rate. They are less similar in violent crimes. Women make up most of the rape victims, but in robbery and assault the female rate is only about half that of the male rate.

Living arrangements affect criminal victimization. Males living alone have higher rates (55.7) than those living with others (24.3) in male- or female-headed households. But women living with others in female-headed households have higher rates (38.7) than those who live alone (20.7). The comparable rates for spouses, however, show that female spouses in male-headed households have a lower rate than husbands in female-headed households (10 vs. 23), and a lower rate than women in any other living arrangement. These data probably reflect the poorer economic circumstances of female-headed households.

Marital status also affects men and women differently. Divorced/separated persons are more at risk than married persons, but the gap is greater for women than for men, especially for crimes of violence. For theft, for both sexes the rates for divorced/separated persons are about twice as high as for the married. But for violent crime the male rates are about three times as high for divorced/separated men as for married man (64 vs. 21) and for women more than five times as high for divorced/separated as for married (57 vs. 11). This may be, again, a reflection of the differential poverty level of divorced/separated women compared to married women, which is greater than the gap for divorced/separated and married men, or it may be the vulnerability of divorced/separated women to assault.

The patterns formed in all these instances are different for women than for men. Women are less subject to crime than men, although their rates are increasing. They are less likely to be attacked by strangers. They are protected more by marriage* than are men and are protected by living in male-headed households. All of this suggests that women have remained in the *Gemeinschaft* world longer than men and thus have been safer from crime, having had less interaction with strangers. (*Gemeinschaft*, a word coined by nineteenth-century German sociologist Ferdinand Julius Tönnies, means a "communal society in which people feel they belong together because they are of the same kind," while *gesellschaft* [see below] is an "associational society . . . in which the major social bonds are voluntary and based upon the rational pursuit of self-interest" [Leonard Broom and David Selznick, *Sociology*, 1956].)

One further pattern must be noted. Under certain circumstances women are more at risk from nonstrangers than are men. The NCS breaks down victimization rates by sex and marital status. The data show that the category divorced/separated is more risky for women than for men as regards nonstrangers crime. Some 64 percent of the violent crimes committed against divorced/separated women are committed by intimates, while only 38 percent of such crimes against divorced/separated men are committed by nonstrangers. Although the overall rate of victimization is slightly higher for men (64) vs. women (57), divorced/separated women are more liable to victimization by people they know (36.5 female rate vs. 24.6 male rate).

Generally, then, as men move more into the *gesellschaft* their vulnerability to victimization increases *as a function of* their further interaction with strangers. However, women who are less attached to the *gemeinschaft* not only suffer increasing attacks from strangers, but also their rate of attack from intimates increases. Women are more vulnerable to the *gesellschaft* because they have less economic and political power to deal with this world. Vulnerability to crime from strangers is largely a function of poverty*, and women are much poorer than men. Additionally, women are subject to attack from male intimates, and here their lesser economic and political power also disadvantages them. (For example, a woman who has means of self-support may leave an abusive husband.)

The NCS data do not fully reflect the reality of female victimization because NCS cannot collect completely accurate data on the sex of *both* victim and offender. The crimes to which women are most subject are crimes which have male offenders. Rape*, wife-battery, sexual harassment*, incest*, and pornography*, all are mostly crimes committed against women by men. Further, NCS does not collect homicide data. FBI data (Uniform Crime Reports, annually) on homicide show that though men are much more likely to be victims of murder than are women, virtually all of the female homicide victims were killed by men. In 1984, for example, of all single offender–single victim homicides where data on sex of both were known, 60.8 percent of the homicides were male offender–male victim, 23.7 percent were male offender–female victim, 12.8 percent were female offender–male victim, and only 2.7 percent were female offender–female victim. Too, research demonstrates that many homicides of men by women are victim-precipitated—that is, the relationship was one with a long history of wife battery.

Wife battery, and the higher incidence of rape, are reflected in the victimization rates for women reviewed above. Male rape rates are so small they are statistically unreliable, and female rates are about 1.6 per 1,000, but there is good evidence that NCS data grossly underestimate rape rates, through a faulty questioning procedure on this one item in the survey (see Diana E. H. Russell, *Sexual Exploitation*, 1984). The higher rates for women for assault from intimates reflect the wife-battery dimensions. The NCS does not measure the offense of sexual harassment; however, it is known that women are disproportionately the victims. They are also disproportionately the victims of incest, but the NCS data do not measure assaults on females under 12 and do not record the form of assault.

Pornography is a final area in which women specifically are victims. A growing body of research indicates that (1) much pornography depicts the bondage, multilation, and torture of women as sexually arousing; (2) exposure to this literature causes its readers to believe women enjoy being humiliated and abused; (3) readers then are less likely to believe any woman can be raped; and (4) there is thus a link between pornography and other female victimizations. Feminists are not agreed that a ban on the dissemination of such literature is appropriate in view of civil liberties questions and are seeking other avenues of redress.

All of the offenses in which women have higher rates of victimization than do men are classically male offenders–female victims crimes, and reflect the status relationships of the sexes, including woman's economic status and her status as a sexual object for men. To the extent that women are able in the future to gain more political and economic power, their victimization rates should lower as a result of enactment and enforcement of laws guaranteeing their safety from sex crimes and as a function of the power of economic security to reduce vulnerability to crime committed by strangers. But since vulnerability to crime is very largely a matter of poverty, those women who do remain economically disadvantaged will continue to have a high rate of victimization, even if women *as a class* improve their situation. Unless the increasing feminization of poverty is halted, woman's vulnerability to crime will escalate until it reaches, perhaps, a higher rate than that of men, in all crime categories.

NANCI KOSER WILSON

W

WAGE GAP. The difference between the average wages of men and women full-time workers. Occupational segregation*, whether brought about by tradition, socialization, or discrimination*, has kept most women crowded into a limited number of occupations and kept the pay for those occupations low. Women college graduates earn less than male high school graduates. Black men earn less than white men, white women earn less than black men, and black women earn less than white women. During the 1980s, women's comparative earnings fell to an average of 59¢ for every dollar earned by men, then rose again. By 1986 women's earnings averaged 64¢ to the men's dollar; in 1988, it was 70¢.

WELFARE. Women are prominent in almost any discussion of social welfare policy in the United States. For example, the most dramatic change in the face of poverty* over the past decade is the *feminization of poverty**. More controversial than the trend itself is the role that public assistance or welfare in the form of cash and in-kind benefits (e.g., food stamps, public housing) has played in its determination. The possibilities are varied. Charles Murray *(Losing Ground: American Social Policy, 1950–1980* [New York, 1984]) has argued that the availability of welfare has contributed to this trend by denying benefits to two-parent families, encouraging unmarried women to bear children out of wedlock, and creating a general attitude of economic dependency* among the poor. David Ellwood and Lawrence Summers ("Poverty in America: Is Welfare the Answer or the Problem?" in S. H. Danziger and D. H. Weinberg [eds.], *Fighting Poverty: What Works and What Doesn't* [Cambridge, Mass., 1986]) dispute these charges vigorously, pointing out that researchers have consistently failed to find a significant correlation between the generosity of AFDC benefits and the percentage of children in single-parent households or birthrates among unmarried women.

The prominence of women in policy debate arises from the basic ideology underlying our nation's social welfare policy. Historically, welfare has been available to those Americans considered to be the *deserving poor*, defined as persons who are poor through no fault of their own. Four demographic groups have been awarded this distinction: children; the aged; the blind; and the disabled. All others (nonaged adults) are expected to be able to provide for themselves through the fruits of their labor, males and females alike. Thus eligibility for welfare benefits is not predicated on gender. Moreover, the ideology implicitly assumes that poverty experienced by nonaged adults is the outcome of inherent character flaws: laziness, instability, dishonesty, etc. To provide economic assistance to such persons is tantamount to rewarding these character traits (*Poverty among Plenty: The American Paradox*, Report of the President's Commission on Income Maintenance Programs, 1969). (Unemployment insurance represents an important exception to this view as it awards benefits to persons unemployed, presumably through no fault of their own. This benevolent attitude expires, however, with the passage of time [normally 52 weeks] as the unemployed are expected to find new jobs.) When first established in 1935, the primary program of cash assistance for the nonaged, Aid to Dependent Children (ADC), was designed to provide aid to poor children living with no more than one parent. At that time the primary target group was widows with children. ADC benefits were paid to the custodial relative assuming financial responsibility for the children, most often the mother. The amount of the benefit reflected only the needs of the children present in the family, however. No provision was made for the adult relative until 1950, at which time Congress amended the law to increase family benefits to cover the essential needs of one needy relative with whom the dependent children were living. The change occurred only after Congress was convinced that it was necessary to ensure that the benefits intended for the children were spent on the children, and were not used to meet the needs of the custodial relative. The name of the program was simultaneously changed in most states to Aid to *Families* with Dependent Children (AFDC). AFDC was further liberalized in 1962 to allow the states the option of extending eligibility to two-parent families in which children were deprived of support as the result of the unemployment of one parent.. Only 26 states have chosen to do so. Most two-parent families are ineligible for benefits. As a result of this restricted eligibility and the low benefits paid in many states, only 63 percent of all poor families with children under 18 received AFDC benefits in 1983. That the vast majority (80 percent) of all families receiving AFDC are headed by females is a consequence of the culturally and sociologically determined role of female as primarily provider of child care which characterizes Western society, not of a gender bias inherent in social welfare policy (U.S. Department of Health and Human Services, 1979).

An additional implication of the rules of categorical eligibility is that there exists a substantial population of poor unrelated (childless) females (4.0 million in 1984) which is not eligible for welfare, other than food stamps, in significant amounts. AFDC families may also be eligible for free medical care under Medicaid; food supplements under the food stamp, school lunch, and the supplemental feeding programs for Women, Infants, and Children (WIC); and for assistance in securing low-cost housing and utilities. Even so, benefits are often inadequate and the combined value of AFDC and the other transfers leaves recipient families far below the federal poverty level. Maximum payable AFDC benefits are less that 50 percent of the poverty line in 30 states. For example, the total value of cash assistance, low-income home energy assistance, and food stamps for an average AFDC family living in Mississippi in 1983 was $3,591, or 43 percent of the federal poverty line (*Social Security Bulletin, Annual Statistical Supplement, 1984–1985*). The combined value of AFDC and food stamps raises a family of four over the poverty line only in Alaska and Hawaii. In 1982, 55 percent of all single-parent families headed by women who received cash and/ or in-kind transfers remained in poverty (U.S. Bureau of the Census, Technical Paper 51, *Estimates of Poverty Including the Value of Noncash Benefits: 1979 to 1982* [Washington, D.C., 1984]). Just as the ideology underlying social welfare policy is gender neutral, so too have been the strategies employed by the federal government to combat the causes of poverty. For example, the major investment has been in general education and training programs with the objective of raising labor market productivity. Although not specifically designed for women, these programs have most benefited women by increasing their hours worked, not by increasing their skills or placing them in better paying jobs (L. J. Bassi and O. Ashenfelter, "The Effect of Direct Job Creation and Training Programs on Low-Skilled Workers," in *Fighting Poverty*). Another major area of investment has been for experimentation with negative income tax programs that would extend eligibility to all poor families and persons. In view of the fact that households with female heads are the demographic group with the highest rates of poverty (24.7 percent in 1983), it seems anomalous that there has not been significant investment in programs designed specifically for them. This anomaly is particularly well illustrated by the Reagan administration's proposals to require welfare mothers to work for their benefits (workfare) without providing concurrently for quality child care*. Thus it happens that the primary routes out of poverty for women family heads are marriage* and receipt of government transfers (M. J. Bane and D. T. Ellwood, "Slipping into and out of Poverty: The Dynamics of Spells," *Journal of Human Resources* 21 [1986]: 1–23). The welfare system does little to help women help themselves and their children.

Further References. I. Garfinkel and S. S. McLanahan, *Single Mothers and Their Children* (Washington, D.C., 1986). H. R. Rodgers, Jr., *Poor Women, Poor Families* (Armonk, N.Y., 1986). R. Sidel, *Women and Children Last* (New York, 1986).

JENNIFER L. WARLICK

WIDOWHOOD, the role assumed by either marital partner upon the death of a spouse, affects all societies where marriage exists, creating individual and social problems that cut across national and cultural boundaries. Although almost half of all adults in the world have experienced or will experience widowhood, in most societies, in both the past and present, widowhood imposes more serious penalties on women than men. And in contemporary society, especially in the West, where female life expectancy exceeds that of males, and monogamous marital traditions dictate that women marry men older than themselves, widowhood is increasingly concentrated among elderly women and persists far longer than in earlier times. That widowhood will be a prevalent and enlarging aspect of the human condition is ensured by the worldwide longevity revolution, in which the number of persons over 60 throughout the world will double by the year 2000.

Severing of the marriage bond through widowhood (and to some extent, through divorce* or desertion) creates certain persistent problems whose resolution has differed according to historical time, place, and other variables. Widowhood alters and disrupts the configuration and functions of the family*, potentially depriving the surviving spouse of sexual consortium, companionship, and assistance in household duties and financial affairs. Frequently, it reduces the economic and social status of women and their families, and often strains the societal fabric, which may be unable or unwilling to care for dependent, elderly widowed women or widows incapable of supporting themselves and minor children. Just as other single women may incur hostility and fear of those who are married, so too may the widow, who becomes an unattached sexual object and potential threat.

Yet unlike divorced women, widows, who become single involuntarily, must also contend with grief and bereavement, as well as with "role loss." One of the most stressful aspects of widowhood in the Western cultural tradition is the impact on the widow's identity of breaking the attachment to the deceased spouse as she makes the transition from being a wife to being a widow to somehow becoming an independent woman on her own. Because so much of a woman's status is intertwined with being married, widowhood creates a sense of loss that penetrates to the very soul of the individual. Nor is the society particularly sensitive to the widow's needs or helpful in supporting her adaptation to a new life.

On the other hand, it is also evident that in some non-Western cultures, where women's social and economic status is less contingent upon the marital relationship, the traumatic rupture of widowhood is mitigated. Further, even in the West, during different historical periods, legal statutes and practices in some instances have empowered widows, providing them with control over property and children which they lacked as married women. For some women who successfully cope with the transition through widowhood to attain an independent status, spousal loss provides an impetus to control their lives unavailable during marriage.

Despite the universality of widowhood, its impact on the individual woman and her ability to cope with it depend on variables that make the experience different for different women. These include (1) the *society itself*, which incorporates social class and cultural proscriptions and practices that influence both appropriate behavior for widows and older women and appropriate grief and mourning rituals; (2) *sex and age ratios* of the population, which affect opportunities for remarriage; (3) *the community* in which the widow lives, which determines the availability of support networks, of economic opportunities, either through savings, pensions, government programs, or paid employment; (4) *family* and *the law*, which affect the nature of marriage and selection of mates, inheritance, and the rights of women to property; (5) *personal resources*, which include friends and neighbors, parents, children and kin, church and social groups, and fellow workers; and (6) the widow's own skills and psyche. Other factors involved in the adjustment to widowhood include age at marriage and at widowhood; circumstances surrounding the husband's death; economic status; the rights and duties of wives and widows in relation to kin and family; and historical context.

More detailed knowledge and more comparative data on the way women in different societies during different time periods have responded to widowhood is needed to determine whether the many responses to widowhood reflect universal behavior or are culturally determined. While recognizing the difficulty of weighting the many factors affecting widows and their ability to cope with widowhood, the one factor that stands out above all others is financial security. Without the assurance of financial security or of knowing that she will be able to gain a living for herself and any minor children, the widow's ability to cope is seriously threatened.

Further Reference. H. Z. Lopata, *Women as Widows: Support Systems* (New York, 1979).

ARLENE SCADRON

WITCHCRAFT is the belief, found in most but not all societies in the world, that humans can manipulate supernatural forces for their own purposes. In most non-Western cultures the power of witchcraft is itself morally neutral, useful for healing as well as harming, capable of bestowing blessings as well as curses. Nevertheless, it is widely feared as a means by which otherwise weak or powerless individuals satisfy their greed, lust, and vengefulness. While most societies believe that men as well as women can be witches, especially where witchcraft entails training in secret lore and bestows elite status, throughout the world the great majority of witches are women.

At the level of popular culture, witchcraft beliefs within the Western tradition closely resemble beliefs in those African and Asian societies in which they are also widely held. They serve as an explanation for the misfortunes and disasters of everyday peasant experience (for example, deaths or illnesses of humans or animals that do not appear to have natural causes), especially if there is plausibly someone in the village with whom one has had a specific quarrel or who has a general reputation for causing trouble through witchcraft.

There is abundant documentary, literary, and archaeological evidence that belief in witchcraft was nearly universal among all social classes in the ancient Greek, Roman, and Jewish civilizations. The triumph of Christianity had a paradoxical double effect, at least among the educated. On the one hand, Christian doctrine emphasized, as Judaism had done, that witchcraft was wholly evil, a turning away from God for low and worldly purposes. Consistent with the early Christian stereotype of the female as spiritually inferior to the male, far more vulnerable to lusts and temptations, the church taught that women were far more likely than men to succumb to belief in and practice of witchcraft. On the other hand, the medieval church adopted Augustine's teaching that witchcraft was not real but rather a devilish illusion, which served to tempt women and men into sin and damnation.

From a few scattered references, we can assume that among the European peasantry witchcraft beliefs (and practices) persisted essentially unchanged. Witchcraft, however, was a very minor concern for the religious and secular authorities during the High Middle Ages. They were much more worried about the heretical movements that emerged at the end of the twelfth century and spread through urban Europe, especially the Rhine Valley, northern Italy, and southern France. In combating the latter, the authorities portrayed heresy as the polar opposite of orthodoxy. It was claimed that the heretics met secretly, at night, for services of worship that were in reality obscene orgies of sexuality. Both ecclesiastical and secular courts also adapted from Roman legal practice the procedures of inquisitorial justice, by which they could circumvent the restraints and protections that the accused enjoyed in customary law. Women were prominent in the heretical movements, and this fact may have enforced the orthodox teaching that they were more prone than men to sin.

In the fifteenth century, popular and official concern about witchcraft intensified dramatically. Especially in the alpine regions of Germany, Italy, France, and Switzerland, there were trials of witches that anticipated features of the witch trials of the sixteenth and seventeenth centuries. For the first time, peasant witches were being hunted out and brought before ecclesiastical or secular courts. At their trials, traditional accusations of harming people, animals, and crops were amalgamated with accusations that derived both from the dark side of the popular folklore—baby-eating, night flying, and the like—and from the church's propaganda against heretics.

In 1486, two Dominican inquisitors at Cologne published a treatise called *Malleus maleficarum* (*The Hammer of Witches*), which synthesized much of the popular and learned opinion into the "new heresy" of witchcraft. The book was one of the earliest best-sellers of the new printing technology. Reprinted 14 more times before 1520, republished frequently during the period of the most intensive witch-hunting in the late sixteenth and early seventeenth centuries, its influence was considerable, although it is difficult to determine precisely what that influence was. Prefaced by a papal bull calling for inquisitorial proceedings against witches, the *Malleus* provided a tacit repudiation of the traditional theology, insisting instead that witches really were heretics who worshipped the Devil and had sexual intercourse with him. Moreover, the book was obsessively and perversely misogynistic, insisting on the inherent weakness and wickedness of women.

The *Malleus* was only one symptom of a gradual intensification of concern about witchcraft. While there were comparatively few witch trials in the 70 years after its first publication, the era also saw the printing of many sermons, pamphlets, and illustrated "devil books" that dwelt on Satan and the horrors that he was working in the world.

The new concern for witches was also incorporated into various statutes and legal codes, notably the *Carolina*, promulgated in 1532 by Charles V for the entire Holy Roman Empire. With the exception of outlying areas like England, Scandinavia, and Russia where the new ideas of demonology failed to penetrate, the European regimes permitted the use of torture and the testimony of people like felons, spouses, and children, which was not allowed in other kinds of trials.

The height of prosecutions, the so-called witch-craze, lasted for a century, from about 1560 to 1660. Its incidence varied widely from place to place. It was most severe in some of the petty states in southwestern Germany and in parts of present-day France and the Low Countries. Somewhat lower on the continuum were Scotland and parts of Switzerland. At the other end of the scale were England, where Roman law never penetrated, and Italy and Spain, where the Roman Catholic Church still controlled witch-hunting procedures and after 1600 reaffirmed the traditional theological doubts about the reality of witchcraft.

Everywhere, witch trials were essentially a local phenomenon. Essentially, those accused and convicted were victims of village rivalries, feuds, and disputes that sometimes went back for generations. At least 80 percent of those executed were women, usually middle-aged or older. Some of them had been midwives or folkhealers, who in popular belief had always been magical practitioners of a sort.

The witch hunts were exacerbated by the religious rivalries of the sixteenth and seventeenth centuries, which saw both Catholics and Protestants insisting that their rivals were in the devil's service. The warfare which was endemic to much of Europe in the period further intensified the sense of instability and spiritual anxiety that found a violent catharsis in the hunting of witches. On the other hand, neither religion nor warfare explains why women should have been singled out so universally.

Historians have recently pointed to three interrelated phenomena as having contributed significantly to women's being the victims of the witch-hunts. First, the witch stereotype as it had evolved since the fifteenth century was the virtual opposite of the male-created stereotype of femaleness. Women were supposed to be passive, to submit to their domestic rulers—fathers or husbands—and to control their passions. In contrast, those accused of witchcraft were routinely depicted by their accusers as being quarrelsome, independent, and unruly. They were frequently economically marginal as well, widowed or unattached to male providers, forced to resort to begging or charity. Very often, their accusers were also women, women who conformed to the interior social status imposed upon them by males and saw in the witches and the anarchic freedom they represented a threat to the security of that status.

In the second place, the judicial assault upon accused practitioners of witchcraft was part of a larger concern for crimes that threatened moral structures of society. In both Catholic and Protestant states, the governments had taken over the supervision of morals that had formerly been the responsibility of the clergy. In much of Europe north of the Alps, this moral crusade entailed prosecution of infanticide*, adultery*, sodomy, and bestiality as well as witchcraft. The authorities saw all of these as threats to religion, the state, and the family*. Implicit in the prosecution of this new genre of crime was what Christina Larner has called the criminalization of women. The private and domestic nature of these offenses meant that women, formerly excluded from the courts, now appeared frequently, both as accused and as accusers.

The third related factor pertains to the development of the modern state, for witchcraft was also a political crime. As pamphlets and treatises insisted over and over, by giving their allegiance to the devil, witches challenged not only God but also the rulers who were his earthly representatives. The very disorderliness of the era of the witch-hunts led those in authority to insist upon the importance of order, as embodied in the governmental bureaucracy. This obsession led them to invest local outbreaks of witch fears and accusations, which usually were directed at marginal women within the villages, with cosmic political significance.

Jurists, preachers, and writers of demonological tracts had insisted since the fifteenth century that there was an enormous conspiracy at work, in which women renounced their proper superiors and the true religion in order to worship the Devil and serve him. Almost all historians now reject the idea that the authorities had uncovered and misinterpreted an ancient religion that worshipped a female god. The only evidence for the contention consists of confessions, generally elicited under torture by male interrogators, and these reflect instead the preconceptions about heresy that had prevailed since the Middle Ages, spiced by various details out of local folklore.

Early in the seventeenth century, officials in various parts of Europe began to have doubts about both the judicial procedures that had been introduced to root out witches and the demonological theories that justified them. Sometimes the excesses of the trials themselves led to questions about them; in addition, some writers began to reassert traditional doubts about the reality of witchcraft or else to inject a healthy skepticism as to the capacity of humans to know the minds of God and Satan as thoroughly as the demonologist claimed.

Ironically, two of the most extensive trials occurred late in the seventeenth century, in places that had formerly been largely immune to the worst excesses. In Sweden, the testimony of children led to a wave of trials that lasted for several years beginning in 1669. In the American colonies, where the pattern of witchcraft prosecutions had been virtually identical with that in England, with occasional trials on the traditional grounds of harming people or animals, claims by a group of adolescent girls in Salem Village, Massachusetts, that they had been possessed by evil spirits sent by witches led to over 100 arrests and 20 executions.

By 1700, prosecution for witchcraft had ended in most of the Western world. It was a more secular and a more pragmatic era, in which authorities no longer were determined to crush moral and religious deviance through inquisitions and prosecutions. Meanwhile, in the rural universe of the peasants, witch beliefs remained essentially what they had been for millennia. And so they remain today.

Further References. J. Klaits, *Servants of Satan: The Age of the Witch Hunts* (Bloomington, Ind., 1985). C. Larner, *Witchcraft and Religion: The Politics of Popular Belief* (Oxford, 1984). J. B. Russell, *A History of Witchcraft: Sorcerers, Heretics, and Pagans* (London, 1980).

CLARKE GARRETT

WOMANIST, WOMANISM, WOMANISH. Terms associated with varied conditions of black womankind. Particularly characteristic of gender-role traits and practices of African-American women, these terms are applicable to all women of African descent. Alice Walker originally introduced the term *womanist* in *In Search of Our Mother's Gardens: Womanist Prose* (San Diego, 1983), yet the ideals behind it have a long-standing significance in black culture. Long before Sojourner Truth's query "Ain't I a woman?" and continuing through contemporary African women's writing, womanism has import.

Womanism, as conventionally employed in black culture, can refer to gender traits or can identify social/political consciousness. Womanism represents an expectation and experience of female knowledge, competence, and responsibilities that are beyond those associated either with youth or with the gender traits traditionally assigned females in Western culture. Its characterization of women as audacious as well as capable contrasts with the image of females under partriarchy* as submissive and inferior. It is significant to note that while black males, regardless of their ages, have been stereotypically addressed as "boys," black females were supposedly denigrated by being referred to as "women" rather than "ladies." However, the connotations of "women" within the black community have become positive ones, asserting and affirming the value in females of adult qualities such as ability, independence, creativity, loving, and strength.

Womanish, then, represents an attitude or orientation toward life of strong-willed, opinionated self-confidence. Within black communities, even young girls are referred to as womanish, that is, behaving like or assuming the responsibilities and perogatives of older, adult females. In fact, black females necessarily assume adult roles and develop a maturity at very young ages.

The form *womanist* identifies someone with a respect for, an appreciation of, and a reliance upon the capabilities of women. A womanist is decidedly pro-woman: an advocate of women's interests, equity, and enrichment within familial, community, religious, educational, economic, political, and social relationships and institutions. This advocacy and activism include an array of matrifocal endeavors, both homosocial and homosexual. Yet as Alice Walker and Chikwenye Okonjo Ogunyemi observe (in "Womanism: The Dynamics of the Contemporary Black Female Novel in English," *Signs* 11 [1985]: 63–80), a womanist is not a female separatist. The concerns of the womanist perspective are the survival, affirmation, and enpowerment of all persons, male and female. Womanism encompasses a black feminism and has also been applied generally to feminists of color. Yet, as Walker asserts, given the complexity and dynamism of black women's lives, womanism has a greater scope and intensity than feminism*. (See BLACK WOMEN AND FEMINISM.) A womanist is spirited and spiritual, determined and decisive, committed to struggle and convinced of victory. A womanist acknowledges the particulist experiences and cultural heritage of black women, resists systems of domination, and insists on the liberty and self-determination of all people.

Further References. P. Giddings, *When and Where I Enter: The Impact of Black Women on Race and Sex in America* (New York, 1984). J. Ladner, *Tomorrow's Tomorrow: The Black Woman* (Garden City, N.Y., 1971).

DEBORAH K. KING

WOMEN'S WORK is a major focus of concern and study among feminists. In the 1980s well over two-fifths of the labor force is female, more than two-thirds of all women, 18 to 64, are employed, and, despite increased representation of women in the labor force and in some male-dominated jobs, over half of all men and women are employed in jobs where at least 80 percent of the workers are of one sex only. Further, it has been predicted that women will continue to work in largely low-paying, sex-segregated jobs in the future. Also, despite important changes, for women of color* occupational race segregation continues to persist.

One consequence of interdisciplinary feminist scholarship has been the expansion of the term *women's work* to include all work women do: domestic labor, child care, and sexual services in the home, as well as wage work in the labor market. Sociology has made important contributions to this endeavor, and both major perspectives in sociology—mainstream and critical—have been significantly affected by feminist scholarship on women's work.

Mainstream sociology traditionally studied women only within the family until the early 1970s, when the focus shifted to include women in the paid labor force. Then, from the study of those factors that affected the individual woman (e.g., education, occupational training, sex-role attitudes, etc.) attention moved to the institutional and structural forces in the economic sector that affected women's occupational position, especially the highly sex-segregated nature of the labor market itself.

Despite serious problems in their theoretical categories and conceptualizations (e.g., although realizing its importance, sociologists were unable to incorporate women's unwaged domestic labor into their analyses of wage work) the mainstream schools contributed two essential features to the study of women and work: first, they helped to demystify and challenge many erroneous assumptions about women, in paid employment and in the home, and, second, they provided a rich and varied base of empirical data on women in the contemporary labor market.

The best known of the critical or radical perspectives in sociology is the Marxist. Although its traditional focus on labor market activities excludes the relationship between home and market all-important for women, Marxist theory has been important in helping shape an understanding of the complexity of the economy, and within it women's lives and work. Marxist study of monopoly capitalism provided a basis for understanding (1) the development of markets that create new types of low-paying, low-status jobs, (2) the processes by which more skilled jobs are broken down into less desirable, more segmented parts and thereby "deskilled," and (3) the processes by which a sex-segregated or sex-segmented labor market develops. These insights help explain the increasing inclusion of women into the labor force in precisely these low-status, low-waged, often deskilled and sex-segregated jobs in an increasingly service-oriented society.

As Marxist scholars developed the implications of monopoly capitalism for the jobs people held, feminist scholars in the critical tradition began arguing for the essential connection between women's domestic and market labor. Marxist feminists argued that the capitalist mode of production* must be understood as a dual system of production that includes domestic unwaged labor as well as wage labor. The unpaid work women do in the home is basic to the reproduction of wage workers (the maintenance and continuation of the labor force) and the production of profits in the labor market. Without it, profits are not possible.

Radical feminists, anticapitalist but not Marxist, argued that the way to end economic class exploitation was to eliminate the primary class exploitation— the domination of women by men, or patriarchy*—on which capitalism rested (in contradistinction to the Marxist feminist position that the primary class exploitation is based on capitalist control over the means of production). Motherhood and housewifery were considered the quintessential partriarchal institutions on which all else rested, including wage labor–capitalist relations. Thus radical feminism* argued for directing women's struggles explicitly against male domination, not class society.

The third group of critical feminists, socialist feminists, took what they considered best from the other traditions, reformulating certain questions and raising new ones to try to bring the analysis of women in late twentieth-century patriarchal capitalism to a new level.

Like Marxist feminists, socialist feminists assume that class relations, in particular capitalism and its construction of women's position in the home, are major causes of the problems faced by women in the labor market today. Thus, because women's domestic labor is unwaged and assumed to be "taken care of'' by the men's paid labor in the market, when women enter the labor market they are generally paid as ''secondary'' workers at wages far lower than men's. (Earnings of fully employed women average about 60 percent of those of fully employed men.) This is true for single women and even more tragically for women heads of households.

Like radical feminists, socialist feminists believe that an analysis of women's problems requires an understanding of the complex effects of the social relations of patriarchy. Thus socialist feminists link radical feminism with Marxism. They argue that capitalist and patriarchal relations operate in both the home and the market, on both material (economic) and ideological (cultural) levels. Only by seeing this dynamic and dialectic system of patriarchal and capitalist relations is it possible to understand women's poor position in the labor market today.

Socialist feminists contribute four key points to the analysis of women's work. (1) Not only is women's home activity economically useful and essential to capitalism, it is also economically beneficial to men: e.g., men, relieved of most of the unwaged labor in the home, are available for the more stable, higher waged, better protected male-dominated jobs in the market. (2) All work women do is the material base of their oppression in society—in the market, and the home, and the community. This work includes such tasks as child care*, cooking, cleaning, shopping, sewing, ego building, sexual servicing, typing, nursing, etc.—both for wages and as unwaged labor in the home. (3) Patriarchal relations operate in the home, and they are a major feature of the capitalist labor market as well. This helps explain why women are exploited in the market and why they are forced into seeking the home as their primary responsibility even when they are wage earners themselves. (4) Not only the social class system but the entire sexual division of labor, both between and within the home and the market, must be eliminated or transformed for the exploitation of women to cease. It is both cause and effect of the social relations of patriarchy and of capitalism in contemporary society.

Finally, many socialist feminists have argued that socialist feminist theory itself must be transformed by the insights gained from women of color: especially that all women's lives in general and work lives in particular are shaped by institutionalized racism. The study of women's work is enhanced by each new challenge.

Further References. B. Reskin and H. Hartmann (eds.), *Women's Work, Men's Work: Sex Segregation on the Job* (Washington, D.C., 1986). N. J. Sokoloff, *Between Money and Love: The Dialectics of Women's Home and Market Work* (New York, 1980).

NATALIE J. SOKOLOFF

WORKING WOMEN. Women who labor in the home, the community, and the workplace. They contribute to the social reproduction of themselves and their families, but they may also do volunteer work and help build communities. Increasingly, they work for wages in formal labor markets nationally and internationally.

Women work, the world over. This is a feature of of women's gender heritage which transcends national, ethnic, and ideological lines. However, not all women globally are involved in the same work, nor is their work valued equally. They share in common work in the domestic sphere*, which includes housework*, child care*, and socialization. And in some parts of the world there is still a fairly close connection between work within the home and the economics of production. For example, black South African women in rural bantustans are a necessary adjunct to the system of labor migration that involves men in industrial work far removed from the area. The women toil and plant and carve out a meager living for their families. Under these circumstances, men are paid a single man's wage even though impoverished families remain behind and in need of their economic contributions. Black South African women must support a community of old people and children largely through their own labor.

In the case of the United States, the growing number of women working for pay is one of the significant transformations in the American labor force. In addition, work within the home and voluntarism are essential elements in profiling American working women. In the past twenty years, the transformation of women's work in these two spheres is noteworthy largely because of the growing number of women working for wages. Women's wage labor has put stress on the volunteer system and the child care system because these both depend on unpaid female labor.

The most frequent adjustment to these changes is a greater workload for women. In fact, women in the United States are increasingly dual workers. They work a double day: first for pay, then as workers for the social reproduction of themselves and their families. This means that child care, cooking, cleaning, the emotional and physical support of husbands, children, and other kin, as well as wage work, are part of their workday. They share this situation in common with many women around the world, as other American women now join the large number of Black American women who have always worked inside and outside the home.

Given women's importance as domestic laborers, analyzing reproduction as well as production is part of any satisfactory explanation of working women.] Furthermore, given the idea that domestic labor is work, some feminists have advocated wages for housework. Yet housework is only one aspect of women's labor within the home. Nurturing, birth, and socialization are also part of the workday. The major point, however, is that working women span both unpaid and paid labor domains.

A second critical area to consider in discussing working women is women as community builders and as volunteers. Women work within their communities. They work with children, old people, and the differently abled. They work in hospitals, churches, halfway houses, and associations. Women type, canvass, run offices, and help elect politicians. They work in all these spheres but not for pay. Increasingly scholars are looking at volunteer work as essential to the maintenance and social reproduction of the community. Although this work is not given value in the traditional calculus of monetary reward as the measure of worth, women and their unpaid labor are the significant dimension in much of the community building of this country. As more women are bound to the double duty of paid labor and unpaid household labor, the issue of collective community responsibility must be addressed.

A third consideration is that the traditional conceptualization of working women refers to those who work for pay. The phenomenon of large numbers of American women in the labor force has been called a revolution by some scholars. Even so, working women in the United States are plagued by sex-segregated occupations, low pay, limited job mobility, and flat age-earnings profile curves. Nonetheless, women continue to enter the labor force in growing numbers, and increasingly, there is some occupational diversity.

Unfortunately, the media image of today's working woman is misleading. She is portrayed invariably as a young, successful white female professional. This is a woman not plagued by double duty, child care woes, sex discrimination* or harassment on the job, or so goes the media hype. In reality, the picture is quite different. American working women are likely to have children, be in their thirties, and not work in a high-paying profession, according to Mary Frank Fox and Sharlene Hesse-Biber (*Women at Work* [1984], 97). They go on to say, "she works, for example, in the typing pool of a large corporation, on the assembly line of a manufacturing firm, or she is a file clerk in an insurance company." She is also likely to provide a service: sell clothes, fix hair, prepare food. In many instances she is likely to be a part-time worker, and often this is not by choice. Part-time work means even lower pay, fewer chances for occupational mobility, and no job benefits. Women accept part-time work most often because there is not affordable child care or no full-time work for them. This is especially true for black woman (J. Malveaux, "Economics and You," *Essence* [November 1987], 116).

If the profile of American working women is translated statistically, it means that by the 1980s more than half of all women over the age of 16 are working outside the home. Elliot Currie and Jerome H. Skolnick point out that "since the 1950s, the labor force participation of married women with no children under 18 has risen by a little more than half, that of women with children aged 6 to 17 has more than doubled, and that of women with children under 6 nearly quadrupled. By 1982, 55 percent of children under 18 had mothers in the labor force, as did fully 46 percent of preschool age children, up from 12 percent in 1950" (*America's Problems* [Boston, 1984], 194. Based on statistics published by the U.S. Department of Labor, Women's Bureau, 1982, 1–2). Since 1982 the figures are even more dramatic for women with young children. In March 1987, 52 percent of mothers with children one year old and younger were in the labor force, and about 60 percent of mothers whose youngest child was between the age of one and six were in the labor force.

Working women's labor force participation rates vary to some extent by race and ethnicity. Somewhat higher proportions of black women, and somewhat lower proportions of Hispanic women are in the labor force than are white women. Black, Filipino, and Chinese women work more than other women of color (E. M. Almquist, *Minorities, Gender, and Work* [Lexington, Mass., 1979]). And black married women are most likely to be juggling the triple load of housework, volunteerism, and formal wage work. Yet even with high levels of labor force participation, black women cluster at the lower occupational levels. Their salaries lag behind white men, black men, and white working women.

A final consideration regarding working women is public policy. Policy changes regarding women, family, and work have been slow to keep pace with the shifting profile of American working women. Their child care needs, health care concerns, and work/family responsibilities have not been clearly addressed in public policy initiatives. Moreover, American private employers have been slow to respond to working women's issues. There is too little quality child care, too little flexible work time, and too little shared responsibility. Since most women are working because of economic need, policies which confront and incorporate women's dual role should be on the agenda. Of the industrial nations, the United States has been slowest in creating national policy initiatives along these lines: maternity leaves, flextime, shared child care, full employment. These issues will not disappear given the large and growing number of working women in this country.

In sum, women are workers. They work within the home, within the community, and within the labor market. Given this, public policymakers nationally and internationally will increasingly have to take into consideration the intersection of community, home, and wage labor in forging policies for working women.

ROSE M. BREWER

Selected Bibliography

A very limited number of bibliographic references are included in many of the articles in the encyclopedia. In addition, a few general works, bibliographies, dictionaries, comprehensive works on women's studies or on fields within women's studies, which may prove useful as a starting point for study, are listed below.

Andersen, Margaret L. *Thinking about Women: Sociological and Feminist Perspectives.* 2nd ed. New York: Macmillan, 1988.

Basow, Susan A. *Gender Stereotypes: Traditions and Alternatives.* 2nd ed. Belmont, Calif.: Brooks Cole, 1986.

Bergmann, Barbara R. *Economic Emergence of Women.* New York: Basic Books, 1986.

Blau, Francine D., and Marianne A. Ferber. *The Economics of Women, Men and Work.* New York: Prentice-Hall, 1986.

Bleier, Ruth, ed. *Feminist Approaches to Science.* New York: Pergamon, 1986.

Boles, Janet K., ed. *The Egalitarian City: Issues of Rights, Distributions, Access and Power.* New York: Praeger, 1986.

Boston Women's Health Book Collective. *The New Our Bodies, Ourselves: A Book by and for Women.* New York: Simon and Schuster, 1984.

Brown, Barbara A., Ann E. Freedman, Harriet N. Katz, and Alice M. Price. *Women's Rights and the Law: The Impact of the ERA on State Law.* New York: Praeger, 1977.

Donovan, Josephine. *Feminist Theory: The Intellectual Traditions of American Feminism.* New York: F. Ungar, 1985.

Fausto-Sterling, Anne. *Myths of Gender: Biological Theories about Women and Men.* New York: Basic Books, 1985.

Fox, Mary Frank, and Sharlene Hess-Biber. *Women at Work.* Palo Alto, Calif.: Mayfield Publishing Company, 1984.

Freeman, Jo, ed. *Women: A Feminist Perspective.* 3rd ed. Palo Alto, Calif.: Mayfield Publishing Company, 1984.

Harding, Sandra, and Jean F. O'Barr, eds. *Sex and Scientific Inquiry.* Chicago: University of Chicago Press, 1987.

Harriman, Ann. *Women/Men/Management*. New York: Praeger, 1985.

Howell, Elizabeth, and Majorie Bayer, eds. *Women and Mental Health*. New York: Basic Books, 1981.

Hrdy, Sarah B. *The Women That Never Evolved*. Cambridge, Mass.: Harvard University Press, 1981.

Jagger, Alison, and Paula S. Rothenburg, eds. *Feminist Frameworks: Alternative Theoretical Accounts of the Relations between Men and Women*. 2nd ed. New York: McGraw-Hill, 1984.

Kanowitz, Leo. *Women and the Law: The Unfinished Revolution*. Albuquerque: New Mexico University Press, 1969.

Klein, Ethel. *Gender Politics*. Cambridge, Mass.: Harvard University Press, 1984.

Kramare, Cheris, and Paula A. Treichler. *A Feminist Dictionary*. Boston: Pandora Press, 1985.

Lerner, Gerda. *The Creation of Patriarchy*. New York: Oxford University Press, 1986.

Loeb, Catherine R., Susan E. Searing, and Esther F. Steinman, with Meredith J. Ross. *Women's Studies: A Core Bibliography*. Littleton, Colo.: Librarians Unlimited.

Ortner, Sherry B., and Harriet Whitehead. *Sexual Meanings: The Cultural Construction of Gender and Sexuality*. New York: Cambridge University Press, 1981.

Powell, Gary. *Women and Men in Management*. Beverly Hills, Calif.: Sage, 1988.

Sapiro, Virginia. *Women in American Society*. Palo Alto, Calif.: Mayfield Publishing Company, 1986.

Searing, Susan E., with Rima D. Apple. *The History of Women and Science, Health, and Technology: A Bibliographic Guide to the Professions and the Disciplines*. Madison, Wisc.: University of Wisconsin System Librarian, 1988.

Shephard, Bruce D., and Carroll A. Shephard. *The Complete Guide to Women's Health*. New York: Signet, 1985.

Sloane, Ethel. *Biology of Women*. 2nd ed. New York: John Wiley, 1985.

Tavris, Carol, ed. *EveryWoman's Emotional Well-Being*. Garden City, N.Y.: Doubleday, 1986.

Tuttle, Lisa. *Encyclopedia of Feminism*. New York: Facts on File Publication, 1986.

Williams, Juanita H. *Psychology of Women: Behavior in a Biosocial Context*. 2nd ed. New York: Norton, 1983.

Index

Page numbers set in *italic* indicate the location of main entry.

Chicano movement, 52, 53

Child abuse (child sexual abuse), 107–8, 188–89, 223. *See also* Domestic violence; Incest

Childbirth (cross-cultural), *53–57*. *See also* Birthing; Birthing alternatives; Couvade; Midwifery; Obstetrics; Parturition

Child Care, *57–59*; of children of imprisoned mothers, 286; policy in Europe, 58; policy in the United States, 58–59

Child custody: of lesbian mothers, 203–4; in Muslim countries, 101

Childe, V. G., 248

Childhood disorders, sex differences in, 333

Children: of concubines, status of, 74; their effect on labor supply, *59–61*; of lesbian mothers, 204; with mothers in the labor force, 394; poverty of, in female-headed families, 282; as social welfare recipients, 382; of women prisoners, 286–87, 289

Child sexual abuse. *See* Child abuse (child sexual abuse)

"Chivalry" in sentencing of females, 257, 288

Chlamydia trachomatis, *61–62*, 349–50

Chodorow, Nancy, 137, 300, 311

Christian church
—regulation of midwives, 237
—rivalries exacerbate witchcraze, 387
—views on: adultery, 14, 15; concubinage, 75; marriage and divorce, 21, 22, 101; witchcraft, 386
—views on and activity against: infanticide, 190; prostitution, 292–93

Chromosomes, determination of sex by, 340

Cigarette: advertising, 10–11, 50; smoking, 49. *See also* Smoke and smoking

Cinderella Complex, The, 91

Circumcision (female), *62–63*

Civil Rights Act of 1964. *See* Title VII

Cixous, Hélène, 90, 331

Clark, Lorenne, 315

Class: differences in school attendance by sex and, 117; exploitation, 391–92; as

one of multiple oppressions, 43, 112; oppression, 351

Clerical occupations, *63–65*; socioeconomic and ethnic status of women workers in, 65, 70

Climactric, *65*, 135–36, 230

Clitoridectomy. *See* Circumcision (female)

Clitoris, 62, 322

Cocaine, 11, 12

Cognitive abilities, sex differences in, *66–68*, 334

Cognitive-developmental theory of sex-role socialization, 338

Cognitive styles/orientation, 67–68

Coitus interruptus, 78

Collins, Patricia Hill, 42

Color, women of, *68–70*; greater risk from cancer, 49; insights to be gained from, 392; multiple oppressions of, 111–12; treatment programs for addicted, 13; wage differentials of, 72. *See also* American Indian women (Native American); Asian women (Asian-American women); Black women (African-American women); Hispanic women (Chicana, Latina, Mexican-American)

Comfort gestures, 251

"Coming out," 180, 205

Commission on Obscenity and Pornography, 281

Common law: disabilities of married women under, 84; property division under, 113, 216

Community builders, women as, 393–94

Community property, *70–71*, 216

Comparable worth (pay equity), *71–73*, 99

Competence, evaluation of, 124–25; women's increase in, in management, 215

Compound family, 129

Compulsive eating, 148

Conception, ideas about, 54

Concubinage, *73–75*, 290; in ancient Rome, 74–75; end of legal recognition

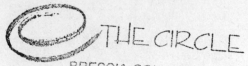

THE CIRCLE

BRESCIA COLLEGE
1285 WESTERN ROAD
LONDON, ONTARIO   N6G 1H2
TEL. 432-8353   FAX 679-6489